European Cinema

European Cinema

Face to Face with Hollywood

Thomas Elsaesser

Amsterdam University Press

Cover illustration: Nicole Kidman in Dogville

Cover design: Kok Korpershoek, Amsterdam
Lay-out: JAPES, Amsterdam

ISBN 90 5356 594 9 (paperback)
ISBN 90 5356 602 3 (hardcover)
NUR 674

Table of Contents

Europe-Hollywood-Europe

Central Europe Looking West

Europe Haunted by History and Empire

Border-Crossings: Filmmaking without a Passport

Conclusion

European Cinema

Conditions of Impossibility?

An Impossible Project

Any book about European cinema should start with the statement that there is no such thing as European cinema, and that yes, European cinema exists, and has existed since the beginning of cinema a little more than a hundred years ago. It depends on where one places oneself, both in time and in space. In time: for the first fifteen years, it was France that defined European cinema, with Pathé and Gaumont educating Europe's film-going tastes, inspiring filmmakers and keeping the Americans at bay. In the 1920s, the German film industry, under Erich Pommer, tried to create a "Cinema Europe," involving France and Britain. It soon floundered, and Hollywood became not only the dominant force; it also was very successful in dividing the Europeans among themselves.[1] For a brief period in the late 1920s, it seemed the Russians might be Europe's inspiration. Instead, from 1935 onwards, it was Nazi cinema that dominated the continent until 1945. The years from 1945 to the 1980s were the years of the different national cinemas, or rather: the period when new waves, national (art) cinemas and individual auteurs made up a shifting set of references that defined what was meant by European cinema. Geopolitically speaking on the other hand, when looking at Europe from, say, the American perspective, the continent is indeed an entity, but mostly one of cinema audiences that still make up Hollywood's most important foreign market.

Looked at from the "inside," however, the conclusion has to be that European cinema does not (yet) exist: the gap between Central/Eastern Europe and Western Europe remains as wide as ever, and even in Western Europe, each country has its own national cinema, increasingly defended as a valuable treasure and part of an inalienable national patrimony. Since the nouvelle vague, French cinema, in particular, insists on its long and proud tradition as the natural home of the seventh art. In the United Kingdom, British cinema (once called a 'contradiction in terms' by François Truffaut) has over the last twenty years been reinstated, re-evaluated and unapologetically celebrated, even if its economic ups and downs, its many false dawns as an art cinema, as well as its surprisingly frequent commercial successes put it in a constant if often covert competition with Hollywood. Germany, having repeatedly failed to keep alive the promise and prestige attached to the New German Cinema in the 1970s has, since unification in 1990, turned to a policy of archival conservation, where museum displays on a grand scale, encyclopedic databases, anniversary retrospectives and an ambitious internet portal all try to heal the wounds inflicted by unpalatable nationalist legacies from the 1940s and by the political-ideological divisions into "German" and "East German" cinema during the Cold War period. Italy, too, nostalgically looks back to both neo-realism and Toto comedies, while discovering the memory of open-air screenings in the piazza under Mussolini or small-town cinemas run by Communists as the true sites of national film culture. Only in Denmark have the Dogma filmmakers around Lars von Trier come up with innovative and iconoclastic ways to stage a national cinema revival that also has a European outlook. In Southern Europe Pedro Almodovar became for a time a one-man national cinema, before sharing honours with Julio Medem and Alejandro Amenábar. But while Medem stands for "Basque cinema" and Amenábar for a successful navigation of the Hispano-Hollywood connection, Almodóvar not only embodied the radical chic of an outward-looking, post-Franco Spain, but with his stylish melodramas and surreal comedies gave international flair and street credibility to such strictly local habitats as the gay and transsexual subcultures of Madrid.

Looked at from outside of the inside, i.e., Eastern Europe, the idea of a European cinema is even more problematic. Knowing they belong to Europe, but feeling all too often left out, filmmakers from Central and Eastern Europe – some of them from the new "accession" countries of the European Union, such as Poland, the Czech Republic and Hungary – are perfectly aware of how much they have in the past contributed to the history of cinema, even during the difficult decades of the 1960s and 70s, when repression and censorship followed the brief opening of the "thaw." This so-called "New Europe" (Donald Rumsfeld), however, is often quite particularist: it expects its respective national cinema to be recognized as specific in time and place, history and geography, while still belonging to Europe. Some of these countries' national cinemas are usually identified by the outside world with one or two directors who have to stand in for the nation, even when this is manifestly impossible.

To give an obvious example: Andrzej Wajda was Polish cinema from the late 1940s, into the 1960s and up to MAN OF MARBLE (1977), until this role fell to Krzysztof Kieslowski during the 1980s and 1990s. Both worked – and were admired – in France, the country of choice for Polish filmmakers in semi-exile. But this is "our" Western perspective: what do we know about the political tensions underlying Polish directors' opposed ideological positions within their own country? What "we" perceived as national characteristics or received as part of the international art cinema, may well have struck Polish critics and audiences not as national cinema but as state cinema: official, sanctioned, sponsored. Yet were Polish filmmakers, along with their countrymen, not obliged to negotiate in less than half a century a world war, occupation, genocide, a civil war, communism, economic stagnation, censorship, repression and post-communism? Given such tensions and polarities, where do Krzysztof Zanussi, Jerzy Skolimowski, Jerzy Kawalerowicz or Agnieszka Holland fit into the picture we have of Polish cinema? Easiest for "us" to treat them as autonomous "auteurs." Similarly, Hungary, for a time, was Miklos Jansco, before it became identified with Istvan Szabo, then perhaps with Marta Meszaros and since the mid-1990s most definitely with Bela Tarr. In the case of former Yugoslavia, which for a time was mostly represented by the brilliant and politically non-conformist Dusan Makavejev, we now have directors carefully advertising their specific ethno-national identity, such as Emir Kusturica's or Danis Tanovic's Bosnian identity. Some "smaller" European countries whose cinematic assets, to the outsider, seem equally concentrated around one director's films, such as Greece (Theo Angelopoulos) and Portugal (Manoel de Oliveira), or countries like Austria, Belgium and Norway prefer to see their outstanding films labeled "European," rather than oblige their directors to lead a quickly ebbing "new wave" national cinema. Michael Haneke would be a case in point: a German-born director with Austrian credentials, who now predominantly works in France. Lars von Trier, together with his Dogma associates, is at once claimed at home as a quintessentially Danish director, and yet his films hardly ever – if at all – refer to Denmark, in contrast to a director from a previous generation, such as Carl Dreyer. Or take Ingmar Bergman, whose films for decades defined both to his countrymen and to the rest of the world what "Swedish" (cinema) meant.

Zooming out even further, one realizes that neither the individual national cinemas nor the label European cinema conjures up much of an image in Asian countries, Latin America or in the United States. A few individual actors (from France or the UK) are known, and once in while a director's name or a film catches the attention. Yet for traditions as historically rich, and for the numbers of films produced in the combined nations

INGMAR BERGMAN

of the European continent, the impact of its cinema on the world's audiences in the new century is minimal and still shrinking. If, in the face of this, there has been something of a retrenchment to positions of preserving the national heritage, and of defending a unique cinematic identity, the question this raises is: defend against whom or what? Against the encroachment of Hollywood and the relentless spread of television, as is the conventional answer? Or against provincialism, self-indulgence and amateurism, as claimed by more commercially successful makers of popular entertainment both inside and outside Europe, as well as by those European directors who have moved to the US?

On what basis, then, would one want to put forward a claim for a European cinema, at once superseding national cinemas and explaining their historical "decline" over the past twenty-five years? Several possibilities open up, some of which will be taken up in the essays that follow. One might begin by reviewing the dominant categories that have guided the study of films and filmmaking in Europe, examine their tacit assumptions and assess their current usefulness. Besides probing the idea of the "national" in cinematic production (once one acknowledges cross-national co-productions and the role played by television in financing them), the other categories demanding attention are that of European cinema as an auteur cinema, which as already hinted at, invariably tends to be implied by the argument around national cinema. Thirdly, one could also look once more at the concept of "art cinema" as a distinct formal-aesthetic style of narration, as well as an institutional-pragmatic category (i.e., art cinema encompassing all films shown at "art-house" cinemas, whether government subsidized or independently programmed, and thus potentially including revivals or retrospectives of mainstream "classics").

Besides a semantic investigation into the changing function of these traditional definitions, the case for European cinema can also be made by pointing out how persistently the different national cinema have positioned themselves in opposition to Hollywood, at least since the end of the first world war, and increasingly after the second world war, when their respective mainstream film industries began progressively and irreversibly to decline. Indeed, in the set of binary oppositions that usually constitutes the field of academic cinema studies, the American cinema is invariably the significant (bad) Other, around which both the national and "art/auteur"-cinema are defined. As my title implies, this more or less virulent, often emotionally charged opposition between Europe and Hollywood exerts a gravitational pull on all forms of filmmaking in Europe, notably in France, Britain, Italy and Germany. Yet if European national cinemas are held together, and in a sense united by their anti-Hollywood stance, there are nonetheless markedly varying degrees of hostility observable in the different countries at government level or among the film-critical establishment. France is more openly hostile than the Netherlands, and Denmark more successful in keeping its own share of domestic production in the nation's cinemas than, for instance, Germany. No country in Europe except France has a quota system like South Korea, but both countries have come under intense pressure by the WTO to reduce or even abolish this form of protectionism. The US cinema is felt as a threat economically and culturally, even though economically,

European cinema-owners know (and let it be known) that they depend on Hollywood movies for bringing in audiences, week in week out. Economically, European films are so weak that they could not be shown on the big screen if the machinery of the blockbuster did not keep the physical infrastructure of cinema-going and public film culture going. This is the germ of an argument that reverses the usual claim that Hollywood hegemony stifles national cinema, by maintaining that Hollywood's strong global market position is in fact the necessary condition for local or national diversity.[2]

The legal ramification of Europe's ingrained anti-Americanism in matters cinema are the various measures taken by successive EU initiatives, intended to bolster the audiovisual sector and its affiliated industries within the European Union. The economic framework that initially tried to regulate world trade, including the rivalry between US and the EU, were the GATT (General Agreement on Trade and Tariffs) rounds, in which audiovisual products featured as commercial goods, no different from any others. While notably France insisted on the cinema's cultural character, and wished to see it protected, that is exempted from particular measures of free trade and open access, the World Trade Organization has never been happy with these exemptions and reprieves. The consequence is that the status of the audiovisual sector remains an unresolved issue, bleeding into questions of copyright, subventions, ownership and a film's nationality. The French, for instance, are proud of their *droit d'auteur*, which gives the director exceptional rights over a film even by comparison with other EU countries, but Jean Pierre Jeunet's UN LONG DIMANCHE DE FIANÇAILLES could not compete for the best French film award in 2005 because it was co-financed by Warner Brothers. Initiatives taken within the European Union to strengthen cinema and create the legal framework for subsidizing the audiovisual industries, include the various projects supported and administrated by the successive "MEDIA" programs of the Council of Europe, which created such European-wide institutions and enabling mechanisms as Eurimages, EDN (European Documentary Network), Archimedia, etc.[3] These, too, despite their bureaucratic character, might be the basis for a definition of what we now understand by European cinema, as I try to argue in a subsequent chapter.

Historicizing the Now

European Cinema: Face to Face with Hollywood implicitly addresses and often explicitly discusses the question of Europe as a political entity, as well as a cultural space, from the distinct perspective of cinema. For instance, the book as a whole stands squarely behind the preserving and conserving tendencies manifest in most European countries with respect to "their" national cinema. Films are fragile, perishable and physically impermanent. They need institutional and financial support; they require technical but also intellectual resources, in order to maintain their existence. Until only a few decades ago, before the videotape and the DVD, a film's presence was limited to the moment of its theatrical release, and for some, this fleeting existence is still part of the cinema's essence. But however passing, transitory and seemingly expendable a particular film may be in the everyday, and however one may feel about the aesthetic implication of such an art of the moment, the cinema is nonetheless the 20th-century's most precious cultural memory, and thus calls forth not only a nostalgic but also an ethical impulse to try and preserve these moments for posterity.

The book, however, does not endorse the view that Hollywood and television are the threats that cinema in Europe has to be protected from. The first section sets out a broad horizon and sketches an evolving situation over the past two to three decades, which includes the asymmetrical but dynamic relationship of cinema with television, re-appraising the division of labour between cinema and television in giving meaning to the "nation". The section on authorship and the one entitled "Europe-Hollywood-Europe" are intended to show how much of a two way traffic European cinema has always entertained with Hollywood, however uneven and symbolic some of these exchanges may have been. What needs to be added is that relations are no longer bi-lateral; the film trade and its exchanges of cultural capital have become global, with reputations even in the art cinema and independent sector rapidly extending across national borders, thanks above all to the festival circuit, discussed in a separate chapter below. Hal Hartley, Richard Linklater, Paul Thomas Anderson, Alejandro Amenábar, Tom Tykwer, Fatih Akin, Wong Kar-Wai, Tsai Ming-Liang, Kim Ki-Duk, Abbas Kiarostami and Lars von Trier have, it sometimes seems, more in common with each other than with directors of their respective national cinemas, which paradoxically, gives a new meaning to regional or local attributes. The argument will be that a mutation has taken place; on the one hand, there is an international art cinema which communicates similar concerns across a wide spectrum of settings, but within an identifiable stylistic repertoire. Partly determined by new film technologies, this style repertoire adjusts to the fact that art cinema directors share with their audiences a cinephile universe of film historical references, which favors the evolution of a norm that could be called the international festival film. On the other hand, the lowering of cost due to digital cinema has meant that films – both feature films and documentaries – are fulfilling functions in the domestic space and the public sphere that break down most of our conventional, often binary categories: first and foremost those between art and commerce, into which the opposition between Europe and Hollywood is usually pressed. But the mutations also change our assessment of the local and the global: in the chapter on festivals, I also argue that signifiers of the regional and the local are often successfully marketed in the global arena, while a more ethnographic impulse and purpose can be detected behind many of the films made in Europe, registering the fact that cinema has become part of culture as a resource for the general good: shared, prepared and feasted upon like food at the dinner table, rather than valued only for the uniquely personal vision of the artist-auteur.

As a collection of essays, the earliest of which were written as film reviews, *European Cinema Face to Face with Hollywood* combines two seemingly contradictory impulses. Writing as a critic, I tried to record the moment and address the present, rather than this or that film's or filmmaker's possible posterity. Other pieces, also addressing the present, set out to develop a perspective of the *longue durée*, or to provide a context that could mediate and historically situate a filmic work or directorial oeuvre. In both cases, therefore, the essays were carried by the conviction that the cinema had a history, which was happening now. The implication being that history might even change, to adapt the catchphrase from BACK TO THE FUTURE, although at the time, I was more under the influence of T.S. Eliot's "Tradition and the Individual Talent," a seminal text in modernist literary history. Perhaps no more is intended than to convey the sense that each film entered into a dialogue with, contested and thereby altered not only those which preceded it, but did so by changing the here-and-now, whenever it brought about a revelatory moment or was an event, usually the reason that made me want to write about them. This makes the book, despite its omissions and selectivity, a history of European cinema since the 1960s, although not in the conventional sense. It does not deal systematically with movements, auteurs, national cinemas, significant films and masterpieces. Rather it is a discursive history, in the sense that the essays carry with them their own history, often precisely because they either directly address the historicity of the present moment, or because they self-consciously place themselves in the position of distance that historians tend to assume, even when they write about the now. Discursive history, also because this historicizing reflexive turn was the raison d'être of many of the articles. Several were commissioned by *Sight & Sound* (and its sister publication, the *Monthly Film Bulletin*) for instance, with the brief to step back and reflect on a new phenomenon, to take the longer view or to contextualize a change. Finally, a history of European film studies because the essays also trace a history of discourses, as the critic in me gave way to the academic, and the academic felt obliged to address fields of debate already constituted, not always avoiding the temptation of the meta-discourse.

Shifting the Discourses and Re-aligning the Paradigms

The more the essays reach into the new century, the more they take reflexive as well as retrospective turns. Not because of any disappointment in the state of European cinema or a nostalgic sense of regretting past glories. There is much to love and admire about the films being made by European directors. With talents as diverse and controversial as Pedro Almodóvar, Lars von Trier, Mike Leigh, Agnès Varda, Danny Boyle, Roberto Benigni, Catherine Breillat, Nanni Moretti, Emir Kusturica, Tom Tykwer, Fatih Akin, Claire Denis, and Jean Pierre Jeunet (to name just a few), the last two decades cannot but strike one as a period where it is exciting to be a working critic. But as my task changed from reviewing films to assuming the role of teacher at a university, establishing film studies degree and research programs, certain constraints imposed themselves about whom one is addressing also when writing, and to what pedagogical end and purpose. Some of the later essays had their origins in lecture notes and position papers, others were given at conferences, and some emerged out of discussions with colleagues and graduate students. Especially crucial were the last three years, when I headed a research group on "Cinema Europe" of about a dozen members, where the issues of European cinema were intensely discussed, sometimes taking a shorthand form, in order to quicker reach a new insight or perspective.

AGNÈS VARDA

There is, however, one common thread or master-trope that seems to run through many of the essays brought together under the various headings. It has to do with an abiding interest in European cinema as it stands in dialogue with the idea of the nation in the political and historical realm, and on the other, with the function that I see the cinema serving in the spectators' identity-formation. This master trope is that of a historical imaginary, but which in the present essays is mostly elaborated around the idea of the mirror and the image, the self and the other. Like a fractal structure, its can and does reproduce and repeat itself at micro and macro-level, it can be analyzed in specific scenes, it shapes the way a national cinema tries to address its national and international audiences, and it may characterize, at the macro-level, the way that the European cinema has been, and perhaps continues to be "face to face with Hollywood."

A few words about this historical imaginary: I am well aware of how contested a notion it is; how it places itself between film theorists and film historians, without necessarily convincing either. I have defined it elsewhere at some length, and given some of the heuristic as well as pragmatic reasons why I employ it as a middle level concept, which allows me to hold in place what I see as related issues.[4] These have to do with my view of the European cinema as a *dispositif* that constitutes, through an appeal to memory and identification, a special form of address, at once highly individual and capable of fostering a sense of belonging. Spectators of European cinema have traditionally enjoyed the privilege of feeling "different", but in a historically determined set of relations based on highly unstable acts of self-definition and self-differentiation implied by the use of terms such as "auteur", "art", "national cinema", "culture" or "Europe". As discussed in more detail in a subsequent chapter (Imperso-Nations: National Cinema, Historical Imaginaries), there seems to be some common ground between my "historical imaginary" and the justly famous concept introduced by Benedict Anderson, that of *Imagined Communities*. While I would not even presume to claim such a comparison, an obvious point of difference can be mentioned nonetheless. My idea of a cinematic historical imaginary (first set out in "Primary Identification and the Historical Subject" [1981] and then again, in "Film History and Visual Pleasure: Weimar Cinema" [1984]) was intended to rely on the distinct properties of the cinematic medium, such as composition and *mise-en-scène*, the architecture of the optical point of view, on-screen and off-screen space, depth of field, flatness and frontal shots as the key indices of a formal inscription that could be read historically. They formed the basis on which to elaborate the properties of a representational system that enabled an individual film, a genre or a body of work to address the spectator as a national or art cinema subject. My topic being initially films and filmmakers from Germany making up a national cinema (in the 1920s and again, in the 1970s), the representational system I identified seemed to me to function across relations of mirroring, *mise-en-abyme* and the figure of "the double as other", in which the self is invited to recognize itself.

Some of the terms were owed to the then dominant psychoanalytical film theories (notably Fredric Jameson's reading of Lacan's concept of the imaginary) and to feminist theory, while the historical-political part came from Frankfurt School-inspired studies of social pathology and the analyses done by Alexander Mitscherlich on collective "personality types". To this already eclectic mix was added an ethnographic dimension. For instance, the mirroring function of such a "historical imaginary" had parallels with Michael Taussig's reading of Walter Benjamin (in *Mimesis and Alterity*); it was influenced by Marcel Mauss' theories about intersubjectivity as a process of asymmetrical power-relations, by Cornelius Castoriades,[5] as well as by Jean Baudrillard's concept of uneven exchange. At the same time, it was never meant to be systematic, but to help answer a particular set of problems: those encountered when trying to explain the repetitions and parallels between two classically European instances of a national cinema, Weimar Germany and the New German Cinema, across the gap and rupture of fascism. In both cases, the significant other was Hollywood, with which this national cinema, in two quite different phases, had established mirror-relationships, in order to work through the displaced presence of an uncannily familiar other: the popular cinema of the Nazi period, framed by two catastrophic histories of self-inflicted national defeat, of humiliation and shame, that of WWI and then WW II. Revisiting Siegfried Kracauer's study of post-WWI films as a national cinema (a term he never uses) had thus to do with a parallel interest in the New German Cinema, in order to derive from it the idea of a historical imaginary, i.e., a concept that was both cinematically specific and historically grounded. This eventually resulted in two books on German cinema, and a monograph on R.W. Fassbinder – all exploring these shifting relations of identification and self-differentiation.

Parallel to this work on German cinema, and in some cases preceding it, I published essays analyzing what in retrospect now appear as similar sets of mirror-relations and over-identifications in France ("Two Weeks in Another Country – Hollywood and French Cinephilia", 1972) and Britain ("Images for Sale", 1984), as well as other essays on new waves, "national identity" and the national self-image. In two more recent contributions, one on "German Cinema, Face to Face with Hollywood: Looking into a Two-Way Mirror" (written in 2002), as well as one about films from the Balkans (from 2003) the same trope appears, differently contextualized and further developed: putting forward the idea of a national cinema (as a theoretical construction) always existing face to face with an "other". Although initially developed in response to a "demand" coming from the "other," namely universities in the United States asking me to lecture on these subjects,[6] I should perhaps mention that much of this work on Weimar cinema and the New German cinema was done while I was teaching at the University of East Anglia, where I had the pleasure of discussing my book on *New German Cinema* with my then colleague Andrew Higson, who went on to write his own essay on national cinema, "The Concept of National Cinema" (1989), which soon became the standard point of reference for all subsequent contributions to this debate.[7]

My own involvement in the national cinema debate, as well as my conscious, but often also unconscious adherence to the trope of the "historical imaginary" and its theoretical configuration, have thus largely determined the selection of the present essays and may explain some of the more glaring omissions, such as a discussion of Jean-Luc Godard, possibly the most "European" director working continuously over the whole of the historical period here considered. The sequence and the structure of the different sections of the book are not chronological. They partly retrace the formation and repercussions of the three dominant discourses that have until recently defined European cinema in the academic realm: "national cinema", "auteur cinema", "art cinema". One could call these the paradigms of autonomy: *National cinema* (the choice of making an auteur cinema represent the nation, rather than the stars-and-genre commercial cinema of a given country). Most national cinemas are (re-) defined as a consequence of self-declared movements or schools (the "new waves", which in Europe started in Italy with neo-realism of the late 1940s, includes Britain's kitchen sink films of the 1950s, the French *nouvelle vague* and other "new" cinemas throughout the 1960s and early 70s in Poland, Germany, the Czech Republic). *Auteur cinema* (the director as autonomous artist and representative of his country) usually goes hand in hand with *art cinema* (the formal, stylistic and narratological parameters which distinguish art cinema from classical i.e., Hollywood narrative, but also the institutional contexts, insofar as art cinema is made up of those films normally programmed in "art houses", a term more at home in the US and in Britain than in continental Europe, where cinematheques, *"art et essai"* cinemas or the so-called *"Programmkinos"* fulfil a similar function). The second half of the collection re-centres and de-centres these paradigms of autonomy. "Europe-Hollywood-Europe" shows how productively dependent the national cinemas of France, Britain and Germany have been on their implied other, while "Central Europe looking West" tries to give some indication of what acts of looking and being looked at have been excluded when defining "European cinema" in terms of its Western nations. "Europe haunted by History and Empire" de-centers "auteur" and "nation" by re-centering them around history and memory, as Europe's colonial past, political debts and troubled ethical legacy are gradually being transformed by the cinema into cultural capital: commodified, according to some into a "heritage industry", capable of creating new kinds of identity, according to others. In either case, by dwelling so insistently on the (recent) past, European cinema distinguishes itself from Hollywood and Asian cinemas. In the essays brought together under this heading, the origins of the new discourse on history in the cinema are traced back to the 1970s and 80s. The section on "Border-Crossings: Filmmakers without a Passport" further de-centers "national cinema" without abandoning the "auteur" by highlighting the efforts – not always successful or recognized – of individuals who have tried to make films either in Europe or addressed to European audiences, from transitional and transnational spaces, including explicitly political spaces. Notably the essays on Latin American filmmakers or on European directors using Latin American topics and settings lead to the final chapter, which traces some of the intersections of European cinema with Third Cinema and World Cinema.

The national cinemas discussed are those of Britain, Germany and to a lesser extent, France. One might object that this hardly justifies the words "European cinema" in the title. And even if I responded by pointing out that there are essays about the Swedish Ingmar Bergman, the Serbian Dusan Makavejev, the Italian Ettore Scola and Francesco Rosi, the Chilean Raoul Ruiz, the Argentinian Edgardo Cozarinsky, the Mozambiquian Ruy Guerra, and that I had to drop my essays on Renoir, Truffaut, Godard, Welles, Bunuel, Chabrol, Pasolini, Fellini, Bertolucci, Visconti and Polanski, one might immediately point out that these essays deal with films from the 1970s and 1980s. Where are the films and film-makers that I claim necessitate the revision of the paradigms of auteur and new wave, of national cinema and art cinema?

In some cases the chapters do not pretend to be anything other than what they are: essays written under different circumstances, for different occasions and spread over 35 years. Since they were not intended to "fit" the categories they find themselves in here, it is evident that even less so, they are able to "fill" them.[8] Yet when making a selection of my writing on the subject of European cinema, these categories made more sense than serving mere taxonomic convenience. They are in each case suggestions of how the study of European cinema since 1945 might be conducted, that is to say, revised, revitalised, recontextualised.

In order to underline the point, the first section was specifically written for this book, as was the concluding chapter. Together, they want to provide an extended introduction, open up another perspective on the material that follows, as well as outline a follow-up for the current phase of European cinema in the global context. The essay on "European Culture, National Cinema, the Auteur and Hollywood" recapitulates some of the standard positions on Europe as a collection of national cinemas. It puts special emphasis on their common love-hate, parasite-host relationship with Hollywood, showing how many intriguing and occasionally even illuminating insights the passion over Hollywood on both sides of the divide can yield, but also how restricted, even narcissistic and self-complacent the "face to face with Hollywood" debate can appear when the horizon is opened a little, and "we" West Europeans either face the other way, or let ourselves be faced and addressed by the East (or the South). In this way the chapter speculates on what basis, other than bureaucratic and economic, a European cinema might build a sense of identity that was neither merely the sum of its parts nor the result of new lines of exclusion and "other"-ing. Might it be time to abandon the search for "identity" altogether, and look for more sovereign markers of European selfhood, such as intercultural competence or the virtues of the family quarrel, interference and dissent? First sketched under the impact of the break-up of Yugoslavia, and the difficulties encountered in even thinking about how to integrate not just the film histories of the former communist states of central Europe, but the memories of its citizens, the chapter is nonetheless cautiously optimistic that there is a common heritage of story types and myths, of deep structures of feeling, genres of symbolic action and narrative trajectories that create recognizably European protagonists and destinies.

The chapter called "ImpersoNations" examines in more detail the fate of the concept of national cinema within film studies, showing how it is structured by successive theoretical assumptions such as essentialism, constructivism and hybridity that characterise the humanities discourse generally, at the intersection and border-crossing of paradigms that run from semiology, cultural studies to post-colonial theory. The debates around national cinema and the conflicting fields of essentialism and cultural constructivism also highlight differences in Europe between cinema and television, popular cinema and auteur cinema, including the difference between imaginary communities and historical imaginaries of post-colonialism and multi-culturalism already touched upon. In all these areas, the idea of the nation and the emotions associated with nationalism have gained new currency since 1989 and the end of the Cold War, without thereby imposing themselves in the manner of the 19th century nation state, or its critique by classical Marxism. On the contrary, it is the crisis of the nation state, transforming itself within the new political framework of the European Union, and being transformed by the demographic and de-territorialising forces of globalisation, that demands a re-assessment of the kinds of loyalties, affiliations but also the conflicting allegiances that bind individuals to their community, territory, region, language and culture, including film culture. A closer look at the idea of the state and the nation, as circulating in the political and historical realm, indicates that the weakened allegiance towards the nation state, so often perceived in the overall context of a lamented loss of civic virtue and refusal of solidarity, is a very contradictory phenomenon, because it is in fact underpinned by new imaginaries of belonging. In this context, the adjective "national" functions both as a catch-all and a temporary place holder, showing its porous fabric in the very gesture of being invoked. But like the family, the nation is a constant battlefield of contending claims and urgent calls for change, yet shows itself remarkably resilient, indispensable even, because questions of identity, allegiance, solidarity and belonging just do not go away.

The obvious question of the role of the media in these changes is posed, but only pursued insofar as it affects the cinema, its place in the new identity politics, but also its self-differentiation vis-à-vis television. From the cinema television took over the social function of addressing its audiences as the nation, a role which in turn drastically changed in the 1980s and 1990s, leaving both cinema and television to redefine their respective modes of address and social imaginaries. The essay on "British Television through the Looking Glass" registers the culture shock of a medium adapting itself from a public service remit to a mainly commercial service provider with, as I claim, decisive changes for our notion of society and the nation. The conclusion reached is that the "national" in European cinema functions since the 1980s at best as a second-order reference, and might well need to be redefined if not replaced altogether. With it, the concept of the "historical imaginary" may also have to be abandoned, less on methodological grounds, but because of the altered socio-historical context (consumer-culture) and media intertext (the increasing dependence of European cinema on public service television). They had made questionable the idea of the nation to which "national cinema" owed its theoretical articulation.

The third chapter draws the consequences of this insight, retaining the focus on national cinema and the auteur as second-order categories. It shifts perspective, however, by suggesting that these labels, and the practices they name, have for too long been abstracted from the historical ground on which they have grown, flourished and in the present conjuncture, re-aligned themselves. This historical ground, I argue, are the European film festivals. Notably those of Venice, Cannes, Berlin, and Rotterdam (at least until the 1990s, since when they are joined by other festivals, such as those of Toronto, Pusan, Sydney and Sundance) have between them been responsible for virtually all of the new waves, most of the auteurs and new national cinemas that scholars often assiduously try to define in essentialist, constructivist or relational terms, though rarely pointing out the particular logic of site, place and network embodied in the festival circuit, which so often gave them the necessary currency to begin with.

The other transformation that the chapter on film festivals tries to name extends the emphasis on site, place and network to include film production. Parallel to the festival site as the place for the discovery of new filmmakers and the moment where individual films acquire their cultural capital also for general audiences, it is location that makes European cinema perhaps not unique but nonetheless distinctive. In particular, cities and regions have superseded auteurs and nations as focal points for film production. Madrid, Marseille, Berlin, Glasgow, Edinburgh, but also the Ruhr Valley in Germany, the Midlands in Britain or the Danish village of Hvidovre have become peculiar post-industrial filmmaking hubs.[9] New media industries have played a key role in enabling certain regions to renew their economic base and reinvent themselves, by moving from traditional industries of producing goods to providing services. Areas once known for shipping, mining or steel production now advertise themselves as skill and enterprise centres for media industries. Cities market themselves on the strength of their photogenic locations or historical skylines, combining high-tech facilities with picturesque waterfront urban decay. Thus, another way of making a case for a distinct European cinema would be on the basis of such "location advantages", in the double sense of the word, as the conjunction of different forms of EU-funded urban redevelopment and new film financing schemes, coupled with a policy of using specific locations which have changed their economic character and their historical associations. Here, too, I present in outline some of the reference points that indicate interesting if also quite contradictory adjustments to globalisation which typify Europe without necessarily distinguishing it radically from other parts of the world.

The final chapter in this section draws some of the consequences for a definition of European cinema from the fact that Europe is usually considered as a special kind of topographic, geopolitical but also demographic space. (Western) Europe's wealth and prosperity over the past fifty years sometimes masks the degree to which it has always been made up of distinct regions, different ethnicities and tribes, many of whom have only relatively recently been brought together into nation-states. These in turn have for 150 years made war with each other, before deciding after yet another catastrophe in 1945 and once more since 1989, to forge the institutions that allow these different regions, languages, cultures, convictions and ethnicities to live in peace. Yet all the while, new demographic movements, at first from the former colonies, then from Southern Europe as cheap labor and finally as refugees, migrants or *sans papiers*, often persecuted at home, or looking for a better life of opportunity and prosperity, added to the mix that called itself the European Union, but which in fact began turning itself into a Fortress Europe. While the first generation of immigrants were mostly too engrossed in the struggle for survival, their children – the second generation – often took to more specifically cultural, symbolic and aesthetic forms of expression and affirmation of identity. Those marginalized or disenfranchised among the ethnic minority groups tend to give expression to their sense of exclusion by resorting to the symbolic language of violence, destruction and self-destruction. But others have also turned to the arts and voiced their aspirations and sense of identity-in-difference as musicians, writers and artists, with a substantial number among them taking up filmmaking. France, Britain and Germany in particular, have seen a veritable filmmaking renaissance thanks to second and third-generation directors from "minority" ethnic backgrounds: names such as Abdel Kechiche and Karim Dridi, Udayan Prasad and Gurinder Chadha, Fatih Akin and Thomas Arslan can stand for a much wider film-making as well as film-viewing community that crosses cultural and hyphenates ethnic borders. In "Double Occupancy" this particular configuration of multi-cultural filmmaking is regarded as typical for the new Europe, at least in the way it can be located at the fault-lines of a very specific European history of colonialism, re-settlement and migration. However, the chapter also sets out to delineate a concept that is intended, at least provisionally, to succeed that of the "historical imaginary", by suggesting that the mirror-relations and forms of "othering" typical of a previous period may be in the process of being superseded, as identity politics through boundary-drawing gives way to general recognition of co-habitation, mutual interference and mutual responsibility as necessary forms of a new solidarity and sense of co-existence. Here, many of the films that have had public success or received critical attention in recent years show themselves in advance of the political repertoire of ideas about European unity, by offering sometimes remarkably astute, moving and often also very witty comments on post-nation subjectivities and communities. In other words, while films such as AMELIE, DOGVILLE, TALK TO HER, RUN LOLA RUN, TRAIN-SPOTTING, HEAD ON or GOODBYE LENIN may seem too auteurist, too commercial or too typical for a given national cinema to count as "European", there is, I am suggesting, another way of reading them as precisely, "New European", in light of certain political scenarios and economic strategies actively pursued by the European Union, its politicians, pragmatists, visionaries but also its critics. They give a new urgency to filmmaking in Europe, which distinguishes it from television, as well as making it part also of world cinema – a perspective taken up in the concluding chapter of the collection.

Europe, Hollywood and "The Rest": The Ties that Bind and that Divide

The essays between the opening section and the conclusion follow to a large extent the trajectory thus charted, examining landmark figures of European authorship, the ever-present and much-resented impact of Hollywood, Europe's own others, and the post-colonial, post-historical legacies. Thus, the section which follows the re-appraisal of national cinema and the emergence of a European cinematic space turns its attention to the Europe-Hollywood-Europe divide, emphasizing the extent to which this usually binary relation of buried antagonisms and resentment actually functions not only as a two-way-traffic, but acts as an asymmetrical dynamic of exchange, whose purpose it is to stabilize the system by making both sides benefit from each other, paradoxically by making-believe that their regular and ritual stand-offs are based on incompatible antagonisms. As in politics so in matters cinema: what unites Europe and America is more than what divides them, not least of all because each needs the other: the insistence on the division often strengthens the underlying dynamism of the system of alliances.

This macro-study is followed by a more micro-analysis of a range of films and filmmakers who could be called independents, if the term still had much meaning, but whom I have grouped together as "films without a passport" – stateless, in-between, one-offs, happy accidents or near disasters, forming new spaces of collectivity and solidarity, and thus symptomatic for the "margins" and the different kinds of metabolism they invoke for the circulation and consumption of European film culture. The films named and discussed in the first sub-section about West European filmmakers and émigrés have to stand for a myriad of others, so that the selection is indeed more arbitrary than what is suggested by my claim of a deeper underlying representativeness. The second sub-section, dealing with films from Eastern Europe, wants to give a sampling of the possible ways in which East European film history may eventually be written together with and as an integral part of West European film history, without simply "adding" names, titles, styles and countries. Instead, their "accession" is a further reason why the entire landscape of European cinema has to be re-mapped. This evidently cannot be done in this collection, although the essays on festivals, on site, space and place have hopefully suggested some conceptual tools that might make it possible. To the three more recent essays on Konrad Wolf, Slavoj Žižek and on films that have come out of the Balkan wars of the 1990s, I have added an older essay on the unjustly neglected Dusan Makavejev, one of the more prescient Yugoslavian directors who acutely sensed both the strains within the Federation when most in the West had little sense of the disasters to come, and of the Western eyes already then felt to be upon the directors from Central Europe.

European Cinema: History and Memory

Makavejev's invocation of the Russian Revolution also makes a convenient transition to the following section "Europe Haunted by History", in which a number of issues are being touched upon which, especially during the 1980s and 1990s, have given European cinema – at least in retrospect – a remarkable unity of preoccupation if not of purpose, across victims and perpetrators, occupiers and occupied: the "working through" of the history of fascism, Nazism and of collaboration, acquiescence and resistance to these totalitarian regimes. What came to the fore was the subjective, often fascinated and even more often traumatized eye cast upon the period, castigated as nostalgic and retrograde by some (*la mode rétro*: Jean Baudrillard), and considered a necessary catharsis and coming to terms by others ("let's work on our memories": Edgar Reitz). While in France, Germany and Italy the concerns were with fascism or the Nazi occupation, in Britain the nostalgic/traumatic core was the loss of Empire, and the so-called heritage film as its compensatory supplement.

The concern with the colonial and postcolonial past was, until the 1990s, mainly reserved for Britain's relations with the Indian sub-continent and the West Indies. Since the 1990s it has surfaced in France as the return of its North-African colonial legacy, but there has also been a dimension of oblique and indirect communication between continental Europe's post-colonial attitude and Latin America, with a German and Italian inflection. On the one hand, it figures itself across a possibly "literary" heritage derived from Borges, Marquez and magic realism. On the other hand, it can also be read as a displaced identification of European filmmakers with Third Cinema as a proxy confrontation with Hollywood, at a time when the direct antagonism seemed to some directors neither accurate nor productive. In the chapter on "Hyper-, Retro- and Counter-cinema", I have picked Werner Herzog (I could have mentioned Wim Wenders' globe-trotting films) and Francesco Rosi (I could have chosen Gillo Pontecorvo), in order to confront them with Raoul Ruiz and Ruy Guerra, in a sort of oblique, indirect dialogue. Their films foreshadow thus the turn of both art cinema and Third Cinema into "world cinema" *avant la lettre*, which seemed an appropriate note on which to close the historical part of the collection.

These different shifts and re-alignments come together in a final chapter, in which I entertain the proposition – often expressed in the negative – that European cinema has become, in view of its declining impact and seeming provincialism, merely a part of "world cinema"- that category under which all kinds of cinematic works, from very diverse temporarily newsworthy or topical corners of the globe are gathered together: the "rest", in other words. My argument will be that, first of all, the category world cinema should be used and understood in its full contradictory sense, which includes the fact that these films, judged by the global impact of Hollywood or Asian cinemas, are precisely *not* world cinema, but a local produce, a token presence in the rarefied markets that are the film festivals or brief art-house releases. But I also want to make a virtue of the seemingly cynical or condescending euphemism that such a label implies, by suggesting a more post-Fordist model of goods, services and markets – made possible not least by the very different forms of distribution and circulation that the electronic media, and notably DVDs, the internet and other types of physical and virtual networks provide.[10] In this context, world cinema does indeed attain a positive significance, and furthermore, it may turn out to be a new way of understanding European cinema in its practice over the past twenty years or so, and define for it a terrain that it can usefully and productively occupy in the decades to come.

(2005)

Notes

1. Erich Pommer's Cinema Europe effort effectively ended with the negotiation of the Parufamet agreement, which however, proved disastrous for Ufa, the company he

headed as production chief. As Tom Saunders has pointed out, creating a united front against the Americans was in any case impossible, seeing how much European cinemas depended on American films: "For companies like Ufa which had partnerships with American firms, friendliness toward Hollywood had very concrete dimensions: they were not prepared to repudiate American liaisons in favor of either a vague European film community or specific, more limited agreements." Tom Saunders, "Germany and Film Europe," in A. Higson and R. Maltby (eds.), *Film Europe Film America: Cinema Commerce and Cultural Exchange* (Exeter University Press, 1999), 174.

2. The best known representative of this position is the economist Tyler Cowen, *Creative Destruction: How Globalization Is Changing the World's Cultures* (Princeton: Princeton University Press, 2003). See also his "French Kiss-Off: How Protectionism Has Hurt French Films, *Reason*, July 1998; accessed March 2005 at: http://reason.com/9807/fe.cowen.shtml

3. Details can be found on the Media website http://europa.eu.int/comm/avpolicy/media/index_en.html.

4. Thomas Elsaesser, *Weimar Cinema and After: Germany's Historical Imaginary* (London: Routledge, 2000), pp. 3-7.

5. Michael Tanssig, *Mimesis and Alterity* (New York: Routledge, 1993). Cornelius Castoriadis, *The Imaginary Institution of Society* (Cambridge, Mass: MIT Press, 1994), in which the Greek-French sociologist, according to the publisher's information "offers a far-reaching analysis of the unique character of the social-historical world and its relations to the individual, to language, and to nature".

6. "Two Decades in Another Country"(American Studies conference, University of East Anglia, 1971), "Primary Identification and the Historical Subject" (Milwaukee Conference, 1980), "Film History and Visual Pleasure: Weimar Cinema" (Asilomar, 1982), "Germany's Imaginary America: Wenders and Handke" (The Clark University-Luxembourg Conference, 1985), "Looking into a Two-Way Mirror" (The Mershon Center, Ohio University, 2002), "Our Balkanized Gaze" (Film Studies Conference, Yale University, 2003).

7. Andrew Higson, "The Concept of National Cinema" *Screen* vol. 30 no. 4, Autumn 1989, pp. 36-46.

8. A list of occasions and places of first publications for the essays can be found at the end of the volume.

9. "'It can be so depressing here in winter,' says our driver, Danish film director Lone Scherfig, as she parks up in the muddy trail outside her office cabin. 'But it's even worse when people put flowers out. It looks like a concentration camp!' This place is Filmbyen, or Film Town, in the Danish suburb of Hvidovre, a thriving movie village that, in its six years, has revolutionised the local economy. One might argue that it has achieved even more. Since November 1997 this has been the central base of operations for Lars von Trier, perhaps the most influential film director working in Europe, and his company, Zentropa Productions.", Damon Wise "No Dane no Gain", *The Observer*, 12 October 2003.

10. On the new world communities of cinephiles, see Marijke de Valck and Malte Hagener (eds.), *Cinephilia: Movies, Love and Memory* (Amsterdam: Amsterdam University Press, 2005).

National Cinema

Re-Definitions and New Directions

European Culture, National Cinema, the Auteur and Hollywood

"The only thing the 238 nations of Europe have in common is America"
John Naughton, *The Observer*[1]

"Living in the 20th century means learning to be American"
Dusan Makavejev[2]

Europe: The Double Perspective

From these two quotations one might derive a somewhat fanciful proposition. What if – at the end of the 19th century – Europe had been discovered by America rather than America being "discovered" by the Europeans at the end of the 15th century? Counterfactual as this may seem, in a sense this is exactly what did happen, because with Henry James, Ernest Hemingway, Henry Miller, Gertrud Stein, Josephine Baker and so many other US American writers, musicians, and artists exiling themselves temporarily or permanently in "Europe," they gave a name to something that before was France, Britain, Germany, Spain, or Italy.[3]

So, there is a double perspective on Europe today: One from without (mainly American), where diversity of geography, language, culture tends to be subsumed under a single notion, itself layered with connotations of history, artworks, the monuments of civilization and the sites of high culture, but also of food and wine, of tourism and the life style of leisure (*dolce far niente, luxe, calme et volupté*). The other perspective is the one from within (often, at least until a few years ago, synonymous with Western Europe, the Common Market countries): the struggle to overcome difference, to grow together, to harmonize, to tolerate diversity while recognizing in the common past the possible promise of a common "destiny." There is a sense that with the foundation, consolidation and gradual enlargement of the European Union, these definitions, even in their double perspective, are no longer either adequate or particularly useful. Hence the importance of once more thematizing European culture, European cinema, and European identity at the turn of the millennium, which in view of US world hegemony, globalization, and the end of the bipolar world model, may well come to be seen as the only "European" millennium of world history.

The cinema, which celebrates its centenary, is both a French (Lumiere) and an American (Edison) invention. A hundred years later, these two countries – as the GATT accords (or discords) have shown – are still locked in a struggle as to the definition of cinema – a cultural good and national heritage or a commodity that should be freely traded and open to competition. That France should take the lead in this is partly due to the fact that it is also the only European country still to possess something like a national film industry *and* a film culture.

National Cinema

It has often been remarked that in order to talk about a "national cinema" at all, one always tries to conjure up a certain coherence, in the first instance, that of the Nation. In this respect, it is quite clearly a notion with a lot of historical and even more so, ideological ballast. A nation, especially when used in a context that suggests cultural identity, must repress differences of class, gender, race, religion, and history in order to assert its coherence, and is thus another name for internal colonization. Nationhood and national identity are not given, but gained, not inherited, but paid for. They exist in a field of force of inclusion and exclusion, as well as resistance and appropriation.

National cinema also functions largely by more or less appropriate analogy. If we take the economic definition, it is like the "gross national product" or the "national debt." But it is also like the "national railway system" or the "national monuments": in the first instance a descriptive or taxonomical category. With the last analogy, however, another meaning comes into view. Like the national opera company, or the national ballet, national cinema usually means that it is or wants to be also an institution (officially, or at least semi-officially), enjoying state patronage and, when defined as culture, often receiving substantial state support. Thus it implies an economic relationship, and indeed, historically, the cinemas of Europe have been part of their nations' political economy ever since the middle of the First World War, when the moving pictures' propaganda value was first seen in action. Since then, governmental measures, encompassing taxation and tariffs, censorship and city ordinances have legalized but also legitimized the public sphere that is national cinema, making both the concept and the state's relation to it oscillate between an industrial and a cultural definition. That this definition has come under pressure since the 1970s is evident: the dismantling of welfare states, privatization, deregulation and the transformation of the media and communication networks under commercial and market principles have been the single most important factors that have put the idea of a national cinema in crisis.

The International Market

What could be said to be the lowest common denominator, the default values of national cinema? It may mean nothing more historically precise or metaphysically profound than the economic conditions under which filmmakers in a given country try to work. It functions as part of an industry required to turn a profit, as artisans selling individually crafted objects in a volatile market, or as artists, sponsored by the state and its cultural institutions, representing a cultural vision.

However, when looked at as an industry, the cinema is not a national, but an international business, in which, as it happens, different nations do not compete on the same terms. For instance, the only cinema which for long stretches of its history has been able to operate profitably as a national one – the American cinema – is not usually referred to as a national cinema at all, but has become synonymous with the international film business, if not with "the cinema" *tout court*. It suggests that "national cinema" is actually not descriptive, but the subordinate term within a binary pair whose dominant and referred point (whether repressed or implied) is always Hollywood. If this international film business draws attention to the economic realities of film production in competition for the world's spectators, the term "national cinema" may disguise another binarism: an auteur cinema as sketched above can be more virulently opposed to its own national cinema commercial film industry than it is to Hollywood films. Such was the case with the *nouvelle vague* or the second generation of New German filmmakers: the *"politique des auteurs"* of Truffaut, Rohmer and Chabrol, or Wim Wenders' and Fassbinder's cinephilia were based on a decided preference of Hollywood over their own national cinema.

Wim Wenders

The paradox arises because national cinema presupposes a perspective that takes the point of view of production – the filmmakers', the film industry's – when promoting or selling films at international festivals. What is generally not included in the meaning are the preferences of audiences, and therefore, the "nationality" of a country's film culture. A moment's reflection shows that no one who goes to the cinema has a "national" film culture; or rather, everyone's national film culture as opposed to a national cinema is both multi-national and cross-generic: high-profile Hollywood block-busters, films on release in the art-cinemas around town, star vehicles and *films d'auteur*. For a country's film culture, national provenance is important in much the same way as the label stitched on my sweater or trainers: I show my brand loyalty and advertise my taste. The situation is altogether different if we were considering television, where there is indeed something like a "national audience," just as there is "national television." But precisely to the degree that one is talking about a "national cinema," one is not talking about audiences, but filmmakers: a fact that runs the risk of leaving one with a one-sided, if not esoteric point of view.

For in the international film business, the idea of national cinema has a very contradictory status: While Hollywood product dominates most countries' domestic markets, as well as leading internationally, each national cinema is both national and international, though in different areas of its sphere of influence. Nationally, it participates in the popular or literary culture at large (the New German Cinema's predilection for filmed literature, the intellectual cult status of French directors such as Bresson, Truffaut, Rivette, Rohmer; the acceptance of Fellini, Antonioni, or Francesco Rosi as Italy's sacred monsters). Internationally, national cinemas used to have a generic function in the way that a French, Swedish or Italian film conveyed a set of expectations for the general audience which were mirror images to those of Hollywood genres. Italian cinema used to mean big busts and bare thighs – and this in films that the more high-brow critics thought of as the glories of Neo-Realism: ROME OPEN CITY, OSSESSIONE, RISO AMARO. As the ubiquitous Guilio Andreotti recommended, when he was Italy's movie czar in the late 1940s: *Meno stracci, pui gambe* (less rags, more legs).[4]

From the perspective of Hollywood, on the other hand, it makes little difference whether one is talking about the Indian cinema or the Dutch cinema, the French cinema or the Chilean cinema: none is a serious competitor for America's domestic output, but each national cinema is a "market" for American films, with Hollywood practices and norms having major consequences for the national production sector. In most countries this has led to different forms of protectionism, bringing into play state intervention and government legislation, but usually to very little avail, especially since the different national cinemas, however equal they may seem before Hollywood, are of course emphatically unequal among themselves, and locked into yet another form of competition with each other when they enter the European market.

Yet paradoxically, a national cinema is precisely something which relies for its existence on a national exhibition sector at least as much as it does on a national production sector; without Hollywood, no national exhibition sector; without a national exhibition sector, i.e., cinemas, whether privately run or state-subsidized prepared to show independent releases, you cannot have a national cinema. This is a truth that some national cinemas discovered to their cost: until an American major had put money into distributing a Wenders or a Herzog film world-wide, their films could not be seen by German audiences. In a sense, they had to become Hollywood (or at least Miramax or Buena Vista), before they could return home to Europe as representatives of their national cinema.

Colonization, Self-Colonization and Significant Others

What could in the 1990s, be at stake in renewing a debate about national cinema? If the struggle over "realism" (the social and political stakes in "representation," whether individual or collective, or the importance of documentation as record and reference) has moved to television, then it is there that the "national" (in the sense I defined it above as exclusion and inclusion, appropriation and consensus) is now being negotiated. As a consequence, the "national cinemas" task may well be to set themselves off even more decisively from their realist traditions, and engage the Americans at their own level: weightlifting onto the screens the mythologies of two-and-a-half thousand years of European civilization, bringing to the surface the collective unconscious of individual nations at particular points in their history (which is what one of the pioneers of the study of national cinema, Siegfried Kracauer, in *From Caligari to Hitler*,[5] was claiming that the Weimar cinema did for Germany in the period between the world wars), or giving expression to the more delicate pressure points of communal life in times of transition, crisis and renewal (as the new waves from neo-realism to the New German Cinema were doing from the late 1940s to the early 1980s).

KINGS OF THE ROAD

In Wim Wenders' KINGS OF THE ROAD, perhaps the finest of films from the 1970s to meditate about a "national cinema," one of the protagonists, contemplating the barbed-wire fence then still separating East and West, half-jokingly, half-regretfully agrees that "The Yanks have colonized our sub-conscious." We can take this perhaps by now over-used phrase in two directions: we can turn it around and say, yes, the national, even in Europe, has become a "colonial" term. Only a state that can admit to and make room for the multi-cultural, the multi-layered within its own hybridities can henceforth claim to be a nation, and therefore only films that are prepared to explore hybridities, in-between states, the self-in-the-other can be in the running for a national cinema. This may finally give a chance to those filmmaking nations at the margins of cultures by which they feel colonized. For instance, the Australian and New Zealand cinema, which in the 1990s has, with CROCODILE DUNDEE on the one hand, and AN ANGEL AT MY TABLE or THE PIANO on the other, quite successfully portrayed the comic and the poignant sides of its *angst* as colonized (cinema) cultures.

The second thought that occurs, when hearing that "The Yanks have colonized our unconscious" is the example of directors like Wenders himself, who was only identified in his own country as a filmmaker with typically German subjects after he had been recognized by his "American friends." But it is not all on the side of the colonizers. If one takes, for instance, Black Cinema in the US in the figure of the filmmaker Spike Lee, or even Italo-American directors like Francis Ford Coppola, one might well be tempted to regard their emphasis on ethnicity as a new national cinema inside the international cinema. However, as Spike Lee has remarked: "If Hollywood has a color problem, it's neither white nor black nor yellow, it's green – the color of the dollar." What he presumably also meant by this jibe is that the chances of blacks making films in Hollywood depend neither on their color, nor their talent, nor even on the size of the black audience: Hollywood's huge budgets have made it so dependent on its exports that for the first time in its history, it can no longer amortize its films on the home market. Yet in its export markets (the largest of which are Great Britain, Italy, France, Germany, along with Japan, Australia and Canada) audiences are apparently very resistant to non-white heroes. Thus, Hollywood has itself been "colonized" by its "European" or "national" audiences, except that Hollywood's dependency on its exports is a fact not exploited by those audiences to put pressure on Hollywood, since they have in common nothing except that they are Hollywood's export markets.

On the face of it, then, national cinema can no longer be thought of in the traditional terms, but only in the context of these place-shifts and time-shifts, the cultural palimpsests that connect the ever-expanding, constantly self-differentiating field of media representations which is the contemporary everyday of movies, television, advertising. In this situation, national cinema becomes a doubly displaced category. It is at best a retrospective effect, so to speak, one that only posterity can confer, as it sifts through the nation's active and passive image bank, hoping to discover the shape of its superego or its id. But national cinema is also a displaced category, insofar as this is a shape, whether monstrous, pleasing or only mildly disfigured, that can only be recognized from without. The label national cinema has to be conferred on films by others, either by other national or "international" audiences, or by national audiences, but at another point in time. Defined by other critics, by other audiences, these mirror images are tokens of a national or personal identity only if this other is, as the phrase goes, a "significant other." Given the mutual dependencies just sketched, Europe (standing in the field of cinema metonymically for European film festivals and the critical or theoretical discourses these produce) is as much a significant other for Hollywood or Asia, as the United States is a significant other for European audiences.

Two European Cinemas: Art-House vs. Genre Cinema, Art-House as Genre Cinema?

In the case of the French film industry, the fact remains that in the period of the *nouvelle vague* of the 1960s, for every Truffaut and Godard, France had to make a BORSALINO (a thriller with Alain Delon), or in the 1970s, co-produce a FRENCH CONNECTION (with Gene Hackman and directed by William Friedkin), and in the 1980s, for every Jacques Rivette making LA BELLE NOISEUSE, and every Eric Rohmer making LE RAYON VERT, there had to be a Claude Berri making a JEAN DE FLORETTE or a Jean Paul Rappenau making a CYRANO DE BERGERAC.

Some European art cinema directors have understood this position of Hollywood and of their own popular cinema as the "significant other" quite well. In fact, one can almost divide European national cinemas between those which in the overt discourse deny it, only to let it in through the back door (such as the Italian cinema in the 1950s and 1960s, or the first wave of the New German Cinema in the 1960s), and those who acknowledge it, by trying to define themselves around it. The directors of the *nouvelle vague* in the early 1960s, who developed the auteur theory not for themselves, but for the Hollywood directors who were their idols like John Ford, Howard Hawks, and Sam Fuller, whom they sometimes used as sticks to beat their own well-mannered gentleman directors with, shouting "Papa's cinema is dead" at the scriptwriter team Jean Aurenche and Pierre Bost, and directors like René Clément, Claude Autant-Lara and Jean Delannois.

In the case of the New German directors of the second wave, they appropriated and acknowledged Hollywood in an even more intimate form: they "adopted" some of the key directors as elective father figures: Douglas Sirk was adopted by Rainer W. Fassbinder, Fritz Lang and Nicholas Ray by Wim Wenders. The twist being that some of these American directors were of course originally German directors who had gone into exile, and Nick Ray was a director who had self-exiled himself from the studio system in the 1960s. Thus, national cinema becomes, on the one hand, a pseudo-oedipal drama around paternity and father-son relationships, and on the other, a matter of exile, self-exile and return. All this acknowledges that a sense of identity for many European film directors since the 1960s has only been possible by somehow re-articulating the debt to Hollywood and the American cinema, by recognizing themselves within the history of this cinema, and identifying with its legacy, if only in order to rebel against it, as did Jean-Luc Godard since the 1970s and Wim Wenders since the late 1980s.

Some among the generation of European directors of the 1990s, on the other hand, neither repress the presence of Hollywood, nor feel filial piety towards it. They play with it, quote it, use it, imitate it – in short, they use it as their second nature, alongside all kinds of other references and styles. They know that image and identity are a slippery pair, traversing and criss-crossing in rather complex ways geographical territory, linguistic boundaries, history, subjectivity, pleasures remembered and longings anticipated. And there is a good historical reason for it, which is also important for our idea of national cinema. For as mentioned above, national cinema does not only refer to a nation's film production, it also must include what national audiences see. Besides a European country's art and auteur cinema, there are the commercial productions, and there is Hollywood, occupying in most European countries the lion's share of the box office. Finally, one needs to add another player, the avant-garde cinema whose filmmakers, however, have almost always refused the label national cinema, because they saw themselves as both international and anti-Hollywood.

Pictures of Europe

Behind the question about the fate of the cinema in the 1990s lurks another one, debated for almost as long as the cinema has existed, aired afresh every year at the film festivals of Cannes, Venice or Berlin, at FELIX award ceremonies and MEDIA initiatives: the future of the European cinema vis-à-vis Hollywood (whether viewed across France's passionate attachment to its cinematic patrimony, or more dispassionately, across the uneven, but nonetheless two-way "talent transfer").

In 1992, a Channel Four program called "Pictures of Europe" neatly assembled all the standard arguments, voiced with varying degrees of pessimism, by David Puttnam and Richard Attenborough, Bertrand Tavernier and Paul Verhoeven, Fernando Rey and Dirk Bogarde, Agnès Varda, Wim Wenders, and Istvan Szabo. One of the least sentimental was Dusan Makavejev, who has probably more reason than most to be wary of the idea of national cinema, but who also needs to believe in the international auteur cinema more than others. Yet he dismissed the suggestion that he might be threatened by Hollywood: "If you can't stand the heat, get out of the kitchen. Living in the 20th century meant learning to be American." On the other hand, Tavernier (whose knowledge about and love of the American cinema is probably second to none, noted the following in his diary for 23 February 1992 about the *César* Awards of that year:

> One grotesque and distressing moment comes when Sylvester Stallone is given an honorary *César* by a sarcastic Roman Polanski. A few days previously, Jack Lang had, in a discouragingly idiotic gesture, made him Knight of Arts and Letters, even going so far as to assert that the name Rambo had been chosen in honor of Rimbaud (Arthur).... The height of irony: I'd be willing to bet that the people who made these ludicrous awards have not the slightest familiarity with the only interesting film that Stallone has directed, the curious PARADISE ALLEY. [6]

Tavernier's final, typically cinéphile remark reminds us that in academic film studies, the Europe-Hollywood-Europe question mediated across the *nouvelle vague*'s love of the Hollywood *film maudit* is almost like the founding myth of the discipline itself. European (French) director-critics discriminating among the vast studio output, according to very European criteria, by creating a canon of Hollywood masterpieces eagerly adopted in turn by American critics and film-makers alike. But the relation between Europe and Hollywood can also be made (and has been made) as a hard-nosed economic case, for instance, in Thomas Guback's chapter in Tino Balio's *The American Film Industry,*[7] or in Kristin Thompson's fascinatingly detailed *Exporting Entertainment,*[8] and most recently, in Ian Jarvie's *Hollywood's Overseas Campaign.*[9] The post-1945 history of the relation was also probed in 1996, at two UCLA- and BFI-sponsored conferences in London and Los Angeles,[10] while the formal case of how to make the distinction has been debated among scholars of "early cinema" such as Noel Burch[11] and Barry Salt[12] around the opposition "deep staging and slow cutting" (Europe) versus "shallow staging and fast cutting" (Hollywood), and it has been argued as a difference of storytelling by, among others, David Bordwell in his influential *Narration and the Fiction Film,* where character-centered causality, question-and-answer logic, problem solving routines, deadline structures of the plot, and a mutual cueing system of word, sound and image are seen as typical for Hollywood films, against the European cinema's more de-centered plots, indirect and psychological motivation and "parametric" forms of narration.[13]

Interestingly enough, even in the television program just mentioned, the formal-stylistic opposition Europe versus Hollywood, art cinema versus classical narrative recurs, but now in the terms in which it has been echoed ever since the 1920s from the point of view of Hollywood, which has always complained that European pictures have no credible stars and central protagonists, or in their editing are much too slow for American audiences' tastes. This point is taken up by many of the European directors and actors who have worked in both industries: Paul Verhoeven and Jean Jacques Annaud see American speed as positive qualities, as do J.J. Beneix, Krzysztof Zanussi, Luc Besson. David Puttnam and Pedro Almodóvar are more even-handed, while Fernando Rey and Dirk Bogarde prefer the slower delivery of dialogue and the less hectic action of the European cinema, as do – not surprisingly – Wim Wenders and Bertrand Tavernier. Among the actors, it is Liv Ullmann who eloquently speaks out against Hollywood forms of action, violence and the externalization of motive and emotion.

Paul Schrader, on the other hand, who has probably thought as deeply about style in European cinema as anyone,[14] argued that the conflict between Europe and Hollywood boiled down to a fundamentally different attitude toward the world, from which comes a different kind of cinema: "American movies are based on the assumption that life presents you with problems, while European films are based on the conviction that life confronts you with dilemmas – and while problems are something you solve, dilemmas cannot be solved, they're merely probed." Schrader's distinction puts a number of pertinent features in a nutshell. His statement might even serve as a basis for teasing out some of the formal and theoretical implications. For instance, his assessment is not that far removed from the view of Gilles Deleuze, who in his Bergson-inspired study of the cinema proposes a more dynamic, and self-differentiating version of Jean-Luc Godard's old distinction between "action" and "reflection" (the opening lines of LE PEITIT SOLDAT), contrasting instead the movement-image of classical cinema with the time-image of modern cinema.[15]

To these different taxonomies of the Hollywood/Europe divide one can reply that the problem-solving model of Hollywood cinema is not intended to characterize a filmmaker's personal belief. It does, however, function largely as the norm that underlies the expectations of both kinds of audiences, American as well as European, when it comes to cinema-going as a story-telling experience. Hollywood mainstream or "classical" films are the dominant because they are made ("tailored" was the term already used by King Vidor in the late 1920s) around increasingly global audiences, while non-Hollywood cinemas have to find their audiences at the margins of the mainstream (the so-called "art-house" audiences), for they cannot even rely on the loyalty of their respective "national" audiences. There is another point, a cliché perhaps, but for that very reason, in need of being stated: European filmmakers are said to *express themselves*, rather than *address an audience*. I do not think that this is in fact the case (I have argued against it at length in a book on *New German Cinema*). For instance, if by following Schrader, one assumes that the European art cinema merely sets its audiences different kinds of tasks, such as inferring the characters' motivations (as in Ingmar Bergman's THE SILENCE), reconstructing a complex time scheme (as in the same director's CRIES AND WHISPERS), or guessing what actually happened and what was projected or imagined in a character's consciousness (as in PERSONA), then the difference could also be one of genre, and thus of the horizon of expectation and the regime of verisimilitude appropriate to a genre. The "tasks" which an art film sets the audience are intuitively recognized by most spectators. That they decide either to avoid them as an unpleasant chore or to seek them out as a challenge, depending on temperament and disposition, is an altogether other matter. It furthermore serves as a reminder that among the audiences watching European art films there have always also been a small but culturally highly significant number of American spectators. In fact, it was the US distribution practice of the "art-house" circuit, which gave the term "art cinema" its currently accepted meaning.

PERSONA

A Map of Misreadings?

But this maybe the rub, and the point where a "cultural" view differs from the cognitive case around narrative comprehension. By the logic of reception studies, it is ultimately the various nationally or geographically distinct audiences who decide how a film is to be understood, and they often take their cue not only from title, poster, actors or national origin, but from the place where a film is shown, in which case, an art film is simply every film at an art-house cinema, including old Hollywood movies, as happens with Nicholas Ray or Sam Fuller retrospectives: the cinema, one and indivisible, as a young Jean-Luc Godard once proclaimed when refusing to endorse these binary oppositions. To claim that European art cinema is mostly a genre, whose identity is decided by the pragmatic decision of where to see a given film and with what internalized expectations, may be something of a lame definition, after all the high hopes invested in such notions as national cinema, "new waves" and the *film d'auteur*. Yet such an argument has at least the advantage that it avoids the (misleading) tautology, according to which a European art movie is a movie made by European artists. Viewing the Hollywood/Europe divide as merely the special case of a more general process of generic differentiation, where films are valued, canonized, or have re-assigned to them identities and meanings according to often apparently superficial or secondary characteristics, can be very instructive indeed. For these characteristics provide on closer inspection a detailed and often sophisticated map of movie culture, which ignores all kinds of stylistic or formal boundaries, but speaks eloquently about the life of films in history.

One could even call it, borrowing from the literary critic Harold Bloom, a "map of misreadings."[16] European films intended for one kind of (national) audience, or made within a particular kind of aesthetic framework or ideology, undergo a sea change as they cross the Atlantic, and on coming back, find themselves bearing the stamp of yet another cultural currency. The same is true of some Hollywood films. What the auteur theory saw in them was not what the studios or even the directors "intended," but this did not stop another generation of American viewers appreciating exactly what the *Cahiers du cinéma* critics had extracted from them.

In such a case, the old idea of European films as "expressive" of their respective national identity would appear to be rather fanciful and even more far-fetched than the notion that European auteurs are only interested in self-expression. It would suggest that "national cinema" quite generally, makes sense only as a relation, not as an essence, being dependent on other kinds of filmmaking, such as commercial/international, to which it supplies the other side of the coin and thus functions as the subordinate term. Yet a national cinema by its very definition, must not know that it is a relative or negative term, for then it would lose its virginity, so to speak, and become that national whore who prostitutes herself, which is, in France or Great Britain at least, the reputation of the heritage film.

Instead, the temptation persists to look beyond the binary oppositions, towards something that defines it positively – for instance, that of a national history as counter-identity. Such might be the case with the films of Zhang Yimou's RAISE THE RED LANTERN or Chen Kaige's FAREWELL MY CONCUBINE, fanning out towards a broader festival and media interest in Chinese, Hong Kong, and Taiwanese cinema since the mid-1980s, where (to us Europeans) complicated national and post-colonial histories set up tantalizing fields of differentiation, self-differentiation and positions of protest. For these films, international (i.e., European) festivals are the markets that can fix and assign different kinds of value, from touristic, politico-voyeuristic curiosity to auteur status conferred on the directors. Festivals such as Berlin and Rotterdam set in motion the circulation of new cultural capital, even beyond the prospect of economic circulation (art cinema distribution, a television sale) by motivating critics to write about them and young audiences to want to study them in university seminars.

One conceivable conclusion to be drawn is that both the old Hollywood hegemony argument (whether justified on economic or stylistic grounds) and the "postmodern" or "pragmatic" paradigm ("it is what audiences make of films that decides their identity and value") tend to hide a perhaps more interesting relationship, namely that of national cinemas and Hollywood not only as communicating vessels, but (to change the metaphor) existing in a space set up like a hall of mirrors, in which recognition, imaginary identity and mis-cognition enjoy equal status, creating value out of pure difference.

Auteurs and Artists

As the longevity of assignations such as neo-realism, *nouvelle vague*, New German Cinema, New Basque cinema proves, the diversity of national cinematic traditions within European cinema is impressive, and there is good reason to study them individually and in their particularity. But this insistence on both national specificity and the (relative) autonomy of film movements since 1945 in European countries nonetheless leaves several factors unaccounted for: Firstly, the national movements and *auteur* cinemas are by no means the only traditions in the countries named. For instance, in the France of the 1960s and 70s, for instance, there were also the cop films with Jean Paul Belmondo, the thrillers with Alain Delon, and Luis de Funès comedies; in Germany the *Heimat*-films, the Karl May films, the Edgar Wallace crime films; in Britain the CARRY ON films, the Hammer horror movies, the James Bond films; in Italy Spaghetti Western and Dino Risi comedies. Are these not part of European cinema?

Secondly, even if we add these to our list of fine European achievements, their impact on the American cinema at the box office is close to zero. In any given year, among the US box office top hundred, less than two percent come from European films of whatever category, be it art cinema or commercial productions. For the American cinema, Europe exists not as so many film-producing nations, but as a market, conceived indeed in single European terms: even if, for the purpose of advertising and promotion, different countries need a little fine-tuning of the campaigns.[17] But Europe is for Hollywood one of the biggest, most important markets, which is why the producers go to Cannes and Venice, rather than Cairo or Hong Kong, for their film festivals. And this is also why the French are so concerned in the world trade negotiations: in 1981, 50 percent of the French box office was earned by French films, in 1991 it was 35 percent with 60% going to Hollywood. Other European countries wish they were so lucky: in Britain 88% of box office is US-earned, and in Germany less than 6 percent of the grosses are from German films, and this includes co-productions.

National Cinema, then, is a notion at the intersection of several quite distinct discourses: to the differential ones already mentioned, one has to add the echoes of the debates around nationhood and national identity in the 19th century, themselves historically inseparable from the rise of the bourgeoisie and its self-styled ideal of a national culture. The latter, usually embodied by literature and print culture, is to this day seen in opposition to mass culture, consumer culture, and therefore by and large, excludes the cinema (as image culture and popular entertainment). This literary legacy gives us another implied semantic field regarding European filmmakers. Those who belong to a national cinema have to strive after a certain status, or demonstrate a pedigree that confirms them as members of the establishment, which is to say as either "artists," "bohemians," or "dissidents," perhaps with a reputation as writers or painters, who via the cinema appropriate or discover another medium for self-expression. Peter Greenaway and Derek Jarman come to mind, or Peter Handke and Peter Weiss, besides the names of the classic European directors: Bergman, Fellini, Antonioni, Wenders, Syberberg, Herzog. Dependent as artists are on state institutions, the art world and the culture industries, such painters, writers, critics, photographers and theatre directors turned filmmakers become *auteurs* – someone who is present both inside and outside his or her creation, by virtue of both a multimedial creative talent and a (self-)analytical public discourse.

I have elsewhere discussed the longevity, complexity, and contemporary transformations of the category of the *auteur*.[18] With some assistance from their American friends, notably Andrew Sarris,[19] the *Cahiers du cinéma* critics effectively helped to rewrite the history of Hollywood, and the view has – despite some violent changes in French intellectual temper between 1968 and 1975 – prevailed to a remarkable degree to this day, identifying the canon of what is considered to be Auteur cinema and its Great Tradition.

The *auteur* theory points to one fundamental property of the European cinema. It has, certainly since the end of the First World War (but especially since 1945), given us any number of portraits of the artist as culture hero, as representative, as stand-in and standard bearer of the values and aspirations of his culture, its better half:

> Every page [of John Boorman's diary] is provocative and stimulating, whether he is talking about his dealings with the Disney executives (that line of Jeffrey Katzenberg's, talking about *Where the Heart Is*: "The trouble is, it's still a John Boorman film. It is not a Disney picture"!) [...]. I'm bowled over by the account of his last meeting with David Lean. How could you ever forget that heartbreaking statement of victory, which Lean muttered to Boorman shortly before he died: "Haven't we been lucky? They let us make movies." And when Boorman answered: "They tried to stop us," Lean added: "Yes, but we fooled them."[20]

This is the image of the *auteur* as Prometheus, defying the Gods. That it should be adopted by a director like David Lean, whom the critics of *Movie* (the British version of *Cahiers du cinéma* in the 1960s) considered the very epitome of their

Cinéma a Papa (from BRIEF ENCOUNTER and GREAT EXPECTATIONS, to DR ZHIVA-
GO and RYAN'S DAUGHTER) shows just how pervasive the self-assessment of the
film director as auteur, and the *auteur* as artist-rebel, has become. Other self-
images that are immediately recognizable comprise Bergman's portraying himself as magician and demiurge, even charlatan in his autobiography, but also in
some of his films; Fellini: a volcano pouring forth a stream of fantastic creatures,
poignant memories amidst life's carnival; Godard: forever engaged in work-in-
progress, to be torn up by his next film; Rainer W. Fassbinder: the cinema is a
holy whore, and I'm her pimp; Peter Greenaway: the film auteur as draftsman,
architect, Prospero, cook, thief and lover; Werner Herzog: Prometheus and Kaspar Hauser, over-reacher and underdog, Tarzan and Parzifal. Under the name
and label of *auteur*, therefore, can hide the artist, the gloomy philosopher, the
neurotic businessman, the conquistador, holy fool, court jester, courtly draftsman, wanderer-between-the-worlds, black-marketeer and go-between. Filmmakers as diverse as Pasolini, Antonioni, Tarkowski, Wenders, Angelopoulos,
and others have given in their work and across their male protagonists more or
less honest self-portraits, inflecting them ironically or inflating them pompously,
using the filmic fable as the mirror for their selves as doubles or alter-egos.

Cinema and Myth

What retains my attention is not the incurably romantic nature of these self-
images, but two structural features: firstly, the contours of the myth they trace,
and the social metaphysics they imply. Secondly, the tacit assumption that the
depiction, however metaphysical, allegorical or self-referential, of the artist and
the labors of creation has a redemptive power for the society, as represented by
the audience and as present through the audience. In the wings of these self-
portraits, in other words, hovers the shadow of sacrifice and the sacred.

First, the contours of the myth, or rather, the family of myths. The European
auteur cinema basically knows three kinds of heroes who are close cousins:
Odysseus, Orpheus and Parzifal – in other words, quest heroes, wanderers who
are often enough prepared to sacrifice a Eurydice on the way, before they –
reluctantly – return to Penelope, who in any case, is really their mother. This is
in sharp contrast to the American cinema which is a relentlessly, obsessively
oedipal cinema, where the hero always engages the father, usually eliminates
him, and eventually sleeps with his mother, though not before assuring himself
that she is his best buddy. The only Oedipal hero in the European cinema, cut in
this mold is perhaps Fritz Lang's Siegfried – and he is felled and pierced by the
paternal spear.

I could phrase the preceding thought somewhat less ironically by recalling that in the Hollywood cinema there are always two plots: the adventure plot and the romance plot (the formation of the heterosexual couple). In the European cinema, we also have two plots: the *Bildungsroman* plot – the story of an education – and the story of the impossibility of the couple. One could even go a little further and say that the Hollywood myth traces and retraces the story of a city builder, a founder and himself in turn a future father. The Orpheus or Odysseus myth, on the other hand, is the story of a survivor, of a son, and even of an orphan who must go home again, who cannot go home again: the heroes of, once more, Fellini, Bertolucci, Wenders, Herzog, and Angelopoulos.[21]

What seems to have happened in the 1990s – on this quasi-anthropological level of narrative and mythic configuration – is that none of these secularized mythologies are still strong enough to support a problematic that engages with contemporary realities. This may be as true of the American cinema as it is of Europe: what we find in Hollywood (especially since Spielberg, but also in Scorsese) is the fatherless society, with male orphans everywhere, or in Robert Zemeckis and Tim Burton, peopled by corrupt fathers without credibility. The European mythology is in crisis, no doubt because it is evidently a historical one, that of losers, survivors of a catastrophe, and also because it is just as evidently a gendered one, and an a-symmetrically gendered one (which is to say, not as "reversible" as in so many Hollywood patriarchal stories, with their perfect symmetries, where in melodrama, horror, and sci-fi the empowered female has made a remarkable showing). In the European mythic universe of both art cinema and popular productions, the social metaphysics of the traditional heroes and of the mythic figures that stand behind them, no longer command assent: which may be no more than saying that they belong to the realm of high culture and the Christian version of redemption and transcendence, rather than popular culture.

But I do not altogether think this is correct. Something else is at stake as well. A popular entertainment form like the cinema must have the loyalties of the masses, however we define them. And the fact is that the American cinema still does (or has once more captured them), and that the European cinema, whether it is the commercial or the art cinema variant, no longer does and has. As explanation, the conspiracy theory, or the colonization and media imperialism thesis do not provide convincing proof. One can think of two other entertainment forms, sports and popular music. They command mass popularity and loyalty, and they are by no means American imports: Soccer is a European and Latin American passion, and a good deal of popular music still comes from Britain rather than the US, though the cross-breeding from blues and rock-n-roll to the Rolling Stones or Eric Clapton is at least as complex a story as that of Hollywood and the European cinema. Why the apparent absence of resonance at the deeper mytho-poetic level, why this exhaustion of the structuring metaphors and cultural narratives the European cinema used to live by?

Auteur, Brand Name, Sacrificial Hero

Since the late 1980s, the image of the *auteur* cinema has changed dramatically. The *auteur* may not be dead, but the meaning of what or who is an *auteur* has shifted considerably: for Europe and America, not self-doubt nor self-expression, not metaphysical themes, nor a realist aesthetic are what makes a director an *auteur*. The themes that still identified an Ingmar Bergman as an *auteur* would today be mere affectations, a personal tic, noted by critics in passing. Instead, *auteurs* now dissimulate such signatures of selfhood, even where they believe or doubt as passionately as did their predecessors. Authority and authenticity has shifted to the manner a filmmaker uses the cinema's resources, which is to say, his or her command of the generic, the expressive, the excessive, the visual and the visceral: from David Lynch to Jane Campion, from Jonathan Demme to Stephen Frears, from Luc Besson to Dario Argente, from Quentin Tarantino to Tom Tykwer, from Lars von Trier to Jean-Pierre Jeunet – *auteurs* all, and valued for their capacity to concentrate on a tour de force, demonstrating qualities which signify that they are, in a sense, "staging" authorship, rather than, as was the case in the days of *Cahiers du cinéma*, earning the title of author as the honorific sign of achievement at the end of a long career that had to emerge in the folds and creases of the routine product which had passed all the hurdles of anonymity of creation, in favor of the stars, the genre formulas and the action-suspense, to reach its public and enrich its studios and producers.

In this respect, however, there is little difference between contemporary Hollywood and the European cinema because *auteurs* today have to be the promoters and salespeople of their own films at festivals, while one or two become pop star role models and idols for their fans. The difference must lie elsewhere, and while the obvious economic answers – the bigger budgets translating into more spectacular production values, the attractiveness of stars, the stranglehold the US majors have on world distribution – are, of course, valid up to a point, they do not seem to me to clinch it. Rather, my hypothesis is that the cinema's mythic dimension plays its part, and that the lack of it in Europe, or rather the lack of European films to be able to embed these myths in the contemporary world is the key reason for the obsolescence of a certain art cinema.

There is the matter of shared conventions, of genres, their breakdown and reinvention. It becomes important when one wants to look again at authorship in the contemporary cinema, both so anachronistic and so important a category of the European cinema. Usually, an author does not create genres (traditionally, he stands in opposition to that term) but he creates shared knowledge (whereas genres codify shared expectations), which the typical European author generates through series (such as making a trilogy with the same protagonist) which are an extension in time, and thus, the author's oeuvre is defined by the way it creates its own memory, its own self-reference and *mise-en-abyme*, or (to speak with Christian Metz) its own "deictic" relationships.[22]

The cinema, in contradistinction to television, is still our most vivid machine for creating memory. As Godard has said: "cinema creates memory, television fabricates forgetting,"[23] which may be no more than saying that the cinema is indeed the space of a certain mythology, the only one in a secular world. It testifies at once to the need for transcendence and to its absence as redemption. The mini-myths of the *auteur* and his vision, the reinvention of romantic figures (along with their self-parodies) even in the most debased forms have probably kept this pact with the ritual sacrifice of the culture hero, and reinstated in the very terms of the protagonist's failure the right of the artist to claim such an exalted role.

Where does this leave us? On the one hand, I have been arguing that some of the enabling fictions of the cinema in general seem to have exhausted themselves. On the other hand, I claim that the consequences – a cinema that no longer commands assent and loyalty of the popular audience – are especially damaging to the European cinema, while Hollywood has managed to renew itself across an anti-mythology, in which death, destruction, violence, trauma and catastrophe seem to form the central thematic core. Perhaps we should be glad that European cinema has not yet adopted these dark fantasies of end-of-the-world cataclysms? Does it therefore matter that there is so little popular cinema in Europe, and none that crosses the national boundaries? I think it does, and to repeat: a cinema that does not have the assent and love of a popular audience and cannot reach an international public may not have much of a future *as cinema*. I am struck by the parallel with contemporary European politics. At a time when so many of the peoples of Western Europe feel neither loyalty to their political institutions nor confidence in the political process, it is perhaps not insignificant that the only European-wide entertainment form besides football is the Eurovision song contest because, for the rest, it is indeed "America" that European countries have in common. On the other hand, it is precisely the history of Europe both East and West that shows how much the last thing we need is a collective mythology or grand fantasies, in order to renew our faith in liberal democracy. But I shall conclude this report on the 1990s by pointing briefly in two directions: to the Past and to the East.

History and Memory

European cinema – European history: who owns it, and who owns the rights to its representation? This question has been posed several times in recent years, not least thanks to Steven Spielberg's SCHINDLER'S LIST and SAVING PRIVATE RYAN, but it has been in the air since Bob Fosse's CABARET and even Robert Wise's THE SOUND OF MUSIC. A whole generation of European directors in the 1970s and 1980s rose to the challenge to re-conquer lost territory: Visconti (THE DAMNED), Bertolucci (NOVECENTO), Bergman (THE SERPENT'S EGG), Syberberg (OUR HITLER), Fassbinder (THE MARRIAGE OF MARIA BRAUN, LILI MARLEEN), and Reitz (HEIMAT) to mention just a few. The British cinema produced its heritage films, adaptions of Jane Austen to E.M. Foster, Shakespeare to Henry James. And after a brief spell revisiting the Résistance (Louis Malle's LACOMBE LUCIEN, AU REVOIR LES ENFANTS, Joseph Losey's M. KLEIN), so did the French: works of Marcel Pagnol, Emile Zola, Edmond Rostand are back on the big screen.

LILI MARLEEN

In SCHINDLER'S LIST, Spielberg has told the story of the Holocaust as a double salvation story: as a Moses out of Egypt story, and as a story of the elect. He has (and this Claude Lanzman recognized quite rightly) "appropriated" the absolute negation of life implied by Auschwitz, by answering it with a kind of Darwinian biologism (how many physical individuals the Schindler Jews have produced as descendants). Spielberg's film, in this respect, is conceived (or can be perceived) as a kind of wager – a triumph of nature over un-culture/ barbarity, and a triumph of synecdoche over literalism ("whoever saves one life, saves the world"). Both, of course, are problematic triumphs, but they cannot be blamed on or credited to a single director or a single film. Nor even can the problem be reduced to the battle Hollywood vs. Europe. The wager is in some fundamental sense inherent in the cinema as a historical and cultural phenomenon. For was this not once the promise of cinema: the rescue and redemption of reality? If we are now accusing Spielberg of arrogance and hubris, because he thinks his cinema can "rescue" history, are we not cutting the ground from underneath the entire debate about the redemptive function of cinema? Or is what is so objectionable for Europeans about Hollywood the fact that now it is rescuing even that which was never real and never history?

The European cinema has always fought its case on the basis of greater realism, it has been committed to a version of both totality and reflection, even where this reality was that of inner feelings, of the mind. Against this we cannot simply contrast a notion of fantasy, of dream worlds and DreamWorks, whether we see the latter as providing harmless or pernicious entertainment. Rather, we have to accept that the cinema generally stands also for forces that compete with reality, that are "invading" or "immersing" reality, and even – as we saw – "colonizing" reality. This fear finds one of its most typical manifestation in the complaint that Hollywood has "taken away our history," and that the cinema is continually eating up history, swallowing the past, only to spit it out again as nostalgic-narcissistic fiction!

Eastern Europe and Europe's Own Others

But who is speaking when claiming the right to "our" history and "our" stories? Let me cite a voice, whose right to speak on the topic of both European cinema and European politics is indisputable, the Polish filmmaker Krzysztof Zanussi, who in a lecture originally given at the Ebeltoft European Film College in Denmark in May 1993 argued that Western Europe is turning its back on the future, just at the moment that the newly liberated countries of Eastern Europe (which from "his" perspective, are "Central Europe") expect to forge a joint future with a cultural community they have belonged to for a thousand years. Just as they are finally taking up their rightful place as Europeans, Western Europe seems to have given up, not only on them, but worse still, on itself. Faced with this loss of faith, Zanussi asked, can the nations of Central Europe, especially Poland and Hungary, infuse a new intellectual and cultural vigor, as they "reform" themselves yet again? [24] The competition for membership and partnership, in times of crisis, however, tends to take an ultra-conservative turn. Witness how the new (cultural) Europe has a right-wing inflection and a siege or fortress mentality: the Lombard League, Neo-fascists in Central Italy, Jörg Haider in Austria, Le Pen in France, Pim Fortuyn in the Netherlands, Christians banding together against the "Ottoman" threat, and on the Balkans, (Catholic) Croats fighting (Orthodox) Serbs, while both are also fighting (Muslim) Bosnians. Some commentators have pointed out the parallels between the fragmentation of a once common (high) culture, and what they see as the re-tribalization of the nation states, after the fall of communism and the end of the cold-war bipolar political world order. Not just ex-Yugoslavia or Russia, or the hostility to ethnic minorities in Western Europe but also the identity politics in the US, with the insistence on being more self-aware of one's racial or ethnic or religious identity. Impossible, though, to affirm a single national or ethnic identity through the cinema: it is more a question of how a country can speak to itself, how it is "spoken" by others, and how the others "inside" speak themselves or ask to be represented. Each national European cinema now produces representations of its own others, reflecting and reshaping its own multi-cultural society. In France, there is the *cinéma beur*, there are films about Turkish communities and by Turkish directors in Germany, and Dutch films about multi-cultural experience are usually the ones recognized as most typical for the Netherlands' independent filmmaking sector. That there is a prevalence of the *Romeo & Juliet/* WEST SIDE STORY motif in such films, of families at war and of lovers seeking to bridge the gap, is perhaps an indication of the mythological narratives which are needed to give such experiences their specific resonance and local truth.

Zanussi is raising issues that go beyond the question of a European cinema: the tasks of creating a (political) Europe, which its populations can recognize as theirs, give assent to and feel loyalty towards, is clearly one that the cinema is neither capable of nor perhaps quite the right place for bringing about. And yet Zanussi touches on precisely this point: the possibility of the cinema to tell stories that may not amount to collective mythologies, but that are nonetheless capable of resonating beyond national boundaries and linguistic borders. Even if mythologies are not the recipe for a renewed faith in liberal democracy or a critique of the market economy, the question of what can be "shared" in such a future European community is important. Whether the citizens of Poland, France, Denmark or Romania (or the Turkish, Moroccan or Afghan communities in Europe's midst) will, in the decades to come, vote only with their wallets at the supermarket, or also with the stories they watch and tell in the movies or on television. This question is one that the crisis of the European cinema in the 1990s at the very least helps to focus on.

(1995)

Notes

1. John Naughton, *The Observer*, 16 May 1992.
2. "Pictures of Europe" Channel Four, television program, 1992.
3. For an inversely related perspective, see Richard Pells, *Not Like Us: How Europeans Have Loved, Hated, and Transformed American Culture Since World War II.* (New York: Basic Books, 1997).
4. Gian Piero Brunetta, *Storia del cinema italiano 1948-1980* (Rome: Einaudi, 1982), p. 34.
5. Siegfried Kracauer, *From Caligari to Hitler: a Psychological History of the German Cinema* (Princeton: Princeton University Press, 1974).

6. Bertrand Tavernier, 'I Wake Up, Dreaming', in Boorman, John and Walter Donohue (eds.), *Projections* 2 (London: Faber and Faber, 1993), p. 311.

7. Thomas Guback, "Hollywood's International Market", in Tino Balio, *The American Film Industry* (Madison: University of Wisconsin Press, 1985), pp. 463-486.

8. Kristin Thompson, *Exporting Entertainment: America in the World Film Market 1907-34* (London: British Film Institute, 1985).

9. Ian Jarvie, *Hollywood's Overseas Campaign: The North Atlantic Movie Trade, 1920-1950* (Cambridge: Cambridge University Press, 1992).

10. G. Nowell-Smith and S. Ricci (eds.), *Hollywood and Europe*, London: BFI 1998.

11. Noel Burch, *Life to Those Shadows* (London: British Film Institute, 1990).

12. Barry Salt, *Film Style and Technology: History and Analysis* (London: Starword, 1983).

13. David Bordwell, *Narration and the Fiction Film* (Madison: University of Wisconsin Press, 1985).

14. Paul Schrader is the author of a film studies classic: *Transcendental Style in Film: Dreyer, Ozu, Bresson* (Berkeley: University of California Press, 1972).

15. Gilles Deleuze, *The Movement Image* (Minneapolis: University of Minnesota Press, 1986).

16. Harold Bloom, *A Map of Misreading* (New York: Oxford University Press, 1975).

17. See the essays by Steve Crofts, such as 'Cross–Cultural Reception Studies: Culturally Variant Readings of CROCODILE DUNDEE', *Continuum*, 6/1 (1992).

18. See my chapter on 'The Author in the Film: Self-Expression as Self-Representation" in Thomas Elsaesser, *The New German Cinema, A History* (Basingstoke: McMillan, 1989), pp. 74-116.

19. See Andrew Sarris, *The American Cinema: Directors and Directions 1929-1968* (New York: DaCapo Press, 1968).

20. Bertrand Tavernier, 'I Wake up Dreaming', p. 266.

21. Besides Orpheus and Eurydice, one finds in European art and avant-garde cinema the reverberations of myths such as that of Echo and Narcissus (Derek Jarman), Empedocles (Jean Marie Straub and Daniele Huillet), or the biblical stories of Cain and Abel, Jacob and Ruth. For a genealogy of Antigone, see my 'Antigone Agonistes: Urban Guerrillas or Guerilla Urbanism', in M. Sorkin and J. Copjec (eds.), *Giving Ground* (London: Verso, 1999), 267-302, also at http://www.rouge.com.au/4/antigone.html. For a reading of Theseus, Ariadne and the Labyrinth, see the chapter on Rivette, in this volume.

22. See Christian Metz, "The impersonal enunciation or the site of film", *New Literary History* 22 (1991), pp. 747-772.

23. Jean-Luc Godard, voice-over in *Histoire(s) du Cinema* (1998).

24. Krzysztof Zanussi, Lecture given at Ebeltoft European Film College (Denmark), *Final Cut*, Fall 1993, p. 52.

ImpersoNations

National Cinema, Historical Imaginaries

> Is there anything more barren than the psychology of peoples,
> this mouldy rubbish-tip of stereotypes, prejudices, *idées reçus*?
> ...And yet, they are impossible to eradicate, these traditional
> garden gnomes with their naively painted nation-faces.
> Hans Magnus Enzensberger[1]

The New Nationalism: A Modern Phenomenon?

As Hans Magnus Enzensberger suggests, it may be fruitless to rail against national stereotypes: they are absurd, unfair, pernicious, and nonetheless so persistent that they probably serve a purpose. When asking where they are most
likely to thrive, one realizes that it is not politics. Set ideas about the national
character or cultural stereotyping are especially vivid within popular culture
and the media.[2] Often, they are diagnosed as potentially dangerous invitations
to racism, or conversely, as accurate, if regrettable "reflections" of widely held
views. But one could also argue that racist incidents in sports or tourism signify
the opposite of the new European racism: a mimicking, a "staging" and an impersonation of prejudice, which tries to exorcise the feelings of fear of the other,
by ritualizing aggression towards the kinds of "otherness" that have become
familiar from life in ethnically mixed metropolitan communities and is thus different from traditional forms of nationalism. By shifting the sites of social representation away from the rhetoric of enemy nations and territorial conquest –
trading jingoism, in other words, for stereotyping and puns – does popular culture fuel the old politics of resentment that were mobilized to fight the wars of
the first part of the 20th century, or are television, tabloid journalism and advertising merely mining a sign-economy of difference, ready-made via a long
history of images and now circulating through the many topographies of consumption? The transformation of the geographic and historical spaces of nationhood and national stereotypes into sign-economies has, however, in no way di-
luted the political value and "emotional legitimacy"[3] of the idea of national

identity. Rather, precisely because no external threat is involved, nationalism has become a major phenomenon of contemporary politics and a focal point in cultural debate. The divisions are no longer only or even primarily across the borders, but have opened up boundaries, zones and demarcations within the nation-states, dividing groups formerly held together by class-interest, economic necessity and religious faith or were forced together by political ideologies, such as fascism or communism. European nation-states, it would seem, are re-tribalising themselves, and in the process, give new meaning to both the nation and the state. The two concepts are no longer bound to each other, as they have been since the idea of citizenship became the cornerstone of the bourgeois world order in the wake of the French Revolution, and Napoleon's attempt to unify Europe under French hegemony.

This suggests that it is the end of the Cold War and the globalization of capitalism, with its free flow of investments and the creation of mobile labor markets that has given the idea of "the nation" unexpected new currency and even urgency, while at the same time, radically redefining its referents. The rise of the new nationalism was unexpected because the societies in question, whether advanced or developing, were coping with the post-1989 upheavals in rather paradoxical ways. In the 1990s, very different kinds of modernization could be observed: the break-up of hegemonies, be they neo-colonial, as in South Africa or ideological as in ex-Yugoslavia; the devolution of democratic decision making to political bodies like regional parliaments, as in Great Britain, or to centralized bureaucracies, as in the European Union; the resurgence of religious fundamentalisms – whether Christian, Jewish, Islamist, or Hindu.[4] None of these re-alignments of authority and legitimation have, as far as one can see, given rise to genuinely new political forms of organization or social bonding (which had been the hope of the "revolutionary" 1960s and the "radical" 1970s when fighting imperialism, racism, and capitalism). On the left, one speaks of post-colonialism and post-Fordism, and on the right of the "clash of civilization" and the "end of history." At the same time, these inward turns of politics seem to have revived a longing for traditional structures of kinship and ethnicity, of family and clan, usually thought of as reactionary, atavistic or even criminal.[5] Many of the various religious fundamentalisms, meanwhile, rely materially and ideologically on substantial and often wealthy diaspora-communities in France, Germany, Canada, Britain and the United States. Even more confusingly, both religious fundamentalism and family- or clan-based business cartels depend as much on the deregulated circulation of capital and labor as do multinational companies, and all take for granted the high-tech world of the mobile phone, the modem and the internet. Nationalism in the forms in which it is "returning" today would thus seem a thoroughly modern phenomenon, exposing how contradictory the processes of "modernity," "modernization" and "post-modernity" have been in the 20th century, and are set to continue to be, now under the new name of "globalization," into the 21st.

Historical Imaginary or Re-branding the Nation?

The concerns in this chapter predate the upheavals of 1989, but they connect directly with this re-figuration of the nation and the national, understood as a *consequence* of modernity rather than as an *obstacle* that modernization had to overcome. For as already hinted at, it seems that the so-called communication revolutions of the past thirty years, together with the media-consciousness of both radical and conservative political groups since 1968, have played a major role in the present resurgence of nationalism, which prompts the question what role culture, and in particular, the media-cultures associated with sound and image technologies (as compared to, say, the leisure industries of tourism and sports) have played. Are they catalysts with an enabling function? Is their effect empowering for some groups and disenfranchising for others? Does access to media representation relativize regional or ethnic difference, or simply create new ghettos? Do cinema and television help foster identities and feelings of belonging, or are they merely parasitic on existing values and attitudes, even undercutting them by playing with their visual and verbal representations, as suggested by postmodern pastiche? Put in these general terms, these questions are endlessly discussed by the media themselves.

Put in more particular terms, the cinema in Europe can be a case for testing contemporary articulations of the nation. First, because among modern imaging technologies, the cinema has had the longest track record. Films have, at least since World War I, been variously credited with or blamed for providing a powerful instrument of persuasion and propaganda, usually on behalf of reaffirming a sense of national identity, by furnishing suitably hateful images of the enemy, or by projecting an ideology of one's own nation under siege and of the home front threatened from without and within. The cinema as propaganda machine and self-advertising tool reached its climax during World War II, among all the warring nations. Its propaganda function has since become attenuated, but as a promotional tool, it has become more powerful, but also more diffuse and opaque. If for the United States, trade (still) follows the movies, for Europe it is tourism and the heritage business that follow the film. The American political media machines of spin and disinformation are widely seen as taking their skills and expertise from Hollywood (e.g., WAG THE DOG, director Barry Levinson, 1997, THE CONTROL ROOM, director Jehane Noujaim, 2004). As an engine of global hegemony, Hollywood is seen to propagate and advertise very specific tastes and attitudes. Declaring this "national" agenda as universal – democracy, freedom, open exchange of people, goods and services – has served America well, insofar as these values and goals ("the inalienable right to the pursuit of happiness") have, until the end of the last century, been widely endorsed and aspired to by peoples who neither share territorial proximity with the United States nor language, faith, customs, or a common history. European values of solidarity, pacifism, the welfare state or the preservation of the past have been less inspirational, and have certainly not translated into the same kind of recognition for its cinema as is the case for Hollywood, even if (as the previous chapter tried to indicate) value systems, and even different "mythologies" can be read off the films made by the national cinemas of Europe since 1945.

However, when trying to understand what this might mean for the future, we may have to change the paradigms that have guided the study of the "national" in European cinema. It used to be assumed – and in more journalistic writing still is – that the films produced in a particular country "reflect" something essential about this country as a "nation." This has been the case, for instance, when talking about German cinema during the 1920s or Japanese cinema since 1945.[6] In Britain, Ealing comedies, the kitchen sink dramas of the 1950s, and even "Hammer horror" have been analyzed and probed for what they say about the state of "England" in the post-war years.[7] The French *nouvelle vague* has been convincingly appraised as belonging to wider and deeper changes in French society and culture.[8] Italian neo-realism has often been read in relation to Italian post-war politics and the delicate balancing act between Catholics and Communists making common front against a common enemy, and – looking "East" (from our often unreflected Western Euro-centrism) – the films and directorial careers of Polish, or (ex-) Yugoslav filmmakers are usually tracked within the parameters of these countries' turbulent history in the last fifty years or so. But also with regard to Hollywood: the presumption that the cinema is a vehicle for transporting a specific ideology dominated the debates in film studies during the 1970s, when the American cinema was deconstructed three times over: because of its political bias, its aesthetics of illusionism, and its gender ideology.

Some of these paradigms are fixed parts of the history of the discipline of film studies. However, they are of little help in understanding the national cinemas of Europe, once one sees them as both separate and interdependent. They do not allow one to study the European cinema in the triple perspective here proposed for the period after 1989, namely as still defining itself against Hollywood (Europe-Hollywood-Europe), as having (since deregulation in the 1980s) to profile itself also against television, and finally, finding itself increasingly defined by others as (merely) part of "world cinema." What this chapter proposes is to look more closely at how the European cinema can redefine its role within this triple conjunction, by suggesting that national identity (or identification with a collective) now figures both above and below the nation-state. Such a perspective is to some extent speculative; it may even turn out to be misleading.[9] But if it can give a new impetus to the field, its purpose of offering a series of concepts-in-progress will have been fulfilled.

The first of these concepts has already been discussed in the previous chapter: that of a national imaginary, in which the "look of the other" is a central notion. Here I want to add the idea of "impersoNation," or "self-othering": including the self-conscious, ironic or self-mocking display of clichés and prejudices. The broadening of the concept is meant to shed light on genres such as the heritage film and more generally, on why the cinemas of Europe have been reworking their respective national pasts as spectacle and prosthetic media-memory. [10] For instance, why do we have the persistence of certain national "images" (Germany and Nazism; France and erotic passion; Britain and dysfunctional masculinity), that are accused of being stereotypes when used in the press or on television, only to be recycled and recharged with emotional resonance in the cinema, provided the context is self-referential, visceral or comic? Do film stars still function as national icons inside and across national borders? Is the casting in international productions of Catherine Deneuve, Gérard Depardieu, Marcello Mastroianni, Jeremy Irons, Kate Winslet, Hugh Grant, Hanna Schygulla, Bruno Ganz, Rutger Hauer, Krystyna Janda, Franka Potente a guarantee that they will be recognized as "typical" for their country by the public? How useful is the cinema as a tool for "re-branding" a nation ("Cool Britannia," "Modern Spain," "la France profonde," the "Berlin Republic"), compared to the re-branding

KATE WINSLET

that can be accomplished through the visual arts (the "successful" campaign by Maurice Saatchi in launching the YBA's, the Young British Artists), a soccer world cup (France in 1998, re-branded as a multi-cultural society) or say, hosting the Olympic Games (as in the case of the Barcelona Games re-branding Catalan identity)?

Media, Nation, State: Another Look at the Discourses

Considered as a subject taught in academic film studies, European cinema is unproblematic: the "impossibility" which I mentioned in the introduction has itself been "institutionalized" and become something of a fixed trope of discourse. As a consequence, despite or because of the difficulties of defining what European cinema is, a growing number of books are being edited and published on the topic since the early 1990s, servicing the needs of the curriculum. Many opt for a pragmatic approach; they either treat Europe as an accumulation of national cinemas, with each getting its turn, or they highlight outstanding authors standing in for the nation and sometimes even for the entirety of a country's film production and filmmaking. What is notable is that the majority of these books originate from Britain, a country whose relation to "Europe" in matters cinema at once reflects and contradicts its population's widely shared Euro-skeptic political stance. Often quick to draw a line between itself and the "isolated" continent, Britain has nonetheless been more successful than any other European country in penetrating this continent with its films. Titles like Four Weddings and a Funeral, Shakespeare in Love, The English Patient, The Remains of the Day, the films of Ken Loach or Mike Leigh, not to mention the James Bond films, Mr. Bean or Monty Python are all familiar to audiences in Germany, France, Italy and elsewhere. Peter Greenaway's work is more welcome in Germany or the Netherlands than he is appreciated in his own country, while Derek Jarman, Isaak Julien and Sally Potter have solid followings in European avant-garde and art worlds. Neither France nor Italy are Britain's competitors, but only Hollywood, where many of Britain's most gifted directors have indeed sought access and found success (Ridley and Tony Scott, Adrian Lyne, Alan Parker and Mike Figgis, to name but the most obvious). The linguistic proximity helps, and British actors – often theatre-trained – have been among the export assets the country has invested in Hollywood (and therefore made internationally known) ever since the coming of sound. But producers, directors of photography, sound technicians and other film specialists have also made their way to Hollywood, increasingly so since the 1980s.[11]

British cinema thus has always been facing the United States, while its back, so to speak, was turned to Europe. So why this interest in European cinema? First of all, it responds to a dilemma, internal to universities, whose departments of modern languages have been under threat. From the mid-1980s onwards, their mainly literature-based language studies of French, Italian, Spanish or German failed to enroll students in sufficient numbers. In many universities the choice was a stark one: either close down departments altogether, or amalgamate them into European studies, and try to attract new students by drawing on cultural studies, media studies and film studies, rather than relying solely on literary authors and texts of similarly canonical authority. Yet the debate about national cinema, and therefore also the thinking behind the books on European cinema, continues a long tradition in Britain. Rather than originating only in the hard-pressed areas of the humanities, the European dimension has accompanied the establishment of film studies in British universities since the 1970s. As a question about what is typical or specific about a nation's cinema, and its obverse: "what is the function of cinema in articulating nationhood and fostering the sense of belonging," the debate owes it productive vitality in Britain to a conjuncture that could be called the "interference history" between film studies, television studies and cultural studies. Several phases and stages can be identified in this history, and they need to be recapitulated, if one is to understand what is at stake also in any substantive move from national cinema to what I am calling "New Cinema Europe," and to appreciate what new knowledge this move can be expected to produce. Paradoxically, it may have been the very fact that by the mid-1990s the discussion around national cinema had – depending on one's view – hardened into dogma or reached a generally accepted consensus around a particular set of arguments that encouraged the desire to conceptualize the field differently, or at the very least to signal such a need.

National Cinema: Essentialism vs. Constructivism

The first signs of a renewed debate around national cinema in Britain took place in the early 1980s, on the fringes of emerging film studies, as part of a polemic about the relation between two kinds of internationalism: that of Hollywood and its universalizing appeal, and that of a counter-cinema avant-garde, opposed to Hollywood, but also thinking of itself as not bound by the nation or national cinema, especially not by "British cinema." At that point the problem of nationality played a minor role within academic film studies, compared to the question of authorship and genre, semiology, the psychoanalytic-linguistic turn in film theory, and the rise of cine-feminism. With the shift from classical film studies to cultural studies, however, the idea of the "nation" once more became a focus of critical framing, almost on a par with class and gender. Broadly speaking, the term "national cinema" thus fed on oppositional energies derived from the avant-garde and the new waves, in parallel to the more sociological attempts to critically identify what was typical about domestic mainstream cinema and the ideology of its narratives. Yet it also responded to the changing function of cinema and television, each "addressing" their audience as belonging to the "nation." These were potentially contradictory agendas, and for a time it was the contradictions that marked the vitality of the debate.

Cultural studies, for instance, took a resolutely constructivist approach to analyzing the nation as "produced" by television, just as it did with respect to gender or race. But from a historical perspective, the classic analyses of national cinemas were on the whole "essentialist," meaning that they looked to the cinema, its narratives, iconography or recurring motifs with the expectation that they could reveal something unique or specific about a country's values and beliefs, at once more authentic and more symptomatic than in other art forms or aspects of (popular) culture. It makes Siegfried Kracauer's study of the cinema of the Weimar Republic *From Caligari to Hitler* (1947) the founding text for such a study of national cinema. Throughout the 1950s and 1960s, his blend of sociology, group psychology, and metropolitan-modernist fieldwork ethnography influenced many studies that purported to investigate the "national" character of a country's cinema, and it yielded some remarkable books on the sociology of cinema, but it also influenced – more indirectly – Donald Richie's volumes on Japanese Cinema or Raymond Durgant's *A Mirror for England*. One could call this the period when *national cinema* connoted a nation's *unconscious deep-structure*, the reading of which gave insights about secret fantasies, political pressure points, collective wishes and anxieties. The danger of this approach was not only essentialism regarding the concept of national identity: it also risked being tautological, insofar as only those films tended to be selected as typical of a national cinema which confirmed the pre-established profile. Grounded in sociology, such studies used the cinema for the distillation of national stereotypes or significant symbolic configurations, such as the father-son relations in German cinema, contrasted with the father-daughter relationships of French cinema.[12] Narratives of national cinema in this sense pre-date the European *nouvelles vagues*, and besides Kracauer and Durgnat, one could name Edgar Morin and Pierre Sorlin in France, or the social anthropologists Martha Wolfenstein and Nathan Leites in the US. From within film studies, these writings stand apart from the aesthetics of "auteur cinema," indeed they are almost diametrically opposed to them, which may be one of the reasons "national cinema" returned on the agenda, when the author as auteur-artist began to be deconstructed in the 1990s, and cinema was seen as a differently generated social text, not cohering around the director.

Three essays in the early 1980s re-launched the debate around national cinema in Britain and the US, broadly in the context of so-called "revisionist film history." The first was by Ed Buscombe, "Film History and the Idea of a National Cinema" (1981), the second was my "Film History: Weimar Cinema and Visual Pleasure" (1982), and the third was Philip Rosen's "History, Textuality, Narration" (1984).[13] Ed Buscombe's short essay from 1981 is still a landmark in the debate. It addressed the problems of British cinema vis-à-vis Hollywood and documented the initiatives taken by the film industry and a succession of Britain's top producers (A. Korda, J.A. Rank and L. Grade) to break into the US market between the 1940s and 1960s. But Buscombe also made clear his own dissatisfaction with the anti-British, anti-national cinema stance taken by the theoretical journal *Screen*. Significantly, perhaps, his essay was first published in the *Australian Journal of Screen Theory*, more sympathetic to Lukacsian Marxism and Lucien Goldman's "genetic" structuralism than to Althusser and Lacan. Phil Rosen's essay from 1984 compared Kracauer's assumptions about national cinema with those of Noel Burch, who had just published a major study on another national cinema, that of Japan, using formal criteria and theoretical concepts quite different from those of Kracauer. Rosen is resolutely constructivist, asking whether it was textual coherence that allowed the national audience to (mis-)perceive an image of itself in the cinema, or on the contrary, if it was the gaps and fissures of the text that were most telling about the nation and its fantasies of identity.

These essays (to which one should add a polemical piece by Geoffrey Nowell-Smith)[14] are in a way indicative of the directions that the national cinema debate in Britain was to take in the following decade. But before sketching this trajectory, it should be noted that a key moment in consolidating the constructivist paradigm was the appearance of a book that seemed to speak to a central doubt, before this doubt was even fully conscious, namely, how decisive finally are the media in soliciting one's identification with the nation and in shaping a country's national identity? Are not other social structures (such as the family), geography (the place one comes from), a particular religious faith (Christianity, Islam) or loyalty to a certain shared past (national history) far more significant? Benedict Anderson's *Imagined Communities* came to the rescue, offering at once empirical evidence, a historical precedent, and an elegantly formulated synthesis of traditional anthropological fieldwork and thorough familiarity with Foucault's *Archaeology of Knowledge*. Anderson's slim book on colonial and postcolonial nation-building and identity formation in what became Indonesia answered the problem, barely posed, about the status of the media in the national identity debate, by making a convincing case for constructivism as a method, and by unequivocally giving the media – in Anderson's case, the print media – a crucial role in narrating the nation. Conveniently for scholars, Anderson also emphasized the power of pedagogy (teachers, bureaucrats, people of the word) in fashioning the nation as an imaginary, but nonetheless effective scaffolding of personal and group identity. According to Anderson: "nations" are constructed by intellectuals, journalists, pedagogues, philologists, historians, archivists who were "carefully sewing together dialects, beliefs, folk tales, local antagonisms into the nationalist quilt."[15]

The book's extraordinary success in cultural and media studies departments may best be explained in terms of the productive misreading and creative misapplications its central thesis lent itself to, insofar as media studies needed Anderson's arguments more than his arguments needed media studies. For even if one disregards the problem of the media in question being quite different (newspapers, books, instead of cinema and television), there was another problem in applying the concept of imagined communities as anything other than a metaphor: Anderson was dealing with the workings of colonial power, which included the bureaucratic, as well as the coercive infrastructure that went with it. So while at one level, not many parallels can be drawn between the introduction of compulsory education or daily newspapers in Dutch East India and, say, home-grown film production in West European countries, at another level, the transformations which European countries were undergoing after the end of the Cold War in the 1990s with respect to their cultures becoming multicultural, their populations transnational and their politics post-national, did make Anderson's historical study of Indonesia appear to be the key to a situation only just evolving in Europe.

Ed Buscombe's essay associated the return to the idea of national cinema neither with a discursively constructed national imaginary, nor with post-colonialism. His ostensible starting point was the decline in popularity and relevance of Britain's mainstream popular cinema. He criticized the rather faltering and – according to him – often misdirected efforts to create a British art- and counter-cinema, and instead, pleaded for a more accessible "middlebrow" British cinema that neither went for the lowest common denominator of Britishness (embodied in the CARRY ON comedies) nor for the structuralist-materialist, Brecht-inspired efforts of the British avant-garde movements, identified with the names of Peter Gidal, Steve Dwoskin, Peter Wollen and Laura Mulvey. Looking at the British cinema that did become successful internationally from the mid-1980s onwards into the new century – the already mentioned "heritage" genre in the shape of Merchant-Ivory adaptations of Edwardian literature, films based on Shakespeare (his plays and his "life"), costume dramas, filmed Jane Austen novels and Hugh Grant comedies – Buscombe's wish for well-made films seems to have come true, maybe with a vengeance. In between, the debate about the British-ness of British cinema flared up several times more. For instance, it became virulent a few years after Buscombe's piece, when it appeared as if, with CHARIOTS OF FIRE winning at the Oscars, and its producer, David Puttnam, embarking on a (brief) career as a Hollywood studio boss, Britain had finally made it into the Hollywood mainstream. This proved an illusion or self-delusion. In 1984, *The Monthly Film Bulletin* commissioned three articles to assess the hangover that followed, with Ray Durgnat, Charles Barr, and myself as contributors. Durgnat, updating his socio-cultural analyses from *A Mirror for England* once more tried to read, in the manner of a more acerbic and canny Kracauer, the national mood from the films. He detected in 1980s cinema a Thatcherite politics of style and status over substance, and noted how middle-class upward mobility covered itself with a mixture of cynicism and self-irony. Barr pointed out how inextricably British cinema was now tied to television, financially and institutionally as well as in its mode of address, and what the contradictory consequences were of artificially wishing to keep them separate. My own contribution to the debate ("Images for Sale") is, as already mentioned, reprinted in the collection here. Focusing on a double perspective – the view from within, and the view from without – it tried to test around the British "renaissance" of the 1980s, the paradigm of self and the (significant) other, first elaborated by me around Weimar Cinema and the New German Cinema.

The idea of a national self-image specific to the cinema and yet with distinct contours in each national media culture is therefore – for better or worse – different from Anderson's imagined communities.[16] If extended beyond the media of print, journalism and bureaucracy, and if aimed at "developed" rather than "emerging" nations, Anderson's scheme would be likely to apply to television more than to the cinema. Indirectly, I tested this hypothesis, too, with an article on British television in the 1980s, written under the impact of deregulation and after the founding of Channel Four ("Television through the Looking Glass"). Face to face with US television and a new domestic channel, both the BBC and its commercial counterpart, ITV began addressing the nation differently. No longer playing the pedagogue, British television found itself at the cusp of not quite knowing whether to address its viewers as part of the national audience (and thus in the mode of civic citizenship), or as members of ever more sharply segmented consumer groups who all happen to live in the same country, but otherwise have different tastes in food and fashion, different sexual preferences, different ethnic backgrounds, faiths and even languages.

From National Cinema to Cinema in Europe

The changing function of television with respect to national self-representation might nonetheless be a useful pointer, when trying to understand the move from national cinema to European cinema. For once one accepts that "European cinema" cannot merely be either the historically conventionalized accumulation of national cinemas (most of which have been in commercial decline since the early 1980s) or the equally conventionalized enumeration of outstanding directors (however crucial filmmakers like Jean-Luc Godard, Wim Wenders, Pedro Almodóvar, Lars von Trier, Peter Greenaway or Krzysztof Kieslowski are in connoting "Europe," above and beyond their national identity) then the criteria for what is meant by "European" have yet to be found and defined. The question is the one that already lay at the heart of the national cinema debate. How representative are films produced in the various countries of Europe for either the idea of nation or state? Alternatively, what role can the cinema play in furthering social goals or political ideals such as European integration, multi-cultural tolerance and a sense of "European" identity that is supra-national but nonetheless committed to common civic values? If the former risks being tautological – for what is a "representative" European film? – the latter may also receive a disappointing answer.

Philip Schlesinger, for instance, has claimed that the cultural argument so often put forward at GATT or WTO meetings about the need to defend the distinctiveness of European audiovisual production against the demand for free trade and liberalized markets, lacks empirical proof and is short on factual evidence. According to him, it is a fallacy to assume that just because the electronic media – notably television – are ubiquitous, they necessarily have an impact on a population's attitudes and behavior.[17] And yet, the "power of the media" has become such a deeply entrenched notion when discussing the future of liberal democracies, the existence of a public sphere, multiculturalism, religion or any other issue of social, political or humanitarian concern, that it poses the question if it is not television that is the barely acknowledged but structuring absence of national cinema, as it loses its representational role. Any future thinking about cinema in Europe would then also have to "face up to" the electronic and digital media, rather than stay "face to face" with the blockbuster, as the constantly invoked "threat" to European cultural identity and national diversity.

More simply put, privileging (national) television as the interface of European cinema in the 1990s suggests a more modest agenda than that implied by the post-1945 national cinemas of *auteurs* and new waves. But it has the advantage of taking account of the actual nature of film production, even in countries that have or have had a viable indigenous film industry. At least since the 1970s, films in most European countries have been financed by pooling very mixed sources, arranged under diverse co-production agreements, with television playing the key role as both producer and exhibitor of feature films. Channel Four in Britain, ZDF's *Das Kleine Fernsehspiel* in Germany,[18] the VPRO in the Netherlands, and Canal + in France have nurtured a European cinema in the absence of a national film industry, allowing such television-produced films the chance of a theatrical release before being broadcast. This model, dependent as it was on the existence of either publicly funded television or on commercial broadcasters with a public service or arts programming remit, proved to be both highly successful if one thinks of the films it made possible, and transitional, if looked at from the increasing pressure from ratings that the remnants of public service television came under in the latter half of the decade. As a consequence, all the bodies just named have drastically scaled back their involvement in feature film production in the new century. Film production in Europe has had to re-orient itself, by looking for another economic model. As will be argued more fully in the next chapter, a different structure of financing, production, distribution and exhibition has become the norm in Europe from that which obtained during the first phase of the new waves, where national and transnational producers such as Pierre Braunberger and Carlo Ponti were able to finance auteurs' films alongside more directly commercial projects. But the current model also differs from the 'cultural mode of production' as it emerged in the 1970s and 80s, when national governments, especially in Germany and France, substantially funded an auteur cinema either by direct subsidies, prizes and grants, or indirectly, via state-controlled television. The new model, for which one could coin the term 'European post-Fordism', to indicate the salient elements: small-scale production units, cooperating with television as well as commercial partners, and made up of creative teams around a producer and a director (as in the case of Figment Films, founded by Andrew and Kevin Macdonald, who teamed up with Danny Boyle to make SHALLOW GRAVE and TRAINSPOTTING, or Zentropa, the company founded by Peter Aalbaeck Jensen and Lars von Trier), originated in Britain in the 1980s, with Palace Pictures (Nik Powell, Paul Webster, Steve Woolley and director Neil Jordan)[19] perhaps the best-known of this brand of high-risk ventures. Since then, similar units have emerged around all the major European directors, such as Tom Tykwer (X-Film Creative Pool, Berlin), Fatih Akin (Wüste-Film, Hamburg) or ex-director Marin Karmitz's MK Productions in Paris.

Post-National Cinema Europe?

Do these small-scale production units amount to a new post-national basis of European cinema? Certainly not by themselves, since many of these units have a national base and are as likely to cooperate with US firms or Asian directors as with other European partners, but they nonetheless constitute one crucial element in the jigsaw puzzle or network system. The other key ingredient is the film festival circuit, discussed in the following chapter, which is indeed transnational and international. The third element to factor in again arises from a national basis, but increasingly follows a trans-national European logic, more specifically that of the European Union, which obliges member states to cooperate with each other in order to benefit from subsidies or protective legislation. Compared to the political rules of the Union, where nations hand over part of their sovereignty to Brussels, in order for Brussels to legislate transnationally, to negotiate internationally (at WTO level) and to subsidize locally (via various supra-national agencies and programs), cinema production in the European Union is lagging behind. The most evident aspect of filmmaking and cinema culture, where the European Union has had an impact is with regard to questions of co-production, tax regimes, copyright and especially on those vital issues of state funding: the European Union has for years been trying to "harmonize" the various national film subsidy schemes and regulate the terms under which individuals from different countries can work in the member states industries and benefit from these schemes. Without unraveling the long and complex history of the relations between cinema and the state in European countries, one can see that what used to be nationally specific protectionism has now become European protectionism, still mostly directed against Hollywood.[20] In these trade disputes, the national is increasingly being invoked by the European Union itself, usually coupled with the concept of cultural diversity or claimed under the heading of devolved national specificity. Thus, in order to buffer directors against the effects of unrestrained market forces, and to cushion the blows from Hollywood competition, the appeal to a "national cinema" gives leverage to a cultural protectionism that cuts both ways. While it tries to shield film production from the full blast of the market, it also obliges national governments to fund filmmaking: either as part of the national cultural heritage and artistic patrimony, or for somewhat more prosaic reasons as a national skills- and crafts-based (or cottage) industry to support the knowledge society of today and its integration into the global information societies of tomorrow. The "national" thereby acquires a different meaning, in that it is neither "essentialist" nor "constructivist" in the sense discussed above, but "post-national", that is, reintroduced for external use, so to speak, while suspended within the European Union.

Having said this, it is worth insisting on a distinction already made earlier. Much of this applies exclusively to the well-established subsidy schemes in Western European countries. In Central and Eastern Europe, the post-Communist states in the 1990s have not only asserted their nationalism as a motor for their cultural identity and political self-determination after the fake internationalism as well as fake nationalism of the Stalinist past. They have also come to the fore with a renewed concern for a national cinema, shadowing the fact that Western Europe underestimated the degree of militancy still inherent in the nationalism in the Balkans and elsewhere. The break-up of Yugoslavia (Slovenia, Croatia, Macedonia, Albania), the re-emergence of the Baltic States (Latvia, Lithuania and Estonia), the split of Czechoslovakia into the Czech Republic and Slovakia), and finally the newly independent states emerging from the former Soviet Union (Georgia, Belarus, the Ukraine) have had more or less catastrophic consequences for these countries' respective film cultures. All of them used to have an official film industry centrally administered. The filmmaker was, in certain crucial respects an employee of the state, and thus did not have to pursue his or her production funds either through commercial production companies or via the box office. Since the end of Communist rule, however, this central funding has fallen away, and the profession has been struggling to re-organize itself along market lines. But since no West European country can sustain its filmmaking activities without the various subsidy systems put in place during the 1970s and 1980s, East European filmmakers are at a disadvantage, not having equivalent schemes to fall back on in their respective countries.

While some filmmakers, notably from the countries of the former Yugoslavia often have a very "post-national" attitude to cultural identity, others still prefer to present themselves also in their cinema as "national." They might be seen in a counter-current to what has been said above, but they are also comparable to the various regional, territorial or ethnic movements, which also in Western Europe claim a distinct cinematic identity.[21] In this respect Hungarian, Bulgarian, or Romanian cinema, along with Basque or Irish cinema is – *mutatis mutandis* – comparable with other parts of the world, where the post-colonial period has seen cultural and ethnic identity-politics join forces with nationalism, to assert autonomy and independence, and a return to local values in the face of a globalized world.

This form of retroactive cinematic nationalism would have to be correlated with, but also distinguished from the way the label "national" in the cinema has come back in almost every European country as a form of branding, a marketing tool, signifying the local – maybe here, too, reinventing the national – for external, i.e., global use. The already mentioned regional or metropolitan labels "Notting Hill" (a popular, ethnically mixed district of London) doubling as film title for a tourist

TRAINSPOTTING

romance, the much-discussed "Scottishness" of TRAINSPOTTING, the Berlin-effect of RUN LOLA RUN, the feisty, feel-good movies with regional appeal (THE FULL MONTY, BRASSED OFF, BILLY ELLIOT), the period piece novel adaptations such as THE END OF THE AFFAIR, THE ENGLISH PATIENT and THE REMAINS OF THE DAY are indicative of this tendency. The films' signifiers of national, regional or local specificity are clearly not "essentialist" in their assertions of a common identity, however much they toy with nostalgic, parodic or pastiche versions of such an identity. The films have developed formulas that can accommodate various and even contradictory signifiers of nationhood, of regional history or local neighborhood street-credibility, in order to re-launch a region or national stereotype, or to reflect the image that (one assumes) the other has of oneself. To call these processes of re-assignment of the nation "constructed" would equally miss the point, insofar as the films openly display this knowledge of second order reference. More appropriate might be to compare this ironic-nostalgic

invocation to the tendency towards auto-ethnography or "self-othering" already noted. Compare, for instance, the phrase quoted in the previous chapter
from Wim Wenders' KINGS OF THE ROAD about "the Yanks have colonized our
sub-conscious" with the scene in TRAINSPOTTING, where Renton despairs of
being Scottish: "We're the lowest of the fucking low, the scum of the earth, the
most wretched, servile, miserable, pathetic trash that was ever shat into civilization. Some people hate the English, but I don't. They're just wankers. We, on the
other hand, are colonized by wankers." Such a double-take on self-loathing is
also a double-take on national identity, and marks the difference between
Wenders' self-conscious assumption of his role as a German auteur, and TRAIN-
SPOTTING's post-national Scottishness. The two films bridge the gap and make
the link between the auteur cinema of the 1970s and the post-national European
cinema of the 1990s, on its way to becoming part of "world cinema" (also, as I
shall argue, entailing some form of self-othering, if mostly less sarcastic). It indicates the extent to which such films now address themselves to world audiences (including American audiences). Post-national pastiche as well as self-
othering represent more fluid forms of European identity, appealing to audiences receptive to films from Britain, France, Germany or Spain. They can play
the role of the non-antagonistic other, against whom a national (or regional) cinema does not assert its identity in difference, but to whom it presents itself as
the impersoNation of "difference."

Beyond Constructivism: Commemorating a Common Past?

There is another, at first glance quite different way in which a more top-down
version of re-instating the "national" as a valid and even vibrant incarnation of
the idea of "Europe" seems to work. It could be seen as the reverse side of the
tendency towards "heritage history" with local color or regional accents, discussed above, insofar as it, too, deals with the past, and with memory. To some
extent, it also refers to how European cinema can assert its difference from television, important for its cultural status but, as we saw, difficult to sustain in
practice, when considering that the vast majority of films made in (Western)
Europe are either initiated, co-funded or co-produced by television.

   The trend I am trying to describe that complements "heritage", historical reconstruction and the nostalgic look at the national past has to do with the increasing Europeanization of what previously were national days of commemoration, as well as adding to the calendar anniversaries with a distinct European
dimension. The day of mourning, for instance, for the victims of the Madrid

railway bombing on 11 March is now widely reported in Europe's media, and 10 May has been mooted as a European day for commemorating slavery. But looming large in this enterprise is the period of fascism and the Second World War, a deeply troubling legacy for Germany, but out of which, it would seem, the whole of Europe is gradually fashioning a common past, in order to project through it an identity and historical "destiny-as-legacy." The moral and perhaps even emotional center of this common past as common identity program is the Holocaust. While thirty years ago, Auschwitz and the persecution of Jews was still very much a catastrophe that the Germans had to show themselves repentant and accountable for in the eyes of the world, the anniversaries of the so-called "Kristallnacht," or the (belated) resistance to Hitler by some of his officers and generals, as well as the liberation of the camps or the end of the war have since become European days for joint acts of reflection and solemn commemoration, where Europe can affirm its core values of democracy and commitment to human rights, while condemning totalitarianism in all its forms. The very negativity of the Holocaust as a human disaster and the lowest point of civilization turning into barbarism, is now the moral ground on which European nations can come together to affirm the statement "never again," but also to admit to a common responsibility for the events that happened more than sixty years ago, by investigating the extent to which all of Europe to a greater or lesser extent colluded with anti-Semitism and the destruction of the Jews in Europe. Hitler, the war and the Holocaust are never out of the news and the media, and Europe has many recurring anniversaries and special dates to draw on: the D-Day landing, the bombing of Dresden, the Nuremburg trials as precursors to the truth and reconciliation commissions or the International Court of Justice. In these commemorations a historical as well as a symbolic Europe are forming themselves, where Eastern Europe shares similar experiences with the West, and where this shared past promises a joint future. It even seems that on such occasions, victims and perpetrators, collaborators and survivors may come together in gestures of reconciliation and mutual recognition.[22]

The cinema has contributed its part to this commemorative Europe, but had to be given a lead – some say regrettably – by Hollywood. Already in the 1970s, German filmmakers complained that the Americans, by making a television series called HOLOCAUST (1978) had appropriated their history. Fifteen years later Steven Spielberg was accused of trivializing the death camps with SCHINDLER'S LIST (1993) and appropriating WWII with his SAVING PRIVATE RYAN (1997). Both films were big successes with the European public, while not faring well with the critics. Yet Spielberg's iconography of death, destruction, loss and suffering can now be found in almost every television reportage on a war or a human disaster. The series HOLOCAUST, it is often pointed out, allowed the German Cinema to reinvent itself in the mid-1970s around films dealing with fascism

(Syberberg, Kluge, Fassbinder, Schloendorff, von Trotta, Sanders-Brahms), thereby for the first time attaining an international public. Similarly, in France (Louis Malle, François Truffaut, Joseph Losey) and Italy (Luchino Visconti, Bernardo Bertolucci, the Taviani Brothers), directors have made major contributions to "mastering the past" in ways that had often less to do with "writing history" and more with the formation of a common European "memory." Films as different as Claude Lanzman's SHOAH (1985) Lars von Trier's EUROPA (1991), Roberto Benigni's LA VITA E BELLA (1997), Roman Polanski's THE PIANIST (2002) and many others have, irrespective of their specific aesthetic merits, put in place an imaginary of European history that lends itself to pious gestures of public commemoration at one end, and to clamorous controversy and scandal at the other. The German cinema, for obvious reasons, is prone to produce both, ranging more recently from Margarethe von Trotta's well-intentioned but embarrassing ROSENSTRASSE (2003) and Schloendorff's stiff THE NINTH DAY (2004) about a resisting priest, to films like ENEMY AT THE GATES (Jean-Jacques Annaud, 2001, about Stalingrad) and DER UNTERGANG (Oliver Hirschbiegel 2004, about the last days of Hitler), where historians rather than film critics find themselves called upon for media comment, earnestly discussing whether Hitler can be depicted as human being. Next to these commercial productions, there are more oblique, often politically risky and "incorrect" works, such as Romuald Karmaker's DAS HIMMLER PROJEKT (2000), Lutz Hachmeister's DAS GOEBBELS-EXPERIMENT (2004), Oskar Roehler's DIE UNBERÜHRBARE (2000), Christian Petzold's DIE INNERE SICHERHEIT (2000) – the last two titles not directly about fascism or the Holocaust, but showing how the ghosts of each nation's past haunt the present, and how important the cinema as the medium of different temporalities can be in showing Europe "working on its memories."

There is, of course, no inevitable congruence between the official calendar of commemoration – often acts of state – and the cinema, re-articulating the national past around different markers of the national. Among these markers, general period settings – Edwardian England, France under the Occupation, Berlin in the early 1930s – are more prominent than specific historical events, and even then, the period often figures in the context of negotiating other issues, such as class, gender or sexual identity. This is the case with some of the films just mentioned, such as Visconti's "German Trilogy," James Ivory's THE REMAINS OF THE DAY, and includes the filmed novels or biographies of Jane Austen, E.M. Foster, Edith Wharton, Henry James and Virginia Woolf. But the new cultural studies or popular memory agendas also change the perspective we now have on the cinema of the 1940s and 50s. Films that according to the traditional canon were previously dismissed as routine and commercial, have become the classics or cult films of contemporary movie lovers, rediscovering the popular culture of their parents (Jean Gabin, the films of David Lean) or even grandparents (BRIEF

ENCOUNTER, Zarah Leander), and making these films the veritable *lieux de mém-oire* of the nation and of national identity. In Germany, a film from 1944 called DIE FEUERZANGEN-BOWLE and featuring the hugely popular Heinz Rühmann, has become just such a rallying point for the retroactive nation. Not only is it broadcast every Christmas on television; university students show it on the big screen in specially hired halls, with audiences dressing up and miming favorite scenes in the ROCKY HORROR PICTURE SHOW manner. The extraordinary reva-luation that the British cinema has undergone in the past two decades is also partly based on such a revision of the criteria applied to the films rather than the choice of films themselves. Coupled with the incessant memory work done by television, through its documentary output (which is, of course, often in sync with the state's policy of commemorative history), media memory is now one of the major ways in which the nation is "constructed," but also spontaneously "re-lived": not least because so much of this tele-visual media memory draws on eyewitness accounts, personal reminiscences, family photos, home movies and other forms of period memorabilia accessible to all. In this respect, televi-sion does work from the "bottom up," weaving together a new synthetic and yet "authentic" fabric of the past, which corresponds to and yet inverts the "quilt" of the nation that Anderson mentions in *Imagined Communities* as patched together by the bureaucratic-pedagogic establishment.[23]

Reconceptualizing National Cinemas

The other extreme of the "post-national" national cinema would be a commer-cial producer's perspective, who like many a European entrepreneur, will uti-lize to the full the EU provisions for subsidies, tax-breaks and other community measures designed to minimize his business risk, in this case, of making films for an unpredictable internal market and with few export sales opportunities other than into the world's niche markets, namely art houses, public service television, and DVD-sales. Films produced in this way, i.e., European in their legal status, insofar as they enjoyed forms of subsidy and are bound to the con-tractual obligations that flow from them, would normally be co-productions, and have the country codes of several states in their production credits. Lars von Trier's EUROPA, for instance, has five of these (Denmark, Sweden, Germany, France, Switzerland), Kieslowski's THREE COLOURS: BLUE has three (France, Po-land, Switzerland), and CHOCOLAT, set in France and directed by a Swede is a UK/US co-production, with no French input. In other words, such films would still have to declare their nationality in all kinds of other ways: for instance, by their stars, their settings and story. For audiences, finally, the criteria of choice are different still: they might recognize the name of a star, say Juliette Binoche, and think of BLUE and CHOCOLAT as French films, belonging together because of Binoche. EUROPA may look to them like a German film, because of its setting and Barbara Sukowa, known from her roles in Fassbinder's films. But what would such a spectator make of BREAKING THE WAVES or DANCER IN THE DARK? British the first, American the second? Then what are Catherine Deneuve and Bjork doing in DANCER IN THE DARK? Cinephiles, of course, will know that these are Lars von Trier films and associate them with Denmark, a nationality label that only the production credits will confirm, but not the language nor setting.

BREAKING THE WAVES

These perhaps exceptional examples nonetheless indicate that national cinema has become a floating designation, neither essentialist nor constructivist, but more like something that hovers uncertainly over a film's "identity." The national thus joins other categories, such as the opposition posited between mainstream films featuring stars, and art cinema identified by a directorial personality; popular genre films versus documentary style and psychological realism. All these binary divides no longer seem to work, since a broader spectrum of possibilities now minimizes the differences between independent cinema, auteur cinema, art cinema, mainstream so that the great loser is national cinema, for which there hardly seems any space, recognition, or identity left at all, when looked at from the audiences' perspective. What may be distinctly European is the seemingly ever-widening gap between European countries' cinema culture (the films their audiences like and get to see) and the same countries film production, where some films are made for the festival circuits and rarely if ever reach other screens, while others are produced by and for television. Only a minority of European productions has the budgets, stars and production values even to try to reach an international mainstream audience, and often enough these films fail in their aim, not least because it means they have to disguise themselves to look and sound as if they were American.

Thus, when differentiating along the classical (mainstream) categories of production, distribution and exhibition, in order to identify what is European cinema, one ends up turning the definition of national cinema upside down, dismissing nationality as the least determining criterion. Rather than rounding up different national cinemas or adding more and more qualifiers, one could start with a concept such as hybridity that immediately makes apparent the essentially mixed or relational nature of the concept Cinema Europe. It, too, would have the advantage of overcoming the conceptual deadlock between essentialism and constructivism that typified discussions of national cinema from the 1960s to the 1980s. But what is served by falling back on the portmanteau words of cultural studies, whose semantics may point in the right direction, but whose formalism risks turning them into empty mantras? If the concept of national cinema is to have any purchase at all, and be of use in understanding the shift from national to European cinema, which in turn communicates with world cinema, then we must be able to explore categories coming from outside the immediate field.

This is to some extent what Stephen Crofts has tried to do, in his useful and much-cited articles from 1993 ("Reconceptualizing National Cinema/s") and 1998 ("Concepts of National Cinema"), where he sets out a number of taxonomies.[24] Crofts, for instance, differentiates between seven types of (world) cinema, ranging from the Hollywood model to Third Cinema. The categories most interesting from a European perspective are those of art cinema, popular indigenous cinema, totalitarian cinema, and regional/ethnic cinema. While such a scheme at first also looks very formalist, it does allow one to draw significant parallels that often cut across geography and social systems, when one thinks how art cinema is a category valid for Sweden as well as for India, and that ethnic/regional cinema can extend from Basque films made in Spain to Maori films made in New Zealand, from Irish cinema to Chicano films in the US, from Turkish directors making films in Germany to Moroccan films made in France or Asian filmmakers entering the mainstream in Britain. It is from Crofts that I have borrowed some of the concepts already briefly introduced, notably the idea of a sub-state cinema.[25] This idea, to which I am adding the sub- and supra-state levels of national identity, will be further pursued in the chapter "Double Occupancy" where specific films will be read against the foil of different political scenarios.

After the Historical Imaginary

As we have seen, much of the debate around national cinema is dominated by two paradigms: that of essentialism versus constructivism, and the paradigm of "otherness," the fact that a sense of (national) identity always implies drawing boundaries, and staking out the visible or invisible lines of inclusion and exclusion. However hard a semiotically inclined mind may find it to abandon the meaning-making power of binary pairs, from what has been said so far, such strict oppositions cannot be maintained without some modification. While the idea of the historical imaginary – which as indicated, runs through most of the essays in the collection – is already an attempt to allow for the shifts and reversals in the relation of self to other, it is evident that this term, too, is dependent on some version of identity as a relation to otherness (at the time intended to combat essentialism, while not yielding to full-blown and ahistorical constructivism). I have tried to include a certain historical dynamic and asymmetry in the power relations at work in the self-other relation, reflected in the section titles, such as "border crossings," "without passport," or the way I trace the relation of art cinema to counter-cinema to Hollywood via the detour of an imaginary Third Cinema of neo-realism as magic realism.

Yet insofar as the essays do have a consistent conceptual-metaphoric basis, it is indeed grounded in this self-other relationship, the cinematic look, the mirror metaphor and the different affective, psychic and political architectures built on it. As already explained in the introduction, the (two-way) mirror is something like the master trope in my thinking about national cinema (Germany, Britain, the Balkans) in relation to Hollywood or the West, but it is equally in evidence in essays such as the one on Bergman and in "Women Filmmakers in the 1980s." While I am therefore not disowning either the underlying assumptions or the analyses thus obtained, I do want to signal that the historical situation of cinema in Europe has changed since the 1990s, or rather, that the questions we put to this cinema have changed, and that in pleading for a new approach I am also revis(it)ing positions put forward elsewhere in the present collection.

I began by looking at the sort of distinctions that are usually made about how the national functions within the body politic (ranging from patriotism, to chauvinism, to racism) and in the media, sports, leisure, and popular culture (print, television, cinema, popular music, football, food, tourism), where signifiers of the national are constantly put in circulation in modes that range from the exotic and the nostalgic, to the patronizing and the provocative. My central question, thus, was to ask what the relation might be between the resurgence of political nationalism in its contradictory, but also very modern or contemporary character, and the increasing ubiquity and political power of audiovisual media, notably television (and to a much lesser extent, the cinema).

The conclusion reached in this chapter has only answered the question above, insofar as it has pointed to the difficulties of moving from national cinema to European cinema with the concepts provided by the discipline of Film Studies. The chapter appears to end on a negative note, suggesting that the debate around national cinema may have exhausted its usefulness for the study of contemporary cinema in Europe. But this also contains the hope that both the essentialist and the constructivist notion of national cinema can be superseded by a new cognitive mapping of the hitherto central categories such as "nation", "state", "identity" and "otherness" without either resorting to the formal-metaphoric level of in-between-ness and hybridity, or the generalized label of postmodernism. If the premise of the present chapter is correct, namely that the relations between nation and state are, within Europe, shifting in particularly paradoxical and countervailing ways, then the concepts of subjectivity and identity, of history and temporality – with which the European cinema has been identified at least since 1945 – are also changing. Such reflections provide more reasons why it may be necessary to revise the concept of the historical imaginary, based as it was on identification and address, and centered on the geometries and architecture of the look, rather than on irony and voice, appropriation and impersonation, painted faces and American accents. The New Cinema Europe, if such an entity exists, cannot be defined as either essentialist or constructed in relation to nation and state, but neither will the mirroring effects of self and other be sufficient to determine its identity. Indeed, the very concept of identity, with respect to self, nation and Europe may no longer be apposite. The hope is that new terms will emerge that can think cinema and Europe, independent of nation and state while still maintaining a political agenda and an ethical imperative. For the former, I shall look at the supra-national organization of the European film business as manifested in the film festival circuit, and the nodes that determine its functioning as a network; for the latter, I will choose a sub-national perspective – above the individual and below the state – to explore how specific films locate their protagonists and narratives in different forms of intersubjectivity and mutual interdependence, while still speaking of inclusion and exclusion. The central concepts will be those of occupancy rather than identity, of interference rather than mirroring. In both these respects – the festival network as a determining factor of contemporary cinema and multiple identities as a determining factor of belonging – European films are not unique, for these are characteristics that they share with films from Asia and the US. Maybe the best reason for calling films European in the global context would finally be their awareness not of what makes them different, but their reflexivity about what makes them able to participate and communicate in the world's cinema cultures.

(2005)

Notes

1.   Hans Magnus Enzensberger, *Ach Europa!* (Frankfurt am Main: Suhrkamp, 1987), p. 105.
2.   Even the sociological question, whether televised sports, ethnic restaurants or mass tourism have – through overexposure and caricature – taken the sting out of the clichés about the national character somehow misses the point.

3. The phrase is from Benedict Anderson, *Imagined Communities: Reflection on the Origins and Spread of Nationalism* (London: Verso, 1993), p. 4.

4. Respectively, in the United States and Russia; in Israel and the United States; in Iran and Algeria; in India and Sri Lanka.

5. British politicians, such as Margaret Thatcher or Tony Blair, routinely appeal to the 'family' as the unit the state is called upon to protect, rather than its citizens. Asian (family) values are deemed essential for the success of multinational capitalism, while mafia-like cartels were apparently needed during the Yeltsin years to turn Russia and the countries of the ex-Soviet Union into functioning market economies, a trend that Vladimir Putin is trying to reverse by reinventing the autocratic state.

6. See Siegfried Kracauer, *From Caligari to Hitler* (Princeton: Princeton University Press, 1947) and Andrew Tudor, *Image and Influence. Studies in the Sociology of Film* (London: Allen and Unwin 1974) for Germany, as well as Donald Richie, *Japanese Cinema: Film Style and National Character* (New York: Doubleday, 1971) and Noel Burch, *To the Distant Observer* (Berkeley: University of California Press, 1979) for Japan.

7. See Charles Barr, *Ealing Studios* (London: Cameron & Tayleur, 1977); Dave Pirie, *A Heritage of Horror, The English Gothic Cinema 1946-1972* (London: Fraser, 1973), Raymond Durgnat, *A Mirror for England* (London: Faber and Faber, 1970).

8. Kristin Ross, *Fast Cars, Clean Bodies. Decolonization and the Reordering of French Culture* (Cambridge, Mass.: MIT Press 1995).

9. The attempts to formulate notions that lie either above or below the concept of the nation-state as the pre-given entity, such as "imagined communities," the "national imaginary," "popular memory," etc., seem at once to attract and repel film scholars. For an intelligent discussion of these issues in the context of Hollywood as a national cinema, see Robert Burgoyne, *Film Nation* (Minneapolis: Minnesota University Press, 1996).

10. The British heritage film has been widely discussed by Sue Harper, Pam Cook, Richard Dyer and especially by Andrew Higson, 'Re-presenting the National Past: Nostalgia and Pastiche in the Heritage Film', in Lester Friedman (ed.): *British Cinema and Thatcherism* (London: University College, 1993) pp. 109-129, and Andrew Higson: 'The Heritage Film and British Cinema', in Andrew Higson (ed.): *Dissolving Views: Key Writings on British Cinema* (London: Cassell, 1996). For French cinema and Europe, see also Ginette Vincendeau (ed.), *Film/Literature/Heritage: A Sight and Sound Reader* (London: BFI Publishing, 2001). For Germany, see the first part of the section 'Haunted by History and Empire', below.

11. Melis Behlil, *Hollywood and its Foreign Directors* (Ph.D. thesis in progress, Amsterdam University).

12. See Martha Wolfenstein and Nathan Leites, *Movies a Psychological Study* (Glencoe, Ill: The Free Press, 1950) and Ginette Vincendeau's "Daddy's Girls (Oedipal Narratives in 1930s French Films)," *IRIS* 8 (1995), pp. 70-81.

13. Ed Buscombe, "The Idea of National Cinema," *Australian Journal of Screen Theory*, no 9/10, 1981, p. 141-153. Thomas Elsaesser, "Film History and Visual Pleasure: Weimar Cinema," now in P. Mellencamp, P. Rosen (eds.), *Cinema Histories, Cinema Practices*. Frederick, MD: University Publications of America, 1984), 47-85; Phil Rosen, "History, Textuality, Narration: Kracauer, Burch and Some Problems in the Study of National Cinemas," *Iris* vol. 2 no. 2, 1984, p. 69-84. All three of us were present at

the "Milwaukee Conference" (held in Asilomar, California) of 1982, where I presented the paper which set out my position, returning to national cinema after auteurism. For a course in the US on "German Expressionist" cinema in 1978, I began with a Foucault-inspired re-reading of Kracauer's assertions about German cinema, replacing "Expressionist cinema" with "Weimar Cinema," which meant a critical engagement with essentialism about the nation, but across the work of auteurs, notably Fritz Lang, G.W. Pabst and F.W. Murnau.

14. Geoffrey Nowell-Smith, "But Do We Need It?," in: Martyn Auty, Nick Roddick (eds.), *British Cinema Now.* (London: British Film Institute, 1985), pp. 147–158.
15. Benedict Anderson, *Imagined Communities* (London: Verso, 1992).
16. See, for an attack on both, the essay by Michael Walsh, "National Cinema, National Imaginary," *Film History*, vol. 8, no. 1, 1996, pp. 5-11.
17. Philip Schlesinger, *Media, State and Nation. Political Violence and Collective Identities* (London: Sage, 1991), p. 143.
18. *Das kleine Fernsehspiel* is discussed in a separate essay elsewhere in this volume.
19. For an analysis, see Angus Finney, *The Egos Have Landed: the Rise and Fall of Palace Pictures*, (London: Heinemann, 1996).
20. For a detailed account of the different film subsidy systems, see Anne Jäckel, *European Film Industries* (London: BFI Publishing, 2004).
21. See Dina Iordanova who in several books has proposed a new territorial identity, namely that of "Balkan cinema".
22. A similar thesis is put forward by Natan Szaider and Daniel Levi in "Memory Unbound: The Holocaust and the Formation of Cosmopolitan Memory", *European Journal of Social Theory* 5(1), 2002, pp. 87-106.
23. At the trans-national level, this memory work is done by the mainly US-controlled, but in Europe also very popular themed channels devoted to history and natural history, in whose programs on human and natural disasters one can see the two categories – history and natural history – increasingly overlap and imperceptibly blend.
24. Stephen Crofts, "Reconceptualizing National Cinema/s", *Quarterly Review of Film and Video* vol 14 no 3, (1993), 49-67 and Stephen Crofts, "Concepts of national cinema", in John Hill and Pamela Church Gibson (eds.), *The Oxford Guide to Film Studies* (Oxford: Oxford University Press, 1998), pp. 385-394.
25. "Concepts of National Cinema", pp. 390-391.

Film Festival Networks

The New Topographies of Cinema in Europe

Markers of Provenance, Strategies of Access

In the previous chapter, I argued that the "national" in European cinema has become a second-order concept ("post-national"), in that it is now generally mediated through the legislative and economic measures taken by the European Union to stimulate the audiovisual industries and promote their role in the preservation of its heritage and patrimony. In the films themselves, references to the nation, the region and the local have also become second-order realities, whenever they function as self-advertisements for (the memorializable parts of) the past, for lifestyle choices or for (tourist) locations. Films made in

Europe (and indeed in other smaller, film-producing nations) tend to display the markers of their provenance quite self-consciously. The emphasis on region, neighborhoods and the local in recent successes such as THE FULL MONTY, BILLY ELLIOT, WOMEN ON THE VERGE OF A NERVOUS BREAKDOWN, CINEMA PARADISO, GOODBYE LENIN, AMÉLIE, provides access-points for the international and global cinema markets, which includes the national audience, thoroughly internationalized through the films on offer in cineplexes and videotheques. The films' attention to recognizable geographical places and stereotypical historical periods thus begin to echo Hollywood's ability to produce "open" texts that speak to a diversity of publics, while broadly adhering to the format of classical narrative.[1]

Two further genres could be called post-national, but for opposite reasons. One are films that appeal to a broad audience, but whose references are not to place or region, nor to the national past. They locate themselves in the hermetic media space of recycled genre formulas from 1960s commercial cinema and 1970s television, spoofed and satirized by television personalities who are popular with domestic audiences but difficult to export across the national or language borders: the French TAXI films or LES VISITEURS would be examples, paralleled in Germany and Austria by the "Bully" Herbig films (DER SCHUH DES MANITU, UNSER TRAUMSCHIFF). The other post-national tendency would be the *cinéma du look*, adopting the style norms of design and fashion. Different from classical art cinema in that it breaks with the conventions of realism, this cinema is not embarrassed by its affinities to high concept advertising (J. Beneix' DIVA, Tom Tykwer's RUN LOLA RUN), nor does it shun accusations of pornography (films like Patrice Chereau's INTIMACY, the work of Catherine Breillat, Michael Winterbottom's NINE SONGS). Style and subject matter ensure that the films travel more easily across national boundaries, and by appealing to universalized Eurochic values of erotic sophistication, adult emotion and sexual passion, they even have a chance to enter the American market.

But there is another way of transcending the national for European films, while at the same time reinstating it as a second-order category, and thus becoming post-national: the international film festival. With respect to Europe, the festival circuit, I want to claim, has become the key force and power grid in the film business, with wide-reaching consequences for the respective functioning of the other elements (authorship, production, exhibition, cultural prestige and recognition) pertaining to the cinema and to film culture. If, as will be argued in the subsequent chapter, television since the 1960s has largely taken over from cinema the task of "gathering" the nation, addressing, as well as representing it, the question broached in this chapter is how the festival circuit, in its turn, holds some of these manifestations of post-national cinema together, giving them a European dimension, at the same time as it makes them enter into global symbolic economies, potentially re-writing many of the usual markers of identity. As such, the film festival circuit presents both a theoretical challenge and a historical "missing link" in our understanding of European cinema, not just since 1945, but since the demise of the historical avant-garde in the 1930s. On the theoretical plane, the answer may well lie not with the traditional concepts of film studies, but in some version of modern system theory. On offer are the auto-poetic feedback loops as proposed by Niklas Luhmann, Manuel Castells' theory of the "space of flows", the "actor-network-theory" of Bruno Latour, or the theories of complex adaptive systems, centered on "emergence", "attractors" and "self-organization."[2] However, here I shall mainly concentrate on the history of the phenomenon and examine in passing some of its systemic properties.

Festivals have always been recognized as integral to European cinema, but they have rarely been analyzed as crucial also for the generation of the very categories that here concern me: the author, national cinema, opposition to (or "face to face with") Hollywood. Characterized by geographical-spatial extensions (the sites and cities hosting such film festivals) and particular temporal extensions (the sequential programming of the world's major festivals to cover the calendar year across the whole twelve-month annual cycle), the international film festival must be seen as a network (with nodes, flows and exchanges) if its importance is to be grasped. Could this network and its spatio-temporal circuits be the motor that keeps European cinema at once stable and dynamic, perpetually crisis-prone and yet surviving, frustratingly hard to understand for the historian and so self-evident for the cinephile?

International Film Festivals

The annual international film festival is a very European institution. It was invented in Europe just before the Second World War, but it came to cultural fruition, economic stature, and political maturity in the 1940s and 1950s. Since then, the names of Venice, Cannes, Berlin, Rotterdam, Locarno, Karlovy Vary, Oberhausen and San Sebastian have spelled the roll call of regular watering holes for the world's film lovers, critics and journalists, as well as being the marketplaces for producers, directors, distributors, television acquisition heads, and studio bosses.

The locations themselves have to be read symptomatically in relation to their history, politics and ideology, that is, in their typically European contexts of temporal layers and geographical sedimentation. Many of the best-known venues are sited in cities that compete with each other for cultural tourism and seasonal events. In evidence are old spas that have lost their aristocratic clientele, and now host a film festival usually just before or after the high tourist season: Venice, Cannes, Locarno, Karlovy Vary, and San Sebastian are the obvious off-season on-festival sites. Other festival cities are indicative of more explicitly political considerations, such as the Berlin Film Festival. It was a creation of the Cold War, and planned as a deliberate showcase for Hollywood glamour and Western show business, meant to provoke East Berlin and to needle the Soviet Union. The documentary festival in Leipzig was the GDR's counter-move, featuring films from Eastern Europe, Cuba and Latin America. It tried to consolidate the "socialist" film front in the anti-fascist/anti-imperialist struggle, while selectively inviting left-wing filmmakers from Western countries as token comrades. Outside Europe, similar kinds of analyses could be made: Pusan, the main film festival in South Korea, was also the result of a "political" gesture in that it began by copying the very successful International Hong Kong film festival, and then subsequently played a major role in reviving Korean filmmaking as a national cinema. Yet for many Western visitors, put off by the sheer size of the Hong Kong festival, Pusan also became the portal for a first contact with the other "new" Asian cinemas in the 1990s. The Toronto festival, too, was a smartly calculated move to consolidate a "national" beachhead that could brave the cultural barbarians south of the border, while rallying Canada's divided Francophone and Anglophone filmmaking communities around a common enemy, Hollywood. Other European festivals are located in industrial cities, some of whom over years, have been trying to repurpose and re-invent themselves as cultural centers: such is the case of the short film festival in Oberhausen which brought film culture to a mining and heavy industry region, while the International Film Festival Rotterdam has greatly contributed to changing this city's image, too: from being identified mainly with its giant container port and a harbor that brings ashore goods from China and Asia while servicing Europe in the past as the point of embarkation for hopeful New World emigrants, Rotterdam has become a center of media, cinema and architecture. It now is an equally important hub and node for other, more immaterial aspect of the experience economy, building bridges between Asian cinema and European audiences, a specialty of the Rotterdam festival for nearly two decades.

The tendency for formerly industrial cities to try and re-launch themselves as capitals of culture is, of course, a much broader trend. It exceeds the phenomenon of film festivals and the continent of Europe. But precisely because of the forces at work all over the developed world to renew inner cities and to infuse new life into the urban fabric (often neglected over the previous half century, or victim of the private motor car, the suburbs and centralized planning), the strategic importance of cultural events in general, and of film festivals in particular for city-branding can scarcely be overestimated. At least two distinct developments overlap and intersect to re-valorize location and emplacement (the "neighborhood" factor) in urban culture. Firstly, there is the phenomenon of "cultural clustering." Following Jane Jacobs' studies of neighborhoods and Sharon Zukin's work on the interplay of cultural and economic factors around New York's loft culture in the 1980s, economists, urban planners and ethnographers of the contemporary city have begun to look at the "locally specific appreciation of the changing interaction between culture (place) and commerce (market) in today's mixed economy of leisure, culture and creativity".[3] As a consequence, companies in the information, high-tech and knowledge industries, now seek "culture-rich environments" for their operational bases, in order to attract the skilled workers and retain the discriminating staff they need to stay competitive and innovative.[4] To keep these companies and their employees, cities feature their perceived location advantages (housing, transport, amenities, infrastructure) by extending them into a total city-concept, in which locality and neighborhood play a special role. Secondly (and not without a certain tension with this idea of the local) the most economically attractive part of the population are not the ethnic clusters of traditional urban neighborhoods, but the yuppies, dinkies, empty nesters, bobos and their likes. Their collective leverage is such that key service industries rely on their purchasing power, leading to something known as the "Bridget Jones economy".[5] To cater for this new economic class, municipal or metropolitan authorities try to endow their city with the sense of being a site of permanent, ongoing events. Complementing the architecturally articulated urban space with a temporal dimension, the built city turns thus into, and is doubled by, the "programmed" – or programmable – city. In this endeavor, major temporary exhibitions and annual festivals are a key ingredient in structuring the seasonal succession of city events across the calendar year. Among different kinds of temporary events and festivals, a special role accrues to the international film festival, at once relatively cost effective, attracting both the local population and visitors from outside, and helping develop an infrastructure of sociability as well as facilities appreciated by the so-called "creative class" that function all the year round.[6] Small wonder then, that the number of festivals has exponentially increased in recent years. There are now more film festivals in Europe alone than there are days in the year. No longer just major capitals, off-season spas or refurbished industrial towns are in the running. Often medium-sized cities, verging on the nondescript, decide to host a film festival in order to boost their tourist attractions or stake a claim as a regional cultural hub (e.g., Brunswick in Germany, Bradford in Britain).[7]

These two components, the cultural clustering of the Bridget Jones economy, and a determination to consider the urban space as programmable and cyclical, provide salient elements for understanding the sheer quantity of film festivals. They do not explain the network effects that international film festivals now realize for the global media markets. Here, the quantity produces consequences that are at first glance contradictory: host cities compete with each other regarding attractiveness of the location, convenience for international access and exclusivity of the films they are able to present. The festivals also compete over the most desirable dates in the annual calendar. But at another level, they complement each other along the same axes. Competition raises standards, and adds value to the films presented. Competition invites comparison, with the result that festivals resemble each other more and more in their internal organization, while seeking to differentiate themselves in their external self-presentation and the premium they place on their (themed) programming. They also need to make sure they follow each other in a pre-established sequence, which allows their international clients – producers, filmmakers, journalists – to travel comfortably from one A festival to the next.[8]

Optimizing its respective local advantages, each festival thus contributes to the global network effect, offsetting the negative consequences of competition (over the finite number of films and timing) with the positive effects of familiar format and recognition value, while giving innovative programmers the opportunity to set trends, or to come up with concepts taken over by others. From the perspective of the films (or rather, their makers) these properties of festivals constitute essential elements in the grid of expectations: films are now made for festivals, in the way that Hollywood during the studio era made its films for the exclusivity release dates of first run picture palaces. Considered as a global network, the festival circuit constitutes the exhibition dates of most independent films in the first-run venues of the world market, where they can gather the cultural capital and critical prowess necessary to subsequently enter the national or local exhibition markets on the strength of their accumulated festival successes. No poster of an independent film can do without the logo of one of the world's prime festivals, as prominently displayed as Hollywood productions carry their studio logo.

Film festivals thus make up a network with nodes and nerve endings, there is capillary action and osmosis between the various layers of the network, and while a strict ranking system exists, for instance between A and B festivals, policed by an international federation (FIAPF), the system as a whole is highly porous and perforated. There is movement and contact between regional and international ones, between specialized/themed ones and open-entry ones; the European festivals communicate with North American festivals, as well as Asian and Australian ones. Some festivals are "outsourced", such as the one in Ouagadougou, Burkina Faso, largely organized and financed from Paris and Brussels, but which functions as the prime space for defining, endorsing and displaying what counts as legitimate African cinema, Anglophone as well as Francophone.[9] Other festivals are festivals of festivals ("bests of the fests"), such as the London Film Festival that brings to the city's filmgoers the pick of the annual festival favorites, but attracts fewer journalists and international visitors.[10]

So tightly woven has this web become, so spontaneously organized are the interactions between the various "network actors," that in its totality the film festival circuit provides the structures and interchanges permitting both chance and routine to operate. Taken together and in sequence, festivals form a cluster of consecutive international venues, to which films, directors, producers, promoters and press, in varying degrees of density and intensity, migrate, like flocks of birds or a shoal of fish. And not unlike these natural swarm phenomena (closely studied by theorists of complex adaptive systems), the manner in which information travels, signals are exchanged, opinion hardens and, consensus is reached at these festivals appears at once to be thrillingly unpredictable and yet to follow highly programmed protocols. The criteria governing selection, presentation, news coverage and awards, for instance, may seem arbitrary and opaque, but patterns are quickly perceived. It suffices to take half a dozen catalogues from different festivals, read the description of the films, or the speeches that go with the prizes, and do a semantic analysis: no more than a dozen or so words make up the evaluative and classificatory vocabulary needed to categorize the vast majority of festival films. This informal lexical stability complements the ever-increasing organizational similarity between festival, and both counteract the temporary nature and variable locations of festivals.

As one of the baselines that allow one to reconstruct the dynamics that today govern the production, distribution and reception of independent films, the festival circuits hold the keys to all forms of cinema not bound into the global Hollywood network. But one can go further: the festival circuit is also a crucial interface with Hollywood itself, because taken together, the festivals constitute (like Hollywood) a global platform, but one which (unlike Hollywood) is at one and the same time a "marketplace" (though perhaps more like bazaar than a stock exchange), a cultural showcase (comparable to music or theatre festivals), a "competitive venue" (like the Olympic Games), and a world body (an ad-hoc United Nations, a parliament of national cinemas, or cinematic NGO's, considering some of the various festivals' political agendas). In other words, festivals cluster a combination of economic, cultural, political, artistic and personality-based factors, which communicate with and irrigate each other in a unique kind of arena. It explains why this originally European phenomenon has globalized itself, and in the process has created not only a self-sustaining, highly self-referential world for the art cinema, the independent cinema and the documentary film, but a sort of "alternative" to the Hollywood studio system in its post-Fordist phase. It first and foremost sets the terms for distribution, marketing and exhibition, yet to an increasing extent it regulates production as well, determined as this is in the non-Hollywood sector by the global outlets it can find, rather than by the single domestic market of its "country of origin". Seeing how they compete for and are dependent on a regular annual supply of interesting, innovative or otherwise noteworthy films, it is no wonder that the more prestigious among the world's festivals increasingly offer competitive production funds, development money as prizes, or organize a "talent campus" (Berlin), in order to bind new creative potential to a particular festival's brand image. It means that certain films are now being made to measure and made to order, i.e., their completion date, their opening venue, their financing is closely tied in with a particular festival's (or festival circuit's) schedules and many filmmakers internalize and target such a possibility for their work. Hence the somewhat cynical reference to the genre of the "festival film", which names a genuine phenomenon but also obscures the advantages that the creation of such a relatively stable horizon of expectations brings. It ensures visibility and a window of attention for films that can neither command the promotional budgets

of Hollywood films nor rely on a sufficiently large internal market (such as India) to find its audience or recoup its investment.[11]

A Brief History of European Film Festivals

The global perspective taken here on the festival phenomenon needs to be contextualized by a brief reference to the history of the European film festivals.
They were, initially, highly political and nationalistic affairs. The Venice film
festival, for instance, as has often been pointed out, was set up as a combination
of a charm offensive on the part of the Italian Hotel Association and of a propaganda exercise by Benito Mussolini in 1932. So strong was the pro-fascist bias of
Venice by the end of the decade, that the French decided to found a counter-
festival:

> In those days, the [Venice] festival and its awards were as much about the national
> prestige of the participating countries as it was about the films. As World War II
> edged closer, the awards began to noticeably favor the countries of the fascist alliance,
> particularly Germany and Italy. In 1939, France was tipped to win the festival's top
> prize with Jean Renoir's LA GRANDE ILLUSION. However, the Golden Lion (known
> back then as the *Coppa Mussolini*) ended up being jointly awarded to a German film
> called OLYMPIA (produced in association with Joseph Goebbels' Ministry of Propa-
> ganda), and Italy's LUCIANO SERRA, PILOTA, made by Mussolini's own son. The
> French were of course outraged and withdrew from the competition in protest. Both
> the British and American jury members also resigned to voice their displeasure at the
> destruction of artistic appreciation by the hand of politics and ideology.[12]

Another festival that owes its existence to political controversy and municipal
rows is the Locarno film festival in Switzerland, which took over from Lugano,
itself founded as a continuation of Venice during the war years. Locarno started
in 1946, just days ahead of the opening of the Cannes festival.[13] The Karlovy
Vary festival, too, was started in 1946, as a direct initiative on the part of the
newly nationalized Czech film industry to have a showcase for "socialist" film
production.

In the post-WWII years, Venice and Cannes came to a more amicable arrangement, joined in 1951 by the Berlin Film Festival, as already indicated, also the
result of a political decision.[14] For almost two decades – until 1968 – these three
A-festivals divided up the year's cinematographic production, handing out
Golden Lions, Golden Palms, and Golden Bears. Typical of this first phase were
the national selection committees, in which the film industry representatives
occupied important positions, because they decided the nominations. They

chose the films that represented their country at the festivals, much like national committees select the athletes who compete at the Olympic Games.[15] Such political-diplomatic constraints notwithstanding, it was at these festivals, and above all at Cannes, that the great *auteurs* of the European cinema – Rossellini, Bergman, Visconti, Antonioni, Fellini – came to prominence and fame.[16] The same goes for two of the grand exiles of cinema: Luis Bunuel and Orson Welles, both of whom were honored in Cannes after low points in their trans-national careers. The Indian director Satyajit Ray won at Cannes and there garnered fame as an internationally recognized *auteur*. Less well known perhaps is the fact that practically all the European new waves also owed their existence to the film festivals. Cannes in this respect has – ever since the festival of 1959 made stars out of François Truffaut and Jean-Luc Godard and created the *Nouvelle Vague* – acted as the launching platform. For instance, it was imitated by a group of mostly Munich filmmakers who declared their own New Wave, the Young German Cinema at the short film and documentary festival of Oberhausen in 1962, while the Dogma group deliberately and self-reflexively launched their famous "vow of chastity" manifesto in Cannes in 1995.

By the mid-1960s, the European festival circuit consisted of half a dozen A-festivals (to the ones already named have to be added Moscow/Karlovy Vary and San Sebastian), and any number of B-festivals, mostly located along the Mediterranean, the Adriatic and the French Atlantic coast. The major changes in festival policy came after 1968, with Cannes once more the focal point, when Truffaut and Godard took their protest against the dismissal of Henri Langlois as head of the French Cinemathèque to the 1968 festival edition, effectively forcing it to close. While Paris was in the throes of the May events, Cannes with its foreign visitors was also shut down, and in the years that followed, sweeping changes were made by adding more sections for first-time filmmakers, the directors' fortnight (*La Quinzaine des realisateurs*) as well as other showcase sidebars. Other festivals soon followed, and in 1971, for instance, Berlin incorporated a parallel festival, the International Forum of the Young Film.[17] But the crucial change came in 1972, when it was decreed, again at Cannes, that henceforth the festival director had the ultimate responsibility for selecting the official entries, and not the national committees. With this move, immediately followed by the other festivals, Cannes set the template for film festivals the world over, which – as mentioned – have largely synchronized their organizational structures and selection procedures while nonetheless setting different accents to maintain their profile and identity.[18]

The shift in the selection process from country/nation to festival director also implied changes in the way the European cinema came to be perceived: while the smaller countries were able to come to international attention via the promotion of a new wave (with *auteurs* now representing the nation, instead of the officials who selected the national entry), the gold standard of the European festivals under the rule of Cannes became the auteur director. But not only for small developing countries or European nations. Thus, for instance, the 1970s was the decade of the young American *auteurs*: Robert Altman, Martin Scorsese, Francis Coppola, along with the Europeans Ridley Scott, Louis Malle, John Boorman, and Milos Forman, all of whom also worked with and for Hollywood. Cannes, in this respect presents a paradox: it is, as the most important French cinema event, often prone to extreme anti-Hollywood sentiment and utterances; but it is also the festival that has anointed more American directors for subsequent status gain back in the US than any other venue. The 1980s saw Cannes anoint German directors (Wim Wenders, Werner Herzog, R.W. Fassbinder) and Krzysztof Kieslowski, who won the Golden Palm in 1988, and in the 1990s, Chinese directors (Zhang Yimou, Chen Kaige). Throughout the decades, Cannes remained the kingmaker of the festival circuit, and retained the *auteur* as the king pin at the center of the system, while stars, starlets and glamour secured popular attention. "Hollywood on the Riviera" also added the film market, at first unregulated and a venue for the growing pornography industry, but from 1976 onwards *Le Marché du film* became more regulated and has not ceased to grow in importance ever since.[19]

Nonetheless, the 1980s saw a shift in the traditional centers of gravity, with the festivals in Asia (notably Hong Kong), in Australia (Sydney), but above all North America (Sundance, Telluride, Montreal, Toronto) gaining in status, eclipsing some of the European festivals and setting the global trends that are followed by other, smaller festivals but which also influence national circuits of distribution and local exhibition: the art houses and specialized venues. Certainly since the mid-1990s, there have been few films without a festival prize or extensive exposure on the annual festival circuit that could expect to attain either general or even limited release in the cinema. The festivals – with some degrees of difference in their ranking – act collectively as a distribution system not so much for this or that film, from this or that country or director. Festivals effectively select each year which films will fill the few slots that art-house cinemas or the dedicated screens of the multiplexes keep open for the minority interest cinema. These are usually the titles that major distributors of "independent" films such as Miramax (USA), Sony Pictures Classics (US), Castle Communications (UK) or smaller ones such as Sixpack (Austria) or Fortissimo (Netherlands) pick up at the festivals. The Weinstein Brothers, founders of Miramax, with their very close ties to the Sundance Festival, are often seen as a mixed blessing, because they have effectively transformed the interface between art cinema, independent distribution, the multiplexes and mainstream Hollywood: beneficial some would argue, by pumping money and prestige into and through the system; baleful as others see it, by ruthlessly promoting their own choices and even buying up films to suppress their being shown.[20]

Together with the winners of Cannes, Venice, Berlin, the Miramax titles thus constitute the season's mini-hits (or "indie blockbuster"), and they often do so, on a global scale, for a world public.[21] For just as one finds the same Hollywood movies showing in cinemas all over the world, chances are that the same five or six art cinema hits will also be featured internationally (titles like TALK TO HER, LOST IN TRANSLATION, ELEPHANT, THE FAST RUNNER, NOBODY KNOWS) as if there is, with respect to cinema, only one single global market left, with merely the difference in scale and audience distinguishing the blockbuster from the auteur film or "indie" movie. The latest medium budget European film will, along with the latest Wong Kar-wai draw – after due exposure at Venice, Cannes,

FAREWELL MY CONCUBINE

Toronto or Pusan – "their" spectators, while in the same multiplex, but for a different screen, audiences will queue to see a Pixar animation film, produced by Disney (who also own Miramax), do battle with the latest HARRY POTTER or LORD OF THE RINGS over who leads the box office on their respective first release weekend. This co-presence confirms that the opposition between Hollywood and the art cinema needs to be mapped differently, with the festival network a key intermediary and interface for both sides. The category "independent" cinema says little about how such films are produced and financed, but acts as the ante-chamber of re-classification and exchange, as well as the placeholder for filmmakers not yet confirmed as *auteurs*. At the same time, the festivals are the markets where European television companies sell their co-productions and acquire their quota of auteur films, usually broadcast under the rubric of "world cinema" or "new (country/continent) wave".

How Do Festivals Work

Given the degree of standardization in the overall feel of film festivals, and the organizational patterns that regulate how films enter this network, it is tempting to ask what general rules govern the system as a whole. Can one, for instance, understand the film festival circuit by comparing it to the mega art exhibitions that now tour the world's major museums? Or does it behave more like a very specialized UPS postal service? Are festivals the logical extension of the artisanal model of filmmaking practiced in Europe since the 1960s, so rudimentary that it obliged filmmakers to organize their own distribution and exhibition circuits? And if so, have festivals "matured" to a point where they fulfill this function, and begin to constitute a viable alternative to Hollywood, encompassing all the traditional parts of the film business – production, distribution and exhibition, while not sacrificing the advantages of the "European" model, with control over the work retained by the film's author? As I have tried to argue, the answer to the latter question is: yes and no. Yes, to the extent that there are some remarkable points of contact and comparison between the increasingly globalized and interlocking "European" model of the festival circuit and the "Hollywood" model of world-wide marketing and distribution. No, insofar as the differences in economic scale and media visibility, not to mention the secondary markets, keep the Hollywood entertainment conglomerates in an entirely different category. Yet the mere idea of the festival circuit as a global network possibly paralleling Hollywood obliges us to think of the traditional categories of European author cinema in different ways. For instance, if films are now to some extent "commissioned" for festivals, then power/control has shifted from the film director to the festival director, in ways analogous to the control certain star curators (rather than collectors) have acquired over visual artists and exhibition venues. Yet the situation is also comparable to the way marketing and exhibition have always determined production in Hollywood, and real power is wielded by the distributors. A delicate but a-symmetrical interdependence is evolving that represents a new kind of social power exerted by intermediaries (festival directors, curators, deal-makers), with implications for how we come to understand what are called the "creative industries".

As Hollywood has changed, so the festival circuit has changed. If at first glance, the logic of transformation of the two system has little in common and obeys different laws, the festival circuit shows parallels to the studio system in its post-Fordist figuration, where outsourcing of certain skills and services, one-off projects rather than studio-based annual production quotas, high profile, "sponsored" cultural events besides stars-and-spectacle glamour form a particular set of interactions. While differing in scale from the studios (now mainly concentrating on distribution and deal-making), the festivals do resemble them, insofar as here, too, different elements are networked with each other. Many of the world's filmmakers are "independents" in the sense that they often act as small-scale and one-off producers who have access to the "markets" primarily and sometimes solely through festivals. Beyond showing homologies at the level of distribution or in the area of theatrical exhibition, there are potentially other points of comparison between the festival system and the studio system (branding, the logo, the personality cults), which should make it even more difficult to speak of them in terms of a radical antagonism, however much this discourse still prevails in the press and among many film festivals' self-repre-sentation. On the other hand, to abandon the direct antagonism Europe-Holly-wood does not mean to ignore differences, and instead, it allows one to put forward an argument for the structuring, actively interventionist role of festi-vals. Further points of comparison with respect to production will be dealt with in the final chapter on "World cinema", while the differences I want to highlight here focus on three sets of indicators – festivals as event, distinction and value addition, programming and agenda setting – that determine how festivals "work" and how they might be seen to reconfigure European cinema in the context of international art cinema, and also world cinema.

Festival as Event

What is a (film) festival? As annual gatherings, for the purpose of reflection and renewal, film festivals partake in the general function of festivals. Festivals are the moments of self-celebration of a community: they may inaugurate the New Year, honor a successful harvest, mark the end of fasting, or observe the return of a special date. Festivals require an occasion, a place and the physical presence of large numbers of people. The same is true of film festivals. Yet in their itera-tive aspect, their many covert and overt hierarchies and special codes, film festi-vals are also comparable to rituals and ceremonies. Given their occasional levels of excess – one thinks of the topless starlets of Cannes in the 1960s and 70s, the partying, the consumption of alcohol, and often the sheer number of films – they even have something of the unruliness of the carnival about them. In anthropology, what distinguishes festivals from ceremonies and rituals is, among other things, the relative/respective role of the spectators. The audience is more active if one thinks of film festivals as a carnival, more passive when one compares them to ceremonies. The exclusivity of certain film festivals aligns them closer to rituals, where the initiated are amongst themselves, and barriers cordon off the crowd: at the core, there is a performative act (if only of being seen – walking up the red carpet in Cannes, for instance) or the act of handing out the awards. Some film festivals include fans and encourage the presence of the public, others are for professionals only, and almost all of them follow ela-borate and often arcane accreditation rules.

Daniel Dayan, a media scholar, was one of the first to look at film festivals from an anthropologist's perspective. In "In Quest of a Festival" he reported on the 1997 Sundance Film Festival, founded by Robert Redford in 1991 and held annually in the Utah resort of Park City. What interested Dayan were two inter-related questions: how did different groups of spectators become an audience, and what were the inner dynamics of short temporary communities, such as they form at a film festival, in contrast to kinship groups' behavior at birthdays, religious holidays or funerals? Having previously studied large-scale media events, such as royal weddings, Olympic Games and the televising of the Watergate affair, Dayan assumed that film festivals were collective performances which either followed pre-established 'scripts' or evolved in such a way that everyone intuitively adjusted to the role they were expected to play. He soon realized that film festivals tolerated a much higher degree of divergence of scripts, that even at a relatively small festival, there were many more layers co-existing in parallel, or even contradicted each other, and finally, that film festivals are defined not so much by the films they show, but by the print they produce, which has the double function of performative self-confirmation and reflexive self-definition, creating "verbal architectures" that mold the event's sense of its own signifi-cance and sustain its self-importance.[22]

A slightly different perspective arises if one thinks of the film festival as an "event", and defines event with Jacques Derrida as a "disjunctive singularity" that can neither be explained nor predicted by the normative logic of its social context, because its occurrence necessarily changes that very context.[23] This highlights and confirms, even more than Dayan, the recursive self-reference, by which a festival (re-)produces the place in which it occurs. Meaning can only emerge in the space between the iterative and the irruption – the twin poles of a festival's consistency as event, which explains the obsession with new-ness: empty signifier of the compromise struck at any festival between the same and the different, the expected and the expected surprise. The self-generating and self-reflexive dimension is what is generally meant by the "buzz" of a festival, fuelled by rumor, gossip and word-of-mouth, because only a part of the verbal architecture Dayan refers to finds its way into print. The hierarchized accredita-tion systems, regulated at most film festivals via badges with different color schemes, ensure another architecture: that of privileged access and zones of ex-clusion, more reminiscent of airports with security areas than either churches for ceremonies or marketplaces and trade fairs. Since varying degrees of access also means that participants are unevenly irrigated with information, the re-strictions further contribute to the buzz. They create a permanent anxiety about missing something important by being out of the loop, which in turn en-courages face to face exchanges with strangers. The "fragile equilibrium" of which Dayan speaks, as well the dispersive energy he notes is thus no accident, but part of a festival's very fabric. It allows dedicated cinéphiles to share the space with hard-boiled deal-makers, blasé critics to engage with anxious first-film directors, and the buying and selling of films to pass for the celebration of the seventh art.

Distinction and Value-Addition

But this "rhizomatic" view probably paints too vibrant a picture of anarchic self-organization. Many invisible hands steer and administer the chaos of a festival, making sure there is flow *and* interruption, and making visible yet another architecture: that articulated by the programming of the films in competition and built upon across the festival's different sections, special events, showcase attractions and sidebars.[24] Cannes, besides the sections "In Competition" (for the Palme d'Or), "Out of Competition" (special invitation), "Un Certain regard" (world cinema), "Cannes classics" and "Cinéfondation" (short and medium length films from film schools) also know the "Quinzaine des réalisateurs" and the "Semaine internationale de la critique". Venice offers similar categories: "Official Selection", "Out of Competition", "Horizons" (world cinema), "International Critics' Week", "Venice Days", "Corto Cortissimo" (short films). Berlin has "Competition", "Panorama", "Forum", "Perspective German Cinema", "Retrospective/Homage", "Showcase", "Berlinale Special", "Short Films", "Children's Cinema." The effects of such a proliferation of sections are to accelerate the overall dynamics, but these extensions of choice do not happen without contradictions. Over the years, festivals, as we saw, were either forced by protests to add these new categories (Cannes, Venice during the 1970s), or they did so, in order to take account of the quantitative increase in independently produced films, as well as the swelling numbers of special interest groups wanting to be represented at film festivals. The rebels of Cannes were accommodated; counter-festivals, such as the Forum in Berlin, were incorporated; and emerging film nations were carefully nurtured, as in Rotterdam, which from its inception in the 1972 began specializing in New Asian cinemas.[25]

In the process, one of the key functions of the international festival becomes evident, namely to categorize, classify, sort and sift the world's annual film-production. The challenge lies in doing so not by weeding out and de-classifying, or of letting the box-office do its brutal work, but rather by supporting, selecting, celebrating and rewarding – in short, by adding value and cultural capital at the top, while acting more as a gentle gate-keeper than a bouncer at the bottom. A festival's professed commitment to artistic excellence and nothing else positively demands a reading in terms of Pierre Bourdieu's analysis of the social mechanisms behind taste and distinction.[26] By broadening the palette of competitive and non-competitive sections festivals are not only democratizing access. New power-structures are introduced and other differentials operate: for instance, delegating the selection for certain sections to critics or to other bodies inevitably creates new forms of inclusion and exclusion, and above all new kinds of hierarchies, hidden perhaps to the spectators, but keenly felt by producers and makers:

If critical capital is accrued from being selected for a prestigious festival, further distinctions are determined through the film's placement within the festival structure. In the case of the non-competitive Toronto festival, the Opening Night Gala slot is often considered one of the prime slots of the festival, and programs such as Galas, Special Presentations, and Masters are eagerly sought by distributors, producers, and filmmakers for the positioning of their films. In this hierarchy, regionally defined programs such as Planet Africa and Perspective Canada are often perceived as ghettos for under-performing work.[27]

There is only so much cultural capital to go round even at a festival, but as we have seen, accumulating it, in the form of prizes, press-coverage or other windows of attention is a matter of life and death for a film. A film comes to a festival, in order to be catapulted beyond the festival. It wants to enter into distribution, critical discourse and the various exhibition outlets. They alone assure its maker of going on to produce another film, be it on the strength of the box office (rarely) or by attracting (national-governmental, international television co-production) subsidy. Films use the festival circuit as the muscle that pumps it through the larger system.[28]

However, value addition operates also as another form of self-reference. As Bourdieu might have put it: All the players at a festival are caught up in the "illusio" of the game. They have to believe it is worth playing and attend to it with seriousness. In so doing, they sustain it.[29] With every prize it confers, a festival also confirms its own importance, which in turn increases the symbolic value of the prize. Cannes, for instance, is not only aware of the seal of excellence that its *Palme d'Or* bestows on a film thus distinguished. It also carefully controls the use of its logo in image and print, down to typeface, angle, color coding and the number of leaves in its palm branch oval.[30] To vary the metaphor yet again: a festival is an apparatus that breathes oxygen into an individual film and the reputation of its director as potential auteur, but at the same time it breathes oxygen into the system of festivals as a whole, keeping the network buoyant and afloat. Film festivals act as multipliers and amplifiers on several levels: first, they provide a privileged public, the press, as arbiters and taste-makers. An ad-hoc stock exchange of reputations is set up, efficiently distributing information with a very short feedback delay. Secondly, with festivals that are open to the general public, such as Berlin and Rotterdam, Locarno or San Sebastian, audiences, whether tourists or locals, act as a control group for testing the films according to very diverse sets of parameters, ranging from cinephile expertise to sensual stimulation for a couple's night out and equally important for a film's eventual identity in the public's mind. Festival visitors, while perhaps not representative of general audiences, are valuable for the gathering of this sort of data, beyond boosting or deflating artistic egos when performing before a "live" audience. Festivals act as classic sites for the evaluation of information, taking snapshot opinion polls and yielding a market research instrument.

Yet because festival audiences are not necessarily representative of the general public, their volatility and collective enthusiasm can also make the unexpected happen. As Chicago film guru Roger Ebert once pointed out, "You can go to Toronto with a film nobody has heard of and you can leave with a success on your hands."[31] The same is true of Rotterdam, which carefully polls its spectators after each screening and publishes an "audience's choice" chart throughout the festival. The results often differ markedly from that of the critics and jurors. Festivals, finally have a crucial role of value addition for films from their own national production, notably in countries whose output does not always meet the international standards. With special sections, such as the "Perspective German Film" in Berlin, or the "Dutch Treats" at Rotterdam, festivals provide ambassadorial or extra-territorial showcases for domestic filmmakers' work. Offered to the gaze of the international press and visitors, whose response in turn can be fed back into the national public debate, in order to shape the perception a specific country has of its national cinema and standing "abroad," such films travel without leaving home. Finally, festivals act as multipliers in relation to each other: most B-festivals have films that are invited or scheduled because they have been to other festivals: the well-known tautology of "famous for being famous" applies here too, creating its own kind of amplification effect.

Programming and Agenda Setting

Festival directors, their artistic deputies and section programmers have to be political animals. They know about their power, but also about the fact that this power depends on a mutual act of faith: a festival director is king (queen) or pope only as long as the press believes in his/her infallibility, which is to say, a festival director is only too aware of how readily the press holds him personally responsible for the quality of the annual selection and even for the prize-giving juries, should their decisions fail to find favor. The complexity of a festival's politicization can be measured by the adamant insistence that the sole criterion applied is that of quality and artistic excellence: "For the rest [our aim is] always to place film at the centre of our acts. Generally, to take nothing into account other than the art of film and the pre-eminence of artistic talent."[32]

But film festivals are not like the Olympic Games, where the best may win according to agreed and measurable standards of achievement. Since 1972, when countries ceased to selected their own films like delegates to the United Nations, taste rules like the Sun King's "L'état c'est moi"(while disavowing the

Zeitgeist and fashion as his chief ministers of state). A festival director is deemed to have a vision – of what's what and who's who in world cinema, as well as a mission – for his/her country, city, and the festival itself. Each of his/her annual "editions" usually stands under a motto, which itself has to be a formula for a balancing act of competing agendas and thus has to be as attractively tautological as possible. The "pre-eminence of talent" then becomes the code word for taste-making and agenda-setting, and thus for (pre-)positioning one's own festival within the network, and among its patrons. These comprise the regular roster of star directors along with talents to be discovered. It also has to include the tastes of those that can most effectively give exposure to these talents: distributors, potential producers, journalists. When one is in the business of making new authors, then one author is a "discovery", two are the auspicious signs that announce a "new wave", and three new authors from the same country amount to a "new national cinema".[33] Festivals then nurture these directors over their second (often disappointing) film, in the hope that the third will once again be a success, which then justifies the auteur's status, definitively confirmed by a retrospective. Such a long-term commitment to building up a particular auteur is typical of smaller festivals such as Rotterdam, Locarno, the "Viennale" or Toronto, preferably but not necessarily with a local/national connection. As Atom Egoyan, Canada's best-known independent director acknowledges: "While it may sound perverse, we benefit from not having a strong internal market. We don't compete with each other over box office share, gigantic fees or star treatment, because it's simply not an issue. This is both a blessing and a curse. As artists, it means that our survival is not set by public taste, but by the opinion of our peers—festival programmers (the most influential is actually called Piers!), art council juries, and even Telefilm."[34]

Art for art's sake suspends these prosaic considerations of cultural politics and national prestige, at the same time as it makes them possible. By re-introducing chance, the fortuitous encounter, the word-of-mouth hot tip, the "surprise winner", appealing to the aesthetic is also a way of neutralizing all the agendas that interested parties are keen to bring to the festival director's attention. The critic Ruby Rich, after serving on many a festival jury, once complained about what she called the "worship of taste" in the international festival discourse.[35] But this is to underestimate the ritual, religious and quasi-magical elements necessary to make a festival into an "event". It requires an atmosphere where an almost Eucharistic transubstantiation can take place; a Spirit has to hover that can canonize a masterpiece or consecrate an auteur, which is why the notions of "quality" or "talent" have to be impervious to rational criteria or secondary elaborations. As Huub Bals, the first director of the Rotterdam Film Festival used to announce defiantly: "you watch films with your belly."[36] Put differently, ineffability and the taste tautology are the twin guardians of a festival's claim to embody an essential, but annually renewable mystery.

Self-affirmation is thus one of the aspects a successful festival director has to keep on the festival's agenda. Yet as any programmer would rightly argue, a film festival has to be sensitive to quite different agendas as well, and be able to promote them, discreetly but efficiently. Yet the very existence of these agendas also breaks with any notion that a festival is a neutral mapping, a disinterested cartography of the world's cinema production and the different nations' film culture. Overt or hidden agendas remind us first of all of the history of festivals. Most film festivals, as we saw, began as counter-festivals, with a real or imagined opponent: Cannes had Venice, Berlin had the Communist East, Moscow and Karlovy-Vary the Capitalist West. All have Hollywood, and (since the 1970s) the commercial film industry, as both their "significant other" and their "bad object". The ritualized appeals are to originality, daring, experiment, diversity, defiance, critique, opposition – terms that imply as their negative foil the established order, the status quo, censorship, oppression, a world divided into "them" and "us". The boom in new film festivals, lest we forget, started in the 1970s. Many of the creative as well as critical impulses that drove festivals to devote themselves to non-commercial films, to the avant-garde and to independent filmmaking are owed to the post-'68 counter-culture of political protest and militant activism.[37] Rotterdam, the Forum of the Young International Film, the Pesaro Festival, Telluride and many others were founded and run by people with political ideals and usually quite ecumenical cinematic tastes.

Thus while public discourses and prize-giving speeches may continue to reflect a commitment to art for art's sake, there are other voices and issues, also pointing beyond the historical moment of protest and rebellion. Film festivals have since the 1970s been extremely successful in becoming the platform for other causes, for minorities and pressure groups, for women's cinema, receptive to gay and queer cinema agendas, to ecological movements, underwriting political protest, thematizing cinema and drugs, or paying tribute to anti-imperialist struggles and partisan politics.[38] Even Cannes, the fortress of the art of film and the kingdom of the auteur, has not remained unaffected. When Michael Moore in 2004 was awarded the Golden Palm for FAHRENHEIT 9/11, probably his weakest film, it would take the jury chair (fellow American) Quentin Tarantino all the blue-eyed boyish charm and ingénue guilelessness he could muster to reassure the festival audience that the decision had been by no means politically motivated and that the jury was in fact honoring a great work of cinema art.

Moore's triumph at Cannes confirmed a point already made by Daniel Dayan about Sundance: "Behind an auteur stands a constituency." Dayan alluded to the following that some directors have at festivals, like pop stars have their fans at a rock concert. But the point is a more general one. The emphasis on the author as the nominal currency of the film festival economy has proven a very useful shield behind which both the festival and its audiences have been able to negotiate different priorities and values. Film festivals thus have in effect created one of the most interesting public spheres available in the cultural field today: more lively and dynamic than the gallery-art and museum world, more articulate and militant than the pop music, rock concert and DJ-world, more international than the theatre, performance and dance world, more political and engaged than the world of literature or the academy. Needless to say, film festivals are more fun than party-political rallies, and at times they can attract public attention to issues that even NGOs find it hard to concentrate minds on. This has been the case in recent years especially with gender and family issues, women's rights, the AIDS crisis or civil wars. The fact that festivals are programmed events, rather than fixed rituals, together with their annual, recurring nature means that they can be responsive and quick in picking up topical issues, and put together a special thematic focus with half a dozen film titles, which may include putting together a retrospective. It sometimes takes no more than the coincidence of two films on a similar topic – the Rwanda genocide, for instance – for a festival, in this case Berlin 2005, to declare itself to be directing the spotlight on the issue, and thus to focus valuable journalists' attention not only on the films (whose artistic qualities sharply divided the critics), but create airtime and make column-space for the topic, the region, the country, the moral, political or human interest issue.

Time and Location Advantage in the New Experience Economy

To sum up some of our findings on how the festival circuit seems to work: Each film festival, if we follow Dayan, consists of a number of cooperating and conflicting groups of players, forming together a dense latticework of human relations, temporally coexisting in the same time-space capsule. They are held together not by the films they watch, but by the self-validating activities they engage in, among which the production of prose struck Dayan most forcibly. My own interpretation – via Derrida and Bourdieu – also stressed the recursive, performative and self-referential dimension, but I associated the various tautologies that result mainly with the processes of value addition: films and festivals mutually confirm each other by conferring value on each other. But film festivals also create a unique kind of audience. Mutually self-confirming and self-celebrating as well, a festival audience has both a very ancient role (associated with the self-celebration of the community at harvest time or the arrival of spring) and a modern – dare I say, utopian - mission (to be the forum where "the people" perform their sovereignty). To both aspects, self-celebration and self-performing, could apply Niklas Luhmann's model of auto-poesis, that is, the tendency of a system to set up close-circuit feedback loops with which it is stabilized internally, while also protecting itself from the surrounding environment.

However, there may also be other ways of reading the organized chaos which is a film festival. A certain degree of dysfunctionality is probably a festival's saving grace, preserving the anarchic element not merely because so many festivals originated in the counter-culture. Just as the big information technology corporations challenge the hackers to attack them, in order to find out where their own weak spots are, festivals accommodate the intransigent artists alongside the film industry suits, in order for the system to self-correct. And as sociologists keep arguing, the urban post-industrial economy needs the bobos (bourgeois bohemians), the Bridget Jones' and the 'creative class' to be the demanding and fussy consumers they are, in order to maintain competitive levels of innovation and flexibility. What these experience-hungry eco systems are to the contemporary city, the hard-core cinéphiles, avant-gardists and auteurists are to the festival economy: the salt in the soup, the leaven in the dough.

But innovation (or "the new") at a festival is itself something of an empty signifier, covering the gap between repetition and interruption, system and "singularity". It becomes the name for the more insubstantial, invisible processes by which a festival's real grand prize, namely "attention" is awarded: gossip, scandal, talk, topicality, peer discussion, writing. These processes of agenda setting borrow their clichés and categories from popular culture or the tabloid press. They are paralleled by other agenda setting routines: those promoting particular causes via the festival programs "pre-cooking" topical issues in their different sections, specials and retrospectives. Hot topics can also emerge bottom up, via participants using the unique combination of place, occasion and physical presence to generate momentum. A third form of agenda setting is the one embedded in the temporal structure of the festival itself and generated by the journalists covering the festival for a broad public. Each year a festival acquires its characteristic themes from the press (or rather, from the competing information flows issuing from the festival press office, the film industry PR personnel and the professional journalists). Together they mediate, mold and mulch the salient topics throughout the week, until by the end of it the flow has hardened into an opinion or become baked into a verdict. Films for instance, initially tend to be reported on in descriptive terms, but halfway through, favorites are being touted, winners predicted, and by closing night everyone seems to know whether the right or wrong film(s) were given the prizes, and whether it was a good or bad vintage year for the festival (-director). There are, of course, losers as well as winners, and to track a winner that turns out to be a loser can be more instructive than the usual festival (fairytale) story of how the underdog became the winner. The Hollywood studios, for instance, are extremely wary which films they send to the big festivals. Some have found out that while winning a European festival prize adds little to the box office draw of a major star vehicle – in contrast to an Oscar (nomination) – bad reviews or a rubbishing at such a festival can do real and lasting damage to a mainstream film.

If a film festival is thus a fairly complex network at the micro-level, it forms another network with all the other festivals at the macro-level. Here the agenda setting has to carry from one festival to the next across their temporal succession, and once more, print becomes the main source of mediation. It might be interesting to track the leading discourses of the cinematic year, and to see whether they are inaugurated in Berlin (mid-Feb) or really acquire their contours and currency only in May ("Springtime in Cannes"), to be carried to Locarno (July) and over into Venice (early September), thence to be taken up by Toronto (late September), London (October/November), Sundance (mid-January) and Rotterdam (January/February). As indicated, these moveable fests and caravans of film cans tend to identify as must-see films (and valorize accordingly) only half a dozen show-case art-house films annually – in recent years with more titles from Asian countries, Latin America or Iran than from Europe – whose fate (or function?) it is to shadow the big blockbusters rather than to present a radical alternative.

For such an analysis one could invoke Manuel Castells' theories of the space of flows and the timeless time, because the *temporal islands, discursive architectures* and *programmed geographies* which are the modern festivals, do not respond too well to traditional metaphors of the kind I have just used.[39] Film festivals are on the one hand typically postmodern phenomena, in their auto-reflexive and self-referential dimensions, but also quite rich in mythic resonance with their performative tautologies. On the other hand, they are clearly a product also of globalization and the post-Fordist phase of the so-called creative industries and experience economies, where festivals seek to realize the time and location advantages we also know from tourism and the heritage industry, but now for other purposes. These purposes have yet to be more clearly defined. For the European cinema, they are particularly uncertain, and likely to be regarded with skepticism if not cynicism, if we insist on keeping the first-order values of art, auteur, and national cinema intact as our guiding principles. However, as I hinted at above, we could also consider the European film festival circuit as special kinds of public spheres, where mediatization and politicization for once have entered into a quite felicitous alliance. We could call film festivals the symbolic agoras of a new democracy – repositories and virtual archives of the revolutions that have failed to take place in Europe over the past 50-60

Dogville

years, but whose possibilities and potential they keep alive merely by the constituencies – Hardt/Negri would call them the multitudes[40] – they are able to gather together each time, each year, in each place. In this sense, film festivals are indeed the opposite of Hollywood, even as they outwardly and in some of their structures appear more and more like Hollywood. On the festival circuit, Europe and Hollywood no longer confront each other face to face, but within and across the mise-en-abyme mirrors of all the film cultures that now make up "world cinema".

Notes

1. For a definition of classical narrative, see David Bordwell, *Narration and the Fiction Film* (Madison: University of Wisconsin Press, 1985), 156-204.
2. These were some of the possibilities explored in our Cinema Europe study group, 2004-2005. My appreciation to Marijke de Valck, Malte Hagener, Floris Paalman, Ria Thanouli, Gerwin van der Pol, Martijn de Waal, Ward Rennen, Tarja Laine and Melis Behlil for their presentations.
3. Hans Mommaas, "Cultural Clusters and the Post-industrial City: Towards the Remapping of Urban Cultural Policy," *Urban Studies*, vol. 41 no. 3 (March 2004), 507-532.
4. The "culture-rich environment" can also be pristine nature, as it is for many of the high-tech companies that in the 1990s sought out Northern California or Oregon for their headquarters: recreation and outdoor sports are firmly part of culture for the "creative class" (Richard Florida). In Europe, culture usually is a combination of an urban environment rich in historical reference: natural and architectural beauty, offering diverse intellectual and artistic resources (universities, museums), as well as entertainment venues and quality shopping.
5. "Helen Fielding (author of *Bridget Jones' Diary*), has drawn someone much more human and recognisable than the elegant and wealthy young New York singles in the TV shows *Friends* and *Sex and the City*. Yet all three portray the people who now dominate and shape the rich world's city life, not just in New York and London, but increasingly in Tokyo, Stockholm, Paris and Santiago: well-educated, single professionals in their 20s and 30s. Moralists fret about them; marketing folk court them; urban developers want to lure them. They are the main consumers and producers of the creative economy that revolves around advertising, publishing, entertainment and media. More than any other social group, they have time, money and a passion for spending on whatever is fashionable, frivolous and fun." *The Economist*, 20 December, 2001.
6. The creative class is a term made popular by Richard Florida: "a fast-growing, highly educated, and well-paid segment of the workforce on whose efforts corpo-

rate profits and economic growth increasingly depend. Members of the creative class do a wide variety of work in a wide variety of industries – from technology to entertainment, journalism to finance, high-end manufacturing to the arts. They do not consciously think of themselves as a class. Yet they share a common ethos that values creativity, individuality, difference, and merit." Richard Florida, *The Rise of the Creative Class* (New York: Perseus, 2002), 7.

7. "An old joke: two mountaineers fight their way up a steep slope. The air is getting thinner, they finally reach a half-deserted mountain village. One says to the other: 'You know what's missing in this place?' – 'No idea,' says the other'. 'It's obvious', retorts his companion, 'a film festival!'" Hans Georg Rodek, "Noch ein Festival", *Die Welt*, 6 April 2005.

8. In 1978 the Berlin Film Festival moved from August to February, in order to be ahead of, rather than following Cannes. This move was dictated by the pressure to "bag" more premieres as well as to cater for the timetable of such important visitors as festival and art house programmers. As Gerald Peary points out: "Berlin is where the annual hunt begins. Each February, film-festival programmers from all over the world start their cat-and-mouse games with one another […]. The hunt continues at other festivals – San Francisco, Locarno, Montreal, Telluride, Toronto, take your choice – with a *de rigueur* stop in May at Cannes." Gerald Peary, "Season of the Hunt," in: *American Film*, Vol. XVI nr.10 (November/December 1991), 20.

9. Manthia Diawara, "New York and Ougadougou: The Homes of African Cinema," *Sight & Sound* (November 1993), 24-25.

10. For an astute analysis of the different functions that such a festival of festivals can fulfil, especially between the industry and the art cinema world, see Julian Stringer, "Raiding the Archive: Film Festivals and the Revival of Classic Hollywood", in P. Grainge (ed.), *Memory and Popular Film* (Manchester: Manchester University Press: 2003), 81-96.

11. The prototypical example of the festival film is Steven Soderberg's *Sex Lies and Videotapes* (1989) whose rise to fame became every aspiring filmmaker's dream story. Made on a modest budget with a handful of (then) unknown actors, it won the *Palme d'Or* at Cannes as best film, plus best actor award for James Spader, then went on to garner prizes at dozens more festivals, was picked up by Miramax which gave it a very clever advertising campaign, and ended making some $ 60m at the box office for a $ 9m investment. It is still a hot favourite on the DVD lists.

12. Benjamin Craig, 'History of the Cannes Film Festival', <http://www.cannesguide.com/basics/> accessed 10 March 2005.

13. "Au debut, dans l'immediat après-guerre, Locarno, petit cité touristique, toute auréoleé de sa notorieté politique et socio-culturelle s'offre en quelque sorte un mini-Venise, ouvrant une "vitrine" cinématographique principalent axée sur le voisinage immediat, l'Italie; et bientot sur le monde. […] Tres vite Locarno devient un lieu de réunion, de rencontre et de spectacle privilegié ou public et professionnels peuvent decouvrir les films les plus importants du moment, dans un cadre à la fois professionel et festif." <http://www.locarnofestival.ch>.

14. Heide Fehrenbach, "Mass Culture and Cold-War Politics: The Berlin Film Festival in the 1950s", in H.F., *Cinema in Democratizing Germany: Reconstructing National Identity after Hitler* (Chapel Hill: University of North Carolina Press, 1995), 234-238.

15. "In the early days, festival films were selected by each country, rather than the festival itself, with the given number of films from any one nation being proportionate to its cinematic output. Consequently, the festival was more of a film forum than a competitive event and the organizers tried very hard to ensure that every film presented went home with some kind of award." <http://www.cannesguide.com/basics/>.

16. Rossellini's *Rome Open City* won the *Palme d'Or* in 1946. Cannes discovered not only Rossellini as an international auteur but inaugurated neo-realism as the key film-movement of the post-war era.

17. For a history of the Forum, see *Zwischen Barrikade und Elfenbeinturm: Zur Geschichte des unabhängigen Kinos: 30 Jahre Internationales Forum des Jungen Films.* Herausgegeben von den Freunden der Deutschen Kinemathek, Berlin, 2000.

18. A fuller account of the history, dynamics and specific organizational profiles of Venice, Cannes, Berlin, and Rotterdam is given in Marijke de Valck, *European Film Festivals* (Ph.D. thesis, University of Amsterdam, forthcoming 2005), which breaks new ground in offering a theoretical model for understanding the festival phenomenon. One of the first critical looks at film festivals within the globalization debate is Julian Stringer, "Global Cities and International Film Festival Economy," in *Cinema and the City: Film and Urban Societies in a Global Context*, Mark Shiel and Tony Fitzmaurice (eds.) (London: Blackwell, 2001), 134-44.

19. Cari Beauchamp and Henri Béhar, *Hollywood on the Riviera: The Inside Story of the Cannes Film Festival* (New York: William Morrow, 1992).

20. This is the argument of Jonathan Rosenbaum, *Movie Wars: How Hollywood and the Media Conspire to Limit What Films We Can See* (New York: A Capella, 2000).

21. Alisa Perren, "Sex, Lies and Marketing. Miramax and the Development of the Quality Indie Blockbuster", *Film Quarterly*, 55, 2 (Winter 2001-2002) 30-39.

22. Daniel Dayan, "In Quest of a Festival (Sundance Film Festival)", *National Forum* (September 22, 1997).

23. Jacques Derrida, "Signature, Event, Context", in *Margins of Philosophy*, tr. Alan Bass (Chicago: University of Chicago Press, 1984), 307-330.

24. See Patricia Thomson, "Clutterbusters: Programmers at Five Leading Festivals Expound on Heady Process of Selecting Films," *Variety*, 18 August, 2003, 47.

25. Rotterdam is also the festival that can be said to have been the one most directly inspired by the post-1968 cultural revolution, since its founder, Hubert Bals, was a lover of avant-garde and independent films, and a keen follower of events at Cannes and Berlin in the preceding years. For a detailed history and analysis of the Rotterdam Film Festival, see Marijke de Valck, "Drowning in Popcorn" in M. de Valck, M. Hagener (eds.) *Cinephilia: Movies, Love and Memory* (Amsterdam: Amsterdam University Press, 2005).

26. See, for instance Bourdieu's famous dictum "taste classifies, and it classifies the classifier". Pierre Bourdieu, *Distinction: A Social Critique of the Judgement of Taste* (Cambridge, Mass.: Harvard University Press, 1979), iv.

27. Liz Czach, "Film Festivals, Programming, and the Building of a National Cinema," *The Moving Image* vol 4, no 1, (Spring 2004), 76-88.

28. Festivals increasingly act also as interface and membrane. A successful film and filmmaker at a festival find that doors open towards the commercial system, which now recruits among "indies". In Europe it is Cannes, in the US, Sundance that are

the turnstiles taking directors into the industry. A typical trajectory, or rather an ideal trajectory for a European filmmaker is: finish film school with a final film that gets a prize at a festival in Europe, is invited to Toronto, or better Sundance, where Miramax takes an option and the majors show interest.

29. Pierre Bourdieu, "The Chicago Workshop" in Bourdieu and Loïc Wacquant (eds.) *An Invitation to Reflexive Sociology* (London: Polity Press, 1992), cited by Mary Eagleton, "Pierre Bourdieu", *The Literary Encyclopedia* <http://www.litencyc.com/php/speople.php?rec=true&UID=501>

30. The official web site of the Cannes Film Festival has eight pages of instruction about proper and prohibited uses of its logo. See rubric "Graphic Chart" at http://www.festival-cannes.fr/index.php?langue=6002

31. Roger Ebert, interviewed by Kendon Polak, *Inside Entertainment*, September 2003, 55.

32. Editorial by the Director of the 58th Cannes Film Festival, Gilles Jacob, on the official website. http://www.festival-cannes.fr/organisation/index.php?langue=6002

33. A recent example of this phenomenon would be the "New Iranian Cinema", for most festival-goers made up of the names of Daryoush Mehrjooi, Mohsen Makhmalbaf, Abbas Kiarostami and Makhmalbalf's daughter Samira. Bill Nichols has written a perceptive study of the agenda setting and meaning-making around the festival circuit which shaped these directors' work into a new national cinema. Bill Nichols, "Discovering Form, Inferring Meaning: New Cinemas and the Film Festival Circuit", *Film Quarterly*, vol 47/3, 1994, 16-27.

34. Atom Egoyan, foreword to Katherine Monk, *Weird Sex and Snowshoes And Other Canadian Film Phenomena* (Vancouver: Raincoast Books, 2002), 2. Egoyan is referring to Piers Handling, the director of the Toronto International Film Festival.

35. B.Ruby Rich, "Taste, Fashion and Service: The Ideology of Film Curating", lecture given at "Terms of Address: A Symposium on the Pedagogy and Politics of Film and Video Programming and Curating", March 7-8, 2003, University of Toronto (Canada).

36. Jan Heijs and Frans Westra, *Que le Tigre danse. Huub Bals, een biographie* (Amsterdam: Otto Cramwinckel, 1996), 216.

37. See Jean-Luc Godard's notorious call "We, too, should provoke two or three Vietnams ...", cited elsewhere in this volume.

38. This applies even more to specialised or themed festivals: "Queer festivals help define what gay, lesbian, bisexual, and trans-gendered cinema is; a festival such as "Views from the Avant-Garde" comments on the state of experimental cinema. The programming decisions amount to an argument about what defines that field, genre, or national cinema." Liz Czach, "Film Festivals, Programming, and the Building of a National Cinema," *The Moving Image* vol 4, no 1, (Spring 2004), 76-88.

39. Manuel Castells, *The Rise of the Network Society* (Oxford: Blackwell, 1996), 442-45.

40. Michael Hardt and Antonio Negri, *Empire* (Cambridge, Mass.: Harvard University Press, 2001), 60-74.

Double Occupancy and Small Adjustments

Space, Place and Policy in the New European Cinema since the 1990s

The famous Strasbourg-born New York political cartoonist and writer of children's books, Tomi Ungerer was once asked what it was like to grow up in Alsace (he was born in 1931), and he replied: It was like living in the toilet of a rural railway station: *toujours occupé* (always occupied). He was, of course, referring to the fact that for more or less four hundred years, and certainly during the period of 1871 to 1945 Alsace changed nationality many times over, back and forth, between France and Germany, and for most of that time, either nation was felt to be an occupying power by the inhabitants.

Double Occupancy: An Intermediary Concept

Toujours occupé seems as good a motto as any with which to confront the present debate about the new Europe and its sometimes siege mentality, when it comes to the so-called "non-Europeans" at its borders or in its midst. By proposing the idea of a permanent occupation, or more precisely, a double occupation, I am thinking of it as a kind of counter-metaphor to 'Fortress Europe', the term so often applied to the European Union's immigration policies.[1] *Toujour occupé* keeps in mind the fundamental issue of the nation states' of Europe's own ethnicities and ethnic identities which, when looked at historically, strongly suggest that there has rarely been a space that can be defended against an outside of which "Europe" is the inside. There is no European, in other words, who is not already diasporic in relation to some marker of difference – be it ethnic, regional, religious or linguistic – and whose identity is not always already hyphenated or doubly occupied. I am not only thinking of the many European sites where the fiction of the fortress, the paranoid dream of *tabula rasa*, of cleansing, of purity and exclusion has led, or still continues to lead to bloody conflict, such as in Bosnia, Kosovo, Northern Ireland, the Basque country, Cyprus, and further afield, in Israel and Palestine. To these, Tomi Ungerer's joke about Alsace may suggest the prospect of a happy ending, insofar as the European Union – founded, let us remember, initially to ensure that France and Germany would never again go to war with each other over Alsace-Lorraine – in this particular instance did provide a shift in the terms of reference by which the conflicting claims of nationality, sovereignty, ethnic identity, victim hood and statehood, solidarity and self-determination could be renegotiated. Indeed, this is the hope of the political elites in the European Union: that these conflicts can eventually be solved, by being given different frameworks of articulation and eventual settlement, after being first bought off with financial subsidies.

I shall come back to what I think these frameworks proposed by the European Union might entail as a political, but also symbolic-discursive space. Yet even outside the internationally notorious territories of overlapping identity-claims and inter-ethnic war-zones just mentioned, it is clear that Europe – however one wants to draw either the geographical reach (south: the Mediterranean, east: the Urals) or the historical boundaries (Mesopotamia, Phoenicia, Greek, Roman or Holy Roman Empire) – has always been a continent settled and traversed by very disparate and mostly feuding ethnic entities. We tend to forget how relatively recent the nation-states of Europe are, and how many of them are the result of forcibly tethering together a patchwork quilt of tribes, of clans, of culturally and linguistically distinct groupings. Those identified with a region have seen a belated acknowledgement of their distinctiveness within the European Union under the slogan of 'the Europe of the regions', but even this opening up of different spaces of identity does not cover the current layeredness of ethnic Europe. One need only to think of the Sinti and Romas, the perpetual "others" of Europe, who because they have neither territory nor do they claim one, resist conventional classifications; they are inside the territorial boundaries of a dozen or so European countries, but finding themselves outside all these countries' national imaginaries. Nor does the Europe of the regions convey the historical "depth" of multi-ethnic Europe, a continent whose two- or three-thousand-year history is a relentless catalogue of migrations, invasions, occupations, conquests, pogroms, expulsions and exterminations.

Thus, the state of double occupancy applies to every part of Europe, and to all of us: our identities are multiply defined, multiply experienced, and can be multiply assigned to us, at every point in our lives, and this increasingly so – hopefully to the point where the very notion of national identity will fade from our vocabulary, and be replaced by other kinds of belonging, relating and being. Blood and soil, land and possession, occupation and liberation have to give way to a more symbolic or narrative way of negotiating contested ownership of both place and time, i.e., history and memory, for instance, inventing and maintaining spaces of discourse, as in the metaphoric occupation of Alsace or the increasing prominence achieved by hyphenated European nationals (German-Turkish, Dutch-Moroccan, French-Maghreb, British-Asian) in the spheres of literature, filmmaking, music and popular television shows. This is not to over-look the fact that there may be good reasons why in some parts of Europe and especially on its current political borders, the recognition of national identity is still a prerequisite to being able to talk about belonging at all, as a consequence of having to cope with occupation, colonisation either directly or by proxy. This seems true for parts of the former Soviet Empire, such as the Ukraine or Belarus, claimed as their spheres of influence by Russia, the US, and of course, the European Union. Even in Alsace, matters are far from resolved: despite the fact that Strasbourg is the seat of the European parliament, Alsace is among the *départe-ments* in France where the Fortress Europe populist Jean Marie Le Pen still has a substantial following, and the incidents of anti-Semitism reported from the region are alarmingly high.

These facts notwithstanding, the present insistence on cultural identity, as that which can most peacefully replace the older, more divisive nationalisms as well as reconcile individual to community, may well have to be re-thought across some other set of concepts, policies or ideas. This is not an easy task, as a quick review of the alternatives suggests. Multiculturalism, the term most read-ily offering itself, has come increasingly under fire: it underestimates the a-sym-metrical power-relations of the various constituencies, and ignores the rivalries among different ethnic communities and immigrant generations. Its notions of a rainbow coalition does not answer the thorny question of "integration" and "assimilation" versus "cultural autonomy" and "separate development" that characterizes the various policies tried or applied within the European nation states. In the European Union, as indeed in parts of the British education sys-tem, cultural identity is being officially replaced by "cultural diversity". Besides the blandness of the term and its tendency to be a euphemism for the problem rather than its solution, I find "diversity" problematic because it, too, leaves no room for the power structures in play, nor does it take account of the imbrica-tion of inside and out, self and other, the singular and the collective. Double occupancy wants to be the intermediate terms between cultural identity and cultural diversity, recalling that there is indeed a stake: politics and power, sub-jectivity and faith, recognition and rejection, that is, conflict, contest, maybe even irreconcilable claims between particular beliefs and universal values, be-tween what is "yours" and "mine". Philosophically, double occupancy also wants to echo Jacques Derrida's term of writing "under erasure", indicating the provisional nature of a text's authority, the capacity of textual space to let us see both itself and something else.[2] One can even gloss it with Wittgenstein's rever-sible, bi-stable figure of the duck-rabbit picture, sign of the co-extensiveness of two perceptions in a single representational space.[3]

Furthermore, I want the term to be understood as at once tragic, comic and utopian. Tragic, because the reality of feeling oneself invaded, imposed upon, deprived of the space and security one thinks one needs, is - whatever one's race, creed or gender, but also whatever one's objective reason or justification – a state of pathos, disempowerment and self-torment. Comic, in the way one considers mistaken identities as comic, that is, revealing ironies and contradictions in the fabric of language and its signifiers. And utopian, insofar as under certain conditions, I shall suggest, it opens up ways of sharing the same space while not infringing on the other's claims.

Perhaps I can illustrate what I mean by the more benign, symbolic and discursive forms that double occupation can take, with a scene from a documentary by Johan van der Keuken, AMSTERDAM GLOBAL VILLAGE (1996). By following the delivery rounds of a courier on a motorcycle, the director follows the lives of several immigrants who have made their life in Amsterdam: A businessman from Grosny, a young kickboxer from rural Thailand, a musician from Bogota who works as a cleaner, a woman discjockey from Iceland, a photographer,

AMSTERDAM GLOBAL VILLAGE

and also an elderly Jewish-Dutch lady, Henny Anke who with her 55-year old son is visiting the flat she lived in during the Occupation, when the Germans came to arrest her husband, deporting him to the Westerbork transit camp, and she had to decide whether to go into hiding with her little boy or to follow her husband to the camp.

The sheer physical contrast of the slight Jewish lady and the woman from Surinam, the discovery of the complete re-modelling that the flat has undergone, obliterating all the spatial memories Hennie might have had, is paralleled by the décor of white porcelain figures and lush green foliage, setting up what might have been a tragic-comic encounter of culture clashes. Yet, as Hennie recalls the terrible years, and re-lives the agony of her doubt about the choices she made, we sense the palpable fact of double occupancy of this domestic, physical and moral space, by two generations who have little in common either culturally or ethnically, but whose succession and coexistence in memory and spoken record, gives a truer picture of a national, but also trans-national history of occupation, colonialism, extermination and migration than either of the women could have given on their own. When the Surinamese mother says she now understands what the old lady has suffered, because she too has gone through re-location and exile, we know and Hennie Anke knows that there are important differences and the respective experiences may not be strictly comparable. But the gesture – even if it is one of mis-prision and mis-cognition – nonetheless sustains the fragile bridge these two women are able to build, establishing an image of transfer and safe-keeping of experience, as they embrace each other for the farewell. In the context of the film's concern with singular fates, diaspora communities and the difficulties of maintaining a multi-cultural Amsterdam, but also following, as it does, harrowing portrayal of ethnic strife, death and devastation in Grosny, the encounter in the Amsterdam flat up the steep stairs encourages the viewer to ponder the possibility of putting space, time and place "under erasure": to see it both yield, erase and keep a memory within a history, while making room for a narrative of double occupancy. But the moment is as fleeting as it is utopian, and appears the more poignant, as one recalls what has happened in the Netherlands since 2001 to its reputation for tolerance and to the consensus model of the social contract, extended to its ethnic communities. After the violent deaths of Pim Fortuyn and Theo van Gogh, each in his way a flamboyant provocateur to the notion of consensus and diversity, this tolerant image is now frayed and seemingly in tatters.

If AMSTERDAM GLOBAL VILLAGE illustrates the utopian dimension, the case of the filmmaker, journalist and television personality van Gogh, who was assassinated as a consequence of making a film deemed by some Muslims to be offensive to their religion, is perhaps more revealing for the tragic dimensions of double occupancy. Van Gogh often argued that his sometimes quite outrageous statements in the media, notably on television and in his newspaper opinion column, was the exact opposite of intolerance, but the expression of his faith in democracy, the law and free speech: by testing the limits, he wanted to safeguard its fundamental principles, very much in the spirit of the famous dictum, (mis-) attributed to Voltaire: "I may disagree with what you have to say, but I shall defend, to the death, your right to say it".[4] Van Gogh's provocation was, in this sense, a mimicking, a "staging" and thus an impersonation of racism, prejudice and othering, by which he wanted to keep alive the emotional reservoir and the very real fund of resentment existing among the population, the better to engage with it. His "activism" sought to expose the sometimes hypocritical lipservice to multicultural ideals in what remains a consensual but deeply conservative society. Perhaps one can think of van Gogh's polemics as a *pharmakon*, a homeopathic cure, way of inoculation and administered to the deeper feelings of fear of the other, "acting out" the aggression towards every kind of "otherness" associated with traditional forms of nationalism and religious fundamentalism. Heir to the radical 1960s, but also part of the performative 80s and 90s, van Gogh saw television, film-making and even tabloid journalism as fields of symbolic action, deploying a language of signs, clichés and stereotypes as the common code of a culture that lives its differences in the realm of discourse, rather than by force. His death at the hands of a self-styled Muslim radical, who grew up in the Netherlands, might indicate that the space for symbolic action had vanished in the aftermath of 9-11 and the "war on terror". Yet van Gogh's assailant not only is literate, fluent in Dutch, "integrated" and adept at using the modern technologies of communication, such as web-sites and the internet: the murder itself, with its ritualistic overtones and easily decodable symbolism, had the performative dimension of other acts of barbarity deliberately staged to produce shocking media images and atrocity events. This would be another meaning of my term "double occupancy" – that semantically, as well as in the performativity deployed, modern media spaces have acquired the force of a first-order reality, by comparison with which the world of flesh and blood risks becoming a second-order realm, subservient to the order of spectacular effects. The privilege of van Gogh's persona, occupying the symbolic space of discourse, became the nemesis of Theo van Gogh the person, brutally deprived of life for the sake of another symbolic space.

A comic version of double occupancy is attempted in another Dutch film, SHOUF SHOUF HABIBI! (Albert Ter Heerdt, 2004), which looks at a dysfunctional Moroccan family living in the Netherlands from the point of view of one of the sons, fed up with his life of petty crime and wanting to make good. Ab (short for Abdullah), too, is fully integrated as well as fully alienated with respect to Dutch society. A duck-rabbit, as it were, even more to himself than in the eyes of others, he knows the cultural codes of both communities, their sensitivities as well as the narrow limits to their tolerance. Like Tomi Ungerer or Renton in TRAINSPOTTING, the young Moroccans, with whom Ab hangs out, direct their best jokes against themselves: "what's the difference between E.T. and a Moroccan? E.T. had a bicycle …, E.T. was good-looking…, E.T. actually wanted to go home." Ab would like to be an actor, but realizes that demand for Arabs as leads after 9/11 is low, a joke that would fall flat indeed were it not contradicted by the film itself, which briefly did make Mimoun Oaïssa into a star, since the film became a big hit in the Netherlands. Sparing neither the Dutch nor the Moroccans, SHOUF SHOUF HABIBI! uses its subaltern humour and television family sit-com setting to appeal to a complicity of ineptitude (another version of double occupancy), which allows for a democracy of bunglers and losers to emerge as the film's political ideal, in the absence of – or while waiting for – better options.

Television and Cinema: Dis-articulating and Re-branding the Nation

Double occupancy, as the co-extensiveness of symbolic and ethnic identities, but also the overlap of media representations, racial stereotypes and day-to-day discriminations, connects directly with the re-figuration of the nation and the national discussed in an earlier chapter. For as already argued, the communication revolutions, together with the media-consciousness and media-skills of diaspora communities, have played a major role in the present resurgence of nationalism and the polarisation of public culture and politics. In some instances, such as militant Islamism, technologies like the mobile phone or the internet are said to have exacerbated the feeling of belonging to quite distinct global cultural formations, having to fight for the space of recognition, if necessary with violent means, at the state or local level.

But this analysis foreshortens considerably some of the key developments both in the media and around the notion of the nation and the state since the 1970s and 80s. As pointed out earlier, and argued elsewhere in this volume, the role of representing the nation is generally assumed to have passed to television. Yet deregulation, privatization and a ratings war between public service and commercial broadcasters has changed the very terms of this representation. For instance, Channel Four in Britain has often been seen as a test case for the shift in paradigm of how the media affect the lived reality of nationhood. In the face of competition from US television imports and needing to profile itself as distinct from both the BBC and its commercial counterpart, ITV, Channel Four had as part of its license remit a new articulation of the nation. In C4's programming Britain appeared as much more diverse and plural than the BBC & ITV had led viewers to believe, with issues of race, of gender, of sexual orientation, as well as region, neighborhood or age (the broadcaster Janet Street-Porter is credited with successfully launching "yoof" culture) coming to the fore. At the same time, these groups were increasingly addressed not as belonging to the same nation, but consisting of interest groups, consumer groups or minorities, rather than being addressed as citizen. Similar developments could be shown to have taken place in Germany, the Netherlands or France, although in some cases with a ten-year delay.

This break up of the nation into segments of consumers, so powerfully pushed by television since the 1990s in every European country including central and eastern Europe, and observed with such despair by those concerned about democracy and the fraying of civic life, must thus be seen to be a thoroughly double-sided phenomenon. It has created spaces for self-representation, even if only in the form of niche-markets, and it has radically de-hierarchized the social pyramids of visual representation, while clearly neither dissolving stereotypes, nor necessarily contributing to a more equitable, multi-cultural society. It is this paradox of simultaneous dis-articulating the nation as citizen, while re-articulating it as a collection of consumers that, I would argue, has radicalized and compartmentalized European societies, but it has also created new spaces, not all of which need to be seen as socially divisive. Yet the manner in which these spaces henceforth communicate with each other, or take on trans-personal and inter-subjective functions, because no longer following the separation of realms into "private" and "public", "interior" and "exterior", has also affected the respective roles played by the cinema and television.

One consequence might well be, for instance, that the cinema, instead of asserting its national identity by opposing the hegemony of Hollywood, has, in truth, national television as its constantly present but never fully articulated "other". The resulting confusion can be read off any number of European films. In a film like LA HAINE, for instance, television is precisely such a constant ubiquitous presence, the visual catalyst for moving from the *bleu-blanc-rouge* of the tricolor of "white" France (on television, still very much state-controlled), to the *black-blanc-beur* of multicultural France (as lived in the streets). Television is despised by the film's youthful heroes for its lies and distortions, and yet they go to extraordinary lengths in order to be featured on it. In GOODBYE LENIN, the "reality" of the disappeared German Democratic Republic is maintained via the simulated television broadcasts, fighting against the billboards increasingly invading the streets, and yet the hero in the end says: "I was beginning to believe in the fiction we had created: finally there was a GDR as we had all dreamt it." Meanwhile, in the British film ABOUT A BOY, television is explicitly cast in the role of the derided "other", against which the Hugh Grant character tries to define a consumerist cool, whose codes, poses and gadgets are – ironically - derived from the very ads shown on the despised box. The confusion is compounded, on the other hand, when one thinks of how the European cinema has developed a kind of retroactive national vernacular, discussed in an earlier chapter as a way of "accenting"[5] the local or the regional within the global context, or packaging the past as heritage industry. A film like Jean Pierre Jeunet's AMELIE was roundly condemned for its fake image of Montmartre, straight out of Hollywood's picture-book Paris, and GOODBYE LENIN has been seen as a shameless pandering towards Ostalgie, i.e., nostalgia for the GDR, conveniently obliterating the stultifying repression, the permanent surveillance, and the wooden language of official hypocrisy its citizens were subject to.

Sub-State and Supra-State Allegiances

A nation is always something smaller than mankind and bigger than an ethnic group or a geographical region. It lives from drawing boundaries, recognizing borders and operating categories of inclusion and exclusion. At the same time, identifying with one's "nation" is increasingly experienced as at once too big and too small to mesh with one's individual sense of (not) belonging. This applies to the disaffected youth in the banlieu of LA HAINE or the drug addicts in TRAINSPOTTING as much as to the cosmopolitan locals of CHOCOLAT, the coma-prone mother in GOODBYE LENIN and the bungling wannabe bank-robbers in SHOUF SHOUF HABIBI!

However, in order to grasp what is happening even in these films of the "New European Cinema", one needs to take a step back perhaps, and return to the origins of the post-national nationalisms, by which the "Fortress Europe" believes it is besieged. For as far as these new nationalisms are concerned, the general consensus seems to be that their contradictory and modern nature can best be grasped if one posits the presence of forces that put pressure on the typical conjunction of nation and state familiar in Europe, certainly since Napoleon and the early 19th century, including the notion of sovereignty that became international law with the Peace of Westphalia in 1648 that ended the Thirty Years War in continental Europe in the wake of the Reformation.

To take the question of the combination of nation and state first: if, for a variety of reasons, in the political balance of modern Europe the idea of "nation" and the idea of "state" are drifting apart, then what we see in the social realm is the formation of "nation" groupings (or senses of belonging) that are either sub-state or supra-state, i.e., that articulate themselves above or below, or next to the nation state. In certain parts of Europe, notably around the Mediterranean and the Adriatic, this has led to separatist movements such as in the Basque country, on Corsica, and to the much more violent ethnic conflicts in the former Yugoslavia. In Britain, the 1990s brought devolution for Scotland, Wales, and Northern Ireland. However, in the sphere of the media, the massive push towards deregulation, privatization, centralization of ownership and global reach, has produced a dynamics of dispersal and at the same time new clustering that is very different from the geographically based, often fiercely blood-and-soil-centered sub-state nationalisms. These latter, paradoxically, are at once *sus*-tained and *con*-tained by the European Union, when we consider how much talk there is, on the one hand, of "a Europe of the regions," and on the other, how all forms of *de jure* separatism, and especially those that go about it by violent means, are countered and condemned. Instead of violence, the European Union supports job creation via regional development and cultural autonomy as the substitutes for political autonomy.

What destabilizes the notion of the nation today, then, are two, apparently contradictory tendencies and yet interrelated challenges. On the one hand, the nation has become an unstable category because more and more so-called sub-state groups aspire to becoming a nation: the Palestinians, the Kurds, the Tamils, the Czechs split from the Slovaks, the Corsicans, the Croats, the Slovenes, the Basques, the Chechens, and so on. On the other hand, many citizens of what for the past two centuries or so have been the nation states of Western Europe no longer feel that it is the 'nation' they owe particular allegiance to. They sense that the nation itself has become too big a category and hence they think of themselves as more represented by their region, by their religion, and in many cases, they prefer to identify themselves by their lifestyle, their leisure pursuits or their professional lives; in the name of which they travel all over the world, they become expatriates in Spain, Tuscany or the Dordogne, work somewhere in the European Union or find permanent positions in Australia or the US. For this group, the notion of Europe as a nation would be an impossibility, but even the idea of a European super-state carries no particular emotional charge.

We could call these the leisure-nationalists, and here the media do play a part. Hence my reference to the arrival of deregulated television, notably in Britain the setting up of Channel Four, which as one of its possibly unintended consequences did to some extent re-articulate the nation as different consumer groups, living in the same country but not necessarily feeling "national" about it. In the "Break-Up of Britain" debate which was conducted in the 1990s, by writers such as Tom Nairn, Linda Colley, or television journalists like Jeremy Paxman, it became clear how differently people, especially in England, perceived the "structure of feeling" (to use Raymond Williams' phrase) that bound them to England. It was no longer class, as it had been for so long, but neither was it nation. What had broken down, in favor of a new sense of social mobility, was the old alliance of working class and region, of internationalist and socialist aspirations on one side of the class divide, opposed to the upper (middle) class elite, living in the city, but celebrating the nation around "the village green, cricket and warm beer," as a former British prime minister once put it. Instructive in this moment of disarticulation of the nation was the recurring, part cynical, part resigned refrain that "we are all becoming more like Americans" – which, of course, does bring us back to matters of the cinema and cultural colonization, except that in Britain it has none of the bitter edge it has in France or elsewhere in Europe.[6]

The consequence of such post-national feelings of allegiance and identification with the nation in some of its parts, but no longer as an organic, deep-rooted totality, may be that we have to revise more fundamentally also the way we think about the social contract that ensures solidarity and defines citizen-ship. For the other, even more commented upon sub-nation, as opposed to su-pra-nation formation is, of course, made up of those who do not feel allegiance to the nation-state in the first place, because they are immigrants, refugees or asylum seekers, and who live within their own diasporic communities and closed family or faith circles, cut off from the social fabric at large through lack of familiarity with either language or culture or both. Also sub-nation in their allegiance are sections of the second-generation diaspora who, while sharing the language and possessing the skills to navigate their society, nonetheless do not feel they have a stake in maintaining the social fabric, sensing themselves to be excluded or knowing themselves to be discriminated against, while also hav-ing become estranged from the nation of their parents. In the best of cases, where they have found the spaces that allow them to negotiate difference, they are what might be called hyphenated members of the nation, or hyphenated nationals, meaning that their identity can come from a double occupancy which here functions as a divided allegiance: to the nation-state into which they were born, and to the homeland from which (one or both of) their parents came. Since all major European countries (France, Britain, Germany, the Netherlands, Spain, but also Italy and Denmark) now find themselves with large ethnic and national minorities, the general disarticulation of the nation state along the lines just sketched, their lack of integration and "assimilation" or their separate iden-tity and cultural autonomy have become major issues of public debate and con-troversy, while also raising the question already touched upon, namely what the limits are of culture as symbolic action in such a context, and under what circumstances do other, more direct forms of agency take over, as in the Nether-lands, where, on the face of it, Theo van Gogh was murdered for making a film, even if, as I have tried to show, the symbolic dimension of the act inscribes itself in a media reality, where tabloid journalism, state warfare and sub-state acts of terrorism differ perhaps more in degree than in kind.

The hyphenation of identity produced by immigration, migration and exile makes those affected by it appear in stark contrast to another group of hyphe-nated nationals, hyphenated at the supra-state level. These are the cosmopolitan elites, i.e., intellectuals, businessmen, entrepreneurs, financiers, politicians, aca-demics, artists, architects, who move freely between London, Paris and New York, or between Berlin, Milan and Warsaw. While their number may be com-paratively small, their influence and role in the world economy is, however, so significant that they are able to set major trends in urban developments, in the labour market and employment, as well as in the spheres of entertainment and leisure. Their activities and movements, thus, also contribute to the social crisis of the nation-states, when we think of them as employees of multinational com-panies, for instance, which operate as states within the state, and are able to move entire industries into other, low-wage countries. Unlike the sub-state hyphenated nationals, the political power of the cosmopolitan elites consolidates the traditional hierarchies of the nation state, rather than flattening them: it even extends the pyramids of power into international institutions and into global spheres of influence.

A Proposal for Defining a New European Cinema

This very general sketch of some of the political ramifications of the many ways in which Europe as a union of nation-states is in the middle of a possibly long and painful process of *dis*-articulating and realigning key aspects of the traditional congruence between nation and state was *inter alia* also meant to underline the difficulty of drawing too direct a parallel between the question of national cinema on the one hand, and the nation on the other. Clearly, the nation state is renegotiating with the European Union question of sovereignty and the principle of non-interference. With its citizen it tries to balance the protection of civil rights against the demands of national security. With its minorities it responds to the challenges posed by different kinds of fundamentalism and by faith communities whose civil societies have not gone through the process of secularization. Yet the cinema – in contrast to television – seems to have a minor role to play in the public debate around these vital issues, not least given the relatively small number of people reached by the films made in any of the European countries on whatever issue, and the unlikelihood of films from one European country finding distribution in another.

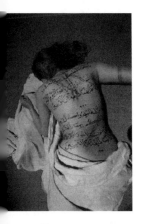

Submission

However, looked at from another angle, two things are noteworthy. First, as indicated, it is surprising how the cinema seems to have become the most prominent medium of self-representation and symbolic action that the hyphenated citizen of Europe's nation states have made their own. Films by Turkish-German directors, by French *beur* directors, by Asian directors in Britain have regularly won major prizes and come to prominence within Europe, though often not beyond. The already-mentioned film by Theo van Gogh Submission,[7] was made with a Dutch member of parliament, Ayaan Hirsi Ali, originally from Ethiopia, and fiercely militant when it comes to women's position under Islam. Not a filmmaker, she resorted to the medium for maximum publicity, which she perhaps over-achieved, in that it led to violent protests, death threats and an actual murder.

Secondly, the European Union does have a film and media policy, with directives, financing and funding structures, fiscally supporting co-productions, for instance, providing all kinds of subsidy, encouraging mixed, i.e., private-public ventures. It also supports technological innovations in the audiovisual sector, such as the digital equipment in cinemas, it subsidized inter-European distribution, it is active in the European film festival circuit, etc. The Media Initiative, started in the mid-1990s, and now in its third four-year period, is part of an important portfolio or directorate, currently that of "Information Society and Media". The directorate has as its brief to strengthen the economic aspects of the sector (too many low- to medium-budget films, too fragmented a market, since European countries are notoriously bad at watching each other's films (with the exception of films originating from the UK). The Media programme also supports training, and indeed, "cultural diversity". But it is equally aware of the function of the cinema in fostering the idea of European unity, cohesion, and its democratic values.

The experiment I have been trying to conduct is the following: I have begun to look at films that, over the past decade or so, have directly or indirectly benefitted from these EU policies, and which have also been "successful" either critically or economically within the markets they intended to reach: those of the US (almost impossible to enter into for European cinema), Japan, Australia and of course, those of the other European countries, usually quite resistant to each other's cinema. In what sense, then, do these films make a contribution to this question of allegiance, how do they address sub-nation or supra-nation communities, their aspirations and anxieties, or to what extent can they be said to be working on the idea of Europe, its professed ideals of cultural identity or diversity, its vision of interpersonal or family values. In other words, is it possible to read the European films since the 1990s, the way Siegfried Kracauer did the German films of the 1920s, Raymond Durgnat read the British cinema of the 1950s and 1960s, or I tried to reconstruct the discourses and modes of address of the New German Cinema of the 1970s and 1980s?[8]

I started from the assumption that it is possible to understand the cinema as a form of symbolic action, rather than as a one-to-one reflection of reality, or even as the construction of socially significant representations. I therefore did not look in the first instance to films that dealt with the representation of minorities or whose narratives directly relate to issues of migration, multi-culturalism or asylum or human trafficking, such as DIRTY PRETTY THINGS, IN THIS WORLD, LILIA 4-EVER or LAST RESORT, important as these films are for defining a new "European" cinema within the various "national cinemas". Instead, I began by examining some of the value structures – the ideology, to use an old-fashioned term – of the European Union, as it might be reconstructed from the various discourses, debates, position and policy papers emanating from the European union, as well as the visions and analyses promulgated by think-tanks, the great and the good and other appointed or self-appointed representatives of the idea of Europe. In short, I wanted to take the European Union at its word.

When inventorizing these "big ideas" of Europe, one realizes just how many different scenarios for the geopolitical future of the Union exist. Focussing on just some of them, for instance, one can distinguish the hope for a European Union as a multi-cultural melting pot along the lines of the former Austro-Hungarian empire; the ideal of a Christian Europe; Europe as the super-nation of the United States of Europe; the Europe of the strong nation states, ceding as little of their sovereignty as possible; Real Europe, i.e., an association of largely economic interest groups under a common legal framework and binding rules of the game.[9]

In the process, I also looked at some of the debates about redistribution and solidarity, i.e. the political as opposed to the moral justifications of the welfare state. Racism and intolerance arise when solidarity no longer even extends to all the citizens of a nation state because it is considered political poison when immigrants, asylum seekers or other non-nationals are benefitting from it. Solidarity also comes under strain with EU budget transfers being made to poorer regions, or now to the new accession countries. What is the relationship between nation-state solidarity (predicated upon a positive concept of national identity) and supra-national solidarity (human rights, international court of human justice, requiring an appeal to some other principle), or when universal human rights supersede the sovereignty of the nation state? I have followed some of the debates around integration and autonomy regarding immigrant and diaspora communities, but I have also tried to keep track of some of the more analytical voices that look at Europe in the broader, global context. Three visions or positions in particular have seemed to me to be worth pursuing with respect to the cinema, although I am not certain that these are indeed the most productive ones.

An "Enlightened" View of Immigration

The first position is perhaps the one most closely tied to the theme of the stranger and the migrant, and here I want to focus on what one might call the Tony Blair-Gerhard Schroeder "enlightened" view on immigration, that is the social-liberal one, which maintains that altogether, immigration is a good thing, and that Europe, and in particular Britain or Germany, have to honor their obligations and responsibilities of asylum. Thus, they make distinction between different kinds of immigrants, legal and illegal, asylum seekers and economic migrants. Among the latter, more distinctions are made with respect to skilled and unskilled ones, and then further distinctions operate, regarding whether the immigrants come from countries that have family values which make all the members economically productive and upwardly mobile, such as the Chinese and the Indians, and those that keep their women indoors and illiterate, and raise their male children in the patriarchal code of macho-masculinity. This vision of distinctions and differentiations, of filters and safeguards, appears as one of the ways the European Union is trying to steer towards a consensus, which it is hoped can lead to legislation or at least to a unified immigration policy.[10]

Such an apparently rational, enlightened and consensus-building strategy, I think, finds itself explored, tested – and finally found wanting – in a film by Lars von Trier which attracted a good deal of critical attention, even if it was not a box office success, DOGVILLE shot in English, and with international Hollywood star Nicole Kidman in the leading role. Here a stranger, Grace, who is being persecuted and threatened with her life, is taken in by a young man in a remote and self-contained village community. Grace makes herself useful, indeed even indispensable, but after a while, her selflessness and goodness provoke the villagers into trying anything on her they think they can get away with. Knowing they can blackmail her, the villagers do what they think serves their own survival. As one perceptive reviewer noted: "The film is focused on an evocation of the independence, privacy, small-mindedness and suspicion of a town's residents, and how they are first charmed and liberated by the thoughtful, and pretty, but needy young woman who makes herself useful through babysitting, gardening, tending a handicapped girl, and spending time with a reclusive blind man. The town's citizens reveal themselves as capable of acceptance, joy, and respect for others, but when they learn more about Grace's relationship to the outside world, they become much more demanding of her, to the point of brutality, degradation, and imprisonment."[11]

However, one can also argue that rather then being petty and small-minded, the villagers show a remarkable community spirit, closing ranks, for instance, or turning a blind eye, when it is a matter of realizing individual advantages (sex, money), which are tolerated, but only insofar as they do not endanger community cohesion. Thus, Ben brings Grace back into the village after taking her money and having sex with her; hence Tom is lying to Grace about how he got the money and to his father about who took the money. Both act pragmatically within the terms of a certain social contract, extending the villager's self-protective shield of disavowal, and thus keeping the public secret, as it were. However, this enlightened self-interest is in the end found wanting. The spectator tends to side with Grace – which is to say, with her father and his brutal gangster methods – when they assert that certain ways of behaving are just not good enough, irrespective of the "real-politik" and its pragmatism. Because of the

American accents and a montage of American Depression photographs, Lars von Trier has been accused of anti-Americanism.[12] Yet as Von Trier himself pointed out, the film was made under the impact of the 2001 Danish elections, when a right-wing anti-immigrant party won 24 percent of the popular vote, obliging the mainstream center parties to come to an agreement with the populist right. Thus, DOGVILLE makes as much sense if read as an allegory or parable not so much of the stranger, but as a model of the ideal immigrant. Preternaturally good, resourceful, adaptable and skilled, she finds herself not only exploited while at the same time becoming the scapegoat and bogeyman, but the hosts – in this case the villagers – by always setting new conditions and making further distinctions around Grace's right to stay, effectively undermine their own ability to act with any moral authority. Von Trier seems to suggest that a community looking for the pragmatic consensus, in the end betrays itself, if it is not at the same time guided by fundamental or non-negotiable principles: "Culture may be what we make of our daily habits and basic social relationships, the ways in which we wake, wash, eat, work, play, and sleep; but civilization, which requires knowledge and organization, is more than the handling of necessities and simple doings—civilization is the result of choices that are willed into being."[13]

My point is not that DOGVILLE is "about" Europe's immigration practices or that it specifically critiques either the rural backwardness become cliché in a certain image of 1930s America (which is its historical reference point), or a kind of social Darwinism to which the liberal market economies of the West seem to subscribe. Rather, the film, in its abstractions and schematism, disengages a certain logic of self and other, the community and the stranger which becomes a tool to think with, especially given the mise-en-scène which dispenses with locations other than a stage set, whose spaces are mostly delineated with chalk marks, and whose boundaries are at once imaginary and real, invisible and brutally enforced. Here, too, space is doubly occupied, insofar as the spectator is forced to superimpose not so much a "realistic" decor on the bare planks, but a different cognitive mapping of what constitutes inside and out, exclusion and inclusion, and even to ponder how an act of inclusion and co-option can be a form of exclusion, if the other's singularity is covered or occupied by fantasy projections.

Europe Cannot Be Defined by Either Faith or Ethnicity

For my second position I draw on Manuel Castells, and his vision of Europe. Castells, best know for his books on the network society, has often argued that he thinks that the European Union will not be able to sustain itself as a viable political experiment if it relies on its Christian values, or its present understanding of liberal democracy around the notion of ethnicity and multiculturalism.[14] What he values in the European Union is the way it reaches decisions by the long-drawn out, seemingly chaotic, opaque and bureaucratic methods of the Commission, the Council of Ministers, the European Parliament, the various consultative bodies apparently blocking each other or reaching only compromises and fudges. Here he sees a novel, even if as yet non-formulatable set of decision making procedures with their checks and balances, which to him will eventually supersede the classic tripartite division of power of Western democracies.

But Castells' main concern is to insist that even with these structures in place, the European Union will not be able to escape the impact of globalization dividing up the world quite differently, namely between those who are networked, connected and 'on-line' and those who are not. Translated into slightly different terms, Castells predicts a world where there are human beings that are useful to the world system as producers and/or consumers, and those who are too poor, too unskilled, too sick, or too destitute to be either producers or consumers, not even of health and welfare services. People who are unable or unwilling to participate in any of the circuits of redistribution and networks of exchange – of goods, services, affective labor or needs – may well be fated to effectively drop out of the human race. In this sense, Castells maintains, not only drug dealers, criminals, traffickers of women or refugees, but also patients in hospitals or a car-thief in prison are more useful to our society than, say someone who grows his own vegetables, is self-sufficient and never leaves his plot of land. Castells even speculates that to be a slave-laborer or a colonial subject might be seen to be preferable to being not even thought valuable enough to be exploited.

What is relevant about this position with respect to the cinema is that it alludes to a state of subjectivity that has been thematized in many of the films coming out of European countries in the last two decades, though they are by no means entirely confined to Europe. One might call this state that of abjection, to use a term made familiar by Julia Kristeva,[15] or the state of 'bare life' in the terminology of Giorgio Agamben.[16] Such abject heroes (or heroines) can be found in the works of R.W. Fassbinder, Agnès Varda's SANS TOIT NI LOI, Aki Kaurismäki, Matthieu Kassowitz' LA HAINE, the films of Catherine Breillat, Mike Leigh's NAKED, Gaspar Noe's SEULE CONTRE TOUS, the Dardenne

SANS TOIT NI LOI

Brothers' ROSETTA, and most recently Fatih Akin's HEAD-ON (GEGEN DIE WAND). In some of the narratives, the protagonists are indeed members of minorities, ethnic others, or hyphenated nationals (French-Moroccan, French-African, or German-Turkish), but these films do not seem to be primarily about race. Rather, they are about human beings that have, for one reason or another, lost the ability to enter into any kind of exchange, sometimes not even one where they can trade their bodies.

The other point to note about them is that they are not victims, at least they do not consider themselves as such, which removes them from yet another circuit of exchange and interaction – that with the victimizer or perpetrator, but also with the one who through charity and philanthropy implicitly or explicitly asserts his moral or material superiority. The protagonist's stories generally take them through this progressive stripping of all symbolic supports of their selfhood, they lose their jobs, their friends, their family, their mind, or their memory, as in the case of Kaurismäki's film, THE MAN WITHOUT A PAST.

These films, in my scheme of things, are the negative equivalent of double occupancy - they are subjects in circulation, but "out of service", to allude once more to Tomi Ungerer's toilet. Or, to vary the metaphor, the subjects of such narratives have been vacated, even by their oppressors, and the space they occupy has been declared a blank. Abject heroes or heroines in European cinema are not only symptomatic for what they tell us about a society and subjectivity that no longer has a social contract about what count as the minimum conditions of value and use, labor and affective work in a given society or community. They may also tell us something about the conditions of possibility of a counter-image of what it means to be human, and thus they approach what I called the utopian dimension of my double-occupancy. In some films, for instance, Fatih Akin's HEAD-ON, after a near-death accident, the male protagonist, having cancelled all obligations even to the proposition of staying alive, eventually agrees to enter into a kind of contract, with an almost equally post-mortem young woman, and the film draws its power, its universality, but also its politics, from the spectator following a human relationship that tries to live by a new socio-sexual contract, an experiment in utopian living, after everything else has failed, but which is itself, in the end, shown to be impossible.

From among many other examples, I could add to my list the hugely successful British film TRAINSPOTTING – a film that is at one level all about the sub-nation and sub-state re-alignment of allegiance that I mentioned earlier (the "choose a life" speech at the beginning and end, or the exchange about the abject condition of being Scottish, already discussed elsewhere). In another sense, the film also touches bottom with regards to the state of abjection in several of its characters, while at the same time hinting at the kinds of communities that only addicts share in, and which have some of the characteristics of anarcho-communist utopias. A similar trajectory is followed by THE MAN WITHOUT A PAST who finds in a group of outcasts and marginals the acceptance of his zombie-state, which in turn allows him to reconstruct a set of mental and affective coordinates that sustain his will to live.

Mutual Interferences

As indicated, according to Castells, the current trial and error process in constructing a European political project is the only feasible option and should be considered as a positive gain. This view is shared, sharpened and reformulated in *The Breaking of Nations* (2003),[17] by Robert Cooper, a British writer and diplomat who provides me with my third vision of Europe, this time centerd on post-Westphalian notions of sovereignty. Cooper argues that the world order—based on liberal democracy—will come to an end, since, as everyone readily acknowledges, we are currently in the middle of a major reconfiguration of geopolitics. He distinguishes four state forms: the hegemonic state or contemporary form of imperialism (USA), the post-modern state (EU), the modern (nationalist, authoritarian) state (Pakistan, Iran) and the pre-modern (failed) state (Sudan, Congo). Cooper maintains that the European system of nation-states and their concept of sovereignty as non-interference in matters of state and religion by outside powers, as formulated in Treaty of Westphalia, will have to give way. According to this view, this balance of power system has been superseded, because the European Union has institutionalized the mutual interference in domestic affairs between nation-states as its modus operandi. Cooper's model of the European Union as a conglomerate of nation-states that are connected with each other through the right and necessity of mutual interference, contrasts with the Franco-German notion of a European super-state, so it will come as no surprise to learn that Cooper is an advisor to the British Prime Minister.

What attracts me to Cooper's notion of the mutual interference in each other's internal affairs is not only that I have some broad political sympathy for the principle itself, with its constant shift of levels from micro to macro and back to micro which seems to me one of the most promising ways of renegotiating the social contract or solidarity based on mutual self-interest that has sustained the European welfare state since 1945, but now freed from its nationalist ideology, while also substantively redefining what we mean by sovereignty. It also provides a legally founded alternative to the American model of pre-emptive strikes by which the current US administration justifies but does not legitimate its unilateral interference in the internal affairs of others. Finally, what I also like about Cooper's notion is that it reminds us of the fact that Europe is present in our everyday lives at precisely this interface of delightful or more often irritating detail. In Britain you now buy your bananas by the metric kilo rather than the pound; what goes into your sausages has been regulated by Brussels, but as an ordinary citizen you can also take your own government before the European Court in Strasbourg and seek redress for something that the laws of your own nation state have not provided for or overlooked. In Amsterdam I noticed that my window cleaner was no longer mounting his vertiginously high ladder outside my bedroom window, but had a fully mechanized and automated moveable platform, working on hydraulic and telescopic principles. When I congratulated him on this, he only muttered that bloody Brussels had forced him to invest in the new, expensive, but evidently safer contraption.

Cooper's model of mutual interference is also suggestive of a number of strategies that can be observed in European films. The already mentioned, and much-maligned French film LE DESTIN FABULEUX D'AMÉLIE POULAIN would offer itself as a prime case study for such an allegory. The heroine, Amélie, a somewhat autistic waitress in a Montmartre café, traumatized in childhood by bizarre parents, and seemingly unable to form normal friendships or heterosexual bonds, not least because she is endowed with rich inner fantasies that always get in the way of waking life, decides – with the death of Lady Di, and the discovery of a shoebox of old toys and memorabilia – to devote herself to the happiness of others. She does so by interfering in their inner and outer lives, mostly for their own good, as she perceives it, but with means that are unconventional, doubtful even, and that have no sanction in law, as it were. They mainly consist of small alterations to the perceptual field of the other, ways of manipulating the everyday surroundings and habits. She fakes, forges, re-writes or re-interprets the reality or intersubjectivity of her victim, entering into their fantasies, phobias and anxieties in such a way that only the tiniest hint or trace is sometimes enough to make their world-picture tip over into a new reality.

Thus I am tempted to see Amélie as the master or mistress of the strategy of double occupancy of site, space and time – in its benign, but by no means unambiguous forms, as well as instantiating Robert Cooper's principle of mutual interference in the internal affairs of others, but again with a caveat, namely that Amélie – at least almost to the end, where there is a kind of enfolding reciprocity – acts for most of the time unilaterally, though with fantasy, rather than force.

The other film to be considered under the aspect of mutual interference, would be Wolfgang Becker's GOODBYE LENIN, a surprise success both in Germany and elsewhere in the world, and which like AMÉLIE, has displeased many critics, looking for a realist depiction of post-wall Germany in general and Berlin in particular. The premise is that in East Berlin, a mother of two, and a stoutly devoted communist, falls into a coma just days before the fall of the wall in 1989. When she comes to, eight months later, her children are told that any shock, especially any changes in her surroundings, might be fatal. So the son decides to recreate for her not only her bedroom, which in the meantime, rather like in AMSTERDAM GLOBAL VILLAGE, has been completely refurbished, but the entire perceptual field of her former pre-fall-of-the-Wall life, mainly by the ruse of simulating with his friend the nightly news broadcast of GDR television. There, all the cognitive and perceptual clues of her surroundings, such as the big banner advertising Coca-Cola are re-figured and re-interpreted within the framework and ideological terms of the GDR, whose citizens, especially those still devoted to the socialist dream, were evidently used to improbable ideological maneuvrings.

Here, too, someone interferes in the life-perception and reality-check of another, for the best possible reasons, and he does so by sometimes minor, sometimes major adjustments to the perceptual field. The physical territory of the GDR has been occupied in the most arrogant and heartless manner by the West Germans, taking over houses, villas, offices and institutions, but as a moral territory it is also still occupied by the feelings, memories, faded dreams and dashed hopes of its socialist inhabitants. As the film progresses, this double occupancy becomes – in the nightly broadcasts – almost literally that duck-rabbit construction of Wittgenstein, so that the son, after a particularly bold and totally convincing re-coding of the West's televisual news images of the fall of the wall, can admit to himself that he is beginning to believe in his own fiction, because it allows that other – utopian – reality to coexist with the new one, that of unification, the capitalist state, and consumerism, as if the ultimate addressee of his manipulation was not his mother, but he himself, and with it, his generation: double occupancy redeems a dream while not being in denial of reality. It is his own trauma/coma that he was able to narrativize and therapize.

On the other hand, the mother's coma also stands for a near-death experience, comparable to the state of abjection or loss of mind and memory already alluded to in my other group of films. What in each case is striking, is how such engineering of mutually sustaining fantasies in GOODBYE LENIN or AMÉLIE is based on the implicit presumption that it is small changes in the everyday which can shift the entire picture. These films at once enact Robert Cooper's political principle of mutual interference in the internal affairs of others, and subtly re-adjust or re-scale it: in the project Europe of the European Union, it may not be a matter of the big idea, the "vision" which is so woefully lacking, as can be seen in the non-debate around the European constitution. Rather, what matters is the

GOODBYE LENIN

small gesture, the tiny detail that at once irritates, surprises and makes us reflect. Ideally, it makes us work on the idea of Europe, which is to say, it has the capacity to politicize us, and who knows, through the bananas we buy or the window-cleaners we pay, turns us from consumers back into citizens, not at the supra- or sub-nation level of the nation-state, but at the trans-national level, as citizens of Europe.

If in GOODBYE LENIN, Europe is thus not the big idea, but the adjustment or alteration in small everyday things that change the semantic, symbolic or moral occupation of a space, a history and a memory, the film also provides us, I am arguing, with a kind of allegorical refiguring of the history I have been trying to tell, namely the respective transfer of representation, address and articulation of nation in film and television in Europe over the last fifty years or so: as projected and articulated by state-controlled television, disarticulated by the consumer society, and then re-enacted, imperso-Nationed by the charade that the dutiful son performs for the mother-country, waking from a coma that is metaphoric at least as much as it is medical. Once again, it indicates the desire for a kind of zero degree, a system re-boot if you like, in the political, social but also subjective-affective imaginaries of the European nation states. Perhaps what is needed is to vacate the all-too crowded and pre-occupied spaces of discourse and debate, as the pre-condition for rethinking both identity and diversity, both history and memory, both the micro-politics of a city and a community and the macro-politics of globalization, including those of immigration, diaspora and exile. As the holiday brochure says: "double occupancy means that the rate is the same whether one or two people stay in the room, providing that they use the existing bedding".[18] Mikhail Gorbachev once spoke about the "house" that was Europe.[19] Maybe we should begin by thinking of it as a "room" and the globe as the "house" we all have to share: could the new European cinema I have tried to sketch in this chapter be the "bedding" that shows us how to make up this room?

(2005)

Notes

1.   Ivan Briscoe. "Fortress Europe Bids You Welcome." *UNESCO Courier*. Sept 2001. 4 May 2005. <http://www.unesco.org/courier/2001_09/uk/doss24.htm.>
2.   Jacques Derrida, *Of Grammatology*. (Baltimore: John Hopkins University Press, 1974).
3.   Ludwig Wittgenstein, *Philosophical Investigations*. New Jersey: Prentice Hall, 1958, 212.

4. Voltaire. *A Treatise on Toleration*. Trans. David Williams. London: Fielding and Walker, 1779. The paraphrase comes from *The Friends of Voltaire*, written by Evelyn Beatrice Hall and published in 1906 under the pseudonym Stephen G. Tallentyre.

5. Hamid Naficy. *An Accented Cinema: Exilic and Diasporic Filmmaking*. Princeton: Princeton University Press, 2001.

6. An excellent review of the debate about the break-up of Britain, with some pertinent analyses of its own is an essay by Jonathan Cook, "Relocating Britishness and the Break-Up of Britain," in Steven Caunce et al. (eds.), *Relocating Britishness* (Manchester and New York: Manchester University Press, 2004)pp. 17-38.

7. <http://www.ayaanhirsiali.web-log.nl/.> or Willem Velthoven. "Theo van Gogh, Submission Part 1." *Mediamatic.net: New Media, Art, Culture, Theory*. 2004. 4 May 2005. <http://www.mediamatic.net/article-200.8323.html&q_person=200.8324.>

8. Siegfried Kracauer. *From Caligari to Hitler: A Psychological History of the German Film*. Princeton: Princeton UP, 1947; / Raymond Durgnat. *A Mirror for England*. London: Faber & Faber, 1970; / Thomas Elsaesser. *New German Cinema: A History*. London: Macmillan, 1989.

9. Paul Hilder, "Which Europe Do You want- A Map of Visions"? 19-03-2003 <http://www.opendemocracy.net/debates/article-3-51-1067.jsp.>

10. See "Towards a Common European Union Immigration Policy" 4 May 2005. <http://europa.eu.int/comm/justice_home/fsj/immigration/fsj_immigration_intro_en.htm.>

11. Daniel Garrett. "This Land is Your Land: DOGVILLE - Reason and Redemption, Rage and Retribution." *Offscreen*. 30 Jun. 2004, 4 May 2005. <http://www.horschamp.qc.ca/new_offscreen/dogville.html.>

12. A. O. Scott. "It Fakes a Village: Lars von Trier's America." *The New York Times*. 21 Mar. 2004, 4 May 2005. <http://www.csudh.edu/dearhabermas/21scot.htm.>

13. Daniel Garrett. "This Land is Your Land: DOGVILLE - Reason and Redemption, Rage and Retribution."

14. Manuel Castells. *The Information Age: Economy, Society & Culture - The Rise of the Network Society*. Oxford: Blackwell, 1996.

15. Julia Kristeva. *Powers of Horror: An Essay on Abjection*. Trans. Leon S. Roudiez. New York: Columbia University Press, 1982.

16. Giorgio Agamben. *Homo Sacer: Sovereign Power and Bare Life* Trans. Daniel Heller-Roazen, Stanford University Press: Stanford, 1998.

17. Robert Cooper. *The Breaking of Nations: Order and Chaos in the Twenty-first Century*. London: Atlantic Books, 2003.

18. "Double Occupancy." *Discount Hotels Hawaii*. 4 May 2005. <http://www.discounthotelshawaii.com/definitions/doubleoccupancy.html.>

19. Mikhail Gorbachev, Nobel Lecture (5 June, 1991). 4 May 2005. <http://www.historiasiglo20.org/pioneers/gorbachev.htm>.

Auteurs and Art Cinemas

Modernism and Self-Reference, Installation Art and Autobiography

Ingmar Bergman – Person and PERSONA

The Mountain of Modern Cinema on the Road to Morocco

The Looming Mountain

On the night between March 25 and 26, 1983, having just finished AFTER THE REHEARSAL, Ingmar Bergman wrote in his workbook-diary: "I don't want to make films again ... This film was supposed to be small, fun, and unpretentious ... Two mountainous shadows rise and loom over me. First: Who the hell is really interested in this kind of introverted mirror aria? Second: Does there exist a truth, in the very belly of this drama, that I can't put my finger on, and so remains inaccessible to my feelings and intuition? ... We should have thrown ourselves directly into filming ... Instead we rehearsed, discussed, analyzed, penetrated carefully and respectfully, just as we do in the theatre, almost as if the author were one of our dear departed."[1] *Images – My Life in Film*, from which this passage is taken, is late Bergman at his most typical where a text is an expertly crafted conjuring trick, altogether worthy of the self-aware, self-confidently tortured master magician. Furnishing his book, as in the passage just cited, with quite a few theatrical trap-doors, Bergman manages to speak as if from beyond the grave, or rather from inside the grave, intently scrutinizing us, the reader, how we react to the sight of the "dearly departed," who is still enjoying the spectacle of hiding and revealing, knowing that there is always another mirror to be cracked, another veil to be torn aside.

For is not Bergman himself the mountainous shadow rising and looming over Swedish cinema, and even contemporary Swedish culture?[2] When he retired from directing with FANNY AND ALEXANDER in 1983, was he tauntingly withdrawing to let a younger generation of filmmakers take up center-stage? Not really, for nearly fifteen years later, no one seems to have dared scale this particular mountain peak or hoist a different flag.[3] Instead, Bergman has continued to be productive, in ways that are particularly remarkable. Not only has he directed several plays and operas, and continues to do so,[4] he also remains in the news thanks to other media: being outspoken about the present situation of the Swedish film industry on television, or publishing his memoirs, reminiscences and recollections are only two ways in which the mountain shows its volcanic force. Indeed, Bergman seems almost incapable of not playing a determining role in his country's film and television productions, making sure they attract national and international attention. Thus, the major Swedish television event of 1991 was THE BEST INTENTIONS ,a four-part historical drama, written by Bergman and directed by Bille August, which, when edited to feature length, was awarded the *Palme d'Or* in Cannes as best film of 1992.

Also in 1992, Bergman's son Daniel made his directorial debut with SUNDAY'S CHILDREN, an adaptation of Bergman's autobiographic novel. In 1996, PRIVATE CONVERSATIONS, the sequel to THE BEST INTENTIONS aired on television, once more shown to large audiences during the Christmas season. Written by Bergman, it was directed by Liv Ullmann, one of the director's favorite actresses, who had already accepted special honors on behalf of Bergman on previous occasions. At the Cannes Film Festival of 1997, celebrating its 50th anniversary, Bergman received another *Palme d'Or*, when he emerged as the favorites' favorite in a poll among all the previous winners of the *Palme d'Or*. This time it was Linn Ullmann, Bergman's daughter by Liv, who took the ovation on the director's behalf, while Eva Bergman, another daughter of his, has completed two films and is set to direct her first full-length feature. Bergman, in other words, represents not only a one-man "culture industry," but he has founded a dynasty where his films, life, and art all seem to mingle, where appearance and reality become merely moments in a continuum, in a torrent of creativity whose energy is carried from person to person, from place to place, from gender to generation. His key actors and technicians have fanned out, in some cases to attain international stardom, as with Max von Sydow and Ingrid Thulin, or cinematographer Sven Nykvist, and at times as directors in their own right, as in the case of Liv Ullmann, who to date has written and directed four films. According to Ullmann, there is also a kind of "pact" in force among the Bergman tribe – Erland Josephson, Max von Sydow and Ullmann making up the core – who assist each other, who act in each other's films, and in this way, pass on the secret and let it circulate.

It therefore requires a special effort to imagine a time when there was no "Bergman" to hover over Sweden, and to remind oneself that the director had to make literally a dozen films before he had a major success with WILD STRAWBERRIES in 1958. Prior to this film and THE SEVENTH SEAL (also 1958), he was valued only among the cognoscenti. Jean-Luc Godard, in an article interestingly entitled "Bergmanorama," conveys the excitement of the emerging French *Nouvelle Vague*, who promptly (and perhaps perversely) championed the early Bergman over the mature director: "When Vadim emerged, we praised him for being up to date when most of his colleagues were one war behind. Similarly, when we saw Guiletta Masina's poetic grimacing we praised Fellini ... But this renaissance of the modern cinema had already been brought to its peak five years earlier by the son of a Swedish pastor. What were we dreaming of when Summer with Monika was first shown in Paris? Ingmar Bergman was already doing what we are still accusing French directors of not doing. Summer with Monika was already And God ... Created Woman, but done to perfection. And the last shot of Nights of Cabiria, when Masina stares fixedly into the camera: have we forgotten that this, too, appeared in the last reel but one of Summer with Monika? Have we forgotten that we had already experienced ... that sudden conspiracy between actor and spectator ... when Harriet Andersson, laughing eyes clouded with confusion and riveted on the camera, calls on us to witness her disgust in choosing hell instead of heaven?"[5]

Reading what Bergman has to say about Summer with Monika (1952) in *Images* ("I have never made a less complicated film. We simply went off and shot it, taking great delight in our freedom")[6], and then watching it recently on video, I could understand Godard's enthusiasm. The film is a glorified home movie, a hymn to a young woman's sensuality, and for the then would-be director of a bout de souffle clearly an open invitation to mix the moral rigor of Roberto Rossellini with the youthful abandon of Nicholas Ray's rebel without a cause.

Reviews in Britain about Bergman in the late 1950s were more cautious and circumspect than Godard. I have before me a page from *The Listener* (9 July, 1959, still folded into my *Ingmar Bergman*, by Jacques Siclier (Editions Universitaires, 1960), where John Weightman (later to become an eminent professor of French literature) "after assimilating a new batch of four films by Ingmar Bergman, made between 1949 and 1953," reflects on the director's "extraordinary unevenness of quality. How can he be at once so subtle and so unsubtle?" Weightman disliked Wild Strawberries and The Seventh Seal, but he, too, liked Summer with Monika, mainly because of its poetic (i.e., neo-realist) qualities. Bergman, according to Weightman, reflects "the instability of the couple's relationship in the changing mood of water and sky," the acting is of "uncanny accuracy," and in a lesson in love and Summer with Monika he identifies "the two young husbands [as] perfect examples of the decent, naive, Scandinavian male who is driven nearly frantic by the vagaries of the female." The last point is ironically offset by Bergman's description (in *The Magic Lantern*) of how he fell in love with Harriet Andersson during the making of Summer with

SUMMER WITH MONIKA

Monika, and how pleased they both were when it turned out that they had to re-shoot most of the outdoor footage because a faulty machine at the laboratory had torn up several thousand meters of negative.[7] But Weightman ended his review on an interesting note: "In putting all these characters and moments of life on to the screen in so many brilliant, if fragmentary episodes, Bergman has done something for Sweden that no one, to my knowledge, is doing for England. But there may be a parallel in France. Two or three young French directors, like Bergman, have deliberately turned down attractive foreign offers and international stars in order to produce films that have a local, home-made or hand-made character. The camera is again being used as a private eye, as a means of expressing a single yet complex view. This return to the artisan tradition is an interesting development, even though some of the initial products have all the defects of first novels ... The cinema is such a rich art form and the poetry of the camera so much more facile than poetry in language, that it is easy for the filmmaker to get drunk on the possibilities of his medium. I think Bergman is slightly drunk in this way."[8]

Reality and Reflection: The Person Behind Persona

When I began writing about Bergman in the mid-60s, my main aim (I think) was to rescue Bergman, the filmmaker, from what I perceived to be his friends, those who saw in him the Nordic sage, a stern spiritualist and philosopher. But I also wanted to defend him against his enemies, my university friends, who idolized Hollywood, and therefore ritually dismissed Bergman's work as mere filmed theatre, pompous, and uncinematic. For me, Bergman became a "classical" (which is to say, also "American") director with Persona (1966), a film I loved for its intelligence, but also for what the film communicated about Bergman's person/persona. This needs perhaps a word of explanation, since in the European cinema, the idea of a personal style has an obviously different connotation from that in the commercial cinema. In the former, personality tends to be defined by a moral vision and a unique aesthetic language, whereas in the latter, it required the "auteur" theory to teach us to detect "personal" traits even in genre films and Hollywood studio productions. Yet paradoxically, the European "auteur" – as if to compensate for the absence of pre-defined genres and stars – requires often a "trilogy" or a steady cast of players in order to have his universe recognized as not just personal but belonging to cinema history. At other times, as in the case of Robert Bresson, Michelangelo Antonioni, or Federico Fellini, it is the entire *oeuvre* that stands for the director, rather than a specific film, in which case, it is the sheer staying power over time that guarantees the work's cultural value. However, since each of these directors is deemed to be a law unto himself, there is a tendency to either like their films or dislike them, according to how sympathetic one feels towards the underlying general conception of "life." Rather than respond to the intrinsic aesthetic qualities of the individual films as such, critics tend to "interpret" such a director's work, launching on thematic exegesis largely on the director's own terms, with blithe disregard for the "intentionalist fallacy."

The point I was struggling with when mounting my own defense of Bergman was not to deal with the work in this way. I wanted to examine whether a cinematic vision which bears so obviously the marks of its creator in all its parts was simply self-referential, short-circuited in a tangle of private obsessions and fantasies, or whether the idiosyncrasies were the result of a self-imposed limitation, the price of a deliberate artistic discipline – in short, a modernist aesthetic. For me, Bergman – despite appearances to the contrary – clearly headed in the latter direction, for the self-reflexivity of the modernist artist was particularly in evidence in the films not generally popular, like THE FACE (1959) whose consistency in theme, characterization and setting allowed a certain world to emerge with exceptional economy as well as clarity. Bergman's films seemed to pose so many key problems of the medium itself, whether the relationship of language to images, or the truth of illusion – and all of these concerns were embodied across the judgment he passed on his characters' self-images, their role-playing and at times sententious verbal self-fashioning. The often pessimistic, possibly sadistic portrayal of human frailty, of the frustrated will to communicate, of remorseless perseverance in moral and psychic self-destruction so typical of his protagonists was, I felt, intimately connected with the peculiarly ascetic mise-en-scène, for Bergman's intensity and intellectual lucidity, as well as the calculated control of audience-response was largely due to a categorical refusal to let any reality (in the sense of unstructured contingency) enter into his films: an absence of "real life," that is, which formed the thematic core of, for example films like A PASSION (1970), but also of THE SILENCE (1963) or PERSONA. Bergman so clearly "fabricated" reality in order to produce situations of artifice, and his particular psychological realism was only effective as a metaphoric language (the

THE SILENCE

predicaments pointing only by extension and extrapolation to the larger situation: a social class trapped in forms of behavior which had become unreal even to itself) because the field of vision had been so carefully delimited and closed. For example, if one looked at the outbursts of violence in Bergman's films, one could see how precise the relation was of what the film said and how (at what price of self-imposed restraint) it said it. In A PASSION, when Max von Sydow swings an axe at Liv Ullmann, the moment transcends the level of hysterical histrionics because Bergman's restriction of the visual field, the avoidance of pans and long-shots, cumulatively engendered a frustration, a sense of unnatural enclosure in the spectator which found its lightning-conductor in the Von Sydow character's furious physical attack. Emotional intensity viscerally transmitted is one of the secrets of the American cinema's sheer physicality. It was only Bergman among European directors who seemed to me to manage a similar tactile immediacy and palpable impact in his films, for he used processes specific to the cinema, such as the manipulation of space, not in order to create intellectual effects, but to convey psycho-physical states (here a sense of claustrophobia) that were integral parts of his moral themes. The barrenness of his island (the setting of this, as so many other films from the 1960s) was the richness of his cinema.

By making this dialectic of visceral impact and spatial restraint both the center and the structuring principle, Bergman had, in my judgment, created especially with PERSONA a uniquely modernist film, where the modernist topos of appearance vs. reality found itself explored across that specifically cinematic mode of meaning-making we call "violence," which is not necessarily the violence *on* the screen, but the always implied violence *of* the screen. It gave PERSONA a different kind of vantage point, for it made an appeal to this fundamental tension of the cinema as a medium of reflection across an assault on the senses, in order to give thematic substance and formal coherence to the logic of its

THROUGH A GLASS DARKLY

images. Whereas some of Bergman's previous films had displayed a discrepancy between the internal truth of the image and the thematic weight it was expected to carry (with the effect that spectators tended to stifle an unintended laugh in THROUGH A GLASS DARKLY [1963] when a big spider crawling along a wall was meant to suggest the presence of God in a schizophrenic woman's mind), PERSONA focused the images and fused them with the dramatic reality of the characters, who develop, expose, hide (and all but destroy) themselves under the silent or aggressive, furtive or direct look (always intensely hypnotic) with which they scrutinize and provoke each other – a look that in essence is the equivalent and stand-in of the spectators' eyes riveted to the screen. Bergman makes this relation quite explicit: the two women face the audience directly whenever the inner, reflective eye that questions perception is to become an element of dramatic importance. As the women's faces are turned to us, their eyes transmit a distinctly probing experience which invariably crystallizes the preceding action.

When Alma, waking up in the middle of the night, sees Elisabet come to her room out of the translucent curtains of the open door, her vision corresponds to an emotion which the entire preceding film has led up to, which is her desire, so ardently expressed in her words and eyes, for friendship, communion, tenderness and understanding with Elisabet. When the women embrace, this desire finds its fulfillment. But as the camera moves closer, the figures disengage from each other, and they turn their faces to the camera, as if they were looking at their reflection in a mirror. Is it possible, the faces seem to ask, that we are really one? And to underline this, Elisabet brushes Alma's hair from her forehead to reveal their striking likeness. It seems obvious that this scene is so memorable because it relates profoundly to the inner movement and dramatic development of the film, that is, because of its structural importance, as much as because it is beautifully photographed (it is the single most frequently reproduced still from the film). The more unsettling, therefore, that the following morning Elisabet denies the very occurrence of this scene, yet this too, is logical, in that it corresponds to the two movements in Alma's character and sensibility: the emotion, the desire that brings the vision into being and makes it materialize on the screen, and the reflection, the mirror-like apprehension that dissolves it again. In such scenes Bergman is concerned with bringing out and establishing the fundamental tensions between emotion, intellect and perception, their necessary relatedness not only in the lives of his characters; these tensions are as present in us, while watching a film, and yet by recognizing the validity of Bergman's themes in terms of our own experiences during the film, we accord general significance to them, as being also part of our lives.

PERSONA as Paradigm: The Mind of the Body

But it was neither for its themes nor for its spiritual uplift that I became a believer in Bergman's genius, because as already indicated, it was not his metaphysics but the *physics* of his films that made me go to the cinema, and write about his work. Although I might not have put it this way, it was the intelligence of the body in Bergman's work that I looked for in the films from the mid-1960s onwards, which made them not necessarily more profound than his "masterpieces" (e.g., THE SEVENTH SEAL or WILD STRAWBERRIES), but distinctly more cinematic and therefore more classical, in the sense that the classical American cinema has always been a cinema of bodily intelligence.

Returning to PERSONA, the story of an actress, Elisabet, who after a nervous breakdown, is nursed back to health by a young woman, Alma, and gradually seems to "absorb" part of the nurse's personality, the question immediately poses itself as to where the film's life and the characters' life-force reside. Is it in the (fragile, unworthy) selves they peel away (and thus in the morality of stripping the soul naked of all pretence), or in these selves' wily and ingenious self-fashioning during the encounters with an "other"? If one looks at the scene which precipitates the nervous breakdown, showing us Elisabet on stage, one can see that the action is at each moment sufficient unto itself. The very way in which the scene is formally organized points to its function, interprets it – indeed explains Elisabet's otherwise so puzzling decision henceforth to remain silent. The disposition of figure and space, of character movement and camera movement convey the urgency of her choice in a manner more immediate and convincing than any verbal explanations given by the doctor. We first see Electra/Elisabet with her back to the camera addressing an audience in a theatre. Gradually she turns round, approaches the camera, until her face is in close-up and she is looking straight at us. The real significance lies not in the verbal commentary (which merely fills in the context) but exclusively in her physical movement. The shot begins with her facing the theatre audience and ends with her facing us, the cinema audience (both audiences are "abstract" as far as one can make out, since the auditorium in the theatre appears in fact to be empty of spectators). This corresponds directly to a process of reflection made manifest in space in that she has quite literally come to a turning point in her life. The transition from an outer world of appearance to an inner revelation of being is given substance by the movement which in a fluid motion joins the two audiences – differentiated as they are by the ontological gap that separates cinematic image and physical reality, and which Bergman has here used to signify the difference between emotional reality (Elisabet's sudden awareness of herself and the emotional involvement of the audience in the film) and external existence (Elisabet's role as actress and the illusory, unreal image on the screen).

This movement from an outer to an inner world is furthermore reinforced, given a concrete spatial embodiment, and hence its ultimate visual reality by the position of the camera. Elisabet is on stage, as a metaphor of a social world, and she turns backstage (where the camera is), to indicate a more intimate and immediate reality. The transition which her movement describes is therefore from an outer, seemingly ordered (but false) world to an inner, often chaotic (but necessary) world. For just as the business that habitually goes on backstage in a theatre is necessary in order to produce the "show," so the chaos of one's inner self may well be the necessary precondition of one's active "social" life (cf. the similar use which Bergman makes of the backstage metaphor in SMILES OF A SUMMER NIGHT [1955], or the juxtaposition of the trailer and the circus ring in the interpersonal dramas of SAWDUST AND TINSEL [1953]).

Where the scene in PERSONA essentially differs from the earlier ones is in Bergman's awareness as to its directly cinematic implication, expressed by the position of the camera and the extreme economy of its use. In this scene, Bergman has not only given the essential movement of this film (its constant dialectic from inner to outer realm), its fundamental theme (the possibility of communicating and living this inner reality) but also vindicated the cinema as a unique medium of revelation and illumination of what is perceptible neither to the naked eye nor to be put in words. By placing the camera backstage with its mechanical eye turned towards the auditorium, Bergman has indicated the ultimately impersonal scope of cinematic art: observing life and giving us its veridical image, the cinema in a simultaneous movement transforms it, recording an inner experience as *action*. In this unique capacity of

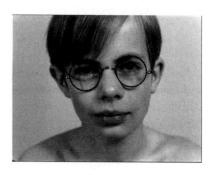

PERSONA

being at once supremely realistic and highly interpretative, even visionary, lies the justification of the cinema, its seriousness, even as it deals in nothing but illusion. The scene described above could serve as a very persuasive argument for the auteur theory – a scene whose minimal overt "content" reveals a maximum of cinematic meaning. It was as if Bergman in PERSONA had discovered the kind of economy of means that seemed to many of us to make the American cinema superior to European art film: the recognition that the cinema is at once the most unreal, the most "faked" and the emotionally most real and most authentic of all aesthetic experiences, and that its fascination resides in the irresolvable oscillation inherent in this contradiction.

Narrative Space

This theoretical-ethical point around which PERSONA is structured is already dramatized in the pre-credit sequence, where a boy with his hands stretched out trying to touch the (projected) image of a woman (his mother?). The image, as it becomes larger and larger is both too close to be clearly recognized and too far to be concretely grasped – it is at once immediately tactile and irredeemably unreal: the boy's longing for his mother, human contact and physical communication remains unfulfilled, for how could he ever bridge the gap between the two planes of reality that separate the body from the image. (To underline this point, and make the didactic-metaphysical implications quite obvious, Bergman lets the boy turn round and repeat the gestures into the camera, obliging the spectator to be both directly related to his predicament and experience it indirectly: we will always remain "unreal" to him, and that means that he – as indeed all the characters in the film – exists only in terms of the role we are prepared to give him, in the act of activating our empathy, our touch, our intellect). In this pre-credit scene of violence and graphic detail, or bodies asleep and bodies in the morgue, of slaughtered sheep and human hands having nails driven through their palms, Bergman clarifies his own position (as if to bid farewell to his early films which, in order to make these points about reality and appearance, had to invent historical fairy tales, (e.g., THE FACE).

Bergman's concern for, and awareness of, the medium is also apparent in his very differentiated and subtle organization of space, that is to say, visual space. This may seem paradoxical, insofar as a certain kind of representational space does not exist at all in PERSONA. There is an almost complete absence of perspective and depth. The women are close to the camera, the background is often indistinct or blurred, and their faces are seen as if from behind glass with flat visual planes with clear outlines, yet without a feeling of roundness and wholeness, thus giving an overwhelming sense of at once claustrophobia and transparency, of constriction experienced in a state of almost hallucinatory clarity. This deliberate one-dimensionality of the image, clearly and essentially belongs to the women's predicament, is achieved by Bergman's refusal to let the illusion of ordinary space develop, substituting instead a properly cinematic space without in any way destroying that sense of psychological realism, so necessary to any involvement in the interpersonal drama unfolding.

The full significance of this floating, translucent space, however, only becomes apparent when contrasted with scenes where there is edge and perspective. For example, when Alma tells her story about the boys on the beach, Bergman gives the room an extraordinary depth, with the two women as focal points, clearly distinguished and surrounded by a particular light which both illuminates and isolates (especially the light near Elisabet). Against the impersonal, flat and even surface of the other scenes, this one has an immediate – but deceptive – quality of warmth and intimacy. The function and significance of this new space is twofold: firstly it clearly separates the two women, isolating Elisabet from Anna's experience, and giving to Anna an emotional freedom, outside their ambivalent relationship. Secondly the deep focus, allowing as it does a fullness of the image and the expansion of the visual space not only corresponds to the sentiment that Alma tries to express, but at the same time associates its thematic value, giving it an interpretation which the story itself does not make evident, which is namely the immensely liberating significance that Bergman wants to convey through Alma's tale, the sensual reality of a warm, expansive day on the beach, the sexual abandon, the physical intimacy, the strangely innocent fulfillment of this impersonal human contact across passion and lust. Thus, the expansion of Alma's self in the narration corresponds to the expansion of the cinematic image, and the reality of her experience becomes materialized in the visual reality of the room in its three-dimensionality.

Where such a reality no longer exists in relation to the characters (as subsequently when Alma breaks down and cries on Elisabet's bed), the space, too, reflects this contraction, becoming indistinct, obliterated. Similarly, the long-shots on the beach, among pebbles and rocks (a landscape present in at least half a dozen of Bergman's films) indicate the total destruction of their relationship, their fundamental discord between each other and their environment. Whereas in his earlier films, these beach scenes often made a somewhat allegorical point about "isolation" and "alienation," the scene in PERSONA has quite a different, wholly specific connotation, because the spatial construction, as I have tried to show, relates to other scenes, and therefore belongs to a specific dramatic turning point.

The film's spatial organization is thus determined by the development of the narrative argument, the power relations and inter-personal struggles, moving from claustrophobic one-dimensional surfaces to focal depth and clarity, or unrelated, forlorn vistas on the beach. Particular importance in this context is given to Elisabet's hospital room. The darkness is bathed in ghostly light emanating from the television set. Terrified by the images of the burning monk, Elisabet tries to escape from the impact of this experience by pressing herself against the wall. The scene is crucial, in that it finds a most apposite visual metaphor for the insoluble nature of her dilemma in the outside world, which she tried to exclude by her silence, but which intrudes the more forcefully as images which quite literally are reflected on her own person. This throws light on her own predicament, and illuminates her inner world from which she cannot escape (though she might have cheated herself, as most of us do, by turning off the set, as she had done previously with the radio). Unobtrusively, yet very powerfully Bergman validates the metaphor of the room as an image of Elisabet's interior world, in which she is exposed to violent conflict. Hence once more the concrete sense of space (which is not a theatrical space) that Bergman gives to the scene. It foreshadows and anticipates a situation of bodily threat and psychic danger repeated later, when Alma is about to pour boiling water in Elisabet's face. If in the first scene it is the reality of an image (the reflection of an external reality) which threatens her, the second scene stages a threat to Elisabet's body image, intended to expose the fallacious purity of her escape into silence. In both cases, the intensity of the emotional conflict depends for its dramatic reality on the justness of its materialization in a visual space.

The importance which Bergman gives to space invalidates a charge made against PERSONA at the time, namely that it examines the relation of the two women in a social vacuum. Not only does the first part of the film show how and why they are gradually taken out of their habitual environment, but the subtle variations of space are partly intended to keep the political dimension constantly present. From the beginning, Bergman stresses the sensual, intellectual (and social) difference between the two women. One notes, for instance, the juxtaposition of the two women going to bed: Elisabet, with her face motionless turned towards the camera, and the image becoming slowly darker and darker – cinematic expression of her essentially reflective nature, while Alma, restless, switching the light on and off is characterized as temperamental and impulsive. At the same time, their common characteristics (from which the dramatic conflict flows) are also underlined. They are both in a "false" position, i.e., both contain within themselves irreconciled contradictions: one by choice and act of will (Elisabet's silence, deliberate negation of her profession as actress and of her middle-class existence), the other by innocence and ignorance (Alma's soliloquies at night as she removes her make-up – a symbolic action, reminiscent of a similar scene at the end of SUMMER INTERLUDE (1950) and contrasted to her seemingly straightforward self-assured day-time manner).

What are these opposites, and what do they signify? As I have already indicated, PERSONA seems to me most meaningful when also considered as a meta-cinematic statement, in which the nature of the characters' drama relates intimately to the specific qualities of the cinematic medium. Thus, Elisabet seems to find in her self-imposed silence a release from her extroverted existence imposed upon her by her profession as an actress. Away from the role that smothered her own self under layers of make-up, she tries to discover an inner dimension, a new intimacy which seem to be the fruit of solitude. To this, Alma brings the necessary – devastating – correction that there may not be a self beneath the mask. On the other hand, Alma, too, finds in this silence a screen upon which she can project all the roles she had always wanted to play. She becomes an extrovert to a degree that seems to surprise even herself, though only to discover in the process that by playing these roles she has stripped herself of all her outward assurance and certainty. By playing herself, and as it were, dramatizing her own existence in front of her silent spectator, Alma becomes an actress, performing before an audience. (The meta-discursive dimension in relation to the cinema is evident, if only by the fact that Alma is of course played by a professional actress: Bibi Andersson).[9] The fictional Alma is nonetheless caught at her own game also by the silence of the spectator Elisabet who makes her lose all control, plunging her into a hysteria that brings her face to face with her own long-concealed anguish. This is precisely the kind of anguish that made Elisabet renounce being an actress – the nurse has become patient, and the patient has become teacher. In this, Bergman seems at pains to remind us of the perverse and at the same time revealing conditions under which (artistic) creativity exercises itself today, which is always on the verge of hysteria, hype, and hypocrisy.

European Art Cinema: The Many Maps of Misreading

Indeed, and this maybe the rub, the point where any interpretation of Bergman's films, any thematic, modernist, or self-reflexive reading comes up against another set of realities: those of production and reception as the obtain in a popular, quasi-universal, but nonetheless capital-intensive medium such as the cinema. After all, it is audiences as well as critics who decide how a film is to be understood, and the former are often cued not by the subject matter or metaphysical dilemmas about reality and reflection, of being and seeming, or the difficulties of the face-to-face in human communication, but by such "cultural capital" as a catchy title, a striking poster, the presence of well-known actors, not to mention such "chance-encounters" as the kind of cinema where one happens to have seen a film, or with whom one saw it. In his time, Bergman was seen as the very epitome of the "art cinema" director.[10]

Today, it makes more sense to put forward the case that the old "art cinema" vs. "commerce" divide, even the opposition Europe vs. Hollywood, or the difference between an "auteur" and a "*metteur-en-scène*" should be understood as a special case of a more general process, where films (or for that matter, most cultural objects and artifacts) have assigned to them identities and meanings according to often apparently fortuitous or superficial characteristics, which on closer inspection, nonetheless provide the only instructive map we have of cultural history, in this case, of film culture. Such a map ignores all kinds of stylistic or formal boundaries, relegates interpretations such as the one I have sketched of PERSONA to the graduate student essay, but speaks eloquently about the life of films and filmmakers in a much vaster history: that of mentalities, taste and sensibilities. One could even call it the only true "map of misreading": In the case of the cinema, this map tells us that many a European film intended for one kind of (national) audience, or made within a particular kind of aesthetic framework, agenda or ideology, undergoes a sea change as it survives the decades (or crosses the Atlantic), and upon its return, finds itself bearing the stamp of yet another cultural currency.

If this is now a commonplace about Hollywood, it is just as true for European art cinema. The qualities for which filmmakers were praised were not necessarily what the audiences liked about their films, and what made them famous was not always what made them successful. In the case of Italian neo-realism, for instance, the aesthetic-moral agenda included a political engagement, a social conscience, a humanist vision. Subjects such as post-war unemployment, or the exploitation of farm labor by the big landowners was part of what made neo-realism a "realist" cinema, while the fact that it did not use stars, but faces from the crowd made it a "poetic" cinema (to come back to Weightman's comments on Ingmar Bergman). Yet as we know, a film like ROME, OPEN CITY (Roberto Rossellini, 1946) which is ostensibly about the bravery of the Italian

THE BICYCLE THIEF

resistance against the German Gestapo, with communist partisans and Catholic priests making common cause against the enemy, represents not only a particular (party-political) view of the resistance and a short-lived compromise among the powers that be, while with established performers such as Anna Magnani and Aldo Fabrizi it was not exactly a film that used lay actors. Or consider why THE BICYCLE THIEF (Vittorio de Sica, 1948), ostensibly about a man who after months of seeking work, finally lands a job, only to lose it straight away because he cannot get to work on time, when thieves steal his bicycle, did well in America not because of the man's social plight ("Why didn't he take his car to work?"), but because audiences loved the story of the man's seven-year-old son, tears in his eyes as he sees his parent humiliated, but in the final shot, slowly clasping his father's hand again, as they walk away into the sunset.[11]

ROME, OPEN CITY became a success abroad for many reasons, including its erotic, melodramatic, and atmospheric qualities. In one often reproduced shot there is a glimpse of Anna Magnani's exposed thighs as she falls, gunned down by the Germans, while in another, a glamorous German female agent seduces a young Italian women into a lesbian affair while also supplying her with cocaine. To American audiences, unused to such explicit fare, the labels "art" and "European" began to connote a very particular kind of realism, to do with explicit depiction of sex and drugs rather than political or aesthetic commitment.

Bergman's films are crucial here, as is the history of his reception and reputation as an artist. Respected in the early 1960s for his films of existential angst and bleak depictions of religious doubt, he was able to have his films financed by Svensk Filmindustri, partly because in the art houses of America such graphic portrayals of sexual jealousy or violence as in SAWDUST AND TINSEL or THE

VIRGIN SPRING (1959), or of a woman masturbating (in THE SILENCE) defined for
the generation prior to the "sexual revolution" what was meant by adult cinema. When in the mid-1960s other filmmakers
in Europe (Denmark, Germany) began to make
films for which the label "adult" was a well-understood euphemism, and when the Americans
themselves relaxed censorship, the art film export as an economic factor for European national cinemas suffered a decline (in Italy, for
instance), although it remained a cultural and
artistic force. Above all, for the subsequent generations of (more or less mainstream) American
directors, from Arthur Penn to Woody Allen
and Martin Scorsese to Francis Ford Coppola,
but also for the academy it was the fact that
without the European art and auteur cinema,
film studies might never have found a home in American universities.

THE VIRGIN SPRING

What can we call this re-assignment of meaning, then, this fluctuation of critical, cultural and economic currency, between one continent and another? A
misunderstanding of the filmmaker's intention? An acknowledgment that as
many Bergmans exist as there were audiences recognizing something of novelty, interest or spiritual value in his films? Or just an integral part of what we
mean by "art cinema" (and, finally, by any form of cinema), where the primary,
economic use-value is either not relevant (because of government subsidies, as
in the case of Bergman), or has already been harvested, leaving a film or a filmmaker's work to find its status on another scale of values altogether? Is this
what forms a "canon" and makes a film a "classic"? In which case, the old idea
of European films as expressive of their respective national identity would appear to be rather fanciful and far-fetched. It would suggest that "national cinema" quite generally, makes sense only as a relation, not as an essence, being
dependent on other kinds of filmmaking (i.e., the commercial/international
mainstream, to which it supplies the other side of the coin and thus functions
as the subordinate term). Yet a national cinema by its very definition, must not
know that it is a relative or negative term, for then it would lose its virginity and
become that national whore which is the heritage film (as in the case of British
cinema from the 1980s onward).[12] This is why the temptation persists to look
beyond relative values, towards something that defines "national cinema" positively, such as "the decent, naive, Scandinavian male ... driven nearly frantic by
the vagaries of the female."

Bergman's carefully staged self-doubt at the end of his active filmmaking life,
together with the sort of qualified, but prophetic faith in his early, poetic films

(as expressed by the review of Weightman quoted earlier) may yet have a common denominator with American audiences' frisson about the "mature" Bergman's candid look at sexual obsessions and violent marital strife. For retrospectively, by a kind of pruning away, these judgments delineate quite accurately the slim ground an auteur like Bergman occupies who also has to signify a "national cinema" (the looming presence I alluded to). He has to have recognizable high culture themes, a stylistic expressivity amounting to a personal signature, a stock company of actors that function as his actual or surrogate family, and that ambiguity or indeterminacy of reference which critics (myself included) used to prize as "psychological realism." By contrast, the French cinema has always been a national cinema with such a diversity of strands and traditions (Lumière, Méliès, surrealism, impressionism, poetic realism), that it makes its famous auteurs (Godard, Resnais, Truffaut, Rivette) almost marginal figures in the overall constellation, dominated as it is by genres, stars, and professional *metteurs-en-scène*.

From Bergman to Corman

With these considerations in mind, re-reading *Images – My Life in Films* left me a little more disenchanted than I was at first glance. One learns about Bergman's dislike of color (because it took away mystery), the importance of lighting (and of Sven Nyqvist), and that some of his early films were devised in order to experiment with complicated camera movements. But he says next to nothing about many of the other things that make Bergman a great *film* director: his use of close-ups, his work on the sound track, the composition of these incredibly complex, yet fluid action spaces within the frame, in both indoor and outside scenes (such as I described them above in PERSONA). Biographical details, childhood memories, moral introspection, the theatre, actors and actresses, music and music-making make up a loosely woven narrative that moves from topic to topic, discards chronology, and groups the films under such oddly coy but perhaps cleverly seductive titles as "Dreams Dreamers," "Jests Jesters," "Miscreant Credence," "Farces Frolics." Often, Bergman confesses of this or that film that he doesn't have much to say about its making. Contrary to the title, there is little about images. Instead, what holds the book together is a daunting effort to account for the process of story-conception, of what mood to be in when writing, what memory to follow up on, what dream to cross-fertilize with an incident he has read about, what well of anguish to tap when the plot seems to wander off in the wrong direction. Bergman is also very self-critical of the final result, often lamenting that a film (like SHAME [1968], or FACE TO FACE [1975]) could have been much better, had he worked more on the script, or recognized in time a fault in the basic construction. It reminds one of how much legitimation and cultural capital Bergman the film director still derives from writing, from being an author as well as an *auteur*, and at the same time, how removed he was from the routines of Hollywood script-writing, from story-boarding or using the script as the production's financial and technical blueprint. In this, Bergman conforms rather precisely to the cliché of the European director: improvisation on the set or on location, the most intense work is expended with the actors, while the film is taking shape as the director penetrates the inner truth of the various motifs that the story or situation first suggested to him.

The notion that Bergman's films are autobiographical has both given his films coherence and authenticated them as important. In a sense, *Images* supports some of the earnest exegeses that exist of his work: one finds the theme of the artist, caught between imagining himself a god and knowing he is a charlatan and conjurer; the motif of the lost companion/partner in an alien city, a war zone, an isolated hospital; the transfer of identity and the destructive energies of the heterosexual couple. But Bergman is also candid about his own compliance with admirers' interpretative projections. *Images* opens with the admission that *Bergman on Bergman*, a book of interviews from 1968, had been "hypocritical" because he was too anxious to please.[13] In a similar vein, he now thinks the notion, endorsed by himself in the preface to Vilgot Sjöman's *Diary with Ingmar Bergman*, that THROUGH A GLASS DARKLY (1961), WINTER LIGHT (1963) and THE SILENCE form a trilogy is a "rationalization after the fact": "the "trilogy" has neither rhyme nor reason. It was a *Schnaps-Idee*, as the Bavarians say, meaning that it's an idea found at the bottom of a glass of alcohol."[14] And yet, as mentioned above, one look at the filmographies of Godard, Antonioni, Truffaut, Wenders, Herzog and Kieslowski shows just how important a prop the idea of the "trilogy" is for the self-identity of the European auteur bereft of genres and star actors.

Brushing *Images* a little against the grain of its own declaration of authenticity ("I was going to return to my films and enter their landscapes. It was a hell of a walk"),[15] it is just conceivable that Bergman's claim to being one of the cinema's great auteurs most firmly rests on his ability to dissimulate, in the sense I suggested above: that the "big themes," the flaunting of moral doubt and metaphysical pain represents not a personal plight somehow transfigured and purified into art (the "romantic" complement of early auteurism), but the doubly necessary pre-text for a cinematic *tour de force*. As Bergman describes making ODE TO JOY (1949), while his second marriage is breaking up and he is full of self-recrimination: "In relation to my profession, I obviously was not suffering from any neuroses at all. I worked because it was fun and because I needed money."[16]

The "big themes" were doubly necessary, I am suggesting, because they helped to define his cinema as "Swedish cinema," and because they allowed him to reinvent himself as a filmmaker: prerequisites for creating a "work" that can be recognized as such at a time when Hollywood still had genres and stars, rather than directors as stars. As to Bergman, the figurehead of a national cinema, *Images* makes clear how many overt and covert threads connect his films to the key authors and themes of Scandinavian literature. Bergman's immense achievement was to have recognized and made his own dramatic situations, constellations and characters echoing those of the great Scandinavian playwrights, especially Strindberg and Ibsen, and using his life-long work in the theatre as both a permanent rehearsal of his film ideas in progress, and as the place to forge the stock-company of actors and actresses who give his films their unmistakeable look, feel and physical identity: Bibi Andersson and Gunnar Björnstrand, Ingrid Thulin and Max von Sydow, Liv Ullmann and Erland Josephson. Even so audaciously private a film like PERSONA uses Strindberg's one-act play *The Stronger* and even so ostensibly an autobiographical work as FANNY AND ALEXANDER borrows, apart from its explicit references to *Hamlet*, several motifs, names and allusions from Ibsen's *The Wild Duck*, and Strindberg's *Ghost-Sonata* and *Dreamplay.*[17]

Beyond their role of giving him a form (the chamber play) and a set of dramatic conflicts (Ibsen's bourgeois family, falling apart through the "life-lie"; Strindberg's couple, tearing each other to pieces in sexual anguish and hatred), the dramatists Bergman is attached to remind one of the importance of the spoken word, of the vernacular, the texture of speech and voice for our idea of a national cinema, and indeed for the European art cinema as a whole. It suggests that one function of the auteur cinema as a national cinema, before the advent of television, was to "transcribe" features of a nation's cultural tradition, as figured in another art form (the novel, theatre, opera), and to "represent" them in the cinema, thereby giving it a haptic presence: often enough only in the eyes of others, other countries' cinema audiences or celluloid tourists, but sometimes also recognized (or gratefully rewarded) by the nation itself.

One can follow this process in Bergman's career, where the films from the late 1950s onwards tend to be more or less self-consciously crafted images, first of the Nordic "character" from the middle-ages to the mid-19th century, and then of middle-class Sweden today. From THE SEVENTH SEAL to THE VIRGIN SPRING and SAWDUST AND TINSEL to THE FACE, from WILD STRAWBERRIES to HOUR OF THE WOLF (1968), from CRIES AND WHISPERS (1972) to FANNY AND ALEXANDER, there is an uneasy acknowledgement of the identity others have thrust upon him, as a national icon and (often ambiguous) national monument. One response is parody or pastiche: is it merely hindsight that discovers in Bergman's big themes often a wonderful excuse for putting on a show? Re-seeing THE

SEVENTH SEAL I was amazed and amused by its Grand-Guignolesque elements, not just the strolling players but even the young girl's death at the stake. Its deftly staged spectacle, its atmospheric touches, its wonderful sleights of hand and sarcastic humor prompted the perhaps blasphemous thought that Max von Sydow's knight back from the Crusades was closer in spirit to Vincent Price in a Roger Corman Edgar Allen Poe horror film than he was to Dreyer's DAY OF WRATH or Bresson's TRIAL OF JOAN OF ARC.

Hence, perhaps, a trauma that seems to have haunted Bergman briefly, even more urgently than his brief arrest by bungling Swedish bureaucrats for tax fraud: the fear of an arrest of his creativity. The tax business resulted in his six year-long self-exile to Germany, and seems to have wounded him to the quick. But so did the pun in a French review of AUTUMN SONATA (1978, starring Ingrid Bergman), suggesting that "Bergman [is not only directing Bergman, but] does Bergman."[18] *Images* in a sense is the record of having laid that ghost to rest, for it gives rise to the theme of an artist becoming a pastiche of himself, a fear he sees confirmed in the later work of Tarkovsky, of Fellini and especially Bunuel, whom he accuses of a lifetime of self-parody.[19] Tying in with the *Schnaps-Idee* of an auteur's trilogy, self-parody is perhaps the fate Bergman believes is in store for all those European auteurs who outlive both the economic and the cultural moment of the national cinema with which they came to be identified. From more recent times, the case of Werner Herzog or Wim Wenders come to mind (though the counter-examples are just as interesting: Rossellini, when he began to make his great historical films for television, or Godard, when he took on video as if to remake and "take back" his own earlier films, commenting on them by way of spraying them with ever more metaphysical "graffiti"). In Bergman's case, the farewell to the cinema was not only the signal to carry on with the theatre, but it also led him to reinvent himself as an autobiographer, novelist, scenarist, and the self-reflexive, slyly exhibitionist essayist he shows himself in *Images*, treating his big themes with an irony, a humor and a detachment not always present when he was turning them into films.

Ghosts and Dreams: Liv Ullmann with Bob Hope on THE ROAD TO MOROCCO

So how does one go about writing Bergman back into the contemporary cinema, and into a film history other than that of the European auteur/national cinema? As indicated, I would probably not start with WILD STRAWBERRIES, but with a film made eight years earlier, which strikes me, for much of its 83 minutes as timelessly "modern" as all great films are: I am thinking of THREE

STRANGE LOVES (1947). Although cast in the form of a journey, rather like WILD STRAWBERRIES – it moves with such a febrile energy, such volcanic eruptions between the characters' past and present predicament, as well as between the various characters to whom the central couple was once or is still emotionally tied, that its extraordinary urgency even jumps off the small (TV) screen, even today grabbing one by the throat.

With THREE STRANGE LOVES in mind, that old art cinema staple, the reality/illusion divide – Bergman's "big theme" not only in PERSONA but in so many of his films, from SAWDUST AND TINSEL to FANNY AND ALEXANDER takes on a new meaning. It becomes part of the heroic effort to wrest from the cinema, that medium of time and space, a logic neither enslaved to chronological time nor to physical space, but instead creating another reality altogether. In his best moments, Bergman manages to render palpable a sense of indeterminacy such as it has rarely existed in the cinema since the great silent European cinema of the 1920s (the films of Murnau, Lang, Dreyer): not psychological, nor psychoanalytical, but "phenomenal." In this sense, Bergman inscribes himself in a universal cinema tradition, as one of those directors whose craft goes into creating a new kind of indeterminacy, making possible those imperceptible transitions between past and present, inner and outer space, memory, dream and anticipation which also give the contemporary post-classical cinema its intellectual energy and emotional urgency. Bergman, in order to achieve this kind of energy, experimented in THREE STRANGE LOVES with an extraordinary fluid camera and complex camera set-ups. Realizing how much more difficult it was to achieve spatial dislocation in the sound film, he did so brilliantly with subsequent films, through the sound track in THE SILENCE, and through the lighting in PERSONA, as well as

THE ROAD TO MOROCCO

shaping through his use of color the floating time of presence and memory, anticipation and traumatic recollection of CRIES AND WHISPERS. In this respect, Bergman's filmmaking is as modern as Godard thought it was. THREE STRANGE LOVES to this day gives one the feeling that this is the cinema that every generation has to reinvent for itself, that the cinema always starts again with this kind of vulnerability and radical openness. If it means being branded an art-cinema, so be it, at least until it becomes prisoner of the double body it seems fated to create for itself – that of an auteur's cinema, pastiching its own cultural self-importance.

One of the most poignant passages in *Images* occurs when Bergman discusses Liv Ullmann's primal scream at the climax of FACE TO FACE: "Dino De Laurentiis was delighted with the film, which received rave reviews in America. Now when I see FACE TO FACE I remember an old farce with Bob Hope, Bing Crosby, and Dorothy Lamour. It's called THE ROAD TO MOROCCO. They have been shipwrecked and come floating on a raft in front of a projected New York in the background. In the final scene, Bob Hope throws himself to the ground and begins to scream and foam at the mouth. The others stare at him in astonishment and ask what in the world he is doing. He immediately calms down and says: 'This is how you have to do it if you want to win an Oscar.' When I see FACE TO FACE and Liv Ullmann's incredibly loyal effort on my behalf, I still can't help but think of THE ROAD TO MOROCCO."[20]

(1994)

Notes

1. Ingmar Bergman, *Images – My Life in Film* (London: Bloomsbury Publishing, 1994), p. 226.
2. "If it is dangerous to regard the Swedish cinema as synonymous with Bergman, it is equally dangerous to dismiss or underestimate his contribution. His work has a universal and continuing importance far beyond that of any other Swedish director." Eva Geijerstam, "All var där utom Bergman" in *Dagens Nyheter*, 12 May 1997, quoted in Rik Vermeulen, *Sweden and its National Cinema* (M.A. thesis University of Amsterdam, 1997).
3. Bo Widerberg, who expended much energy on polemics against Bergman's vision of Sweden, neither inherited nor survived him – he died in May 1997. On the feud between Widerberg and Bergman, see Peter Cowie, *Scandinavian Cinema* (London, Tantivy Press, 1992), p. 147.
4. According to Rik Vermeulen, *loc. cit.*, Bergman was to direct a play, written by P.O. Enquist, called *The Makers of Images: Memories from the World of the Silent Film*), set in the 1920s and dramatizing an encounter between the writer Selma Lagerlöf and the actor/director Victor Sjöström.
5. Jean-Luc Godard, "Bergmanorama" *Cahiers du cinéma*, no. 85, July 1958 [reprinted in T. Milne (ed.), *Godard on Godard* (New York: Da Capo Press, 1967), p. 77-78].
6. *Images*, p. 295.
7. Ingmar Bergman, *The Magic Lantern* (Harmondsworth: Penguin Books, 1988), p. 169.
8. *The Listener*, July 9, 1959, p. 12.
9. As David Thomson once dryly noted: "Bergman's films are about actors and artists playing actors and artists." David Thomson, *A Biographical Dictionary of Film* (New York: Alfred A. Knopf, 1994), p. 60.
10. "Many people of my generation... joined the National Film Theatre in London to see a retrospective... of Bergman's early films after THE SEVENTH SEAL and WILD STRAW-

BERRIES had come to represent 'artistic' cinema." David Thomson, *A Biographical Dictionary of Film* (New York: Alfred Knopf, 1996) p. 60.

11. In Italy, for instance, directors like Fellini (also fated to be popularly remembered for his sexually most explicit film, LA DOLCE VITA) or Antonioni could make their films because directors like Sergio Leone and Sergio Corbucci were turning out profitable Spaghetti Westerns with Clint Eastwood and Klaus Kinski which were seen by millions in Italy, Spain, France, Germany, the US, Asia, and Latin America. When, in the early 1970s, kung fu movies with Bruce Lee, and made in Hong Kong ousted Spaghetti Westerns as the world's favorite action and adventure movies, the Italian art cinema of director-auteurs vanished at the same time, deprived of its (hidden) economic base.

12. Andrew Higson, "Nostalgia and Pastiche in the Heritage Film" in Lester Friedmann (ed.) *British Cinema under Thatcher* (Minneapolis: Minnesota University Press, 1992), pp. 109-129.

13. *Images*, p. 11.

14. *Images*, p. 245.

15. *Images*, p. 15.

16. *Images*, p. 277.

17. See Egil Törnqvist, *Between Stage and Screen: Ingmar Bergman Directs* (Amsterdam: Amsterdam University Press, 1995), pp. 137-145 and pp. 174-187.

18. *Images*, p. 334.

19. Ibid.

20. *Images*, pp. 80-82.

Late Losey

Time Lost and Time Found

> *Tel qu'en lui-même, l'éternité le change*
> Mallarme

A year after his death, a new Losey film opens in the cinemas. STEAMING raises special expectations: Is it a sort of testament? Or did Losey, as a director, with more than 30 feature films to his credit, die – so to speak – intestate? STEAMING, Losey's only film after returning from French exile, is in some ways a work in the "minor" genre of the filmed play. One thinks of the American Film Theatre productions (for which Losey did GALILEO), and Altman's SECRET HONOR, or COME BACK TO THE FIVE & DIME. It would have been more satisfying, if for the sake of symmetry at the very least, if Losey had directed Pinter's BETRAYAL, instead of the all-female cast of Nell Dunn's successful stage debut.

Joseph Losey: Time Lost and Found

JOSEPH LOSEY

Nonetheless, STEAMING could be seen as a parable of English society in the Pinter mode. The Turkish baths are after all, a sort of microcosm, a refuge and place of comfort, but also of decay. "This Empire-rich society provided edifices of marble with beautiful fixtures." That it should be demolished, to make way for a car park, is a fitting, though perhaps slightly too obvious an allegorical hint. On the other hand, the situation is also typical of many Losey films: the home, the refuge that turns into a beleaguered fortress. It recurs regularly, from THE PROWLER to THE SERVANT, from BOOM and SECRET CEREMONY to THE ASSASSINATION OF TROTZKY and A DOLL'S HOUSE.

Usually it is a guest, regardless of whether invited or not, whose presence disrupts a precarious equilibrium, bringing into the open or engineering the tensions that lead, after a brief flash of self-awareness, to inevitable mental or physical self-destruction. The intruder who disturbs the peace this time is not a policeman (THE PROWLER), an insolent stable boy (THE SLEEPING TIGER), an

au pair student (ACCIDENT), a self-styled angel of death (BOOM), a German gigo-
lo (THE ROMANTIC ENGLISHWOMAN), a Jewish Resistance member (M. KLEIN) or
a ruthless nymphet (THE TROUT), but a less symbolic or mysterious provocation
– property speculators hiding behind a London borough council. The mundane
occasion, the modest ambitions could themselves be an ironic comment on the
Losey legend, or on the bathos beneath the rhetoric in contemporary Britain on
the Falklands and Whitehall, on Greenham Common, Greenpeace, and the
GLC.

What is different in STEAMING is that the protagonists are women and that
division leads to solidarity. But as in the other films, the threat from outside
provokes via a series of cathartic and violent encounters a moment of self-recog-
nition. Though unlike the mostly solitary or male counterparts, the women do
not expend their passion and intelligence on self-destruction as in THE SERVANT,
FIGURES IN A LANDSCAPE, LES ROUTES DU SUD, or THE TROUT: An access of defi-
ant self confidence makes them triumph and claim victory. In the gloomy
brown fittings and the gleaming white tiled baths, overarched by a glass dome,
the women symbolize what is alive and vibrant.

But STEAMING will disappoint those expecting a definitive statement from
Losey rounding off and closing a work that spanned four decades and three
national film industries: Hollywood, Britain and France. For connoisseurs of
Losey's darker side, the optimism will seem superficial, the issue too slight to
bear the allegorical weight, the commitment to the cause (of women? of public
services in the Welfare State? of endangered civic architecture?) too external and
distanced.

It will even displease those with no particular interest in Losey as such and
who expect to see in the film what the play set out to do: "show women fighting
for their own identity and, in the process of coming together, finding the
strength to alter their lives." For Losey seems more interested in the reticent
performance of Vanessa Redgrave and her statuesque beauty than in the dramatic interplay between the women. This may, however, be a limitation inherent in the play. It develops each woman in turn by a virtuoso scene of self-expo-
sure, confession, or near-hysterical outburst rather than by actual confrontation
and mutual revelation.

One weakness of the play, the somewhat stereotypical and over-anxious division of the women according to class, age, background and race is turned by
Losey to advantage: some figures stay very much in the background, and the
interest shifts between the three central characters, who become more or less
aspects of one person, a decision which Nell Dunn might have endorsed: "There
is some of me in all the women in the play." In the film this composite portrait is
focussed on Vanessa Redgrave by the sheer force of her screen persona.

As a consequence, Losey, no doubt deliberately, accentuates the spectator's ambivalent position between claustrophobia and voyeurism. One is aware of being an uninvited guest not by any suggestion of erotic lubriciousness, nor because the women confide in each other things they might not say when dressed. It is more a matter of feeling oneself put in the metaphoric position of the intruder, who of course throughout the film remains not only faceless (as was the helicopter crew in FIGURES IN A LANDSCAPE) but absent. Unlike a film such as George Cukor's THE WOMEN, where one might argue that in a very ambiguous fashion, it is the men who structure the absence around which the action turns, STEAMING presents a more complex case. Through Vanessa Redgrave's melancholy, the optimistic trajectory of the film is considerably darkened, for no longer does it seem as if the women join their respective talents. Rather, the confrontations over class, over career versus children, education versus street-wise experience, over sex or self-respect are endlessly circular oppositions, which do not lead to "identity," either individual or collective, but to the insight that whatever one's position, the logic of the mutually exclusive will always manifest itself. In the mirror of the Other which the women hold up to one another, only the same divided self can appear.

The spectator is thus not simply responding differently according to gender, however much the film might provoke reflection about individual identity. Losey, more strongly than in many of his films, links the issue of spectatorship with that of aggression, but also, more subtly, associates self-realization with exhibitionism. The question is furthermore whether one is prepared to accept as a properly aesthetic emotion, the tact and delicacy communicated by the camera as a celebrated director films celebrated actresses in a state of nakedness that is both intimate and anti-erotic, and therefore marked by intimations of mortality even as the fable moves towards a liberating orgiastic finale. Losey's last image is of white balloons rising like effervescent champagne from the hot bath. But the spectator knows that their ascent is checked by the glass roof, protecting the women but also enclosing them like a sealed bubble.

Such thoughts about STEAMING might be the starting point for a revision of one's first impressions and could lead to view the film more abstractly but also more personally. A testament after all? It might also be the starting point for reviewing the fate of late Losey, the British cinema's most prodigal son whose career seems to have ended in the wilderness.

As so often with Losey, upon reflection or with the passage of time, his films gain in complexity what they initially appeared to lack in subtlety or spontaneity. During the final decade, each Losey film confounded the expectations raised by his name, and his work was met with polite interest often disguising frank disappointment. The public too either stayed away or was not given a chance to find out. THE ROMANTIC ENGLISHWOMAN, M KLEIN, LES ROUTES DU SUD, THE

TROUT are all either unknown in Britain or barely remembered. Even DON GIOVANNI, Losey's only international success in his last years, had very mixed notices both in France and Britain precisely because it seemed to be made for a public of opera lovers who do not usually like the cinema. It became a cultural occasion; reviewers noted the sumptuous spectacle and the star cast but on the whole did not ask themselves what place the film had in Losey's work or what it meant for the cinema.

The disappointment was mutual. It emanated from Losey the man as much as it was the prevailing reaction to his later films. Disappointment on Losey's part above all about the careless handling of his films by producers and distributors. This was in itself nothing new in his career. In 1959, BLIND DATE was bought by Paramount, but because of a McCarthyite article in the US press, was only re-leased much later as the bottom half of a double bill. The complaint of interfer-ence and gross negligence, voiced by Losey at the NFT in 1964 about the Hakim Brothers' treatment of EVE, seems not to have been mitigated by subsequent experience. MGM was so little convinced of THE GO-BETWEEN that they tried to stop it being entered officially at Cannes in 1970. In the event it won the Golden Palm. The reason Losey was ready to leave France to return to England, he told his audience at the London Film Festival in 1982, was that distribution and ac-cess to international audiences had to be better in London than they were in Paris. THE TROUT, the film he presented, was never released in Britain.

Within the film industries in America or Europe, Losey never achieved the position of a producer-director. None of his films made the kind of money that allowed Hitchcock, Billy Wilder, or Stanley Kubrick to enter the market as an equal partner with a distribution company. Hence the anger, frustration, and occasional self-pity of a man who had to spend much of his time in the ante-rooms of people he despised.

Losey's other source of disappointment was that although he belonged to the very few great directors of world cinema, the world was reluctant to give him the recognition he deserved. Comparable to the best American directors of his generation he nonetheless remained at the margin of both the commercial film industry and the art cinema. In Europe he knew himself to be the equal of the symbolic fathers of the different national cinemas: Bunuel, Bergman, Visconti, Resnais, Wajda, but his reputation was never as assured as theirs, nor did his prestige seem to matter enough to his chosen home, Britain, to warrant either the financial or institutional support he would have needed as the figure at the artistic center of a national cinema. Worse still, to a critical establishment jud-ging serious films by their literary merit, he was not an original artist, but de-pendent on the quality of his scripts and in particular, on the genius of Pinter. Paradoxically, Losey thus worked during the last phase of his career under the double shadow of his own past reputation and the present one of his collaborators.

No wonder Losey is so often cited as a negative example of how a Hollywood career interrupted by political machinations came to be at the mercy of international co-productions and the vagaries of film distribution; how a director's unrealized projects might turn out to be more significant for his filmography than some of the ones he did make; how difficult it is to work in a tradition of British cinema that is not simply parasitic on certain literary models or cultural cliches, but critical; and finally, how impossible it is to be an auteur in Britain. Hence the sad irony of seeing lesser men make the films he had worked years to prepare: his Conrad project failed, UNDER THE VOLCANO made by Tony Richardson, a German porn film producer doing Thomas Mann's THE MAGIC MOUNTAIN and bitterest disappointment of all, Volker Schloendorff directing A LA RECHERCHE DU TEMPS PERDU. Pinter at least was able to publish his screenplay when their Proust project fell through, but Losey's work was wasted. Hardly a film was made at the time it was first conceived: THE GO-BETWEEN took seven years, THE TROUT originally planned with Brigitte Bardot and Dirk Bogarde took eighteen years, and GALILEO from 1947 to 1974.

As an enemy of promise Losey is only comparable to Orson Welles, with whom he shared the sheer endless string of aborted projects, but towards the end also the physical bulk and a face in which a feminine sensibility was permanently at war with an all too male sensuality. Showing the ravages of many passions, the intolerable periods of dissipation between the waiting and the discipline of concentrated work, Losey however, tended to see himself as victim: a difficult position for a man as physically imposing, who knew himself to be a master in his chosen craft. The French critic Alain Masson, reviewing Michel Ciment's *Joseph Losey*, comments on Losey's politics: "Lucid about his illusions, Losey entertains a fair number of illusions about his lucidity."[1] It might apply to other areas of his life as well, for unlike Welles who acted the buffoon and the ham even with his own tragic career, Losey never quite seemed to see his tragedy without showing some rancor or bitterness.

Given the many abandoned and frustrated plans, it is easy to see Losey's work as uneven, or to single out preferred films or a preferred period, such as the Pinter collaborations and explain away other projects by the accidents of circumstance. Losey himself sometimes seemed to endorse this view. THE ROMANTIC ENGLISHWOMAN he claimed not to care about. Perhaps following the example of John Ford, he may have been too proud to confess to liking a film, which the public had rejected. But eliminating certain films from the canon does not resolve the uncertainty about the nature of Losey's achievement as an auteur or director. In this respect his standing promises to be similar to that of Fritz Lang, whose reputation seems to hover over his work while never quite becoming identified with more than two or three films. This would be the supreme irony: Losey was the man whom Seymour Nebenzahl had hired to remake M, a sacrilege for which Lang never forgave the producer and was not prepared to acknowledge the director as belonging to the profession.

Losey's M, a remarkable film in its own right, might almost stand as an emblem for something about his career that merits more attention, which is the curious sense of *déja vu* about many of his later films, or rather the impression of Losey having chosen subjects and genres, styles and themes, to which other directors either before or after him had managed to give a more definite shape, or who had simply had more luck in making them popular and successful. Why is it, one may ask, that when one sees Losey's later films they so often evoke the after-image of their non-identical twins?

STEAMING brings to mind both THE WOMEN by Cukor and COME BACK TO THE FIVE & DIME by Altman if only because these are also based on plays about a closed world of women, but one also remembers DEEP END by Skolimowski, irrelevantly perhaps but surely not accidentally, because of Diana Dors as the baths attendant. The guest as intruder and catalyst is a theme shared with Pasolini's TEOREMA. DON GIOVANNI appeared virtually at the same time as Bergman's version of THE MAGIC FLUTE. Now it stands in the shadow of Forman's popular hit AMADEUS. LES ROUTES DU SUD, with a script by Jorge Semprun and starring Yves Montant as a left-wing writer haunted by his revolutionary past during the Spanish Civil War, recalled only too obviously for some critics Resnais' LA GUERRE EST FINI, while the figure of the son seemed to come straight out of Chabrol's NADA. M KLEIN, made well after the crest of the wave of Nazi nostalgia and French retro-fashion, was compared to Visconti's THE DAMNED, Bergman's THE SERPENT'S EGG, films about the French Occupation by Malle and Melville and was eclipsed in the public's mind by Truffaut's LE DERNIER METRO. The opening scene of THE ROMANTIC ENGLISHWOMAN reminded one critic of the train in Bergman's THE SILENCE, the park scenes in Baden-Baden recalled LAST YEAR IN MARIENBAD, and the drug trafficking was reminiscent of Bunuel's THE DISCREET CHARM OF THE BOURGEOISIE. Stoppard's script was seen as an attempt to parody Pinter, possibly at the expense of Losey. A DOLL'S HOUSE was released the same year as Fassbinder's version of the same Ibsen play (NORA HELMER), the invisible helicopter crew in FIGURES IN A LANDSCAPE had been anticipated in Spielberg's cult movie DUEL, THE GO-BETWEEN invited comparison with Renoir's LA REGLE DU JEU, SECRET CEREMONY recalled Polanski's REPULSION, BOOM – with the Burtons in the lead – was compared to WHO'S AFRAID OF VIRGINIA WOOLF. And MODESTY BLAISE, while wittier and more elegant was outshone and outdone by the James Bond films that soon followed.

It was similar with Losey's actors and actresses. From the decision to cast Michael Redgrave as the alcoholic father in TIME WITHOUT PITY to letting Dirk

Bogarde play a young lout in THE SLEEPING TIGER, Losey's conception of character implied a systematic play with the stereo-typical and atypical in an actor's screen persona. Jeanne Moreau in EVE is conceived as anti-Malle and anti-Antonioni, as well as anti-Truffaut. To have set her against Stanley Baker created a powerful interplay, not only between two acting styles, but further extended Baker's traditional range, after BLIND DATE and THE CRIMINAL, as if already to prepare his part in ACCIDENT. Delphine Seyrig, in ACCIDENT, brings with her Resnais, but then Bogarde in Visconti, Resnais and Fassbinder brings with him the universe of Losey. THE TROUT, pursued by its own phantom of two decades earlier, was also an exploration of the possibilities inherent in Isabelle Huppert's persona. In contrast to Donald Sutherland's lean CASANOVA, Ruggero Raimondi's DON GIOVANNI becomes a portrait of the seducer not as the artificer of desire, as in Fellini, but of its mask and mirror, hiding an all too heavy body. Glenda Jackson in THE ROMANTIC ENGLISH-WOMAN is anti-Schlesinger, while Helmut Berger in the same film is a Visconti reference, as well as a memory of Alain Delon from Rene Clement's PLEIN SOLEIL, whereas in M KLEIN Delon recalls the films with Melville. Delon and Romy Schneider in THE ASSASSINATION OF TROTSKY bring their off-screen personal life into the film, as do the Burtons theirs in BOOM. If Yves Montand is borrowed from Resnais, as it were, he is also used against the spirit of Costa-Gavras, and against Godard's own anti-Gavras Montand in TOUT VA BIEN. Jane Fonda and Delphine Seyrig in A DOLL'S HOUSE implicitly refer to their political lives outside the film, while Vanessa Redgrave's portrayal of the upper-class abandoned

A DOLL'S HOUSE

wife in STEAMING relies for its effect on the clash of associations between her roles in films such as JULIA, and the high moral stance she takes in her politics.

This catalogue of cross references is neither exhaustive nor rigorous. It would be frivolous and irrelevant if it was offered as evidence of Losey's lack of originality. On the contrary, such placing and positioning of surface echoes all along the work, and in late Losey from his own work to that of others, seems more an aspect of his political as well as cinematic intelligence, than a sign of decline. The doubling effects are relevant in an altogether different perspective: they do not affect the integrity of his work, and only trouble a certain conception of the auteur for which coherence is a matter of hermetic closure, self-reference, or the accumulation of the signs of a private ideolect.

At the height of Losey's fame, after THE SERVANT, FOR KING AND COUNTRY, ACCIDENT and MODESTY BLAISE the notion of him as an auteur in this sense gained ground. While Losey was alternating projects which had an art cinema appeal with projects for a wider mass audience, and in the spirit of rebuilding a national cinema, he explored different genres and experimented with different styles, his coherence seemed assured by the continuity of his themes. The auteur could express himself in his work, or be dispersed across it, as long as he was always readable, he remained identical with himself, recoverable in the mirror of metaphor and critical hyperbole.

In Britain, the price for being considered a serious artist was that Losey's films were seen as moralizing fables. Critics during the 1960s looked for the

SECRET CEREMONY

allegorical meaning of his work, and searched for profundity and depth, often disappointed when he seemed to be engaged in a mere exercise of style, as in MODESTY BLAISE or when he became flamboyantly baroque, as in SECRET CEREMONY. After THE GO-BETWEEN, they increasingly commented only on the repetition of his stock moral dilemmas, treated in stories and styles of an evermore unpredictable eclecticism. It seemed to indicate a lack of control, an inability to impose on his material or on his working conditions the stamp of his personality and the force of his will.

Embarrassed by the signs of very conventional good taste and the impeccable accessories of a well-to-do lifestyle taking up more and more room in his films, many former admirers suspected unconscious self-parody. They missed the nervous Bohemian intellectuality of Losey's first British films, or considered the true Losey to be the director of social satire, of the sharply observed rituals of self-immolation among the British upper classes, as in the films with Pinter. What was not always appreciated was that Losey as an auteur had probably been more complex than the allegories he was constructing, and that the relation of his moral preoccupations to his films was not at all straightforward. It was the very notion of necessary self-identity that fostered the impression of a decline, as the echoes from his own work became progressively fainter and were replaced by different inter-texts and stronger interferences, the more so since some of these parallels were coincidences, the arbitrary gags of chance, so to speak.

Yet Losey, perhaps precisely because of his having had to come to terms with being an exile from the film industry and the art cinema, in Britain as well as France, may have drawn a particular lucidity from his disappointments. He was aware that a national cinema had to be an international business, in which the values traded and properties exchanged were national stereotypes, the names or events of recent history, the cinema's own history. The composition of audiences had changed so radically in the 1970s, television had become such an important client that the constant inter-text of any European or national film industry had to be television's own version of art, culture and reality. Having failed to become a national institution himself, Losey for a long time toyed with the idea of getting "half a dozen or ten of the world's most important directors" together and found a production company, which could present the majors with a united front. The project, of course, came to nothing. In an interview from late 1976, Losey said: "I'll soon have to go to England and talk about it once more, even though it's too late. There is no longer a British film industry, and they don't know how to go about it. My idea was a chance to get back into business, but the chance was wasted. There still is an opportunity, if they really wanted to. Give directors the sort of possibilities they would have had if they had united, with financial loans from the government."

In a sense, Losey has remained true to this conception, even if it meant that he had to do it by himself. His films from the last decade with their constant references to other "texts" – whether these are actors, directors, personalities and works from the stage, from literature or opera – are a sort of preview of what a European art cinema would be in the 1980s, when it is no longer an auteur's image and self-identity that provides a public with the pleasure of recognition, but the images of a common cultural identity. Losey may have been ahead of his time in this, or rather, his single-mindedness of purpose was misconstrued as merely a combination of time wasted and missed appointments with the Zeitgeist.

This does not mean that Losey has not also remained true to his themes as an auteur. There are two complementary moments in late Losey. That of the individual protagonist, abruptly and in the midst of life, as it were, confronting the Double he has always tried to avoid. What had mistakenly appeared as a point of self-realization and fulfillment, turns into the awareness that his inner life, his past, and his achievements have crumbled away and vanished. It is, if one likes, Losey's Conradian theme (the figure of Decoud in *Nostromo*, Kurtz in *Heart of Darkness*, *Lord Jim*), part of his Midwest Edwardian heritage, an echo of T.S. Eliot's "Hollow Men"). Losey's GALILEO, his M KLEIN, Yves Montand in LES ROUTES DU SUD, Don Giovanni, almost all the male characters in THE TROUT, Michael Caine and Glenda Jackson in THE ROMANTIC ENGLISHWOMAN and, finally, even Vanessa Redgrave in STEAMING: they are all prototypes embodying the same quintessentially bourgeois configuration. Often the Double is symbolized by an encounter between the generations, between fathers and sons, as is only to be expected in a society as obsessed with Oedipal relations as ours.

The other moment, equally important in the later films, is that there is no longer any confrontation with this Double other than as an endlessly reflecting mirror which brings the void of pure surface, and is thus endlessly fascinating and seductive. To make it stay, and at the same time to master this phantom self, the characters are themselves constructing fictions, duplicating the situations they find themselves in by an additional mise-en-scène. This is most obviously the case in THE ROMANTIC ENGLISHWOMAN and DON GIOVANNI, but just as true of the characters in THE TROUT or LES ROUTES DU SUD – and indeed, in STEAMING: for all we know, the whole film may be the mise-en-scène of such an absent and deferred confrontation. However, while this doubling of the fiction from within may itself seem a very traditional feature of cinematic modernism, it is, as I have tried to indicate, itself mirrored by the accidental or deliberate doubling effects on an external level: that of the national-international film industry.

Even more personally, one can now see Losey's work and his professional preoccupations under a double aspect, as well: as the "tragic" defeat of an artist in quest of unity and coherence, and on the contrary, as the no less serious attempt to stay on the surface, constructing contexts and subtexts so intricate and dense that the *auteur* could disappear, or at any rate hide, in order for the work to be everywhere in its echoes but nowhere in its essence.

Losey wanted to make the Proust film very badly, and one can understand why. It was not only because he had been working on it in virtually every film at least since THE GO-BETWEEN, but also because in it, the displacements in time and space, of exile, bad timing and duplication, so irritating in his career and so disappointing to the man, might actually have found their thematic realization and perfect formal equivalent.

In Proust's writing, Disappointment is the key emotion that sets off memory, and all but inspires the sensations most fertile for self-analysis. It may have played an even more central role in Losey's life and work than I have suggested. Pinter reports that what guided him and Losey in adapting Proust for the screen was "that the architecture of the film should be based on two main and contrasting principles. One, a movement, chiefly narrative, towards disillusion, and the other, more intermittent, towards revelation, rising to where time that was lost is found, and fixed forever in art." One will recall that in *Le Temps retrouvé*, the final volume of Proust's epic, Marcel, the hero, says that he is now able to start the work. But, of course, "he" has already written it. Could it be that Losey, after all, did not have to make the film of *A la Recherche du temps perdu*, because "Losey" had already made it?

(1985)

Note

1. Alain Masson, review of Michel Ciment, *Le Livre de Losey,* Paris: Ramsay, 1986 (French translation of *Conversations with Losey,* London: Routledge, Kegan and Paul, 1985), *Positif* August 1986.

Around Painting and the "End of Cinema"

A Propos Jacques Rivette's LA BELLE NOISEUSE

There are films about painters, films that feature paintings in the plot, and there are films about particular paintings. In the first category, the centenary has given us several van Gogh movies (directed by Paul Cox, Robert Altman, Maurice Pialat), and in Derek Jarman's CARAVAGGIO we had the anti-myth to the myth of the creative genius tormented by his Art. In all of them, what remains, one way or another, is the "agony and the ecstasy," whether embodied by Kirk Douglas, Tim Roth, or Nigel Terry.

Paintings, and especially painted portraits abound in what has been called the women's paranoia cycle of Hollywood melodramas from the 1940s, but they also star prominently in some celebrated "films noirs" of the 1950s: one thinks of REBECCA and SUSPICION, LAURA and WOMAN IN THE WINDOW, THE TWO MRS CARROLLS and STRANGERS ON A TRAIN. Hitchcock, as one can see, is particularly fond of them, but so are Germanic directors like Lang and Preminger. Such portraits activate a host of associations, partly historical (they often connote a period setting and a genre: the Gothic), partly social (in a world of objects and people, a painting is always extravagant, excessive in that it is both object and person), partly economic (whoever owns a painting has surplus value to display, which means it also often functions as a signifier of class), and finally, the connotations are inescapably sexual (Beauty and Fatality, Perfection, Woman, the Unattainable Object of Desire). Sometimes they are the very epitome of patriarchy, as Joan Fontaine's father disapprovingly looks down on her choice of Cary Grant as husband in SUSPICION.

JACQUES RIVETTE

Films featuring series of paintings are mostly "European," and they seem to belong to the 1980s: Godard's PASSION, Raul Ruiz' HYPOTHÈSE DU TABLEAU VOLÉ, and – stretching the term painting a little – Peter Greenaway's THE DRAUGHTSMAN'S CONTRACT. In each case, what is explored are tableaux vivants, though to different ends. Greenaway sees social hierarchies mirrored in the pictorial geometries, both of which fail to contain the more elemental or anarchic forces set free by (female) sexuality (of which the moving image becomes an ally); in Ruiz, the *tableaux vivants* tell of all the narrative possiblities – all the possible movies, in other words – locked up in static images, and of interpretation games far more devious but also more interesting than the analytic master-narratives of Marx or Freud. For Ruiz, the relation between cinema and painting raises the question of pictorial realism generally, meaningful only if read as allegory – a point to which I will return. In Jean-Luc Godard's PASSION finally, the stillness of the tableaux is not only juxtaposed to the machine noise on the factory floor and the noise cluttering up personal relationships; the scenes taken from Velasquez, Rembrandt, Ingres, Goya – even while depicting violence and destruction – suggest the possibilities of existential confrontation not afforded any of the protagonists. Painting, it seems, provides a vanishing point from which to view a world in the process of disintegration, but at the price – as in Kafka – of excluding its protagonists from both.

It is not immediately clear what category Jacques Rivette's LA BELLE NOISEUSE belongs to. Attention seems equally divided between the artist, the portrait that gives the film its title, and the painting as material artifact and commodity. Emphasized as in no other film is the process of creation itself, the artist's labor-intensive hard grind (or "scratch," since it is pen-and-ink-on-paper we mostly hear), and the bone-crushing, limb-twisting postures the model is subjected to. Rivette's story is simple enough: A famous painter, Eduard Frenhofer (Michel Piccoli), suffering from a prolonged fallow period, is persuaded by his dealer, Porbus (Gilles Arbona), to take up again a canvas which he, Frenhofer, had abandoned ten years earlier – the "Belle Noiseuse" of the title – with the help of a new model, Marianne (Emmanuelle Béart), the girlfriend of Nicolas (David Bursztein), an aspiring young painter. The couple happen to be visiting the area where Frenhofer has made his home, not least because Nicolas wants to know what the great master has been up to in his country refuge. Outraged at first, Marianne consents to be Frenhofer's sitter, and over a space of five days, the painting is completed. Hovering in the wings is Frenhofer's wife, Liz (Jane Birkin), his erstwhile favorite model and the original "Belle Noiseuse," who is both eager for Frenhofer to get over his creative block and afraid of being replaced. But she knows that *"Frenhofer est un gentleman,"* and indeed, he has no sexual interest in Marianne, except that the casual, sometimes brutal and in the end quite sadistic regime he inflicts on his model during the sittings do seem to unnerve the young woman, her poise and cool temporarily breaking under the strain. Both couples go through an emotional crisis, deeper and possibly more serious for the older couple, since it seems to convince Liz that not even the completion of the painting will release either of them from their living death. Porbus, however, wants to celebrate "La Belle Noiseuse," and a picnic in the grounds of Frenhofer's estate serves as a kind of coda, with the young couple also departing, though not before Nicolas tells Frenhofer that he is not too impressed by the new work. What he does not know is that the painting on display is not at all "La Belle Noiseuse," but one which Frenhofer had done in one all-night session, not even bothering with the girl as model. In voice-over Marianne tells the audience that what happened after they got back to Paris is another story.

Arguably, Rivette means us to take his drama as just that: Frenhofer's struggle to conquer his anxiety, to wrestle with his muse and angel, in order to bequeath to posterity some essence of his vision, the work that says it all. "Faster, faster, mach one, mach two" he explains to Marianne, as if death was already too close for any mere terrestrial motion towards a goal. Cloistered away in his somber studio, while outside Nature is vibrating to a Mediterranean mid-summer heat, the tragic irony would then be that in spite of subjecting himself and those around him to the most intense pain and sacrifice, there can only be a masterpiece that nobody sees, and one that brings neither redemption nor transcendence. Frenhofer is then the modernist after modernism, the antithesis of Cezanne (who would not have tried painting the view from Frenhofer's tower and balcony), but also the opposite of Picasso, for whom the painter and his model/lover/wife became the emblem of how to renew his art by dramatizing through this relationship every conceivable vital and venal, violent and voyeuristic impulse. Just such a sketch evoking Picasso can be found among Frenhofer's discarded canvasses stacked on the studio wall, perhaps because, as Rivette mentions in an interview, his friend Claire Denis bombarded him with Picasso postcards depicting this motif while Rivette was hesitating whether to undertake the project at all. In the end, Frenhofer is more like Beckett's comment on Bram van Velde in *Four Dialogues with Georges Dutuit*: "nothing to paint, nothing to paint with, and yet nothing left to do but paint."

The success of LA BELLE NOISEUSE – winner of the Grand Prix at Cannes in 1991 – and the fact that it is by far Rivette's most accessible film since LA RELIGIEUSE, makes it plausible that audiences see a qualified but nonetheless comforting reaffirmation of the values not only of art with a capital "A", but also of the European art cinema. Indeed, perhaps Rivette (until now mostly an enigmatic outsider even in his own country) wanted to try his hand at the genre better known through Eric Rohmer. LA BELLE NOISEUSE could well be one of those "*contes moraux*" which have become Rohmer's trademark and quality guarantee. Rivette's tight plotting, the film's many formal symmetries and neat ironies, the division into clearly felt scenes and acts, the respect for the unities of French classical drama all recall Rohmer, both theme and setting making one think of LA COLLECTIONEUSE or Rohmer's homage to Matisse, PAULINE À LA PLAGE. The opening of LA BELLE NOISEUSE, with the young couple pretending to be strangers who succumb to lust at first sight, in order to shock two dowdy tourists from England is pure Rohmer, if it wasn't also vintage Rivette (comparable to the opening of *L'Amour par terre* where a solemn group of men and women is led through back streets and courtyards up several flights of stairs into a Paris apartment to become eavesdropping witnesses to the infidelities and domestic complications of an executive with a wife and a mistress, before the spectator realizes that these are down-at-the-heel actors who have invented not street theatre but apartment theatre).

To be familiar with other Rivette films certainly helps to make sense not only of this opening; quite naturally the temptation is to regard LA BELLE NOISEUSE in the light of the director's other films. If there are still any auteurists out there, here is a chance to practice the old skills of recognizing personal themes and formal obsessions, of spotting allusions and putting together the cross-references and inter-texts: in other words, precisely, to salute the artist and his inimitable signature. What in the earlier films had been the structuring principle, namely to use the theatre, a performance to be rehearsed, a show to be put on, in the course of which the characters find out some – inevitably painful – truth about themselves is here the function of painting, in each case setting off art versus life, the classical versus the vagaries of personal relations, formal order vs. the anarchies of *l'amour fou*, the destructiveness of self-obsession. Rivette himself has called this principle *"la vie parallèle,"* and virtually all his films take one text and overwrite or underlay it with another.

LA BELLE NOISEUSE is unquestionably an auteur's film, but the very fact that it advertises this status so insistently suggests that we may have to regard it as something that no longer can be "taken as read." Perhaps the very principle of *"la vie parallèle"* has assumed another meaning, and makes its own contribution to a particular polemic: A film about an artist (what more overdetermined a choice of actor for this part than Michel Piccoli?), a female star (Emmanuelle Béart, fresh from her success as "Manon des sources"), and the difficulties of fixing a representation. It also counts as a move in what seems to be a *"Kulturkampf"* raging in France over the meaning and definition of French cinema. In this cultural battle, "painting and cinema" has become a kind of code, though it is, at least for an outsider, far from clear exactly where the lines are drawn. This is certainly no longer the line between the *"tradition de qualité"* and the *"Nouvelle Vague."* From Truffaut to Rohmer, from Tavernier to Pialat, including even Carax and Besson, directors seem to have made their peace with a fairly capacious version of the "great tradition" of the French cinema, preferring to rework its stock situations and stable constellations, rather than inaugurating radical breaks.

What, then, is the evidence for assuming that a film about painting made in 1991 may have a special topicality? Since the mid-1980s there has been a steadily increasing number of (excellent) books about cinema and painting by leading French film critics and academics: Rivette's scripterwriter, Pascal Bonitzer's *Décadrages: peinture et cinéma* (1985), two scholarly conferences devoted to the topic at Quimper and Chantilly in 1987, Jacques Aumont's *L'oeil interminable* (1989), Marc Vernet's *Figures de l'absence* (1990), Raymond Bellour's collection of papers from one of the conferences, *Cinéma et Peinture: Approches* (1990), his own *L'Entr'Images* (1990), presented at a seminar and a lecture at the NFT in 1989, and finally, in 1991, an international colloquium at the Paris Louvre, on "Le portrait peint au cinéma," documented in a special issue of the journal *IRIS*.

While not mentioning either a battle or even a crisis, many of these essays raise the point whether one should not look at the cinema from the vantage point of painting? This, in a sense, takes one back to the art-historical or filmological debates of the 1940s and 1950s, to Elie Faure and André Bazin,[1] whose implicit question was: is the cinema an art, and if so, how does it relate to the other arts? Instead, should one not assume this battle to have been won? Is it not time to reverse the angle, and look at painting from the vantage point of cinema? Aumont calls this an "analecture," a retrospective reading of (the history of painting) in the face of the existence of the cinema and its impact on pictorial questions of spatial disposition, framing, expression, lighting, the representation of time (the "pregnant moment"), and above all, the spectator's role and place in front of a "view." Cynics may say that this is merely a rather arcane debate over the direction of academic film studies, in the wake of disenchantment with ciné-semiotics and psycho-semiotics: a swing of the pendulum away from the literary-linguistic foundations of "serious" film analysis to an equally respectable "art-history" discourse, with the cinema still looking for a pedigree. One might even contrast what is happening in France unfavorably with the situation here. In Britain it was, among others, John Berger's *Ways of Seeing*[2] (and its polemics with Kenneth Clark) that helped fuel a debate about the boundaries between fine art and popular culture. Against the history (of capitalism) that both were seen to be implicated in, an alliance emerged which led in the 1980s to the confluence of art history, film and TV studies, feminist theory, merging in the cultural studies courses at universities, art colleges and polytechnics. In France, the terms of the debate, at least from the focal point of the cinema, do not appear to be high culture versus popular culture, nor does it look as if any overtly political agenda has made inroads in the curriculum and emerged as something akin to cultural studies.

Most instructive for bringing some of the undercurrents to the fore was Raymond Bellour's[3] lecture in London just cited, where he compared what is happening in the realm of cinema and the image to the "revolution in poetic language" of which the writer Mallarmé was the messenger, when he lectured in Oxford in 1894 on the theme of *"on a touché au vers,"* meaning the breakdown of meter in French poetry and thus of the radical difference between prose and verse. Bellour, half-jokingly, half-seriously suggested that he too had a message to bring to London: *"on a touché à l'image."* The divide for him seemed to run between "cinéma" and the *"nouvelles images,"* the latter itself a complex historical phenomenon, obliging us to see Nam June Paik taking the first Sony portapack into the street, Christian Metz[4] writing his first film-semiological essay, and Godard making LE MÉPRIS as all belonging to the same moment in time. In other words, the "crisis" which in Britain since the mid-1960s concerned the fate of popular culture, the avant-garde, high culture, and high tech, working its way through the debates as the issue of representation, consumption and "spectatorship" was in France a debate about the material, linguistic and psychic support of cinema – all driven by the fact that the photographic image could no longer be taken as the medium's self-evident basis, and therefore doing away with any indexical relation between reality and the image. It is against this background that in a fundamental sense, painting could become a metaphor for the cinema (as the medium associated with the history of photography) in contrast to the electronic or the digital image. Given its longer history, painting was to provide a certain vantage point on this rupture.

Thus, behind the equation "cinema and painting" other (dialectically intertwined or deeply antagonistic) pairs are lined up: cinema and architecture, cinema and video, cinema and television. What "painting and cinema" seems to signal is not necessarily where one stands in the divide, but rather indicates how one proposes to go about articulating that stand: perhaps *"reculer pour mieux sauter,"* or putting together an inventory. Aumont's book is typical in this respect: it takes a historical view for the cinema according to him, is quintessentially the 19th century reaching right into the middle of the 20th, and he sees his book as a kind of janitor's job, tidying up after the show is definitely over, making sure the building is secure and everything is in its proper place.

To this one could add a more local issue, the struggle over the critical heritage of *Cahiers du cinéma*, and the right to interpret the history of its influence. A two-volume chronicle, Antoine de Baecque's *Les cahiers du cinéma, l'histoire d'une revue*[5] apparently sent many ex-contributors and collaborators to their word-processors for rectifications, amplifications, justifications. In short, almost all aspects of French film culture seem to be involved in a major film-cultural stock-taking. One of the most brilliant *Cahiers du cinéma* critics of the late 1970s and early 1980s, Serge Daney, gave up his job at the magazine in 1987 when he became media critic of the daily *Libération*, discussing television, advertising, commercial video with an erudition and critical wit not seen before in French journalism or criticism.[6]

Daney is perhaps the most radical among those who think it is time to repay the cinema its due: it has taught us how to look at the world, now we have to learn how to look at the other arts and media through the lens of the cinema, but a cinema so naturalized, so culturally internalized as to be nowhere in particular and yet everywhere. In its near-hundred year history, it has become a kind of truth, namely our truth. What Daney had in mind was strikingly confirmed in a recent BBC2 *Moving Pictures* item devoted to the memory of Jean Vigo. Bernardo Bertolucci, asked to talk about L'ATALANTE, quite spontaneously described the film not as a film, but as a reality existing in its own right, a reality existing next to other realities. He ended up talking about what he called "liquid cinema," a notion especially suggestive. Bertolucci's way of celebrating Vigo contrasted with a no less enthusiastic Lindsay Anderson in the same program, for whom there were masterpieces like ZÉRO DE CONDUITE which had inspired him in IF.., and, even more importantly, there was an "artist" with a "personal vision," an entity to which he admonished all young filmmakers to remain true. Bertolucci not only paid homage to Vigo by reworking a scene from L'ATALANTE he particularly liked in THE LAST TANGO IN PARIS. At the Canal St. Martin, a life-belt with "L'Atalante" written on it is tossed to the couple in the water, only to sink like a

L'ATALANTE

stone. By giving the cinema a dense materiality, Bertolucci's ultimate compliment to Vigo was to speak of his film as existing in the real world, like a building or the Canal St. Martin itself, landmarks we can all visit and inspect. Martin Scorsese, also has this exact attitude. Gone are the days when love of cinema meant talking about "film as film" – works with their own aesthetic texture, structure and textuality (as the first generation of film scholars, say, Robin Wood[7] or Victor Perkins[8] had to do in order to legitimate studying the cinema at all). Like Bertolucci or Daney, we may need to treat films as events that have happened to us, experiences that are inalienably ours, and thus as material facts. The cinema has helped carry the burden of history, or has given the illusion of carrying it, but it has also bequeathed a kind of double or parallel life, shadowing another, perhaps ever more shadowy life, as our culture's real past become its movies.

That Rivette's films – "*scènes de la vie parallèle*" – appear to hold in many ways key positions in the more specifically French debate is not in itself surprising when one remembers his beginnings. Probably the most intellectually precocious of the young Turks around Bazin and the early years of *Cahiers du cinéma*, Rivette was nonetheless – along with Godard – one of Bazin's more unruly sons when it came to deciding whether he belonged to those who "believed in reality" or those who "believed in the image." Championing Hawks and Hitchcock, and also Fritz Lang, Rivette always oscillated between the classical cinema of Wyler and Preminger beloved by Bazin, and a more offbeat Hollywood. He preferred the "improbable truth" (the French title of Lang's BEYOND A REASONABLE DOUBT) to Rossellini's "things are there – why tamper with them"?

The reference point, then, for LA BELLE NOISEUSE may well have to be Godard's PASSION, which proved to be a key film of the 1980s. As so often, God-

PASSION

ard sensed the tremors announcing the landslide earlier than most, and in PASSION and the accompanying television program, *Scenario de Passion* he began to redefine his cinema, but maybe also *the* modern European cinema generally (Wenders certainly seems to follow in Godard's footsteps, though in a grandiosely overblown manner, in UNTIL THE END OF THE WORLD). Godard, precisely, went back to painting. But in PASSION, cinema is the vanishing point between painting on one side, and the video screen and monitor on the other: it is a "film" shot with a big Mitchell camera that the Polish director is unable to finish, and it is perhaps no accident (for the genesis of Rivette's project) that PASSION features Michel Piccoli as the patron and patriarch, lording it over not only his employees, but his wife, who is the lover of Jerzy, playing the director (and used by Godard because he was the "Man of Marble" from Andrzej Wajda's film), now unable to muster the "solidarity" needed to still make cinema.

Seen as part of this dialogue of French film culture with itself, we have to assume that LA BELLE NOISEUSE's "classicism," its well-lit sets and carefully composed shots, its "logical" editing rhythm and shot changes, its balanced alternations between indoor scenes and the dappled outdoors, it day-times and its night-times, and thus its apparently solemn affirmation of the spiritual values of great art, is less a polemical re-statement of the *"politique des auteurs,"* and a rather more subtle or nuanced intervention in present-day cultural politics. Rivette has made an auteur's film, but one in the full knowledge that it has to be an auteur's film, for reasons of survival, not only as bulwark against the anonymous output of TV, but also so it can be shown at Cannes. Festivals are the places where films financed by television receive the world's endorsement that they nevertheless still count as cinema, by a process that Godard has called "giving a film its passport" – a phrase already used several years ago by Peter Wollen, describing his own work as "films without a passport."

A number of distinct aspects of Rivette's film come to mind in support of reading it as just such a statement about the impossibility of the auteur and yet the necessity of being one. First, there is the question of authenticity and the original. What at first sight is curiously old-fashioned if not naive about LA

BELLE NOISEUSE is its belief in authenticity and the original throughout most of the movie, until Frenhofer, coolly and methodically, fakes himself by hiding the "Belle Noiseuse" forever, while passing off a painting quickly daubed during one late night session as the fruit of ten years' creative agony. Apart from the three women in the know (who do not speak out), nobody so much as suspects the fraud and the substitution.

Second, an argument about Authorship, Style and Signature. If LA BELLE NOISEUSE is indeed the parting self-portrait of the author as a cultural icon of authentic art, signature itself substitutes for style. In Rivette's film, this signature comes from beyond the grave. One is reminded of Wenders' THE AMERICAN FRIEND, where the importance of the paintings sold by Dennis Hopper was that they were forged, but by the painter himself, who was played by Nicholas Ray, the film auteur par excellence of the *Cahiers* group, and of whom Godard once wrote: "if the Hollywood cinema were to disappear, Nicholas Ray would single-handedly reinvent it." In one of the most dramatic scenes of the Rivette film, Frenhofer's wife enters his studio at night, looks at the painting of "La Belle Noiseuse" (which we never see – except like a fetishist spying a piece of thigh, we catch a glimpse of carmine red, when the covering sheet is accidentally lifted for an instant). Frenhofer's wife, evidently shocked by what is on view, walks round the painting, and next to his signature on the back, she paints a cross, as if to confirm that this has been painted by a ghost. The gesture turns LA BELLE NOISEUSE into something close to a horror film, halfway between the gothic tales around painted portraits mentioned in the beginning, and Roger Corman's TOMB OF LIGEA or FALL OF THE HOUSE OF USHER.

Third, an argument about craftsmanship, labor and duration. Much of the film is taken up with the act of painting itself. The fact that in LA BELLE NOISEUSE all that effort, all that painful scratching of pen on paper, the sketches, the posing, the crucifixions that the model's body undergoes, seems in the end to have been produced merely to be hidden forever, is perhaps a more oblique comment than one at first assumes, on what can be the relation between the labor that enters into a work, and its value or effect. The discrepancy between labor and value was already the subject of Whistler's argument with Ruskin, and thus stands as a crucial debate at the threshold of the modern era, signaling the end of correlating the value (exhibition or social use) of a work of art with the labor (read: personal pain or mental anguish) invested in producing it.

Fourth, the contest between cinema and painting over "representation." The artist-painter's torment in the cinema is always slightly ridiculous, because it is betrayed by the cinema's facility in rendering what the painter is striving after – this particular quality of light, that particular painterly effect, this particular likeness. Hence, any canvas actually shown in a film invariably turns out to be either bad art or a fake, the cinema always seeming to mock painting at the same time as it defers to its cultural status. One of the most shocking moments in John Berger's *Ways of Seeing* was when he walked up to a Botticelli in what looked like the National Gallery, took out a Stanley-knife and cut a sizeable square out of the priceless canvas. After such knowledge, no painting can survive its representation in cinema: one more reason why "La Belle Noiseuse" must remain hidden at the end.

Finally, an argument about different kinds of time. Well before German directors like Syberberg and Reitz opted for length to make themselves heard, and cut a sizeable chunk of time out of the media landscape of television, Rivette produced monsters of extended time, from L'amour fou to Out One. It is, apart from anything else, a response to the need of European art films to counteract the blockbuster media-blitz of Hollywood. Yet the length of Rivette's films also foregrounds the spectator's place, and the experience of viewing – not excluding boredom. Rivette is a more experimental director than most, opening his films to varying degrees of attention and attentiveness, and by making painting his subject he is able to enact a certain kind of viewing: contemplation, exploration, negotiating distance and proximity, occupying a different space, and yet "entering into a picture." The emphasis on both process and product reinforces this parallel, so that over long stretches of the film, the spectator is, as it were, alone with his thoughts, "watching paint dry" – itself an aesthetic statement in the age of media-instantaneity and electronic images.

L'Amour Fou

But La Belle Noiseuse also enacts this different form of spectatorship concretely, carving a "spatial form" out of the time it takes to view it. Length becomes one of the auteur's weapons in his battle against so-called "dominant cinema": the film lays and splays itself across television's time slots and scheduled evanescence, as well as breaking down a first-run cinema's two or three evening performances. La Belle Noiseuse is four hours, carefully segmented internally into dramatic acts, but also externally, by a break that the film itself announces. Thus, when the model in the film gets giggly from exhaustion, and several times grabs for a cigarette, the film advises patrons in the cinema to take a break as well and come back for the next sitting. La Belle Noiseuse is nothing if not aware of the kind of special occasion contract it has with its audience, and although TV's archetypal moment of disjuncture, the commercial break, might fit just as well, one wonders how the two-hour TV version manages to convey this double articulation of duration.

All this may be no more than saying that La Belle Noiseuse can be and must be read as allegory, or rather, as that particular form of allegory known as *mise-en-abyme*. This is perhaps the more surprising, since the film is, in its narrative as well as its mise-en-scène, one of the most "classical" films imaginable, respecting at all times the ground rules of cinematic realism. But rather than being conformist, this classicism functions as an act of resistance. Looking at Rivette's oeuvre, it is possible to argue that his films have always anticipated another technology – that of video, of the video recorder and of electronic images, especially in their obsession with parallel realities, with going into dream-time and paranoia-time, with layering one text with another, confronting theatre and life in a modulated commentary on Anna Magnani's question in Renoir's LE CAROSSE D'OR: "where does the theatre end and life begin"? But the tension and pathos of Rivette's films, their quality of clairvoyance and hyper-alertness actually depended on the resistance which the medium "film" offers and imposes on both filmmaker and viewers in differentiating and resolving this layering: these strainings after representing twilight states, these superimpositions of parallel worlds need a realist medium, need the solidity of celluloid. Similarly, in LA BELLE NOISEUSE, the pay-off of all this labor comes when Frenhofer takes out the unfinished canvass of ten years' earlier, in order to paint the new picture over the old, seemingly obliterating his wife-as-model by the young woman, the two merging and mingling, the face of the first gradually but only partially, hidden beneath a veil of blue crayon. It might be a video-effect, and yet it crucially must not be a video-effect.

Ultimately, it is this capacity to be a "realist text" and allegorical at the same time that makes LA BELLE NOISEUSE contemporary, and to my mind, an "intervention" rather than a conservative restatement. One might cite Borges and Roland Barthes: Rivette is re-writing a classical (readerly) text as an allegorical (writerly) text. As in the case of Barthes most famous allegorical rewriting of a realist text, Balzac's novella Sarrasine in *S/Z*, so the realist text of Rivette is also a novella by Balzac, *Le*

LA BELLE NOISEUSE

chef-d'oeuvre inconnu. From it, Rivette takes the initial situation where the young Poussain offers his mistress to the master Frenhofer as a model, in order to spy on Frenhofer and get a glimpse of the one painting Frenhofer refuses to put on show, "La Belle Noiseuse," reputed to be a masterpiece, the chef-d'oeuvre inconnu. In Rivette's film, the title of the painting is itself thematized, by what may well be no more than a piece of folk etymology: *noiseuse* comes from *noix*, nuts, and in Quebecois slang, it means a woman who is a "pain in the ass."

Deliberately and bluntly, LA BELLE NOISEUSE parades a world of men who enter into a kind of bargain or exchange whose object is a woman. Not only is the young painter's girlfriend offered as bait or gift, she is also intended as a substitute for Frenhofer's wife, regarded by Porbus as the cause of Frenhofer's creative block. But the twist and thus the film's central allegory, or re-reading of Balzac, is that Rivette makes of Frenhofer the Minotaur, a creature both powerful and baffled, half-man, half-beast. It brings the Frenhofer figure once more close to Picasso, for whom the Minotaur was a central reference point. But more importantly, it emphasizes the different role the young woman has as the sacrificial victim, offered by the men to appease the man-god/ man-beast of artistic genius. And the question which the film raises in that last voice-over is whether Marianne is in fact a kind of Ariadne, venturing forward so that the wily, but also cowardly Theseus can follow, to slay the Minotaur, or at any rate, to take away his power. What in Balzac is an Oedipus story becomes in Rivette a Theseus myth, or rather an Ariadne story.

This suggests two things, by way of conclusion. I would see in LA BELLE NOISEUSE Rivette's decided plea for cinema, but not as a simulacrum of painting, nor of its cultural status or commodity value: rather the plea for a cinema where the virtual realities and parallel worlds are created by the fact that you can believe in what you do not see, in contrast to a Hollywood cinema where you can see what you cannot possibly believe (thanks to special effects), and a television which can do neither, and only asserts. Yet it also suggests that the change from the photographic image to the digital image is more than a change in technology, or delivery system, but will entail a long and protracted struggle not only over the interpretation of this or that film, but over the meaning of the cinema altogether. This debate, hardly begun, seems figured in the allegorical *mise-en-abyme* into which "La Belle Noiseuse" so definitively disappears. The painting is finally what one suspected it to have been: a mirror, but a mirror standing for "the visual," through which our civilization seems destined to step, rematerializing on the other side as something quite different. Rivette, perfectly agreeing with Daney's analysis, might take exactly the opposite position. Once the painting has vanished and the guests have departed, we hear the sounds of the village: a baby crying, the voice of a woman answering, the noises of people at work – a world outside once more coming alive, though now perhaps we have the inner eye to finally see it.

(1992)

Notes

1. Elie Faure (1873-1937) was a French art historian, whose important essay on the cinema, "De la cinéplastique," originally appeared in *L'arbre d'Eden* (1922). André Bazin published a key essay on "Peinture et cinéma" in *Qu'est-ce que le cinéma*, vol. 2,

"Le cinéma et les autres arts" (Place: Éditions Cerf 1959), pp. 127-132; translated into English as "Painting and Cinema", in Gray, Hugh, *What Is Cinema*, Vol. 1 (Berkeley: University of California Press 1967), pp. 164-169.

2.   John Berger *Ways of Seeing* (Harmondsworth: Penguin Books, 1972). Based on a BBC television series, it became one of the most influential books of the decade.

3.   Raymond Bellour, Lecture at the National Film Theatre, September 1989. The talk appears as the title essay in R. Bellour, *l'Entre-Image, Photo Cinema, Video* (Paris: Edition La difference, 1990).

4.   Christian Metz, "Le cinema: langue ou langage", *Communications* 4 (1964), pp 52-90.

5.   Antoine de Baecque, *Les cahiers du cinéma, l'histoire d'une revue* 2 vols.(Paris: Editions de l'Etoile, 1991).

6.   Serge Daney's work is, among others, collected in *Ciné-journal* (Paris: Cahiers du cinéma, 1986); *Le salaire du zappeur* (Paris: P.O.L., 1988) and *Devant la recrudescence des vols de sac à main: cinéma, télévision, information* (Paris: Aléas, 1991).

7.   Robin Wood, *Hitchcock's Films* (London: Zwemmer Books, 1965) .

8.   Victor Perkins, *Film as Film* (Harmondsworth: Penguin Books, 1972).

Spellbound by Peter Greenaway

In the Dark ... and Into the Light

On Leaving the Century of Cinema

In his brief essay "Painting and Cinema," André Bazin, after sharing the general dissatisfaction with films about artists and paintings, nonetheless remarks that, "the cinema, not only far from compromising or destroying the true nature of another art, is, on the contrary, in the process of saving it."[1] About half a century later, and a full century after the first presentation of the Cinématographe Lumière, it is tempting to read in Bazin's phrase a question that reverses the terms: is another art in the process of saving the cinema? This question makes sense, I believe, but only if one concedes that what prompts it is the very success of cinema, an "art" now so ubiquitous as to be all but invisible. Here I am posing it as a possible vanishing point for looking at a series of strategic steps – sideways steps, as they must seem – that Peter Greenaway has taken in recent years in his career as a filmmaker, by curating exhibitions and directing operas. As it happens, the steps fit into a project he has called *The Stairs*:

> In 1986 I wrote a film script called *The Stairs* which ... speculatively hoped to discuss the provocations *ad nauseam* of the business of putting images with text, theatre with architecture, painting with music, selfishness with ambition. Stairs became the architectural motif and the general metaphor of the potential film (not ignoring the appropriate pun on a good hard look) ... it was to present a platform for display, like a theatre stage raked high for excellent visibility.[2]

Needless to say, the film was never made. But as "architectural motif" and "general metaphor," the stairs have a symptomatic role, not only in the Greenaway shows, mounted in Geneva and Munich under that title. They point in the direction of what Greenaway has had in mind for some time, namely "taking the cinema out of the cinema."[3] It turns out that the period of his greatest triumphs as an established, indeed sustaining pillar of the European art cinema, from THE DRAUGHTSMAN'S CONTRACT (1982) to THE COOK, THE THIEF, HIS WIFE AND HER LOVER (1991), has coincided with his greatest restlessness and dissatis-

faction about this medium and its history: "Just now that cinema celebrates its
first centenary and is a medium ripe for
the re-invention of itself, there is evidence
to believe that all art moves towards the
condition of film."[4] If the "birth" of the
cinema more or less coincided with the
height of European Wagnerism, when
Walter Pater could claim that all the arts
aspired to the condition of music, and
Stéphane Mallarmé – apparently contra-
dicting, but in fact merely refining this

The Cook, The Thief, His Wife and Her Lover

dictum – quipped that the world existed in order to become a book, it is hard to
resist the irony at work in the thought that, a hundred years hence, the Zeitgeist
seems to have changed its mind to such an extent that much of life is now lived
in order to fit into a film.

Such a universalized "condition of film" would, however, provide the appropriate conceptual horizon against which the paradox of ubiquity and invisibil-
ity, of "taking the cinema out of the cinema" in order to "save" it, might come to
make sense, and for Greenaway's stairs/steps to be more than a flight of fancy. It
might even make possible to ask – once more with Bazin – "what is cinema,"
though – against Bazin? – one would not necessarily go in the direction of either
"specificity" (the modernist obsession) or "ontology" (the realist paradigm),
and rather follow Erwin Panofsky's program of "perspective as symbolic
form," except to note that whatever the cinema's "symbolic form" might turn
out to be, it is unlikely to be, academic film studies notwithstanding, "perspective."[5]

To get the measure of this claim, though, one would have to be able to get out
of the cinema, leave the 24-hour cinema in front of one's eyes, in the streets, in
the home, and assume a space, or step into an episteme from which a symbolic
form could be defined, in the way that the ruptures introduced by Cubism allowed Panofsky to "see" perspective as something both more and less than a
system of pictorial representation. The cinema after one hundred years, is finally achieving not the status of "the seventh art" it so often appeared to crave – at
least not in Europe – but emerging as the Archimedean point, around which a
culture turns without being aware of it, or actually disavows, like a blind spot.

One exit from the cinema at the top of Greenaway's stairs might be a museum, a film museum, the NFT for instance, in order, for instance, to ponder
once more D.W. Griffith or Abel Gance, Paul Sharits or Jean-Luc Godard, an
Antonioni film from the 1960s or a Hölderlin film by Straub and Huillet. All
other exits lead in the direction of the traditional arts: opera, theatre, gallery art,

where, of course, much on view bears the unmistakable imprint of cinema. Nothing more obvious, then, than to observe closely a painter turned film-maker, returning from forays into television and dance, as he presents an installation reflecting on "a century of propaganda for the cinematic experience"? I am particularly thinking of his contribution to "Spellbound," a centenary show installed at the Hayward Gallery between February and May 1996 in London.

Greenaway and the visual arts: each of his feature films has an old master, a style, a single picture as its figure or ground, self-consciously, explicitly, performatively introduced and sign-posted.[6] But a wider compass on his work, and his installation at the Hayward suggests that Greenaway is actually travelling the other way, as it were, not towards examining what the cinema might have in common with the visual or performative arts, or even, in the manner of some recent French films by Rivette or Pialat, dealing with painters or the act of painting, to make canvas and brush suitably ironic metaphors for the disappearance of celluloid and the *camera-stylo* from image-making. Instead, it is to purge the cinema, confronting it both with itself and its "others," recalling or insisting on a few conceptual features, which might rescue it from its self-oblivion, by theatrically staging it across painting, sculpture, dance, music, drama and architecture.

How would the Greenaway oeuvre look from such a vantage point? Broadly speaking, two kinds of meta-commentaries flank the central art film panel of the five features that constitute his cultural capital, or in his words, his European "platform for display ... raked high for excellent visibility." The early experimental work, culminating in the anti-films A WALK THOUGH H (1978), THE FALLS (1980), and ACT OF GOD (1981), took the cinema into the worlds of maps and archives, Borges and Calvino, missing persons and Babylonian libraries, stripping character and motive out of the narrative, and confronting film – across the voice-over-of-God embodied by BBC announcers and the Central Office of Information – with its mythically documentary origins. The work for television (including A TV DANTE-CANTO 5, 1985, M IS FOR MAN, MUSIC, MOZART, 1991) and PROSPERO'S BOOKS (1991) one could call post-films, in the sense that their concerns are neither narrative nor iconic-photographic. Instead, and unlike the early pseudo-documentaries, whose investment in place made them turn on the referential illusion of mainstream film, the later work, in keeping with the new technologies it deploys, is graphic, having to do with trace and body, with surface, rather than with space and (absence of) body, as in the case of the art films.

To these conceptual pillars, one now can add, by way of a pantheon, an impressively proportioned project consisting of a series of installation-exhibitions, such as *The Physical Self* (Rotterdam, 1991), *Les bruits des nuages* (Paris, 1992) and the already mentioned *The Stairs* (Geneva 1994, Munich 1995) – the latter keeping Greenaway, until the millennium, at work on public commissions from some of the world's major cities. Commenting on a typical preoccupation of the 1980s with large urban projects (the Lloyds Building, the London Docklands, François Mitterand's *Grands travaux* in Paris, such as the Bastille opera house), Greenaway has chosen cityscapes and civic architecture as the medium against which to "project" the cinema, fashioning a series of interrogatory building-signs or ironic sign-buildings that could well be his "Year 2000 – A Space-Encyclopedia."

This focus on the city is worth retaining, I think, because it announces an interesting and possibly crucial transfer. Much of Greenaway's work, I would argue, belongs to a British tradition of land(scape) art, an idiom not only intriguing for its long history embracing as it does an interest in shrines, gardens, vistas, secret paths and other invocations of the *genius loci*, but also offering a sophisticated conceptual vocabulary of trace, mark and index with which to think perennially topical problems of aesthetics and rhetoric, aesthetics and semiotics. If Greenaway's art films, in their "excessive Englishness"[7] inscribe Britain as a set of replete signifiers into the Europe of the 1980s, so the city installations (so far planned and executed mainly in such "European" cities as Rotterdam, Vienna, Geneva, Munich, Barcelona) transfer a specifically "English" language of landscape, site and history into urban environments, which are conceived, unlike, say, Christo's combination of land art, landmark, and building site, as "immaterialities": mobile traces, roving points of view, as metaphors not of the city, but of the cinema, and of a cinema, once more on the move.

A Postmodernist Turned Modernist?

Inevitably, one is tempted to ask whether Greenaway, in both his cinema and installation work, is maintaining his faith in modernism, or should he be regarded as one of the cinema's post-modernists? And if a modernist, does he belong to the American tradition of minimalism and conceptual art, or to the modernism that has, in poets and critics like T.S. Eliot or Ted Hughes, revived a "metaphysical" or "Jacobean" world of the extravagant conceit, of violence and masculinity? Already about THE DRAUGHTSMAN'S CONTRACT, Greenaway said: "My film is about excess: excess in the language, excess in the landscape – which is much too green."[8] But this may be to underestimate the force and diversity of the British/English concern with landscape which has proven remarkably resilient and flexible, capable of accommodating the most diverse strands of modernist thought, almost all of them shadowed by versions of pastoral, from which only the expatriate modernists (T.S. Eliot, Ezra Pound, Wyndham Lewis) were apparently able to shake free but which held in thrall the indigenous left and right, as well as the Irish and the Celtic fringe, if we think of Hugh McDermaid or Seamus Heaney.[9]

Thus, it is possible to draw a genealogy for Greenaway, and to situate him in the major post-war British tension between "art school" modernism (David Hockney, Peter Blake and Richard Hamilton, the Marlborough Gallery)[10] and "art history" modernism (the Courtauld Institute, Anthony Blunt's Poussin, Nicholas Pevsner, Anthony Powell and William Golding) with its English gardens, the landscapes of neo-Romanticism, country houses set in ample grounds, stuffed with curio-cabinets and private collections. The tension also runs through the depiction of coastline and water, prominent in Green-away (cf. Greenaway's films *Drowning By Numbers, Fear of Drowning* or the early short *Water Wrackets*), but difficult to place with any precision within British art and litera-ture, for so much – from Henry James and Virginia Woolf to Michael Powell and Derek

DROWNING BY NUMBERS

Jarman – is haunted by the seascapes of Kent, Sussex and East Anglia, or ob-sessed with off-season resorts, when not more recently "learning from Black-pool."

These British modernisms – assuming they can count as such – of landscape and land art are, famously, only some of the 20th-century's modernism, and arguably not the ones that proved most fertile for the cinema, or vice versa. The other side of the British divide alluded to, the modernism of art school "pop," its own brand of whimsy firmly plugged into the energy of commercial art, posters, fashion and design for the emergent mass-market – is probably the real partner in dialogue with the cinema, if not its out and out rival for consideration as the century's most prominent symbolic form. Pop and advertising certainly produced a generation of British filmmakers whose international – read "Holly-wood" – influence is undeniable and inestimable. It brought the top end of Brit-ish advertising agency talent into direct contact with the Hollywood main-stream, and contributed not insignificantly to revitalizing Hollywood itself in the 1980s. The sarcasm and contempt of the generation of Alan Parker, Ridley Scott, Adrian Lyne for Greenaway is remarkably uninhibited, as was that of Jarman for both Greenaway and British Hollywood, a facet that is itself worth exploring further.

Whether any of this has ever troubled Greenaway is not at issue. It nonethe-less seems that his work since THE COOK, THE THIEF, HIS WIFE AND HER LOVER presents a kind of meditation not only on the impossible dilemmas of a Thatcher-style Britain, but a British cinema, between America and Europe. Even as he works with digital technology, Greenaway's mock-Victorianism sits uneasily with the pop-energies of a Hockney, also experimenting with electronic images and a digital paint box.[11] Greenaway's TV DANTE is in better company with land artists such as Richard Long's or Hamish Fulton's visible and invisible walks, where space, place and trace make up a perfect geometry in not three but four dimensions, than to Hockney's laser-printed portrait-photographs (though Hockney's treatment of California suburban swimming pools is nothing if not a search for the *genius loci*). Greenaway has talked about how he once buried a hundred ball-bearings in precisely marked sites, calculated to coincide with the grid pattern of Ordinance Survey Maps.[12] If this is the spirit of code-cracking Bletchley, where land art and the computer first met on Alan Turing's operating table, Greenaway also has an eye for the pastoral's down-market, heritage version: the green wellingtons variety of gothic, the Agatha Christie universe of eccentricity and whimsy, the exacting world of bird-watchers and Stonehenge solstice worshippers. This dual legacy takes one's reflection on cinema after cinema, of cinema out of the cinema in two directions: a postmodern "multiple-choice multiplex" and an ironic-modernist "precision optics."

The Hayward Show, or: The Cinema as Kit – Expanded or Exploded View?

Morbid or cynical musings on the end of cinema, the death of cinema, or as Greenaway put it, on its "sterility of concept, uniformity of execution"[13] are not in short supply among British and other European filmmakers. But when so much cinéaste ambition has had to write itself small and withdraw into the sulk corner of late-night television, Greenaway's successes have given him a chance to choose a larger canvas. He, too, starts with a skeptical assessment:

> It is too late. Cinema is a one-way traffic: the best that can be hoped is to change the street furniture and the traffic-lights in readiness for the next attempt."[14]

Nonetheless, a centenary is neither the worst occasion for the attempt to reinvent the cinema, nor is Greenaway a stranger to the magic of one hundred, the figure having served him well, for instance, as the narrative architecture of DROWNING BY NUMBERS. Since then, he has taken "100 Objects to Represent the World" to Vienna, "100 Stairs" to Geneva and "100 Projections" to Munich. Even if in the London show the hundred is folded in half, as it were (for logistical and financial reasons, one assumes), a play of symmetry and seriality is nonetheless essential to the project.

And the idea of the "fold," the pleat, the package and the box is not altogether inappropriate for a project that translates a temporal experience like the cinema into a spatial sequence and an "artifically arranged" (to cite Georges Meliès) display. The order is reversible, the steps retraceable, and this film can be rewound. What enfolds also unfolds. The labeled boxes, the white screens, the projections onto the buildings (Munich), the display tables and wall mounts (Rotterdam), the maps, the instruments of vision and dissection (Geneva) which so predominate in Greenaway's installations so far, evoke a number of robust antinomies around removal and unpacking, storage and retrieval, inside and outside, before and after, evidence and argument, with both the cinema and the other arts alternately furnishing the *mise-en-abyme* into which each in turn is Chinese-boxed (or taxonomied).[15]

On a visit to the Hayward, another comparison also came to mind. The Museum of the Moving Image, that modestly boastful monument to the movies' ubiquity, with its Zoetropes and fantasmagorias, its agit-prop trains and blue-screens, its Western set and BBC newsroom, pays permanent homage to "expanded cinema." The Greenaway exhibit, so conveniently adjacent as to provoke the pun, might well aspire to the label "exploded cinema." A delayed/deferred detonation, a freeze-frame blast, or perhaps an explosion in the technical sense, of parts pulled apart or removed for closer inspection and identification, as in a car mechanics' manual or an engineer's drawing, used for demonstrating the workings of a carburetor or a self-regulating servo-system.

What does the visitor see? A large space lined with steeply racked cinema seats from a disused movie house. In the middle, long wooden tables piled high with props in neatly sorted piles, evoking film genres and movie stories. One's path is blocked by Plexiglas trays, on which the daily newspapers accumulate, kept since the opening day. The smell of rotting food directs one's gaze to dinner plates on which sauces slowly dry and mashed potatoes accumulate mold. At the far end, a series of glass showcases, as in expensive boutiques, housing live humans in rigid poses. Huge loudspeakers resonate with periodic bursts of sound-collages, rumbling through one's solar plexus as one tried to shield one's ears from the assault, as if an aural fireball or the call to the dead for the Last Judgment was rolling overhead.

If we view Greenaway's installations as exploded cinema in this technical sense, then our attention must be at once on the individual parts or specified constituents, and on the fact that their arrangement is neither fixed nor arbitrary. Rather, they move along a number of determined axes, which represent their alignment of thought, their conceptual architecture. For his London cinema kit, Greenaway proposed nine elements: "artificial light, actors, props, text, illusion, audience, time, sound, changing imagery." Some of these I would see as the "working parts," laterally displaced, others as the imaginary axes along which they flee the center of what we normally understand by the cinema machine. The challenge is of course not to give away too soon which is which, in this deconstructionist's graphic depiction of all-too familiar icon and objects from the cinema we grew up with – whether Mickey Mouse or Marilyn – now at once mummified and merchandized in the MOMI's adult toy shop, but to provoke new reflections through novel juxtapositions. The props Greenaway has put together, in their profusion and surrealist incongruity also seem to nod and wink at the spectator. But despite their comforting, archetypal associations, they are more like gremlins, bent on mischief and ready to bite, or the not-quite-functioning plot parts of a melancholic Dada meta-mechanic's dictionary of British cinema.[16]

The reason why a gallery space seems appropriate to such an exploded view of cinema is that the installation is partly designed to render to some of these elements a new materiality, or to recall an original, resisting "corporeality," especially if one regards the cinema's biggest crime as having divested the world of its physicality and substantiality.

> Cinema's low ratio of physicality and corporeality is relevant to the physical relation-ship it has towards time.[17]

Temperature, texture or touch are aspects of bodies and objects that do not seem to "matter" to either the world of cinematic projection, or that of the commod-ity, casting its spell as sign, desire and promise: both live by the transparency of artificial light, and both are parodied by a flashing electric torch that in a gallery – as Marcel Duchamp's ready-mades have taught us – invariably is at once an "empty" sign and a "full" object.

The second dimension, central to the cinema's repressed other, is also pre-served or reinvented by the gallery space: that of a cinematic spectacle as live performance, and yet fundamentally different from theatre, where body and voice always have to pretend to the presence of destiny. Greenaway "explodes" this nexus, by having actors in "showcases, vitrines and small theatres," but as in cinema, separating body from voice, and also making sure that each day has another program. The latter recalls a crucial dimension of (early) cinema as a performance. At first, when films were bought and sold rather than exchanged or rented, the options were at once "materialist" and "conceptual": either the same film to a different audience, or different films to the same audience, each becoming a function, or aggregate state of the other, in a more or less precisely calculable equation. If historically, the principle of "different film/same audi-ence" won the day, to the extent of creating the unique commodity that is film (whose value depends on materializing a time advantage and a location advantage), Greenaway's installation recalls that this may not be inevitable, especially if one is calling into question all the other material parameters of cinema.

Less obvious, but no less essential to the project of an exploded cinema is the materiality of time, of sound, of light, an interest central to both the American and British film avant-garde of the 1970s.[18] To take the case of temporality.

> Film as substance gains nothing by becoming old …. It gains no patina, no *craquelure*, makes no valuable chemical interaction with its environment, and its requirements for preservation, like its requirements for exhibition, are demanding. But in preservation it is invisible.[19]

Greenaway's different materialities play along the axis of absence (the photographic tense of the past-praeteritum, the once-having-been-there of Roland Barthes) and presence (body-voice-space, the theatrical performance as *"kairos,"* time filled with destiny), but also along the axis of decay (of food, daily changing, gently rotting) and the perishable (the newspaper in a museum, daily changing, and because of it, flagrant embodiment of the obsolete by its fetishism of the instant). Both absence/presence and instant decay are at the heart of the cinema's ambiguous inscription of temporality, its ridiculously relentless life and its terrifying un-deadness, TERMINATOR II and BRAM STOKER'S DRACULA.

Dislodging the Frame: The Future of Projection, Scale and Ratio

Perhaps the most important reason, though, why for Greenaway it seems the (European) cinema has to pass through the art gallery if it is to "reinvent" itself is that constant irritant, the "rigour of cinema's insistence on the rectangular frame, and that frame's fixed aspect ratio."[20] Something must surely give:

> The ever decreasing choice imposed by commercial and industrial standards has tightened the frame-ratio to such a point that it must – in the same way as other tightening strictures have operated in other fields – explode. Painting, as always, has set the pace ... the last three decades have seen [the heavily framed painted image] largely evaporate."[21]

Interestingly enough, it was Bazin in the already-quoted essay who provided one of the most often commented on distinctions between the cinematic and the pictorial frame.[22] Bazin uses a rather traditional account of the picture frame to argue his well-known view that the outer edges of the cinema screen are not strictly speaking comparable to a frame at all, but instead function as a "piece of masking that shows only a portion of reality ... part of something prolonged indefinitely into the universe." But he then goes on to say that "a frame is centripetal, a screen is centrifugal," thus bringing us not only back to the idea of the "exploded cinema" of Greenaway, but also leaving open the possibility that modern painting (having abandoned the "centripetal" frame Bazin mounts his argument on) can indeed redeem the cinema, if only to the extent of restoring to it the function Bazin claims for it: "Thanks to the cinema and to the psychological properties of the screen, what is symbolic and abstract takes on the solid reality of a piece of ore."[23]

Here we have the "materiality" Greenaway misses in cinema, although its source of value is not anchored in the economic metaphor of Bazin's realism, emerging as it does instead from any object's status as "work," once placed in the gallery space, the latter now performing in its institutional role as the gilded frame. Precisely insofar as it is the cinema's ubiquity that makes it invisible, the question of the frame, now in the sense in which it has been problematized by post-Duchamp art and the gallery space, becomes central to the future of the cinema, even though the way in which these problems may be worked out cannot be those of modern art.[24]

Greenaway contests and tests the frame in a number of ways. One of the most interesting moves is what I see as the shift from "wall-oriented, frontal-parallel-perpendicular" projection and display, to a horizontal plane (the table tops, as "screens" that need a different bodily engagement), and multi-dimensional screens "behind" screens, showing not an image but the cone which cinematic lighting cuts into space. The installation at once suggests the complex geometry of the cinematic apparatus, and acts as a projection-in-waiting where the upright screen becomes a "box" to be filled rather than a surface to reflect an image and absorb a viewer. The glass vitrines, on the other hand, become cubic/cubist screens, on which the actors' roles – all the adulterers or kings they have played – unfold and are enfolded. This means a whole film in a box which is also a screen, without losing that ambiguity of objects/living things behind glass: "don't touch, I'm valuable," and "don't touch, I'm dangerous." Here, too, we may have come full circle from the time when Orson Welles compared American filmmaking unfavorably to European cinema, by saying that Hollywood treats the cinema picture like a shop window behind glass, always stuffed to bursting.[25]

The thematics of tilting the image, of renegotiating the relation of horizontal to vertical around the issue of the frame is as old as the cinema, and a crucial feature of early cinema.[26] It is a preoccupation that I think, one also finds in Greenaway's film, both literally (VERTICAL FEATURES REMAKE) and metaphorically. Almost too insistently, from THE DRAUGHTSMAN'S CONTRACT and DROWING BY NUMBERS to A ZED AND TWO NOUGHTS and PROSPERO'S BOOKS, the sustaining fiction turns out to be paranoid "fictions within a fiction," passageways to salvation or self-advancement become trapdoors to the ontological void, his heroes invariably "framers framed" by some fearful symmetry. THE BELLY OF AN ARCHITECT, for instance, is a good example of such radical dislodging the frame, since the problem of both Kracklite and his hero Boullée, is precisely one of "framing," of sorting out the different time-frames and scale-frames, deciding in the end to take the plunge ...[27]

The question of dislodging the frame in the cinema, however, seems urgent not so much because of the realist/illusionist problematic of Bazin, or the materialist preoccupations of the modernist avant-garde, but because it opens up that other dimension, perhaps the most crucial for Greenaway, that of the audience. His worry about the frame as a function of the size and proportion of the screen, which at first glance looks like the familiar grumble about cinema having given in to television's aspect ratio, may well touch the nub of his enterprise, because the question of the frame implies scale, and via scale, the issue of cinema as architecture, as public art.

The European art cinema began, historically, in a defensive move, claiming "film" had to aspire to the status of art, in order to reclaim the purity of its modernist forms. If now, according to Greenaway, "all art aspires to the condition of film," the paradox is that this seems to happen at just the moment of the art cinema's historical demise. What went wrong? We hear that it is the audiences who deserted the cinema. But this is manifestly not the case. We know how the American cinema gathers its audiences, even in Europe, especially in Europe. The economic arguments are strong, but they do not altogether explain why audiences have deserted the European film. Might this have something to do with the fact that European cinema has a rather traumatized relation to the notion of audiences, just as European democracies have a traumatized relation to the notion of a public art (say, architecture – but also advertising)? The historical experiences of totalitarian regimes – experts at both the cinema and public art – have made discussing the issue doubly difficult, with the avant-garde able to claim the moral as well as the aesthetic high ground.[28] My sense is that Greenaway seems prepared to engage in a debate about what could be a public art, and what could be its audiences, just as postmodernism on a broader front has reopened the discussion around the spectacular in art.

Body-Measure, Body-Mass

Does this mean that Greenaway should be counted among the postmodernists after all? Yes, if by postmodern we understand not only – as is so often stressed – the border-crossings of high and low culture in both directions, but – a more crucial and critical point – a willingness to engage in a debate about what might be the place of art in contemporary public space, and what it is called upon to perform.

Greenaway no doubt comes with the right credentials, and his consistent interventions at the crossroads between urbanism, installation-art and the gallery/ museum space have as their vantage point the only truly public art of our times, the cinema, however problematically it is itself placed between architecture, advertising, media-event and style-file.

"To turn an event – any event – into a performance, all we need is an audience."[29] Audiences (not as mass but qua concept) have become noticeably important in Greenaway's oeuvre, to the point that they not only feature prominently in his most recent films, especially PROSPERO'S BOOKS, A TV DANTE, M IS FOR MOZART and DARWIN, but are their veritable subject. THE BABY OF MACON, for instance, is about what the limits, if any, are to an event, an action, once one assumes that being observed by an audience makes something an event. Here, the specularization of contemporary social interaction is put to the test, as it were, stretched beyond the limit, in order to see whether indeed "events not witnessed by an audience are not only non-performances but non-events," and setting out to prove whether anything attended by an audience becomes a performance, and what this might mean for our notion of the real, the possible and the tolerable (these "limits of representation" are a major concern of modern cinema, from Pasolini to Fassbinder, from Godard to Oshima).

Less traumatized perhaps by history and fascism, Greenaway, too, tests the limits of representation. But unlike the structuralist-materialist avant-garde of the 1970s, he goes into the gallery not for an intimate space but for a very public space, the last of the big spaces. And like the big spaces of the 1930s and 1940s, or the Paris big spaces of the 1970s and 1980s, he goes to spaces that are not just public but based on the power of the state, art and power, the state and power, the state and art. These are dangerous themes and provocations to confront, not least of all for a filmmaker who saw his country in the grip of an autocratic political caste the likes of which it had not seen since Churchill's War Cabinet. For Greenaway's dissenting voice in the Thatcher Era 1980s could be heard loud and clear well before THE COOK, THE THIEF, HIS WIFE & HER LOVER.

At the same time, Greenaway's investment in installation art may be understood as a move to use the gallery again as a gallery in the literal sense, as a passage way, an architectural feature to get from one space to another, protected from all manner of inclemencies: think of the democratic Athens of Plato. For unlike much of the filmic avant-garde of the 1970s, Greenaway does not seek refuge in the gallery in order to find an intimate space for his media-meditations, but tries to occupy it as a public space, one of the last agora-spaces of our overlaid, overcrowded, and interfering public domains.

He wants to turn the separating wall, the protective skin and delicate membrane that is the gallery outwards, in order for the city itself to be experienced as an intimate space. What he wants to reach via the gallery is the city, sites and places that are public, because already traversed by different kinds of audiences, forming instant, transient and transparent communities – shoppers, strollers: "a man taking a dog for a walk, a dog biting a man, a man biting a dog."[30] Greenaway has denounced the pseudo-community of today's cinema attendance, averring that even television scores higher as a form of sociability. It almost seems that he has decided that there is no point in making (European) cinema, unless one understands what it is that creates not just audiences – "audiences ... the watchers watched" – but sociable or public audiences, even under the conditions of the "society of the spectacle."

THE PILLOW BOOK

How to put this society "in the picture"? For a start, by reversing the marks of mobility and stasis, as in his installations, whether "The Stairs" or that of "Spellbound." Then, by applying the principles of the engineer to the tasks of the Cubists, once more reconstructing the moving (sound) image "from scratch." At first he enlarges the frame, projecting it onto the dimensions of any space whatsoever, as in the Hayward Gallery, then he compresses and shrinks it, as in his video-films or quick-time movie inserts. The extreme case is THE PILLOW BOOK (1996), where the triad city-text-skin is constantly tested against the scale, ratio, proportion and endurance of the human body, as if it was a matter of finding the new "golden means," the proper "aspect-ratio" of our electronic and virtual environments.

Not until there is a new definition of the visual event and its time-space ratios, will there be the "material" conditions for a new cinema. Moving events and not just moving pictures, but also not just monuments and mausoleums. Are there spaces, he seems to ask, between the museum and cyberspace, comparable to the previously mentioned *Grands travaux* of Mitterand or the headquarters of multinational banks, an agora of our visual age the way the book and library once were, nonetheless funded by the state or cultural institutions, as part of the general good, rather than relying on the marketplace?

In this sense Greenaway, at the top of "The Stairs", "In the Dark and Into the Light" might just offer a vision of a new, eminently civic, maybe even democratic, but in any case, yet to be realized, public function for the cinema. It is as if, because of digitization or in spite of it, a battle is on for a new kind of presentational or representational space, which we need not be ashamed to call "cinema." The frame for this is not renaissance perspective, with its fixed, individualized eye of the beholder, confirming "him" as subject, but the mobile mass of audience and spectators, whose social body is at once the new "vanishing point" and "frame" of (audio-)visual culture. In this fashion, film art renews itself across the modes and spaces of the traditional arts but not, as was once thought, in order to upgrade the cinema as art, but to preserve the cinema for its audiences, which is to say, not for art's sake, but for politics' sake.

(1996)

Notes

1. Andre Bazin, *What is Cinema*? Essays selected and translated by Hugh Gray (Berkeley and Los Angeles: University of California Press, 1967), p 168.
2. Peter Greenaway, *The Stairs* (London: Merrell Holberton, 1995), p. 11.
3. Ibid., p. 9.
4. The passage continues: "Painters, writers, playwrights, composers, choreographers – creators indeed who we could say should know better – have eager aspirations to make films, and if not to make them, then debate endlessly the possibilities of making them." *The Stairs*, p. 13.
5. See for instance, Phil Rosen (ed.), *Narrative, Apparatus Ideology* (New York: Columbia University Press, 1987), especially the essays by J.L. Commolli, J.L. Baudry, C. Metz, and S. Heath, arguing the cinema's imbrication in the ideology of monocular vision, camera obscura specularity, and classical perspective's relation to the bourgeois, transcendental subject. Recently, this view, however, has come under attack. See M. Kemp, *The Science of Art* (New Haven: Yale University Press, 1990) and J. Crary, *Techniques of the Observer* (Cambridge, Mass. MIT Press, 1992).
6. A brief reminder: Vermeer (*Zed and Two Noughts*), Breughel (*Drowning by Numbers*), Piero della Francesca (*Belly of an Architect*), and Frans Hals (*The Cook, the Thief, His Wife and Her Lover*).
7. See Peter Wollen, "The Last New Wave" in Lester Friedman (ed.), *Fires Were Started* (Minneapolis: Minnesota University Press), p. 46.
8. Quoted by Wollen, in Friedman, loc. cit., p. 45.
9. It is interesting to note that for both Greenaway and Derek Jarman – in most other respects, diametrical opposites – Shakespeare's *The Tempest* proved a crucial text/test of Englishness.
10. Wollen among others has argued that Greenaway fits this (1960s, painter-poet-filmmaker) avant-garde model perfectly: "At heart, Greenaway, like Kitaj is a collagist, juxtaposing images drawn from some fantastic archive, tracing erudite coincidental narratives within his material, bringing together Balthus and Borges." Peter Wollen, in Friedman, loc. cit., p. 44.
11. David Hockney, *Secret Knowledge* (London: Phaidon, 2000).
12. See, for instance Stephen Bann's remarks on Richard Long in 'Introduction', *Edge of Town* (Exhibition Catalogue, Hartford Art School, 1995).
13. *The Stairs*, p. 26.

14. Ibid., p. 22.
15. Greenaway himself refers to Borges' famous Chinese encyclopedia quoted by Michel Foucault in *The Order of Things*. Greenaway, Prospectus for "In the Dark."
16. "Although a list of archetypes might be conceived in a larger number... 100 of them have been chosen for consideration, to be recreated by actors... with all their relevant attributes, props and gestures, in showcases, vitrines and small theatres... The purpose is not only to celebrate the disciplined richness of this consensus collection, but to make connections and associations between the various ways the different media have established these hundred characters, and the limitations that might have ensued in the visual language necessary to identify and exploit them." Greenaway, Prospectus for "In the Dark."
17. *The Stairs*, p. 25.
18. See P. Adam Sitney, *The Film Culture Reader* (New York: Praeger, 1970), David Curtis, *Experimental Cinema* (New York: Dell Publishing, 1971), Standish Lawder, *The Cubist Cinema* (New York: New York University Press, 1975), or Peter Gidal, ed., *Structural Film Anthology* (London: BFI, 1976).
19. *The Stairs*, p. 26.
20. Ibid, p. 19.
21. Ibid.
22. "Just as footlights and scenery in the theatre serve to mark the contrast between it and the real world so, by its surrounding frame, a painting is separated off not only from reality as such but, even more so, from the reality of what is represented in it... This explains the baroque complexity of the traditional frame whose job it is to establish something that cannot be geometrically established – namely the discontinuity between the painting and the wall, that is to say between the painting and reality." André Bazin, *What is Cinema*, p. 165.
23. *What is Cinema*, p. 168.
24. The battle over verticality and horizontality of the picture plane in American modernism has recently been described by Rosalind Krauss (*The Optical Unconscious* (Cambridge, Mass. MIT Press, 1993), by arguing that Andy Warhol mimetically moved Jackson Pollock's drip paintings picture plane (produced on the ground but crucially designed to be vertical, upright, eye-level), to the horizontal plane, putting canvases flat on the ground, to be stepped on, dripped on, pissed on...
25. Quoted in James Naremore, *The Films of Vincente Minnelli*, Cambridge: Cambridge University Press, 1993, p. 1.
26. See, for instance, *The Ingenious Soubrette* (Pathé, 1902), featured in Noel Burch's *Correction Please*, the story of a maid miraculously hanging pictures by defying gravity and walking up the wall. The effect, of course, turns on an imperceptible switch of the plane of vision, casting radical doubt on the viewer's habitual verticality.
27. Kraklite throws himself off the Victor Emmanuel Monument in Rome. Bouillée, according to Greenaway, was "an architect on paper only, but of monuments of impossible scale..." (*The Stairs*, p. 12).
28. This makes the case of the British ex-ad directors in Hollywood so intriguing, as intriguing as the brief love affair between America (Coppola) and the New German Cinema – Herzog, Syberberg, Wenders, and Fassbinder.
29. *The Stairs*, p. 23.
30. Ibid., p. 32.

The Body as Perceptual Surface

The Films of Johan van der Keuken

Introduction

Of Dutch filmmakers whose works I have some acquaintance with, none has left me with more suspended emotions and unresolved moral chords than Johan van der Keuken. This has an autobiographical origin: Van der Keuken was the first director I met in person when I moved to the Netherlands from London in 1991. It was an instructive meeting, leaving me with the feeling that it would be good, one day, to reply to the questions that stayed unspoken in the air. This encounter or perhaps I should say, this near-miss collision with Van der Keuken happened in 1993. We had just moved into a new house by one of the canals, when the Canadian scholar Ron Burnett came to visit, while attending IDFA, the International Documentary Festival in Amsterdam. Burnett was also a friend of Van der Keuken, having published one of the first essay-interviews in English on the director back in 1978.[1]

What could be more natural than to get us together, and so we invited Johan and his wife Nosh for drinks in our garden and they came. Johan looked around the house, and then asked what I was doing in Amsterdam. When I told him that I was trying to set up Film Studies at the University of Amsterdam, he shot back: "And what do you know about Dutch cinema?" Somewhat taken aback but deciding to be honest, I replied: "Not as much as I would like to." When I added that the University had hired me, rather than a Dutch national, because they wanted the program to have an international dimension, I realized too late that this was not a very diplomatic remark. Johan quizzed me some more about which film of his I liked best, and how much money I was making in this job. Ron tried to intercede, explaining that I was a writer of some standing in the international community, but Van der Keuken became visibly upset. He soon insisted on going, taking his wife with him, and leaving Ron no other option but to join them.

A Life and a Work

Johan van der Keuken was born in Amsterdam on April 4, 1938. His grand-father introduced him to photography when he was twelve, and in 1955, he published his first photo book, *We Are Seventeen* (years old). The book consisted of a series of portraits of his friends at school, and although Van der Keuken

himself thought of it as a sober record in the classic Dutch tradition, it was hailed as the manifesto of a new era, as well as chided for the somber and cheerless image it managed to give of Dutch adolescence. With hindsight one can see how it was part of the world-wide genera-tional revolt we associate in other countries, such as Brit-ain, with The Angry Young Men, in Germany with the *Halbstarken*, in France with the *Nouvelle Vague*, and in the United States with Marlon Brando, James Dean and Elvis Presley. In the Netherlands, the angry young men of the arts called themselves the *Vijftigers* – the Fifties. Van der Keuken became one of their prominent mem-bers, along with the writer Bert Schierbeek, the poet and painter Lucebert, and the Rimbaldesque poet-rebel Re-mco Campert. All of them at one point or another worked with Van der Keuken or had films dedicated to them, for instance, Bert Schierbeek (THE DOOR, 1973) and three films with and about Lucebert (LUCE-BERT, POET-PAINTER (1962, short), A FILM FOR LUCEBERT (1967, short), LUCE-BERT, TIME AND FAREWELL (1994, short), after his friend's death.

JOHAN VAN DER KEUKEN

After *We Are Seventeen*, and still hesitating between photography and film, Van der Keuken won a grant to study at the Institut des Hautes Études Cinéma-tographiques (IDHEC) in Paris, the Mecca of many a budding cinéaste not only in the late 1950s. Although he later confessed that he found the atmosphere stultifying, he must have been there during the same period as future directors such as Volker Schloendorff, Costa Gavra, and Theo Angelopoulos. Feeling like an outsider, he continued with his photography, emulating the tradition of Brassai, André Kertesz and Cartier-Bresson, and eventually publishing a book of photographs entitled *Paris Mortel* (1963). By that time, however, Van der Keuken had befriended two Americans, James Blue and Derry Hall, also at ID-HEC, and together they made PARIS À L'AUBE (1960), a short film about Paris in the early morning, at once in the tradition of Marcel Carné's PARIS QUI DORT (1925) and reminiscent of the Joris Ivens' Paris film (LA SEINE A RENCONTRÉ PARIS, 1957), and certainly very much in tune with the first films of the *Nouvelle*

Vague, if we think of the early work by Godard, Truffaut or Rivette's PARIS NOUS APPARTIENT – all films that have Paris as their chief protagonist.

Returning to the Netherlands in 1960, he made a series of portrait films, with a preference for exceptional children, exceptional sometimes for the way they coped with physical handicaps (BLIND CHILD,1964; BEPPIE 1965; HERMAN SLOBBE, BLIND CHILD 2, 1966). He continued with his portraits of artists, paint- ers (A FILM FOR LUCEBERT) and musicians (BIG BEN WEBSTER, 1967), for which he received international acclaim, though again, less so at home. For instance, a number of commissioned films involved him in controversy, notably THE SPIRIT OF THE TIME (DE TIJD GEEST 1968) and VELOCITY 40-70 (1970). BEAUTY (1970), a film of high artifice verging on camp, but strangely powerful and in its stylized violence utterly compelling today, was particularly misunderstood.

As with so many other European filmmakers, the late 1960s inaugurated also a new period for Van der Keuken, producing often very oblique, but also quite angry and aggressive films, in which a general anti-Establishment stance had to signify political engagement. Sensing the dead-end of such polemics, and also the narrowness of the political discourse in the Netherlands, Van der Keuken undertook a remarkable series of projects, beginning with DAGBOEK (DIARY, 1972), followed by THE WHITE CASTLE (1973) and THE NEW ICE AGE (1974) – films later shown together as a trilogy under the title NORTH-SOUTH. The period ended with A FILMMAKER'S HOLIDAY (1974) and THE PALESTINIANS (1975), a short film made in Lebanon, on the eve of the outbreak of civil war, about Pales- tinian refugees. An openly partisan film, commissioned by the Dutch Commit- tee for the Recognition of Palestine, the film is perhaps the closest Van der Keuken came to making a *cinema verité* or *direct cinema* documentary. But it was also so openly pro-Palestinian that it lost him many friends, especially among the left-wing Jewish-Dutch filmmaking community.

In 1978, the director returned to a subject closer to home, focusing on what one might call the micro-politics of the Netherlands as both very local and yet tied into the global economy. The film is called THE FLAT JUNGLE (DE PLATTE JUNGLE, 1978), and is about the coastal region, the Waddenzee and its inhabi- tants, former fishermen who now make a living digging up worms on the sea- shore at ebb tide, picking and packaging them for sports fishers all over the world. THE FLAT JUNGLE introduces a new Van der Keuken, at once lyrical and sharply analytical, with an eye that takes in the colorful plastic bottles that pol- lute the countryside at the same time as it documents the myriad manifestations of coastal micro-life, each leaving its transitory trace between land and water. Aware of the fragile nature of the ecosystem, while paying homage to the taci- turn stoicism of the locals, in the tradition of John Grierson or Robert Flaherty's MAN OF ARAN, the film is a masterpiece, awaiting to be rediscovered in the age of globalization and ecological sensibilities. THE FLAT JUNGLE led to recognition by the French cinephile community, with an article by Serge Daney in *Cahiers du cinéma* consolidating his fame in France. It paved the way for his international reputation, with Ron Burnett's article from the same year the first sign of his new pre-eminence.

In 1985, Van der Keuken became seriously ill, but recovered from what was diagnosed as intestinal cancer. Experiencing this recovery as a special gift, freeing him from the need to either explain the world or change it, he undertook another remarkable series of projects that took him to India, Thailand, Tibet, Central Africa and Latin America. In Hong Kong he made I Love $ (1986), catching the city in a feverish phase of transition. But as with other directors before him (one thinks of Renoir, Rossellini and Louis Malle, for instance) it was India that helped resolve a crisis and stabilized his own identity in transition. For Van der Keuken, Madras in particular was the catalyst, giving him a vision of human life, where opposites not only coexisted, but where the contradictions actually gave access to a deeper understanding of what it is we are meant to do, to see and to bear witness to, during our brief stay on earth. The Eye Above the Well (1988) was the first result of this wisdom, which discovered a new value in the weight, as well as gravity of tradition, religion and ritual. As he himself acknowledged: "To show that this tradition is not part of a perfect world, I included a sequence in which everything falls into chaos; you see crumbled steps and crippled people. [But] I found a way of editing to show both. That was new to me. It released me from the guilty look."[2]

There followed three films – Face Value (1991), Brass Unbound (1993) and Amsterdam Global Village (1996) – which confirmed that Van der Keuken had indeed discovered a way of finding the world in a face, a posture, a phrase like *Bewogen Koper* (brass in motion), the original title of Brass Unbound. The faces might betoken lost worlds, as in Face Value's little girl, made up in the costume of the Dutch Golden Age, or in the bridal photo, taken in Rochlitz, 14 April 1990, a small town in what then was still the German Democratic Republic, only months before unification. Or the worlds he documented might be becoming-worlds. These becoming-worlds, Van der Keuken found above all in Amsterdam, turning his attention to his hometown, in a gesture at once generous and proud, all-embracing and meticulously particular. Amsterdam Global Village is a tribute as well as a triumph, a film that finally reconciles one of the city's most famous sons to the fact that the city remained, for much of his life all but indifferent to his existence in its midst. A young Moroccan courier speeds on his motorbike through Amsterdam, delivering photos to clients all over town, linking different lives that Van der Keuken follows into their living rooms, their work spaces and coffee shop hang-outs, but also into their past lives and faraway places of birth or homelands. A Chechan businessman takes us to bombed-out Grosny, his mother and a 110-year-old relative. A Bolivian musician, now working as a cleaner, returns to his village in the Andes. We meet a female DJ, a fashion photographer, a Thai kickboxer and his family, and a Dutch Jew revisits the house where she lived before her husband was deported to the transit camp Westerbork, as well as the family where her five-year-old son survived, while she went into hiding. Van der Keuken has spoken of how the circular form of the Amsterdam canals (the *Grachtengordel*) had inspired the structure of AMSTERDAM GLOBAL VILLAGE. But I am also reminded of Gilles Deleuze's description of Amsterdam as a rhizomatic city,[3] in which the spirit of Leibnitz had become architectural form.

In 1998, Van der Keuken was once more diag-nosed with cancer. This time, he decided to make it known, and to undertake a journey with uncertain outcome. The result was his last completed film, THE LONG VACATION. Together with his wife Nosh, who had done the sound on his films for the past twenty years, he filmed while he traveled and traveled while he filmed, returning to Africa, Asia, and other places that had given him images which became his, just as he had given them a place in the memory of the world. THE LONG VACATION was the highlight of IDFA 2000, where he was indeed celebrated and feted like the prodigal son, finally come home.

THE LONG HOLIDAY

Photographer, Filmmaker, Artist, Auteur?

So what kind of film director was Van der Keuken? Although it may seem as if the still photographer and the filmmaker were forever competing with each other, he knew how to catch the instant (the gift of the photographer), while making us feel how this instant belonged in a continuum, a movement, a process. Consider a still that he took on holiday in Spain (Sierra Terade, Andalusia 2000), and which he captioned for his monthly picture column (*From the Life of a Small Self-Employed*), a task he fulfilled for nearly thirty years for the film magazine *Skrien*. It shows a bend in the road, cut into rocks and is taken from the slope of a mountain. The caption reads: "The spirit of Hitchcock has just passed and disappeared around the corner. But in his absence he still commands the scene." Homage to a master of montage from another master of montage, Van der Keuken sees a view and sees the movement in it, he sees a view and sees the fiction in it.

It was perhaps this permanent and fruitful tension between filmmaker and still photographer, which predisposed him to all manner of other productive interferences, not just as here, blurring the distinctions between documentary and fiction, the holiday snap and the *objet trouvé*. It also allowed him to transcend genres and styles, giving him scope to mingle the sensory registers, as well as the different aggregate states of the moving image, alternating quite consciously between static viewer/moving image, still image/ mobile viewer (museum), moving image/ mobile viewer (installation) as well as all other possible permutations. It is thus not surprising that he himself, while never experiencing the photographer and the filmmaker in conflict with each other, did finally regard the big installation work he undertook in the late 1990s – THE BODY AND THE CITY (1997-2001) as a form of reconciliation and higher synthesis. Like any true auteur, his work coheres around a few consistent themes. Besides the tension between still and moving image, and possibly quite closely connected with it, there is his the abiding fascination with the human face, from *We Are Seventeen*, his photo-portrait book from 1955, via the Lucebert films all the way to FACE VALUE and THE LONG VACATION (2000).

A third recurring strand, vibrating with tension and conflict is the one he himself named, when he called his installation work THE BODY AND THE CITY. The city is a central reference point – starting with his first short film in and about Paris, his photo book *Paris Mortel*, and then his films and photographs about global cities, including New York and La Paz, returning him eventually to Amsterdam, but its relation to the body remains troubling: a disconcerting clash of flesh and stone, on might say, to paraphrase Richard Sennett's title.

The Documentary Tradition

On the face of it, then, Van der Keuken is a very Dutch filmmaker, especially considering that one of the strengths of Dutch filmmaking has always been in the field of documentaries. Van der Keuken had no difficulties in seeing himself in the tradition of Joris Ivens: "We met in Paris in 1968. With immense generosity he was willing to watch my films with me. It was the first time I was able to show my work to someone with international standing, who carries with him the myth of a "world filmmaker," a status I still find irresistible. In a period of intense searching for a new link between aesthetics and politics, he seemed to recognize what I was trying to do, and in a completely unpretentious way gave me advice, in a way no-one in the Netherlands would have been able to. Although I realize that I never made an "Ivens film", his way of thinking about the position and stance of the filmmaker had an enormous influence upon me. Ivens was to have this place in my life for nearly twenty years."[4]

There is a certain poetic justice – frequently commented upon and perhaps for that reason also a little too neat and orderly – in the fact that Van der Keuken received the final accolade in his own country in the form of the Bert Haanstra oeuvre prize, and this at a festival whose main prize is called the Joris Ivens Award. Haanstra, one may recall, was the outstanding Dutch documentary director of the so-called "second generation" (Ivens being the first). The award, in fact, made Van der Keuken enter the generational paradigm, effectively anointing him as the official heir to a noble lineage, and this two months before his death!

Three generations, thus, reconciled and reunited at last in the work of Van der Keuken, who seems to have struck a perfect balance between the politically very exposed (and some would say, dangerously extreme) Joris Ivens (later, Van der Keuken himself made some critical remarks on that score), and the much more humorous, sardonic, and even facetiously playful Bert Haanstra, who with FANFARE and ZOO made two of the best-loved (that is, by the Dutch themselves) films about the Dutch, their foibles, their peculiar sense of humor, but also their Calvinist self-restraint and self-censored affective lives. Haanstra celebrates the ridiculous moments in life, observing ordinary people, picking their noses or just loitering. In ZOO, for instance, he draws scurrilous comparisons between the humans who visit zoos and the animals they stare at, showing the humans through bars and behind fences, and thereby the animals to be so much more human. Haanstra's films hold up a mirror to the Dutch – even if it is a bit of a fairground distorting mirror, but with whose reflection they can live. This in contrast to Ivens, whom for most of his life the authorities rejected totally, to the point of temporarily depriving him of his passport and citizenship, and also in contrast to Van der Keuken, to whom as we saw, recognition and respect came late, and in whose work, as far as one can judge, the Dutch do not recognize themselves. Nor would, I think, Van der Keuken want them to.

However, this idea of generational succession is a very ethnocentric, perhaps even parochial way of looking at Van der Keuken, too reminiscent of the Dutch House of Orange (not unlike the British house of Windsor) worrying about when the reigning monarch might abdicate and pass the throne to the heir apparent. It also fits Van der Keuken too neatly into the boxes and drawers that open up when one pronounces the word "documentary," a designation that Van der Keuken detested. Not only was he, as we saw, keen to maintain his double vocation of photographer and filmmaker, to which one might add the poet-essayist and pen-and-ink draftsman, but he also found it most tedious to get involved in the debates over the different kinds of documentary: the French *ciné verité* school (Jean Rouch) versus the American direct cinema (Pennebaker,

Leacock or Fred Wiseman), the politically committed filmmaker (where, as he often complained, ugliness and shoddy work had to guarantee hard-line political correctness) versus the film essayist (Godard, Chris Marker, Harun Farocki, Straub-Huillet). In fact, there are at least four reasons why any of these classifications would leave Van der Keuken and his work short-changed and wrong-footed:

- His close involvement with poets, painters and musicians, as well as his own artistic personality as a multi-talent made him first and foremost an artist. So much so, that the distinction between documentary and fiction made no sense to him, because, as he argued: what is central, as with the painter, is the "image" (which, of course, for him included sound, words and movement).

- If anything, the path to approaching his filmic form would be that of a piece of music. As one critic said: Van der Keuken's films are like classical music – one has to see them many times in order to take it all in, it offers something new with each viewing.[5] Similar remarks can be found throughout his life, and while Van der Keuken might balk at the suggestion that it is classical music that most inspired him – he was forced to learn the cello as a boy and resented it – the free improvisation of jazz, as well as contemporary orchestral and symphonic music attracted him and led to fruitful collaboration with many musicians and composers, from the "serious" concert music of Louis Andriessen (also a collaborator of Peter Greenaway), to the free jazz and even folk-inspired music written and performed for him by Willem Breuker for so many of his major films.

- His politics were very different from both the Dutch documentary tradition, and from what one might call the Dutch mainstream dissident tradition, while nonetheless having, of course, contacts and connections. His film DE TIJD GEEST (THE SPIRIT OF THE TIMES, 1968) casts an acerbic look on the Dutch establishment as well as on the protest movements, and was hated by both sides. DE WEG NAAR HET ZUIDEN (The Way South, 1980) begins with the violent squatters' protests at the 1980 Royal Wedding in Amsterdam, but soon leaves the Netherlands behind, both geographically and metaphorically. It seemed to him that the Dutch political gestures of dissent often amount to little more than "*ik ben boos*"("I am angry"), obliging him to take on a scope that even in the European context was, if not unique then nonetheless exceptional: that of the North-South Divide, at a time when the East-West Cold War divide was still the determining factor of European politics.

- Secondly, his ethnographic interests, which he may have taken from the French *cinéma vérité* school, was "politicized" by his sharp eye for contradiction, an eye he learnt to trust more and more, until as he put it, he had overcome the "guilty look" with which the Western, European gaze falls upon the poverty, misery, suffering and injustice that stares at us everywhere in the world, once we leave our secure boundaries and habitual tourist comfort zones.

– Finally, and this would be my strongest argument for placing him in the Dutch context by radically re-situating him, I think there is a "way of seeing" in Van der Keuken's work that deserves special attention and patience, and which I have called, provisionally: "the body as perceptual surface."

Dutch Ways of Seeing: The Art Historical Tradition

What would it mean to speak of typically Dutch ways of seeing, within which Van der Keuken could be placed and *dis*-placed at the same time? For such a scheme, one has to step outside the bounds of cinema and resort to analogies and examples from painting, even at the risk of establishing a very rough-and-ready, indeed cliché form of categorization.

There is, first of all, the tradition of the rebus picture in Dutch art, the illustration of proverbs and figures of speech, as in Hieronymus Bosch or Breughel the Younger, and which comes into the Dutch Golden Age with some of the more enigmatic, allegorical or duplicitous genre pieces, still lives and interiors, as we know them from Pieter de Hooch, Gabriel Metsu or Jan Steen. Svetlana Alpers has developed a whole theory of art history around what she perceived as the crucial difference between the Northern Renaissance and its image tradition, and the various Italian schools.[6] Clearly, it is not my place here to enter into the debates that her theories raised. But there is a more light-hearted look at this tradition, through Sister Wendy, an eccentric English nun from Norfolk, the eastern province of England. In the 1980s, Sister Wendy was a popular figure on British television, because of her infectious enthusiasm in matters art and art history, treating the viewers in one particular episode to a GRAND TOUR OF THE RIJKSMUSEUM: there, she stopped to explain ter Borch's famous *Paternal Admonition*. For several centuries it was taken for a scene where a father admonishes his daughter to be more modest in her clothing and demeanor, but now the painting is generally recognized to depict a brothel scene with money changing hands, and a madam taking her cut. Such sly reversals, or rather, such an ability to balance a representation on the cusp of meanings that flatly contradict each other is something we can also find in Van der Keuken, in his group portraits and figure compositions.

Then, there is the gaze of Rembrandt, not only the one of the Rembrandt lighting, so influential on Hollywood in the 1920s and so-called German Expressionist cinema, but the rather colder, more clinical and therefore often almost unbearably intense gaze of the *Anatomy Lesson of Dr Tulp* or *Dr Deyman*. I want to argue that some of the most shocking and most bodily absorbing images in Van der Keuken have this quality of a steadfast, unflinching gaze at something that is almost too cruel in its stark confrontation with ultimate and unbearable truths about the human condition, such as the scenes of the Grosny dead in Amsterdam Global Village.

Thirdly, there is the tension between the gaze of a van Gogh, with its swirling vortices or vertigo-inducing energies of colour, light and line, as in *Starry Night*, contrasted with the quite different lines and grids of a Piet Mondrian. Van Gogh's way of seeing returns in Van der Keuken in the form of repeated meditations on the effects and reflections of light on water. As Van der Keuken tells it, the idea for Amsterdam Global Village originally came to him by looking out of his window onto the canal, and seeing the morning light creep over the water towards a blue houseboat, as one finds them moored in several of Amsterdam's main canals. The Mondriaan references are a little more oblique, but I sense a deliberate and sarcastic pastiche of Mondriaan's grids in the final scene of Van der Keuken's film about a journey to Russia, Animal Locomotion (1973), showing the now-desolate blocks of a suburban housing estate, still bearing traces of the once pastel-colored windows arranged in constructivist surfaces and squares.

And finally, returning more directly to the cinema and the eye of the camera, there is the very Dutch way of using windows in their domestic and urban environment. I am referring to the ostentatiously reticent display of virtue and property, going back to the window tax in the 17th and 18th century that Simon Schama, in his famous book on the Dutch Golden Age, *The Embarrassment of Riches* had already made so much of. To this day, it gives one that very schizophrenic experience in Amsterdam, between the large domestic widows overlooking the canals, neither veiled nor graced by curtains, located right next to the almost uniquely Dutch or Flemish feature of prostitutes displaying their bodies in glass cases, at street level and theatrically lit by gaudy neon strips, a merchandise-metaphor once deftly deconstructed by performance artist Marina Abramovic in the 1970s. From these contradictory signals of "look, I have nothing to hide" and the quite open invitation to the seemingly most depraved and shameless forms of sexual voyeurism, the Dutch cinema has distilled its own kind of visual humor, nowhere more in evidence than in the work of fellow filmmakers and men of the theatre Alex van Warmerdam's Abel, Frans Weisz or Gert-Jan Reijnders' Oude Tongen (1994).

My argument would be that we can also find echoes and evidence of all these ways of seeing in the work of Van der Keuken, though often in a transmuted form, be it by a reworking of the very terms of reference, as in the rebus pictures we get in A Film for Lucebert or in the very direct citation of the woman in the window in AMSTERDAM GLOBAL VILLAGE. But even more starkly present are Dutch ways of seeing the human face, as already mentioned, in Van der Keuken's take on the tradition of the portrait. The un-veiled, naked gaze emanating from a face, in the last decade such a powerful trope in contemporary photo-graphy from Thomas Ruff, Nan Golding to Rineke Dijk-stra, runs right through the work of Van der Keuken, but it brings us also back to the frank and yet so disturbing gaze with which the subjects of classical Dutch painting so often return our look. There, the self-confidence of having nothing to hide implies a provocation that is little short of intensely physical and even erotic, as many an admirer of Vermeer's *Girl with the Pearl Earring* has noted, now made perhaps over explicit by a novel of that title, subsequently turned into a film. Controver-sially, Van der Keuken in his later photographic works, especially as incorporated in his installation *The Body and the City*, dwelled on the female nude in ways that have not always been appre-ciated in the context of his abiding interest in the human face and the provoca-tive eye.

LUCEBERT

The Body as Perceptual Surface

I could go on, by introducing yet another argument, this time borrowed from David Hockney and his re-discovered passion for the Delft, Ghent, and Bruges schools of painting, over those of Florence, Venice and Rome, around the ques-tion of the *central perspective*, and its Northern variants. I would have cited Van der Keuken's repeated forays, notably in his photo-essays for *Skrien*, into ques-tions of perspective and point of view, where he thought aloud about his own poetics, especially his use of montage principles, or the purpose of the frame, to come to grips with the problem of multiple vantage points inscribed in the same image or sequence, and the increasing obsession with how to account for the power of that slightly anamorphic, off-center or out of focus vanishing point he discovered in his own pictures and those of others. Particularly instructive in this respect are his photo essay *Women and Children in Madras* (April/May 1988), and a text he wrote for a photo book by Eddy Posthuma de Boer, entitled *The Peruvian Woman* (1996).

But instead of exploring this tradition further, I want to try and center – and re-center – Van der Keuken, by introducing my title, and what I provisionally call "the body as perceptual surface." I am referring by this, first of all, to a powerful sense that in the past twenty years the cinema of whatever provenance – mainstream, avant-garde or art house, as well as the art world that has finally found in the moving image one of its main resources for renewal and self-reflection – has made a pre-occupation with the body its central concern. From action spectaculars with Bruce Willis or Sylvester Stallone, to sexually explicit, semi-pornographic thrillers by Paul Verhoeven, Catherine Breillat, by Brian de Palma or Jane Campion; from the body art of a Stel-Arc and Marina Abramovich to high-street tattoo parlors and body piercing; from slasher exploitation films by Tobe Hooper or Wes Craven, to video art by Bill Viola and Gary Hill; from the films of David Fincher to the diasporic videos of Mona Hatoum, it seems that visual culture in the Western world has put aside the metaphors of window and mirror, of door and vista, of frame and screen that have dominated high art for four hundred years and the cinema for its first eighty to hundred years. They seem to have been smashed or have melted away in favor of making skin, flesh and the body in the first instance the *materia prima* of their art, and in the second instance, turn them into so many surfaces upon which to project. Project images, project aggression, fantasies, desires, project violent thoughts and desperate acts, embody and body forth anxieties of the dying and wasting body in films concerned with AIDS, to perhaps equally anxious but pathological fantasies of the indestructible body in combat films and computer games.

I am sketching this obsession with the body in deliberately broad brushes and perhaps even garish outlines, just so as to have a quick change of scenery also for the work of Van der Keuken, by shifting the backdrop from the previously painted canvas of (Dutch) documentary, framed by (Dutch) art history, towards one where the differences between background and foreground, high art and street culture, frame and horizon can hardly be assumed to be present at all. What in other words, would Van der Keuken's work look like when seen against this "ground" of the body in all its states and stages? What space might it occupy, what energies might it put in circulation?

My point of reference would be the article by Serge Daney in *Cahiers du cinéma* 290/291 from July/August 1978[7] that I already mentioned, which introduced Van der Keuken to the Paris cinephiles, and helped him to international recognition. In an essay entitled "The cruel radiation of that which is"[8] Daney zeroed in very quickly on what he thought made Van der Keuken so remarkable: for instance, he noted that there were in his films many protagonists that were either children or people with handicaps, as in BLIND CHILD I, HERMAN SLOBBE and BEPPIE. In THE NEW ICE AGE (about a family of workers in an ice-making factory in Northern Holland) an almost surrealist dimension is added by the fact that several of the family are deaf, which Van der Keuken initially

chanced upon, almost by accident, but which comes to determine the means and manner of communication finally
structuring the film as a whole. Then there are others, such
as the farm workers and fishermen in THE FLAT JUNGLE
whose "handicap" is more subtle, and often merely the reverse side of their special gift. Their marginal position in relation to the ordinary world means that they have a much
more penetrating and thereby also defamiliarizing perception of what passes as "normal." Hence the recourse in Van
der Keuken's films to blindness, deafness, and blocked
senses, because they work as magnifying glasses on the broken, blocked and fragmented relation we all have to so-
called reality, except that we rarely allow ourselves such an
admission, preferring to pretend that we know what is
what, and are in control of the bigger picture.

THE FLAT JUNGLE

I want to concentrate on this insight of Daney's and maybe expand it a little
further, by suggesting that the presence of protagonists with handicaps, and the
observation by the camera of how they cope with their environment, immediately changes the viewer's center of gravity, as well as his or her perceptual
focus. What is at work in Van der Keuken's films, I would argue, are two fundamental principles: one is what Van der Keuken himself calls "asymmetry," that
sense of imbalance, of uneven exchange, contradiction even and injustice, which
any long, hard look at human affairs reveals. But asymmetry also of forces,
power and the latent potential for conflict, that is necessary for any work of art
or of the imagination, any narrative or fiction to
emerge, to come to life and engage the intellect,
the emotions and the senses. The second principle which I detect in his films, is, if you like, the
happier, more serene stance vis-à-vis this same
asymmetry: the always present possibility of a
compensatory principle, in which the loss or
impairment of one sense-organ or faculty of
perception, is compensated by the more ecstatic
and exalted acuity of another: the blind having
a special sensory capacity for hearing, the deaf
or mute developing a hyper-active, richly varie-

BLIND CHILD

gated sense of touch, those with a speech impediment becoming endowed special flashes of insight or possessing a particularly attentive sense of spatial relations and human dynamics.

The two principles, in their counter-current and ambivalences are already
fully present in Van der Keuken's first films, BLIND CHILD and HERMAN SLOBBE

(BLIND CHILD II) from 1964 and 1966 respectively. For BLIND CHILD, Van der Keuken spent two months in a special home for blind children, observing a world difficult to visualize: how young human beings, deprived of sight, struggle to stay in touch with reality. Whereas the first film trains a very lucid eye on the pain and anger that sensory deprivation imposes on these children kept in an institution, however well-tended and well-intentioned, while also showing their ability to create worlds as rich as anything accessible to a sighted child, the second film, taking one of the most rebellious and recalcitrant boys from the first film, is an astonishing celebration of the human spirit in adversity. We see how the lust for life makes Herman Slobbe burst out of any kind of restraint, and fashion a universe, triumphantly asserting not only his right to be, but his unique contribution to the world as *we* know it, sense it and see it. No wonder that van der Keuken signs off at the end of the film by addressing us and his protagonist: "everything in a film is a form. Herman is a form. Farewell, dear form."

A similar principle organizes the films around Lucebert, the painter-poet, here portraying man of extraordinary talents, but in a sense also asymmetrical, excessive, unbalanced if you will: forcing our perception of shape, color, form – especially with regards to the human form and face – into regions of mental extremity and risk, from which the artist brings back a sense of vibrancy, immediacy and lightness that spares us the human cost such piercing perception undoubtedly and invariably entails.

A no less-powerful, but in its power also problematic, asymmetry obtains around the body, skin and sound. From the bigness of Big Ben Webster, whose tenor saxophone converts his bodily bulk into matter as light as a feather, and whose glistening black skin is lit as if to reflect back and make resonate the vibrato of his instrument, to the tuba players in BEWOGEN KOPER whose bronze skin folds are like the sound pockets reverberating with their tuba's lower registers, Van der Keuken managed to find images that are sounds, or rather, he understood how to orchestrate a soundscape with images, making them the tactile, visible equivalent of its sonorous envelope. As he explained in an interview: "I've often drawn the comparison with playing the saxophone, or the trombone when it comes to zoom shots. For me, the camera has three features: the musical instrument aspect, in which you play your part, improvise, when you're directly implicated; the second is boxing, with the camera's striking power; and the caress, because the slight movements that graze the skin of beings and things interest me a lot."[9]

Evidently, Van der Keuken is not the only filmmaker in recent decades who has practiced what one might call *an aesthetics of sensory asymmetry*. Jane Campion's THE PIANO has a mute heroine, and the film gorges itself on a palette of tactile sensations. Krzysztof Kieslowski, in THREE COLOURS: BLUE makes the heroine's skin her most sensitive, vulnerable and perceptive sense organ. Lars von Trier built all of his most powerful films – from Europa (language), Breaking the Waves (hearing voices) to Dancer in the Dark (blindness), Idiots (mental infirmity) and Dogville (invisible walls) around protagonists with handicaps or sensory dislocation. And before him, Jean Luc Godard, in Passion had one of his characters, played by Isabelle Huppert, suffer from a recurrent stammer, for which she is blessed or cursed with an intensely tactile response to her human surroundings and the natural environment.

What comes to mind in these, and many similar instances in modern cinema is a literary trope, more than a hundred years old: Arthur Rimbaud's "de-reglement de tous les sens," as he wrote in the famous *Lettre du Voyant* to his friend Paul Demeny in 1871.[10] Again, we could invoke a whole romantic and postromantic genealogy of synaesthesia, going back to the Ancients, revived by Keats or Novalis, and after him by Baudelaire, Rimbaud and the surrealists. There, the synaesthetic effect is similarly produced not by a concert of the sense perception, but various verbal and *ekphrastic* techniques of clashes and blockages that rub the sensory associations of words against each other, rather than attempting to harmonize them. It was these sensory discords that surrealism enriched or aggravated with further semantic and visual clashes between tenor and vehicle, squeezing heightened perception out of cognitive dissonance as much as sensory derangement.

Yet to see Van der Keuken's film-aesthetic derangement of the senses in this particular tradition of synaesthesia would cut it off from other sources of both inspiration and of influence. As already indicated, I think a major impulse in Van der Keuken is to find ways for the eye of vision to displace itself, look, as it were, behind its own back, from other vantage points, a reference itself to the body in different mappings, and for the body to develop a third eye. I already mentioned the possible function of the nude in Van der Keuken, notably in the sketch called "Cyclops," made in the 1970s, but published by him in his column in *Skrien*, with its art historical references to Courbet's *L'Origine du Monde* as well as Picasso, but also to the raunchier kind of lavatory graffiti.

First of all, the displacement of the eye, be it in its ability to assume vantage points that fall outside or circumnavigate the central perspective of Western painting, or in the direction of the parodic, prosthetic and pornographic proliferations of eyes across the body, its orifices and apertures, is only one aspect of the matter. That a demotion of the eye is under way in our culture is hardly in doubt, and one can ask oneself whether the rule – or some would argue – the tyranny of the eye, has now, three-and-a-half centuries after Descartes, come to an end. Martin Jay, in his *Downcast Eyes*, certainly provides some telling evidence that this is indeed the case.[11] Theories why this should be so are not difficult to come by: a pyramid is being overturned, a Panopticon is being stormed, the single eye on the dollar bill must learn to shade its arrogant stare, look inward and reflect, rather than outward and dominate.

Another, more ethnographic or anthropological perspective will tell us that we are only beginning to realize the full implication of the double shift that has taken place during the 20th century in the Western world with respect to the body: whereas the first half of the 20th century has made the hand obsolete in the productive process – replacing manual labor, physical dexterity and the many skills that handmade objects have indexed, archived and stored – the second half of the same century has, more or less in every sphere, made the eye equally redundant. Visions machines and war machines, satellites and computers, tomography and scanners have taken over the "work" of the human eye in anything from medicine to traffic control, from data processing to draughtsmanship. If Walter Benjamin is the eloquent analyst and chronicler of the hand's obsolescence, with his elegy on the gambler's hand throwing the dice to the arsonist striking the match, then we are still awaiting an equally acute analysis of the decline and fall of the eye and its epochal significance. Yet we already have elegies of sorts in and through the cinema, precisely of the kind that Van der Keuken proposes. What may be happening, in other words, is less the deregulation of the senses or the obsolescence of vision, but a new mapping of sensory perception for which the body provides the projecting surface, but surely cannot be the foundational ground. Indeed, it may be the constant demonstration of its unsuitability for such a task that makes it be so prominent in our visual culture.

For in Van der Keuken, the senses are also at war, they are in competition, they fight over territory, autonomy and identity, and they remind us that they have their own origins, their own domain, their local habitat and sphere of reach, and they are not giving way that easily. In particular, the sense of touch has gained a new prominence, as if, in the face of the complete visual over-stimulation that our in practice redundant eye is now the target of, the filmmaker's or visual artist's role has also changed. His is the task to teach the eye new skills, and in particular, to develop the eye into an ear, and extend the ear to become a "hand." It would mean seeing the world around the tactile register and learning to experience the body less as a container, and more as a surface. It would be a surface not bounded by frame and view, and instead a permeable and vulnerable membrane, combining the properties of screen and filter, veil and curtain, as well as the softness of flesh with the hardness of lacquer.

In other words, in Van der Keuken's later films, it is no longer actual physical blindness that brings to the fore the tactile qualities of hand, touch and weight, but rather it is as if the world as a whole had gone blind, having looked into the bright sun of too many images, too much sensory-ocular stimulation. If filmmakers now train the hand – or rather the hand as symbol of the sighted touch

– then it would have to be as a sense organ with an ethical sense, capable of negotiating proximity and distance, developing the intimate touch, but also replacing hierarchy with contiguity and coexistence, making us aware also of what is at stake politically in the new proximity and ethically at what risk (the racist usually hates the other because of the smell of his food or his body-language, i.e., sensory affronts signaling the anxieties of proximity and intimacy with the other). In this respect, touch would indeed be the sense necessary to "grasp" what is meant by the seemingly seamless, imaged surface of our lives and the new politics they demand.

That such concerns preoccupied Van der Keuken in the last years of his life is particularly evident in AMSTERDAM GLOBAL VILLAGE. There, for instance, the motif of the hand and touch – running so strongly through his films, from BLIND KIND to one of his last photo-commentaries – is almost like a structural constant, perhaps as strong a bonding agent in the film as the circular construction of the Amsterdam canals, and the clockwise trajectory of the motor-cycle courier. The Thai kickboxer film shows us how the poor of this world still have to live by hand and fist, the latter particularly paradoxical in the setting of the gentle Thai village where he comes from, just as Van der Keuken dwells at great length on the finger-printing of Asylum seekers as they are processed in transit camps. Or consider the interview with Borz-Ali Ismaïlov, the Chechen businessman. He is introduced with his hand on the steering wheel of his car, a mobile phone in the other, and there is hardly a shot at Borz-Ali's home, where the camera does not concentrate on his hands, as if this was the place where his troubled life-story could come to rest, after the camera has scanned his face for a clue to the sometimes poetic, sometimes enigmatic utterances he makes. Once we are in Grosny, a grieving mother, cradling her dead child, is also first introduced not through her face, but via the hand holding the little corpse, moving to her other hand stroking over its terribly still, eerily serene face, as if the vigor of a working woman's hand might mould the pale body back to life.

Perhaps one needs to think of the revolt against the Eye of Enlightenment as a re-ethnicization of the senses: re-locating, re-localizing their respective territory, negotiating a place in a space as yet to be determined, in which skin, flesh and the body are as much sensory organs as they are support for the senses that refuse to be reigned in under a universal and universalizing authority. In Van der Keuken, there is a non-negotiable boundary, which the contest of the senses has to acknowledge, a price to be paid for making the body the main perceptual surface, that is, the body in the "cruel radiance of its there-ness when all life has left it," when the body has become a corpse.

Or is there a more positive reading? Where body and memory, history and temporality, space and place can surface in a way that illuminates the particular perceptual potency of the body, in all its markings of race, age and gender, but also in its ability to transcend those limits and pass on something else? Just as the senses are in uproar, demanding their separate identity and "embodiment" as a sort of "ethnic" political autonomy (cf. Shakespeare's *Coriolanus*), so in Van der Keuken's films there is a sense of the senses warring with each other over the body, including the a-symmetrical body politic of the North-South divide and of the world's global cities. But conversely, there is in the latter, especially in AMSTERDAM GLOBAL VILLAGE an equally strong feeling that the senses might not only be compensating for each other, but in their diversity developing new forms of interdependence. One takes away from his films the hopeful sign that if the senses no longer fit under the authority of the eye, then the kind of asymmetry that the director speaks about may yet lead to a state where the same space can be occupied by several senses, and deploy their possibly separate but nonetheless coextensive presence. AMSTERDAM GLOBAL VILLAGE has for this a fitting image that can be extended as a parable for the whole, breaking both the rule of the center versus the periphery as well as the global local divide. This is the scene where the Dutch-Jewish Hennie Anke and her son are visiting the house where she lived during the German Occupation with her young son and which is now inhabited by a Surinamese woman with her little boy.

Although the flat has undergone such extensive rebuilding as to have done away with all the physical memories Hennie might have had, the encounter is deeply significant. As Hennie recalls the terrible years and the deportation of her husband, in this space we sense the lingering presence of two generations who have nothing in common either culturally or ethnically, and yet, whose succession and coexistence in memory and spoken record illuminate in a single image Dutch history of the 20th century, from occupation to deportation, from colonialism to post-colonial immigration. Even if the fate of a Dutch-Jewish "onderduiker" (a person in hiding during the Occupation) and of a Dutch-Surinamese immigrant are not strictly comparable, but amount to another asymmetry, the gesture of their farewell embrace shapes a fragile bond across the cultural differences, establishing an image of double occupancy, as well as of life's transience that lends an almost utopian hope to these stories of exile, migration, and necessary homelessness told in AMSTERDAM GLOBAL VILLAGE.

This then, might be the very specifically "European" lesson that Van der Keuken's films can bring us, in the context of our current concerns with multicultural communities, ethnic clashes and "radical" confrontations: we shall all have to learn to take a leaf out of Hennie Anke's and the Surinamese woman's book, learning to make a place both yield and keep its memory while practicing a form of double occupancy.

As a foreigner and an exile living in Amsterdam, and after a less-than-happy meeting with the man in the flesh, I think I have come to appreciate the wisdom of Johan van der Keuken, if not always in his life, then in his films. There, in a very Dutch way, he shows what it means to practice global citizenship, he show us the spaces, physical as well as mental, of the present and of memory, that we as human beings must be able to occupy together. If Europe is to be more than a vain dream or a bureaucratic nightmare, then it will have to become a place where such double occupancy is the norm: a form of citizenship we can all aspire to. It makes Van der Keuken's cinema, that body of perceptual surfaces, hold out the promise of a new political, but also ethical map of Europe, part of the globalized world, rather than its panoptic apex.

(2004)

Notes

1. R. Burnett, "Johan van der Keuken," *Cine-Tracts*, vol. 1, no. 4. 1978, 14-21.
2. Interview with Max Arian, *De Groene Amsterdammer*, 2 February, 2000.
3. Gilles Deleuze, *The Movement Image* (Minneapolis: University of Minnesota Press, 1986).
4. Serge Daney, Jean-Paul Fargier, "Entretien avec Johan van der Keuken," *Cahiers du cinéma* no. 290-291 (July/August 1978), 63-67 (65).
5. Fred Camper, "The Way South", *Chicago Reader*, http://65.201.198.5/movies/capsules/17372_WAY_SOUTH
6. Svetlana Alpers, *The Art of Describing* (Chicago: University of Chicago Press, 1983).
7. Serge Daney, "La radiation cruelle de ce qui est." *Cahiers du cinéma* no. 290-291 (July./August 1978), 68-72.
8. This is a quote borrowed from James Agee and Walker Evans' *Let Us Now Praise Famous Men* (Boston: Houghton Mifflin, 1941).
9. Serge Toubiana, "Le monde au fil de l'eau. Entretien avec Johan van der Keuken." *Cahiers du cinéma* no. 517 (October 1997), 44-55.
10. Arthur Rimbaud, *La lettre du voyant*, (15 May 1871, à A. P. Demeny).
11. Martin Jay, *Downcast Eyes. The Denigration of Vision* (Berkeley: University of California Press, 1993).

Television and the Author's Cinema

ZDF's *Das Kleine Fernsehspiel*

As far as the European cinema goes, the 1970s belonged to Germany, or more exactly, to the "New German Cinema." Breaking through the commercial and critical twilight of the post-war period, a handful of internationally well-exposed star directors – mainly Fassbinder, Herzog, Wenders and Syberberg – briefly illuminated a notoriously bleak filmmaking landscape. Looking back, however, one realizes that this blaze of light left much territory underexposed, not least by obscuring the ground on which some of these talents grew. For besides the New German Cinema of auteurs and festivals, to which we owe THE MARRIAGE OF MARIA BRAUN, AGUIRRE, HITLER – A FILM FROM GERMANY or KINGS OF THE ROAD, there existed another New German Cinema that functioned almost exclusively within West Germany itself, and which, in its own terms, was as successful as its better-known half.

Both New German Cinemas have in common one very material fact: a radical change in the way films were made and financed in West Germany. From the late 1960s onwards, the Bonn government had stepped in with grants and subsidies, distributed by the *"Gremien"* of the Filmförderungsanstalt in Berlin, which opened up a chance to projects and personalities that no commercial producer would have risked. But this federal funding system, which Herzog once called his life-support machine, was a mere drip-feed compared to the blood transfusion and oxygen boost given to the patient after the so-called "Television Framework Agreement" of 1974. It obliged the various West German broadcasters to co-produce feature films and to set aside additional funds for transmitting independently made films first shown in the cinemas. With one stroke, independent filmmakers had gained access via television not only to a breed of producers and co-producers who wouldn't go bankrupt in mid-production or run off to the South of France; they had also acquired the next-best thing to a distribution and exhibition guarantee: audiences. This was especially important in a country whose cinemas were either controlled by the American majors, or owned by people convinced that a German-made feature film emptied seats more quickly than a colony of mice released at a children's matinee.

While both kinds of New German Cinema benefited from television, the auteur cinema was understandably anxious to play down this helping hand, preferring to attribute the films' existence to individual genius. The other, less well-known New German Cinema, by contrast, actually seemed to thrive on the possibilities as well as the limitations presented by being partnered with television. One can see why, when this partner turned out to be ZDF's *Das Kleine Fernsehspiel*.

Yet what made German television decide to pump some 17 million Deutsch Mark into feature films, especially when so many of the projects were either submitted by directors with little previous fiction film experience, or had no wide public appeal? The answer has partly to do with the structure of West German television, which in those days was still wholly publicly owned, funded by a license fee and thus under political control: when their paymaster spoke, the broadcasters had to listen. But they put up little resistance, because the deal also promised them some tangible benefits.

To start with, German television, which in the previous decades had desperately tried to find forms of programs and types of drama that distinguished it from both theatre and the cinema, had hit on the *"Fersehspiel"* as its cultural flagship, and from the mid-1950s onwards, invested substantial amounts of money and prestige in this particular form of live drama. However, there had always been a shortage of good in-house-produced drama, and by the late 1960s, the flagship had more or less run aground when it was abandoned by its audiences because of relentlessly high-brow aspirations, and it had been pushed, because of its minority interest, further and further into the late night schedules. Perhaps, television executives argued, a generation of young, ambitious filmmakers might well have the new ideas so sorely needed.

Secondly, certain regional broadcasters, notably Westdeutsche Rundfunk, were looking, as a consequence of taking quite seriously its public service obligations, for more topical and socially relevant material, but also for programs, which did not fall neatly into either documentary or fiction. The chance to make feature films appealed on both these counts, revitalizing the Fersehspiel by new formal approaches, and allowing more controversial issues to be given fictional treatment. The latter was especially important. By claiming a filmmaker's authorial right to self-expression, producers could bypass the stipulations of political balance and neutrality which usually attached itself to factual programs dealing with socially or politically contentious issues. To this bold move, the New German Cinema owes, for instance, the so-called "Arbeiterfilme (workers films)" of Ziewer, Fassbinder, Lüdcke, and Kratisch which the WDR produced in the early 1970s.

Finally – and this brings us closer to *Das Kleine Fernsehspiel* – the Second German TV Channel (ZDF) was set up in order to commission much of its programming from outside producers, thus keeping overheads low and schedules flexible. This meant that independent filmmakers could, in principle, join other freelance or commercial producers in the queue for ZDF commissions. A system was thus already in place that allowed the Framework Agreement to be implemented on the back of an existing production structure. Last but not least, ZDF's Head of Drama and Film during the period in question, was Heinz Ungureit who himself began as a film critic and was a staunch supporter of the New German Cinema. He, in turn, had the good sense of putting in charge of *Das Kleine Fernsehspiel* an equally committed champion of independent cinema in general, Eckart Stein. Stein recognized early on that the twin directions agitating the debate about the future of cinema and television – convergence of the two media and self-differentiation – had also exposed certain niches and gaps in the scheduling policy which his department at ZDF was ideally placed to exploit.

Das Kleine Fernsehspiel

According to Stein, the idea behind *Das Kleine Fernsehspiel* was to create a "forum for witnesses to the age" and a showcase for new talent who would be given the opportunity to express a singular vision, without being bound by either issues or format. The intention may have initially been to build up a kind of filmic archive of the *Zeitgeist*, but Stein also knew that the films had to address two kinds of audiences at one and the same time:

> maybe half our audience watches regularly to see what this week's program is like, and the other half has a group interest in what we are doing. A film about homosexual teachers will attract primarily a homosexual public or viewers involved in education; or take the women's films ... we might have a mainly female audience.

In Stein's hands, *Das Kleine Fernsehspiel* not only became a precious source of finance for first-time filmmakers, it also proved the most fertile ground for new narrative forms: "the small TV play" became a double misnomer, since the films could be as long as three hours, and they were rarely confined to television. Given its late broadcast slot, time was less critical, and given Stein's brief to make unconventional programs, the films were often more formally innovative than the idea of the "single play" encompassed, but they could also be unconventional solely thanks to their subject matter, using a documentary or semi-fictional approach, which again, redefined the old label "*Fernsehspiel.*"

It was these niches and open spaces which formed the basis of a sort of tacit agreement between filmmakers and commissioning editor where, at least for a while, each party's needs worked hand in glove with the other. For the director, the chance to do a film falling right outside the commercial cinema's range proved attractive, especially since *Das Kleine Fernsehspiel* could offer budgets and production facilities somewhat above the finance raised when one is dependent on family, friends and a bank overdraft. Knowing that there would be an audience, and furthermore, an audience who might never go to the cinema, seemed to outweigh the knowledge that this audience was small: it might just include a critic who would write a glowing review, giving the film a chance for a follow-up in the specialized cinemas, or another tv showing at a slightly better time.

For the ZDF, on the other hand, getting a director of unlimited enthusiasm and perhaps a talent to match, was a good investment. If the film was exceptional, as many of the films made for *Das Kleine Fernsehspiel* undoubtedly were, the network acquired cultural capital and a reputation for being a patron of the arts: over the years the weekly programs comprised documentaries and feature films, by first-time filmmakers and established ones, both German and foreign. Directors known for their avant-garde fiction films such as Raoul Ruiz, Steve Dwoskin, Jean Pierre Gorin, Theodore Angelopulos, and Jim Jarmusch all made films for the ZDF, and by all accounts were given virtually *carte blanche*. Often, the films could be sent to international film festivals, and many came home, showered with critical acclaim. Even if the film did not quite come off – which also happened from time to time – the network still managed to fill its slot at a cost below the average opera transmission or drama commissioned from a professional writer.

Furthermore, with *Das Kleine Fernsehspiel* the ZDF was able to legitimate itself socially, too. During the politicized 1970s, the insistence of minorities or special interest groups to benefit from the principle of *Öffentlichkeit* as defined in the statutes of German broadcasting, and to have their views represented in a public medium, grew louder than ever before. It gave rise to an enormous demand for films on a whole variety of social issues, films which by their very nature were needed by television, but which, when "signed" by a director-author, could nonetheless count as part of the (by then, famed) New German Cinema. Titles that would normally form part of television's factual or current affairs output, often had, thanks to *Das Kleine Fernsehspiel,* the status as authored, personal works. In other words, films dealing with social issues such as racism, juvenile delinquency, drug abuse, the yellow press, the penal system, state surveillance, prostitution, urban redevelopment, or unemployment would be directed by auteurs such as Helma Sanders-Brahms, Ulrike Ottinger, Michael Klier, Sohrab Saless, Alexander Kluge and Edgar Reitz.

One "minority" which might be said to have especially benefited from this compromise between giving new talent a chance and fulfilling a social or cultural brief, were women – both women as filmmakers and women as target audiences. In a very real sense, *Das Kleine Fernsehspiel* marked the first time that women had more than a token presence among Germany's leading directors. For them to gain access to television, in order to do a feature film required a very precise conjunction indeed, since as long as women directors were type-cast, and assigned only to do documentaries on women's issues, they found it virtually impossible to obtain a comparable space for feature film projects. The turn to autobiography in the women's movement generally provided for many a point of entry into the fiction film, allowing feminists to respond to a demand for self-expression as self-representation, and thus combining the "personal" with the "political." *Das Kleine Fersehspiel* welcomed this autobiographical approach.

Women turning to the ZDF, even with very little experience in filmmaking, also had *carte blanche*, as Jutta Brückner was to find out: "I am completely self-taught. I had never been to a film school or been an assistant. When I decided to make my first film ... I just wrote a script outline and sent it off to all the TV stations, and ZDF – one of their departments, that is, *Das Kleine Fernsehspiel* said they wanted to do it. I was so surprised, I really didn't know what to do and I just phoned some friends and said 'I'm making a film' – they all thought it was a good joke. I said, 'No, really, I already have the money' and they were dumbfounded."

The result was a film which fused the autobiographical impulse so strategically important for the women's movement with a formal structure as innovative as it was ingeniously simple. TUE RECHT UND SCHEUE NIEMAND consists of photographs from August Sander's "Menschen des XX.Jahrhunderts," matched on the soundtrack with Brückner's own mother's hesitant and muted narrative of her life. The film becomes the story of an older woman, whose personal reminiscences, anxieties, and deeply melancholy disappointment with life underline the ideology of her class. It makes her, for the spectator, a representative, indeed a historical document of the German petit-bourgeoisie of the 20th century. At the same time, this very realization modifies our view of her as an individual, while sound and image powerfully fix her as unique and particular. From the tension between these two conflicting perceptions the film derives its pathos, freeing the look to embrace the banal and even treasure it, under the aspects of its imminent disappearance. Hovering between historical document and personal reminiscence, Brückner is able to generate the kind of emotional intensity one associates with fiction films.

TUE RECHT UND SCHEUE NIEMAND is a good example of the paradox which made Eckart Stein's experiment so valuable to women filmmakers because, whereas in the case of documentaries and current affairs, television usually controls quite tightly the forms such programs take, *Das kleine Fernsehspiel*, especially in the area of feminist filmmaking, commissioned subjects which, on the strength of *Das Kleine Fersehspiel*'s reputation, could enter film distribution, thus giving television, usually the grave of feature films, the role of acting as a preview theatre for cinema films. On the other hand, the fact that films such as

Brückner's TUE RECHT UND SCHEUE NIE-
MAND, or Elfi Miekesch's ICH DENKE OFT
AN HAWAII (about women in an old people's home) originated from within a television program that covered the whole
spectrum from avant-garde experiment
to social case history, from American independents to Herbert Achternbusch,
made it easier for female directors to es-

TUE RECHT UND SCHEUE NIEMAND

cape the sort of ghetto implied by a term such as "women's film." *Das Kleine
Fernsehspiel* thus did much to democratize not only the distinctions between the
sexes in filmmaking, it also democratized the differences between formal avant-
garde and fictional narrative, and finally, it helped demystify the difference between artistic and technical input, giving those whose project Stein liked the
practical training or assistance needed to bring about its realization.

What is clear is that the *Das Kleine Fersehspiel* recognized the potential and the
need for new kinds of narrative feature films, and by sponsoring them in an
international context, it allowed women filmmakers such as Brückner, Miekesch, Ottinger, and Sanders-Brahms to find a forum as well as a form. The role
that radical subjectivity has in these filmmakers' worlds of fantasy, trauma and
violence furthermore belonged to a recognizable tendency within feminist film
generally, where excess, display, masquerade and spectacle became the political
stances of a new cinematic investment in the female, the maternal, the aging
and the androgynous body. This might be said to be one of the aesthetic legacies
of *Das Kleine Fernsehspiel*, even if the extent to which the signature of *Das Kleine
Fernsehspiel* had an impact on the *Frauenfilm* as a genre is impossible to decide.

The director, however, whose work most fully epitomizes the complex dynamic implicit in *Das Kleine Fernsehspiel* is undoubtedly Werner Schroeter, the
New German cinema's greatest "marginal" filmmaker. Schroeter's "total cinema" is one which devoted itself to the areas where painting, music, dance,
narrative and performance intersect, making him one of the most unlikely filmmakers ever to be officially recognized. While it was television which alone had
the financial power, the organizational base and the programming niches to
support (but in a sense, also to exploit) his unique talent, Schroeter also had to
keep his distance from television's promiscuous pluralism as well as its ephem-
erality: he did so, not so much by any "Brechtian" distance, but by presenting
"beautiful" images, while at the same time undermining the very aestheticism
of the beautiful by obstinately beautifying marginal and discarded phenomena.
Obliged to almost always work for *Das Kleine Fernsehspiel* and its late-night
slots, Schroeter thrived more than other filmmakers in, but also suffered more,
from the spaces Eckart Stein managed to keep open. Often uncredited, films

such as WILLOW SPRINGS, DER TOD DER MARIA MALIBRAN or DER BOMBERPILOT, however, became the prototypes not so much for television programs, but for almost all the varieties of experimental feature film practiced in Germany in the 1980s, whether feminist, gay, avant-garde or as in the case of Syberberg, the historical film essay. It makes Schroeter the "secret" or "missing" link between the one kind of New German Cinema – the authors' cinema – and the other, in which minorities and marginal voices moved center-stage. While ZDF and Stein signaled Schroeter's importance as a filmmaker to the cinema, he in turn highlighted the importance of *Das Kleine Fersehspiel*: proving that television can provide the possibilities of forging a chain not between film and television, but between cinema and cinema.

(1992)

Touching Base

Some German Women Directors in the 1980s

The Basis Film Verleih

A recent event at the ICA, featuring the work of a Berlin distribution and production company, the Basis Film Verleih, has again highlighted the current dilemmas of independent cinema on the Left, battling against an unfavorable cultural climate, increasing difficulties with funding, and the competition from denationalized and deregulated television markets. The history of Basis, however, also demonstrates, amidst an atmosphere of near-despondency, the position of (relative) strength from which women filmmakers in West Germany can take stock and address the changing situation. The audience at the ICA was on the whole skeptical about the lessons to be learnt, given the different (and considerably worse) starting point in Britain, but in the way Basis proposes to respond to the crisis, it is adding a new chapter to the history of the *cinema d'auteur*.

Basis Film Verleih was founded in 1973, initially in order to promote and distribute a number of television films (DEAR MOTHER, I'M FINE, SNOWDROPS BLOOM IN SEPTEMBER) which Christian Ziewer had produced and directed about shop-floor conflicts, strikes, and their repercussions in the home, the so-called *Arbeiterfilme*. Basis' intention was to bypass the commercial (and moribund) system, by taking the films directly to a working-class audience, into factories, trade-union meetings and social clubs. When Ziewer hired Clara Burckner as his production manager and director of Basis, the company expanded its operations, using subsidy money, production grants, and distribution aid to build up revolving capital with which to co-produce and distribute films from mainly Berlin filmmakers, the Berlin School. With the decline of the *Arbeiterfilme*, in the wake of party-political pressures and more cautious television editors, Basis was able to move more strongly into an emergent area of independent work: it attracted funds for projects by women filmmakers, and over the years has added to its distribution list films by directors as diverse as Helke Sander and Ulrike Ottinger, Helma Sanders-Brahms and Ula Stöckl, Helga Reidemeister and Ingemo Engstrom, Jutta Brückner and Alexandra von Grothe,

Cristina Perincioli and Marianne Rosenbaum. Where do all these filmmakers come from?

German Feminism and Film Culture

In West Germany, films by and for women have to be seen against two historical factors: The internal developments of the women's movement in late 1960s (the realization that feminist issues did not have a natural home inside the Marxist students' movement), and secondly, the cultural shifts which made television take up women's issues (creating from within the institution new spaces for their representation). But the feminist film culture, which by the early 1980s was associated internationally with the names of Margarethe von Trotta and Helma Sanders-Brahms, had also benefited enormously from the initiatives of women like Helke Sander, who had gained access to the media and who, rather than making a career as individual auteurs, had campaigned for political and institutional support structures which could discriminate positively in favor of

REGINA ZIEGLER

first-time women filmmakers and women film collectives. Sander, a prominent member of the radical student left, but also a tireless organizer, brilliant polemicist and a filmmaker since 1966, had initiated, together with Claudia Alemann, the first international women's film seminar in 1973 and in 1974 founded the influential journal *Frauen und Film*. Equally as crucial as Helke Sander and Clara Burckner were Regina Ziegler (Head of Regina Ziegler Filmproduktion), Renee Gundelach (producer and managing director with Road Movies) and Erika Gregor (co-director of the Friends of the German Kinemathek and the International Forum of Young Film). Their role in the production, distribution and exhibition sectors gave women directors (though not only them) the adminstrative and often legal expertise essential for survival in the complicated funding and public subsidy system that was the backbone of the German film renaissance during the 1970s.

The West German women's movement shared with the first phase of the student movement an anti-authoritarian bias, but the struggle for women's rights on particular issues, above all abortion, soon understood itself as "autonomous" and even mobilized – however briefly – a strong social base. Politically active women came to film not least because they had, from direct and practical experience, a very clear sense of the uses of the media in publicizing demands and pressing for their recognition: Helke Sander, Erika Runge, Ingrid Oppermann's early interventions, taking mostly the form of didactic docu-dramas, investigative or observational films, dealt with experiences specific to women (DOES THE PILL LIBERATE?, SHOULD WOMEN EARN AS MUCH AS MEN?, WHY IS FRAU B. HAPPY?, WOMEN: AT THE TAIL END OF TRADE UNIONS?). But the uniqueness of the German situation was that women directors also tackled wider social issues (e.g., Helma Sanders-Brahms' first shorts, the fiction films of Marianne Lüdcke, or the documentaries about education, Turkish immigrant families and working class communities made by graduates of the Berlin Film School (Suzanne Beyeler, Gisela Tuchtenhagen, Marlis Kallweit).

In one sense, these feminists provided clear examples of filmmaking relying for its primary audiences on the existence of politically motivated spectators. On the other hand, their work also highlighted certain institutional double-binds. The major source of funding for women came from television, which, with its voracious appetite for issues, discovered the women's question around 1975 much as it had discovered the working class around 1971. Through its current affairs slots, TV magazine features and documentary departments television created the need for in-depth reports and analyses where the individual touch or grassroots involvement were attractive assets. Some of the "topical" themes even of the more cinema-oriented feature films in West Germany (Margarethe von Trotta's first films, for instance, or those of Jeanine Meerapfel) also reflect this proximity to television.

As a reaction, some of the women directors who had come to film via militant struggles (a tendency encouraged by the entrance requirements and the syllabus of the Berlin Film and TV Academy), preferred to make films intended mainly to raise the self-awareness of those directly affected, through interviews, or by asking them to act out semi-fictional situations (for instance, Helga Reidemeister's BUYING A DREAM, 1977 and WHO SAYS "FATE"?, 1979). Such issue-orientation and intense local involvement may also explain why, perhaps earlier than in Britain or the US, this conception of women filmmaking was felt to lead to an impasse, especially after the social need for alternative information began to diminish, or was taken up in more consumable forms by television itself. Yet in order not to be swallowed up by television, women directors needed another forum: an independent producer or distributor with access to cinemas or at least to outlets that gave the films the kind of exposure which would result in newspaper coverage, discussions, invitations to present the work in person. Basis Film Verleih came to specialize in this thankless but vital area. It complemented that other tangible result of the high film-political profile women had achieved as a professional association spanning the film and television industries and embracing women film-technicians as well as directors and actresses.

The *Union der Filmarbeiterinnen* (Union of Women Film Workers), by demanding parity at all levels forcefully challenged the notion that women could be successful filmmakers only by either specializing on women's issues (and thus be ghettoized in television) or as *authors* (and thus become competitive, make it on the international festival scene, in order to achieve a better bargaining position at home).

The result was a redefinition and revitalization of the Autoren-film as practiced by Basis which was cooperative at the level of production, but individual at the level of exhibition. As Clara Burckner put it in her position paper at the ICA: "The more the film industry debases the filmmaker to a mere deliverer of a consumer product ... the more important it is to fight for the recognition of film as a cultural property ... with an author whose rights must be protected and whose artistic freedom is inalienable ... For Basis the question of the survival of the *film d'auteur* is the question of the survival of a national film culture. That is why, in the face of ... a television industry which floods the networks with images, we wish to continue helping our filmmakers ... New ways for bringing the films to the audience are being tested. First experiences as, for instance, how to re-conquer the cinema as a "cultural space" have been made." What scope does this program give the filmmakers? Does it result in new forms, and thus new potential uses? The example of four women filmmakers, all at one time associated with Basis, may give a clue to the options open in the 1980s.

Helma Sanders-Brahms

Initially making shorts and features about the economic situation of working-class women and men, before taking up explicitly feminist subjects, as in SHIRIN'S WEDDING (1976) Helma Sanders-Brahms won several festival prizes which secured a basis for further work in cooperation with ZDF and WDR, the two most generous German television networks. Yet from 1977 onwards, her films reflect the changing trends within the New German cinema as a whole rather than the issues emerging from the women's movement. HEINRICH (1977, produced by Regina Ziegler) and GERMANY PALE MOTHER (1979, much more successful internationally than in Germany) illustrate two major tendencies in 1970s German Author's Cinema, the filmed literature/costume drama (example: Fassbinder's EFFI BRIEST, 1974 or Herzog's WOYZECK, 1978) and the "turn to history" (Syberberg's OUR HITLER, 1975, Fassbinder's MARRIAGE OF MARIA BRAUN, 1979). Nonetheless, Sanders-Brahms' films could be seen to follow major developments within the women's movement, discovering in autobiography a key to history, and testing official history for its often contradictory repercussions on private lives and the personal sphere. HEINRICH is based on the writer Heinrich von Kleist's letters, detailing a suicidal liaison with his half-sister, and GERMANY PALE MOTHER offers an autobiographical investigation of a mother-daughter relationship. NO MERCY NO FUTURE (1981), the case history of a young woman schizophrenic takes the disintegration of the bourgeois family into the present, the Berlin of immigrant workers, American soldiers, old people's homes and mental hospitals. The success of GERMANY PALE MOTHER and the relative (critical and commercial) failure of NO MERCY NO FUTURE may have led Sanders-Brahms in the direction of the European art cinema, by then increasingly in conflict with the political themes and aesthetic counter-strategies of German cine-feminism. Her recent films have featured well-to-do middle class couples, often with stars from the German and international cinema THE FUTURE OF EMILY, with Brigitte Fossey, Ivan Desny and Hildegard Knef, and LAPUTA with Krystyna Janda (from MAN OF MARBLE) and Sami Frey (from, among others, Godard's BAND À PART).

Ulrike Ottinger, Jutta Brückner: Spectacles of Self-Estrangement

A different redefinition of the *auteur* and of the "political" in the wake of autonomous feminism can be studied in filmmakers who turned to that area of experience where women felt most alienated from themselves. In the words of Heide Schlüpmann and Carola Gramann: "the women's movement started simply and materialistically with what was nearest, the woman's body, and from there tried to disentangle the violation of women's rights and their subjection." Yet some of the films most directly concerned with "what is nearest, the woman's body," such as Jutta Brückner's HUNGER YEARS (1979) and Ulrike Ottinger's TICKET OF NO RETURN (1979) devastatingly show that this body is much too near, too real to serve as a vantage point for a "materialist" critique. On the contrary, it is as if in these films, once the body comes into view, all perspectives crumble.

HUNGER YEARS

HUNGER YEARS is structured as a repetition of moments and situations around which the trauma forms that eventually reduces the adolescent heroine to bouts of, alternately, anorexia and bulimia. An autobiographical case history, Brückner wanted, through the film, once more to "identify with myself."

Although such a desire for self-exploration and self-identification is fairly typical of the auteur cinema generally, formally HUNGER YEARS cannot be assimilated into a tradition. Also, the self with which the heroine tries to identify is the mother. The film shows how her inaccessiblity (as love object, as a source of the confirming gaze) makes the young woman direct the most intense aggression against her own body, subjected to and subjecting it to the terrible regimes and violent rhythms of hysterical bleeding, compulsive eating and self-induced vomiting. The images are marked by a violence which is only rarely present in the characters' actions. Mostly it is the violence of the mise-en-scène itself: a lugubrious half-light, as in the closing scene, shots held for a painfully long time, episodes that make the viewer aware of the actors' own discomfort, images difficult to watch in their naked privacy, stripping away the self-protection of a fictional role. Similar observations apply to Brückner's ONE GLANCE – AND LOVE BREAKS OUT (1987), a film made up of successive performance pieces, where different heroines stage over and over again, in a compulsive rhythm reminiscent of Pina Bausch's dance theatre fantasies of desire, lust, self-humiliation and aggression.

Ulrike Ottinger

In TICKET OF NO RETURN the central fantasy is one of self-oblivion. Single, wealthy and beautiful, Ulrike Ottinger's heroine makes Berlin the destination of her final binge, the "ticket of no return." However, alcohol is merely a convenient figure signaling an urge towards self-annihilation similar to that of Brückner's films and Sanders-Brahms' NO MERCY NO FUTURE. The body has become an intolerable carapace and prison, but infinitely available for disguise and display. Unlike Brückner and Sanders-Brahms, Ottinger makes no concessions to elemental imagery or the rawness of the flesh: every surface is polished, mirrors and metal gleams with a precise and cold reflection. Even the heroine's attempted suicide/murder becomes a choreographed ballet of open razor blades against an impeccably coordinated bathroom wall.

Nonetheless, Ottinger's subject similarly revolves around a process obsessively repeated but ultimately failing, that of discovering a self through the other. Yet in TICKET OF NO RETURN, as in FREAK ORLANDO (1981) and DORIAN GRAY (1984), the process is treated exclusively through characters hyperconscious of their self-image, whose quest to lose themselves is intertwined with the discovery of a double in the outcast and the freak or his/her lustful creation (and destruction) in and through the media/the cinema. In TICKET OF NO RETURN this "other," so unlike the heroine and yet the very image of her own degradation and liberation is the bag lady Lutze, who joins her on her drinking bouts, pushing a supermarket shopping cart and mumbling obscene imprecations. In contrast to the heroine, adorned by fashion, dressed to kill and giving her body fantastic forms, the old lady is a shapeless bulk, grotesque and neglected. In tolerating Lutze, she succumbs to a fascination whose object one imagines to be, here too, the body of the mother. Empathy towards the face of decay and imminent death becomes almost a nostalgia for the self's own future, and not free of its own form of aggression. Yet the real violence is directed against the heroine herself, the very stylization and beauty of Tabea Blumenschein's appearance displayed as if to hurt the eye.

With films such as Ottinger's or Brückner's, Basis has come a long way from the *Arbeiterfilme* and sociological documentaries. In TICKET OF NO RETURN three female figures, their severity and eccentricity underlined by hounds-tooth dresses, accompany the heroine like a chorus. Called "Common Sense," "The Social Problem," and "Reliable Statistics" they take her alcoholism literally, and are the ironic stand-in for those presumed and intended audiences who expect films to show them how to change their lives. Brückner's emphasis in ONE GLANCE – AND LOVE BREAKS OUT on the differing function of the gaze for men and women, and thus of cinematic identification, points in a similar direction. The cutting edge of their films is not (yet another form of) realism, but a mise-en-scène of perversion, paranoia or schizophrenia: modes of perception and consciousness to which the cinema lends itself as no other art form.

Helke Sander

In contrast to Helma Sanders-Brahms or Margarethe von Trotta – two examples of the woman filmmaker as auteur – Helke Sander remained committed to a more narrowly defined constituency in Germany itself, and also to a consistently socialist and feminist perspective. One of the very first students of the Berlin Academy, her career can also be read symptomatically in the way that it quite deliberately documents the women's movement and its impact on the private as well as public lives of her characters, at once autobiographical and representative.

On one level these themes are historicized and made concrete in the context of West Berlin and the fate of the German left; on another, they become quite rigorous questionings of issues of representation and aesthetic form. Instead of the "personal" being subsumed under the "political," or directly opposed to it (as tended to happen in the *Arbeiterfilme* and the early feminist documentaries), Sander came to reject any such bi-polar conflict model. The subjective factor in her film of that title, for instance, is not some ineffable personal essence, but seems much more the frictions and dissonances attendant upon the incoherence of the signs surrounding the heroine, and her resistance to the publicly circulating records of events, such as photographs or material from the sound archives which constantly revise, reposition and retouch her own memories. It is the non-convergence, registered painfully as loss or comically as a gag, between these realities which constitutes the personal in the political.

In short, Sander radicalized the genre most readily available to women, that of the diary and the autobiographical narrative. Between the effacement of the "personal" in left politics and its lust- or painful exhibition her films try to chart a different course, insofar as they neither pursue nor disavow either side of the equation. Instead of, as it were, staging the deficit of identity with exhibitionism and masquerade, her characters dramatize the loss of self as a sort of "bad timing," as for instance in LOVE IS THE BEGINNING OF ALL TERRORS (1984) where the heroine's sharply divided loyalties, when trying to live with an unfaithful lover, stand for a more fundamental recognition of the impossibility of separating "self" from "other." Transposed into another register – the irreconcilability of "here" and "now" – it is objectified in the film by snatches of opera sung by a female voice. Sander here at times comes close to conceiving of the problem of female identity and the staging of its impossibility (coded as love) in terms as much reminiscent of the music-spectacles of Werner Schroeter as of the political-feminist discourses in her earlier films. In REDUPERS ("The All-Round Reduced Personality," 1977), it will be remembered, Berlin as divided city and the woman divided between artist-and-mother symbolized the social and historical dimensions of gender. Yet within her own work, the splitting of body from voice, as one of the ways in which difference is articulated in LOVE IS THE BEGINNING OF ALL TERRORS is a logical development from REDUPERS and THE SUBJECTIVE FACTOR, especially in their investigation of the divisions of the female self in the various apparatuses of male power.

CHINA – THE ARTS, EVERYDAY LIFE

Sander, Ottinger, Brückner are not popular directors. Even though their work has been awarded prizes, they are mainly known for making difficult, and often even painful films. Sander, who does not like to work for television, has not made a film for five years. Ottinger's latest film, CHINA – THE ARTS, EVERYDAY LIFE was financed by television, which only showed a cut version, treating the film almost as raw material for a travel feature. Brückner, whose previous film, KOLOSSALE LIEBE, also made for television, had one late-night airing before disappearing into the vaults, decided to make ONE GLANCE – AND LOVE BREAKS OUT in Argentina, on a shoestring budget largely advanced by the Goethe Institute. This inevitably raises the question whether such films are their author's "cultural property," as Clara Burckner would see it, or the nation's "cultural commodities." Basis Film Verleih at home, and as guest of the ICA, works hard to ensure that the filmmakers can still "touch base" with their audiences.

Margarethe von Trotta

Touching base in a different sense is how Margarethe von Trotta, perhaps Germany's most successful woman director and not part of the Basis Film Verleih, entered filmmaking. She started as an actress – for Fassbinder, among others – then became a screenwriter, working on the films of Volker Schlöndorff. Together they directed THE LOST HONOUR OF KATHARINA BLUM (1975), but by 1977, she had achieved a breakthrough as a solo writer-director of THE SECOND AWAKENING OF CHRISTA KLAGES. The story of a nursery teacher and her two male companions who rob a bank, in order to raise enough money to keep their daycare center going, it is based on a *fait divers* and has echoes of the early days of the "Baader-Meinhof Group".

Feminist thriller, social issues film, Euro-pudding, lesbian romance, and docu-drama about post-'68 Germany, CHRISTA KLAGES was immensely successful. Coming after KATHERINA BLUM, and made in the same year as GERMANY IN AUTUMN, Von Trotta's film formed part of the broad sweep that led the German cinema directly into political issues, at a time when public discussion about the Red Army Fraction, the assassination of Schleyer, the hijack and Special Commando rescue of hostages at Mogadishu airport, and the suicides in the Stammheim security prison had polarized the country into dangerously dogmatic either/or positions.

All the major motifs of Von Trotta's later films are already present in CHRISTA KLAGES: violence for a good cause, female friendships, isolation and suicide, mothers and daughters. Von Trotta is a feminist, but as she once said, she "cannot imagine making a film that does not have a direct bearing on our situation in Germany." This also means that she has always aimed at the largest possible public, not shunning formula plots, emotional manipulation, and sentimentality. THE GERMAN SISTERS (1981), her best-known film abroad, was accused of sensationalism in Germany. As the barely fictionalized story of Gudrun Ensslin, one of the members of the "Baader-Meinhof Group", told from the perspective of her sister, a journalist working for a feminist magazine, the film borrows the investigative plot of the thriller, works with conventional suspense techniques and positive identification figures. In Hollywood or France, this aesthetics of the mainstream would make Von Trotta a commercial director working within the established film industry. But since in Germany such an industry had not existed for the last thirty years, she is in fact an "independent."

In her stories, social or political conflicts are personalized, and the narrative is charged with resolving them, at least metaphorically, by providing the necessary elements of closure. Binary oppositions, symmetrical situations, repetitions and visual parallels are structural features much in evidence. In CHRISTA KLAGES, the daycare center cannot survive because the landlord wants to open a sex shop; Lena, the bank teller, is both a double of Christa's school friend Ingrid and, in another context, symmetrically related to Christa's own young daughter. In SISTERS OR THE BALANCE OF HAPPINESS, the heroine Maria has a double in the severe matron presiding over the typing pool, and Maria and Anna are echoed in the blind old woman, always shouting at her sister. Miriam is interested in Maurice who gets Maria, and Robert is interested in Maria but gets Miriam. In THE GERMAN SISTERS, Marianne the terrorist has presumably thrown bombs that have wounded innocent people; her innocent small son becomes the victim of a hideous arson attack when someone finds out who his mother is. Juliane works for a feminist magazine, but the editorial meetings are distinctly authoritarian, and so on.

On the other hand, the form connects to the themes: all of Von Trotta's films are about role reversals, mutually sustaining projections and dependencies intertwined like daisy chains. They are about sisters – blood sisters (SISTERS, THE GERMAN SISTERS), or female bonding (CHRISTA KLAGES, FRIENDS AND HUSBANDS, 1983). In each case, an identification across difference is the base line of the story, with a third woman (or a child) acting as the catalyst or mediator. In SISTERS, where the paradigm appears in its purest form, Maria finally accepts the Anna within herself, ending the process of repression and disavowal that effectively killed her sister. Despite its historical basis, THE GERMAN SISTERS follows this pattern very closely. Here, too, Juliane ends up "becoming" the dead Marianne, finding her way back to her own rebellious youth, while making a more positive commitment to life than her sister, by raising Marianne's child. In neither film do the men have any significant role, and if they help to bring the issues into the open, they are dropped as soon as the conflict proper gets under way. The distinctive feature of both films is the return to the past, in the form of flashbacks to the sisters as small girls, and through visits that bring into play the looming presence of mothers and absent (dead, denying) fathers.

What distinguishes Von Trotta's films from those of other German filmmakers is that her social ethos has its roots in the German Lutheran Church, over the centuries perhaps the most durable home of bourgeois humanism and liberalism, with its own tradition of political nonconformism, social work, education, child care and, more recently, a principled anti-fascism and anti-nuclear militancy. This is the moral and ideological milieu in which her observations are uncannily apt and her stance most consistently intelligent and generous. The conflict is between a sense of impersonal duty towards a common good and the almost inhuman isolation it entails. In SISTERS, Maria's solitude becomes a temptation to use moral righteousness as a weapon in an essentially psychological struggle. And in THE GERMAN SISTERS, the elitism of unmediated spiritual suffering that makes Protestantism so strong is also what emotionally explains – even if it does not justify – the radicalism with which terrorist violence and direct action rupture the social contract. This rich tissue of moral and historical complications and nuances is what Von Trotta catches in her images, the brusque or rapid gestures of the women, their energy that can take cold and brutal forms or suffuse the films with a particular emotional flow. These are qualities of the mise-en-scène, more interesting than the linearity or diagrammatic neatness of her narratives.

Personalizing conflict as Von Trotta always does, might be seen as a reduction of the political to psychological categories, but her strength may still be in finding the psychological in the political, and the political in the personal. If political terrorism is ostensibly about macro-politics – imperialism, capitalism, patriarchy – Von Trotta's strategy is to transform these themes into micro-politics (daycare center, a rural commune, giving a child a home). This is both a feminist position and a sound audience strategy for a popular filmmaker. But it also plays safe because Von Trotta always *scales down* the issues she takes on in her films. A bank robbery for a daycare center rather than for an arms deal or for forged papers: CHRISTA KLAGES is about a little bit of terrorism and for an unambiguously good cause. Through an attention to detail, a density of visual texture and mood, her films locate a certain truth about her characters, building up the emotional resonance, irresistible and corny at the same time. She succeeds supremely well in making comprehensible a chain of motivations and situations that "leads" an individual to extreme acts: but in the process she makes the radically other into the familiar, the extreme into the logical, by balancing everything out with symmetries and parallels – rather than, as do the other feminist filmmakers discussed, insisting on the otherness of a person or a motive, and deriving emotional force from obliging the spectator to acknowledge difference, without providing the categories or emotions that translate difference into recognition and "making sense."

Yet empathy is precisely the thematic center of her films, and hence something that remains contradictory and problematic for her. One of the catchwords of the 1970s was *Sympathisanten*; sympathisers. From the point of view of the government and the police, it designated all those who overtly – in the form of demonstrations, writings, and speeches – expressed sympathy or agreement with "terrorists or extremists," and thus anyone who had a word of explanation or reflection to offer on the emergence of this type of radical militancy and desperate violence. For having written the story of KATHARINA BLUM, for instance, novelist Heinrich Böll found himself called a terrorist sympathizer by the Springer press. Such a strategy of isolation, exclusion, and expulsion towards those who dissent or merely think differently imposes on the writer or

filmmaker a quite distinct task – to create the possibility of understanding through sympathy, not at least by dramatizing the psychological mechanisms of disavowal, projection, and identification. Von Trotta's cinema – "classical" and conformist as it may seem when viewed formally – has, in its intense preoccupation with identity, doubling, splitting, and the transference between self and other, a political dimension both within and outside her feminist positions. In the context of a tradition of liberal humanism that in Germany as elsewhere in the 1980s seemed threatened by authoritarian conservatism, she not only reclaimed herself from the mirror projections of erstwhile fans. She also made films mirroring a Germany that is still in search of its image.

THE LOST HONOUR OF KATHARINA BLUM

(1987)

Europe-Hollywood-Europe

Two Decades in Another Country

Hollywood and the Cinephiles

In a "history" of the impact on Europe of American popular culture, the systematic elevation of Hollywood movies to the ranks of great art would make an intriguing chapter. Legend has it that the feat was accomplished almost single-handed by motivated and volatile intellectuals from Paris sticking their heads together and pulling off a brilliant public relations stunt that came to be known as *Cahiers du cinéma* and *Nouvelle Vague*.[1]

The legend bears some relation to the facts, but only insofar as it has allowed a very simple version of a very complicated cultural phenomenon to gain widespread or at least topical currency. Today, at a time when film criticism is again increasingly oriented towards theory, the more controversial sides of the episode seem to have been put to rest.[2] Nonetheless, two implications deserve to be studied more closely. One is the feedback which Hollywood's European fame has produced in the United States, and the value now attributed by Americans to their indigenous cultural assets in this field. It is noticeable, for instance, that after a very fitful shift, when news from France was greeted with derision and incredulity in New York and Los Angeles, the Hollywood cinema, especially the films of the 1930s, '40s and '50s, has come to be recognized and often nostalgically celebrated as a (if not *the*) truly original contribution of the United States to art and aesthetics in this century.[3] The fact that there exists an American Film Institute,[4] and that courses are being taught on the American cinema at countless universities, indicates a change of attitude quite as decisively as do the antiquarian labors and pastiche work of Peter Bogdanovitch (cf. THE LAST PICTURE SHOW, WHAT'S UP DOC? and PAPER MOON) and the many New York movie houses which are taking notice of the "director's cinema" when billing their rerun double features, while even five years ago only the stars would have been the attraction.

The other question is prompted by a more general reflection: what does enthusiasm for Hollywood tell us about intellectual or scholarly interest in popular culture, and particularly American culture? There is little doubt that this enthusiasm is, within Europe, predominantly and characteristically French. Critics in Italy, Spain, and even Poland have subsequently taken their cue from the Paris line, but as an example of highbrow interest in lowbrow culture the phenomenon only makes sense if one concentrates on France. This is not to deny that Britain produced the most important pro-Hollywood journal outside France,[5] or that as a consequence an ideologically significant, though brief debate flared up in the early 1960s between the "aesthetic Left," the "Left" and the "liberal Right" in England. But historically, the important piece of evidence to keep before one's eyes is that after the Second World War, a number of French cinephile intellectuals (some of whom – but by no means all – went on to found an eventually very influential platform for their views, the said *Cahiers du cinéma*)[6] began to apply a highly literate sensibility and a sophisticated appreciation of aesthetic problems to a body of films (roughly the Hollywood output from 1940 onwards) which on the face of it appeared impressive mainly by its quantity. This output had previously existed in "serious" writing, with the exception of a handful of films by Welles and possibly Ford, only in the wide meshed grid of sociological generalization, the more so, since on another level the promotional activities of the film industry were deemed to speak for themselves: the star system, gossip columnists, fan clubs and other accessories of the showbiz machinery proliferated the image of crass commercialism, unspeakably vulgar, sensationalist, and turning out on celluloid and in newsprint a never-ending flood of cut-price fantasies. Or so it seemed to the educated European. And it rendered the products of such efforts beneath contempt – until, that is, rumor got round of how in France they thought differently.

To understand the change, we need a brief historical flashback: in the 1920s the cinema, including the American cinema (Griffith, Stroheim, Chaplin), enjoyed an enormous intellectual prestige, condensed in many a weighty volume on film aesthetics and theory published during the decade.[7] They unanimously hailed a new art, which they assumed to have almost magical possibilities. With singular optimism, Elie Faure would attribute to the cinema the power to transform the traditional arts, and Bela Balazs would sketch a new vision of man which the screen was to project and communicate to the masses. Reading their books today, one becomes aware that the cinema seemed to promise at once a new aesthetic religion and social revolution, the regeneration of a tired civilization. Apart from such slightly millennial hopes, which can also be found in the writings of Delluc, Eisenstein, Arnheim, Pudovkin and Vertov, avant-garde artists such as Leger, Artaud, Dalí and Cocteau were equally spellbound by the medium.

The invention of sound at the end of the 1920s dashed this euphoria once and for all. Worried by the way the cinema was more and more forcefully developing in the direction of a realist representational medium given over to narratives of dubious merit and originality, artists in the modernist vein came to regard the cinema as aesthetically reactionary, a throwback in fact to the nineteenth century. Film criticism throughout the 1930s did not recover from the blow, and the decade which witnessed an unprecedented economic expansion of the film industries in Europe and America also saw critics only too willing to conclude that popularity automatically spelled aesthetic nullity. The new art of the talking picture came to be written off as irredeemably "commercial," peddling to nothing but escapist entertainment, or worse still, pernicious demagogy.[8]

Because it displayed commercialism and bad taste with gusto and little sense of shame or selfconsciousness, Hollywood had to bear the brunt of the disappointed expectations which quickly relegated the cinema from a potentially major artistic force to a conveyor-belt dream factory. This did not prevent some of the most well-known directors in Europe from emigrating to California, and although most of them left for good political reasons, especially from Germany, not all felt themselves to be heading for dire exile: Ernst Lubitsch, F.W. Murnau, Fritz Lang, Max Ophuls, Otto Preminger, Douglas Sirk, Robert Siodmak and Billy Wilder became established as successful Hollywood directors; René Clair and Jean Renoir made important films in America, and so did Alfred Hitchcock. The case of Hitchcock is particularly instructive, since he left England under no political pressure and at the height of his fame at home.

Faced with this massive exodus from Europe, critics rarely if ever used the opportunity to reassess their idea of Hollywood and their judgement of the films it produced. More apparent was the way they gave vent to disillusionment and ill-temper which made the emigrés seem deserters to the cause and hucksters of their talents. The reception of Hitchcock's American films in Britain can stand for many similar attitudes: "SPELLBOUND and NOTORIOUS [are] classic examples of brilliance run to seed... heartless and soulless "ingenuity,"[9] or about THE MAN WHO KNEW TOO MUCH: "a vulgar and debilitated remake by Hitchcock of his splendid Gaumont-British melodrama, demonstrating once again the pernicious effect of the Hollywood system on a once-brilliant entertainer."[10] Even VERTIGO, a film of rare subtlety and as hauntingly intense as any romantic masterpiece, was the object of a scurrilous and misinformed attack by the leading film journal of the day.[11]

Among the chorus of nostalgic voices bitterly bemoaning better days and pouring scorn on Hollywood, a few French critics, notably Roger Leenhardt and subsequently André Bazin, stand out for their lucid seriousness and moderation. Bazin, in an article he first published in 1945 and later gave the imposing title "Ontologie de l'image cinématographique,"[12] translated this difference of tone and emphasis into a critical position with a theoretical basis. His ambition was nothing less than to rethink the dichotomy between silent and sound film, European cinema and Hollywood. The first had paralyzed film theory since the 1920s, and the second had made film criticism a stagnant backwater of highbrow prejudice, condescending occasionally to being amused by "entertainers." Bazin's system, as far as one can constitute it from his journalism and the numerous pieces of more sustained criticism[13] based itself on an altogether different distinction, that between directors who "believe in the image and those who believe in reality."[14] Directors who believe in the image, according to Bazin, believe in it as a representation of some concept or idea, and their method consists in using the representational nature of the moving image to construct a synthetic reality of the intellect, in short a rhetoric or iconography, to serve an analytically conceived purpose or message. By contrast, those who believe in reality treat the image as a means to "illuminate," "explore" etc. the thing represented; they are committed to the aesthetics of *Anschauung*. Instead of montage techniques, superimposition and collage effects, their main aesthetic resources are depth of field (i.e., compositional tensions within the frame), camera movements (tracks, pans, lateral travelings which produce levels of ambiguity and multiple points of view), and finally long takes which allow an action to develop its own dramatic momentum while accumulating the kind of energy inherent in duration itself – as opposed to "cutting up" a scene into snippets of action and reassembling them in the editing.

ANDRÉ BAZIN

However impartial Bazin's system might have appeared, in practice it implied a strong value judgement in favor of what he himself called the "phenomenological" approach to filmed reality. Applied polemically, his crucial argument was intended to separate those film makers who, like Eisenstein, Pudovkin and Vertov, "tampered" with reality because of their didactic intentions, from those who "respected" the continuity of action as it appears in "real life" and who deployed the temporal narrative dimension of the cinema instead of searching out and experimenting with its conceptual analytical possibilities. In Bazin's mind the "phenomenological tendency, evidently the one he preferred, was associated with the work of Stroheim, Dreyer, Murnau, Flaherty and Renoir during the silent period and Wyler, Welles, Bresson, Rossellini and again Renoir since the 1930s and the advent of sound.

One can see that Bazin was at least as anxious to dissolve the European-American dichotomy as he was to posit a continuity and tradition of aesthetic conception, bridging the supposed gulf between silent and sound era. In effect, he was able to acknowledge theoretically, and consequently to validate the historical development which had pushed the cinema towards becoming a predominantly narrative medium (the very development which had disaffected the intellectuals), but only at the price of virtually "outlawing" the modernist strain and formulating for the sake of clarity and sharpness of definition an either-or position which in its turn distorted a good deal of the evidence at hand.

What deserves to be remembered is that Bazin's efforts were directed to "naturalizing" the compositional techniques of the feature film, which implied playing down the artificiality and manipulative nature of all filmed reality. In this he went against modernist and post modernist suspicion about the status of fiction and fictions. Bazin's line of argument, conservative though it may seem in a literary context, could however claim to be empirical in that it made sense (even if limited) of the predominant historical development in the cinema, without having to retreat to a sterile rejection of the narrative film or indulge in fashionable pessimism about the evils of commercial mass culture. Implicitly, it came near to giving a negative definition of "popular" cinema, rejecting the kind of self consciousness about medium and means of expression that constitutes the level of truth and authenticity in much 20th-century art. The material basis of popular art is different: stereotypes, formulaic plots, cliches, melodramatic emotions and situations ensure a high degree of recognition, and the unabated popularity of gangster movies, Western, thriller, comedies and musicals confirms the expediency if not the value of this basis.[15] On the other hand, in order to show that the end product was different from the ingredients, Bazin had to resort to a philosophically quite demanding hypothesis about the nature and origin of the cinema, which makes a case for Hollywood only by subsuming it under the category of "phenomenological realism," and thus a perfectly legitimate species of traditional (i.e., highbrow) art. The American cinema found itself culturally upgraded, and rather than presenting it as a specifically popular art with a corresponding analysis of popular aesthetics, Bazin in fact explained and interpreted it by a recourse to Husserl, Sartre, Merleau-Ponty and French Catholicism.

It is altogether characteristic of Bazin's position and the influence he exerted not only on French film critics, that in some important respects he by-passed very smartly the debate about art and entertainment, popular and avant-garde, to which the options usually boil down. He did this by focussing on a director such as Renoir (who was as familiar with Marivaux or Flaubert and Zola as he was with modern painting, the novels of Georges Simenon and the midinette music hall ambiance of Montparnasse), and on the American side, putting heavy emphasis on Wyler (born in Germany) or Welles, the most avowedly intellectual director to have come out of the Hollywood studio system. For Bazin, Welles was an innovator (along very European lines) and to be preferred to a more genuinely "representative" director like John Ford, the very epitome of the seasoned practitioner and virtuoso professional in the popular movie idiom.

Although these correctives and the balancing of emphasis within the appraisal of Hollywood were subsequently supplied by Bazin's disciples on *Cahiers du cinéma* (the "Hitchcoco-Hawksiens" as they were called), the tendency towards validating the "genre"-oriented narrative cinema in terms of high art became, if anything, even stronger in the magazine, with, as I shall hope to show, consequences that revealed significant contradictions. Bazin, because of his philosophical vocabulary, his Christian existentialism, his abstention from any kind of political controversy, helped in the main to soften up the prejudices of the educated middle-class viewer towards the American cinema by making him aware of the beauties in a Boetticher Western or a Hitchcock thriller, and ranging their films as equals alongside those by Mizoguchi, Fellini, Renoir, or Bergman. Despite his strictures against Eisenstein and the Russians, it was Bazin's catholicity of cinematic tastes and his "textual" approach to individual films that made his criticism enduring and which compensated for the equivocations that surrounded his notion of what defines artistic achievement of a specifically popular kind.

The problem will perhaps be clearer if we look at Welles, whose early Hollywood films (CITIZEN KANE, THE MAGNIFICENT AMBERSONS) created a sensation in Europe, as indeed in the United States, though there for somewhat different reasons. As I have already hinted, in Europe he tended to be hailed as an innovator, the man who was finally, giving some artistic stature to the American talkie, who had invented the aesthetics of the deep focus shot, revitalized flashback techniques and dramatic montage, pioneered narrative ellipsis and the use of Freudian imagery to give his characters psychological depth. But Welles' case furnished arguments both for and against Hollywood: married as he then was

CITIZEN KANE

to the pin up idol of American GIs, Rita Hayworth, and making "genre" films like LADY FROM SHANGHAI and THE STRANGER, he nevertheless very convincingly played the part of a persecuted genius, misunderstood and thwarted by the Hollywood system. To any dispassionate observer he appeared to be facing Hollywood, as it were, with one cheek flushed by boyish excitement ("the biggest and most expensive electric train set that anyone was ever given to play with"), and a half-ironic, half-sardonic smile on the other. His films breathe a sarcasm that was confusingly directed against himself as well as the people he was working for – just the kind of attitude that recommended him to interested but skeptical (about Hollywood, that is) European intellectuals, but not at all to a popular audience. Welles' later career bears out just how atypical and in many ways deeply antagonistic he was – not only to the working conditions imposed by even so flamboyantly nonchalant a studio boss as Howard Hughes at RKO, but to the whole Hollywood way of thinking about movie making and popular entertainment. Welles was, and remained, indifferent if not hostile particularly to the missionary idealism paired with a sound business sense which runs through the generation of producer studio heads who had shaped the Hollywood of the 1930s and '40s. Like Cecil B. de Mille, Irving Thalberg and Samuel Goldwyn before them, Meyer, Selznick, and even Zanuck possessed a curiously explicit "ideological" outlook on their work, and a by no means crude understanding of the media and their audiences made them self-appointed apostles of their country's often contradictory aspirations and ideals. In the films they commissioned and approved from their directors and scriptwriters they were as concerned with reinforcing specifically American socialization processes and synthesizing the overall patterns of American history (always seen, to be sure, from the point of view of the economically and socially most dynamic groups) as a Henry James or Edmund Wilson was concerned with finding out what constituted American identity and American culture.

The conflict of East and West Coast, industrialization and agriculture, the Frontier, the Civil War, urbanization, the immigrant experience, the Depression have all been reflected, and often in a highly critical manner by Hollywood films, as indeed have social evils – from prison conditions and corruption in local and state government to racism, right-wing republicanism or such old favorites as extortion and protection rackets in boxing or baseball. That the dramatic pattern inevitably engineered a "personalized" solution to social problems and that they distinguished only with difficulty the dividing line between the moral and the political is a matter that affects a lot of social thinking in America. The fact remains that the standard genres from Western to psychological thriller and soap opera melodrama have evolved on close analogy to underlying psychological and social tendencies, and the far from innocuous comedies of Tashlin or Billy Wilder have consistently dramatized the internal contradictions of representative American social experiences.[16] Not only is Hollywood ideologically transparent in the way films aim at internalizing and psychologizing the public and social issues of American history, but their aesthetic and stylistic devices arc geared towards locating the value and purpose of that experience in recognizably commonplace situations and everyday contexts, mainly by means of a visual dramatic rhetoric, a strategy of persuasion as "classical" and subtly adaptable as any which past civilization have produced in periods of hegemony. During the apogee of Hollywood, even the most outlandish adventure story or musical extravaganza had to build its dramatic structure and narrative development on a familiar, easily identifiable subsoil of emotional reactions, drawn from the basic psychological dilemmas of the age. It is this emotional proximity to the viewer maintained across an immense variety of subjects, situations and filmic genres that one has to reckon with in any argument about the nature of popular culture in the cinema. And Welles, although his first four films or so (before his Shakespearomania took over) were squarely within the national quest for the American psyche, was nonetheless in his stylistic approach far too idiosyncratic and "expressionist" ever to achieve or probably ever to aspire to the powerfully emotional realism of the commonplace, for the sake of which Hollywood directors, producers and script writers fashioned iconographic stereotypes, infinitely recycling plots, psychologically one-dimensional characters, and a completely codified, carefully sifted image of the American (moral, social and geographic) landscape. By sheer force of repetition it imposed itself successfully as a symbolic system of notation within which very differentiated statements could be articulated, and it also constituted a dramatically acceptable, and for a long time ideologically accepted set of conventions by which to picture the dynamic interplay of reality and fantasy that Europeans find so characteristic of l'homme americain moyen sensuel.

These aspects of Hollywood and the resolutely "popular" aesthetics underpinning them were not on the whole given much attention in the heyday of Cahiers criticism. Support of a different kind for the American cinema came at about the same time from surrealist groups, who let their love and admiration for American "pop" – the comic strip, science fiction, pin-up eroticism, pulp fiction – generously embrace Hollywood movies, first somewhat ambiguously ransacking them, especially the B productions of the smaller studios, for conscious or involuntary sublimities in the way of visual or emotional shocks and for that elusive quality of the insolite by which imaginative authenticity could be gauged. Several "genres" received their special attention, thus the horror movie and exotic adventure film (le merveilleux et le fantastique – both terms were and still are used as descriptive categories), gangster movies and thrillers with a strong romantic flavor (le film noir), musicals and "low-brow" comedies (e.g., Jerry Lewis). In all cases, what was stressed was the subversive element in "pop," where Hollywood could provide additional firepower in the revolt against bourgeois notions of appeasement, sobriety and taste in art.

It is obviously essential to keep the middle class, consciously intellectual approach to the American cinema via Welles, Wyler and the Catholic Left around Bazin, distinct from the militant anti-bourgeois, anti-academic enthusiasm of the surrealists. However, since their differences had the good fortune to be brought out into the open and ripen with the years into sharp antagonisms, the invaluable effect was to generate committed and partisan debates, thus putting pressure on the trenchancy of the arguments: the Hollywood cinema during the mid-1950s in France decidedly prospered on the crest of waves agitated by highly polemical clashes of opinion in the Paris magazines, carried into the country on the groundswell of the cine-club movement which had already made France the most cinematically literate country in Europe. Another factor that can scarcely be overestimated was Henri Langlois' Cinematheque, begun during the war in association with Georges Franju and Jean Mitry, but which only after the war became the unique film archive that it is today, unique mainly because from the start Langlois did not operate any form of pre selection, least of all one dividing cinematic "art" from "entertainment." He tried to preserve all the celluloid he could lay his hands on, and presented in the rue d'Ulm, as at the Palais de Chaillot, a collection from which each faction could draw and build its own tradition and genealogy of cinematic art. Given the transitory nature of film viewing, Langlois played a crucial role as a democratizing and stimulating force, since it was only because the films were around and could be seen and re-seen that critical engagement was possible and disagreement worthwhile.

If this had been all, the vogue for Hollywood movies might not have amounted to more than a passing intellectual fad. What can't be ignored, however, is the special relation which French literary culture entertained with American writing, and the attitude of official France towards America in the first decade after the Second World War. The years of German occupation and the Vichy Regime had given the Americans the halo and aura of liberators. They had rescued Europe from fascism, they had handed France back to the good French, and even left-wing circles for a time looked upon the United States, its political system, its democratic institutions, its productivity and prosperity with something resembling respect. Jean-Paul Sartre visited America on several occasions and published long, guardedly appreciative or occasionally enthusiastic pieces in *Les Temps Modernes* and elsewhere.[17] Since the 1930s, French intellectuals had taken pride in having "discovered" modern American literature, as Baudelaire had "discovered" Poe: not just for France, but for the rest of the world and especially for Americans themselves. Malraux wrote with real knowledge and insight about Faulkner at a time when Faulkner had barely left the tutelage of Sherwood Anderson, and in his famous preface to the French edition of *Sanctuary* he spoke of it as "the incursion of Greek tragedy into the detective story."[18] Sartre's articles on *The Sound and the Fury* were long regarded as definitive statements on Faulkner the "modern" novelist,[19] while Gide waxed enthusiastic over Dashiell Hammett's *Red Harvest*. Dos Passos, Dreiser, Steinbeck, Lardner, Caldwell and O'Hara were as seriously discussed and as widely read as Scott Fitzgerald, West, and Hemingway. Last but not least, the mainstay of every station bookstore and newsagent in the country was American thrillers in translation: a good deal of – the famous "serie noire" publications were American or modelled on American novels, and they popularized an image of America – violent, individualist, bitter with the cynical cool of idealism gone sour, though energetic and vibrant; a fabrication compelling enough to do without a philoso-phical commentary and still register as the concrete embodiment of existential alienation, "Angst" and the nihilistic *acte gratuit*, seemingly lived on the scale of an entire nation. At this level of projection, and drawing on similar inspiration, the American novel and the cinema naturally reinforced each other to produce an image in which America figured largely as a state of the imagination, a frame of mind, much in the way it had served an earlier generation of European intel-lectuals – those in Germany during the 1920s, for instance, of whom Brecht is probably the best-known exponent.

But the kind of revolution in aesthetic standards and attitudes to popular cul-ture that was under way in France by the end of the 1940s is equally well illu-strated by the book of a literary critic and scholar published in 1948, and which for the first time attempted to fuse the literary and philosophical interest in American fiction and culture with the grass-roots popularity of the movies: Claude-Edmonde Magny's *L'age du roman Americain*, extremely original in its conception, was able to catch in argument and example the climate of informed opinion as well as the general pro-American bias accurately and eloquently en-ough to become an instant classic. What is interesting is the glimpse it gives of the evaluative criteria that made a study of the cinema a worthwhile intellectual activity. Her thesis is briefly this: The modern American novel – and here she means mainly Dos Passos, Steinbeck, Hemingway and Faulkner – is exemplary in two ways. It has managed to break through the distinction between high-brow and low-brow fiction, and it has at the same time assimilated into narra-tive forms some of the important aesthetic achievements of imagism and sym-bolism, such as objectivity, neutrality of tone, a reliance on description, a decep-tively non-introspective use of language and speech or syntax that possessed the muscularity of action. Yet this was not the result of studying the symbolists or Flaubert, Joyce, Gide or Proust, but because American novelists had willingly entered into a reciprocal relation with the movies and filmic techniques, learn-ing from them what they could. Considerable space is devoted to Hammett, whose methods of description and characterization Magny analyzes in some detail. This she uses to argue against the middle class bias in French fiction, and she proceeds to sketch an alternative history of the modern novel, approached through a terminology borrowed from the cinema: there are chapters on mon-tage and cutting in film and novel, on ellipsis and narrative structure, on scenic presentation of character and spatial form. The summing up of the first part of her argument is particularly instructive:

> We are here concerned with a new convergence of the same kind as that which has already been discussed – a convergence between the results of psychoanalysis, beha-viorism, and sociology and the new vision of the world that the movies and the novel communicate to us almost unconsciously, by virtue of their technique alone. It is no

longer a question of a kinship between two forms ... but of one between the abstract themes that haunt contemporary thought and the conclusions that are suggested by the evolution toward an epoch of purely aesthetic techniques belonging to the domain of the emotions rather than of the intellect ... But this is not the only reason for its (i.e., the American novel's) success: it also gives us a more simple and direct, and therefore more universal vision of man than that proposed by our traditional literature. Through its masterpieces we glimpse the promise of a new humanism. If its major importance is its content, however, why is it its technique that is most imitated? To use Sartre's apt phrase, it is because the technique is pregnant with a whole metaphysics.[20]

One has to read this passage in its historical context: the reference to Sartre, to a new humanism, to an immediate, because emotional truth are not fortuitous. Magny lends her voice to the same guarded social optimism which during the post-war period led Sartre to modify his philosophy in the direction of dialectical materialism, but one can also see how a more "theological" existentialism might be attracted to American literature and the movies – that of Andre Bazin for instance, and reflected in the tenor of the early period of *Cahiers du cinéma*. What French intellectuals expected from things American were works of fiction that could serve as creative models, representative of their own situation and embodying specifically modern tensions – between intellect and emotion, action and reflection, consciousness and instinct, choice and spontaneity. It is remarkable for example how many of the film critics who rallied behind the Bazin-*Cahiers* line did in fact go on to make films themselves, using their knowledge of the Hollywood cinema as a constant reference point in elaborating their aesthetics. The names are too wellknown to need much comment: Chabrol, Godard, Truffaut, Rohmer, Rivette, Melville, Doniol-Valcroze and others.

Magny's book, with its copious references to films, also brings striking confirmation that the French were ready and able to draw on a cinematic literacy in a general debate about aesthetics which would have been unthinkable anywhere else in the world. She is not at all selfconscious or apologetic about mentioning movies like Curtiz's Angels with Dirty Faces in the same breath as Faulkner's *Light in August* to illustrate a point about narrative ellipsis and indirection, or to compare favorably techniques of anti psychological characterization in Hawks' Bringing Up Baby with those to be found in Camus' *L' Etranger* or a novel by Aragon. In her book the cinema exists, and not just as the potentially vital art form of the future (in the way it had done for so many theorists of the 1920s), but by virtue of actual and contemporary films that were deemed to hold their own in a comparison with writing and literature.

Consequently, what gave *Cahiers du cinéma* its impact and made it known abroad was the dedication with which its contributors put the prestige of French highbrow culture behind their enthusiasm for Hollywood. With benign self-confidence they made the cinema appear in almost every respect on an equal, if not a superior, footing with contemporary literature, and often enough with the great art of the past. "Griffith is to the cinema what Bach is to music"[21] and "Fuller is to Welles what Marlowe is to Shakespeare"[22]: these were the kind of opening gambits that made Anglo-Saxon critics very nearly choke with indignation. But the recklessness of such claims was not simply *pour épater* those who preferred to keep their art clean or resented cultural trespassers. It was part of an effort to analyze film history and thereby consolidate critical standards appropriate to the medium: "Stendhal is superior to Losey up to the point where the subject of his description passes from intention and mental rumination to its incarnation in a universe of bodies and forms. At this precise instant, Losey becomes incommensurably superior to Stendhal."[23] The references across

GIANT

the arts were ultimately only a means of establishing priorities and a scale of evaluation within the cinema itself. This becomes clearest where *Cahiers du cinéma* criticized films that didn't come up to what one could expect from the director or the genre he was working in: George Stevens's GIANT, a hugely successful epic of the 1950s and James Dean's last film, is found wanting because "its eclectic morality leaves no room for that spirit of satire, of severity too, nor for the sense of the grand-

iose, the tragic, the perilous which comes so naturally to countless American films. No comparison between the complaisance with which the characters here cultivate their clear conscience and the beautiful generosity of Nicholas Ray's heroes.[24] However partially *Cahiers* critics judged films, their great merit was to judge them by criteria derived from other, comparable films and not from idealist notions of what "art" or the cinema ought to be like. Yet since they were committed to the idea of the director as the creative center, they had to retreat by necessity to a relatively tiny area of cinematic specificity, fortify it intellectually and proceed from there to conquer the whole territory of interpretation and evaluation. Given the fact that in Hollywood the director often had no more than token control over choice of subject, the cast, the quality of the dialogue, all the weight of creativity, all the evidence of personal expression and statement had to be found in the mise-en-scène, the visual orchestration of the story, the rhythm of the action, the plasticity and dynamism of the image, the pace and causality introduced through the editing. This is why the mise-en-scène could transform even the most apparently conventional Western into a profound and nuanced statement about personal guilt, redemption, existential choice, divided loyalties, and moral growth (as in Anthony Mann's work), or a multi-million epic could explore the dialectics of personal commitment and moral distance, passionate spontaneity and short-sighted rashness (e.g., Otto Preminger's Exo-DUS).[25]

Both concepts, however, that of the *auteur* and mise-en-scène on which was founded the *Cahiers*'s revaluation of Hollywood popular art, operated not only as aesthetic value judgements and hermeneutic principles of exegesis; they also had in the historical context a polemical edge: the notion of the "auteur," the temerity of assuming his very existence at the heart of the vast Hollywood machinery was intended to counter the dismissal of American films as impersonal, standardized consumer products and to militate for the attitude where every film is to be viewed on its own merits according to criteria evolved historically and empirically from actual films and the conditions under which they were made. Nonetheless, the *Cahiers du cinéma* position on Hollywood and its directors was, for all the virulence and conviction with which it was argued, a fragile one. The polemical edge cut both ways, and the contradictions that resulted from constantly trying to play both ends against the middle became in time more and more noticeable. By the early 1960s it had become all but untenable: *Cahiers* defended Hollywood and the studio system, but made a cult of the individual artist that was suspiciously intellectual and European; they recognized the uses of genre formulations and conventions in a medium with universal appeal, but they praised in preference those films that managed to subvert the conventions and transcend the limits of the genre; they approved of the aura conferred by a star (*Charlton Heston est un axiome. Il constitue a lui seul une trage-die*),[26] and they made great play of the fact that films appeal to the emotions and the senses rather than the intellect, but their own system of interpretation required a highly sophisticated, aesthetically conscious sensibility; they were fond of underlining the cultural significance of Hollywood films, but their main critical plank, the idea of mise-en-scène, meant at the most obvious level "form" to the exclusion of "content," and in the hands of more skilled critics, an inordinately high regard for the strategies of aesthetic distance by which a director could transform overt content into a coded message accessible to the initiated.

For a time these contradictions were fruitful, especially where they produced the kind of friction which made the stylistic differences between Wyler and Ford, Fuller and Losey, Hawks and Anthony Mann live issues which sparked off debates about fundamentals. The *Cahiers* line remained creative as long as these tensions were felt to be intellectually challenging and a useful weapon in another struggle closer to home: that against academicism in filmmaking and literary-mindedness in criticism. To militate for a "pure cinema" of mise-en-scène was to fight against the stodgily theatrical cinema of Delannoy and Cayatte, and enthusiasm for American mass culture was meant to defy the growing embourgeoisement of popular entertainment in France and Europe. That *Cahiers*'s criteria were "only" aesthetic and their mode of appreciation elitist highlights sharply the conflict of the intellectual when trying to articulate the values inherent in non-intellectual art, or indeed any art that grows from different cultural and social preconditions: doomed to resort to his own language, he necessarily distorts his own intuition and transforms the object of his study into a metaphor. France's relations with American culture are very much a case in point. If it took existentialism to make American fiction intellectually respectable, and if it took the occasional histrionics of the Orson Welles persona to give artistic luster to Hollywood, it is scarcely surprising that a literary critic like Magny feels the need to appeal to the "universally human" as the proper antidote to the exclusively middle-class orientation of the modern French novel, and that film critics are tempted to vindicate their interest in the action movie or the melodrama by an occasional recourse to Jansenism, phenomenological vocabulary and a theory of concrete universals.[27] The dilemma of finding a non-metaphorical critical discourse is endemic to all contemporary intellectual inquiry, even where this is Marxist or structuralist in inspiration. Historically, *Cahiers du cinéma* suffered from its internal contradictions as soon as its position began to harden into a dogma, and when the struggle on the home front brought victory in the shape of the *Nouvelle Vague* and the journalistic ballyhoo created around it. By entrenching themselves in the all-importance of the mise-en-scène, they were continually forced to soft-pedal the more political implications of their preference for such "ultra" directors as Hawks or Ford, and they were unable to bring out such significant American attitudes as the conservative radicalism of, say, Walsh or Fuller. And this is where their sharpest opponents, the critics around the magazine *Positif* and inheritors of left-wing surrealism scored most of their points. In two famous articles,[28] the Bazin-*Cahiers* aesthetics of an optimum of continuous time and space, of integrated narrative and action, directorial indirection rather than expression, drama through depth of field rather than montage etc., was mercilessly dismantled and declared to be an ideological smoke screen disguising political timidity and impotence. At the height of the Algerian war, Bazin's "liberal" aesthetics of ambiguity was denounced in no uncertain terms as a "sitting on the fence, as the cunning tergiversations of conservatism, as the reactionary deviousness of Catholic obscurantism: ."...*cette mechante eglise de campagne qu'est le systeme de Bazin.*"[29]

In many ways this attack was grossly overstating a valid enough case. It was unfair if one looks at the ideological complexion of the two or three directors whom Bazin praised most warmly: for instance Renoir and Rossellini. The latter was closely associated with neo-realism which of course at the time was considered very much as an artistic movement of the Left, and Renoir, a prominent member of the Popular Front, could by no stretch of the imagination be called a dyed-in-the-wool conservative. In this context, the Hollywood films that Bazin liked were absorbed into that floating populism – generous, emotional but also rather nebulous – which many French intellectuals, and especially those of the Catholic Left, had taken away from the days of the Resistance.

What was suspect to *Positif* was Bazin's theological terminology and the failure of his disciples to bring their political options explicitly to bear on their critical system. The ambiguously metaphoric status of *Cahiers'* commitment to Hollywood made their search for a cinematic tradition at the same time creatively productive and intellectually confusing, and once the critics had become film makers in their own right, Hollywood lost much of its use as a club to swing at the establishment, thus giving some substance to the charge made by *Positif* that it was all a rather sorry spectacle of bad faith and rationalization.[30] For *Positif*, though equally accepting the importance of Hollywood, argued from quite different premises: by and large they too subscribed to the notion of a "director's cinema" and to a similarly textual approach, but their pantheon of directors was determined by an overall interpretation of American culture and society. Coming from an explicitly Marxist left, their inclination was to look for a comparable equivalent to European left-wing thinking, and they believed they found it in the predominantly liberal or ex-Marxist left, present in Hollywood through directors such as Huston, Losey, Kazan, Mankiewicz, Rossen and some of the directors around the producer Mark Hellinger. *Positif*'s interest in Hollywood during the 1950s might be said to have inversely mirrored that shown by McCarthy and the House of Un-American Activities Committee's special investigation. *Positif* maintained that the American cinema became an ideologically significant index of the "state of the union" precisely because of the dialectical interplay between the directors' quest for specific statements in a cinematic language designed to level off personal expression in the interest of communicability, and the economic pressures to market a product that fulfils as nearly as can be the already existing expectations of the greatest possible number. More historically minded than *Cahiers du cinéma*, *Positif*'s staff were interested in the American cinema because they were interested in America, and not the other way around. Hollywood being a means rather than an end, they were able to remain "faithful" to it when the tide began to turn in the mid-1960s.

The same cannot be said of *Cahiers* whose line was not only internally unstable, but extremely vulnerable to the historical developments at large. The cinema on whose chosen masterpieces they had lavished such eloquent praise became during the same time embarrassingly powerful and economically dominant, so much so that many of the *Cahiers* critics turned film makers were suddenly confronted with the more materialist side of their aesthetics, namely the stranglehold which American production companies and distributors had on the European scene and on finance: the late 1960s and early 1970s were marked by the successive stages of an extremely successful move to corner markets, buy out competitors and invest capital and thus build up control in the national film industries in Britain and on the Continent. *Cahiers* found it difficult to cope with this evidence, to which must be added the growing malaise among European and especially French intellectuals about American influence in world affairs – military, economic, social and cultural. Their response was to assume a heavily nostalgic tone, the films that came out of Hollywood didn't please as well as they had done, and even though it was obvious that the American film industry was undergoing a decisive internal evolution, their critical system proved inflexible and unresponsive. It had to be maintained intact, or broken. And when the rise of television began to starve the cinemas of their mass audiences, and Hollywood production companies dissolved their studios at home and moved to Pinewood, Cinecitti or some village in Spain or Yugoslavia, *Cahiers* thought they could detect an altogether different product, with which they were impatient and bored, and they felt justified in speaking of the Hollywood cinema in the past tense.

The more, therefore, historical events threw into prominence the interventionist role of the United States in world politics, whether by force of arms, monopolizing markets or cultural exports (which the film industry spearheaded long

La Chinoise

before the rock/pop/beat scene created a quite different European-American interdependence with its own vast commodity market), the more evident it became that praise of Hollywood could and did lend indirect but influential support to American ideology abroad. The events of May 1968 made the *de facto* break with the American cinema which began in 1963 *de rigueur* for the *Cahiers* contributors, and the magazine holds today an extreme left position of Marxist-Leninist persuasion, thus severing itself from its own past as radically as from Hollywood itself. Godard's press release for his film LA CHINOISE (1967) rang the changes for everybody to hear:

> Fifty years after the October Revolution, the American industry rules cinema the world over. There is nothing much to add to this statement of fact. Except that on our own modest way we too should provoke two or three Vietnams in the bosom of the vast Hollywood-Cinecitti-Mosfilm-Pinewood empire, and, both economically and aesthetically, struggling on two fronts as it were, create cinemas which are national, free, brotherly, comradely and bonded in friendship.[31]

If the decline of Hollywood in critical esteem among a certain section of European intellectuals can be seen to have such an explicitly political side to it, responding with considerable swiftness to the increase of anti-American feeling in social and political thinking, one is tempted to conclude two things: one, that the rise of Hollywood was equally affected by a specific ideological situation, which I have briefly sketched, but which the first line of *Cahiers* critics managed to displace onto the purely aesthetic level. The second point is that the episode of Hollywood in another country contains the lesson that any critical system or aesthetic discourse which is unable to refer to and reflect upon the social and economic conditions under which the medium or the art in question produce and maintain themselves is liable not only to be incoherent and distorted, but to remain ignorant about the nature of its own activity. The cinema, with its curious status, halfway between an art form of self-expression and a capital intensive industry of international importance, may put this into particular relief, but it is a sobering thought that it might be equally true of less "popular" manifestations of modern culture. The French intellectuals who championed Hollywood by raising it to the level of high art, in order to snatch it from the clutches of the sociologists had to discover that they were themselves the victims of the ideology they had affected to transcend.

(1975)

Notes

1. The term *"nouvelle vague"* started its life as a journalists' tag at the Cannes Film Festival of 1959, when a dozen or so new French films by unknown, though not always particularly young directors got rave reviews from the international press. Among the films were works by Chabrol, Godard, Truffaut (who won the Festival Prize for *Les Quatre Cent Coups*). See on this an important but highly critical study: R. Borde, F. Buache, J. Curtade *Nouvelle Vague* (Paris) 1962.
2. Recent writing on the cinema tends again to follow the French lead and seems to concentrate on "the processes of signification" and the linguistic-semiotic status of the image as sign. See C. Metz, *Langage et Cinéma* (Paris) 1971. In English, some of the main issues are set out in P. Wollen, *Signs and Meaning in the Cinema* (London) 1969, which also contains a chapter on the "Auteur Theory."
3. The writer who has done most to popularize the French view of the American cinema in the United States is Andrew Sarris. Under his editorship *Film Culture* devoted a special issue to Hollywood (no.28, Spring 1963). In January 1966, Sarris brought out the first issue of an ambitious though short-lived publishing venture, *Cahiers du cinéma in English*. The controversy over Sarris's appraisal of Hollywood directors can be studied in two issues of *Film Quarterly*: Pauline Kael's "Circles and Squares" (Spring 1963) and Sarris's reply "The Auteur Theory and the Perils of Pauline" (Summer 1963). See also the Introduction to Andrew Sarris, *The American Cinema. Directors and Directions 1929-68* (New York) 1968.
4. The American Film Institute was inaugurated in June 1967.
5. *Movie Magazine*, whose first issue appeared in 1962.

6. *Cahiers du cinéma* was founded in 1951, as the successor to *La Revue du cinéma* (first issue in 1946). Its editors were André Bazin, Jacques Doniol-Valcroze, and Eric Rohmer.

7. See for instance: Ricciotto Canudo, *L'Usine aux images*, Paris 1927; Louis Delluc, *Ciné et Cie*, Paris 1929; Germaine Dulac, L'Art Cinématographique, Paris 1927; Elie Faure, *L'Arbre d'Eden*, Paris 1922; Béla Balasz, *Der Sichtbare Mensch*, Vienna 1924; V. Poudovkin and L. Kouleshov, *Film Regie und Film Manuscript* 1929; Sergeii M. Eisenstein, *Film Form* (London) 1949 and *The Film Sense* (London) 1948; Rudolf Arnheim, *Film als Kunst*, 1932; Raymond Spottiswoode, *A Grammar of Film* (London) 1935.

8. The best-known example of this school is of course S. Kracauer, *From Caligari to Hitler* (New York) 1947.

9. *Sequence*, Winter 1947.

10. *Sight and Sound*, Summer 1956.

11. *Sight and Sound*, Autumn 1958.

12. Originally entitled "Problemes de la Peinture," in *Esprit*, 1945.

13. André Bazin, *Qu'est ce que c'est le cinéma*. 3 vols. Paris 1958-61.

14. L'Evolution du langage cinématographique' op. cit. vol. 1, p. 132.

15. "De 1930 a 1940, c'est le triomphe a Hollywood de cinq ou six grands genres qui assurent alors son (i.e., the American cinema's) écrasante supériorité." op. cit. vol. 1, p. 136.

16. See Jeffrey Richards, *Visions of Yesterday*, London 1973, especially the chapter on Frank Capra and Populism; also Raymond Durgnat, *The Crazy Mirror*, London 1970.

17. See J.-P. Sartre, *Situations III* (Paris) 1949.

18. See A. Malraux, "Une Preface pour *Sanctuary*," *Nouvelle Revue Française*, November 1933.

19. See J. P. Sartre, *Situations I* (Paris) 1947.

20. Claude-Edmond Magny, *The Age of the American Novel* (New York) 1972, p. 100-101.

21. *Cahiers du cinéma* no. 70, April 1957, p. 43.

22. Quoted in Richard Roud, "The French Line," *Sight and Sound*, Autumn 1960, p. 167.

23. *Cahiers du cinéma* no. 107, May 1960, p. 24.

24. *Cahiers du cinéma* no. 70, April 1957, p. 44.

25. For a comparable approach in English, see R. Wood, "Exodus," in *Movie* no.2, 1963, and T. Elsaesser, "Exodus" in *Brighton Film Review* vol. 2, no.5, 1969.

26. *Cahiers du cinéma* no. 107, May 1960, 24.

27. For example "William Wyler ou le jansénisme de la mise-en scene" in *Qu'est ce que c'est le cinéma*, vol. 1, p. 149.

28. *Positif*, nos. 46, 47 (June, July 1962).

29. *Positif*, no. 46, 59.

30. See *Positif* no. 122, November 1970, R. Benayoun, "Les Enfants du paradigme," p. 7.

31. Quoted in Jean Narboni and Tom Milne (eds), *Godard on Godard* (London 1972), p. 243.

Raoul Ruiz's L'HYPOTHÈSE DU TABLEAU VOLÉ

Imagine Peter Greenaway, on leave from the Central Office of Information, accepting a commission from the Arts Council to do a documentary on Anthony Blunt, and turning in a filmed interview with John Gielgud (playing a collector) who sets out to prove that Landseer's paintings are full of scatological references to mid-Victorian society scandals. Translated into French terms, this would yield one – but only one – layer of Raúl Ruiz's THE HYPOTHESIS OF THE STOLEN PAINTING (1978), the story of a collection of paintings by Tonnerre, a French academic painter of the mid-19th century, whose rather undistinguished works, with no consistency in style or subject matter, are said to have provoked a major but mysterious society scandal. However, to complete my hypothetical analogy, one would have to add that Ruiz has made the state of exile (in turn mimicking and mocking France, his host country, with equal conviction) the starting point for an erudite but nonetheless highly ironic study of the difference between filmic and pictorial rules of representation which leaves one wondering until well into the middle of the film whether Ruiz might not, after all, be serious with his conceit of these paintings bearing a dangerous secret.

THE HYPOTHESIS OF THE STOLEN PAINTING

What Ruiz has in common with Greenaway is a gift for mimicry as travesty (Ian Christie, talking about Ruiz's television work, once referred to "the strategies of parody and literalism"), which is to say, a sharp awareness of the tacit assumptions underlying the conventions of non-fiction film and television. Followed to the letter by a determined director, these television conventions of the filmed interview have the same disruptive effect on our sense of reality as a work-to-rule of post office workers has on our mail delivery. Ruiz once indicated that he might actually be an admirer of Greenaway ("Seeing THE FALLS, I found there my own hatred of British television, of the BBC with all its artificiality, the false efficiency that people are now trying to copy in France"), but he makes quite un-English use of the deliriously straight-faced British approach to wildly improbable narrative premises.

For whereas parodies of television manners in Britain tend to beget either the rather fussy elegance of Greenaway, or the funny but sometimes facile nihilism of Monty Python, Ruiz's parody of tasteful French connoisseurship (in the tradition of André Malraux, for instance) in THE HYPOTHESIS OF THE STOLEN PAINT-ING leads, on admittedly playful and labyrinthine paths, straight to the moral-philosophical tales of Eric Rohmer or Jacques Rivette. This, of course, may itself be a ruse, since HYPOTHESIS, together with SUSPENDED VOCATION, was the visiting card for Ruiz's gaining admittance to the still quite limited circle of Francophile foreigners accepted as honorary Paris intellectuals, and thus permitted to use – occasionally even misuse – the funds of the national television channels.

The story, with its fanciful premise of a series of paintings linked obliquely to each other (and thereby protecting an embarrassing secret) by a random alternation of formal devices, mythic motifs, esoteric references and hidden clues, is a typical example of a *récit emboîté*, or shaggy dog story. It makes of THE HY-POTHESIS OF A STOLEN PAINTING a very literary meditation on the subject of parallel worlds, of messages disguising themselves as accidents and coincidences revealing the hand of fate. Ruiz courteously pays tribute to Jorge Luis Borges, Italo Calvino and the paranoid histories of Thomas Pynchon. But like Umberto Eco's *The Name of the Rose*, it is also a detective story. The clues, pointing as they do to a conspiracy and a cover-up "out there" in the world of history – on the side of the referent, so to speak – shape themselves even more convincingly into an allegory of "in here", i.e., of reading and the mind's need for sense-making. The conspiracy is that of the sign, which can overturn one's hold on the real, simply by opening up a gap and positing a missing link: in this case, a supposedly stolen painting, removed from the series to make the rest indecipherable and random. Here, forming a hypothesis, in itself an insubstantial and unsubstantiated conjecture, is enough to plant the seeds of both doubt and possibility, and instantly instill the oppressive quiddity of some banal paintings with an air of mystery and suspense – not by presenting fresh evidence, but by repressing, subtracting evidence, or if you like, adding an absence. The English translation (referring to a stolen *painting*) is deficient, because what Ruiz's original title refers to are not paintings but *tableaux*, in fact *tableaux vivants*, which he subjects to several readings, varying the context or isolating a detail.

Once cued to these dual and triple registers, the film can be enjoyed as a sophisticated play with the narrative possibilities contained in static images, the stories that linger within or at the edges of a visual representation. And as an exercise in perverse readings, demonstrating both the necessity and the impossibility of interpretation, HYPOTHESIS gives more than a passing nod in the direction of Roland Barthes, Jacques Derrida, and theories of textual deconstruction. For instance, one of the *tableaux* even refers to the ambiguous role of an androgynous figure, "the principle of indefinition," which is an allusion not only to Pierre Klossowski's novel *Baphomet*, but also to a central motif in Barthes' *S/Z*.

The openness of the film, however, is ultimately more apparent than real. Ruiz moves rather systematically through different modes of interpretation, while cunningly suggesting there is a progression from *tableau* to *tableau* which will eventually establish a coherent whole. Symbolic, allegorical, mystical and historical readings follow each other not in pursuit of a final truth, but rather to demonstrate, in the manner of practical criticism and close reading, the range of Russian formalist criteria of pertinence, signification and meaning. If this sounds dry and pedantic, the film itself is too much second cousin to Orson Welles' F FOR FAKE (1974) – and too caught up in the pleasures of telling tall tales – not to want to milk the lore of Freemasons, Rosicrucians, Crusaders and other secret conspiracies for all the surreal encounters they can yield (in the spirit of Max Ernst's pseudo-narrative collages). Thus, the society scandal finally revealed, the reading of the *tableaux* "correctly" turns out to be itself possibly no more than a ploy to disguise an even more dastardly plot – the revival of a secret military sect or brotherhood.

Two possibly contradictory aims contend with each other. Ruiz's fascination with the underworld of meaning indicates a healthy skepticism towards the interpretative strategies of this century's dominant "secret societies" in the empire of signs – Marxism and psychoanalysis, of which Ruiz has said that they are "Gothic systems: an exterior facade and an enigma buried within", always aiming to produce the same master text. As an exile, living in the interstices of several cultures, dogmas and systems, Ruiz evidently prefers to consider interpretation mainly as a matter of staging most effectively the chance confrontation of one text with another. If a particularly anodyne family portrait can be made to seem riddled with mystery and scandal when passages from a mildly

pornographic 19th-century novel are made to connect with its grouping of figures, then the enigma resides in neither the *tableau* nor the novel, but in the surreal match between voice and image.

A wholly imaginary world comes into being which owes little to reality or fiction, and much to the cinema's power to conjure up presence from absence. The philosophy implicit here evidences a total skepticism about cinema's supposed realism. In one *tableau*, the voice-over commentary points out that respect for the

THE HYPOTHESIS OF THE STOLEN PAINTING

laws of perspective may simply be a concession to the vulgar pleasures of recognition and identification, the better to mask that other message and purpose of the painting, which is to be part of a chain: its linking elements are a number of purely formal devices (light/shade, circle/crescent/sphere) which end up reducing the representational content to a mere support function.

The literary pretext of THE HYPOTHESIS OF THE STOLEN PAINTING, however, is a novel by Klossowski, commentator on de Sade, actor in Bresson's AU HASARD, BALTHAZAR (1966), brother of the painter Balthus and himself a painter of some distinction. His pictures are erotic mainly through the unchaste gestures and gazes by which the figures communicate with each other in an otherwise quite prosaic setting. Klossowski's literalism has to do with Sade's *Philosophy in the Boudoir*: making men and women enact, rather than represent, certain philosophical positions and moral postulates. Klossowski's fascination with the power relations embedded in the language of abstract speculation – which he parodies by illustrating them in explicitly sexual terms – fits in well with Ruiz's skepticism regarding the relation of word to image and image to reality. But the switch from abstraction to the literal in Klossowski's scenarios of philosophical debate undermines traditional notions of interpretation that want to move from realism to the symbolic, or inversely, from the hidden to the manifest (as in biblical or psychoanalytical discourse). There is, as the tempting but fraught "resolution" to this conundrum, the religious if not outright Catholic belief in the sanctification of the body by the word. Subjecting flesh to the logic of thought and language is ultimately to conduct a discourse that is both pornographic (writing desire with and on the body) and metaphysical (seeking the incarnation of the word). It is this latter dimension, typical enough of French modernism and postmodernism, which is absent from Ruiz's film. More interested in the problems of cinema (what is the relation between the *tableau* as a static image and the sequence that makes up the filmic flow?) and the problems of narrative (what determines the story potential of a visual configuration, and how does one get from one configuration to the next, without imposing on the image a text – a single fiction – which would arbitrarily limit those possibilities?), Ruiz plays the compliant agnostic even to Klossowski's iconoclastic Catholicism. "Every time that a general theory or a fiction is elaborated I have the impression that ... there is a painting stolen, a part of the story or puzzle missing. The final explanation is no more than a conventional means of tying together all the paintings. It's like the horizon: once you reach it, there is still the horizon."

(1984)

Images for Sale

The "New" British Cinema

The Thatcher Years: Hard Times, Interesting Times

The British cinema industry during the 1980s – the Thatcher years – enjoyed a Renaissance. Indeed, early on in the decade even Hollywood helped to celebrate its rebirth: Oscars for CHARIOTS OF FIRE (Hugh Hudson, 1981), the appointment of its producer, David Puttnam as Director of Production at Columbia Pictures, and more Oscars for GANDHI (Richard Attenborough, 1983). The 1980s also saw notable hits on the art cinema circuit with LETTER TO BREZNEV (Chris Bernard, 1985) and MY BEAUTIFUL LAUNDRETTE (Stephen Frears, 1985), recognition for auteurs like Peter Greenaway, John Boorman, and Nicolas Roeg, plaudits in Berlin for heretic iconoclasts like Derek Jarman, and commercial successes for international directors like Stephen Frears, Ridley Scott, Adrian Lyne, and Alan Parker. A more hard-bitten, controlled professionalism among directors eclipsed the volcanic and fizzing talents of a Ken Russell and a Lindsay Anderson from the previous decades. This group, by and large, opposed the ideological rigidities of Thatcher, matching the Iron Lady's temperament with an equally steely determination not to whine or indulge in left-wing romanticism.

During the decade, more British films were made than at any time since the 1950s, or at least more British films attracted international awards and coverage. In Britain, the cinemas were filling up again, albeit for American blockbusters; but whatever the attraction, a revival of audience interest might just, in the long run, be good for British movie business as well. One could begin to talk of a "British film culture" without having to invoke François Truffaut's famous quip about "British" and "cinema" being a contradiction in terms. Movies were also helped by the lively interest television took in the cinema, thanks to a popular preview program like Barry Norman's *Film* on BBC1, the retrospectives on BBC2's "Film Club" and "Moviedrome," the South Bank Shows devoted to filmmakers, the "Media Show" on Channel Four, and the co-production/co-financing or in-house filmmaking of television, especially BBC's "Screen Two" and Channel Four's "Film on Four" series, with a helpful hand from the BFI

Production Board. Out in the streets, however, the scene became further depleted: fewer and fewer cinemas even among the Rank/EMI-Cannon duopoly, and a dying out of independent neighborhood cinemas as well as art houses.

In the country at large, millions of Britons were living through hard times during the Thatcher era. Others found them interesting times, because her government brought about polarizations in the body politic not seen since the late 1920s: the definitive break-up of a social consensus which had maintained a common discourse about what was important to the national interest across the political spectrum. With Thatcher, the very terms by which to voice dissent were challenged, a point of some importance when considering the different political styles that emerged: from Arthur Scargill's Miners' Strike to David Owen's Social Democrats, from the Militant faction on Liverpool City Council to Nicholas Ridley on Germany. In the cinema's case, the different filmmaking styles (too readily lumped together as "postmodern") broke with the consensus idiom par excellence of "realism." In short, the Thatcher years implicitly and explicitly asked what it meant to be British – or English, Scottish, Irish, Welsh, to be from the North, the Midlands or the South. The decade also questioned what it meant to be a British filmmaker.

The polarizations along lines of class, of race, of region, nationality and language, recalled similar break-ups elsewhere in Europe. They make the 1980s a period of momentous social shifts well beyond Thatcherism and support the view that violent social tensions are often the best soil for the flowering of resilient, contesting and confrontational arts, obliging artists to rediscover themselves as social counter-forces and moral consciences.

An obvious topic would be to investigate whether one can trace the break-up of the consensus also in the cinema of the 1980s. Yet equally relevant is whether the kind of self-questioning of national identity just hinted at can be distinguished from another response, no less prominent in the 1980s: self-promotion, also pursued in the name of national identity. Given the increasing dependence of the arts on money (a condition always true of the cinema), and the fact that those granting money increasingly demanded that the arts demonstrate their usefulness, what might be the status of such a national identity, especially where it defines itself in economic terms: as competitive edge, conquest of markets and brand name awareness, while nonetheless relying on images and stories rather than goods and services for its meaning and substance.

Not Another British Cinema Renaissance ...

Screenwriter Colin Welland's cry of "The British Are Coming" at the Oscar ceremony for CHARIOTS OF FIRE set the tone for the decade, releasing a flood of
pent-up emotion and producing acres of print about the British Film Renaissance. But whenever the word Renaissance crops up in the context of the British
Cinema (as it seems to do at least once every decade), one needs to be wary.
Chances are the film industry is in deep trouble. This was the case around 1984/
1985 when, still flushed with the success of CHARIOTS OF FIRE, a string of media
events culminating in the British Film Year of 1985 persuaded the public to see
not the small acorn but the mighty oak tree, in other words, basically ignoring
the continuing decline of an indigenous film industry, the decreasing share of
British-made films in British cinemas, and an exodus to Hollywood of directors,
cinematographers and specialists in many filmmaking crafts (especially sound,
sets and animation).

Scanning the titles trumpeted as New British Cinema at the 1984 London Film
Festival, one wonders if what took place was a large-scale re-labeling of the
goods, a quick-fix for the deep- seated structural ills of mainstream filmmaking.
Suddenly, half the drama output of British television found itself named "cinema." While some "Plays for Today" deserved to be called movies (RAINY DAY
WOMEN, 1984, scripted by David Pirie, for instance), even more television films
should never have been showcased in the cinema, although co-production deals
(sometimes with foreign companies) made this obligatory. Thus, Chris Peachment could write about LOOSE CONNECTIONS (Richard Eyre, 1984):

> what we have here is something that would not be diminished by showing on video.
> Which may be perfectly acceptable to its director ... but is not what one would hope to
> say about something consciously made for the cinema.[1]

More damning still, Jeremy Isaacs, then Head of Channel Four, thought the efforts by the independent filmmaking sector fell between both stools: "too slight
for the cinema, too slack for television" [2], while for the critic John Brown a major
vehicle of the film industry, THE DRESSER (Peter Yates, 1984), despite its "elabo-
rately promoted status (The Royal Film, the Oscar nominations) as a big screen
movie [could not disguise the fact that it] operates as a big screen extension of
television traditions."[3]

A renaissance implies a renewal. What was it that was stirring, moving,
breaking through frozen ground? Talent? Commercial success? Big Themes?
Big Names? The organic metaphors flowing from those panegyric pens homo-
genized divergent if not contradictory phenomena. In the case of the British cinema in the mid-1980s, these ranged from fiscal changes affecting investment

depreciation (the end of tax shelters, in short), to judicious programming (film critic Derek Malcolm's term of office as Director of the London Film Festival proved particularly rich in this respect), to taking in an anniversary (50 Years of the British Film Institute in 1983), to the trial-and-error period of a new television network (Channel 4's buying and commissioning policy), and to the low rental rates of home video recorders and pre-recorded tapes (making Britain by the early 1980s "the largest home video market in Western Europe," according to *American Film*, May 1983).

Talk of a renaissance, however, rekindled the question of what could be a national cinema, what has it been, and who needed it? The British film industry always had problems asserting itself economically against overpowering Hollywood competition. Interestingly, in the periods when it held its own, or whenever a discernible strategy emerged (during the war years, or the 1950s), its success sprang as much from an ideological move as from an economic boost. This is what one learns from the classic studies. *A Mirror for England* was the programmatic title of Raymond Durgnat's influential book,[4] and Charles Barr[5] showed in what elaborate ways "Projecting Britain and the British character" was Michael Balcon's motto at Ealing Studios. In other words, whether during the war or immediately after, propaganda, patriotism and "projection" have functioned as integral parts of a successful national cinema.

Reporting on the 1981 Berlin Film Festival's retrospective of Balcon's work, David Robinson marveled at "just how rich the British cinema was in the 1930s and 1940s," and concluded that it had to do with:

> craftsmanship and a sure and determined sense of a national identity ... The films have a sort of confidence that they can sell themselves without recourse to vast budgets, or running after "international" (that is American) appeal.[6]

Robinson was not alone in thinking that an "emphasis on British themes gives... films the sinew of authenticity." The writer Alan Bennett put it equally succinctly:

> Behind a lot of the questions that are raised lurks an unspoken one: how do we make it big in America? Risking being hauled before Colin Welland in the Barnes Magistrates Court, charged with insulting behaviour, I'd like to ask why do we want to? ... the European directors I admire ... don't eat their hearts out because they're not big in Arkansas. Why should we? Mrs. Thatcher has the answer, but does she know anything about films?[7]

To which one might reply that she may not know much about films, but her speech writers knew a thing or two about self-promotion. She projected "British themes" and the "sinews of authenticity" pummeled out of flabby jingoist nostalgia, or more humbly put, she constructed new national myths out of the bric-a-brac of history, xenophobia, and paranoia.

Thatcher's Britain: An Invention of the Media

The dilemma when writing about cinema in the age of Thatcher is quite simply this: The Thatcher years were an invention of the media, or at the very least, the result of a complex and often collusive love-hate relationship between the Thatcher government, the press, and television. Most commentators agree that the connection between politics and television – not just in Britain – has become too close for comfort for democracy. But since the connection between film and television have become even more inextricable, it is almost impossible to construct for the cinema during this decade a straight opposition between confrontational artists and compliant public opinion, nor indeed for those working in the audio-visual media, an opposition between the hard times for some and the interesting times for others.

What remains most vividly about the decade is the so-called Saatchi effect. In politics, it pinpointed the close ties between the Conservative Central Office and a well-known advertising agency: the massive deployment, from within No. 10, of the Prime Minister's press secretary Bernard Ingham, and the promotion and preferment of flamboyant industrial entrepreneurs or "boardroom buccaneers" such as Lord Hanson (of the Hanson Trust), Lord King (Chairman of British Airways), and Lord Weinstock (Chairman of GEC). These men, a newspaper once pointed out, Margaret Thatcher rewarded as Queen Elizabeth I once rewarded Francis Drake. For the cinema, the Saatchi effect blurred the lines between the different kinds of self-awareness: that which probes and that which promotes. When Norman Stone,[8] writing for Rupert Murdoch's *Sunday Times*, made his much-publicized attack on filmmakers like Derek Jarman and Stephen Frears, he quite simply hated what they showed. Clearly alien to Stone was the idea that a filmmaker's shocking or disturbing images might be essential to making a certain reality visible, not just to the eye but to one's moral and emotional senses. Stone could assume, without questioning it, that at issue was England's image in the world, since national cinema worked like advertising: the agency should look after the client.

On the other hand, as the high-risk business for self-made men and buccaneers par excellence, the film industry should have appealed to the Thatcher philosophy. Yet even Puttnam and Attenborough found it hard to catch the Prime Minister's ear when it came to mitigating, with the help of central funds, the effects of abolishing the Eady levy, the tax write-offs and other economic measures detrimental to the film industry. In one sense, of course, the film industry in any European country always looks towards state support, as did the New German Cinema, or the French government's massive aid to its film industry. In Britain, government perceived the film lobby as looking for "hand-outs," and thus anathema to free-marketeers. But equally in the pursuit of new (and this means American) markets, British cinema should have enjoyed the government's benevolence on a par with Plessey, Westlands or Rover Cars. After all, Britain under Thatcher became a nation of national brand names, company logos, icons and slogans: identity under the reign of "The Image."

STEPHEN FREARS

How then can one read the relations between the British cinema and Thatcherism? When neither official rhetoric nor central government supported the small but nonetheless real impact of British films internationally, the whole spectrum, from Alan Parker to David Puttnam, from Dennis Potter to Peter Greenaway, from Derek Jarman to Stephen Frears turned scathingly anti-Thatcher. But did this necessarily mean that Britain in the 1980s had either a critical, self-questioning or a combative, society-questioning cinema?

What "We" Can Sell to "Them"

The answer must be both and neither. Both, insofar as one can easily name dozens of films highly critical and satirical, somber and desperate about the state of Britain. Neither, insofar as the terms of the debate about the cinema shifted sufficiently to make "critical" and "combative" almost irrelevant notions. Superficially at least, the debate on both sides concerned markets, box office, image and impact. As to "why we want to make it big in America," for instance, film journalists had no doubt. Perhaps the Thatcher ethos was well-understood and accepted. More likely, the home truth had sunk in that no successful European film industry can make films for its own market alone. Investment calculated on a purely national revenue basis makes the home-grown product look too cheap to be attractive to domestic audiences, those who vote with their feet for pictures with production values. On the other hand, journalists like Margaret Hinxman thought that "precisely the qualities that have made CHARIOTS OF FIRE such a hit across the Atlantic" were the ones apparently advanced by Rank, Lord Grade and EMI for turning David Puttnam down when he approached them for financing: "It has no name stars in it, its subject was sport, above all, it was too British."[9] Here, then, appears another dilemma – they were either too British or not British enough. Yet this presents too easy a juxtaposition. At issue is what kind of Britishness "we" could sell to "them," in turn balancing an appeal to "insider knowledge" about England and Britain with what the world knew, or thought it knew about Britain.

Such a proposition raises a number of further points. Firstly, we must differentiate between the projection of what one could call a "social imaginary" of Britain and the projection of a "national imaginary," one for "us" and one for "them." The distinction might even mark off television productions from film productions, with the latter necessarily destined for an international audience. Mamoun Hassan rightly points out that, as far as television goes, "international sales provide the jam" because the bread-and-butter is a national audience. The BBC has to justify its license fee, while the paymasters of commercial television are "the advertisers, [who] wish to sell their goods ... in Birmingham, West Midlands, and not Birmingham, Alabama."[10] But he underestimates the quite tangible "commercial goodwill" which tourism, the publishing trade, luxury cars, or British quality knitwear and leather-goods derive even from the relatively paltry sums changing hands between American PBS stations and ITV for *Upstairs Downstairs* or *Brideshead Revisited*. From television to films, and from style magazines to record sleeves, the Thatcher years taught the British media a crucial lesson: the importance of an image culture, rather than a film culture.

Film Culture: A Foreign Import?

I once argued that Britain lacked a film culture from the grass roots up, as in France, by which I mean, a large number of filmgoers who could recognize a traveling shot by Vincente Minnelli or a sequence edited by Sam Fuller. Equally important, I thought, was a generation of cine-literate as well as cinephile writers and directors. Hence the early enthusiasm for Chris Petit (a film critic turned director), whose reputation as a director always seemed slightly higher among the cinephiles than their judgement of his films, and the high praise for David Pirie (a film critic turned script writer):

> RAINY DAY WOMEN is a film... highly conscious of its choice of vocabulary, operating within un-fashionable dialects in the face of a dubious art-house accent from draughtsman to ploughman, putting its energy into story-telling and discovering its themes in the process.[11]

But I now wonder whether an emphasis on a film culture which, with the advent of television, risks becoming either scholastic or antiquarian, if it insists on filmmakers being cine-literate (knowing the "language of cinema") or cinephile (quoting from John Ford or Jean-Luc Godard) misconstrued the role of a tradition. During the years between 1968 and 1975 when a new generation of British film critics struggled to have the study of film accepted as a valid intellectual endeavor, the dialogue of the deaf between a certain journalistic establishment and the university film theorists narrowed the options of a film culture. On one side, was the demand for a "materialist" practice and a counter-cinema, on the other the condemnation of semiology and psychoanalysis as the Screenspeak of "pod-people."

One could also think of another kind of divide – perhaps more appropriate for the age of media globalization – that between the insider's and the outsider's view of Britain, where the outsider could well be from Scotland, Ireland, or Liverpool, and the insider from Hollywood. Historically, the "outsider-as-insider" view of Britain has often proved most memorable. So in Joseph Losey's films, especially in his collaborations with Harold Pinter, which epitomize an image of Britain in the 1960s that still survives, even if it never achieved cult status. To the Losey/Pinter partnership one should add Roman Polanski's REPULSION (1965) and CUL DE SAC (1966), as well as Jerzy Skolimowski's DEEP END (1970): films where the pastiche element has, over the years, taken on a patina that gives them a truth sometimes missing from the films of Lindsay Anderson or John Schlesinger.

The precise relation of Britishness to a (cinema or television-based) film culture is important, even if one argues that a strong national cinema must feed on its predecessors and thus stand in a vampire relation to what has gone before. Identity and pleasure in the cinema remain connected to questions of narrative, the art of repetition and recognition. One strategy of both television and the cinema as socially significant forms of self-representation might well be the energy either medium puts "into story-telling and discovering its themes in the process." [12] But film culture partakes also of the pleasure of the quotation and the in-joke, the reworking of known styles, genres, idioms and themes. Imitations, irony, remake, pastiche, parody – so many modes of sustaining a sense of cultural identity or a myth of the nation.

National Audiences, or ...

What of the national audience for either British television or British cinema, insofar as the cinema still has such an audience? Does it care about national identity when it comes to entertainment? For viewers in the North of England, the lifestyles in *Dynasty* or *LA Law* are about as real as the lifestyles of the Yuppie stockbrokers living in London's Dockland or the Home Counties. Is the "national cinema" question then, more than a figment of someone's (the critics') imagination, or a promotion ploy of doubtful use for products not marketed by way of genre or star? The unclassifiability of a production range drawn from television drama, film/TV co-productions, commercial feature films, and ex-film school debuts is self-evident. But it is equally self-evident that the mid-1980s "Renaissance" was tied up with the showcasing of large numbers of British films at jamborees like the London Film Festival.

Film festivals are the Olympics of the show business economy, and not all are as market-oriented as the Cannes Festival. What competes at festivals are less individual films than film concepts, film ideas, sales angles, or what Stephen Heath called a film's "narrative image."[13] Created by the press back-up, by promotional activity that suggests several sources of appeal or cultural access in a film, these images can be generated by sheer numbers (if diversity is tied together with a label) or, more frivolously, by emphasizing a newsworthy item either in a film or surrounding it. What counts at festivals is novelty, discovery, the element of surprise. With the paying public afterward, it is more a matter of what they already know or recognize, the familiar, which they discover in the different. A native public, therefore, may be flattered by the attention that others – other critics, other media, other audiences – give to the home-grown product or talent, as was the case with A FISH CALLED WANDA (Charles Crichton, 1988), making the most celebrated heroes at home those who win their highest accolades abroad.

Critics thought the hype surrounding the British contingent at such festivals was rather over the top:

> The current rash of hyperbole about the new British cinema will fade. Of course much of the TV drama "showcased" at the London Film Festival was merely routine. The pendulum always swings too far at first. [14]

Yet bulk remains crucial in launching a national cinema. The New German Cinema emerged internationally at the 1974 Cannes and 1975 New York festivals, mainly from the sheer number of films by three or four directors. These filmmakers' earlier work fed distribution demands, which in the case of Rainer W. Fassbinder amounted to some ten or twelve films. Producers or directors must have sufficient films, for demand once generated must be met quickly. Hence the close interdependence of film and television as delivery systems, neither of the same narrative material nor of a necessarily different experience, but of two distinct cultural discourses continually implying and pointing to each other. In the case of British films in the 1980s, the persistent danger was that if films never circulated outside television, then the associations evoked by the label British Cinema would fade; if the label exists successfully, but the industry cannot provide enough product to fit it, then television will offer its product under the label: "British", with possibly diminishing returns for the idea of a national cinema. The objective conditions for the renaissance, therefore, were not so much the existence of Channel Four and its commissioning policy, but the co-existence of Channel Four, the BFI Production Board, the National Film Finance Corporation, and two or three risk-taking producers (David Puttnam, Simon Perry) and production companies (Virgin, Chrysalis, Palace) living "inside the whale" of all the available sources of film financing. Their films – by the very heterogeneity of cultural and economic values that entered into the filmmaking process – were open texts, changelings rather than bastards, traveler's checks rather than forgeries in the currency markets of film culture.

Therefore, as far as a "brand image" is concerned, Britain faced an interesting dilemma. In its efforts to promote a particular national cinema, it stood somewhere between Germany and France. Despite the *Nouvelle Vague*, French filmmakers over and over define themselves (positively or negatively) by reference to their own cinematic traditions, their cosmopolitan international film culture, and a heavily theorized cinephilia. Think of Eric Rohmer and Betrand Tavernier at one end, and of JEAN DE FLORETTE and CYRANO DE BERGERAC on the other. In West Germany, where an idea of a national cinema imposed itself only in the 1970s, diverse directorial talents accumulated enough films to appear before an international art-house audience as a group whose work reflected back on the country from which they came. What could Britain offer in the way of either image or group identity to an art cinema audience? In Germany, it was invariably a director/star combination (Fassbinder/Hanna Schygulla; Herzog/Klaus Kinski; Wenders/Bruno Ganz) or "trilogies" that provided genre association; in Britain, films are one-offs, with an Oscar-winning engine to pull a few others in its train. Could this add up to a national cinema? On the other hand, British media products, in terms of an industrial infrastructure, are poised not between competing European cinemas, but between commercial Hollywood and commercial television, with the independent sector in both film and television up until the mid-1980s (prior to the quota) much more marginalized than the French or Italian art cinema. The British film industry rests on a strong technical base and unrivalled craftsmanship in certain specialized areas – heavily used by the Americans as long as sterling was weak against the dollar. Its television industry is highly competitive and sufficiently funded to buy what talent and services it needs from the theatre, the film industry or the literary establishment.

The real crisis for a new British cinema, therefore, came in the distribution and exhibition of material produced for television as well as for the cinemas. Without the tradition of an art cinema, British society only slowly incorporated the institutions (Regional Film Theatres, film magazines) necessary to create a coherent image for different kinds of film at their point of reception and consumption. The two major distribution/exhibition chains always preferred to handle American films, partly because they could acquire, in addition to the film, the advertising, promotion and marketing directly with the product. Such films prove much easier to handle than something which needs not only a market but an image as well. By contrast the biggest French distributor, Gaumont, undertook a vast diversification program which made it both desirable and necessary for a distributor to invest in the production even of art-house films, something which Rank and EMI have been notoriously reluctant to do and for which the stakes in Britain may be indeed be too high.

Gaumont expanded and diversified into new areas of filmmaking only to the degree that it could distribute these films adequately – be it by exporting to Italy, Germany, and the US, or by splitting their Parisian and provincial theatres into ever more mini-units. It gave the company a higher turnover of films, but also allowed them to keep a "sleeper" in repertory without clogging up the schedules for their blockbusters. Gaumont's extraordinary monopolistic position and strong vertical integration meant that this policy benefited both production and exhibition. In Britain, it seems that the smaller, London-based distributors/exhibitors (Artificial Eye, the Screen group and the Gate cinemas) tried something very similar: to acquire enough venues to enter the market as a biggish buyer, which in turn gave them the number of films that makes programming policy respond to variable and unpredictable demand.

... National Imaginaries

With this mind, we might return to our topic: national cinema. If we exclude what I earlier called the "social imaginary" of television and concentrate on the "national imaginary," the cinema of the 1980s stands in a highly instructive relation to what precedes it, while it also helps us to identify how the cinema under Thatcher is distinctive. We can read a number of motifs, narratives and images as a kind of identikit rather than an identity of Britain, and can construct from them mythologies, or mythemes. But does such an emphasis on the recycling and recombining of already existing images not risk collapsing filmmaking entirely with that obedient manipulation of images and references one now identifies as the curse and legacy of the Thatcher image culture? Perhaps. Yet what would it mean to oppose this image culture with a stern recall to realism and a search for that favorite catchword of the New German Cinema, "authentic images"? In Britain's case, this would be a call for images of misery and degradation, of unemployment and urban blight, of pollution and police harassment, of violence and racism. But is this not a retreat to another kind of conservatism, no less nostalgic than Heritage England or Edwardiana, and no less demagogic than the Enterprise Culture?

British cinema celebrates its renaissances with such regularity because it always functions around another polarization – what one might call an "official" cinema and an "unofficial" cinema, a respectable cinema and a disreputable one. The renaissances always signal a turning of the tables, but only to change places, not the paradigms. Official: Basil Dearden, Noel Coward, David Lean; unofficial: Powell/Pressburger, Gainsborough melodrama. Official: Ealing comedies, unofficial: "Carry On" comedies. Official: ROOM AT THE TOP (1958), SATURDAY NIGHT SUNDAY MORNING (1960), THIS SPORTING LIFE (1964); unofficial: Hammer horror, FOR KING AND COUNTRY (1964). Official: SUNDAY BLOODY SUNDAY (1971), unofficial: SECRET CEREMONY (1968). One could go on ... official: THE PLOUGHMAN'S LUNCH (1983), unofficial: BRAZIL (1984); official: CHARIOTS OF FIRE, GANDHI, unofficial: HOPE AND GLORY (1988). Sometimes it appears as if the same films get made every twenty years or so: LOCAL HERO (1983) a remake of WHISKY GALORE (1949) and THE MAGGIE (1954); THE PLOUGHMAN'S LUNCH a remake of ROOM AT THE TOP (or as Charles Barr has pointed out, of DARLING, 1965), and CHARIOTS OF FIRE a remake of IN WHICH WE SERVE (1942).

THIS SPORTING LIFE

This Jekyll and Hyde, yin-yang quality of the British cinema, first analyzed by Raymond Durgnat, has in its "realism versus romanticism" version become one of the orthodoxies of academic film studies. Its deeper psychic economy, as it were, rests in the fact that for every mythic or cliché image of Britain, there is a counter-cliché. Rare are the films that let both myth and counter-myth assert themselves, which is why BRIEF ENCOUNTER (1945) has such a special place in the canon. One of the main changes in the 1980s is that more films meshed the traditions: under Thatcher, reality itself became fantastic, for some a fairy tale (A ROOM WITH A VIEW, 1985), for most a nightmare (JUBILEE, 1976, THE LAST OF ENGLAND, 1988, SAMMY AND ROSIE GET LAID, 1988, NO SURRENDER, 1986). Others saw the future as high-tech and shabby at the same time: BRAZIL, for instance, a very British film by an American director (Terry Gilliam), not dissimilar from BLADE RUNNER, a very American film by a British director (Ridley Scott).

For much of the 1980s, the *mythemes* remain in place. On one side: home counties, country house, public school, sports, white flannel, rules and games;

Edwardian England, Decline of the Empire, Privilege and Treason; male bonding, female hysteria. On the side of the counter-myth: Scotland, Liverpool, London; dockland, club-land, disco, football, punk, race-riots, National Front; working class males, violent and articulate, working class women, sexy and self-confident. No one would mistake this as realistic, yet the films that fit the scheme range from LETTER TO BREZNEV to THE DRAFTSMAN'S CONTRACT, A PASSAGE TO INDIA to THE LAST OF ENGLAND, MY BEAUTIFUL LAUNDRETTE to ANOTHER COUNTRY, THE LONG GOOD FRIDAY to EDUCATING RITA. Most of these images of Britain sell better in Birmingham, Alabama than Birmingham, West Midlands, because they encapsulate what "we" try to sell to "them." But on closer inspection, one sees the films that did well in both places, whether coming from the "official" or the "unofficial" cinema, gave the myths a special edge, mixed the stereotypes in unexpected ways, or enacted the cliché to poignant perfection. Thus, they re-

THE LONG GOOD FRIDAY

leased a rich cultural sediment of meaning by which members of a national and historical community explain themselves to themselves and express themselves to others. In effect, the density or cross-hatching of such (self-)references has assumed the place of "realism." Consider, for instance, how little relation to the historical facts the prevalence of stories about public school spies and traitors has. It is not only that the advent of satellites has made spies less relevant to information gathering or to national security. Yet because the complex of playing fields, Oxbridge, homosexuality is able to articulate and negotiate such a number of important oppositions and contradictions (traitors to one's class/traitors to one's sex/traitors to one's country) its reality to Britain is of a different order than merely historical or sociological, and therefore we can expect some version of it even to survive the end of the Cold War.

Materializations of the Image

During the 1980s, British films and television have successfully marketed and packaged the national literary heritage, the war years, the countryside, the upper classes and elite education. In a sense, they emulated the British record industry, rock musicians and the rag trade, a lesson the Americans learnt quickly after the Second World War, when commerce started following Hollywood rather than the flag. That the communication and media industries participate in the commodity exchange systems of capitalism should not surprise anyone who knows about ownership and control in these industries, and that images, clichés, narratives are now fully caught up in the same game simply takes commodification to its logical conclusion. Like the natives in Third World countries who impersonate themselves for the sake of the tourists, Britain appears the victim of its own sophisticated media-making, the materialization of its own imaginary. Feeding from the myth and the counter-myth in equal measure, the images give a semblance of verisimilitude to its public life by the sheer diversity of recognizable stereotypes.

Such a circulation of representations is useful politically (as the Thatcher government knew full well) insofar as it fixes a complex and shifting reality (e.g., nationhood and social cohesion at times of crisis and decline) into images commonly accepted as true and meaningful as soon as they crop up everywhere, forcing even the opponent to do battle on the same terrain. Britishness in the cinema may thus be a synthetic myth, but it remains no less powerful for that because it is held in place by binary oppositions and polarities that attract each other. Due to the violence of the social tensions which the uneven distribution of the wealth generated by North Sea Oil brought to almost all regions and communities of the British Isles, Britain during the 1980s was probably the most colorful country in Europe. In this respect, the 1980s were a rerun of the Elizabethan or the Victorian age, if only by virtue of the immense contrasts between rich and poor, energy and waste, violence and ostentation. But when history returns, to paraphrase Marx, it usually does so not as tragedy but farce. No wonder, perhaps, that Dickens was the author most often adapted on television during the period, or that, when Margaret Thatcher finally resigned the main evening news program was followed by a montage of the day's images to a text made up of quotations from Shakespeare's history plays.

One tends to imagine little effective political opposition to Thatcher, but in the years to come we may recognize the wealth of talent in writing and journalism, which etched the decade's image in acid. Much of the talent found its way into television, less into the cinema. But film, after all was not about documentation, information, investigation, or even satire (all the province of television), and rather about myth and the stereotype, both beyond realism and fantasy, and closer to allegory and to games played according to the rules. Yet both the myths and counter-myths of the British cinema strongly speak of Britain as a class-society, maybe even a caste society. In this respect at least, less has changed during the Thatcher Years than might at first appear. While her social policies broke up one kind of consensus, another was formed, one using the same elements but striking from them a different coinage. Hence the impression that in the New British Cinema the sum of the parts, at least for now, is greater than the whole. The cinema under Thatcher contributed greatly to an unmistakably British image culture, but perhaps not so much to a film culture. Once more, talking about British cinema implies a look at British television, for the national imaginary hides, but also implies the social imaginary. But that is another story.[15]

(1984/1993)

Notes

1. Chris Peachment, "London/Munich Loose Connections," *Sight and Sound* 53 (2), 1984, pp. 151-52.
2. Jeremy Isaacs, "If We Can Sustain the Impetus...," *Sight and Sound* 53 (2) 1984, p. 118.
3. John Brown, "Home Fires Burning," *Sight and Sound* 53 (3) 1984, pp. 188-90.
4. Raymond Durgnat, *A Mirror for England*, (London: Faber and Faber, 1970).
5. Charles Barr, *Ealing Studios*, (London: Cameron and Tayleur, 1977).
6. David Robinson, "Berlin Festival Report," *The Times*, February 27, 1981.
7. Alan Bennett, "My Scripts, Where Wheelchairs Make Up the Armoured Division, Are Not Ready-made Movie Material," *Sight and Sound* 53 (3) 1984, pp. 121-22.
8. Norman Stone, "Sick Scenes from English Life," *Sunday Times*, 10 January 1988.
9. Margaret Hinxman, "British Cinema," *Daily Mail*, 31 January, 1982.
10. Mamoun Hassan, "Journalism and Literature Use Words..., *Sight and Sound* 53 (2) 1994, p. 116.
11. John Brown, "Home Fires Burning," *Sight and Sound* 53 (3) 1984, pp. 189-190.
12. Ibid., p. 190.
13. Stephen Heath, "Narrative Space," *Questions of Cinema*, (London: Macmillan 1981).
14. Gavin Millar, "I for One Am Not Going to Wait Around," *Sight and Sound* 53 (2) 1984, pp. 120-21.
15. See "British TV through the Looking Glass," elsewhere in this volume.

"If You Want a Life"

The Marathon Man

The Loneliness of the Long Distance Runner

In 1962, a film appeared that left a permanent impression and may have changed my life. I saw Tony Richardson's THE LONELINESS OF THE LONG DISTANCE RUNNER in a cinema in Brighton, shortly after moving to Britain in 1963. The lean and bony features of Tom Courtney's face instilled in me an intense yearning of wanting to belong to the English working class, one of the true aristocracies of the human race, as it seemed to me: noble in spirit, brave in adversity, resolute in action. The feeling is long gone, but its memory returned when I saw a young Tim Roth in Mike Leigh's MEANTIME many, many years later. What made Tom Courtney special, though, was that he was a runner. As one reviewer put it: "You can almost smell the wet leaves of the forests and hills, and feel the cold of the morning air as you follow Courtney on his daily jog. England, with its crummy weather, declining manufacturing economy, post-imperial history and hugely varied terrain, is particularly well-suited to the sport. Distance running is primarily a solitary activity, designed for bona-fide introverts, obsessive individuals who do not mind pain, and in some cases, may actually enjoy it."[1]

Courtney plays Colin, a Nottingham boy in his late teens, who is sent to borstal for robbing a bakery. In the reformatory school he is spotted as a "natural" by the upper-class governor with a mission. He gives Colin special privileges because he wants to groom him as a runner to lead the prison team in a much-anticipated long-distance race against a local public school. The ensuing conflict of whether Colin can be bribed into betraying his class, or would a victory be his alone, had a lot of resonance in the early 1960s, when – in the wake of the writings of Richard Hoggart and the education policies of the new Labour Government under Harold Wilson – working-class boys began entering British universities and the professions in significant numbers. "To join the establishment or to jinx it?" could have been the motto of Britain's "Swinging Sixties." In the film, Courtney decides on the latter, and when – far out ahead of his public school opponent (James Fox in one of his first roles as the archetypal upper-class cad) – he simply coasts to a stop within view of the finish line, casually dashing the ambitions of the governor as well as his own. Is the moral of the tale that "one is reminded that, in truth, there's no real losing, only degrees of winning," or do we witness "that essentially English state of mind, where it is better to fail than to succeed as long as you have chosen to fail?" True enough, for a first-year undergraduate reading Sartre and dreaming of Juliette Greco, the images of Courtney running through the open Nottinghamshire countryside were like long riffs by Django Reinhardt in one of cellar clubs of St. Germain-des-Prés: the confusion was no doubt helped by the film's beautiful jazz score, complete with trumpet solo by John Addison.

The Marathon Man

A little more than ten years later, another memorable runner made it into the movies and into my life. This time, a Hollywood production, set in New York, but it, too, directed by an Englishman. Instead of Angry Young Man Tony Richardson, it was the turn of Angry Young Man John Schlesinger to direct THE MARATHON MAN (1976). And instead of (Sir) Michael Redgrave as the governor, we have (Sir) Laurence Olivier as the older man, opposite the hero, played by Dustin Hoffman. His "Babe" in MARATHON MAN is not altogether different from Courtney's Colin. As David Thomson describes Hoffman: "his screen character is reticent but stubborn. He is small and often timid, but a nucleus of hard identity never wavers .... A wary liberalism lurks in his anticipation of suffering at the world's rough hands."[2]

In MARATHON MAN the rough hands are those of Olivier as Dr. Szell, a former Nazi SS dentist, once known as "The White Angel" of Auschwitz, who after hiding for decades in South America, has come to New York to retrieve a cache of ill-gotten diamonds, once he learns that his brother, who kept the (other) keys to the safe, has been killed, but not before telling someone compromising secrets about Szell. In this convoluted tale of Nazi villains, CIA agents and New York Jews, better not ask how "Babe," who is a graduate student at Columbia University, gets into the act. Rather, what matters to the viewer is how he gets in (and out of!) Dr. Szell's dentist's chair, in a scene that nobody, absolutely nobody, who has seen the film will ever forget. Say to someone: "so, tell me ... is it safe? Is it safe?!" and chances are, they'll twist their jaw in a grimace of agonized pain.

Whether MARATHON MAN – despite SS war criminals, Auschwitz, Jewish survivors and teeth – qualifies as a Holocaust movie is questionable, but it has one of the most stunning running sequences on film, as Hoffman puts to good use his stamina, gained through long hours of training for the New York Marathon, and weaves through the traffic on the interstate freeway, successfully outwitting his pursuers. No jazz score this time, but a Manhattan cityscape every bit as gritty as that of Martin Scorsese's Taxi Driver, and almost as jazzy as Piet Mondrian's Broadway Boogie Woogie.

Chariots of Fire

The 1980s, too, can boast of a runner's movie. Mention *its* title, and most people will grimace, trying to hum its theme tune. The three or four chords that make up Vangelis (Papathanassion)'s score have stayed in people's ears longer than they cared for, and now are probably as (in)famous as Beethoven's "ta-ta-ta-taa." This film is, again, set in Britain, even based on historical characters, and it involves class, race and ethnicity in politically correct proportions. Chariots of Fire tells the story of two British track athletes, competing in the 1924 Paris Summer Olympics. One, Eric Lidell, is a devout Scottish missionary who runs for God, the other, Harold Abrahams, is a Jewish student at Cambridge's Caius College, who runs mainly to prove himself in front of the college snobs, and to escape anti-Semitic prejudice.

Chariots of Fire

The plot runs their two stories in parallel, until they compete against each other, and the stakes for each of them are shown to be similar. Both are inspired by higher principles that underscore their dissidence, while giving them the outsider's position in their respective peer groups. The Presbyterian Scot Lidell has to explain to his sister who wants him to quit: "I believe God made me for a purpose. But he also made me fast, and when I run I feel His pleasure. To win is to honour Him." The orthodox Jew Abrahams has a showdown of his own with two Cambridge dons who question his "esprit de corps." He defends himself by saying: "I want victory as much as you do. But you want it achieved with the apparent effortlessness of Gods. I believe in the relentless pursuit of excellence." For after losing to Lidell in the qualifying heats, he had accepted the offer of a coach, Sam Mussambini: a decision that the Establishment considers un-gentlemanly, and a choice – Mussambini is not English – that further hardens racially biased resentment against him. Abrahams is the moral center of the film, as one viewer clearly noted: "The film is anchored in the character study of the introspective, brooding, and complex persona of Harold Abrahams, wonderfully portrayed by Ben Cross. Here is a man with all of the outward trappings of success: academic achievement, unparalleled athletic ability, wildly popular with his peers, yet tortured by an inbred inferiority complex and driven to lash out at the world in response. In the end, he conquers his inner demons through hard work, sacrifice, understanding of his fellow man, and the love of a good woman, to whom he opens his heart." CHARIOTS OF FIRE was a huge success in 1981, ensuring for its producer, David Puttnam, a significant, if brief Hollywood career as studio boss, a prominence not given to a "Brit" since Alexander Korda in the 1940s, though Korda, a naturalized Briton, was in fact a Jew and a Hungarian from Puzstaturpaszto!

It is not hard to see that running in CHARIOTS OF FIRE once again serves as a metaphor for changes in British society, as it had done twenty years earlier in LONELINESS OF A LONG DISTANCE RUNNER. Abrahams already represents the new meritocracy of the Thatcher Years, where city gents, bank managers as well as politicians learnt to their cost that they could no longer rely just on the old school tie and the amateurism of the landed gentry, but needed to surround themselves with experts, think tanks and (if necessary, foreign) advisers. Slyly identifying this new professional (business) ethos with Jews – Margaret Thatcher famously had promoted several British Jews to cabinet rank – CHARIOTS OF FIRE is prepared to attack amateurism as a now obsolete instrument of class warfare, no matter how disinterested it may present itself in the arena of sports, which thanks to television is, of course, now one of the least amateurish branches of global media entertainment business. The fact that the only other prominent sportsmen in the film are Americans delivers this message loud and clear – and the Oscars the film garnered show that it was well-received.

There are some exquisitely staged running sequences, not least the opening one by the seashore, choreographed and cut like a Pina Bausch ensemble piece. Yet although the film makes distinctions, and even establishes something like a morphology of runners – Lidell is called a "gut runner, digging deep" – my sense is that CHARIOTS OF FIRE (or maybe just Vangelis on the Walkman in Central Park) did finally more for jogging than for running.

Run Forrest Run

If only things had remained so simple. Clear ethical choices, running as a metaphor for social change, underpinned by the affirmative trajectory of self-transcendence, with "winning" standing for an act of rehabilitation or the removal of a stigma in the arena of social acceptance. But in the 1990s, a film appeared – now once more coming from Hollywood – that also features running at a pivotal point in the hero's life, in circumstances so much more enigmatic. Robert Zemeckis' 1994 FORREST GUMP, starring Tom Hanks, is more of a puzzle than its commercial success would indicate, or the contempt of its enemies would be prepared to admit. A Vietnam veteran, decorated for rescuing the commander of his platoon, tells the story of his life to anyone who cares to listen, sitting on a bus-stop bench somewhere in the Deep South. It turns out that Forrest played a key role in practically all of the events of the Sixties and Seventies: The inven-

tion of rock'n'roll, the assassination of John F. Kennedy, the Civil Rights Movement in Alabama, the Kent State shootings, the anti-Vietnam protests at the Washington Monument, the Watergate break-ins. Forrest was always there, as we can see from the newsreel pictures cut into his flashback narrative. There is only one problem: Forrest does not seem to have a clue about the significance of these events. His sweet personality and home-spun wisdom turns everything that has happened to him or that he was instrumental in bringing about, into an illustration of his Mother's motto: "life is a like a box of chocolates – you never know what you find inside." For those who loved the film, here finally was a conciliatory version of America's most troubled two decades in modern history. For those who felt offended, and there were many, the pro-

FORREST GUMP

blem was not only that FORREST GUMP wiped the historical slate clean of all the struggles, sacrifices and the fight against injustices, to which a whole generation had given its activism and dedicated its idealism. FORREST GUMP also used the latest technologies of digital re-mastering to fake the historical record, by inserting Tom Hanks into "authentic" television footage of Kennedy, Lyndon Johnson, and the Black Panthers.

How aware is the film of what it is doing? There is a period in Forrest's life when he becomes something of a Messiah, following his decision to run across America, several times, all by himself. At first, people start lining the route where he passes, but then more and more imitate him, because of the mysterious saintliness that seems to radiate from his determined, unstoppable run from coast to coast, from Alaska to Baja California and from Maine to New Mexico. Perhaps in contrast to the pathetic jogging that US Presidents ritually perform in front of news cameras – the film pointedly shows Forrest passing a television shop, just as the now famous footage of Jimmy Carter's morning jog can be seen, when suffering from heat exhaustion, he collapses in the arms of one of his aids – Forrest Gump is like the original Marathon Man. He bears a message for his people, though it remains unclear whether of victory or defeat. After three years of perpetual running, and finding himself in the middle of Monument Valley, trailed by a group of devotees, whom he has never addressed, Forrest suddenly decides to stop running, and returns home, much to the consternation and then contempt of his followers.

No explanation for his decision is given. It could be that he remembered the scene from his youth, when, still a boy with leg-braces and severely handicapped, he is pursued by a group of bully boys on bicycles. At this point, his childhood sweetheart Jenny – herself abused by her father – comes out of the door and shouts to him "run, Forrest, run." Miraculously, he picks up speed, the braces fly off, and Forrest is now free – running, running, running. Perhaps he realizes that this was in fact the true motto of his life, but that he had never figured out the direction of his running: was he running away or running towards something? This indeterminacy, this radical openness of his running, without origin or goal may have been his saving grace, the secret of his saintliness. Now was the time to return to Jane, the evident mother-substitute, and found his own family, which he does, except that it is too late. Jane, having just given birth to a boy, is dying from a mysterious virus. And so, Forrest is once more in a loop, a time warp, for which the bus-stop is as useful a metaphor as was the leafless tree in *Waiting for Godot*. With Forrest Gump, the passion for running had left the world of linear-chronological narratives, of teleological life-plans or self-improvement. The fact that he stopped in the middle of Monument Valley, that archetypal Western landscape, seemed to signal the end of the *grand récit* of America's frontier myths, even in mainstream movies. But what was the film hinting at?

Run Lola Run

Just as in FORREST GUMP, the coordinates of historical chronology begin to bend, as the hero's spectral body is present in every historical event, while his soul has time out, running across America or waiting on the bus-stop bench, so the runner's film for the new century – though dating from 1999 – opens up the time-loop across the metaphor of running. I am referring to Tom Tykwer's RUN LOLA RUN. This time, it is a young Berlin woman, who gets a phone call from her boyfriend, Manni, somewhere in the city, and is told to run, Lola, run. He is in deep trouble with a drug dealer, and needs to replace the 100,000 DM he carelessly lost in the Berlin *S-Bahn*, and to do so within the next 20 minutes, otherwise he's dead. Three times we see her start on her "race to the rescue," each time one slightly different micro-incident radically changes the course of events. The first time she arrives too late and Manni is killed by the police, the second time, she is killed trying to shield him, and the third time, she arrives in time, and Manni himself has found the money he had lost to a tramp. It is like winning the jackpot in a computer game that re-sets itself after each bout, but here balanced by the agonized pillow-talk between Lola and Manni separating the segments: "Why do you love me? – Why me?" Lola asks, to which Manni

Run Lola Run

can only reply "why *not* you?" Running becomes a modality of being-in-the-world, to counter such epistemological skepticism as besets Lola about never being able to know what goes on in "other minds," however familiar their bodies may be. The techno-sound of her pounding heartbeat ensures lift-off to another realm of possibility, shifting gears between the unique event and the "what if" of the "rippling consequences of chance": "Tykwer illustrates how the smallest change in what a person does can alter the rest of their life (not to mention the lives of others, including complete strangers she passes on the street)." Lending her athletic body to the sense that every act forecloses an alternative reality, and by that very possibility, makes it both preciously special and potentially meaningless, Lola's running bends time's arrow, to render obsolete that distinction between being "last" and being "first" in life, once one is aware of all the forking paths and all the roads not taken.

"I wish I were a beating heart that never comes to rest." Compared to Lola running, powered by an urgency due not just to Manni's predicament, the usual city jogger to my mind resembles nothing more than a donkey on the water wheel with the eternal return of the same. Running, too, as we have seen, may be without where-from and where-to, but its intensity to the point of in-direction, and its acceleration to the point of movement in multiple dimensions makes for that repetition and reversibility which ensures that the last can be the first, and the first will (not) be the last: the further the runner runs, the closer he or she is to the point we all have to start from, up against ourselves. For the runner, distance and proximity fold inwards, suspending and even sublimating the very idea of "first" and "last" in an altogether different topography of being and becoming. The Marathon Man is a Moebius man and as long as he is on the move, the actual and the virtual, the inner and the outer are the perfectly joined recto and verso of a figure, whose singularity is also a token of its infinity. Or as Emil Zatopek, the Czech Olympic champion of Helsinki in 1952, and perhaps the world's greatest marathon man ever, was fond of saying: "If you want to run, run a mile. If you want to experience a different life, run a marathon."

(2003)

Notes

1. Taken from THE LONELINESS OF THE LONG DISTANCE RUNNER, "User Comments," The Internet Movie Database, accessed June 2002.
2. David Thomson, *Biographical Dictionary of Film* (New York: Knopf, 1994), p. 343.

British Television in the 1980s Through The Looking Glass

For the study of European cinema, the 1980s are a particularly significant decade, because they saw the final demise of the commercial film industry in all but one country, France. By contrast, Britain, Germany and Italy, each in very particular ways, found that it no longer had a domestic market that could sustain indigenous feature film production on the Hollywood model. Films continued to be made, but on a different economic basis, with different institutional partners or commercial participation, and for a different public. The 1980s signaled the fact that cinema in Europe could no longer be looked at or studied in isolation. Decline has to be seen in the context of a shift, an opening up, a re-alignment: for the decade also witnessed a radical transformation in the overall media landscape: the deregulation of state-owned broadcast television, the arrival of video and the VCR, the rise of the Hollywood event movie or "blockbuster," and the weakening of "new wave" art, avant-garde, and counter-cinemas, pushed further to the margins.

How these transformations and shifts could best be studied was a major preoccupation for academic media studies from the mid-1980s onwards, which saw the emergence of television studies and cultural studies, at the expense, some would argue, of film theory and film history. Under the label of "postmodernism" a new agenda for critical engagement arose which also implied a shift: from an emphasis on aesthetic, hermeneutic and historical questions, to an intense debate about the value, relevance and function of popular culture, a foregrounding of identity politics (gender, class, ethnicity) within the social formation, in place of a politics of radical action against society, and perhaps most momentous of all, a fresh evaluation of consumerism and the culture industries. In these moves, television – and television studies – became paradigmatic for studying all media, including the cinema, which had indeed found in television its greatest ally and life-saver, rather than its arch-enemy, as it had been seen in the 1960s and 1970s.[1]

While at first film theory and cultural studies became the disciplines that set an agenda for television studies within the humanities, opening up a space for debate next to media sociology and communication studies 'the traditional disciplines for the press and broadcast media' television studies soon developed its own identity, greatly helped by the kind of tacit knowledge both students and teachers brought to the subject by the mere fact of watching a lot of television and enjoying it. A pleasure in search of legitimacy is not a bad start for an interesting debate, and it must have found the availability of powerful critical discourses propitious. But if 1970s film theory was one of the preconditions for television studies becoming so quickly assimilated in the teaching and research schedules of academic institutions in Britain, the much more important factors were the changes taking place in British broadcasting itself, epitomized though not exhaustively explained by the founding of Channel Four in the early 1980s.

At least this is how the situation presented itself to me. What first drew me to "teaching television" was less a long-standing tele-addiction in need of rationalization, but the fact that students brought to classes a wholly different film and media culture, evidently shaped by television. But equally decisive was the conviction – or confirmation – that in some sense our (critical-hermeneutic) literary culture had "passed through the looking glass." The catalyst for this confirmation was indeed Britain's Channel Four, which despite its modest ratings (an average of 7-9 percent of the national audience) had, within a few years, an incalculable effect on program makers across the networks, not least by going on the premise that television can be judged by television, and needs neither the support of high culture nor of the ratings to know when it "works." This was itself a paradoxical position, since Channel Four's appearance in 1982 coincided with the beginning of British television's own crisis: the Conservative government's push for "deregulation" under the pressure from media conglomerates and new technology. While instant nostalgia began to celebrate the 1970s as British television's golden age, I began to gorge myself on "quality television," sampling its menu as if it was an ethnic neighborhood restaurant about to be demolished to make way for a fast-food franchise. Except that I soon realized "quality TV" was itself a fast-food franchise cleverly made up to resemble a neighborhood restaurant.

The looking-glass effect thus has two sides: television in love with television, and supremely confident of itself as "cultural form," and television as a vernacular into which everything can be translated, a paradoxical "global demotic" which can make much of our literary culture appear a mere mandarin ideolect. And precisely because television showed off its own self-assurance as a mode and a textuality, it in turn not only changed the balance of power across the media as a whole, but brought into being a new "materiality." This insight is what, among other things, I also take from a passage by Fredric Jameson:

> It is clear that culture itself is one of those things whose fundamental materiality is now for us not merely evident, but inescapable. This has, however, been a historical lesson: it is because culture has *become* material that we are now in a position to understand that it always *was* material, or materialistic in its structure and functions. We ... have a word for that discovery ... and it is of course the word medium, and in

particular its plural, media, a word which now conjoins three relatively distinct signals: that of an artistic mode or specific form of aesthetic production; that of a specific technology, generally organized around a central apparatus or machine; that finally, of a social institution. These three areas of meaning do not define a medium, or the media, but designate the distinct dimensions that must be addressed ... It should be evident that most traditional and modern aesthetic concepts – largely but not exclusively, designed for literary texts – do not require this simultaneous attention to the multiple dimensions of the material, the social, and the aesthetic.[2]

The triad named by Jameson as essential prerequisites for any adequate discourse about the media is not new, but it is a convenient historical benchmark for the various critical moments that have dethroned literature as the core of the humanities. Indeed, the triad marks important stages in the development of film studies itself (traditionally author-, genre-, and text-oriented and thus determined by a literary hermeneutics), which became influential over the last ten years, for instance, to the degree that it was able to construct a common framework out of the implications of two brilliant moves: that of Jean-Louis Comolli and Jean-Louis Baudry about technology, the apparatus and realism, and that of Christian Metz, Raymond Bellour, Laura Mulvey, Stephen Heath and others about narrative, specularity and sexual difference.[3] Both these moves made subjectivity and spectatorship central to film theory, tying them inextricably to the coherence effect (illusionism) of the text, and the subject to his/her ability to signify and symbolize itself in language. However, the force of the model depended on the fact that the cinematic apparatus, narrative, and sexual difference were conceived as interlocking, mirroring and mutually reinforcing manifestations of the same Symbolic, whose material or historical diversity was suppressed in favor of identifying, for instance, the transcendental subject in whose mirror the spectator was constituted (and from whose position the theorist, too, was necessarily speaking).

Film studies' move into television has meant that scholars are once again interested in the materiality and heterogeneity of this Symbolic, speaking from the side of the Imaginary and therefore invariably complicating the genealogy according to which television could be construed as the inheritor of the cinema. Film and television share genres (melodramas and soaps; crime films and cop shows), narrative (the ubiquity of its basic structures and narrational modes), and both are shaped by the wider context of capitalism, in particular, the industrialization of show business and leisure. The continuity is strongest perhaps when one concentrates on the financial infrastructures, on ownership of the sites of production, or on the relation between the technologies involved and the "product" needed to exploit them commercially.[4] The key area of divergence, on the other hand has been the spectator. For as soon as one looks at the strategies of the two media for gathering audiences, for binding them or "constructing coherent subject positions," the differences are palpable: television has a different "apparatus," a different psychic investment in the image, a different treatment of sound, different definitions of the shot or the sequence, different forms of suture and textual closure, a different (non-existent) concept of off-screen space. To put it briefly, whereas film studies locates the spectator in the text, television studies locates the text in the spectator (what the spectator does with the text).

The case of the cinema and television sharing a common destiny and yet being fundamentally different is one that confronts us, regardless of whether we work in film studies or television studies. It may even be that the process of how one medium "inherits" another, or by its very existence changes another, needs a mode of analysis not found in either discipline. This could be the basis for the claim that cultural studies is the true successor to film studies. With its emphasis on commodity consumption under capitalism, Jameson's conjunction of the material, the textual and the social becomes axiomatic to cultural studies' method. The focus on how individuals (especially in sub-cultures and marginal groups) make sense of or draw identity and pleasure from mass-produced objects and everyday life under capitalism has undoubtedly energized the field of media studies with new theories of power, resistance and struggle. Cultural studies has tried to define for the popular "an artistic mode or specific form of aesthetic production," exploring subcultures' relation to style, or returning to Levi-Strauss' concept of "bricolage" and Michel de Certeau's idea of "tactical knowledge."[5]

From the perspective of cultural studies, television has a rather weak claim to being treated as an autonomous object, despite the fact that television confronts us most directly with evidence that materiality, textuality and apparatus belong together. Yet television is also too parasitic (on radio, cinema, show business, on events and interests generated elsewhere) and too transparent (the way it blends with politics, journalism, the advertising of goods and services, or functions as display case of curios, artifacts and the national heritage) for it to appear as wholly distinct from the rest of "culture." At the same time, cultural studies also scores over film studies insofar as right from its inception, it took seriously the idea that cultural production today is in large measure "post-production," the appropriation, transformation, the collage, montage and sampling of ready-made objects and discourses. It takes as given what elsewhere is still contested territory: that capitalist economies today are organized around consumption, and less and less around production. The advantage over an older critical paradigm – that of the Frankfurt School, for instance, and its concept of mass-culture as mass-deception, of commodity fetishism and false consciousness – is that cultural studies clearly shows how many of these concepts were dependent on models of production: an ideal of material production derived from a notion of non-alienated labor, and an ideal of aesthetic production de-rived from the negativity and minimalism of high modernism, itself a nostalgic-heroic evocation of a mode prior to the division between mental and manual labor.

However, to argue from the de-facto reversal of production and consumption in societies which do not produce for need and use, but create need as desire and use as semiotic play, is a tactical advantage that may itself come to be seen as the blind spot of cultural studies' critical system, as it comes up against two historical changes: in Eastern Europe, the reshaping of both high and popular culture's role in the struggle for national identity and social democracy in the wake of Stalinism, and in Western Europe, where in the name of deregulation and harmonization, a realignment of the production apparatus is proceeding apace, which models culture (its objects and its forms of reception) on the com-modity and the service industries: no longer Adorno's Culture Industry, but the "culture industries" dedicated to generating diverse forms of consumption (dif-ferent material and immaterial aggregate states of the "work" or "text": videos, CDs, T-shirts, badges, toys), in order to sustain production.

One casualty of this process may be the various theories of spectatorship. Cultural studies, aiming to rescue the popular-as-progressive from radical theo-ry's disenchantment with both high culture and mass-entertainment, has rightly emphasized the sophistication and discrimination (the traditional hallmarks of educated taste) of popular reading strategies, as well as their subversive, inter-ventionist and deconstructive potential.[6] Cultural studies, at least in Britain, conspicuously circumvented or abandoned the psychoanalytic paradigm, stres-sing instead the openness of any cultural text towards different meanings and pleasures, and the social, ethnic and gender diversity of spectators, whose dy-namics are often group-oriented, family-centered or collective rather than invol-ving the subject's (individualized) desire and its symbolizations.[7] The fact that – despite notions of struggle and contradiction – cultural studies lacks a concept of the unconscious as an operative term, may well be one of the reasons why it appears often in danger of becoming entangled in the discipline from whose embrace it tried to free itself, namely empirical sociology. At the same time, theories of film spectatorship developed around the sign and symbolization, as well as the psychic and the unconscious (identification, subject, gender) have tended to be so heavily centered on the specular that their relevance to televi-sion – a predominantly verbal and aural medium, with its direct address, its performative modes, its multiplication of voices, its manipulation of the image – has become too problematic to be ignored.[8]

In the following I want to take up some of these points, but perversely per-haps I want to argue that, despite the increase in the "instrumental" side of tele-vision viewing through the VCR, time-manipulation, the remote control, the push-button choices, it may still be useful to think of television viewing as a practice situated in an imaginary, an imaginary to which correspond certain manifestations of the symbolic. For the crisis in both film and television theory may well stem from the recognition that we are unable to construct a unifying symbolic which would hold in place the various imaginary subject positions typical of television and cinema: bourgeois ideology, renaissance perspective, the cinematic apparatus and patriarchy no longer seem to provide the single coherent articulation they used to give to film theory. At the same time, with the collapse of socialism in Eastern Europe it is difficult to maintain a historical or theoretical reference point from which capitalism could be named as the uni-fied symbolic, however much it continues to be, in Jameson's phrase, an "un-transcendable horizon." How, then, to figure the relationship between a practice situated in the imaginary (say, that of television, become total, global, self-refer-ential and self-validating) and the symbolic underpinning it, which may well be heterogeneous, fractured, but as global capitalism, possesses its own material-ity?

As many theorists of television have pointed out, flow and interruption are dialectically intertwined as necessary constituents of television's spectatorial re-gime.[9] And even if one feels that desire – in the way feminist theory understood the term – is not an appropriate concept for analyzing television viewing, I would suggest that mis-cognition is still a key dimension of television spectator-ship. For it is here that I detect one of commercial television's most powerful subject effects: namely, the answer to the question "why does television talk to *me* as if I were part of *us*?" The question can be mapped onto a formulation that I think gives us a clue to the nature of television's symbolic: "Television does not deliver programs to audiences, but audiences to advertisers."[10]

I would like to think of this syllogism as something of a Lacanian formula-tion, insofar as it posits a double structure of mis-cognition symmetrically re-lated, much along the lines of Lacan's schema *"objet petit a"* for the structure of the subject (S) in relation to the Other (A). S would stand for audiences, A for advertisers, in relation to which the program or television text situates itself as a – a, the axis of the Imaginary. In trying to account for the nature of desire in television, without direct recourse to film studies' concept of (male) oedipal identity, I would take issue with cultural studies' notion of "subversive plea-sures" and instead argue that television does not produce a commodity at all, but instead cements a relation – that of mis-cognition, and thus one charged with psychic investment quite different from that associated with "desire as pleasure."[11]

In order to pursue this further, a detour may be necessary. I want to return to where I started, namely the particular paradox facing anyone thinking about British television. The simplest way may be to say that television, whether commercial or under state control, has been identified predominantly with what has come to be known as "public service broadcasting," meaning that regardless of the revenue basis, British television is constrained to operate within a framework of public accountability and social responsibility often summed up in the phrase that television's function is to "inform, educate and entertain." Whereas the "progressive" side of the public service remit has been to give us "quality television" (well-made drama, comedy and light entertainment, a qualified news service, documentary films on every conceivable subject of public concern), and high-tech standards and production values, the drawbacks were always seen to reside either in a certain paternalism about what's good for the viewer (the famous "Reith" ethic of the BBC), or in the underlying consensus model of society, meaning that social life is represented on television as white, heterosexual, middle class and English (rather than British).

The arrival of Channel Four seemed set to change all that, in that it actively promoted an image of Britain as multi-cultural, regionally and nationally diverse, but also divided by class, race, opportunity and living standards. In other words, Channel Four's programming not only addressed the viewer differently (socially aware, politically informed, media-literate and sophisticated in his/her reading practice of social texts, in short: "postmodern"), but it seemed to construct a different symbolic – that of an intolerant, greedy and self-devouring society ("Thatcher's Britain"), of which the Channel's projection of a tolerant, caring, enlightened televisual community (its implied or constructed audience) was the representation, its imaginary.

However, this transformation of the public service remit (a process obviously more complex and contradictory than I am able to sketch here) occurred during a time when the entire duopolistic structure of British television was beginning to be dismantled. Indeed, public broadcasting came of age in Britain at precisely the moment it was about to disappear altogether. Not because it was abolished by the State or deserted by its viewers, but because it had changed its status: the public service remit, from being the symbolic underpinning a certain range of viewing- and subject-positions, it became itself an imaginary, held in place by another symbolic. This symbolic is the axis audiences-advertisers, but as I shall try to suggest, not in any direct way definable as a question of ratings.

Perhaps I can illustrate what I mean with an incident which left quite an impression: seeing Dick Cavett in a commercial for a micro-wave dinner during my last visit to the United States. Why was this such a culture shock?[12] In the early 1970s, when I first came to the US, Cavett was my television hero, or rather his chat show on PBS was the link (along with "All Things Considered" and the *New York Times)* to reality, meaning Independent Television News, the BBC World Service, *The Guardian* newspaper: Cavett was, in a way, nothing less than my transcendental signifier. When coming from Britain, American television, experienced on its own ground rather than in select program slices as it appears on the world's screens, is an odd experience because it seems to be a permanent, competent, and straight-faced impersonation of something else (or possibly of itself): at any rate a discourse not usually in need of a referent.[13]

With Dick Cavett – a person I had associated with the "real world" – suddenly being part of this impersonated reality of television, it became almost ontologically impossible to sustain not so much the naive idea that television was a window on the world, a representation of the world, that television went "out there" and bring something "in here." What the terrible smile with which Cavett was biting into his television dinner did was pull the rug from under the mode by which I had consciously or not understood British television

Dick Cavett

and the great British quality debate: that television was, give or take this or that aberration or excess, a serviceable representation, if not of the real, then of the social.

When I learned that Cavett had in fact begun his career as a magician and had been a stand-up comedian before becoming a talk show host, which in turn was only one episode of his varied showbiz life, it occurred to me that watching Cavett on PBS I had been caught up in the imaginary of American television because I was reading it across another, different, imaginary – British television, though until then unaware what the nature of British television's imaginary actually was. If in the 1970s I mistook Cavett for a person who was on television because of his place within the "social," was I not in the 1980s mistakenly assuming Channel Four's function to lie in being a representation of the social, rather than being in the business of making television? For what Channel Four in my mind shared with both the BBC and the commercial network was precisely the notion of television as the social bond that holds the fabric of the nation together, as the big story-telling, narrative generating machine, realigning the fragmented subjectivities we necessarily are with our previous selves, our political institutions, our cultural past, our collective memories, in short, in Raymond Williams' phrase, with our "whole way of life."

Similarly, what seemed to sustain (British) television and media studies in general was the belief that just as print culture had changed the way we think about the world and our place in it, so audio visual culture was beginning to change us. As usual, there was a trade-off of gain and loss, but perhaps one needed to take the longer view. In which case, a certain logic became apparent whereby the public spheres, the social worlds which the great bourgeois revolutions had passed on, were being transformed by this new cultural mode of being, for which television could stand not only as the central metaphor, but as its living form and embodiment.

The fiction British television sustained was that democracy, welfare, education, information, history, popular memory, the arts are in safe hands, so long as they are on television. Television in Britain during the Thatcher years had become the glue that still held it all together, while a large part of the population was un- or under-employed and politically disenfranchised by living in poverty ghettos, while the inner cities decayed, while the developers disfigured the countryside, while the public services broke down, while the education system ground to a halt, while health care was bankrupted and the utilities such as gas and electricity were sold off at bargain basement prices to financial speculators. A new articulation of the interplay of the media and social life gave rise to the idea of television as a stand-in and stand-for society, as the storage medium and storage modes by which to pass on cultural capital and to socialize future generations. One defended television – government controlled as well as commercial – as in its own way a great historical achievement, a very British institution, deeply imbued with the ethos of the welfare state, in the triangle made up of what was most at risk under Thatcher: the health service, the education system and the freedom of the press.

Of course, other formations into which television inscribes itself (that of the shopping center, the theme park and the film and music industries), were also present on British television: many of the quality programs are actually made for export and in order to boost tourism; conversely, British television depends on a large number of US imports, on game shows and quiz shows, American football and Australian soaps, on reruns of Hollywood movies and international entertainers. But this happens under the heading of diversity and representativeness, of popularity and demand. It does not stop British television from legitimating itself as the social bond, in its programming and scheduling for instance. Much of it still modulates the times of day, while simultaneously conjugating the generations, classes, the social groups, their interests and pleasures. Television sees itself in its own self-definition as the microcosm of society, it constantly reinvents this society, and even though it does so in its own image, this is the mode and model according to which it operates, and therefore one on which it can be challenged and ultimately held accountable: it *stands for* society.

From this perspective, American television appears not as a *stand-for* television but perhaps a *stand-by* television, like the muzak one gets when dialing a WATS number and while you are kept on hold. US television is "event-driven" insofar as it takes a Challenger disaster, the Ollie North hearings, an earthquake in San Francisco, the fall of the Berlin Wall, or a Gulf War, in order for the beast to spring into action, in order for it to deploy the "electronic sublime" of global omnipresence.[14] One is reminded that the history of television as inheritor of radio, become the first global entertainment medium has imperceptibly merged with that other history – of aerial photography, of spy satellites, of bank and supermarket surveillance cameras: all on stand-by, all modeling "empty time."[15]

Now, if empty time is television's raw materiality, broadcast television organizes it by segmenting the televisual flow around a temporality which mimics the presumed time experience of its preferred or targeted addressees. But as cable television proves, modeling the temporality of lived experience is not the only way of programming television. On the contrary, the channel-hopping couch potato as well as the CNN addict, cultivate a television experience in direct opposition to any naturalized temporality. Such a perspective might allow us to understand how it is that the viewer is able to tolerate the level of frustration, interruption and deferred gratification so central to a psychoanalytic theory of televisual desire. If in Britain the notion of television as a more or less adequate representation of the social imaginary, as a cultural form and a "service" to the viewer still has some semblance of plausibility, American television appears in the business of producing a commodity: that commodity is not the programs, but the viewers. Yet precisely for that reason, American television is superior to British television, because it already contains within itself, as one of its aggregate states, that particular use which I have called "stand-for television," which – if it wanted to or if it was profitable – American television could "customize": indeed, it does so, at the local or regional level, and on PBS. Dick Cavett as talk show host was already the staging of a television genre (debate and argument about politics and current affairs) rather than the stand-in for the social. From this apparent paradox one could thus develop British television's specific textual unconscious, whereby quality television – say, in form of documentaries or current affairs – does not bring a social discourse (political awareness, informed choices) to audiences, but audiences to a social discourse, not interpellating them as subjects, but coaxing them as willing participants (not unlike quiz and game shows).

What I suspect is that the idea of television as authorless, plurivocal "cultural texts" open to all kinds of reading is quite problematic, because it ignores that these readings, however diverse, are all secured by the strategy of flattering the viewer and making him/her a participant in a "knowing" discourse, which in turn has to do with confronting the problem of finding an optimal solution to the structural imbalances between buying power and numbers, between educational-cultural privilege and the notion of a mass-market.[16] Quality television, in other words, is one of the answers to the problem of the rich getting richer and fewer, and the poor getting poorer and more numerous.

For some time now, it has been common knowledge that advertisers do not necessarily demand from program makers mere quantities of viewers but differentiated, carefully segmented sub-sets of audiences: multipliers, taste makers and trend setters, viewers whose high incomes are matched by high entertainment/information expectations. The paradox then, is not only that British quality television as embodied by Channel Four addresses a community in the know: made for an audience and in a country that assumes a high degree of cultural identity, of shared references, modes of discourse (humor, allusion, irony, understatement), agreed linguistic, visual, aural, material referents that can be used as signifiers, that can be put in play. The paradox is that it is these very "cultural" qualities which make such an audience commercially sought after as the advertisers' ideal target group, a confirmation of this new televisual symbolic/imaginary relation I have been trying to define.

Channel Four's liberal ideology of a multi-cultural society is thus actually welcomed by advertisers in that it helps segment audiences, creating televisual sub-cultures whose loyalty is one of the Channel's main assets. It is therefore not surprising that its programs have "quality" written all over them, and here we re-encounter Dick Cavett. While his British equivalent can sell high-culture or post-modernism, Cavett has to sell fast food, which suggests that quality television is not the endangered alternative to commercial television that it appears in the public debate, but rather that it is stand-by television's finest hour: a proposition illustrating quite well Horkheimer and Adorno's "dialectic of enlightenment," and suggesting that their "critical theory" may have the last laugh over "cultural studies".[17]

Thanks to Dick Cavett's Television Dinner then, the stand-for model (the cultural studies argument) now seems to me as untenable as to defend "quality television" on the grounds of discrimination, taste and superior morality (the high culture argument which cultural studies set out to dismantle): in either case one speaks from a position that risks mistaking a set of subject positions and recognition effects for an objective representation of the social, be it consensual, militant or multi-cultural. To hold up quality television as social bond, social therapy and cultural memory may invert the "critical" paradigm of television as an ideological state apparatus, but it ends up identifying as the effects of a symbolic (the profit motive) what is in fact another imaginary, whose symbolic is not the commodity, but a historically specific capacity to *mobilize* audiences, whether mass audiences or target audiences, audiences as consumers or audiences as sophisticated postmodernists, whether minority audiences or multi-cultural audiences.

It is this symbolic of mobilizing audiences while segmenting them into differently desiring subjects that seems to me not addressed by the theories of television spectatorship currently derived from either film studies or cultural studies.

For television to be a medium in Jameson's sense, it has to occupy and be present in all "three dimensions" of its system of coordinates: the television apparatus' power to gather audiences, the schedules' power to invest television viewing with an imaginary dimension, and finally, the programs' power to construct pleasurable and meaningful viewing positions.

The common denominator of these coordinates is usually "The Ratings"; but such a view disguises first of all that the ratings are ultimately no more than a set of conventions, agreed to by the parties involved at a time when purely quantitative methods did not seem too crude a measurement of "the market." With the demand for ever more finely calibrated categories of viewers, however, the rating system has itself entered a crisis and may eventually give way, as the gold standard did, to a more fluctuating and uncertain "exchange rate mechanism," with a "speculative" viewer economy of television in the global context existing alongside the old "ratings wars."[18] In the speculative economy, prime time programs, expensive to make but with a mass-market audience (*Dallas, The Cosby Show*) compete with quality programs for highly defined minority

HILL STREET BLUES

audiences, also expensive to make but which attract high rates for off-peak time programming (*Hill Street Blues, LA Law*), while cheaply made programs (game shows, talk shows) ensure a less affluent but more numerous audience for daytime viewing: each, furthermore, with different revenue prospects in different international markets. Such variables increase when one adds the role of media events or political crises: the upheavals in Europe in 1990, the Thatcher resignation in Britain, or the Gulf war make news programs or news channels more attractive to advertisers, but the cost of news coverage of, say, a war or a popular uprising in remote parts of the world can put networks under severe economic strain, as was the case of the BBC which has had to reduce budgets for other programming by up to 5 percent for 1991 because of the unexpected expenses incurred during its coverage of Eastern Europe so soon followed by the Gulf war.[19]

On the other hand, since the power of gathering audiences is always a political power before it is an economic one, it is perhaps "the market" which ensures that this political power is not outright totalitarian.[20] The increasing concentration of the ownership of television in the hands of already very powerful media conglomerates, such as News International, and the political pressure to which publicly funded broadcasting is often subject, suggests, however, that the market cannot be regarded as safeguarding democracy,[21] in a system fundamentally and necessarily based, as I would argue, on a set of structural relations organized around mis-cognition and uneven exchange.

This mis-cognition would be twofold; firstly, in the way viewers relate to programs as if their function was to entertain them or to provide information, that is as if they were meant for *them*, when programs are more like "sensors": meant to identify, provide feedback and consolidate audiences; secondly, mis-cognition characterizes the nature of the contract entered into by the viewer with the program maker or television channel. Instead of paying for the screening of a film, or the rental of a video, we know that we pay for television in a more indirect way in the form of a license fee, or by being solicited by commercial breaks and the sponsor's message. This too, however, misconstrues the nature of the relation; license fee television is as much a prisoner of the ratings as commercial television, while advertisers do not pay for programs, they pay for time (attention time and location time, e.g., prime time), they pay for the status of the viewer (in terms of disposable income),[22] and for the accuracy of a program in identifying this status (the often quoted example of *Hill Street Blues* or MTM).[23] Yet I would argue, it is this mis-cognition, which ensures that television engages with the viewers' subjectivity.

For assuming that television's political and economic conditions can thus be called a "symbolic," it would allow one to see its different articulations correspond to historically specific "imaginaries": ways in which the television spectator engages not so much with the individual text but with the institution television as a whole. Its most obvious – because most discussed – imaginary is that of the family, and television studies has made it its task to analyze both texts and audiences in terms of the family as the social and psychic identity around which programming policy, mode of address and programming content cohere. If there is debate, it has been primarily about the class nature, ethnic misrepresentation and patriarchal ideology of family television, and secondly, as to whether this imaginary is constructed by the genres and texts or by the viewing situation and domestic context.[24] It was in this spirit that, earlier on, I tried to suggest that under pressures which might be enlightened and liberal but which might equally be "merely" economic, the imaginary of the family in British television, has been supplemented (though not displaced) by a different "simulation of the social," in the shape of Channel Four. Less oppressively consensus-building around the white middle class family and more multi-cultural, stand-for television suggests a mobile and less monolithic imaginary, but also one more likely to deliver differently packaged audience segments.[25] At the other extreme, the part that television is said to have played in the revolutions in Eastern Europe, can perhaps best be understood as generating "imagined communities"[26] which for a brief time, coincided with geographical-national ones, but which soon began to diverge quite sharply.

Yet precisely because of shifts in the "symbolic" – i.e., the structures that secure the television apparatus' functioning in the economic and political world (deregulation of the broadcasting industries, availability of satellite television in Europe or of cable television in the United States) – neither the family nor a generalized idea of sociability continue to function unproblematically as the dominant imaginary around which viewers construct their spectator identity. A historical line of development is beginning to become apparent about how to understand television spectatorship within the overall history of the audio-visual media and their audiences. Involving similar variables of time advantage and location advantage as were used to segment cinema audiences in the 1920s and 1930s, television's symbolic imposes on program makers choices between "open texts" (allowing "dominant" or "deviant" meanings to be made at the point of reception) and "restricted texts" (addressed to the viewer-in-the-know). Both kinds of texts are nonetheless comparable in that they require a high degree of (cultural) intertextuality and (media) self-reference: television through the looking glass.

What I am arguing, then, is that the crisis in film and television studies is connected to a double loss: the loss of a unified symbolic (which, in the form of Screen theory, made film studies productive) and the loss of a unified imaginary (which, focused on the representation of the family, inspired television studies). The bored couch potato watching everything on offer, the restless "prospector" zapping through the channels "in search of gripping images,"[27] or the viewers hooked on *Miami Vice, Neighbours* and *Twin Peaks* are ultimately a challenge to the industry (but also the discipline of television studies) not only because of "guerrilla raids" on diegetic coherence, and narrative closure by spontaneous sampling and montage techniques, or because such viewers "activate" texts with subversive or aberrant readings, but perhaps because it is not altogether obvious what kinds of imaginary identities, if any, the relentless search of the industry for "quality" (as opposed to quantifiable) audiences actually produces.

"Television," one of my students once rebuked me as I held forth on the pre-oedipal and post-oedipal personality of the television spectator, "is not about fantasy at all, it's about detail." This acknowledges that television allows for more diverse subject positions than both filmic and "culturalist" theories of spectatorship had led us to assume: accommodating the casual viewer, the tele-addict, the remote-control junkie, the family audience and other fantastical beings – including not needing any viewer at all (in the stand-by mode I alluded to earlier on). [28] But television is about detail also because it thrives on the fragment, the perpetual combination of isolated elements, the sheer semiotic power of decontextualizing and recontextualizing the everyday.[29]

Yet perhaps most crucially, my student may also have wanted to insist that the fan, the addict, and the aficionado represent typical ways of engaging with television texts today, based not on those shared imaginaries of the family, of oedipal identity, oral rage or social cohesion, but requiring and gratifying the ability to focus on the part at the expense of the whole, to deploy intimate knowledge, to be an expert – of maybe nothing more nor less than an expert of television itself, its genres, its codes, its manners and modes. No longer viewers driven by lack, but by redundancy and plenitude,[30] desire when watching television becomes manageable and meaningful by making not morons, but specialists of us all.

How often do we not use television to register the minutest tremors in the emotions of our favorite soap opera characters, detect hidden abysses in the bland and dead-pan questions of the talk show host, enjoy guessing the price of coffee makers or tumble-dryers along with the contestants of game shows. The same applies to the news: we do not watch President Bush or Margaret Thatcher for the information they convey, for the message they bear, but for the surplus message that escapes their make-believe. We watch in the endlessly renewable hope that politicians and celebrities will give us the "psychopathology of public life," when a momentary hesitation, a sideways look, an unguarded gesture, an awkward stride will unmask them as impersonators and impostors, catch them out as players and performers. What orgies of finely honed attention to detail could be indulged when Richard Nixon tried to justify himself on television,[31] when Ollie North took the witness stand, when Margaret Thatcher was forced by her own supporters to resign, and General Schwarzkopf was grilled by CNN![32]

Given the objectives pursued by the program makers, such viewing positions and spectator-identities have their own logic. If advertisers are indeed targeting ever more select groups of consumers, programs have to capture spectators who, while not displacing themselves physically from the home, may nonetheless no longer feel themselves part of the family context or even the nation when watching television.[33] In command of their own set, they are television monads; operating the remote control, they are television nomads. While television viewing has always been a peculiar combination of isolation and communality, television programs in the speculative viewer economy of sports channels, news channels, movie channels or quality television necessarily aim to convert these monads/nomads into groups, members of a collectivity though not defined by anything as physically concrete or geographically precise as race, color, neighborhood or nationality. In this respect, the fan, the cult follower, or the armchair expert are ideal compromise formations for identities that are at once global and local, instantaneous and iterative, mobile and yet loyal: so many "discursive formations" nestling within mainstream culture.[34]

The fan and expert viewer, in contrast to the family viewer, forms part of trans-national communities via different entry-points, focused on particular features of a program, even seemingly arbitrary ones attached to the show's form or format.[35] Hence the (critical and commercial) importance of cult audiences, needed not least because advertisers are increasingly trans-national and global companies.[36] Even when gay men get together in someone's home once a week to watch *Dynasty*, they may be deconstructing a popular heterosexual text, but insofar as they constitute a spontaneous community of individuals, they bring to the program what advertisers expect it to deliver: spectators united by common attitudes or life-styles. The deconstructive, ironic or camp modes of reading a popular text thus do not affect its efficacy in binding spectators to what can be called television's post-social and post-national symbolic, especially since negotiated and oppositional reading strategies no less than dominant ones, aim at maintaining a pleasurable relation to the text: *Dallas*, the show you love to hate.

There is undoubtedly much work to be done on the textual implications of these subject positions and reading strategies emerging around the fan, the expert, the viewer-in-the-know, all attending to detail at the expense of closure, grasping the rules that obtain without the need to be immersed in diegetic worlds, and thus without the need to experience the kind of gendered subject coherence traditionally attributed to the cinematic text. Perhaps one of the most interesting rhetorical strategies to study in this context is not irony, excess, pastiche or parody, but that of *complicity*, first suggested by John Ellis as typical for television.[37] It may well prove capable of further theoretical elaboration, as a splitting of the subject not along the dual Lacanian lines of the mirror phase, but in terms of the triadic yet constantly shifting relation between viewer, presenter and event. If, as in my example of Dick Cavett, the presenter *is* the event, the viewer is confronted with an impersonation, while an event without a presenter requires a viewer-in-the-know – the complicity consisting in the credibility gap maintained between presentation and representation, each calling attention to the other as a performance, and visibly pleased with it.[38] Against the specular, voyeuristic mode of cinematic identification, televisual complicity functions like the Freudian joke, told at the expense of someone else: a latent structure of aggression, an uneven distribution of knowledge, a mechanism for inclusion/exclusion that could be democratic, populist but also fascist.

This suggests a final thought. Since program makers only *appear* to be looking at the audience eyeball to eyeball, but have their sights fixed behind and beyond the viewer on the advertisers, it is possible to see a curious analogy between the cinematic apparatus as described by Baudry or Metz, and the televisual apparatus, at first sight so different from the basically 19th-century optico-mechanical projection machinery mimicking Plato's cave. Yet if we think of the television apparatus not only as an electronic circuit but as the *dispositif* I have been sketching, in which the triangulation of desire is not organized along the path of light beam, screen and lens, but via cognitive double-binds, such as "I know that you know that I know," then the *mise-en-abyme* of Dick Cavett impersonating Dick Cavett, or television's ability to be always pleased with itself, mimics in its mode of address, the structure of any program as it looks at us, while making signs at the sponsor.[39] One is reminded of the famous scene in Alfred Hitchcock's REAR WINDOW, when Grace Kelly, caught in Thorwald's apartment, tries to stare out the suspicious Thorwald, while triumphantly flashing the deceased Mrs. Thorwald's wedding ring behind her back in the direction of James Stewart's window. I wonder if television viewers will ever get as angry as Thorwald and menacingly confront the sponsor? Probably not, at least not as long as they think they are in on the joke.

(1990)

Notes

1. The canonical texts for the relation between film studies and television studies are John Ellis, *Visible Fictions* (London: Routledge, 1982) and Robert C. Allen, (ed.), *Channels of Discourse* (Chapel Hill: University of North Carolina Press, 1987); for cultural studies and television studies, see Raymond Williams, *Television: Technology and Cultural Form* (London: Fontana, 1972) and Stuart Hood, *On Television* (London: Pluto Press, 1980). More recently, there has been John Fiske, *Television Culture* (London: Methuen, 1987). Larry Grossberg's writing on television (e.g., "The Indifference of Television," *Screen* 28/2, Spring 1987) might stand for the postmodernist approach to television studies – all of which have been challenged by communications theory, among others. See Susan Boyd-Bowman's "Biennial Report on the Third International Television Conference," *Screen* 30 (3), 1989, pp. 140-43.
2. Fredric Jameson, "Reading without Interpretation: Postmodernism and the Videotext," in Fabb, Attridge, Durant and MacCabe (eds.), *The Linguistics of Writing* (Manchester: Manchester University Press, 1987) p. 199.
3. See Philip Rosen, (ed.), *Narrative, Apparatus, Ideology* (New York: Columbia University Press, 1986) for a representative reader on these debates.
4. While it is easy to see how the individual film text can be considered the "product" of the cinema (though the standardization of this product is by no means self-evident, and has a history of its own), it is far less clear what the "product" of television might be. Hence, the idea of television as a service rather than a commodity industry.
5. See Michel de Certeau, *The Practice of Everyday Life* (trans. Steven F. Rendall, Berkeley: University of California Press, 1984).

6. The most eloquent and elegant proponent of this approach has been John Fiske, e.g., in *Understanding Popular Culture* (Boston: Unwin Hyman, 1989).
7. See Charlotte Brunsdon and David Morley, *Everyday Television: Nationwide* (London: BFI Publishing, 1979) and David Morley, *Family Television: Cultural Power and Domestic Leisure* (London: Comedia/Routledge, 1988).
8. See Sandy Flitterman-Lewis, "Psychoanalysis, Film and Television," in Robert C Allen (ed.), *Channels of Discourse*, pp. 172-206.
9. The terms were first introduced by Raymond Williams, *Television: Technology and Cultural Form*, John Ellis, *Visible Fictions*, and they are elaborated in a psychoanalytic perspective by Beverle Houston, "Viewing Television: the Metapsychology of Endless Consumption," *Quarterly Review of Film Studies* vol. 9, no. 3, Summer 1984.
10. An adaptation of Richard Serra's TV-broadcast 1973 Television Delivers People, it is used by Nick Browne in "The Political Economy of the Television Supertext," *Quarterly Review of Film Studies* 9/3 (Summer 1984), 174-82.
11. See also note 4, above. For a historical account of the cinema as commodity, see Charles Musser, "The Nickelodeon Era Begins" in *Early Cinema: Space Frame Narrative*, pp. 256-273. For a theoretical discussion of desire and commodity fetishism, see Mary Ann Doane, *The Desire to Desire* (Bloomington: Indiana University Press, 1987), pp. 22-25.
12. When academic visitors from Britain (or France) come to the United States, they often experience a surge of critical insight, a brief but often violent defamiliarization, which sometimes results in a kind of productivity I attribute to the culture shock. Raymond Williams' "television as flow" axiom which has proved so influential, was conceived, as Williams tells us, during a sleepless night in a Miami Hotel after a sea voyage across the Atlantic (*Television: Technology as Cultural Form*, p. 92). There is also Umberto Eco's *Travels in Hyperreality*, or Louis Marin's visit to Disneyland, which changed the author's perception of the Court of Versailles under Louis XIV. One could cite *America*, where Jean Baudrillard, with some anxiety, recovers the founding moment of his own immensely productive theorizing about media culture, only to encounter his own concepts staring back at him. Finally, it could be argued that Wim Wenders' most popular films – ALICE IN THE CITIES, THE AMERICAN FRIEND, and PARIS, TEXAS – all record the reverberations of carefully nurtured culture shocks occasioned, respectively, by American television, by the Hollywood film industry, by an American marriage.
13. Someone once referred to this as "honest American bullshit." Perhaps this is what Larry Grossberg means when he says television "presents images of the indifference of meaning, fantasy and reality" or talks of David Letterman's "pose-modernism" and quotes a Jules Feiffer cartoon of a woman in front of TV: "Ronald Reagan talks to me on television. No nonsense...and sincere. Who cares if he's lying?" Larry Grossberg, "The Indifference of Television" *Screen* 28 (2) (Spring 1987) pp. 42-43.
14. One might venture the hypothesis that whereas texts produce subjects as readers, events produce audiences as viewers, which is to say, we may be in a historical transition between a text-based model of television and an event-driven model.
15. See, for a rapid overview, Paul Virilio, *Logistique de la perception* (Paris: Cahiers du cinema, 1985).
16. The Late Show (BBC2) is a good example of the kind of television, which in its style is self-consciously indistinguishable from the glossy and witty ads which so fasci-

nate non-British viewers on a visit. The sophisticated ad has in some sense become the stylistic norm for arts and culture programs, as they bleed into MTV type music programs. Thus even where advertising is economically not the motor force, as in the case of the BBC, it effectively drives both the sign economy and the textual economy of television. This can be also be seen, for instance, by the trailers run by the BBC for its programs, or by looking at its news broadcasts, punctuated by breaks, recaps, and intermissions.

17. Horkheimer and Adorno, it will be recalled, already in the 1940s predicted that the fate of high culture would be to help segment and target markets more efficiently. "The Culture Industry," *Dialectic of Enlightenment* (New York: Herder and Herder, 1972).

18. The recent merger, in Britain, of two satellite operations, Rupert Murdoch's SKY TV and BSB, its erstwhile arch rival, under economic conditions where both were incurring huge losses, might be an example of such a speculative viewer economy, especially in light of the truly Byzantine financing strategies of Murdoch's News International.

19. See "Global News" Media Show (Channel Four), 16 Sept 1990.

20. What the example of the fascist public sphere shows is that, as the Nazi regime knew, the mass media can be used to gather audiences, consolidate ideological communities and generate desiring power, without directing this power to commodity consumption regulated by a market economy, and instead, towards a world war. I have tried to discuss this different desiring economy in "Fassbinder, Fascism and the Film Industry," October 21 (1982), pp. 115-40.

21. That numbers per se are decisive neither to the market nor to parliamentary democracy can be seen in British politics over the past decade where whole groups of citizens below a certain income have, because of demographic factors, become irrelevant to the major political parties as voters to be wooed, just as advertising is increasingly targeted only at those able to afford frequent changes in life-styles.

22. This is not altogether different from what we pay for in the cinema. See my discussion of this point in T. Elsaesser, ed., *Early Cinema: Frame Space Narrative* (London: BFI Publishing, 1990) p.166.

23. Jane Feuer has introduced the term "quality demographics" which she defines as "the idea that ratings must correspond to particular (high-consuming) audience segments rather than to the amorphous mass audience... Around the time that *Hill Street Blues* emerged as a "quality hit program," this idea of demographics rather than numbers was refined even further. Certain programs could become "quality" or "demographic" successes in that, although their overall numbers were relatively low, both the demographics and the "q" scores were compensatingly high among those urban young professionals most likely to desert the networks for pay and cable television." Jane Feuer, "Producer/Industry/Text" in Jane Feuer, Paul Kerr, Tisa Vahimagi, *MTM: Quality Television* (London: BFI Publishing, 1984), p. 4.

24. For a full discussion of the domestic viewing context, see David Morley, Family Television, and Philip Simpson, ed., *Parents Talking Television* (London: Comedia, 1987).

25. Channel Four is in the business of making television, and it would be easy to confuse this function with the ideology around which it was established: that of catering to minority audiences. For this ideology is perfectly compatible with being pop-

ular (to a diverse but devoted audience not divided along high culture/mass culture lines) and of delivering "imagined communities" which is to say fictions, narratives, forms of entertainment and discourses that make groups of people identify with certain life-styles and self-definitions (in turn associated with certain objects, activities, values, and tastes).

26. I take this phrase from Benedict Anderson, who sees the (post-colonial) nation state and nationalism as the product of print culture. Benedict Anderson, *Imagined Communities* (London: Verso, 1991).

27. D. Marc, *Demographic Vistas* (1984), quoted in John Fiske, *Television Culture*, p. 99.

28. A point also made by Dana Polan, in reviewing Ien Ang's Watching Dallas: "Ang's study shows a diversity of viewing practices ranging from identificatory immersion...to ironic distancing in which the spectator makes the television show an object for parody and explicit commentary. Moreover... Ang suggests how this variety... can coexist, even in the same subject. In a spiral of involvement and disavowal, the mass-culture spectator can move in and out of various positions, suggesting perhaps that it is precisely this weaving of contradictory positions, rather than the achieved assumption of any one position, that may constitute much of the power and pleasure of the operation of mass culture." Dana Polan, "Complexity and Contradiction in Mass Culture Analysis," *Camera Obscura* 16 (1988), p. 193.

29. There may be a continuum, rather than a radical distinction, between MTV or CNN doing the "zapping" for you, and your daytime soap inviting you to "graze" with the remote control in hand, or wandering off to the tea kettle or the telephone. Alternatively, one might argue that having control over what to skip greatly increases one's cognitive pleasure of guessing or inferring the missed parts.

30. "One of the great mysteries of life is why young people watch Neighbours until they pass out. In "Soap Down Under" Barry Norman sought an explanation from a high-priced media consultant in a stripy shirt. "Its greatest weakness" opined this cove, "is its greatest strength – which is that nothing very much happens." This theory was confirmed by consumer interviews with Oxford undergraduates. "One of the enchantments of Neighbours," said one, "is that you know exactly what's going to happen next." (John Naughton, in *The Observer* 6 January 1991, p. 60).

31. See Umberto Eco, "Strategies of Lying," in Marshall Blonsky, (ed.), *On Signs* (Oxford: Basil Blackwell, 1985) pp 3-11.

32. Days after the resignation, the televisual highlights had already been set to stirring passages from Shakespeare's histories and tragedies. A similarly potent imaginary is, I think, present in quality news programs and in-depth analyses such as the "McNeil-Lehrer Report" or the BBC's "Newsnight." They secure our attention for the most abstruse issues by making the viewer into an instant expert: "Something should be done about amateur field marshals like Peter Snow of "Newsnight," whose gung-ho enthusiasm for discussing military tactics with superannuated brasshats has become positively obscene. He was at it again last week, playing in his sandpit with Corgi tanks and miniature mines." (John Naughton, The Observer, January 6, 1991). This jibe is reminiscent of a famous 1989 "Spitting Image" sketch where another well-known British television anchorman, Alistair Burnett, in full combat dress, is shown orchestrating the invasion of Poland by Germany in 1939 from his television studio.

33. Dave Morley's *Family Television* represents probably the most complete and searching anatomy of a specific use of television about to become marginal: family viewing which, as he shows, is completely dominated by the uneven division of labor between the sexes and the male breadwinner's increased amount of leisure time spent within the home.

34. The phrase is taken from Ernesto Laclau and Chantal Mouffe's *Hegemony and Socialist Strategy* (London: Verso, 1985). But what I want to suggest here is that the simulacrum of the social and its history, as found on British quality television, may indicate the imperceptible transformation of social cohesion based on traditional, geographic or national references into the new model of the mobile, transnational imagined communities held together by shared media references (watching Dallas, the Olympic Games or the Gulf crisis), so important to advertisers. What Laclau and Mouffe have in mind, of course, is that discursive formations will be important as the agency that mobilizes people for any future socialist politics.

35. What makes Dallas compulsive watching for many "sophisticated" viewers is its dead-pan but encyclopaedic playing out of dramatic or rhetorical clichés recognizable from classical Hollywood film melodrama. The fact that Dallas takes itself seriously makes it available for camp appropriation, which turns this lack of irony into pastiche.

36. I want to signal here in passing the attention cultural studies and film theory have in recent years been devoting to the fan and cult audience, pointing to its elaborate, highly structured, ritualized, self-conscious codes of behavior and differentiations. From a psychoanalytical perspective such subject positions are also interesting, insofar as the fan "negotiates" identification differently from the "ordinary viewer." While fandom may represent a much more direct identification with the object of pleasure, an often vast and detailed knowledge about the program or performers also ensures that "attention to detail" traditionally associated with high culture reading formations, becomes a source of pleasure.

37. John Ellis, *Visible Fictions* (London: Routledge, 1982), pp. 163-9.

38. "In commercial art, the personality portrayed, whether it be portrayed by a model, an actor or a gang of vegetables, has to look pleased with itself, and especially pleased with its association with the product. Pleased with itself means that the personality has a limit, a property and stays within that limit, that property," Matthew Klein, "And Above all, do not disturb," in Marshall Blonsky, (ed.), *On Signs*, p. 484.

39. What complicates this structure is the program makers' "pre-engagement" with the audience, a set of assumptions about the social and demographic consistency of this audience, but also their values, sensibilities, politics and aspirations. For the notion of "audience pre-engagement," see David Barker, "St. Elsewhere: The Power of History," *Wide Angle* vol. 11 (1), 1989, p. 33.

German Cinema Face to Face with Hollywood

Looking into a Two-Way Mirror

The patterns of competition, cooperation, and contestation that characterize the Hollywood presence in the German film business from 1945 to 2000 can be outlined, I think, across three different phases and three types of narrative. The first one is broadly economic-political, the second is governmental-institutional, and the third is cultural-authorial. Depending on which narrative one prefers, the periodization will also shift slightly. The cultural and legal models often prefer the phases 1945 to 1962, 1962 to 1982, and 1982 to 2000, while the economic periodization is somewhat simpler: it knows two cycles that run from 1945 to 1974, and from 1974 to today. The first period marks the apparent apogee, but in fact reflects the gradual decline of Hollywood hegemony (what might be called "Dominance in Disarray"); the second period marks Hollywood redux ("Dominance through Dispersal"). Since I shall be mostly looking at the issues from a German rather than Hollywood perspective, I shall keep the triple period division. However, for reasons that I hope will become clear at the end, a fair amount of overlap and blurring of these boundaries is inevitable, since I also want to contrast an orthodox account with a "revisionist" account, where the latter takes a European perspective, in contrast to the primarily national – in our case, Germano-centric – emphasis of the canonical story.

Traditionally, the economic model has been applied mainly to the first phase, from 1945 to 1960: it is the story of how Hollywood attained hegemony in the German film market, through a policy of divide and rule. It focuses on the dismantling of the heavily centralized prewar film industry, the forced regionalization of German production units, and the dumping practices of American distributors in order to saturate the market with Hollywood films.[1]

The second phase is generally given over to the cultural model, typified by strong governmental intervention and a legislative framework. It relies on the notion of the *Autorenfilm* and the New Waves: for Germany, this means the Young German Film, followed by the New German Cinema. It stands under the sign of oedipal revolt: *Papa's Kino ist tot*, long live the *Autor*, which is why the cultural model could also be called the oedipal-generational approach to succession, filiation, and transmission. As I have shown elsewhere, the New

German Cinema's relation to Hollywood is largely a function of this generational revolt – with interesting consequences at the cross-cultural level of identification and projection, producing some of the strategies of othering and mirroring-effects alluded to in my title. During these years between 1962 and 1982, Hollywood's presence on the German cinema screen, with one or two exceptions that I shall return to, is of relatively little consequence for the cultural model. By contrast, American-produced shows on German television, notably in 1977 and 1979, were to be of momentous consequence for the New German Cinema.

The third phase encompasses the period since the early 1980s, when Hollywood returned in force to the German big screens with its blockbusters and must-see "event" movies, changing both the priorities of production and the patterns of exhibition (urban multiplexes, the CinemaXX chain), thus radically altering the cinema-going experience. At the same time, some of the brightest talents in filmmaking, production, and distribution – though not only there, but across the whole media sector – could not enter into business with Hollywood and US companies fast enough.

In what follows, I shall attempt to nuance this picture somewhat, above all, by trying to apply the double focus – economic and cultural – to all three periods just outlined, in order to put up for discussion in what sense film relations with the US are invariably both economic and cultural, mediated by the state more than by the market. That this has always been the case is one of my subtending contentions: I argue that the complex *cultural* relations in matters of moving images and visual icons between Europe and the US since 1945, with Germany perhaps representing a special case, are actually a replay of the *economic* relations during the 1920s and early 1930s, so that US-German film relations show great continuities across the whole of the last century.

The question this raises for our present century, then, is whether the stereotypical binary divides, in which Europe stands for culture, and America for commerce, still hold, or if we can perceive, and conceive, of a somewhat different alignment. Here are, for quick reference, some of the implicit items of conventional wisdom, as they characterize not only the cinematic divide: Europe stands for art, and the US for pop; Europe for high culture, America for mass entertainment; Europe for artisanal craft, America for industrial mass production; Europe for state (subsidy), Hollywood for studio (box office); European cinema for pain and effort, Hollywood for pleasure and thrills; Europe for the auteur, Hollywood for the star; Europe for experiment and discovery, Hollywood for formula and marketing; Europe for the film festival circuit, Hollywood for Oscar night; Europe for the festival hit, Hollywood for the blockbuster.

An additional interest in presenting this table is to ask whether in all this juxtaposition and polarization, there might be a hidden dialectic that we film scholars have not yet figured out, but where our colleagues from other disciplines, notably economic and political historians, might usefully offer suggestions.

But first, to flesh out briefly the economic history of Hollywood hegemony: the phase from 1945 to 1962 was characterized by the US State Department directives to prevent another Ufa empire from arising during the post-war reconstruction period of the *Wirtschaftswunder*, while fully benefiting from the boom in consumption and leisure, by keeping the enormously important German market wide open for American films.[2] In effect, an economic imperative (free market non-protectionist film policy for US product) and an ideological-political imperative (re-education and democratization of the German people) happily coincided, to the benefit of Hollywood, preventing post-war West German cinema from being more than a cottage industry operating in an assembly line economic environment. This happened not without internal contradictions or resistance even in the US. Let me cite two instances. In a famous speech from 1947, Spyros Skouras, head of 20th Century Fox, argued that

> it is a solemn responsibility of our industry to increase motion picture outlets throughout the free world because it has been shown that no medium can play a greater part than the motion picture industry in indoctrinating people into the free way of life and instil[ling] in them a compelling desire for freedom and hope for a brighter future. Therefore, we as an industry can play an infinitely important part in the world-wide ideological struggle for the minds of men, and confound the Communist propagandists.[3]

Thomas Guback has detailed how, despite these fine and patriotic sentiments, the Hollywood film industry was able to hold the Military Government to ransom over the use of American films for re-education and propaganda purposes. Only when the Motion Picture Export Association, headed by its powerful and indomitable president Jack Valenti, was satisfied that its earnings on the German market could be converted into dollar-holdings and there were no restrictions on the free movement of capital did Hollywood follow its words with deeds. This happened when the US Senate passed the Information Media Guarantee Program in 1948, which effectively gave the go-ahead for the commercial exploitation of the German market:

> The reluctance of American companies to send films to West Germany ... was a result of concerns with revenue. Even the Military Government's objective, to re-educate Germany, was not sufficient incentive for the companies. The event which turned the trickle of American films into a torrent was, clearly, the initiation of guarantees by the American government. That the IMG program was lucrative to Hollywood was ap-

parent when ... Congressman H.R. Gross attacked film industry lobbying in Washington and the IMG, declaring that ... the "Motion Picture Export Association has been given a pretty good ride on the Informational Media gravy train ...".[4]

By 1951, over two hundred American films were released annually in the three Western-occupied zones. For the German cinema, trying to re-establish indigenous film production out of the ruins of what had, from the 1920s onwards, been one of the most prosperous and technically advanced film industries, this saturation of the market proved a permanent handicap.[5]

However, in light of recent empirical research, this story needs revision. According to Joseph Garncarz, for instance, the German commercial cinema, despite several crisis cycles, actually survived and occasionally thrived during the years 1947 and 1970; it was economically viable, even if it had little critical prestige and virtually no export chances.[6] What kept it respectable was its domestic market share of spectators, with German films year-in, year-out outperforming Hollywood titles at the box office until 1970.

The still-unanswered question is why West Germany could not develop the mixed model of an art cinema and a commercial cinema that Italy and France maintained throughout the 1960s and well into the 1970s, or develop along the British model by retooling its studio-capacity to provide US offshore production facilities, specialist craftspeople for Hollywood companies, as in the James Bond films or for the STAR WARS saga, and exporting its popular culture (the Beatles films, swinging London comedies) to America's youth. Italy, it must be said, also experienced a collapse of its film industry similar to that in Germany around 1972-1973, when the spaghetti western – Italy's own coming to terms with Hollywood – ceased to attract audiences, and domestic comedies with Toto or Fernandel became relics of a bygone age.

As in the case of Germany, was it new technologies, such as the videotape revolution, that killed off German genre cinema? Was it television? Was it the new marketing strategies of the Hollywood blockbuster? None would be specific to Germany, so an additional factor might have to come into play, such as the particular paradoxical and politically complicated generational transfer in West Germany. It would point to a cultural, rather than an economic, legacy that at least for a period seems to have inflected the US-German film axis, but it did so across an inter-German conflict situation.

With this we enter the second phase: the years from the Oberhausen Manifesto in 1962 to the Hamburg Declaration in 1977, and from the "German Autumn" of 1977 to the death of Rainer Werner Fassbinder in 1982, which coincided with the end of the social-liberal coalition of the Brandt-Schmidt years.

The Young and New German Cinema had very distinct attitudes toward Hollywood, ranging from total hostility to ambivalence, and from playing off one good auteurist America-Hollywood, against another, bad imperialist America-

Hollywood. Despite some harsh words from directors like Wim Wenders about "the Yanks having colonized our subconscious," we know that Wenders in particular was probably the classical Hollywood cinema's greatest and most knowledgeable fan among New German directors. But Wenders already belonged to the second generation. The Young German Cinema of Alexander Kluge and Edgar Reitz – that is, those born ten years earlier – was more or less solidly anti-American from the start; their oppositional stance against commercial mainstream (German) cinema extended to Hollywood, probably under the double impact of seeing their entry into filmmaking blocked by ex-Nazi directors still dominating the industry, and seeing the entry of their independently made films into the German cinemas blocked by US distributors, who were of course supported by cinema owners, even where these were German-owned (their numbers dwindling as the 1970s wore on).

Also significant in the shaping of the image of Hollywood was the role of journalists and critics around the Munich-based monthly *Filmkritik*. Here, too, the second generation (among whom could be found future filmmakers such as Wenders and Rudolf Thome) proved more pro-Hollywood than the first and the third. After the initially exclusive aesthetics of neorealism (anti-Hollywood), there came to prominence, from the mid-1960s onwards, a faction who took over from the *Cahiers du cinéma* the reevaluation of the Hollywood director as auteur. These critics (including Enno Patalas and Frieda Grafe) made clear distinctions between the 1960's American productions they mostly detested, and the classic Hollywood of the 1930s and 1940s by American auteurs whom they celebrated: John Ford, Alfred Hitchcock, and Howard Hawks. A special place was reserved for the Germans working in Hollywood: besides the 1920s émigrés Ernst Lubitsch and F.W. Murnau, they championed the political exiles Fritz Lang, Billy Wilder, Max Ophuls, and even such commercial contract directors like Robert Siodmak, or later, the Hollywood B-movie director Douglas Sirk (after the British had "rediscovered" him).

The ambivalences characterizing the New German Cinema directors vis-à-vis America (the label and thus the distinction "New German Cinema," incidentally, was also invented by Anglo-American critics and scholars) can be described by several mutually interdependent identity formations. I have called it the oedipal matrix, where I distinguish the colonial paradigm, the elective paternity paradigm, and the no-contest or "American friend" paradigm.[7]

Both the colonizing cliché and the oedipal dimension of conflict and contest come very directly out of the post-war German generation's experience of Hollywood hegemony and the re-education effort, which had an impact not on the first but second generation. While their parents may have been obdurately high-culture in their tastes and outlook, preferring Sartre or Camus to Steinbeck and Reader's Digest while shunning the cinema altogether, the generation of

Wenders, Fassbinder, and Werner Herzog not only grew up with but embraced American cinema, AFN radio, and Disney comics, finding in them a liberation and refuge from the stultifying, repressed, and dishonest atmosphere of the parental home during the Adenauer years. Wenders's perhaps over-quoted line about American colonization from IM LAUF DER ZEIT (released in English under the title KINGS OF THE ROAD) needs to be balanced against his other famous remark, where he called rock and roll his "lifesaver" as an adolescent, at a moment in which American popular culture provided the antidote to "twenty years [of parental amnesia ...]; we filled it with Mickey Mouse, Polaroids and chewing gum." Thus, "the Yanks have colonized our subconscious" points in several directions at once, and in the narrative-filmic context in which it occurs, it functions both approvingly and critically: one of the two protagonists cannot get the lyrics of a pop song out of his head. Furthermore, the site of the scene is also important: an abandoned US patrol hut at the German-German border. Faced with this barbed-wire border, it seems preferable to have one's subconscious colonized by American rock music than to be an actual colony of the Soviet Union, like the other Germany the two young men can see from the US Army lookout. In other words, the protagonists allude to America at a juncture in their journey where they are forcibly reminded of the historical events that had brought the Americans to Germany in the first place, and in what role (as liberators from Nazism, and as buffer from Stalinism). Not unimportant for the structure and ideological work of the film is also the fact that the remark is made at a point in the two men's wary friendship, when a growing intimacy and regression to childhood threatens their sense of separate and (hetero-)sexual identity. It indicates in Wenders's *oeuvre* the homoerotic undercurrent, associated in his mind with American popular culture, which eventually became his way of resolving the oedipal confrontation with the fathers via the two-buddies-on-the-road or two-angels-in-the-city solution.

Without detailing here the discursive texture and filmic embodiments of these different positions among the leading figures of the New German Cinema, one can nonetheless observe that across the split between past Hollywood grandeur (of classic auteurs and maverick outsiders inside America) and the present – that is, the 1960s and 1970s imperialist US superpower, operating, as it was perceived, repressively outside its borders – the German directors tried to reconstruct their own national imaginary between the liberal traditions of the Weimar Republic and the totalitarian horrors of the Nazi period. Filmmakers regularly "adopted" good elective fathers, in order to reject their own bad (Nazi cinema or natural) fathers. One finds, for instance, very strong elective paternity suits by Wenders (Nicolas Ray and Sam Fuller) and Fassbinder (Douglas Sirk, Raoul Walsh, and Michael Curtiz). But one cannot help being disconcerted by the extraordinary anti-Hollywood diatribes of an Edgar Reitz and Hans Jürgen Syberberg. Thus, Hollywood came to function as a complex signifier – both catalyst and stick with which to beat the opposition – in the post-1968 German intergenerational confrontation, which culminated politically in the Red Army Fraction and cinematically in *Germany in Autumn*. The "return to history" among the art-cinema directors found its echo in the "Hitler Wave" of the popular media and the retro-fashion films from Italy, France, and Germany (Ingmar Bergman filming in Munich-Geiselgasteig), and yet this typically European or even German obsession with the recent past was itself not unaffected by the 1972 American hit movie *Cabaret*, with its stylish revival of 1930s fashion and iconography.

West Germany's cinephile identity formation around oedipal paradigms was broken up with the screening of the US-television series *Holocaust* in 1978 and 1979. Such was the shock at discovering American television "appropriating" *the* German subject par excellence that the New German Cinema "responded" with films by Volker Schlöndorff (THE TIN DRUM), Kluge (THE PATRIOT), Syberberg (HITLER - A FILM FROM GERMANY), Fassbin-

THE TIN DRUM

der (THE MARRIAGE OF MARIA BRAUN), Margarethe von Trotta (THE GERMAN SISTERS), Helma Sanders Brahms (GERMANY PALE MOTHER), culminating in Reitz's 1984 HEIMAT.[8] This so-called mastering-the-past debate gave the New German Cinema its internationally defining identity, but it left a notable gap: the whole debate around the television series *Holocaust* kept the issue of German-Jewish relations (i.e., anti-Semitism) prior to Kristallnacht and after Auschwitz out of the German directors' pictures. Excluding one or two of the films of Fassbinder, Kluge, and the little-known Herbert Achternbusch film DAS LETZTE LOCH (1980), the omission was hardly noticed as significant – except by American critics. How can you represent somebody or something whose disappearance you do not acknowledge, whose presence you do not miss?[9]

These, then, would be some of the markers or terms for reconstructing a particular cultural line of transfer and transmission, wherein Hollywood, time and again, played a role in catalyzing, exacerbating, or profiling German film culture's relation to its own identity. One could say that after denial and disavowal in the 1950s, and opposition and rejection in the 1960s, we find in the 1970s patterns of reverse identification with America and even over-identification with Hollywood. In other words, the coherence, purpose, and identity of the

New German Cinema, during the brief period in which it was experienced as both new and German, was founded on a series of fantasies that involved Hollywood literally and metaphorically, materially and as the imaginary other. Furthermore, almost all the aesthetic debates as well as the film-politics focused on German cinema as a national cinema during the 1970s and 1980s were displaced versions of antagonism and competition, of oedipal rivalry and submission to Hollywood: perverse in Syberberg, disingenuous in Reitz, geographically dislocated in Herzog, disarmingly devious in Fassbinder, and filial-fraternal in Wenders.

In terms of a cross-cultural exchange, these fantasies are eminently readable: first, they belong to a very traditional German history in which America has so often served as the screen of self-projection and self-alienation.[10] But the fantasies of *Fernweh* and homecoming can also be read as a fairly precise account of acts of self-creation (by the *Autor*) in a specific film-historical conjunction, by a cinema that wants to be national and representative, but because it disavowed its own popular cinema (both *Papa's Kino* of the 1950s and the Ufa genres of the 1940s), had to go to Hollywood to legitimate itself. In the course of this, it staged a revolt as well as a submission, and then rewrote this dependency into a Kaspar Hauser foundling story (in Herzog, Wenders), an exile story (Herzog's Kinski figures), and into the return of the prodigal son (Wenders again, Syberberg, and the opening scene and repeated motif in Reitz' HEIMAT): both stories together made up West Germany's own myth of a "national" and "independent" cinema, in a movie business that by then had become global and interdependent or not at all.

Possibly realizing the artistically productive, but economically crippling, miscognitions in this self-understanding of a national or auteur cinema in a rapidly globalizing environment, a segment of Germany's filmmaking community turned away from such tormented love-hate relationships with Hollywood in the mid-1980s. Instead, they transformed the encounter with an imaginary America, mirroring an introspective and retrospective Germany still in thrall to

its recent history, into a more or less straightforward exchange. Abandoning imaginary over-identification and virtual exile, these directors and directors of photography (Wolfgang Petersen, Michael Ballhaus, to name the two most prominent) practiced a deliberate and open emulation of Hollywood: their dream was to make films that either found a large popular audience or pleased an American distributor, in order then to set off and emigrate to New York and Los Angeles.[11]

AIR FORCE ONE

If for much of the 1980s, it was the multiply refrac-
tured, projected, and introjected Hollywood that gave
the work of Wenders, Herzog, and Fassbinder its precarious German identity, the names associated with
emulation and subsequent emigration are, besides
Petersen (IN THE LINE OF FIRE, OUTBREAK, AIR FORCE
ONE, THE PERFECT STORM), Roland Emmerich (STAR-
GATE, INDEPENDENCE DAY, GODZILLA, THE PATRIOT),
and Uli Edel (LAST EXIT TO BROOKLYN, BODY OF EVI-
DENCE), all of whom have been making films in Hollywood itself, but for global audiences. Instead of the Lacanian mirror-phase, of "colonizing the unconscious,"
or acting out a Kaspar Hauser complex, the talk is now
of tax shelters, package deals, talent scouts, product re-
purposing, and corporate synergies.

THE PATRIOT

Considered from the German side, however, this third phase is not without
its own mirroring effects. First, in some respects it repeats and mirrors the transatlantic movie trade of the 1920s, with German directors, such as Ernst
Lubitsch, Fritz Lang, and F.W. Murnau embracing Hollywood production
methods and genres already when working in Germany (as did Petersen, Edel,
and Emmerich in the 1980s when they started in Germany), prepared for being
offered Hollywood contracts. Petersen and company were joined by Michael
Ballhaus, Fassbinder's former cameraman, who became the Karl Freund of his
generation, with credits (besides working for Petersen) on films by Martin
Scorsese and Francis Ford Coppola, such as GOODFELLAS, THE AGE OF
INNOCENCE, BRAM STOKER'S DRACULA, GANGS OF NEW YORK. These German
film people are singularly successful in adapting themselves, at least compared
with their fellow filmmakers from the same generation, such as Schlöndorff,
Percy Adlon, and Wenders, who also made films directly in the US, but whose
sojourns were brief and for whom Hollywood in retrospect appeared to be a
career detour rather than the chosen destination.

Second, the mirroring effects extend to the films themselves, especially when
one switches perspectives and looks at the mirror from the other side, that is,
from Hollywood. The picture so far implies that during the second phase – from
1960 to 1980 – Hollywood had already let its dominant position slip not only in
Germany but had lost its grip on audiences worldwide. To some extent, this is
true. Although Hollywood experienced its deepest domestic crisis in the 1950s,
as the Paramount decree demanded de-cartelization, and television took away
its core clients (the family audience), the impact on foreign sales only manifested themselves fully in the 1960s. The old formulas no longer worked; not
even new technologies such as Cinemascope, epic subjects, or lavish musicals

could keep audiences or attract the younger generation, especially abroad. Thus, the springtime of the new waves all over Europe – not just in Germany, which was a latecomer when we think of Britain, France, Poland, and even Brazil – resulted in part not from the strength of the European auteurs but from the weakness of Hollywood itself.

Nonetheless, the long years of structural changes in America's audio-visual entertainment sector gave Europe breathing space. While Hollywood was in disarray, Europe made some inroads that have permanently changed the film cultural landscape. The 1970s, for instance, were the time of the growing importance of the film festival circuits, which emerged as a new force in European cinema, developing an alternative system of promotion, distribution, exhibition (and sometimes even an alternative production model), coexisting with Hollywood. The festivals – Cannes, Venice, Berlin, Toronto, New York, and Sundance – provided the launching pads for auteurs and national movements, not least for Germany. The programming of these regular venues throughout the year became, together with the Goethe Institutes, the institutional base from which German independent directors benefited, especially during the 1980s.

While film festivals took on a new importance for art cinema auteurs and independent productions worldwide, the reorganization of the American film industry was also largely completed by the middle of the Reagan years. New ownership patterns in the production sector (Hollywood's old studio facilities turned over to making television series), a new business model of the delivery systems (the rise of cable and the pre-recorded videotape market, for instance), and synergies in repackaging content (culminating in the Time Warner deal) were some of the economic changes that led to the remarkable revival of Hollywood as the world's premier provider of mass entertainment. The new cultural hegemony, on the other hand, was in part due to new branding and advertising methods, which in turn relied on the reorganization of Hollywood's global markets through distribution agreements among the studios. They formed cartels for their overseas distribution, by acquiring worldwide outlets and thus the ability to program thousands of first run cinema the world over for opening a film widely, which is to say, to schedule carefully coordinated release dates and thereby reap profits from theatrical release very quickly, within two to three weeks. The rise of the blockbuster as a new marketing concept (tie-ins, merchandising, the Disney and Dreamworks high concept movies that now dominate popular entertainment) thus represents a gradual and complex story, based economically on re-establishing so-called vertical integration and culturally on the return of family audiences to the new multiplexes, the capturing of the youth market, notably with movies that appeal to young women as well as men. The blockbuster concept also racked up the cost of such movies to unprecedented levels, generating the need to suck in venture capital but also multiplying the risk to investors, with the not unwelcome side effect of excluding most European countries (with their delicate balance of state funding, television production money and weak box office for their audiovisual sector) from being able to afford a commercial film industry.

Important for our topic is that Hollywood in the age of the blockbuster is servicing global audiences, with often very different tastes. Just as it had done in the 1920s, it has thus been interested in recruiting filmmakers and film personnel from all over the world who can deliver these global audiences. Thus, the 1990s saw an unprecedented influx of foreign talent to Hollywood, among whom the German contingent forms a substantial but by no means exceptional part. Once one thinks of the Netherlands, which with Paul Verhoeven and Jan de Bont also supplied two top blockbuster directors, or remembers France, where Luc Besson and Jean Pierre Jenet have made the trip to Los Angeles (and back to Paris) several times, not to mention Finland (Rene Harlin), Spain (Alejandro Amenábar), and Ireland (Neil Jordan), then the success of the German directors mentioned above no longer seems so exceptional. It is dwarfed, for instance, by the stream of talent from Australia (Peter Weir, Phil Noyce, Mel Gibson), New Zealand (Peter Jackson, Lee Tamahori), and Great Britain, where John Boorman, Ridley and Tony Scott, Alan Parker, Adrian Lyne and Mike Figgis led the way in the 1980s, with a veritable invasion, and where a British producer, David Puttnam, actually occupied the position of studio head of a major Hollywood company (Columbia Pictures), albeit briefly.

This 1980s and 1990s influx of directors was itself the succession of an earlier migration or trickle, partly caused by the thaw in Eastern Europe in the late 1960s – Milos Foreman, Roman Polanski, but also including Louis Malle and even, briefly, Michelangelo Antonioni, the Wim Wenders of his generation in this respect, if you pardon the anachronism. The Russians, too, after the collapse of the Soviet Union, provided some new talent to Hollywood (Andrej Konchalowsky comes to mind), but many more continue to come to Hollywood from East Asia, India, Mexico.

An economic perspective thus sees the 1990s under the sway of the American model: providing global markets with entertainment by buying up international talent and content, while controlling distribution and exhibition, by exporting the multiplex cinema, complete with merchandising and popcorn. Across its three post-war phases – Hollywood hegemony, Hollywood in disarray, and Hollywood redux – the studio system with its constant striving for vertical integration has remained remarkably stable over a very long period. It proved adept at adapting itself to new technologies, to new demographics and business models, emerging as a global force, despite bankruptcies, takeovers by foreign interests, and other challenges, such as the video cassette, digitization, and the Internet. This American model of popular culture, as we know, is still making vast inroads, even in areas of the globe where other aspects of American values and especially American foreign policy agendas are sharply condemned or encounter violent and bloody resistance.

Europe – and especially Germany – was not able to either reverse-engineer the American model successfully (as did Hong Kong, for instance, and Bollywood, India's popular cinema) or to counter it with a film industry model of its own (as did Egypt in the 1980s and Iran in the 1990s). Within Europe, as indicated, France and Britain were much more successful than Germany. France excelled in the area of what one might call cultural prototypes: French films have been remade in the US, sometimes by another director (THREE MEN AND A BABY), sometimes by the same one (NIKITA). Yet thanks to journals such as *Cahiers du cinéma* in the 1950s and 1960s, France also provided much of the theory by which America now evaluates, celebrates, and appropriates its own cinematic heritage and the history of Hollywood. Britain was most successful in the area of popular music, playing back to US audiences their own ethnic and regional music: bands such as the Rolling Stones, the Beatles, and the Animals systematically repackaged as youth and re-branded as pop, American rhythm and blues, rock and roll, country music, gospel music, and other forms of ethnic popular music.

Nothing of this kind can be said of Germany, whose impact on America's popular culture has only been in the area of automobiles: from the VW beetle, via the BMW, to the luxury division of Mercedes and Porsche. Compared to this, the New German Cinema – whether with commercial or art-house films – cut a very poor figure even in its heyday, and economically played no role at all. However, this is where the broadly cultural parameters of my analysis may well offer some compensation and correction: what I earlier described as the generational or oedipal model, and which I here call the two-way mirror model of cultural transfer, applies (as I have just tried to indicate) also the other way round, namely, to America itself. The case of Britain and pop music, and of France and critical discourses, are both based on a sort of mirror function: Europe appropriates something from the US, reprocesses or rearticulates it across a European sensibility and then plays it back to the US, whose dissident intellectuals, maverick artists, and sometimes even popular audiences are happy to perceive themselves thus culturally upgraded and recognized in the mirror of their European fans and admirers. Just as the American novel of Faulkner and Hemingway after 1945 found itself accepted as serious literature by the appreciation of André Gide, Jean Paul Sartre, or Claude Edmonde Magny, so Martin Scorsese, Francis Ford Coppola, Paul Schrader, and Steven Spielberg learned to love their own past Hollywood cinema across the panegyrics penned by François Truffaut, Claude Chabrol, Jacques Rivette, and Jean Luc Godard. One might say that both the British and the French have, in their different ways, been playing at being American without losing their own distinctive cultural inflexion. As American signs, icons, and values are retranslated twice over, they produce not so much the Chinese whisper effect of surrealist *cadavres exquis*, nor the hybridization so vaunted by postcolonial theorists, but an amplification effect that knows its own noise and interference yet offers a sort of dialogue across the Europe-America divide that seems to have added cultural capital to the cinema rather than pushed it down-market.

The German case is somewhat different and more complex. It is different in that West Germany never had the popular culture appeal of working-class Britain; it had nothing to compare with the Beatles from Liverpool (who got their start in Hamburg), the Rolling Stones from suburban London, and the Animals from Newcastle. The best Germany could offer was the internationalization of the *Heimatfilm*, but that was THE SOUND OF MUSIC, a Hollywood production, of course, set in Salzburg, Austria. Nor did Germany have the high-culture discourse of Parisian cinephiles. On the contrary, its dominant post-war intellectual idiom, the Frankfurt School critical theory, was notoriously hostile to American popular culture, comparing it more than once to Nazism.

Yet precisely because of the legacy of Nazism, the situation is also more complex than in France or Britain. For Adorno and Horkheimer rightly recognized that Nazism had produced one of the most seductively modern and mediatized forms of populism, with a strong iconography of styling and design, the political equivalent of marketing a brand. I therefore may need to modify what I said about Germany only marketing its automobiles as popular culture. As already hinted at, its other export to the US in the 1970s and 1980s were narratives and images of its national disaster. The New German Cinema became critically successful and culturally significant when it began to "represent" its terrible history in the form of stories about Nazism and the war. Virtually all of the films still remembered from the New German Cinema have this twelve-year period and its aftermath as their direct or indirect topic (THE TIN DRUM, OUR HITLER, THE MARRIAGE OF MARIA BRAUN, LILI MARLEEN, THE GERMAN SISTERS, GERMANY IN AUTUMN, THE PATRIOT, THE POWER OF FEELINGS, GERMANY PALE MOTHER, HEIMAT, and WINGS OF DESIRE). We may think this is because of the quality of the films or the gravity of the subject matter, but in the US it is Nazism that carried a special recognition value for the signifier "Germany" within popular culture. It has been and still is

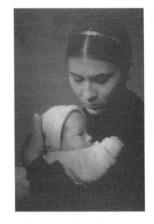

GERMANY PALE MOTHER

a taboo-breaking, transgressive signifier, emotionally, ideologically as well as libidinally, besides having – in these films – the high-culture appeal necessary to make some impact in the American public sphere. That a

political and human disaster with unimaginable individual tragedies, where in-
describable crimes and atrocities were committed by men of unremitting evil,
should be a subject that "played well" in both the popular mass media and in
high-brow culture may be an observation of egregious callousness. So let me
phrase somewhat differently what seems to be at stake. Seen as another moment of cultural transfer and transatlantic transmission, two aspects of "fascinating fascism" and its cinematic representations call for comment: first, the
construction of the meaning of Nazism and the Holocaust for Germans themselves and between Germany and the rest of the world; and second, the generic
coding of heroes and villains in popular culture generally, where their function
is to test through transgressions the social norms of a community, and the
boundaries of what it means to be human.

The representability of the Holocaust and the interpretations of Nazism have
remained to this day not only a topic among professional historians. They are
probes for the state of public debate, and the possibilities of cross-generational
and inter-cutltural dialogue, fuelled by unresolved issue of victims and perpetrators, survivors and the second generation, and of their mutual claims upon
each other, their self-images and representational spaces. In this respect the
somewhat embarrassing statements of Hans Jürgen Syberberg,[12] or the seemingly naive remarks of Edgar Reitz[13] in reply to Elie Wiesel,[14] were nonetheless
tokens of such a dialogue and exchange, however truncated, just as the role of a
Francis Ford Coppola in giving the films of Syberberg and Herzog American
art-house and "special event" distribution greatly enhanced their visibility, not
by bringing them to Hollywood but to San Francisco, and Berkeley's Pacific
Film Archive instead.

How this entrepreneurial activity of Coppola fits into his own self-image of
the Shakespearean over-achiever in love with grandiose failure is an aspect of
my topic I cannot fully enter into here. But it helps me build a bridge to the
second issue at stake, as well as to yet another two-way mirror effect, attached
to my third phase, that of German-born filmmakers in Hollywood since the
1990s. For this emulation-emigration generation, I would venture that a similar
pattern obtains, where reflections of Nazism are, despite appearances to the
contrary, still an issue. Petersen made his name in the US with DAS BOOT, an
action film (i.e., a typically American genre) on a topic (war) and with a theme
(male bonding under pressure) that for the post-Vietnam generation proved to
capture the right mirror of otherness, while still servicing the image Americans
associated with Germany: the war, Nazis, automotive machinery. Petersen, for
his part, has admitted that he liked making films in Hollywood not only because of the state-of-the-art facilities and a worldwide public but also because it
gives him the opportunity to make political-patriotic films of a kind he could
never make in Germany. What is missing there are not the budgets as much as

the ideological climate. His favorite topics – leadership, courage, and individual initiative – are still too sensitive in Germany, while they are the very stuff of the Hollywood hero.

Roland Emmerich profiled himself already in Germany as a sci-fi director. He, too, is an expert in terrestrial and extra-terrestrial disasters, making movies that could easily be said to reflect the legacy of war-like or emergency scenarios. In this sense, Petersen and Emmerich are true to an earlier pattern, where non-American Hollywood directors had to be both European in their view of America, and at the same time capable and willing to make 110% American films. With DAS BOOT, DIE ENDLOSE GESCHICHTE, CHRISTIANE F. – WIR KINDER VOM BAHNHOF ZOO, DAS ARCHE NOAH PRINCIP and JOEY, Petersen, Edel, and Emmerich proved that they were at home not so much in the American genres of sci-fi, fantasy, children's films, and action pictures, but that they had primed themselves for the myths, conflicts, and anxieties that power these genres in the media-event and prosthetic-memory culture of the American cinema of the 1990s. Defeat and rescue, childhood helplessness and omnipotence, man-made and natural disasters, wars and invasions, the legitimacy or corruption of power, innocent perpetrators and the guilty who get away with it: these are perhaps universal themes, but blockbuster cinema has given them such allegorical elaborations that their meanings can be extracted by audiences everywhere, while still referring unmistakably to an America between Vietnam and 9/11. It is too early to tell what exactly the cultural significance is of Hollywood's dominant ideologies in the 1990s – Michael Rogin has tried to read Emmerich's INDEPENDENCE DAY in this light[15] – but that non-American directors have made a major contribution to their visual feel as well as their narrative fabric seems already evident. Even the works of Verhoeven and de Bont can be said to belong to this genre of disaster films after disaster: Verhoeven, for instance, has had a lifelong obsession with Nazism, which goes back to his experience of German occupation of the Netherlands and its immediate aftermath when he was a child after the liberation. TOTAL RECALL or STARSHIP TROOPERS make perfect sense against this historical foil. Their portrayal of action heroes and intergalactic disasters also fit into a postclassical Hollywood preoccupation with traumatized males and reactive automatons, with questions of power and sovereignty, obedience and legitimacy, or the fine line between demented heroism and dedicated patriotism.

Thus, the metamorphosed legacy of the war and Nazism in today's Hollywood can be seen as yet another form of cultural transfer, a manner for Europe and America each looking into a two-way mirror. With films like INDEPENDENCE DAY, STARSHIP TROOPERS, IN THE LINE OF FIRE, AIR FORCE ONE, THE PATRIOT, and several others, it is as if the German and European directors mentioned are "reading" America for Americans, in a way not all that different (though in a different idiom and register) from how Lubitsch, Stroheim, or Hitchcock read Vienna, Paris, and London for Americans in the 1920s and 1930s, or how the German emigrés from the 1930s – Lang, Ophuls, Wilder, Siodmak, Bernhard, and Ulmer – helped create film noir by reading American nightmares of urban malaise and male insecurity across their experience of the feverish energy and dark excesses of the final days of the Weimar Republic. The compliment was returned some twenty years later, when French and German directors in the 1960s and 1970s used Hollywood gangster films and B-movies to read post-war France and Germany, while yet another twenty years later, a Quentin Tarantino would read his own Los Angeles suburban subcultures as if they were located in Godard's Parisian *banlieux*.

Without dwelling on all the paradoxes involved, I hope to have indicated just how layered the *cultural* (as opposed to the economic) factor can be, even when seen in the film industry context in the narrow sense, not to mention popular culture in the wider sense. However, there is one paradox I do want to highlight, because it brings us back to our economic analysis. One of the reasons why these directors are in Hollywood, I argued, is that Hollywood needs to address global audiences, because it is now economically dependent on them, a fact that has not always been the case, certainly not in the 1950s. But another reason why especially the German directors are in Hollywood – beyond their choices as creative individuals and possibly auteurs with a personal thematic signature – is the vision and resolve of a single individual. He is, however, not a director in the usual sense, but the epitome of the entrepreneur, the impresario, and the producer, very much the German equivalent of, say, the more flamboyantly cigar-stomping David Puttnam who engineered the British invasion of Hollywood in the 1980s.

His name is Bernd Eichinger, and outside specialist circles, he is relatively little known. Born in 1949 and thus roughly of the generation of Wenders and Fassbinder, Eichinger went to the Munich film school, directed some none-too-successful literary adaptations in the mold of Schlöndorff, and began his career as a producer in 1978, by buying up the once prestigious but by then moribund distribution-production company Constantin. Eichinger brackets as well as bridges the 1970s and the 1990s, and he furnishes all the ingredients for an alternative history of the New German Cinema in the 1980s. Standing apart from both the state-subsidized, television-funded author's cinema, and the old German film industry chiefs, like Atze Brauner, Horst Wendlandt, and Luggi Waldleitner, he produced the early films of Petersen (DAS BOOT and DIE ENDLOSE GESCHICHTE), but also films by Doris Dörrie and Söhnke Wortmann. He is thus largely responsible for the much-derided turn of German cinema to comedies (*Beziehungskomödien*) and the building of German movie stars out of television personalities. Yet he always pursued a double strategy, servicing the German market and making European co-productions out of high-brow but popular no-vels, such THE NAME OF THE ROSE, directed by a Frenchman, Jean-Jacques Annaud and starring Sean Connery, or THE HOUSE OF THE SPIRITS, directed by a Dane, Bille August, and starring Jeremy Irons and Meryl Streep. Eichinger's own brand of European internationalism was designed to get him into the American market, and from there back into Europe, Asia, and Latin America.[16]

However, Eichinger is not only a less visible David Puttnam or a successor to the Italian international producers Carlo Ponti, Dino de Laurentiis, or the Italo-American James Bond franchise owner, Albert Broccoli. Eichinger epitomizes for me the economic equivalent of the two-way mirror, and of the various mu-tual interdependencies that come with Hollywood hegemony: he is what I would call the embodiment (or with respect to the film business maybe even a pioneer) of the principle of strategic "inward investment" in the US, where what is invested is not only capital but cultural capital, and not only manpower but brainpower and talent.

In this sense, Eichinger fits into a wider set of shifts in the relations between Europe and the US, after GATT, after protectionism and cultural exceptionalism of the French variety, and after state-funded filmmaking of the German sort. In Germany one can put him next to and following on from one of his rivals, Günter Rohrbach, the chief of Bavaria studios in the 1980s, a former television producer who tried to become a global player by building up a studio base – that of Munich-Geiselgasteig, one of the oldest production facilities in Germany. Eichinger, on the other hand, came into the business from distribution, and im-mediately adopted the post-studio system of the New Hollywood, based as it is on the package deal, on outsourcing and subcontracting, in short, on post-For-dist methods of flexible production and reduced plant and personnel over-heads.

At the same time (and thus making up yet another internal German rhyme or mirroring effect), Eichinger pretty well followed the strategy and fulfilled the role in Germany in the 1990s that Erich Pommer had pioneered in the 1920s in-side Ufa, when he created a Cinema Europe, while always also keeping one foot firmly planted in Hollywood. Pommer was pushed by Ufa twice, the second time in 1933 for racial reasons. Yet such is the irony, but also the logic, of the German film business in its dealings with America that Pommer came back in 1946, now in a US Army uniform, and as the US Government Chief Film Offi-cer, entrusted with de-Nazifying, rebuilding and re-licensing the German film business, which he started to do in no other place than Munich's Geiselgasteig Studios. That Pommer eventually had to give up, vilified and sabotaged by the Germans he tried to help (but no less frustrated and disappointed by the Holly-wood lobby in the State Department, who would not allow him to build up a centralized viable production base even in the American zones) is a story well worth telling, because it, too, gives a more nuanced and revisionist account to the one I began with about Hollywood's "divide and rule" policy after 1945.[17]

But back to Pommer's historical double from the 1980s, Eichinger. The larger picture to which Eichinger belongs is not only the history of the German film industry face to face with Hollywood in 1925, 1933, 1945, and the 1990s, or of the European film industry since GATT and beyond. The associations I tried to invoke, by calling his method "strategic inward investment," is of course meant to call to mind also the likes of Jürgen Schremp, head of Daimler-Chrysler, Leo Kirch, founder of Kirch Media – until 2001 a global player with a film library, television interests, and publishing assets who modeled himself on Rupert Murdoch, Ted Turner, and Silvio Berlusconi – and Thomas Middenhoff, the now deposed CEO of Bertelsmann, whose rise and fall in turn mirrors that of Jean Marie Messier of Canal+ and Vivendi-Universal in France – the very company that, under the name of Compagnie Générale des Eaux, bought the old UFA/DEFA Studios in Neu-Babelsberg and hired none other than Volker Schlöndorff to be the new company's production head, which makes Schlöndorff, at least in this respect, a failed Bernd Eichinger.

What could be the moral of this story, or rather, what might be the hidden dialectic I was hoping would emerge out of shaking up the obsolete polarities of *Kunst* and *Kommerz*, art and show business, high-culture and pop? The first hidden dialectic is, of course, that there is no dialectic. At best, there are a set of differentials, of shifting terms and relations that have to be tracked individually and closely, if they are to yield any kind of reliable knowledge or illuminating insight. But in another respect, and despite the spectacular failures of the likes of Middenhoff, Messier, Kirch, and Eichinger's success with DER UNTERGANG in 2005, something suggests to me that a hidden dialectic becomes visible when – once more calling upon our mirror metaphor – we adopt the position of the Americans, but look through the mirror with our European eyes, namely the very European perspective of the avant-garde as research and prototype. Except that this avant-garde today is located in the US and not in Europe, if one agrees (with Walter Benjamin) that a given artifact should be judged avant-garde only when it embodies the most (technically) advanced practice and employs the most experimental, risk-taking practitioners.

Looked at from this avant-garde American point of view, we have another binary scheme, no longer based on the art versus commerce opposition, but structured around the terms we now associate with globalization: space/place, mobility/ubiquity, mapping/tracking, etc., but where the pairs do not line up on a positive/negative scale, and instead represent different modalities, aggregate states of varying intensities. In such a line-up, both Hollywood and Europe would no longer mark distinct territories, and more states of mind, or modes of thinking about the same practice or phenomena. Thus Hollywood would connote "differential," and Europe "dialectical"; Hollywood would be inclusive, and Europe exclusive; Hollywood hybrid, relational, while Europe autonomous, essentialist; Hollywood multipurpose and mixed media, Europe specific and monomedia; Hollywood deterritorialized and rhizomatic, Europe territorial and hierarchical; Hollywood time is "real time", European time is history; Hollywood space is site (access for all, from anywhere), European space is place (local, geographically, linguistically bounded).

While this new Hollywood hegemony probably implies that the US operates politically as an empire, this too is a mirror that looks both ways. "It is a dangerous world out there," George Bush likes to warn his fellow Americans, but there is an irony that may have escaped his speechwriters: the very success of America as an idea, and of Hollywood as a state of mind means that – at least as far as movies, popular culture, and mass consumption are concerned – there is no longer an "out there" by which we mean that all the world – for good or ill – is already "in here." Bush's threat to "America's enemies," in other words, also pertains to a promise. Hollywood spectators everywhere have a right to hold the president to the promise that they, too, are part of America.

With this, I may have come to the end of the useful life of my two-way mirror metaphor. For what my revisionist account suggests is the possibility of inward investment extending beyond financial capital to a certain kind of cultural capital. Complementing the identity politics of marking boundaries would be the identity politics of cultural mimicry – of the always already "inside" of culture, after universalism, but also after multiculturalism. My look at film history has shown that almost as many Americans love to play at being European as Europeans love to play at being American. My hidden dialectic suggests that besides the discourse of anti-Americanism and of counter-Americanism, we may have to find the terms of another discourse: let me call it, in a provisional gesture of Euro-de-centrism, the discourse of karaoke-Americanism – that doubly coded space of identity as overlap and deferral, as compliment and camouflage.

(2003)

Notes

1. Kristin Thompson, *Exporting Entertainment* (London: BFI Publishing, 1986).
2. Reinhold E. Thiel, "Was wurde aus Goebbels' UFA?" *Film Aktuell*, 2 (February 1970).
3. Thomas H. Guback, *The International Film Industry* (Bloomington, IN: University of Indiana Press, 1969), p. 112.
4. Ibid., p. 135.

5. See Klaus Kreimeier, *Kino und Filmindustrie in der BRD. Ideologieproduktion und Klassenwirklichkeit nach 1945* (Kronberg: Scriptor, 1973) and more recently Heide Fehrenbach, *Cinema in Democratizing Germany: Reconstructing of National Identity After Hitler* (Chapel Hill: University of North Carolina Press, 1995).

6. Quoted in Peter Krämer, "Hollywood in Germany, Germany in Hollywood," in Tim Bergfelder, Erica Carter, Deniz Göktürk (eds.), *The German Cinema Book* (London: Routledge, 2003), pp. 227-37, quoted here p. 236, note 35.

7. Thomas Elsaesser, "American Friends," in Geoffrey Nowell-Smith and Steve Ricci (eds.), *Hollywood and Europe* (London: BFI Publishing 1998), pp. 142-55.

8. Peter Märthesheimer and Ivo Frenzel, *Der Fernsehfilm Holocaust. Eine Nation ist betroffen* (Frankfurt: Fischer, 1979).

9. For a further elaboration of this seeming paradox in German postwar cinema, see Thomas Elsaesser, "Absence as Presence, Presence as Parapraxis," in Tim Bergfelder, et al. (eds.), *The German Cinema Book* (London: Routledge, 2003).

10. "You have to go away in order to come home," Louis Trenker's old school teacher tells him in the 1934 film THE PRODIGAL SON, before he leaves for New York, while Peter Handke noted that "America is for [my] story only a pretext, the attempt to find a distanced world in which I can be direct and personal... At the same time, there is no other place except America which provokes in me such depersonalization and estrangement." Thomas Elsaesser, "Wim Wenders and Peter Handke," in Susan Hayward (ed.), *European Cinema* (Birmingham, 1985), pp. 31-52; quoted here p. 33.

11. Thomas Elsaesser, "German Cinema in the 1990s," in Thomas Elsaesser and Michael Wedel (eds.), *The BFI Companion to German Cinema* (London: British Film Institute, 1999), pp. 4-5.

12. Hans Jürgen Syberberg, "The Syberberg Statement," *Framework* 6 (Autumn 1977), pp. 12-15.

13. Edgar Reitz, "Arbeiten an unseren Erinnerungen," *Medium* 5 (1979), pp. 21-22.

14. Elie Wiesel, "Trivializing the Holocaust," *New York Times*, 16 April 1978.

15. Michael Rogin, *Independence Day* (London, BFI Publishing, 1998).

16. Elsaesser and Wedel, pp. 73-74.

17. Ursula Hardt, *From Caligari to California* (Providence: Berghahn Books, 1996).

Central Europe Looking West

Of Rats and Revolution

Dusan Makavejev's THE SWITCHBOARD OPERATOR

Many Western European tourists take the motorway through Zagreb and Belgrade to Greece, Turkey or holiday in Dubrovnik, but not many can claim more than a superficial knowledge of the actual social reality and the human conflicts of the country called Yugoslavia. Although we are familiar with the figure of Tito, with his part in post-war history, and know about the economy's acute problems and shortcomings, the human reality in which this defective system operates probably escapes us as much as it is ignored by most of those who know the country merely as tourists.

Any opportunity to acquaint oneself with the representation of this society in the cinema deserves our special attention. It gains an importance, which goes beyond the specific aesthetic value of the individual film, or even the reputation of a director, whose work, given our general ignorance about Eastern Europe (to which our curiosity ought to be inversely proportional), acquires the status of documentary evidence and sociological essay. In Dusan Makavejev's THE SWITCHBOARD OPERATOR (1967), we are presented with the image of a society whose presence is both direct and critically reflected.

DUSAN MAKAVEJEV

After an opening scene, in which a scholarly sexologist delivers a lecture on sexual liberation, illustrated by art works and cult objects that document phallic worship across the centuries, the title character and female protaginst Isabel (Eva Ras) talks to her girlfriend Ruza (Ruzica Sokic) about her erotic-romantic fantasies. She subsequently meets the municipal rat catcher, Ahmed (Slobodan Aligrudic) and the two start an affair of sorts. Disorientingly, the film cuts to a murder scene with police discovering the body of a young woman. Another lecture follows, this time by a criminologist explaining the history of murder weapons for domestic crimes and crimes of passion. The viewer fears the worst for Isabel, whose romance with Ahmed is slow to blossom. Switching back and forth between the lovers becoming intimate with each other, and the history of Soviet Communism, from the fall of the Romanov tsars, via the abolition of the church, to the Yugoslav government's program to control rat infestation and agricultural reform, Makavejev contrasts the upbeat political narrative with the downbeat and eventually doomed love affair, condensed in the scenes of the mortuary and the autopsy of Isabel's body, while she and Ahmed are still trying to work things out.

At first glance, THE SWITCHBOARD OPERATOR seems thus a bitter and disillusioned statement about failure of the Communist Revolution in addressing the emotional and personal problems of those it was supposed to liberate. Makavejev sharply contrast the two worlds existing within one social reality, in the story of Isabel, the switchboard operator, and Ahmed, the health officer, whose love affair suddenly disintegrates after the intrusion of guilt and misunderstanding, and finally ends in Isabel's accidental death.

To one world belongs the intense joy, the brief moments of enchantment as the two discover each other and experience the liberating intimacy of a sexual relationship. Juxtaposed to this is another universe altogether, the public world of abstract didacticism and cold rationality (the sexologist, the criminologist), in short, a society that produces the kind of bureaucratic barrenness and willful ignorance one associates with Eastern Europe. Inevitably, it is the latter that destroys the couple, leading Isabel to infidelity and Ahmed to bouts of drunken stupor.

Yet there is a third world which puts in relief both the new Enlightenment of the officials and the inability of the couple to sustain a permanent relationship: the memory of the Russian Revolution and of Tito's national liberation war, evoked in the photos, banners, music and film clips. The significance of, for instance, repeating Hanns Eisler's song *Vorwärts und nicht vergessen* about the coming of the Commune, or the sequence from Dziga Vertov's SYMPHONY OF THE DONBAS which shows the Russian revolutionaries tearing down the false idols of the Orthodox Church, lies in their being a (relative, and ironically countered) reference point, by which to judge and illuminate the present. It would be a misinterpretation to see in these allusions to past promises simply derisive laughter directed at the pathos and the sentiments expressed in these works of art. Their very seriousness acts as a moving frame, giving the present a double focus.

By referring to the Revolution in terms of the art it has produced, Makavejev not only situates his own activity as a filmmaker in a revolutionary perspective, but also stresses that the Revolution is – in terms of the film's own reality – on a different plane, distinct from both that of official Yugoslavia and of the couple itself, thus retaining (if not emphasizing) the moral force of the revolutionary ideals, while criticizing their historical degeneration.

This emerges most clearly in the scenes where Makavejev fuses his emotional commitment to his characters with his ideological stance: certain "happy" moments of the couple's life are underlined with Eisler's revolutionary music, notably the one where Ahmed returns with a record player, and in which the camera follows Isabel from the courtyard as she climbs the stairs to greet him, the slow pan and crane upwards strongly reinforcing the uplifting sentiment of the music. In another scene, Isabel's pride in her own skill as a housewife (she bakes a magnificent strudel) is celebrated with the same musical accompaniment. Celebration and (self-)mockery have rarely been as closely linked.

The film's bitterness, on the other hand, is also extreme. Unmitigated by the scenes of fragile bliss just quoted or the pervasive tone of irony, the sarcasm reflects the disillusion of a generation who seems to suffer from an exhausted aimlessness, coupled with intense emotional difficulties of adapting to modernity and its mores. Having been told that socialism would liberate the individual and emancipate the sexes, this couple sullenly waits for the promised goods, utterly unprepared to grasp their own personal process of maturation as a necessary stage of social liberation. In the socialist countries the legal emancipation of women in society and the world of work seems to have traumatized the relations between the sexes and accentuated the still-persisting imbalance of emotional needs. To problems which theoretically should not exist (viz. the sexologist's amiable lecture), solutions are the more difficult to apply.

Makavejev's critique is therefore essentially an auto-critique of Communism and its backwardness in recognizing human emotional needs and gender problems. He shows two struggling and rather helpless individuals within a society, which is at once too impersonal, too abstract and schematic either to preserve the revolutionary idealism or to provide a basis for a meaningful existence for those who live in it. In order to achieve the proper complexity of his story Makavejev intercuts the narrative of the romance with a series of "lectures" on the one hand, and the minute account of the autopsy of Isabel in the morgue. This technique enhances the desperate irony of the film, at the same time as it increases the pathos of their brief mutual happiness. But it also associates the didactic content of the lectures with the cold, clinical sterility of the morgue. The film's satire carries an additional polemical point: it is the "scientific" attitude to human problems as displayed by the criminologist and the sexologist, which is ultimately responsible for there being a corpse on the dissecting table at all.

This stark juxtaposition of private and public, of the emotional and official realms of existence is also borne out by the direction. The fixed, cool and distant camera of the interpolated pieces alternates with sequences of very fluid movement in the domestic scenes; and finally, the jagged rhythm of the hand-held sequences at the end are intended to convey the emotional turbulence that leads to the accident. The two styles merge at a significant point, namely when Ahmed, exercising his profession of rat catcher, is seen carrying a box full of dead rats to the rubbish tip on a building site, whereupon the camera freezes as he poses for an official photo, presumably intended to celebrate his heroic fulfillment of the socialist plan.

With this style of self-mockery alternating with sarcasm, Makavejev has chosen (for a Western audience) a difficult stance. His black-joke irony, between pathos and satire, makes his own perspective and position quite obvious. Exploring this tale of betrayal of two individuals by scientific socialism and a didactic paternalism risks perhaps too simple a dichotomy. It could be argued that in this respect, the intercutting technique gives the film an all too obvious, moralizing intent, which works against its own aesthetic complexity. For instance, the final deterioration of the characters happens so rapidly, one feels, mainly for the sake of the moral fable, which makes it less plausible than the characters actually deserve.

Makavejev's montage, this formal device that is meant to recall the heroic style of the Soviet cinema, partly obliterates the more subtle analysis of the characters' own ignorance about themselves, their (self-protective) self-deception, which, however, cannot save them. The gap is illustrated very startlingly in the scene where Isabel sings about "man is not made of wood" while Ahmed writes his report about rats in slaughterhouses, toilets on building sites, and domestic cellars. Her spiritual nature, finding its purest expression in the song, must always remain incomprehensible to him, so long as he is obsessively fixed on his task of exterminating rats – symbol of a repressed and chaotic psyche. The parallel, then, which the metaphoric structure of the film draws, is between the apparent clinical order of the morgue (standing for an antiseptic, dead society) and Ahmed's fastidious, orderly personality: both cover an infested, diseased substrata.

This psycho-pathological significance of the rats as the untidy, contagious, and repressed element of the social body, however, lends the fatal-final scene by the well a magnificent structural aptness. For the well – even more clearly – represents the descent of the characters into their own troubled psyche, to which the sexual connotations of the well are evidently linked. Isabel's death is both necessary and logical, indicating the tragic way this divided society is coping with its problems: by rejection, repression and (self-)destruction, drawing rigid boundaries that not only run between people, but within each individual.

(1968)

Defining DEFA's Historical Imaginary

The Films of Konrad Wolf

(with Michael Wedel)

Introduction

Nearly a decade after the demise of DEFA (Deutsche Film A.G.), East Germany's state-controlled film company, can we begin to think of an "integrative" history of GDR cinema, at once within German film history, and of German film history within the international debates around "national cinema"? After the fall of the wall, the task of "integrating" not only territories and people, but also the arts and cultural life was evident. Equally evident was the danger of simply appropriating them or rewriting their differences. In the area of cinema, the GDR film culture posed special problems, since – compared to the literary life – it had remained terra incognita for the West German and Western public. Where it was considered, it either figured in relation to the old BRD-cinema as representing a parallel "commercial" cinema (under the special conditions of state capitalism), or as a parallel "auteur cinema" (Konrad Wolf, Frank Bayer, Heiner Carow etc. as the "equivalents" of Kluge, Reitz, Herzog, Fassbinder, etc.). The result were rather skewed symmetries. Nor was it really feasible to conceive of East German cinema as a "counter-cinema" in the sense that the political cinema of Jean-Luc Godard in the 1970s, the films of Glauber Rocha, or the New Brazilian cinema were once referred to as counter-cinemas.

Thus, the exact "placing" of GDR cinema must remain an open issue, one that this essay will not be able to accomplish. When looking at how the mapping of GDR cinema has been explicitly or implicitly tackled, one notices that in a number of (traditional) film histories the approach tends to be "paratactic," which is to say, the DEFA/GDR cinema is "added to" to the existing cinema(s) of the Federal Republic, as if the problem was one of "filling in" the blanks and "white areas" on the cinematic and cultural map. But such a map is no more than the guide to a minefield as soon as someone steps into the territory itself. It is a minefield of contending discourses, normative judgments and prescriptive debates. We cannot presume to do more here than state this fact, but our paper wants to affirm the necessity of opening a new agenda.

Examining these largely contextual or meta-textual questions requires a broad canvas. We have nonetheless chosen to concentrate on one director, Konrad Wolf. In fact, we propose to base ourselves on what is ideally a close textual reading of individual works. Our thesis will be that some of Wolf's best known films offer the viewer surprising moments of recognition: of other cinematic idioms, of unsuspected echoes, of striking parallels to styles, signatures and motifs known from national and European film history. The working hypothesis we derive from these moments of recognition (which are necessarily also moments of mis-cognition) is not intended to furnish a new reading of all of Wolf's films, nor will it provide a master strategy for approaching the DEFA output in general. On the other hand, the viability of our points about Wolf would clearly be strengthened if they were found to also resonate in other GDR films.

Yet as already indicated, the aim is to show how the conceptual inclusion of GDR cinema into German film history not only re-situates the place and discursive spaces of GDR cinema. "Adding" GDR cinema necessarily alters our conception and perception of not only West German cinema, but rephrases the whole question of the "identity" of German cinema, and in particular the filmic articulation of its breaks and continuities, its constructions of genealogies and traditions, its master-narratives, the relation of mainstream and margins, of alternative and oppositional practices. It would, in other words, try to overcome the apparently straightforward and seemingly ineluctable ideological binary divisions according to which the historical contiguity of East and West German cinema has resulted in two separate cultural developments within two politically and socially antagonistic systems.

For pragmatic reasons a few references to Konrad Wolf's LISSY, DER GETEILTE HIMMEL, ICH WAR NEUNZEHN, and SOLO SUNNY will have to suffice to put our hypothesis to the test. But we will start with another extract, from West German television, which seems to us to instantiate, firstly, the nature of televisual intervention in our debates. Secondly, the explicit "politicization" of the institutional apparatus "television" during the processes of unification should keep us alert to (and self-critical of) the delicate problematics of speaking about GDR cinema in the first place. It cautions one against assuming that there can be a position to speak from "outside" which is not already "inside" another political and discursive formation.

"*Siegergeschichte*": The 1990 TV Broadcast of Wolf's DER GETEILTE HIMMEL

On the evening of 3 October 1990, Konrad Wolf's 1964 film DER GETEILTE HIM-MEL was broadcast by the regional TV station Nord 3, and introduced by the popular West German announcer Hanni van Haiden with the following words:

> N3 now presents the GDR film DER GETEILTE HIMMEL, which was made by Konrad Wolf in 1964. It is a film that is considered by many film critics to be the very epitome of GDR film art in the 60s. An outstanding production, carefully arranged images, and on top of it, a script based on the novel by the poet Christa Wolf. What else could one ask for?
>
> Since the last Berlin Film Festival, however, audiences have become familiar with other [GDR] films from that period, films which right after their completion, were immediately banned, such as DIE SPUR DER STEINE by Frank Beyer, or DENK BLOSS NICHT, ICH HEULE, directed by Frank Vogel. Both films are exciting [topical] state-of-things descriptions of a society longing for change. How different in this respect the film of Konrad Wolf. In the guise of an alleged love story, the director manufactures one ideological cliché after another, mouthed cartoon captions, more un-erotic and inane can scarcely be imagined. In this respect, however, DER GETEILTE HIMMEL is an extremely revealing document, testifying to the kinds of intellectual adjustments necessary for a film to make it into the GDR cinemas in 1964."

Leaving aside the bizarre, almost willful ignorance that such a description betrays of Wolf's film itself, it is of course itself "an extremely revealing document," for it demonstrates the difficulties of dealing with films from the former GDR at a point in time when it had just ceased to exist. What Hanni van Haiden's words illustrate is the fact that to speak of this heritage in a unified Germany inevitably means to enter an ideologically and politically charged cultural battlefield which, far from belonging to the past, has become, after German unification, a painful process of negotiation and redefinition.

In this process, Hanni van Haiden's moderation makes a significant intervention, significant in its double positioning towards the film (offering both an auteurist and a political reading), but above all, in its attempt to undertake a retrospective rewriting of the DEFA canon, which, in the light of the freshly uncanned so-called *Verbotsfilme* of 1965, quickly dispatches a film that was once regarded as the very icon of Konrad Wolf's auteurist credibility and DEFA's status as a company prepared to invest in politically controversial projects.

What the particular constellation of Hanni van Haiden (as TV "authority"), Konrad (and Christa) Wolf's DER GETEILTE HIMMEL, shown on the day of German unification can usefully stand for is a self-fulfilling prophecy, ideologically supported by a retrospective teleology. As such, the occasion might serve as an allegory of the coincidences and over-determinations, which all to often seem to haunt the history of German cinema, making evidence and ideology, intentional malice and an involuntary slip hard to disentangle, while nailing, in this instance, a whole period to the cross of the two date-posts – 1965 and 1990. By constructing the forbidden films as being at once a moral, an aesthetic and a historical vantage point, from which GDR cinema could now be surveyed and judged, West German television reasserts its putative role in helping the GDR's citizens to gain their political and economic freedom, but now also adding to the spoils its cinema, "liberated" in 1989, by revealing to the public of both the east and west the hidden and thus necessarily authentic, better part of the GDR. A more exemplary case of Walter Benjamin's assertion that "history is always written by the winners" (*Siegergeschichte*) is difficult to imagine: it is as if the *Verbotsfilme*, had they not existed, would have had to be invented by the West, so perfectly did they fit into the re-writing strategies of the West German cultural establishment, with respect to GDR culture in many of its aspects.

"Normalization" and "Internationalization"

It would be interesting to examine whether this particular version of *Siegergeschichte* has since become widely accepted among West German film critics, some of whom enthusiastically welcomed the *Verbotsfilme*, using them as a convenient excuse for not paying the obligatory "GDR-bonus." Certainly, they unexpectedly provided the film world with an historically documented variation of the public exorcism which their literary colleagues had administered to the likes of Christa Wolf and Heiner Müller. At the same time, the discovery of the *Verbotsfilme* may have offered necessary ideological openings towards the West to the so-called *Wendehälse* (turncoats) in the film business, for whose post-unification fresh starts the forbidden films could function as proof of politically neutral ground at the very heart of ideology (were the *Verbotsfilme* not evidence "of a society longing for change"?) What is certain is that such easy passages from difference to indifference, from rejection to appropriation cannot and should not satisfy historians of the German cinema.

But what are the alternatives? What perspectives or options can current film historiography put at our disposal? Our initial appeal was to the so-called New Film History, in order to speak of the former East and West German cinemas without falling back on ideological positions and foregrounding the different political interests. The New Film History might help us "normalize" this period of German cinema history, in the sense of giving due weight to the institutional aspects, the comparative dimension, and the definition of the kind of "public sphere" cinema in general represented in the former GDR. In short, what is meant by this at first glance highly ideological term "normalization" is the desire to "internationalize" our object of study, which means refiguring the problematics of particular film historical periods or national cinemas, in order to render them present in several discursive registers and visible on several interpretative planes.

In opting for this approach, we hope to find ourselves broadly in line with most of the positions and approaches taken by scholars of GDR cinema in recent years. For instance, the specific *institutional context* and industrial mode of GDR film production and distribution, film finance and audience reception has been most impressively re-investigated, notably for the early years of DEFA, by historians such as Christiane Mueckenberger, Thomas Heimann and Gerd Dietrich, sometimes basing their re-readings on information freshly unearthed in the archives.

A complementary strategy involves the reconstruction of the *public sphere* in which the cinema found its place among the arts and leisure activities of GDR citizen, requiring the historian to take account of the broader film and media-culture, and including questions of foreign film import, the actual percentage of DEFA's share of the domestic market, as well as tracing international influences feeding back into production, or identifying changing reception patterns and expectations attached to the cinema as distinct from television, itself a key public sphere of the GDR, because – although illegal – most GDR viewers had access to West German television broadcast since the 1980s. As the two Cologne catalogues of all the films screened in cinemas on the territory of the former GDR between 1946 and 1990 has shown, there was a substantial presence of West German popular genre films on GDR screens in the mid- and late-50s, followed by their virtual absence in the decades to follow. This went hand in hand with a slow whittling away of import embargos in respect of West European and even Hollywood productions during the course of the 1980s.

Another area where new insights can be expected about the GDR cinema's place in people's minds and the public sphere are the studio histories of DEFA-Babelsberg. By highlighting the influence of non-GDR stars and personnel, or charting the history of international co-productions one can identify unexpected points of industrial continuity and artistic cross-fertilization. This work has recently been undertaken by, among others, Ralf Schenk, Wolfgang Gersch, and David Bathrick. They all have reminded us of the large number of former Ufa studios personnel, as well as West German and West European personnel in the DEFA studios until at least 1960. Of related interest for the reconsideration of a less monolithic public sphere in which DEFA cinema operated are the increasingly numerous "auteur" studies – biographies, documentations, and interviews – extending beyond directors, to encompass scriptwriters, actors, musicians. These often point to rather conflictual patterns of influence and orientation which, as we shall try to suggest in the case of Konrad Wolf and the filmmaking elite of his generation, involved at the very least the double agenda of, on the one hand, belonging to a filmmaking collective obliged to define a domestic filmmaking practice while, on the other hand, having knowledge of and participating at international festivals in the contemporary international cinema, as it mutated after 1945 from neo-realism to the *Nouvelle Vague*, and from Ingmar Bergman or Antonioni as representatives of their respective national cinema, to East European directors fulfilling this function, such as Andrei Tarkovsky, Andrzji Wajda, Istvan Szabo, not to mention East German filmmakers' exposure in the 1970s and 1980s to the New German cinema and to New Hollywood. In a turn known from the other arts and public media (literature, theatre, and the visual arts), the GDR's film culture's access to travel permits, foreign currency, international contacts acted in a way that was similar to GDR sports personnel: as "performance-enhancing drugs" for the artistic elite.

Finally, another model of internationalization, which has inspired our own approach in this paper, is to look at the films of a particular *national cinema* not so much across its auteurs, individual masterpieces, or underlying national mythologies, but *across popular genres and modes of representation*. In the past few years, this position has been programmatically formulated by Barton Byg with respect to GDR cinema, but it is also mirrored in a number of other recent publications, which either take a fresh look at popular musicals, fantasy films, comedies, and GDR Westerns (the so-called *Indianerfilme*) or challenge accepted views about DEFA's massive and varied output of documentaries, and its well-recognized vanguard position in the genres of the children's film.

Why Konrad Wolf?

Having said this, why then choose Konrad Wolf, who of all the GDR film people is probably *the* most prominent "auteur," GDR figurehead and "official" cinematic representative. As such, his films have usually been read across a personal, if not autobiographical matrix, in which poignantly political comments refract institutional discourses about class, family and national identity – almost always positioning his heroes or heroines in-between, a figuration easily decodable against Wolf's background as a German educated in Moscow, and as a Communist, burdened with the legacy of (Nazi) Germany. So, when we claim *not* to be concerned with either these conflicting fields of negotiation, or with the aesthetics of a subjective consciousness reflecting and thereby commenting upon "official" versions of this history and reality – what do we mean? In what sense can Wolf's films be said to raise questions usually applied to popular (in Western terms: commercial) cinema and address issues of generic conventions, the continuity of stylistic traditions and the presence of international cinematic codes?

First of all, Wolf seems an appropriate choice in a negative sense: if it is possible to show an acknowledged "auteur" to have the international cinema, in both its mainstream and art cinema idioms as his intertext, then our point about GDR cinema in general being less *sui generis* than assumed gains a credibility it could not have if our examples were merely drawn from popular genre films, well represented in the GDR cinema.

Secondly, Wolf while a recognized DEFA auteur, cannot easily be construed as an oppositional artist in relation to the regime, given his prominence as high-profile emigré, his official assignments as Party member and Chair of the Artists' Union, President of the Academy of Arts (East, 1965-1982) and member of the Central Committee of the ruling Socialist Unity Party (SED, 1981-1982). This point is also illustrated by the fact that the one Wolf film not released at the time of its production, SONNENSUCHER (1958/71), was banned not for fear of a possible corruption of public morals or threat to interior security as was the case with the *Verbotsfilme* of 1964/65, and instead for diplomatic reasons on the international scene. At the time of its completion, the States of the Warsaw Pact were negotiating an agreement with the US, a process which was suspected of being irritated by the release of a film about the Soviet-run Uran mining in Wismut.

Thirdly, Wolf seemed especially suited for testing our hypothesis because, despite all their diversity, the bulk of his films are to a greater or lesser degree representative, if not symptomatic of the two genres of DEFA cinema on which its claim for the foundation of an alternative tradition is built: the genres of the "anti-fascist" film and the *Gegenwartsfilm*. This fact should make the more visible our attempt to open up the cinematic inner lining, so to speak, of these two genres, as well as Wolf's seemingly personal obsession of shuttling back and forth between the breaks in Germany's recent past and the problems of GDR present reality shaped by this double legacy of a socialist and a fascist working class.

Finally, Wolf has himself suggested that his films be read against the grain of authorism, when, admittedly in a somewhat different context, he once stated: "I don't really care whether in 20 years my films will be read as expressions of one auteur, or merely as documents of an epoch."

"History as Film History": The Films

In this at once specific and extended sense, and thus different from the way it is usually asserted, we take Wolf's films to be symptomatic of significant tendencies and characteristics of GDR cinema, at the center of which is a problem well-known from other European national cinemas, namely the projection of a national identity across cinematic modes of representation. To come to the point, and thus also to the denominator common to most European post-war cinema, including that of the GDR, in our opinion, what is at issue is the capacity of a national cinema to conceive of, and in the event, to be able to re-figure national history credibly *in terms of*, or simply *as* national film history. With Hollywood the clearest example of a nation continually rewriting its history as film history, the emphasis shifts to the films' generic identities and intertextual relations, thus giving less prominence to the more traditional questions of European art cinema, namely to notions of "realism" or to the high culture intertexts, connoted by film culture's reference to artists, auteurs and filmed literature.

Melodrama and Pastiche: LISSY

It has often been noted that, while standing as the foremost examples of DEFA's continuation of the tradition of the "anti-fascist film," Wolf's films of the 1950s sometimes tend to fall back on "compromised" cinematic formulas, popular genres such as the *Heimatfilm* and the doctors' film, melodramatic stylizations

STERNE

and plot constructions. Critical attention to these films has mostly cast the trajectory from EINMAL IST KEINMAL (1954) and GENESUNG (1956) to SONNENSUCHER (1959) and PROFESSOR MAMLOCK as a slow but steady process of artistic maturation towards "realism," and only rarely invested itself into the ambivalences so visibly marking this body of work.

About STERNE (1958), for instance one could point to the fact that only after German cinema found a mode to narrate the Nazi past via the melodramatic, was it recognized abroad. Wolf received an award at the Cannes festival for STERNE, and when in the 1970s, the New German Cinema began to have its brief moment of international acclaim, it was once again largely thanks to the melodramatic forms it found to deal with the family under fascism (THE MARRIAGE OF MARIA BRAUN, HEIMAT, GERMANY PALE MOTHER). A line can thus be drawn from Konrad Wolf to Rainer Werner Fassbinder, as well as from STERNE to SCHINDLER'S LIST; STERNE, furthermore, is an archetypal melodrama of the victim and victimization, which in a typically German pattern predating both Wolf and Edgar Reitz, casts women as victims, in order to test the men as to their capacity for change, and the women as to their ability to endure the suffering. With its ending, where the man, despite his best intentions, comes "too late" to rescue the woman he loves, STERNE invites a more thorough comparison with many of the "self-pitying" or "apologetic" moments in both Ufa/Nazi cinema and in post-war West German mainstream cinema than it has thus far received.

Yet the feature this points to is not in the first instance Wolf's own ideological attitude or possible "complicity," but the kind of foreknowledge present in his audience, who are used to encountering moral dilemmas in this particular generic constellation, directing our attention to the similarities of the two public spheres east and west, and possibly Wolf's uncertainty about his audience at that point in his career. Hence, a film historian today might justifiably be more interested in the film's ambivalences about reorganizing its conflictual visual material and codes of representation in the form of melodrama, rather than to test how politically correct or patriarchal Wolf's film now strike us. His own "solution" to the ambivalences of his public sphere seems to have been a style that is at once genre-bound and original, but whose originality lies in the mastery of past idioms (or idioms of the past), showing a talent for historical pastiche which paradoxically, seems to have ensured the film's reception as "authentic" in the context of a film festival like Cannes where critics "recognized" and honored in Wolf at once the "auteur" and the spokesman of the "better Germany."

This quality of pastiche of stylistic traditions and perfect mimicry of generic conventions is if anything even more striking in LISSY, made the year before (1957). The film, based on F.C. Weiskopf's 1931 novel, tells the story of Lizzy, a woman from a proletarian background, and her husband Freddy, who both lose their jobs in the socio-economical whirlwind of the *Wirtschaftskrise*. Prior to this, on the verge of financial breakdown, Freddy has a sort of epiphany from which he emerges as a Nazi sympathizer and party member, soon climbing up into the higher echelons of the SA. While the effects of the couple's economic misery are aggravated by the existence of a newly born child, the general crisis of working class solidarity and identity is exemplified in the fate of Lissy's brother Paul, a former communist and pickpocket, who finally joins the Nazis, but soon turns against the Party, disappointed by its attacks on communists rather than capitalist industrialists and businessmen. Paul is the victim of a shooting, for which his erstwhile communist friends are held responsible. But it is unintentionally admitted by Freddy's party mentor Kascmierczik, that the murder was actually committed by the Nazis in their efforts to rid themselves of an awkward witness. At the official Nazi funeral, Lissy is so disgusted by the hypocritical speeches that she storms out of the Church, leaving the viewer to infer that she is ready to forsake her newly acquired domestic comforts, in order to once again fight on the side of her true comrades.

Much of the film's uncanny fascination resides in its ability to reconstruct the period of the early 1930s, achieved mainly by the many sequences one feels one has seen before. The film is replete with citations of the Weimar's left avant-garde cinema, from Piel Jutzi to Slatan Dudow, which is most evident perhaps in Freddy's door-to-door salesman montage sequence and the kitchen scene with Lissy and Freddy which are modeled on the job-search motif and Mata Hari sequence in KUHLE WAMPE. This has led commentators, who can also point to the use of an off-screen narrational voice framing the dramatic events (which occurs in almost all of Wolf's early films), as Wolf's step towards Brechtian modes of distanciation. However, an equally plausible inter-text for this kind of narrational commentary can be found in contemporary mainstream filmmaking in West Germany, where the films of Kurt Hoffmann, this cinema's most successful and prolific representative at the time, often have a similarly "ironically" commenting voice-over.

What is even more striking about LISSY, however, is how painstakingly the film attempts to negotiate the troubled cinematic heritage of the time between the point of the narrated and the moment of narration in its reconstruction of the historical detail of city life (newspapers, street cafes, shopping arcades) and the social and emotional states of the protagonists. In this sense it can perhaps be seen as a longingly detailed, somewhat fetishistic reconstruction of the moment before the political fall (Sündenfall) which today may almost appear as a postmodern pastiche of history through its modes of representation, deploying cinematically stereotypical plot situations and social spaces (Berlin backyards, typically petit-bourgeois interiors), character identities well known from the popular cinema of 1920s and 1930s, or female subjectivities caught in-between the two worlds of "new woman" self-emancipation and "new order" consumerism, a split captured admirably by Wolf in mirrors and reflective shop windows. The representation of social mobility on the side of the male character Freddy doubles as a particular anxiety about the narcissistic "petit-bourgeois" in German cinema, whose epitomization from the 1930s to the 1960s became Heinz Rühmann. Whereas, Freddy's ambivalences, in the scene of his anti-Semitic outburst in front of a billboard, for example, point to parallels in the "fascinating fascism" films of Visconti or Bertolucci from the 1970s.

In the light of these parallels out of time and place, the strong melodramatic ending of the film, in which Lissy turns from the carefully choreographed, shadowy space of the church to a symmetrically framed tree-lined avenue, is less of a stylistic break with the "proletarian" cinema of the 1920s, than the necessary complement to perfect the pastiche as a variation on the typical look of a Sirkian melodrama or the somber mise-en-scène of funeral rites in a Gustav Ucicky or Veit Harlan melodrama from the early 1940s, raising the issue of how to represent German fascism without having recourse to its iconography some 20 years before it was put on the agenda by Fassbinder and the New German Cinema.

Subjectivity and the Divide: Der geteilte Himmel

It has frequently been argued, that the early 1960s signaled a break in GDR cinema, marked by a more restrictive import policy towards Western production and new demands for contemporary subjects engaging critically with problems of industrial production and everyday reality for which the so-called Bitterfeld programme has become synonymous. With regard to Wolf, this break is said to reverberate strongly in Der geteilte Himmel which was both controversially received by its domestic audiences, while immediately appreciated abroad.

The film, as was already mentioned earlier, is an adaptation of a novel of the same title by Christa Wolf's (who also worked on the script). It is set during late-1960, early-1961 and the time of the Berlin Wall, and is told from the perspective of Rita who, after a nervous breakdown, looks back on her relationship with the chemist Manfred who left the GDR, where his revolutionary process of dying cloth was rejected by the state-owned manufacturing industry. Manfred opted for the FRG, in order to see his invention put to use, while Rita, who trains as a school teacher and also works in a train wagon factory during her holidays, is torn between her love for Manfred and the solidarity towards her two fatherly mentors, her teacher, Professor Schwarzenbach and the veteran worker Meternagel. After a brief visit to Manfred in West Berlin, she decides to return home to the GDR, hoping for a fuller life among her "own kind."

In speculating about the possible reasons for the controversies the film provoked, it may be of significance that these centered not on the hot topics of *Republikflucht* and the national divide (after all, quite a few films were made in the GDR about the wall before Der geteilte himmel), but concerned the film's formal characteristics and its difficult, avant-garde mode of narration. Indeed, it makes

Der geteilte Himmel

sense to refigure the problematics of DER GETEILTE HIMMEL around its mode of narration, marked as the film is by several parallel spatio-temporal narrative strands, by a complex use of montage and reframing, and an obsessive return to a few recurrent spaces, made up of metaphorical landscapes and city spaces, "interior monologue" flashbacks and subjective point-of-view structures.

As a film immediately reminiscent of other current cinematic modes – stylistically, as well as thematically close to the international art cinema – it features lonely couples, caught in nameless anomie, generational conflicts and painful inscriptions of social and historical realities across the focusing consciousness of female subjectivity. DER GETEILTE HIMMEL thus situates itself somewhere between Marguerite Duras' films with Alain Resnais, or an early Antonioni film with Monica Vitti. In the context of a generic approach to the films of Wolf, these features would suggest that the shift between the 1950s and the 1960s also refigures a change in the public sphere. The identity politics connoted by the different cinematic idioms place Wolf's film at the heart of a typically Western, "capitalist" malaise, in which physical well-being can go hand in hand with spiritual anxiety and desolation. But these associations serve Wolf as a space in which to inscribe a much more historically specific, German malaise while giving the "German-German problem" a voice that could be heard within the international art cinema. To represent the GDR topic of *Republikflucht* through the looking glass of HIROSHIMA MON AMOUR and LA NOTTE, puts a film like DER GETEILTE HIMMEL in the same discursive dimension that at around the same time, Alexander Kluge (with ABSCHIED VON GESTERN, or ARTISTEN IN DER ZIRKUSKUPPEL: RATLOS) and Edgar Reitz (with MAHLZEITEN) tried to add to the Young German Cinema. Seen in this context, Wolf's film takes on a new historicity, but also an avant-garde quality within German film history which makes the 1990 comment by Hanni van Haiden seem the more ideologically grotesque.

Authenticity as Simulation: ICH WAR NEUNZEHN

A similar reading of Wolf's subsequent film, ICH WAR NEUNZEHN (released in 1968), would at first glance be more problematic to establish. In the subjective temporality of a filmic diary, ICH WAR NEUNZEHN revisits two weeks of historical time between 16 April and 3 May 1945, the last days of World War II. The film's loosely structured narrative is focalized through the subjectivity of the 19-year-old Gregor Hecker, born in Cologne, who has returned to his native country in the uniform of the Red Army. As such, he temporarily becomes commanding officer in the small town of Bernau, and functions as a translator for diplomatic negotiations, but is mainly responsible for ideological agitation at the front, his weapon of choice being not a Soviet tank or Kalashnikov rifle, but a mobile audio van with loud-hailer, microphone and amplifier. His companions are the Germanophile officers Vadim (a teacher of German from Kiev who knows Heinrich Heine by heart) and Sasha, who has a special predilection for German folk music and *Schlager* records. The film's structure further consists of an allegorical prologue, and is at two points early into the narrative intercut with historical documentary footage. It is carefully arranged around a number of encounters and key situations of recognition and misrecognition between Gregor and his German countrymen, whose mythical subtexts extend onto its poetic geography of dark labyrinths (in the sequence set in the catacombs of the Spandau citadel) and wasted landscapes, most saliently in the film's final sequence staged around a Brandenburg farm.

As a filmic reworking of Wolf's own experiences as a 19-year-old returning from exile in a Red Army uniform, and because of the way in which the film breaks with classical modes of narration and spectatorial address, while taking formal recourse to contemporary Russian films such as Ballad of a Soldier (Grigori Chukhrai, 1959), Nine Days in One Year (Romm, 1961), or Tarkovsky's Ivan's Childhood, 1962, Ich war neunzehn is generally regarded as Wolf's most frankly autobiographical work, an expression of personal vision, individual integrity and historical authenticity.

What caught our attention upon re-viewing the film some 30 years after its first release, was how this "authenticity-effect" is accomplished by the film's acute awareness of cinematic traditions from around the time in which it is historically set, and which it rewrites. This dimension of "authenticity as simulation" is perhaps most visible when after the last shot of the interview with a concentration camp employee taken from the 1946 production Todeslager Sachsenhausen/ Deathcamp Sachsenhausen and identified as documentary footage, the film cuts directly back to the fictional interview with the landscape architect, where the viewer is for a moment disoriented before he is able to identify the fictional characters and thus the status of this sequence. What is demonstrated here quite clearly is, however, only the tip of an iceberg of strong intertextual undercurrents, powerfully running through the visual representation. To name only some of the most prominent sources, one can easily recognize Roberto Rossellini's Paisa (and not only the citation of its "dead partisan sequence" in the opening), the nowhere Berlin of the same director's Germania anno zero, and in the Spandau citadel sequence an ironic citation from Jean Renoir's La grande illusion. Additionally, it distinctly foregrounds how in the cinema an "authentic" public sphere is constructed in terms of its "media reality" through the mediation of human and technical communication devices, such as bi-lingual translators and mono-microphones, popular *Schlager* and folk music records, Schellack recordings of classical music from Bach through the

Prussian "Hohefriedberg March" to Ernst Busch's Spanish Civil War song "Rio Guarama." At the same time, the literary references from Heine's "*Ich hatte einst ein schönes Vaterland*" (itself the title not only of the memoirs of one of German cinema's seminal film histories, Lotte Eisner, but also of a number of German films since the 20s), and the Reclam edition of Kant's works (from which the landscape architect deduces his apologetic monologue) to the American comic book which Gregor devotes himself to while listening, double this investment in the mediality of history. Wolf succeeds in using the cinema as a time machine of historical simulation, in which "authenticity" follows the course of an inward spiral, not so much one of personal memory and biographical reconstruction, but an inward spiral into (propaganda) media and (popular European) cinema history as public memory, where history returns as film history in similar ways as it was forcefully to return in the New German cinema a decade later. Indeed, the fact that since Ich war neunzehn was made, Germany's past has been re-written into, and *as*, media history in, e.g., Edgar Reitz's Heimat I & II, the films of Fassbinder or Godard's Allemagne neuf zero suggests a common paradigm bracketing several phases of post-war cinema in Germany, and lets us begin to see the terms of the integrative history we outlined as a necessary agenda and a possible goal.

Such a shift in perspective regarding Ich war neunzehn would also suggest a less symmetrical and more implicated reading of the German-Soviet matrix around which Wolf has spun not only Ich war neunzehn, but also the earlier Sonnensucher and the subsequent Mama, ich lebe, when set against the German-American axis so prominently figuring in Wenders, Reitz and Fassbinder. Would it be too far fetched to think of the common basis of several directors' cinematic versions of national foundation films as rooted in the classical movie tropes, such as the "frontier" with its definition of national identity and otherness, its geography of "homelands," "enclaves of civilization" and "minority reservations"? What the road movie is for Wenders, the family Odyssey for Reitz and the female melodrama for Fassbinder emerges in Wolf as a keen appreciation of the classical Western, in the manner of John Ford, Robert Aldrich, or even Sam Fuller! In this light, Gregor, the hero of Ich war neunzehn, is perhaps best understood as the typical Western figure of the "Indian scout" (rather than a returning Ulysses), allowing us to trace the ways in which Ich war neunzehn redistributes "otherness" in complex but significant ways between Russians, Germans, Wehrmacht soldiers and SS-members, or how the geographical organizations of the Western's classic plot situations and spatial set-ups from Stagecoach, Apache or Run of the Arrow recur in Ich war neunzehn, adding a quite distinct cinematic mythological layer to the more classical mythology of Styx and Lethe, also evoked in Ich war neunzehn by the river landscapes and symbolic crossings staged in a Mark Brandenburg that has all the harsh solitariness, but also the resolute solidity of an East Prussian outpost of the "Germanic" pioneer spirit.

Performing the Everyday: SOLO SUNNY

The last example illustrating our argument comes from SOLO SUNNY, released in 1980. The film, set in the GDR present, portrays the nightclub singer Sunny, member of a touring band but longing for a solo appearance, who is replaced after refusing to sleep with the band's saxophonist Norbert, just as she refuses throughout the film to enter into a sexual relationship with her faithful admirer, the cab driver Harry. Earlier on, Norbert who had his lips injured in a fight, is himself temporarily replaced by the philosophical amateur-saxophonist, whose quiet, secluded life-style exerts a strong fascination on Sunny, but who himself is very casual about their relationship. After she has accidentally caught him in bed with another woman, she has a major crisis which ends in attempted suicide. The film concludes with Sunny, following her recovery, presenting herself as the lead singer in another band, visibly of a younger generation.

With SOLO SUNNY one is struck by another related discursive level on which a comparative or integrative historiography might generate a useful set of terms in order to redefine some of the driving forces be-hind postwar German cinema. It concerns the repre-sentation of female subjectivity not across sexual lib-eration (in this respect Sunny needs no liberation, her autonomy is established in the very first lines of the film – "going to bed with me comes without breakfast in the morning, and no argument" she says at one point), but through the mediation of the public sphere of show business, signalled via the stage, microphones and amplifiers, self-exhibition and spectacle. In German cinema this tradition of fe-male self-representation as spectacle was most mem-

SOLO SUNNY

orably as well as ambiguously exploited by Ufa films of the 1930s and early 1940s: Zarah Leander and Marika Rökk being the best remembered instances. As we know, by the time SOLO SUNNY was made, this particular model of "per-forming" female subjectivity via exhibition and spectacle was rewritten by di-rectors associated with New (West) German cinema, most eminently perhaps in the films of Rainer Werner Fassbinder, who himself not only rewrote Ufa show vehicles (in LILI MARLEEN), but like so many other European filmmakers of the 1970s, took the female artiste as a metaphor for linking fascism and show-business, while negotiating the concept of identity above, rather than through political, ideological, or gendered choices. If one situates SOLO SUNNY within this very controversial field of reference, at the outer vanishing point of the triangular constellation of writing and rewriting, there emerges another film, as a kind of relay for all three cinematic modes across historical time and national boundaries: this film is Bob Fosse's 1972 CABARET, and its heroine Sally Bowles directly evoked several times in SOLO SUNNY, and thus all the more important as a catalyst for the German cinema in respect to its controversial cinematic and national past, worked through in relation to female subjectivity, popular culture, and the public sphere.

What precisely this particular constellation (Nazi cinema, Hollywood, Fassbinder, SOLO SUNNY) adds by way of another, meta-critical dimension to the film's engagement with contemporary GDR reality is something we refrain from speculating on, but there are a number of possibly fortuitous points of contact which such a transversal reading of aspects of Wolf's films establishes with West German, European, and Hollywood cinematic practices and generic codes, so that the question of their relevance seems to us, at the very least, a legitimate one, and perhaps even one that makes a comment like Hanni van Haiden's a little more difficult in the future, not only in film classes but even on German television.

Conclusion: Wolf and Fassbinder 1982/1992/1997

With SOLO SUNNY we have in some sense come full circle, focusing with Sunny as with LISSY on the female heroine, and the question of cinematic representations of history around the legacy of Nazi cinema, national stylistic traditions and international genres, with the vanishing of the historical referent and the narrativization of present and past realities giving the imaginary mode of the cinema a special function. In such an integrative and international history of the German cinema, Konrad Wolf and his films appear to provide something of a missing link, representing a work no less challenging and controversial than that of any of the other German directors we have long acknowledged. To take note of the work of Konrad Wolf would also mean that the Oedipal break which has so strongly marked the politics and the theorization of West German cinema, the gap between directors born before 1920 such as Kurt Hoffmann, Rolf Hansen, and Veit Harlan, but also Käutner, Staudte, Wicki, and the directors of the Young and New German Cinema born in the mid-30s and 40s, would have to be re-addressed. For instance, it is worth noting that not only Wolf, born in 1925, but most of the other directors of the so-called "second DEFA generation"

– Heiner Carow (b. 1929), Egon Günther (b. 1927), Joachim Kunert (b. 1929), Günter Reisch (b. 1927), Frank Vogel (b. 1929), Ralf Kirsten (b. 1930), Konrad Petzold, Gerhard Klein (b. 1920) – were all born between 1920 and 1930 and constitute a generation virtually absent from West German cinema.

By way of concluding, however, we want to return to the Fassbinder/Wolf constellation. 1982, the year of the untimely death of both filmmakers would surely mark one of the most likely dates around which an integrative history of post-war German cinema would have to constitute itself. The attraction of this coincidence is of course a symmetry, which only covers up a number of asymmetries. Because just as telling and symptomatic might be a look at the commemorative culture that has sprung up around the two iconic dead directors: the fairly asymmetrical balance between the "10 years after" Fassbinder retrospectives of 1992, and the events upon the same occasion for Konrad Wolf: Fassbinder was celebrated with a huge exhibition at Alexanderplatz, extensive cinema and TV retrospectives, publications. Wolf, on the other hand, commemorated with only films on TV, but an evening at the West (!) Berlin Academy of Arts, with Wim Wenders beginning his memorial speech with the words: "Actually, I am the wrong guy in the wrong place ..."

What if there was a way of approaching GDR and FDR filmmakers, and thus post-war German cinematography in general, from a vantage point that is less concerned with the obvious political and historical asymmetrical symmetries? It is clear that Fassbinder and Wolf could stand for two different (but in each case far from "official") versions of national history: Fassbinder's panoramic and Balzacian attempt at delivering a complete social representation from the late-19th century to the post-war years, with the focus on individual strategies of negotiating existing social frameworks, a cinema of long-term shifts and historical continuity; countered by Wolf's retrospection obsessively zooming in on the same breaks (the *Machtergreifung* 1933, World War II, the so-called zero-hour), which put his characters in between two world, moments of personal "trauma" and political "decision," but which leave the significance of these historical points of discontinuity untouched. Yet despite these differences, it is equally clear that the historical imaginaries of Fassbinder and Wolf could bring the filmic heritage of both Germanies into a productive dialogue. That such a dialogue is not taking place throws into even sharper relief the fact that both the New German Cinema and GDR cinema are united in their absence from today's cinema screens, as absent as they are from the current debates about the present state of German film culture. In the light of this, the need to resituate both cinemas – west and east – becomes even more pressing, in order to make a discourse about German film history possible at all.

(2001)

Under Western Eyes

What Does Žižek Want?

> When I had delivered a lecture on Hitchcock at an American campus, a member of the public asked me indignantly: How can you talk about such a trifling subject when your ex-country is dying in flames? My answer was: How is it that you in the USA can bear to talk about Hitchcock?
>
> Slavoj Žižek[1]

A Lacanian Subject

It must be said straight away: Slavoj Žižek is no Lacanian. If he were, not only would he be furnishing the master's text with the sort of commentaries scholars usually give to Biblical exegeses; he would also be unlikely to retain our attention for very long. Rather, Žižek is a Lacanian "subject." The difference is not negligible. Having long ago activated within himself and then turned outward the peculiar structure of the Lacanian psyche, Žižek seems now in possession of a formidable instrument of cognition, a laser-like intelligence that cuts through layers of ideological tissue, revealing malignant growths, but also unsuspected connections all over the body politic. Another way of putting it is to say that Žižek has honed to a needle point the paranoid dialectic practiced by Jacques Lacan, extending it into two areas the master wisely refrained from occupying, namely philosophy and cultural theory. The latter may not take much courage, though more skill than is usually credited to the practitioners by their detractors, but to have elevated paranoia to a philosophical discourse is no small achievement. Žižek would argue (I think, rightly) that he is simply taking up a tradition, that of the philosophy of mind, consciousness and self-consciousness, which might lead one to identify him first and foremost as a Hegelian, who has come to the teachings of Jacques Lacan via Alexandre Kojève and Louis Althusser. But this could be a misunderstanding.

Of course, it is true that Žižek knows his Hegel (as he knows his Marx), and he makes approving nods in the direction of those who in recent years have tried to re-read Hegel, in order to rescue his notion of "*Aufhebung*" from its notoriety as the worn-out piston of a 19th-century engine-room historical necessity, reinstating its relevance for a contemporary way out of the collapse of binarisms. But, perhaps surprisingly, Žižek's master-philosopher is in fact Immanuel Kant, and in particular, his *Metaphysical Foundations of Morals*, which preserve a negativity, the force of an injunction and a finitude which Spinoza's *"sub specie aeternitatis"* wanted to do away with.[2]

Žižek's other philosophical points of reference are Schlegel and Kierkegaard – what we might think of as the tradition diametrically opposed to Hegel. At the same time, it is equally clear that Žižek's ontological-ethical project distances itself forcefully from the Nietzsche-Heidegger-Derrida triad as it has dominated continental philosophy for the past thirty years, while also examining (and finding them wanting in both ethics and political philosophy) the deconstructivists' partners in transatlantic dialogue, for instance, Richard Rorty's neo-liberal pragmatism or John Rawls' distributive justice.

But what interests me here is Žižek the "theorist" and cultural critic. As a Lacanian subject, he is totally aware of the Other, knowing that he can only constitute himself as subject in the field of an Other. The various manifestations of this Other, and the many configurations of the symbolic order we call our social reality, give Žižek his foremost theme, indeed it sometimes seems, his only theme. And among the various contested territories where the Other manifests itself to the Lacanian subject, there is one that Žižek has privileged access to. This field is the one which "we," the West, the liberal democracies living under capitalism at once constitute and occupy, and against which "the East," Central Europe, the post-communist world (the deliberate speaking positions of Žižek's discourse) have – since the fall of the Wall – attempted to become "subjects."

Thus, Žižek has fashioned for his speaking self a complex and oddly "representative" subjectivity, an instrument that registers many of the fine tremors or gaping fault-lines that today traverse our political and intellectual culture. In other words, subtending his books is a geopolitical, but also temporal divide across which he addresses us. And this divide informs everything he says, it is what gives his words both their energy and their urgency, their slightly shocking cheekiness and at times desperate irony. Yet Žižek also knows that far from being an impediment to communication, it is this divide that assures him of our attention, because both

Slavoj Žižek

named and erased, it exerts a considerable fascination on us. So, in almost all his books, and invariably right at the start, there is an answer, in the form of a question: "Why was the West so fascinated by the collapse of Communism?" or

"I would like to begin by calling into question the hidden implications of the request made of me to give a report on recent ethnic conflicts in the exotic place I come from, Slovenia" – questions by which he teasingly lets *us* know that *he* knows why we are so fascinated by him, why we have made him into such a star on the academic lecture and conference circuit.

Žižek, no doubt, delivers.[3] Even as he deconstructs the nature of our interest in Central and Eastern Europe, he satisfies our curiosity about what – and how – some of the intellectuals behind the former iron curtain are thinking, and whether they have been "hibernating" all these years. Yet what Žižek gives us is not an ideological critique of Stalinism, no account of its economic failure, its ideological bankruptcy, its human cost, or other stories of victimization. Rather, Žižek tells of its "success," especially its success in libidinally binding so many individuals for such a long time to its undeniable but utterly psycho-(patho-)logical monstrosity. As we read Žižek explaining why, once the wall was down, the whole Stalinist terror/bureaucracy crumbled so quickly and totally, part of our thrill derives from watching the process of Stalinist zombies come back to life, mutate into nationalists, then merge and morph back into Communists.

Knowledgeable about totalitarian make-belief, Žižek, however, also knows only too well what it means to have the eyes of the West upon him.[4] At one point, he quotes Kurt Vonnegut: "we are what we pretend to be, so we must be careful what we pretend to be."[5] As he gratifies a moral and intellectual curiosity he no doubt considers to be partly pornographic (we want to see the other's desire), as well as literally obscene (our media's need to pull into the limelight all kinds of local and regional politics that had for decades remained off-stage), he not only detests the demands we make on him. He also, ever so politely, reads us the riot act on them, for the "desire" we are so keen to see in the citizens of Central and Eastern Europe is "their" desire for "us". Perhaps not literally, as in a porn film or with a prostitute, but similar enough in structure: the desire for our consumer goods, our freedoms, our democracy. And while we patronize this desire, we are also gratified by it, because we know that such a desiring other is "safe." Comfortable in the knowledge that what they desire does not threaten us (we have plenty of consumer goods, business advisers and experts to sell to them), since they simply want to "catch up" with us, we look at them with generous benevolence. After all, they want our past as their future. More than that, through their eyes we can enjoy the innocence of our own past, making them the perfect object of our sentimentality, our nostalgia, for we can love in them the wide-eyed child of democracy we once were. Thus, in answer to why we were at first interested in what was happening in Eastern Europe, Žižek replies that the East's political and economic "reforms" allow us once more to inspect our own value system, in which we have lost all faith or conviction: liberal democracy and free market capitalism.

However, not least with the civil war in the former Yugoslavia, that situation has changed, bringing Žižek to the bitter conclusion that "the emergence of ethnic causes [broke] the narcissistic spell of the West's complacent recognition of its own values in the East: now Eastern Europe is returning to the West the repressed truth of its democratic desire." And as in the first world war's hurrah-patriotism, when the Left could only look on in passive fascination, because the working classes couldn't get to the frontlines fast enough, now Western Europe, faced with all the nationalisms and fundamentalisms, can only wring its collective hands. The "kernel of enjoyment" being precisely what remains the same in many a transition from one paradigm or episteme to another (in this case, from totalitarian rule to the new societies, or from the "evil empire" to "our partners in the East"), Žižek obliges us to recognize a point he never tires of making: we enjoy the "other" only when he consents to either mirroring us or to playing the victim. Woe to him who shows us his desire when it's no longer constructed in our image! Žižek indelicately points out the peculiar logic by which (one country's) freedom fighters become (another country's) terrorists, or (today's) victims become (tomorrow's) fundamentalist fanatics. We, after all, know where to draw the line.

Žižek himself is more circumspect: he speaks our language, speaks our problems, he tickles and at the same time thrashes our narcissism, refusing to play the role we have allocated to messengers from Eastern Europe – to plead with us for sympathy, for understanding, for compassion. At the same time, Mephisto-like he seems to know us better than we know ourselves, by speaking to us about all the problems that give us fitful dreams: the new racisms and "political correctness," fundamentalism and the aesthetics of violence, identity politics and the culture of complaint. Between satisfying our curiosity and castigating it, Žižek keeps us fascinated, aware that he is the first post-'89 theorist to address post-'68 pessimists, giving a "political" reading that doesn't use the language of politics, but of philosophy and psychoanalysis. Thus, the master-trope of Žižek's discourse, but also the fulcrum which gives it leverage, is the gaze to which he feels himself exposed as he speaks about a historical experience we have barely begun to look in the face. What can one say, he seems to ask, to the patronizing gaze from the Right, complacently mistaking the velvet revolutions as a vote for themselves, and to the fascinated gaze on the Left, wanting to hear that the dissidents should have held on to socialism, or looked for the "third way."[6]

Exposed to this most powerful of Althusserian "interpellations" which construct for him a seemingly ineluctable double bind, Žižek compares the East as it used to be ("official obeisance, private cynicism"), to the West as it has always been ("officially we're free, privately we obey, and because our cynicism is empty, we only function through our conformism"). He then finds that they have much in common, and comes to the ironic conclusion that "the enemy is not the fundamentalist, but the cynic."[7] Fortunately, he doesn't leave it there, but via what looks like an extended detour, tries to break open this double bind, by holding up a mirror – Medusa's mirror, perhaps – so that we might recognize a more painful truth about ourselves in its anamorphic representations.

Learning from Hollywood: The Movies are Not Fooled

Žižek has had no trouble recognizing these Western eyes upon him, constituting him as a subject and robbing him of his desire: this gaze is analyzed at length in Lacan's *Ecrits*, but it also traverses the work of Alfred Hitchcock. Before commenting on this further, a propos a book, edited by Žižek, that makes precisely this connection (in English: *Everything you always wanted to know about Lacan ... but were afraid to ask Hitchcock*, and in German: *Ein Triumph des Blicks über das Auge*),[8] I want to ask why the mirror he holds up to us is popular culture, or more specifically, the movies. While citing them all the time, nowhere, as far as I am aware of, does Žižek "justify" his references to the cinema, say, in the way that Siegfried Kracauer, in *From Caligari to Hitler*, made a case for reading the movies of the Weimar Republic as the manifestation of a knot of fears, desires and premonitions, making the German soul toss, and eventually turn towards totalitarianism. And yet, when T.W. Adorno emigrated to the US, he used his traumatic experience of fascism as a kind of probe, in order to interpret and indict American popular culture and Hollywood (in the famous "Culture Industry: Mass Culture as Mass Deception" chapter of *Dialectic of Enlightenment*). Although no refugee in this sense, Žižek, too, attaches extraordinary cultural weight to the movies, and one might be forgiven for drawing a parallel between him and these members of the Frankfurt School, when one sees what good use Žižek makes, for instance, of the Lacanian "between two deaths," or "the two fathers," in order to illuminate at one time Stalinism and at another, Hollywood movies. And yet, not only the conceptual framework where Lacan can meet Hitchcock, but also the purpose for which Žižek has recourse to cinema in the first place is so different from Adorno's that one hesitates to pursue the analogy any further. It is precisely because Žižek probably started with the same question as Adorno, namely how could so many accommodate their libidinal economy to a totalitarian regime, that their answers are so far apart. While Adorno, reflecting on mass culture and fascism (which "only" lasted twelve years), could still believe in a kind of heroic resistance and refusal, by assuming ideology and the psyche to be similarly structured, Žižek's view is both more

tragic and more "enlightened," after seeing what fifty years of Soviet-style totalitarianism could do to break up any correlation between ideology and subjectivity. In his analysis of East European dissidence – the difference between
Vaclav Havel and Milan Kundera, for instance – Žižek is able to redefine resistance and opposition in a way that makes much of the Frankfurt School's ideological critique of the culture industry obsolete. [9]

The question thus remains: what precisely can philosophy, politics and culture "learn from Hollywood"? Perhaps, after architecture has "learnt from Las
Vegas," the problem no longer poses itself: in the slipstream of postmodernism,
we have all accepted as irrelevant not only the distinction between high culture
and popular culture, but also that between popular culture and commercial culture (a distinction on which cultural critics as far apart as Adorno and Raymond
Williams had put much weight). Or is it that Žižek sees in the very superficiality
and commercial opportunism of popular culture a certain "truth," one indicating that the unconscious is not something deep and hidden, but plays on the
surface of the social text?[10] More polemically, Žižek does have a theory of popular culture, though neither a sociological nor a postmodern one. It turns partly
on the notion of enjoyment ("*jouissance*") and partly on the idea of the "truth of
error." The cinema, it would seem, allows Žižek to make a number of distinctions: having, in *The Sublime Object of Ideology* dismantled the traditional notion
of ideology as deception or illusion, in short, as a problem of perception, he
turns what he calls "the representationalist paradigm" on its head, by suggesting that especially in the cinema, we always have ideology-as-fantasy-frame underpinning, as well as placing ideology-as-discourse, the former not only impervious to even the most well-founded ideological critique or deconstructive
reading, but also never fooled by ideology in the first place! On the contrary, it
is those who utter ideological critiques in the name of authorative non-error,
who are most thoroughly duped by it, according to the famous Lacanian pun:
les non-dupes errent! (try saying *that* in fluent French). The fantasy-frame, on the
other hand, is one of the symptoms of enjoyment, that key term of Žižek's,
around which his whole theory of culture ultimately turns, at once secreted (or
do I mean ex-?) by and exceeding ideology. Enjoyment, as the laughter of derision, but also the unbearable, unrepresentable core of psychic existence, obliges
Žižek to make, via the cinema, a second distinction: that between, bluntly
speaking, collective ideology, individual identity and subjectivity, or in more
Lacanian terms, to renegotiate the relation between the Imaginary and the Symbolic, in favor of investigating, ever so tentatively, the much more terrifying
relation between the Imaginary and the Real.

For anyone familiar with contemporary film theory, such use of Lacan for a
critique of ideological criticism is not without irony. More obvious than either
the Frankfurt School or postmodernism as the link connecting Žižek with the

movies is indeed Lacan, and in particular, his distinction between the Imaginary, the Symbolic and the Real, a triad – or rather, a triangular geometry of displaced and superimposed binary pairs – crucial in Lacan for understanding both the structure and the ontogenesis of consciousness. Thanks to the notion of the "mirror-stage" and the importance attributed in it to the look, Lacan's theory of the formation of subjectivity (i.e., how human beings enter into the symbolic order, such as language, or experience themselves as separate individuals in the sphere of the inter-personal), has had an enormous impact on film theory since the 1970s. At first sight, Žižek seems to follow quite closely French and Anglo-American film theory's approach to the so-called "classical" cinema (especially the films of the 1940s and 1950s), the critical focus being on deconstructing cinematic realism, narrative and gender. Interminably analyzed in these Lacanian categories of the subject, Hollywood melodramas and musicals, Western and detective thrillers seemed to confirm Althusser's notion of ideology as "interpellation" and Lacan's theory of the imaginary as the subject's necessary "mis-cognition" of itself.[11]

But Žižek's approach is cleverer than that. After more than a decade of the mirror phase, of voyeurism, scoptophilia and fetishism, with film scholars exhaustively discussing the "male gaze" and wondering why women still enjoy going to the movies when they can only be the object of this gaze, Žižek starts elsewhere, or at any rate, he complicates this simple structure of seeing-seen, of looking and being-looked-at. Although not the first to do so, he mounts his oblique critique by returning to Lacan, and his cardinal distinction, so often conflated in psycho-semiotic film-theory, between the look and the gaze.[12] For Lacan, as for Žižek, look and gaze are placed asymmetrically to each other, in the sense that the gaze is always on the side of the object, marking "the point in the picture from which the subject viewing it is already being gazed at. Far from assuring the self-presence of the subject [i.e., the gaze as instrument of mastery and control], the gaze introduces an irreducible split: I can never see the picture at the point from which it is gazing at me."[13] The eye is thus always already observed: *esse est percipi*, but with that extra dimension into which the first look and the second look are folded, an en-folding of looks that induces a kind of ontological vertigo, making us doubt not what we see, but the very possibility of there being a place from which to look. With this critique of the gaze and the look, Žižek is able to re-read classical cinema in a subtly different but decisive way: Hitchcock, for instance, becomes the director whose work constantly opposes the gaze (invisible) and the eye (the over-elaborated mise-en-scène of characters looking and being looked at), the latter serving to dissimulate the former until that crucial point, the moment of the uncanny when the sheer force of the gaze overwhelms the eye, exposing it to an almost unbearable terror: the eye looks, but cannot see.

Mindful of Žižek's half-ironic, half-paranoid thematization of his own position under Western eyes (as in the passage at the beginning), one can understand more clearly why there are mainly two kinds of cinema that interest him: the films of Hitchcock and those tales of male paranoia and narcissism which for lack of a better word we have come to call the "film noir" genre. It is not, however, the cult figure of Humphrey Bogart in a trench-coat and fedora pulled over his eyes that interests Žižek. Rather, it is as if, in order to get his bearings, Žižek is reconstructing the vantage point, or more accurately, the vanishing point which can catch our post-Cold War vertigo, and arrest that sense of being sucked into deep space as he leaves the compression chamber not of Stalinist ideology, but of Stalinist subjectiv-ity. This vanishing point, at the far end of the picture plane, so to speak is the West's own post-(modern), post-(Oedipal) subjectivity, in the sense we have now defined it: suspended between look and gaze, shattered between paranoia and narcissism. Žižek finds in the New Hollywood, in the post-classical cinema of David

The Elephant Man

Lynch (The Elephant Man, Blue Velvet, Twin Peaks), Ridley Scott (Alien, Blade Runner), Martin Scorsese (Taxi Driver, The Last Temptation of Christ, Cape Fear) and Alan Parker (Angel Heart). Its genealogy, however, goes back to Hitchcock (Notorious, Vertigo, Rear Window, The Birds) and to the hard-boiled detective/gangster films (The Big Sleep, Farewell My Love, The Big Clock), behind which stands Raymond Chandler, and beyond him, Herman Melville, Edgar Allen Poe, Charles Baudelaire, and Franz Kafka, in short, the American male as American Psycho, Stalinist (and modernist) Europe's (and also Žižek's) *mon frere, mon semblable*.[14]

Before me are the English and German editions of *What you always wanted to know about Lacan ... but were afraid to ask Hitchcock*. As it happens, their respective covers summarize rather accurately the difference between two ways of theorizing the cinema according to Hitchcock. The German edition (published in Vienna) sports a green cover with a narrow vertical slit through which we can discover a black and white photo on which Alfred Hitchcock is peering at us, astride a ridiculous mountain bike. In the English edition (published in New York and London), the piercing stare of Jacques Lacan extrudes a series of concentric circles made up of the words "... but were afraid to ask Hitchcock," spiraling outwards towards us, then downwards, finally moving in close to the right ear of Hitchcock, who seems to be in the process of being strangled by his own left hand.

Clearly, the German cover reproduces the idea of Hitchcock's as above all a voyeur's cinema, and the cinematic apparatus constructed as a camera obscura in which the world is mirrored as an illusionist trick, thanks to a cranking, pedaling mechanism of transport and transmission (let's call it "film theory's Hitchcock"). The English cover, by contrast, invites a rather fuller exegetic treatment, to be read both literally and figuratively, allegorically and anagogically.[15] Literally, the script spiraling outwards links these two heads, as though suggesting that if you squeeze or press Hitchcock hard enough, out comes the lesson of Lacan. Alternatively, one might say that the cover shows how that popular and easily accessible entertainment which is the cinema is about to be strangled by one of the most oblique, and as some would claim obscurantist thinkers, and thus allegorizing the threat of high theory for low culture. In whichever case, Hitchcock and the cinema become a kind of semantically crowded textual and visual surface, on which a number of theoretical motifs form interpretable arabesques (let's call it "Žižek's Hitchcock").

American Psycho

In order to understand what Žižek means by "Hitchcock" and "film noir," we therefore have to see these terms in such a semantic field where they function as

PSYCHO

both complement and contrast to each other. A number of linked complexes make up this field, ultimately centered on the figure of the father (if we remain within the Oedipal terminology of Freud and Lacan), or – more generally – the symbolic order (the big Other, in Žižek's terms) in which subjectivity regulates itself.[16] The word "psycho" gives a clue to one aspect of the complex. For Hitchcock's PSYCHO might be said to be the single most important film to have articulated this subjectivity, already back in the 1950s.[17] Turning the tough guy of the hard-boiled thriller inside out, it ushered in a cinema of sex murder and the serial killer, of the psychopath and seemingly gratuitous or senseless violence, making Hitchcock the director of a "world out of joint," with no one in sight to set it right. At least Sam Spade and Philip Marlow gave the semblance that "down those mean streets, where a man must go" not only death, but also (self-)knowledge might lie in wait.[18]

One trait, therefore, that differentiates Hitchcock from film noir, is what Žižek calls "the big Other's benevolent ignorance" as it refers to Hitchcock, and "between two deaths," as it applies to film noir. The latter, one finds in Billy Wilder's DOUBLE INDEMNITY, Tay Garnett's THE POSTMAN ALWAYS RINGS TWICE or Rudolf Maté's DOA: DEAD ON ARRIVAL, three films using the typical film noir convention of voice-over and flashbacks, to signal a hero, who at the end of his quest, instead of being reconciled to his symbolic community (stereotypically, the final kiss leading to marriage), is unable to represent himself to himself, and thus to symbolize himself. Effectively, he dies twice over: physically, and in the minds of those who might remember him. Without a consistent identity in the field of the big Other (society, peer group, posterity), he has recognized, as Žižek puts it, that "the game is already over" (when for us, his life/the film is just beginning).[19]

The big Other's benevolent ignorance is the counterpart to the noir hero's sense of doom. It is at work in such typical Hitchcock scenes as the election meeting in THE 39 STEPS, the Nazi society ball in SABOTAGE, the auction scene at Christie's in NORTH BY NORTHWEST, or the final escape of Cary Grant and Ingrid Bergman from Claude Rains' mansion in NOTORIOUS. In each case, the hero and his adversary try to score against one another in full view of an audience which does not know/must not know what is truly at stake in the confrontation; protagonist and antagonist have to execute their moves so as to preserve appearances and be "covered" by the etiquette of polite society. Three kinds of looks are involved: that of the hero making the move; his opponent who clearly recognizes the move's meaning, but who can only observe it helplessly; and thirdly, the ignorant Other, the bystanders and members of the public. The structural condition of this interplay is not only the Other's ignorance, but its "benevolence," i.e., the fact that the social fabric is still intact. For us spectators, bearers of the fourth look enveloping them all, the fact is of course a fiction, and we remain, alternating between laughter and horror, suspended in ethical and ontological mid-air.[20]

As soon as the big Other, however, loses its benevolence and assumes features of a hostile or paranoid agency, we are in the world of "noir," or rather, in the 1980s revivals of "noir": the world of the Tyrell Corporation (BLADE RUNNER), Hannibal Lector (THE SILENCE OF THE LAMBS) and "Frank" (the evil genius of BLUE VELVET). Hitchcock films like PSYCHO and THE BIRDS are precisely on the cusp of this mutation in the status of the big Other, its failings balanced between seeming comic and sinister. In the "new noir" universe, however, the adversaries have become nothing but sinister. Constrained neither by their inherent evil, an unstoppable and seemingly indestructible "life" or "intelligence," nor by the symbolic order, these creatures become indistinguishable from the big Other, whose presence is signaled neither by benevolence nor ignorance: only indifference still "frames" events, which is the very absence of frame and gaze. If in the 1970s paranoia thrillers starring Robert Redford, Warren Beatty or Dustin Hofman (e.g., ALL THE PRESIDENT'S MEN, THREE DAYS OF THE CONDOR, THE PARALLAX VIEW), a suitably ambiguous father figure would still emerge ("Deep Throat," or seasoned hero-villains like Max von Sydow, anticipating Donald Sutherland in JFK), one looks in vain for them in such neo-noir classics as Terry Gilliam's BRAZIL, or Joel and Ethan Coen's BLOOD SIMPLE.

The other pertinent trait in the oscillation between Hitchcock and film noir is what Žižek calls "The Trouble with Harry" (after the Hitchcock film of that title, a black comedy set in a small town where a dead body gives rise to farcical complications as everyone suspects everyone else of having had reason to kill the unfortunate victim of a heart attack). As in TWIN PEAKS, David Lynch's neo-noir television soap opera, it is this very network of presumptions (of guilt, of complicity, of crime and corruption) that keeps the community together, an idyll of doughnuts-and-coffee, "beyond good and evil," disturbed only when an outsider, Detective Dale Cooper, is still brazen enough to want to get at "the truth."[21] PSYCHO was already less the confrontation of an idyll (the hotel love-making) with its dark underside (the motel shower-murder), than a film about average American alienation, of furtive lunchtime sex, of egregiously vulgar wealth and white collar crime. In the fatal encounter between Marion Crane (Janet Leigh) and Norman Bates (Anthony Perkins), the hysteria of everyday capitalist life is confronted not with cathartic release, but meets an even darker, psychotic reverse side. However, this reverse is less the nightmare of pathological crime than a world that has embalmed the rituals of rural life, that still rigidly clings to the moral and ideological precepts of the American dream, when everyone else has long since accommodated to flouting the law, practicing double standards or getting by with bare-faced cynicism.

What is so decisive about PSYCHO is that the process whereby the intersubjective "public space" of discourse loses its transparency can be observed *in status nascendi*, and step by step. Gradually, the neutrality of the symbolic order as the ultimate guarantee for any sense of reality, however provisional it may have been, gives way: the ground caves in, like the swamp behind the Bates motel into which Marion's car disappears. The true "noir" world starts just beyond this point, where such irony as Norman Bates' attentiveness to clean sheets and solicitousness about freshly cut sandwiches has ceased to be irony, and becomes quite clearly that mad supplement, "the Thing," that fantasy Žižek calls the "kernel of enjoyment," to which shreds of the symbolic order are still attached, senseless and contextless, and yet essential in order to hold our subjectivity in place. Žižek here return to the register of the visual and visuality, calling these moments "anamorphoses," in analogy to Lacan's famous description of Hans Holbein's painting *The Ambassadors*, where a light smudge, like a blur or a shadow, conceals a death's head, drawn so obliquely as to lose its representational identity, unless viewed, not *sub specie aeternitatis* (as one would expect from a *memento mori*), but sideways and from the ground up. The stain, the blot, the oblique angle lead Žižek to argue that for the post-Cartesian subject, the normal world only functions because something/the symptom/the sinthome is lodged at the heart of it. Yet it is to this "thing" that we necessarily have an anamorphotic relationship, be it of "enjoyment," horror, violence – the nature of which Hollywood movies and popular culture are not only "not duped" about, but according to Žižek, are singularly prescient and astute about.

This gives me the clue to a further examination of the cover of *Everything you always wanted to know*: the spiral now runs from philosophy to popular culture, but also in the inverse direction: not just high theory "explaining" the movies, but popular culture speaking a truth about philosophical motifs, even where it appears to be most farcical or gruesome. Figuratively, what becomes important about the spiral is the reversible or quasi-palindromatic quality of the title. But it is the piercing eye and cusped hand of Lacan turning into the ear of Hitchcock strangling himself that provides perhaps the most suggestive reverberations for our theme: "you never speak/look from where I listen/see you" were two of Lacan's most famous dicta, so that, on this cover, Lacan and Hitchcock, neither knowing or caring about each other, nevertheless constitute themselves as the other's Other: reading the cover anagogically, they suggest that across this gap of their mutual ignorance, they make each other into subjects, thus allegorically reproducing the process whereby the Lacanian subject "Žižek" communicates with the Hitchcockian subject "American psycho." Having thus started with Žižek's *Hitchcock*, I seem to have arrived at Hitchcock's *Žižek*, whose "re-subjectivized"[22] psycho can now lend us his eyes, to look afresh at "Eastern Europe," and in particular, at what we have always wanted to know, but were afraid to ask Žižek: "Bosnia." Next time, instead of asking that fatal question: "how can you talk about Hitchcock ...," we will demand "tell us more about Hitchcock," knowing that the subject he analyzes will be himself looking at us, so that we can look with Western eyes at an Other which is and isn't "our brother, our likeness."

(1995)

Notes

1. Slavoj Žižek, *The Metastases of Enjoyment* (London: Verso Books, 1994), p. 1.
2. "In contrast to [Spinoza's] universe of pure positivity in which nothing is to be punished and only pure causal links are to be grasped, Kant introduces the radical responsibility of the subject: I am ultimately responsible for everything; even those features which may seem to be part of my inherited nature were chosen by me in a timeless, transcendental act." Slavoj Žižek, *Tarrying with the Negative* (Durham: Duke University, 1993), p. 218.
3. Beween 1989 and 1994, Slavoj Žižek published no fewer than five books in English: *The Sublime Object of Ideology* (London: Verso Books, 1989), *Looking Awry* (Cambridge, MIT Books, 1991), *Enjoy Your Symptom!* (London: Routledge, 1992), *Tarrying with the Negative* (Durham: Duke University, 1993), and *The Metastases of Enjoyment* (London: Verso Books, 1994). Since then, he has added at least two more per year [note: 2005].
4. "It is as if the totalitarian Leader is addressing his subjects and legitimizing his ower by... saying to them: 'I'm your Master because you treat me as your Master'." *The Sublime Object of Ideology*, p. 146.
5. *Enjoy Your Symptom*, x.
6. Slavoj Žižek, "East European Liberalism and its Discontents," *New German Critique* 55 (1992), pp. 27-31.
7. *Enjoy Your Symptom*, x.
8. Slavoj Žižek, (ed.), *Everything You Always Wanted to Know about Lacan... But Were Afraid to Ask Hitchcock* (London: Verso, 1992); Slavoj Žižek, (ed.), *Ein Triumph des Blicks über das Auge, Psychoanalyse bei Hitchcock* (Wien: Turia & Kant, 1992).
9. *The Metastases of Enjoyment*, pp. 62-64.
10. "The idiot for whom I endeavor to formulate a theoretical point as clearly as possible is ultimately myself... I am convinced of my proper grasp of some Lacanian concept only when I can translate it successfully into the inherent imbecility of popular culture. In this full acceptance of the externalization in an imbecilic medium, in this radical refusal of any initiating secrecy – resides the ethics of finding the proper word." "Appendix: A Self-Interview," *The Metastases of Enjoyment*, p. 175.
11. For a brief summary of recent theories of cinema, Lacan's Imaginary and male identity/male subjectivity, see my "American Graffiti" in A. Huyssen and K. Scherpe, (eds.). *Postmoderne-Zeichen eines kulturellen Wandels* (Reinbek: Rowohlt, 1986) pp. 305-310.
12. See Jacques Lacan, *The Four Fundamental Concepts of Psychoanalysis* (London: The Hogarth Press, 1977), pp. 104-109. Jacqueline Rose (*Sexuality in the Field of Vision*, London: Verso Books, 1989) and Joan Copjec (*Apparatus and Umbra*, Cambridge, MIT Press, 1991) had already taken film theory to task for conflating the concepts of look and eye in Lacan. More recently, Kaja Silvermann has also argued the distinction: *Male Subjectivity at the Margins* (London: Routledge, 1992), pp. 125-156.
13. "The Ideological Sinthome," *Looking Awry*, 125.
14. Žižek argues the affinity between Stalinism and PSYCHO more explicitly in "In His Bold Gaze My Ruin Writ Large," *Everything you always wanted to know*, pp. 218-222.

15. Žižek himself alludes to this biblical model of exegesis when discussing the generally unsatisfactory theories of film noir. *Enjoy Your Symptom*, p. 187.

16. "How the Non-Duped Err," *Looking Awry*, pp. 69-79.

17. Within film studies, Hitchcock is one of the very few canonical authors, and perhaps the director around whose work the discipline has acquired both academic legitimacy and a high level of theoretical self-reflection. Thus, a number of "strong" readings of Hitchcock exist, by filmmakers, critics, and theorists such as Francois Truffaut, Jean Douchet, Robin Wood, Raymond Durgnat, Peter Wollen, Raymond Bellour, William Rothman, Stephen Heath, Tania Modleski, and now Žižek.

18. One key feature of film noir, the femme fatale, is extensively discussed by Žižek under the heading "feminine enjoment" and the "obscene father" in *Enjoy Your Symptom*, especially chapters two, four, and five.

19. "The logic-and-deduction story still relies on the consistent big Other: the moment at the novel's end, when the flow of events is integrated into the symbolic universe, narrativized, told in the form of a linear story, when... the detective reconstructs the true course of events, [and] order and consistency are reinstated, whereas the noir universe is characterized by a radical split, a kind of structural imbalance, as... the integration of the subject's position into the field of the big Other, the narrativization of his fate, becomes possible only when the subject is in a sense already dead, although still alive, when... the subject finds himself at the place baptized by Lacan "the in-between-two-deaths" (l'entre-deux-morts)... The putting into words does not bring about pacification, reconciliation with one's symbolic community, but rather gives rise to a mortal danger." *Enjoy Your Symptom*, p. 151

20. Here Žižek's notion of "the big Other doesn't exist" is very similar to Gilles Deleuze's discussion of "The Powers of the False," especially in the importance both theorists attribute to Orson Welles, Alfred Hitchcock, and Fritz Lang, filmmakers who for Žižek and Deleuze represent the "modern" within classical cinema. Gilles Deleuze, *Cinema: The Time Image* (Minneapolis: University of Minnesota Press, 1989), pp. 126-155.

21. At one point, Jean Renault, one of the locals, says to Dale Cooper: "Before you arrived, life in Twin Peaks went on quietly and smoothly, we were selling drugs, we organized prostitution, everybody was content – once you were here, everything went wrong." At least this is how Žižek quotes the scene in *Enjoy Your Symptom*, p. 163.

22. The term plays a major part in Žižek's analysis of what he calls "drive" creatures in the contemporary popular cinema (i.e., man-machines like Robocop, Replicants or Terminators, programmed by an external agency, but gradually finding that they have "implanted" in themselves such bits of subjectivity as personal memories, sense of loss, nostalgic yearnings. See "The Real and its Vicissitudes," *Looking Awry*, pp. 22-39.

Our Balkanist Gaze

About Memory's No Man's Land

Speaking Positions

Anyone addressing issues of representation in the ethnic and political conflicts of the Balkans cannot but be aware of the precarious position from which he or she is speaking and writing. The very title of this symposium – No Man's Land, Everybody's Image – aptly reminds us of what is at stake. Images, especially media images of conflict, have a way of being appropriated. Possessing the image is to possess what it refers to. The primitive magic still seems to work in our high-tech world. Often enough, as competing claims for property, possession, and thus interpretation are being fought over, it is the human lives that have registered in these images that risk becoming no-man's land, terra incognita.

Perhaps not in the geographer's or ethnographer's sense: rather, an image implies someone who looks, and a look that responds to this look. No man's land might be when neither of these looks meet or engage, and when instead, another gaze is present. If we follow the logic of the images that we have of these wars in ex-Yugoslavia, much of what happened or rather, what we were given to see as happening, stood under the sign of a third gaze, for whose benefit, however this benefit is defined, the various competing narratives were being constructed, which accompanied the warring sides and factions. In this paper, I want to look at what sort of territory, what sort of "land" the speaking positions, the listening positions and the exchange of looks map out as this conflict's media-scape, and to ask what contribution the cinema has made to "re-claim" not only the images, but the looks that can give them a place, from which they can speak.

It is perhaps an observation not capable of being generalized, but when watching media reports of wars or disasters, I often fail to take in what I see, and instead have a heightened awareness of my surrounding, as if trying to assure myself of a "place," before being able to place an otherwise unimaginable event. Living in Amsterdam, but not being from it, I witnessed the Bosnian war through a double displacement: although it was taking place in the heart of

Europe and its proximity shocked me, its ferocity made it also very remote. I could not locate the events, because I could no longer locate myself, since both the geographical closeness and the political intractability shattered the relatively comfortable identity of the cosmopolitan European I had begun to take for granted. Then came a set of events that allowed me to witness, at close quarters, a kind of *mise-en-abyme* of the Balkan conflict, bringing it close to the very place from which it seemed so remote. Not being Dutch, I saw – and sensed a concern I could share – how the Dutch public tried to wrestle with the Netherlands' own part in the Balkan tragedy. Not simply because of the International Court of Human Rights in The Hague, with its ongoing war crime trials of Serb, Croatian, and Bosnian detainees, including Slobodan Milosevic himself, but because of a much closer connection with one particular incident from the Balkan Wars.

As may be known, ever since the summer of 1995, the Dutch have been agonizing over their role, or rather, that of their government and army, in the fall of the Bosnian enclave of Srebrenica, where one of the most appalling acts of ethnic cleansing occurred right under the eyes of United Nations peacekeeping troops, dispatched by the Netherlands, the so-called Dutchbat. These peacekeepers not only did not prevent the Bosnian Serbs from entering the town, but actually were said to have helped the troops of Radovan Karadzic and General Mladic separate the women and children from the men and boys, who were then rounded up, driven away, shot and buried in mass graves – some 7000 of them in two days.

Three governmental commissions later, and a four-volume report of some 3500 pages, not counting the appendixes, by the NIOD, the National War Documentation Institute presented to the then-Prime Minister Wim Kok, (who – together with his entire cabinet – resigned over the report's findings), the Netherlands have still not been capable of coming to a final resolution. Commentators continue to argue whether their government had acted naively – the good intentions to assist the international effort far outstripping the military and strategic capabilities of keeping the enclave a safe haven (the French, for instance, knew it was hopeless and withdrew) – or whether there had been a conspiracy among the army top brass, to hide the facts as known on the ground, and thus delay ringing the alarm bells, both back home in the Netherlands and at the UN Headquarters in New York.

The trauma for the Dutch is not that their troops committed crimes or even that they were guilty by omission. Rather, the traumatic core seems to be about what to do with an accountability within a complex national/international chain of command, where military considerations and political priorities continually seemed to have tripped each other up. And on the other hand, how to square this formally structured military-bureaucratic accountability with an unstructured, spontaneous, and self-defined responsibility, on behalf of the Dutch people via its government, to offer humanitarian assistance, and then – bringing sharply to light the incommensurability of the two – not having been able to prevent the death of so many people. It is similar to the situation so often described by Slavoj Žižek, namely that in our postmodern world order, where supposedly everything goes, it is not that "we" no longer have norms and values, but on the contrary, that we are constantly raising the stakes of the ethical norms we think we ought to live up to, with the result that we invariably fail, and then are traumatized by this failure. As Žižek puts it: "Dostoyevsky was wrong. Not: 'if God is dead, everything is permitted' but rather, since God (or the bourgeois symbolic order) is dead, everything is forbidden (the pitfalls of political correctness)."[1] The paradox of postmodern subjectivity would then be, that because everything one does infringes on someone else's rights, the only thing that becomes universal are universal guilt feelings, and the near-universal vying for victimhood, as the only safe-haven of subjectivity.

In this situation, according to Žižek, a sinthome can appear, a quite trivial event can occur, or an object can emerge almost by chance, which gathers upon itself or condenses all the obsessive phantasms, which fill the gap of the non-existent "God" and the social symbolic. The object-event slots into place, and allows the subject or the collectivity to manage these guilt-feelings, give them a concrete, touchable shape. And sure enough, such an object did turn up, in the case of the Srebrenica inquiry as well: for months and months – in fact for three years – a discussion raged around a roll of film ("*het rolletje*" as it came to be known) that had mysteriously disappeared on the way from the staff photographer in Srebrenica to Army Headquarters in the Netherlands. What exactly was supposed to have been on the film was never clearly established (shots of dead Muslims, with Serb soldiers standing nearby), but what was established was that the film had disappeared, possibly spoilt in the developing bath: was it human error (there was talk of the man in the lab having been on a drinking spree the night before), or was it a cover-up, ordered from above? Everything focused on this bit of film, as if the solution to the riddle of why and how the mission had gone so badly wrong, might have been fixed on this strip of celluloid. The loss for the government, you might say, was the gain for the film scholar.

The desire to locate all one's uncertainty, emotional anxiety, or moral misery in one single object as source and origin, and from it derive the subject position of the victim, or to master the anxiety by naming – or shaming – this source, is of course, one of the lessons that Žižek has been trying to hammer home, when he argues the duplicity of the gaze that the "Western" media cast on the wars, and how that gaze is in turn used as a "prop" (in both senses of the word) by the contending factions and their fight for territory, which is as much a fight for the territory of representation and of images. By making the spectator identify with the victims ("imaginary identification"), and by making the victims "perform" their victimhood for the camera, the camera reproduces in this gaze upon them also the distance of that gaze (the "symbolic identification"), which is to say, the hidden knowledge that – as victims – these Bosnians (or whoever) pose no threat, make no demands, stake no claims (political, economic, religious) other than that of being treated as victims, which automatically reconfirms the West's position as benefactor, i.e., secure and powerful enough to

No Man's Land

be in a position to help. And it was this fiction which the failure of the Dutchbat's mission in Srbrenica punctured and destroyed for the Dutch people as spectators.

On the other side, to represent oneself "successfully" as victim to this Western media gaze was to retain the power of negative interpellation, to keep the spotlight "in place" – the media moonbeam, so to speak, on which attention traveled. With attention came – not so much aid, succor and practical solutions (almost all films made from "within" seem to be equally scathing about peacekeepers, UNPROFOR and other agencies – think of Tanovic's No Man's Land). This is why the irony in the Dutchbat debacle was indeed the discrepancy between the inflated self-importance these troops projected back to the Dutch public, and the sober-cynical assessment the Bosnian Muslims – not to mention the contempt the Bosnian Serbs – had for the effectiveness of these troops, and which, once the mission failed, led to equally exaggerated Dutch soul-searching and display of shame and guilt. Rather, because of this "realistic" or "cynical" estimation of outside intervention (at least during the Bosnian war, perhaps the case of Kosovo was different), media attention appeared to function internally, among the warring parties, as a bargaining counter in the political stakes, to gain advantages in the propaganda war. Although it is probably easy to exaggerate the importance of this media coverage, if one is to believe what one reads about the deal-making at Dayton, where success seemed to have had mainly to do with who was still alert enough at four a.m. to outfox the others. However, for those whom the war deprived of home and belongings, who lost their loved ones, and who witnessed the utter destruction of their lives, the (foreign) media played a much more ambiguous role, and one which seems to me to exceed the simple vying for victim status.

Time, Place, and Media Space

In other words, I want to use this incident of the roll of film, and my Žižekian reading of it, in order to turn it round, and so to alter the premise. Rather than explore further its phantasmic function as a fetish-object, to bridge a gap in the Dutch subjects' relation to their national imaginary, I want to pursue further its perhaps no less fantastical indexicality: in other words, why – in an age of instantly transmitted satellite-beamed video-images, and the even faster and heavier traffic of digital images, should a roll of undeveloped 35 mm celluloid come to such prominence? Why this incredibly old-fashioned mise-en-scène of diplomatic couriers, developing baths and physical destruction, if not because it also allegorizes some other form of disappearance and loss? Perhaps it helps us to grasp what is at stake in the massive intervention of media images, of cinematic representations in our traditional concepts of public history, personal memory, trauma, mourning, healing. I don't have the answers, but I do want to ask: are there other ways of understanding this structuring of the "Balkanist" (my appropriation of "Orientalist") gaze? Have there been attempts to re-function this gaze of the media or the camera at either end – by the filmmaker, and by those being filmed? In other words, given this over-inscribed, constantly thematized gaze of the other, the outsider – the visitor, the traveler, the helper and the meddler – and its reflection, deflection and inflection "inside," can one envisage, apart from self-objectification, exhibitionism and self-exoticism, other modes of neutralizing and negotiating it, for instance, by a more homeopathic sort of treatment of the gaze, i.e. inoculate it with itself?

For this, I want to briefly sketch three examples or cases, all of them highly self-reflexive in the way they take this supplement of the duplicitous gaze into their film. One is the tactic that is perhaps only open to a fiction filmmaker, who mirrors and repeats the distance just mentioned and thus tries to collapse it; the second is the strategy employed by a documentary filmmaker, who tries to minimize the distance, but shows us the bodily effort, strain and even physical danger this minimization takes, and the third example would also come from a documentary filmmaker, but one who is concerned to precisely sustain the distance and maintain it in place – in order to examine whether the transitionally "empty" space thus opened, gives the persons filmed a different relation to their own speaking position and subjectivity.

What I want to pursue with this exercise is to test a broader hypothesis, which has to do with memory and place, and involves a kind of topography of memory that seems to be substituting for, or at least supplementing the traditional "theatres of memory" (cemeteries, statues, shrines, altars, framed photographs, pilgrimages, and rituals). On the side of the spectator of memorable events – such as disasters, atrocities, and traumatic shocks – this topography re-locates (perhaps in *synthome*-fashion, perhaps not) the perception of an event by an awareness of the place from which one witnesses its medial representation or rather, their repeated re-play. In other words, a shift from the indexicality of perception ("what I see is real") to an indexicality of experience ("I am seeing this 'now' and 'here'"), that is to say, an awareness that not only memory, but perception itself has a metonymic side to it, and functions around the axis "where were you when" (which is related, but also different from mere embo-died perception) and that this is an important aspect of "postmodern" or media-saturated social subjectivity, to which may respond, on the side of those who experience something traumatic, and who are then confronted with the media images of that experience, an equally metonymic displacement of their subjec-tivity. Seeing oneself seeing, or seeing one's phantom self (the "having also/once/just been there" self) seeing. One may remember the TV-guy in Richard Linklater's SLACKER, for whom a stabbing he witnessed hadn't really happened, because he could not replay, fast-forward or otherwise manipulate it on his vi-deo recorder/monitor.

Emir Kusturica vs. Radovan Tadic and Heddy Honigman

But now, briefly let us turn to my Balkan examples. The first case – the strategy of mirroring and multiplying the distance of the gaze of the other and thus trying to collapse it – would indeed be Emir Kusturica's UNDER-GROUND, which has been read as an exemplary case of the postmodern "nothing is what it seems," with layers and layers of referentiality both piling up and peeling away, illustrating the palimpsest nature of Balkan history, where every site, every sentence, every emotion is doubly and triply occupied by incarnations of the self and the other.

EMIR KUSTURICA

As you may recall, Žižek reads UNDERGROUND as the drama of Yugoslav nationhood – its emer-gence, consolidation and collapse – as staged and performed for the eyes of the Big Other.[2] Yet one can also see, more conventionally perhaps, UNDERGROUND as a combination of the Italian operatic mode of Visconti, Fellini, and Sergio Leone (with characters larger than life, viscerally driven by the demands and needs of the body), and the inverted operatic, melodramatic mode of Fassbinder, as for instance in THE MARRIAGE OF MARIA BRAUN and LILI MARLEEN (to which UNDERGROUND explicitly alludes), where war, occupation, totalitarianism are also linked to show-business and the black market, each feeding off the other as the recto and verso of keeping, from a political point of view, a consumer-economy going, and from an ethical perspective, keeping a libidinal economy going, where it is the shared unspoken secrets – the double standards – that keep a totalitarian (but why only totalitarian?) regime in place. Kusturica borrows from Fassbinder (and others) also the collusion between the cinema as a world of make-believe, and the world of politics as a world of propaganda, self-deception, and dis-information.

What Kusturica adds – his satiric mode – is that he hyperbolizes despotism, by performing its arbitrariness out in the open. This might also be called his post-colonial, "magic realist" heritage, made famous by writers such as Gabriel Garcia Marquez and Mario Vargas Llosa, but also Salman Rushdie, who, referring to Marquez, once wrote that "truth [in Latin American political life] has been controlled, to the point at which it has ceased to be possible to find out what it is. The only truth is, that you are being lied to all the time."[3]

This seems relatively benign, if we interpret Rushdie still positing "truth" as a possible or desirable default value. If, on the other hand, we translate his sentence into the terms of the ubiquity of video-images and permanent surveillance, practiced once again, completely out in the open, then politics in Latin America is still this mode's avant-garde: think, for instance, of the surveillance tapes recorded, over a period of several years, by Vladimiro Montesinos in Peru under the Fujimori regime, when he was bribing state officials and media tycoons, telling them – on camera! – that he was filming them, and then laughing out loud, saying "I'm only joking, you know I'd never stoop so low." This scene is worked into an extraordinary film, called EYE SPY, by Sonia Goldenberg, and it is as if Montesinos had wanted to illustrate Žižek's theory of the double-bind of the enjoying super-ego, for which he sometimes quotes Groucho Marx: "I tell you, he may look like an idiot, he may talk like an idiot, but make no mistake – he is an idiot." Montencinos may be telling you he is taping you, but make no mistake, he is taping you.

In Kusturica, one gets the sense that this slipping away of all ontological grounding is still mapped onto an "intact" idealist-cynical topography. The tunnels and underground passages, nostalgically recalling, but also sarcastically over-writing the heroic period of the partisans from, for instance, Andrzj Wajda's KANAL, also seem to allegorize the cinematic dispositif of Plato's cave, except that above ground, of course, his characters are still inside the cave (the film within the film metaphor, so often called in also by other Balkan filmmakers to support the simulacrum). The trap doors, banana-skin trip-ups, or crazy careening through the corridors or tunnels in oversized prams and undersized trunks, then, become part of that darker and more cruel world of falling, drifting and breaking away, indicative of a post-Tito despair of not being able to "locate" either personal or national identity, to inhabit either a space/place or a politics/ethics, unable to find a home either in homo-social/friend/neighborly trust or in heterosexual wife/lover/mother-of-your-children fidelity – and hence, the ridiculous, carnivalesque "grounding" of life in eating, fornicating, physical sensation: unable to perceive life as heroic-tragic, the characters are condemned to see it as a comedy, with life stupidly just going on, even beyond – especially beyond – (individual) death.

In its disappointed and disoriented idealism – the fact that it still has an implied reference point to the spirit of revolutionary socialism, UNDERGROUND might usefully be compared with a small, but not uninteresting film that also constructs a relatively straight vanishing point, against which to map the layeredness of reference and the opaque politics of place of the 1990s. It too, uses the Latin American experience, but this time the heroic tradition of Fidel, Ché and Salvador Allende, itself nostalgically doubled by the Spanish Civil War and the International Brigades. I am referring to a film made by a Hungarian woman filmmaker, Ibolya Fekete, called CHICO (2001), and which would be a more documentary instance of this "looking-glass" world-inside-out perspective on the Balkan Wars, trying to map the internationalism of the revolutionary-without-frontiers onto the re-nascent nationalism of the Croats (and Hungarians), making the case for what are in fact a gang of mercenaries, as genuinely errant souls, looking not so much for a cause as looking for a place. Generically, it its the Balkan travelogue and visitor's tale narrative, but in its lack of closure, dissociated-ness and direct address to the camera, it is a very effective portrayal of the co-extensiveness, in discourse, memory and perception of multiple identities, while both acceding to and subtly reducing ad absurdum, the demand (and the desire) of "taking sides."

The film is fully aware that each piece of ground is already colonized and layered with images, references, memories and identifications: witness the moment, when the hero, finding himself as a reporter for a Spanish newspaper in Albania, is reminded by the landscape – the striated hills, the grazing sheep, the poverty of the people lining the market place – of nothing so much as Chile. And when he decides that the Croats are "it" for him, it is because he finally meets people there, who touch each other the way he had not seen since he left Bolivia.

Set mostly in the Croat border region with Hungary and Serbia, near Osijek and Vukovar, CHICO seems to me a film also in search of a different kind of indexicality, where places recall images rather than images referring to places, but where the "layers" of a place are also what makes it significant. Thus, one of locals explains that he is taking up arms to defend the village, not because it used to be Hungarian or because he is a Croat nationalist, but simply because the village has been there some 800 years, and it's those 800 years he wants to defend. This is why he also tells the international mercenaries that he will not be fighting outside or beyond the village boundaries, whether for Croats, or against Serbs.

But my second case study – where the filmmaker tries to minimize the distance of the gaze, showing us the physical effort, and a non-intimate proximity would be THE LIVING AND THE DEAD OF SARAJEVO/LES VIVANTS ET LES MORTS DE SARAJEVO by Radovan Tadic, made "outside," in France, in 1993, by an insider, indicative of the dual existence, globalized perspective, and multi-national working conditions of most Balkan filmmakers today.

Ostensibly, Tadic's film tries to convey the effect of the war on the daily routine of civilians in Sarajevo. He follows a handful of characters, among them a young, newly married mixed couple, a Bosnian Serb who is wounded and has both his legs amputated, a surgeon, a staff nurse and a permanently trembling patient at the hospital, and finally a young boy who scavenges for water and firewood for his family. Tadic's intention seems to be to simply show how these individuals experience the war on a very basic, day-to-day, matter-of-fact, how-to-keep going and survive level.

But what struck me – as indeed most viewers I have talked to – is a "three-minute scene in which Tadic has the camera perched at an intersection. The viewer watches as pedestrians coming from the market or on errands stop at the intersection, hesitate, turn around, face the intersection again, look up and down the street, run across with the occasional sound of sniper fire in the background, and then continue walking, accustomed to the risk." Here we have the filmmaker adopt the vision mode of the surveillance camera, formalizing, in other words, the gaze by folding it into a way of seeing that produces "operational" images, motivated by something other than human curiosity, voyeurism or empathy. The scene contrasts and yet is complemented by the hand-held shot, "following the young boy around as he tries to find water, walking across town, over the open bridge, outrunning sniper fire, to an empty tap. On the way back the boy hesitates at the bridge. When asked why, he replies that his older brother was killed there and continues across."

It is as if Tadic refuses to contemplate the human depth of his characters' lives or the political complexity of their situation. No show of empathy, no parading of victims, no testimonies by witnesses. Instead, the camera resolutely sticks to the surface, deliberately flattening the images as well as the verbal exchanges. With an artless, and for that reason, troubling literalness of exertion and embodied presence, the camera pursues the boy as he pursues the hunt for water. What we see is not the boy, or the success or failure of his quest: we see "real time," which is to say, the camera is recording time, in which everything and nothing can happen, but rather than those hand-held shots, the raw footage from the scene of the action, where the cameraman runs, weaves and ducks with the demonstrators or stone-throwing Intifada youths, and we the spectators secretly thrill to the possibility that these might be the last shots this cameraman will ever see through his viewfinder, Tadic merely registers the "here" and "now," as it modulates the time it takes the boy to cross the bridge or pass along abandoned factories to find his rusty tap. The fact that sniper fire can be heard, and that the terrain is visually open to the Serb positions, simply emphasises that this is a film not about images or a geometry of imaginary or actual lines of sight, but about intervals, pulsed duration, the cling-film of a different kind of indexicality, perhaps that of the digital video image, whose materiality – as everyone says who uses it – is dense, opaque, without depth or spatial extension. Instead of representation, we have authentification – of a unique, particular segment in time, but rather than a return to the indeterminacy and ineffable depth of the neo-realist image, say, in PAISA, we have the digital image of the camcorder or the surveillance camera, an actual or virtual time-code marking this as an act of registration rather than as a moment of revelation.

O AMOR NATURAL

Perhaps here is where my last example should come in, a film made by the Dutch documentarist Heddy Honigman, known for films such as METAL E MELANCHOLIE, about taxi drivers in Lima, and O AMOR NATURAL about elderly people in Brazil reading into the camera passionate and even pornographic love letters they wrote or received as young men and women. She, too, made a film called UNDERGROUND, about musicians busking in the Paris metro (THE UNDERGROUND ORCHESTRA). Music, as the "somatic supplement" of her character's life-experience is a typical feature in her films and forms the explicit topic of her film about, among others, Dutchbat officers in Srebrenica, called CRAZY (2000).

The film that interests me here, though, is a video work she made in Bosnia, GOEDE MAN, LIEVE ZOON (A Good Husband, A Dear Son, 2001), which to my mind exemplifies the third strategy I mentioned, i.e., the one that marks the distance of the gaze as a distance, sustaining it in order to maintain the possibility of the images finding their own "location," and where an event is neither narrated, performed nor negated, but spatially arranged and displayed, as it were.

The question that Honigman seems to put to herself is: what is the role of showing and telling, when lives have been so totally shattered and devastated, how to re-assemble even the most basic reference points of time and place, when your wife has been murdered, your children are either dead or in a militia unit, hiding in the hills, and your home has been burnt down by your neighbors? At this liminal point, clearly, narrative is no longer an option, even assuming linguistic, educational or cultural barriers were not operating. Honigman's camera, whom her interviewees are able to address, actually preserves the dissociation, the fracturing, the inner and outer ruin, with which trauma, loss and incomprehension mark the discourse. The sense of searing irreplaceability of the loved one, the fact of being stuck in the actual moment of shock, or the fragment of perception that keeps coming back, seem to occasion a kind of mnemonic adjustment. It is not a theatre of memory, not a narrative of experience, but an apparently erratic topography of commemoration, except that even commemoration is the wrong word, rather a sort of repertoire or catalogue of gestures and acts, whose inner logic is what the film seeks to find and tries to trace.

Not Victim, But Survivor?

Honigman, I shall claim, presents survivors, as opposed to victims. Being a survivor is, when one thinks about it, quite a complex role and paradoxical subject-position. A survivor, in a sense, is somebody who should have died, yet somehow did not. What makes him a survivor is that something near him or in him, has died. This is why, conversely, it is possible for a survivor to be already dead, except he does not know it (as in Kusturica's UNDERGROUND). Thus, the state of survivor ties you to a moment in the past, but in the form of a perpetual present, that is in the mode of contiguity and dissociation (as opposed to repression or the compulsion to repeat), but it might equally well be the subject-position of the corpse (if one pardons the oxymoron). A survivor, in other words, is a subject of ambiguous agency, not least because there is a remainder he/she is not master of, but the survivor is also an active agent, actively constructing himself in ways that the victim is not.

HEDDY HONIGMAN

In Honigman's film, but I do not want to limit it to her, the subjects are confronted with a task: the active construction of a different topography of memory (in the absence of traditional theatres of commemoration and *lieux de mémoire*). It is their response to the despoliation of their communal or individual sites of memory, of the desecration of the places, the destruction of the homes and houses, or sometimes (Srebrenica, Ground Zero) the re-assertion of agency when faced with the incomprehensibility of the sheer number who died in one spot, all at once. How to begin to put together a rudimentary architecture of emotion and affect, how to lay a path to yourself and to the ones you have lost?

What Honigman's camera observes is that people seem to operate a sort of freeze-frame on the objects, the activities and the moments (they have kept the watch which stopped at the moment of a loved one's violent death, they preserve the tools he used on his last job, they repeat a gesture, or they stroke a coat that still hangs in the closet). This makes the act of showing and telling to the camera no longer one of narrative integration or psychoanalytic mastery. Rather, it becomes a sort of surrogate burial, not of bodies but of acts, objects and gestures, where the cinema, the moving images become kind of a virtual mortuary, or a permanently open grave, yet one which – in contrast to the forcibly opened graves, the humiliating in-difference of mass graves, the anonymous seriality of mass reburial, or the body bags stored in forensic morgues – despite its immateriality and virtuality is more impervious to de-individualization and more protected from violation, even as the accidental indices of a son's, a brother's, or a husband's existence are presented to the camera's gaze.

One might say that the screen (once more) becomes a kind of virtual shroud, providing the "real time" support for a new indexicality of death, a sort of thanato(po)graphy. Especially if we think of the moving (video) image as having put itself in the place of – and therefore demanding a re-articulation of – the uncanny ontology of the photographic image as we find it variously theorized in Walter Benjamin, Roland Barthes, Siegfried Kracauer, André Bazin, Susan Sontag and Annette Michelson. To return to my opening, we need to re-theorize celluloid "*het rolletje,*" the roll of film that went missing in Srebrenica.

For such a new thana-topography of memory and presence also has implications for the outside gaze with which we started. It redefines this gaze, by either entrusting it with the duty of recording and preserving from forgetting, with the task of the archivist or the conservator, or by making it a gaze from beyond the grave, which also positions the "traveler-viewer" in a different temporality, at once "no longer there," but also deferred: "not yet there," as if by placing it there, it was in patient anticipation of an eventual judgement day. Instead of the human rights demand for war-crime trials, instead of liberal-democratic demand for "dialogue" (the proof of whose impossibility requires no Lacan: thanks to the rules of media performativity, every schoolchild knows how skewed an offer this usually is, in favor of the demanding party), or instead of the Judeo-Christian talking cures of therapy, confession or mourning work, – and in the absence of a truth and reconciliation initiative – this placing, re-placing and displacing is enacting a deferral prepared to await a different sort of justice, of which the foreign gaze becomes a temporary placeholder.

My argument is that video and digital images, perhaps less by design than by default, are taking over a very particular cultural role, in which the supposed indexicality of the photographic image is being re-negotiated in yet to be specified ways, in respect to temporality (as *Nachträglichkeit*, "deferred action" time, but also as "real time," registered time), and in respect to space as "site," which is of course different from place, since "site" is at once archaeological and virtual, and in respect of identity, discourse and subjectivity (from truth to trust, or rather, "from the lie to the self-reference of the lie," according to the Greek paradox, where "all Cretans are liars" – says the Cretan).

This would indicate that the space/time of traumatic events is changing through the media images in ways we are only just beginning to understand. Except in very specific cases, momentous or traumatic events no longer seem to be an occasion for seeking explanations (our popular media have largely given up asking "why," in order to harvest witnesses and testimony; only intellectuals and "experts" have the dubious honor to interpret, contextualize and what Fredric Jameson used to call "historicize"[1]). In this respect, we may, however, already have passed the peak of what I have called the "vying for victimhood." The collusive gaze, the duplicity analyzed by Žižek, might complicate itself (or should I say, simplify itself) by subjects now thinking of themselves as "survivors," which is to say, in a different temporality, which also implies a different agency and identity. As spectators, subjectivity (i.e., the imaginary relation to the "truth") is no longer confirmed in the act of "seeing with one's own eyes," nor in the capturing (memorizing, narrativizing) of an event as eye-witness or narrator-focalizer "mastering the event" through emplotment. In place of this therapeutic or self-help mode, the aim is to negotiate the position of the survivor who is no longer in mortal danger, and not yet out of harm's way. In this sense, the media make survivors of us all, whether we want to or not. If I am right this can imply a dauntingly "ethical" spectator-position, making once again demands upon us that necessarily skirt and court failure. But the alternative is that the survivor is just the corpse, who does not know it yet.

The desperate double occupancy of space and place is not atavistic, but post-postmodern, because this is what the future of the past, the future of memory is going to be all about: to mark the sites, but now no longer in their pristineness, but precisely in their layeredness – only sites that are "archaeological" will be perceived as authentic, remediated sites if you like, multiply inscribed, like video-overlay, or multiply occupied, like land claimed by several owners. An authentic historical building will be seen as a fake, where a ruin, with bullet-holes and shot to pieces will strike us as authentic, because it is a material representation of its multiple existences, its realities as well as its virtualities. This is the paradox of why the wars in ex-Yugoslavia were at once unfinished business from at least WWI and WWII, but why they are also heralding the 21st century, and are thus very contemporary. It is the media's role that is at stake: their role in the active competition in the construction of a memory. How, we have to ask, is this past wrapped not in a shroud, or put in coffins and graves, but onto layers and layers of video, images piled upon images? The task is to make visible, not the prurient fascination with the sites where great crimes have been committed, the so-called atrocity tours, but the sites, where the non-visibility of these crimes, but also of the lives such crimes blight or put an end to altogether, can be placed and marked, remembered and commemorated.

(2003)

Notes

1. Slavoj Žižek, passim, but see *The Plague of Fantasies* (London: Verso, 1997), p. 77.
2. Slavoj Žižek, in *De Groene Amsterdammer*, 31 May 1995, pp. 14-15, and in *The Plague of Fantasies*, pp. 60-64.
3. Salman Rushdie, *Imaginary Homelands: Essays and Criticism* 1981-1991, Granta, 1992, p. 303.
4. Fredric Jameson, *The Political Unconscious* (Ithaca, NY: Cornell UP, 1981).

Europe Haunted by History and Empire

Is History an Old Movie?

It's Show Time

It all started with CABARET ... suddenly, the Third Reich had become a subject for feature films, in fact, for a while it seemed to be, especially for European filmmakers, *the* subject. Luchino Visconti's THE DAMNED, Ingmar Bergman's THE SER-PENT'S EGG, Bernardo Bertolucci's THE CONFORMIST, Lina Wertmuller's SEVEN BEAUTIES, Louis Malle's LACOMBE LUCIEN, Lilian Cavani's THE NIGHT PORTER, François Truffaut's THE LAST METRO, Joseph Losey's M. KLEIN: the 1970s were the decade of films exploring what Susan Sontag had termed "fascinating fascism." The combination of kitsch and camp, the cult of death and the ambiguous celebration of style which had made Nazi imagery, colors and iconography lead a second life, first in

CABARET

garish comics and then in coffee-table books, surfaced in the movie mainstream, to join the growing number of biographies, monographs and scholarly publications devoted to the period.

German directors were at first slow to catch the trend. For obvious reasons, the topic carried a special burden, not to be shouldered lightly or irresponsibly. But in 1979, when HOLOCAUST, the six-part television series made by NBC provoked unprecedented public commotion in West Germany, filmmakers felt duty-bound to respond to or protest against what Edgar Reitz, in a memorable phrase, was to call "the Americans ... taking away our history." After Hans Jürgen Syberberg's OUR HITLER (1977) and Rainer Werner Fassbinder's DESPAIR (1978), there appeared in quick succession Helma Sanders-Brahms' GERMANY PALE MOTHER (1979), Alexander Kluge's DIE PATRIOTIN (THE PATRIOT, 1979), Volker Schlöndorff's THE TIN DRUM (1979), Fassbinder's LILI MARLEEN (1980), and finally, in 1984, Edgar Reitz' eleven-part HEIMAT. These are still among the titles most immediately associated with the New German Cinema, its identity apparently rooted in a brooding return to Germany's troubled past.

But clearly, more was involved than Germans claiming the right to speak up for themselves, and of coming to terms with Hitler's legacy. At stake seemed to be history itself, and the cinema's way of dealing with it. What mattered, many of these films argued, was the subjective factor, the individual experience, with the cinema only truthful where it concentrated on the personal, on private, often sexual obsessions, while the public sphere remained a colorful but often clichéd backdrop. In the case of the German films, they tended to show how fascism had affected the (bourgeois) family, and family relations: especially mothers and daughter, mothers and sons, more rarely husbands and wives.

The realization of a rather radical change in attitude to German and Italian fascism, to the Occupation and Resistance in France – or merely the fact that these films were very popular – spawned a number of theories, the most original perhaps being that of Jean Baudrillard. He detected in the general retro-fashion a distinct "retro-scenario": the peoples of Western Europe, locked into political stasis, nostalgically imagine through the cinema a time where their country's history still meant individual villains and victims, causes that mattered, and decisions of life and death. One attraction of such a history was the excuse for still telling stories with a beginning, middle and an end, which would give the illusion of a personal or national destiny: a need fascism had tried to gratify on a collective scale. The return to history in the cinema was therefore for Baudrillard not a move towards coming to terms with the past, but the fetishization of another trauma altogether, located in the present. What the female ankle or laced-up boot is to the foot fetishist, fascism is to contemporary imagination, namely the last permissible sight that can be possessed as object, prior to the trauma barred from sight and consciousness: the absence of history altogether.

Baudrillard's thesis may well explain the orgies of reconstruction, of lovingly recreated period detail, the fixation on authenticity (the source of which turns out to have been a book of glossy photographs by luminaries such as Brassai or August Sander) that gripped the movie and television screens. Instead of history, we have archive footage as action replay, and a media-made present of authentic sound, digitally remastered. After Vietnam – the war in your living room, terrorist hijackings for the benefit of TV cameras, or the hard sell of US Presidents, it seemed to Baudrillard that all the direst predictions of the May '68 Situationists about the "society of the spectacle" had come true.

It suggests that the cinema of the 1970s essentially confirmed a melodramatic view of history: spectacular in the public sphere, a family soap opera in the home. For if Baudrillard is right, then even in films like HEIMAT or GERMANY PALE MOTHER the insistence on the family was something of a fetish, because it too clung to an unexamined notion of "personal experience" as somehow a quality that could be recovered and represented on film. Was Heimat really sixty years of Neighbours condensed into sixteen hours, or on the contrary – to use a term introduced by Foucault into the French retro-debate – an important part of "the struggle over popular memory"?

Taking Back Neo-Realism

What seemed clear was that reintrodu-cing fascism as a film subject also sig-nalled the end of the European cine-ma's post-1945 dedication to "realism" and a critical "reflection" theory. Vis-conti's The Damned, Bertolucci's No-vecento, or Fellini's Roma had, in a sense, "taken back" neo-realism (which of course, in such classics as Rossellini's Rome Open City or Visconti's Osses-sione could itself be quite melodra-matic). And with it went the Bazinian notion of what the morality of cinema was ("truth 24 times a second" as

The Damned

Godard put it, who, though, also knew two or three things about the difference between the real and media-reality). If one looks at the German cinema, one notices that a number of key films are in fact rewrites, pastiches or decon-structed remakes of other films. The once much-despised *Heimatfilm* became the generic basis for Heimat, but Reitz shows no rural, pre-industrial idyll, and instead, makes much of the fact that his heroines go to the movies, and his heroes dabble with ham radio sets, take photographs, and are active as cinema-tographers on the Eastern front.

In the case of Fassbinder, The Marriage of Maria Braun, for instance, quotes scenes from a ponderous but well-meaning *Trümmerfilm* of the late 1940s (Harald Braun's Zwischen Gestern und Morgen), but it is also a take on Michael Curtiz' Mildred Pierce and a homage to Douglas Sirk's A Time to Live and a Time to Die. Yet Fassbinder, apart from being an inveterate cine-phile, also held a deconstructionist's view of the vanishing historical referent. The analogy sometimes made between his films about Germany (from Effi Briest, via Berlin Alexanderplatz, Bolwieser, Lili Marleen, Lola, Mer-chant of Four Seasons to The Third Generation and In a Year of Thir-

TEEN MOONS, he covered virtually every decade between 1890 and 1980) and Balzac's *Comédie humaine* is only apt if one allows for the fact that his ambition to present all social strata and classes was no longer founded on the belief in the documentary character of the novel (or, for that matter, film). Fassbinder's Germany is one where rewriting its history means also rewriting this history as film history.

THE MARRIAGE OF MARIA BRAUN

More particularly, Fassbinder's cycle of films about the 1930s and 1940s tend to foreground those aspects of Nazism which make it a subject for filmmaking. The connection between fascism and show business, for instance, appears to be the implicit (critical) perspective in LILI MARLEEN, LOLA and VERONICA VOSS. What emerges from these films is that the cinema can deal most effectively with history, where this history has made its pact, on a grand scale, with make-believe, deception and self-deception. Fassbinder's characters are caught up in show-business and the entertainment world, or they take drugs; which contrasts sharply with the films about ordinary folk (or "the personal as political") under fascism (HEIMAT, GERMANY PALE MOTHER), but it also differs from the *film noir* atmosphere with which some of the immediate post-war films wanted, rather naively, to "expose" the evils of the political system, enmeshing individuals in guilt, crime or madness (e.g., Wolfgang Staudte's THE MURDERERS ARE AMONG US, 1946).

LILI MARLEEN was not the first film that broke the post-1945 taboo of representing fascism as spectacle, and therefore involved with desire, pleasure, libido. However, of all the films that in the 1970s and early 1980s had fascism as their subject (including those made in Italy and France), it was LILI MARLEEN that took furthest the alignment of fascism and show business, seeing Nazism as a "modern," self-consciously political organization of mass-entertainment. By splicing together in one narrative the second world war and the buoyant entertainment industry of radio and the phonograph, via a female star performer and patriarchal oedipal melodrama, Fassbinder focuses on the transformation of totalitarian power into a spectacle redolent of cinematic fascination, showing how "hard" military and logistical power gets commuted into erotic glamour, by way of three related themes: mobilization of the masses, the productivity of a war machine, and the consumption of spectacle. The staging of immediacy and presence, symbolized by the song of the title being performed, recorded, played over and over again, erases the boundary between the material and the immaterial, so that the reality of hunger and deprivation gives way to the intoxication of seeing technology in action. Not coercion, but the war machinery side by side with the technology of sound and image reproduction is the drug that keeps the population vital and productive.

Syberberg's OUR HITLER

In Fassbinder's LILI MARLEEN, fascism is shown as a form of show-business, which exploits for its own ends the capacity of a popular song (and by extension, of popular culture) to arouse intense emotion in millions of individuals, and act as a mirror of their subjective longing and of a collective utopia: in this case, as it happens, a song about loss and death. Fassbinder here implicitly replies to Syberberg's OUR HITLER, where the proposition that modern show-business is in some sense more fascist than Nazism, informs much of the argument by which Hollywood cinema, and Hitler are bracketed together. For one of Syberberg's central points is that the Nazi deployment of radio broadcasts, live transmissions, mass rallies, and civilian mobilization campaigns turned the State into a twelve-year state-of-emergency, experienced by many Germans as communality, participation and direct address (a notorious complaint, by disgruntled citizens in the 1950's was that "in the old days, under Adolf, there was always something going on").

That the cinema has an especially ambivalent role in the representation of Nazism derives not least from the fact that German fascism has left a more complete account, in sight and sound, in visual records and staged celebrations, of itself and its version of history than any previous regime. But Leni Riefenstahl's TRIUMPH OF THE WILL is not so much the record of the 1934 National Socialist Party Congress in Nuremberg as it is its visual, dramatic, aural mise-en-scène *in action*. What makes the ambivalence and fascination emanating from this film survive all ideological deconstructions of its message is that through television, we have come to live with its underlying aesthetics: that public events are often staged, that news is made rather than simply happens, that public life is a photo-opportunity. In this respect, Syberberg's ironic pastiche provides a problematic but also apt reflection on the wider relationship between history and the cinema, for he points to the surplus meaning carried by any audio-visual or photographic record when used in film as (self-) "evidence." Syberberg's point is that Hollywood cinema and now television, in the name of democracy and the right to consume have made the Riefenstahl aestetic the international norm: a perpetual festival of there-ness, action, live-ness, where spectacles of destruction, or feats of prowess and the body beautiful are feeding national or individual fantasies of omnipotence.

While OUR HITLER, as part of a trilogy, also continues Syberberg's theme of false prophets and false prophecies, which to him characterize the cycles of German history, his concern is not just Germany. If the Nazi ideology of *"Volk"* and *"Lebensraum"* could only gain credibility, because radio was able to put on a daily electronic simulacrum of "The People united behind the Führer," it was not a lesson lost on post-war political leaders. There is thus for Syberberg a continuity between fascism and the modern entertainment business, precisely because he sees a continuity between one kind of capitalism trying to solve its crises by building up a war economy, and another kind of capitalism trying to solve its crises by enticing people to buy, spend, and consume. What in fascism is the will towards self-representation (perversely, the anticipated promise of genuine democracy) has in post-war societies become the narcissism of the consumer. In consolidating the mirroring structures of spectacle, and making them invisible, cinema has played a crucial role towards bringing about such a transformation. The show is democracy's tribute to totalitarianism, not only because the past can always be revived by becoming a movie, but because individual or collective experience is no longer passed on other than as an object of consumption, in the visual system of identification, projection, mirroring and doubling that is the cinema and television.

Such a bleak message certainly seems to throw the baby out with the bath water. Nonetheless, with hindsight, OUR HITLER is recognizable as the high-water mark of a certain post-'68 anti-Americanism, while the critique of Hollywood can also be found in Godard's demand for "two or three Vietnams, in the heart of the Hollywood-Mosfilm-Cinecitta-Pinewood Empire," or in the British avant-garde's calls for a "cinema of unpleasure."

The Return of the Mummy Complex?

Yet it is perhaps the unmitigated pessimism about the Holocaust having been forgotten because of HOLOCAUST which makes Syberberg's film itself a historical document. What happened in Germany, and in the name of Germany between 1933 and 1945 is still so incomprehensible, so far from being settled, that the questions – what lead up to it, how was it possible, how does it still affect Europe – refuse to go away. Almost every week, there is a documentary on television which reminds us of Josef Mengele and his Auschwitz research programme on identical twins, the "forgotten Holocaust" of Southeast European gypsies, the John Demjanjuk trial, alleged Nazi war criminals in Scotland, but also of the collusions and the compromises: the "British Betrayal" of the Cossacks in Yugoslavia, the Red Cross' refusal to act on information about the death camps, or Tom Bower's documentary about the "Operation Paperclip," which in 1945 spirited Werner von Braun and other leading Nazi from the V2 rocket research center in Peenemünde to Mexico, and from there into the top echelons of NASA, the US space program. In many of these films, it is not the wealth of visual material that is surprising, but how much is still hidden in archives, in the interstices of secretive bureaucracies, but also, how many men and women are still alive, willing to speak and give testimony, not always to their advantage. Above all, one thinks of Marcel Ophuls and LE CHAGRIN ET LA PITIE, MEMORY OF JUSTICE, HOTEL TERMINUS, where each time, Ophuls turns his camera and microphone on people whose self-deception is only rivaled by their self-importance. He also turns himself into a character, not afraid of playing the clown, or having a door slammed in his face like a traveling salesman. Dissimulating his own feelings and convictions, in order to make (some minor protagonist of) history "speak," he likes to compare himself to Peter Falk's Columbo, the awkwardly stooping detective, and indeed, there seems no end to the conspiracies and turpitudes still needing to be "uncovered."

Rather than regretting that so much personal or public history has vanished into its representations, into family-snaps and archive footage, some filmmakers seem to welcome this fact, because it has renewed their faith in cinema. Syberberg, for instance, has found in his rejection of narrative and realism a whole new aesthetic of cinema, neither fiction nor documentary, neither enacted drama nor talking heads, but back-projections and stage props, dolls, dummies and soliloquists. Ophuls and others have gone out to find the "authentic" voices that speak to the images we may have seen too many times. Still others create an overwhelming presence of history out of the very absence of evidence.

One of the consequences of living in an image world is that these images that connote "history" have taken on not only a new solidity, an almost immutable reality in their own right. Whoever deals with them, takes on a new kind of responsibility, if necessary, to show what they do not show. The dilemma is nowhere more starkly in evidence than in Claude Lanzmann's SHOAH. The dialectic of material and immaterial, of who speaks and who is silenced in an image, becomes here the very core of the enterprise. Lanzmann's care over bureaucratic detail, the exact description of place and circumstance, the way he goads the memory of surviving prisoners, guards of concentration camps and farmers who merely looked on, suspend all preconceived narratives and explanations. SHOAH does not invalidate them, nor does it complement them. Instead, it confronts us with the sheer enormity of the numbers of victims and their total disappearance, even in the minds of those that helped or were present at their death. Appalled and intrigued by the industrial scale and methods used, one is also overwhelmed by the particularity and physicality of annihilation, pondering how little survives of a life compared to the mass of data, information, administration – truths not preserved in political, economic or even psychological discourses about the "Final Solution." In the end, the dead defy any viewer to imagine a history that could contain the palpable reality of their death, but also spurning the notion that film or photographs might somehow preserve their memory or signify their lives. It is a sobering reflection, when trying to console oneself with the thought that among the many ways mankind has tried to prolong and preserve life beyond death, the cinematographic might not be the worst. So much for André Bazin's "mummy complex."

In other words, does the cinema have a conscience? Not merely about the Holocaust and its history, but about its complicity and precise role in the dilemma of our media world, first stated by Walter Benjamin, namely the dialectic which makes the act of recording also an act of destruction, a Faustian wager: a memory, an experience, in exchange for a moving image and recorded sound. The problem with many of the discussions about cinema and history is that whether we talk about accuracy and authenticity, of recovering the past "as it really was," or whether we take the other side of the coin: film necessarily betraying the past to illusionism, nostalgia. What makes of history an old movie reflects the awareness that the cinema is more than vehicle for conveying or containing something that has happened elsewhere. For the consequence of the dialectic of recording as destroying (the obverse being Kracauer's "redemption of physical reality") is that instead of imagining the cinema more or less accurately representing a reality or event outside itself, it is a historical force in its own right, and finally needs to be understood as such, which is both more and less than what is usually meant by "media-reality."

Syberberg, for instance, explicitly refrains from restaging historical events in OUR HITLER, and puts on a puppet show. Like Fassbinder, he, too, recognizes no "outside" to the world of showmanship, make-believe, or in his case, massmedia manipulation, in contrast to Reitz, who for much of HEIMAT, still holds on to an unfashionable, but maybe for popular film and television necessary belief in historical recreations.

By treating fascism and the cinema not at the level of the referent (how accurately can a film present fascism, its horror or seduction) but engaging with what the French would call their (technological, social) *dispositifs*, Syberberg and Fassbinder deserve credit for having drawn attention to one particular history of the cinema's (and television's) power-potential: for creating a public sphere ("mobilization") and for affective/emotional engagement ("subjectivity"). Where they differ is in their estimation of whether this history is an inevitable one.

Eros and Mourning Work

One question, which I think all the feature films from the 1970s ask themselves is this: why – despite everything we know – do we instantly recognize ourselves in the fascist self-image? It's not so much that the clothes and haircuts look sexy again, or that the pseudo-classical sculpture make a perfect backdrop for modeling swimwear or suntan lotion. Thematized as sex and death in virtually all of the Italian films, it is this fatal identification which in Fassbinder and Syberberg becomes a question of the cinema's strategies of identification per se.

Fassbinder, as a director of the 1960s and 1970s, invites comparison with two other directors: Pasolini, and Oshima. All three filmmakers come from countries which espoused fascism as their way of "modernizing" a feudal society, and all three took fascism as the historical key to understanding the formation of their country's present, but even more so to explore social marginality, in fact, their own subjectivity and sexual identity. Although Fassbinder never made a film as direct as Pasolini's SALO or Oshima' EMPIRE OF THE SENSES, he shares with them the conviction that one does not have to "believe in reality" (Bazin, again) in order to know that the historical referent can indeed be seized in the form of resentment, hate, desire, in short, at the level of a psychic "perverse" investment which can overturn the existing order: the promise of revolution, existential, sexual, and a long way from the quietist slogan of the personal as political.

In this respect their heir in the 1980s is Derek Jarman, who in some of his films, most notably in his EDWARD II deconstructs class-war and history (understood as the recording, remembering and passing down certain versions of power and masculinity, and not others), setting against them the investment of sexual love, hatred and jealousy.

These very different filmmakers – Fassbinder, Pasolini, Oshima, Jarman, Ophuls, Lanzmann – who care passionately about both history and about the cinema, all share a kind of direct personal commitment, often one of anger, outrage, but there is also an aesthetic commitment, usually to a non-realistic, operatic, or minimalist style, among the documetarists. For them, the cinema does have a morality – not of truth, but of representation, including the representation of loss or excess. There is no doubt that Syberberg, too, has such a commitment which is both moral and aesthetic. He has called it *"Trauerarbeit,"* work of mourning. This Freudian notion (from *Mourning and Melancholy,* 1926) of working through the processes of grief by way of introjection (blaming the self) and projection, when faced with apathy (about one's own fate) and anger (towards the loved one one has lost) after bereavement was popularised in Germany by Alexander Mitscherlich. Mitscherlich had attempted to explain why so few Germans felt remorse after the defeat of Nazism. Historicizing Freud's concept, he suggested that West Germans suffered from a particular kind of self-alienation, the "inability to mourn," which meant, they were also unable to love, either themselves or others.

In Syberberg, "mourning work" assumes, apart from its meta-psychological meaning, an aesthetic dimension. Noting how it posits an active, conscious coming to grips with historical experience, on terms that imply a self-distancing, but also self-abandoning stance towards the "other," in view of being able to acknowledge loss and absence, Syberberg conceived it as a direct counterpart to the processes of primary narcissism and identification, whether with a political leader or a movie star. As a consequence, his films eschew filmic space, and set up associations, network of cultural references, emblems, historical sign-posts and musical echoes, which appeal to memory and conscious recognition. This opposition between "mourning work" on the one hand, and the unconscious identification-projection mechanisms of the classical fiction film on the other, structures all of his films, and ultimately determines the kind of role he sees for his cinema as a counter-cinema, sketching a poetics of plastic toys, image debris, clichés, quotations that is inspired by Benjamin's book on baroque tragedy, itself influenced by the surrealists.

But "Trauerarbeit" became a catch-word among German directors making films about history, not least because it could be connected to an elegiac tradition in German intellectual culture, especially since Hölderlin and the Romantics. OUR HITLER makes one of these elegiac mourning works explicit: a section is named after Heinrich Heine's Deutschland ein Wintermärchen, a satirical poem written from exile in Paris in 1844, on the eve of yet another failed German revolution. "Trauerarbeit," in this tradition, signals the particular love-hate relationship of German post-war writers and filmmakers towards the Federal Republic, which they felt alienated from, but nevertheless represented, especially abroad.

In its heyday in the 1970s and 1980s, international spokesmen of the New German Cinema like Herzog, Syberberg and Wenders saw themselves as just such ambassadors of the good Germany, often taking the moral high ground. They did public penance if and when required, and on occasion, were not afraid to bite the hand that fed them (the Bonn Government and its film-funding system).

However, this right of the (literary and film) authors to speak on behalf of Germany and German history, now appears to have been one of the casualties of unification. A complex process of reassessment has begun, perhaps not yet of German history, but of some of those who have been its artistic custodians. With it, the idea of Trauerarbeit itself as an authentic stance of both separation and engagement now sounds a little hollow: not least because it over-values the political importance of the aesthetics of moral rectitude. Abroad, snickering remarks can be heard about "the world-record holders of breast-beating self-accusation," while in Germany, some cultural high-priests of yesterday are openly being referred to as "harmless nut-cases." The populace, it seems, is not in the mood for being schoolmastered: not by their politicians, not by their press and television, and least of all, by their state-financed avant-garde filmmakers. Syberberg, who has played the part also in a number of books, has had to endure his share of ridicule.

Die Schuld lassen wir uns nicht nehmen (we won't let them take away our guilt") once read the caption to a West German cartoon of Chancellor Kohl laying a wreath at a concentration camp memorial. It maliciously echoes Edgar Reitz's phrase "they're taking away our history." At a time, when history has returned to Germany and places its own kind of burden on the future, while the legacy of Nazism in Croatia, Serbia, and elsewhere has to be confronted by the whole of Europe, it cannot possibly be "our history," just as it need not only be "our mourning work." If making spectators identify with the "other" is finally the goal of every European director, it remains to be seen how German filmmakers come to represent to Germans the kinds of otherness of a common history.

(1986)

Edgar Reitz's HEIMAT

Memory, Home and Hollywood

When the NBC series *Holocaust* was aired on German television early in 1979, it started a heated public discussion about the ethics of turning this episode of national disgrace into a family melodrama and thriller. But, so the verdict ran, if a tearjerker manages what no documentary film, no literary account, and not even a show trial like that of Adolf Eichmann had achieved, namely to bring home the horrors of Nazi rule and to open locked doors of memory, conscience and personal history – as *Holocaust* did for millions of Germans – why quibble over points of detail or aesthetics? And why had German filmmakers not tackled the subject themselves in a format accessible to the general public instead of waiting for Hollywood? The American series had crossed, inadvertently or not, a certain taboo threshold for the West German media; and Reitz's HEIMAT, begun around March 1979, responds to the challenge by entering into a sort of dialogue not only with *Holocaust*, but with its reception in Germany and the "retro" fashion in general.

Reitz, in fact, had participated in the debate quite directly, with an article he published in the May 1979 issue of *medium*, entitled "Let's work on our memories." It conceives the issues from a partisan aesthetic perspective, as befits a film-political activist and co-signatory of the 1962 Oberhausen Manifesto: "If we are to come to terms with the Third Reich and the crimes committed in our country, it has to be by the same means we use every day to take stock of the world we live in. We suffer from a hopeless lack of meaningfully structured, aesthetically communicated experience... One should put an end to thinking in categories, even where this terrible part of our history is concerned. As far as possible, we must work on our *memories*. This way, films, literary products, images come into being that enlighten our senses and restore our reflexes."

What stands in the way of this, according to Reitz, is the economic hegemony of Hollywood in the entertainment market, which translates itself directly into a dominance of aesthetic forms. European national cinemas or individual "film languages" are always at a disadvantage, since their product not only reflects the material difficulties of making films at the margins of the system, they are also judged according to the so-called "international aesthetic criteria" set by the seasonal blockbusters:

The difference between a scene that rings true and a scene written by commercial scriptwriters, as in *Holocaust*, is similar to that between "experience" and "opinion." Opinions about events can be circulated separately, manipulated, pushed across desks, bought and sold. Experiences, on the other hand, are tied to human beings and their faculty of memory, they become false or falsified when living details are replaced in an effort to eliminate subjectivity and uniqueness ... There are thousands of stories among our people that are worth being filmed, that are based on irritatingly detailed experiences which apparently do not contribute to judging or explaining history, but whose sum total would actually fill this gap ... Authors all over the world are trying to take possession of their history ... but they often find that it is torn out of their hands. The most serious act of expropriation occurs when people are deprived of their history. With *Holocaust*, the Americans have taken away our history.

Reitz was appalled by the alacrity with which the German critical establishment jumped on the bandwagon:

Along comes the Uncle from America, pulls *Holocaust* out of his pocket, millions watch the box, thousands phone in, ten thousand break into tears: "don't expect us to be the spoil-sports and wheel on critical objections! We have to join the crowd" ... This sort of reasoning means that even after 35 years, the Nazis' anti-intellectual propaganda still shows through. Our Arts Page critics, such as ([Wilfried] Wiegand) are afraid of being found in the company of the unsuccessful, so they make off to the villas while there is time, hoping that the rich will let them piss with them. Their longing for a "blockbuster" is like the petty bourgeois' yearning for a "Führer" – even today.[1]

Is Reitz settling old scores, not afraid to name names, as Syberberg had already done in OUR HITLER, which has a *Kultur*-inferno peopled with German film critics? The only inveterate and unrepentant Nazi in HEIMAT is called Wiegand; the most opportunist Nazi is an ex-madam of a brothel whose ambition in life is to own a villa; and when the uncle from America arrives after the war, she can't wait to pin the Stars and Stripes on her hat and shed crocodile tears over her adulation of prominent Nazis. Or is it that for Reitz nothing much has changed? It would explain why in the film fascism and pro-Americanism are so closely allied, since both are judged mainly in relation to a persistent petty-bourgeois hero worship.

In contrast to simply "replacing" one authority with another, and the "falsifying" of memory and experience by someone like Lucie, most characters in HEIMAT have "irritatingly detailed experiences," giving history a local habitation and a name. But Reitz's engaging plea for a cinema of memory directly communicating individual experience, unprocessed as it were, which would amount collectively to history, does not translate easily into practice, and neither is it his own. It is true that in keeping with many films of the New German Cinema, HEIMAT is poor on plot and suspense, and rich on incident, episode, atmosphere: for a German audience, there must be literally hundreds of details and scores of incidents that feel absolutely "right," that spark off personal memories, and allow an audience to recognise themselves in the guise of the "other" up there on the screen or right there in the living-room. But the strength of the American cinema, for instance, is precisely that it has established certain gestures, a certain landscape, a certain manner of speaking as unmistakably, typically American: what audiences recognize and respond to in Hollywood films is the pleasure of always returning to something already seen and experienced. It may not be the authentic, irreducible experience of history Reitz has in mind, but it is experience all the same, and not, as he claims, the pushing back and forth of opinion: Reitz's polemic somewhat over-shoots its target.

HEIMAT itself is a fairly complexly layered film, full of references to other visual material, other films, current cultural contexts of which the dig at Wiegand the critic is perhaps the least important. Inadequately translated as "Homeland" (which is why the title has been left in the original for international release), "Heimat" is an intensely emotional concept, always implying a return to (imaginary or real) origins, roots; it has predominantly rural associations and is therefore close to the land and "soil," to a particular landscape or a region. As such, it has been much abused by German nationalists from the Romantics to this day: every expansionist or annexation policy in German history has been justified by the slogan *Heimat* or, as under Hitler, "Heim ins Reich."

In addition, Reitz includes an extract from a very popular 1938 Zarah Leander vehicle called HEIMAT (directed by Carl Froelich). In 1937, Detlef Sierck had made a film called DIE HEIMAT RUFT, following his 1936 Zarah Leander hit, ZU NEUEN UFERN, a title which itself evokes the symmetrical complement to "Heimat," i.e., *"Fernweh."* This is in fact the subtitle of the opening episode of HEIMAT, in which Paul returns home, only to be seized by an irrepressible yearning to leave "for new shores." Zarah Leander is a crucial reference point for several characters in HEIMAT, for the women who stay home (and dream of Spain, Italy, the Mediterranean), as well as for the men on the Front (who dream of returning home): a movie star becomes the convergence of several (asymmetrically placed) fantasies.

In spite of his diatribe against Hollywood, Reitz is clearly aware that in our century, to talk about memory is to talk about audio-visual representations of events. None of us can escape the force of the images that always already exist, and to build a counter-memory from scratch, that is without recourse to photographic images is as heroic as it is impossible (or at least, so it seemed, until Claude Lanzman set about to do just that in SHOAH). One might even go so far as to say that Reitz's film is not so much a review of German history as a review of German *film* history, a summa and recapitulation of the German Cinema, its achievements, its themes and images, as well as its battles with critics and producers. This is no criticism of either Reitz's theoretical position or his film: on the contrary, it is a measure of his achievement as a commercial director that he may have founded – building on the work of others and his own previous films – the visual and narrative bases of a new film language for narrating the nation.

Episode 1: *Fernweh/The Call of Faraway Places (1919-28):* Returning from a POW camp in France to his native village of Schabbach in the Hunsrück, Paul Simon decides to abandon the traditional family craft of blacksmith. Through the hard currency dealings of Wiegand, mayor of the village, he is able to build his first wireless set. Yearnings for a life elsewhere unite him with Apollonia, a servant girl ostracized by the villagers. She is pregnant by a soldier of the French occupying army but in love with Paul, whose courage to run away with her fails at the last moment. Instead he marries Maria, daughter of Wiegand. They have two sons, Anton and Ernst, and Paul returns to the blacksmith's shop alongside his father. Eduard, Paul's elder brother, unfit for military service or work because of weak lungs, starts prospecting for gold in the river. When he and his sister Pauline take the nuggets to a jeweler in the nearby town, the gold turns out to be copper oxide, but the jeweler falls in love with Pauline and marries her. One night, Paul is woken by a marten in the chicken coop. The next day, he sets a trap, puts on his hat, and walks away. Maria and his family look for him in vain.

Episode 2: *Die Mitte der Welt/The Center of the World (1928-33):* Eduard has contracted tuberculosis from standing in the river. His father sells land to send him to Berlin for treatment. He recovers and, on an evening stroll, is invited by three young women into a brothel where he meets Lucie and marries her. They return to Schabbach on the day Pauline and her husband pay a visit in their new car. Things are evidently looking up, and only Katharina Simon, the mother, refuses to celebrate Hitler's birthday; instead she visits her brother in Bochum, where she witnesses a dawn raid in which her nephew Fritz, a communist union organizer, is arrested and deported. She returns to Schabbach with Fritz's young daughter Lotti.

Episode 3: *Weihnacht wie noch Nie/The Best Christmas Ever (1935):* Lucie, anxious to see Eduard succeed, ingratiates herself with the Nazi Gauleiter, who takes an interest in Eduard's amateur photography. With a loan from a Jewish banker, the couple build a villa in the village next to Schabbach, where Eduard becomes mayor. When Maria's younger brother Wilfried returns from Berlin in his new SS uniform, Lucie persuades him to get a delegation of Nazi officials to have lunch at her house. At Christmas, the Simon and Wiegand families attend mass in the church. Only old Wiegand stays at home, listening to the *Horst Wessel Lied* on the radio.

Episode 4: *Reichshöhenstrasse/The New Road (1938):* Six thousand men from Todt's labor brigade arrive in the region to build a new road. The chief engineer, Otto Wohlleben, is billeted with the Simons and takes an interest in Maria's younger son, building him a model airplane. After an evening at the movies with Pauline, Maria confesses that she'd like to start all over again somewhere else, and the two women dress up as Spanish dancers. Otto has an accident at work, and while he is being looked after by Maria, the two fall in love. Alone in their villa, Lucie and Eduard are glad of a visit from Martina, one of the women from Lucie's Berlin days. They toast the New Age, and Eduard wishes things would stay like this forever.

Episode 5: *Heimat /Up and Away and Back (1938-39):* A special delivery to the Simons brings a letter from Paul – now owner of an electrical company in Detroit – announcing his visit. Amid the rejoicing, the shattered Maria, realizing she is no widow, breaks with Otto. Traveling to Hamburg with Anton, Maria catches only a glimpse of Paul, who has to remain on board ship even though the Simons have lived as Protestants in Schabbach since 1650, records show an ancestor called Abraham, and Paul needs an Aryan certificate. Maria returns just in time to hear war being declared on Poland.

Episode 6: *Heimatfront/The Home Front (1943):* With most of the men at the front, the women are helped in the fields by French POWs. Wilfried Wiegand has become the local SS commander. When an English pilot breaks his legs parachuting into the woods, Wilfried shoots him "trying to escape." Anton, who had stayed in Hamburg, has been drafted, and sends his pregnant fiancée, Martha, to live in Schabbach. Maria has a four-year-old son, Hermann, whose father is Otto, now a bomb disposal expert for the Luftwaffe's home front airfields. By chance, Otto comes across Ernst, a trainee pilot, and learns about Hermann. Anton, a cameraman with a propaganda unit on the Eastern Front, meanwhile arranges a proxy wedding ceremony with Martha. While the village celebrates with ersatz *gateau*, Anton's "I do" is filmed by his colleagues for the weekly newsreel. Ernst commandeers a plane, flies to Schabbach, and drops a bouquet of red roses for Martha.

Episode 7: *Die Liebe der Soldaten/The Love of Soldiers (1944):* As the Eastern Front collapses, Anton's propaganda unit covers the retreat by filming executions of Russian prisoners, disguised as partisan warfare. Contriving to visit Schabbach, Otto spends the night with Maria. With Allied bombers overhead, war has come to the Hunsrück. The prospect of private happiness makes Otto over-confident, and on his next demolition assignment, the bomb explodes under him. When the Americans move in a few months later, Lucie is busy fraternizing, despite having her villa requisitioned as the area HQ.

Episode 8: *Der Amerikaner/The American (1945-47):* Trying to find a doctor for her wounded husband, Martina dies in the crossfire during the battle for Berlin, while back in Schabbach people have already accepted their new masters. Paul turns up in a chauffeur-driven limousine, showing off his wealth with gifts and a lavish party. Lucie is in her element, but for Maria, Paul is a total stranger. As he prepares to leave again, his son Anton returns, having walked home from Russia via Turkey and Greece. Ernst is also safe, according to Klärchen, whom he sends to join the household. Paul stays long enough to attend his mother's funeral and to help Anton realize his dream, the founding of an optical instrument factory on his grandfather's land.

Episode 9: *Hermännchen/Little Hermann (1955-56):* Ernst has acquired a US Army helicopter which he uses to transport lumber for his father-in-law's sawmills. He is visited by Hermann, his precociously gifted stepbrother, on whom Maria lavishes unfulfilled love and thwarted ambition. Hermann is the first of the family to receive a grammar school education, which makes him attractive to Klärchen, for whom he writes poetry and plays the guitar. Although almost twice his age, she becomes Hermann's great love, but decides to leave after having an illegal abortion to protect him. Jealous at the idea of losing her son, like her husband, to a "dark" woman, Maria persuades Anton to threaten prosecution, but merely succeeds in alienating Hermann from home and family.

Episode 10: *Die Stolzen Jahre/The Proud Years (1967-69):* Anton's factory is the object of a takeover bid by Belgian industrialists, but after consulting his staff Anton refuses to sell, unlike Paul, whose "Simon Electric" has been acquired by IBM, giving him leisure to tour Germany accompanied by a young nurse. He is closest to Hermann, who is about to conduct a performance of his first major electronic composition after studying in America. The concert is broadcast live, and in Schabbach everyone gathers round the publican's hi-fi radio. To Maria's embarrassment, most of the villagers leave, and only the village idiot claims to hear Hunsrück birdcalls and the sounds of nature.

Episode 11: *Das Fest der Lebenden und der Toten/The Feast of the Living and the Dead (1982):* Maria is on her deathbed. Most of the family is assembled, including Paul and even some relatives from Brazil. Ernst is now a dealer in farmhouse antiques (his men are hovering in the village) and only Hermann has yet to arrive from Munich. At the funeral, a downpour scatters the congregation, and as Hermann drives into the village the abandoned coffin suddenly looms before his windscreen. During the wake, the latent hostility between the brothers climaxes in Anton boarding up the house to stop Ernst or his men from entering. His firm is in the red and he is anxiously awaiting promised government subsidies. At the annual village fair, most of the funeral guests find grief turning into dissolute levity, even though Paul nearly dies and Anton suffers a mild stroke that leaves him temporarily deaf. No one notices that the village idiot, who seems most shaken by Maria's death, is in agony. He dies as a full moon rises over Schabbach and the noise of the fair can be heard in the church-yard.

Filtering public events through their private repercussions is very much what television is good at, both in Britain and elsewhere in Europe. In West Germany, it is also a film genre, and virtually imposes itself whenever fascism, the War or the post-war period are dramatized: GERMANY PALE MOTHER, THE MARRIAGE OF MARIA BRAUN, and for the events of the 1970s, GERMANY IN AUTUMN and THE GERMAN SISTERS. The word "Germany" is very much in evidence in these titles, and HEIMAT, a project Edgar Reitz spent over five years writing, research-ing and directing, has as its logo a milestone bearing the inscription "Made in Germany," which is what it was to have been called. The greatest danger of the genre, therefore, is an all-too-ready symbolism: Germany is linked to the femi-nine, motherhood, sisterhood; the land, the regions, the seasons come to stand for the nation, and History along with women and the family are reclaimed as Nature. As it happens, none of the films actually endorses unequivocally such a metaphoric construction of its female characters. But it is a misunderstanding that critics had already inflicted on Brecht's *Mother Courage*, and which Reitz must have known he was laying himself open to, when he made Maria – the patient, life-sustaining central force of HEIMAT – a woman born in 1900, so that one of the characters can say of her, "she is our living calendar."

HEIMAT's exceptional length of nearly sixteen hours makes it difficult to clas-sify. Produced by two television channels, it was obviously conceived with an eye to being shown as a mini-series, but Reitz insists that it is a film for the big screen. A project of this size inevitably has to be exploited in both media; and there are now sufficient precedents, in Germany and elsewhere, of either very long films already shot in segmentable episode form (KAOS, ONCE UPON A TIME IN AMERICA), or television series for which a condensed cinema release version was anticipated (Fassbinder's BERLIN ALEXANDERPLATZ, Bergman's SCENES FROM A MARRIAGE), to make Reitz's chosen format viable, if still risky, since he is adamant about not cutting the cinema version down to even Syberbergian length.

Seeing as I did, the first five parts in a cinema, and the remaining six on tele-vision, HEIMAT produces distinct experiences, not only because of the different degree of involvement in the image. On television, the series is a chronicle; the episodes, quite loosely joined at times, are introduced by Glasisch, a sort of good-natured village idiot, shuffling through a stack of photographs which serve as a recapitulation of the story so far and a reminder of the previous epi-sode. For each update he changes the emphasis because he picks different snap-shots. This storyteller stance fosters the cozy ambience of anecdotes come to life from a family album, especially since the comments and reflections of Glasisch are delivered in the broadest Hessian dialect. The fact that some characters disappear, that minor ones have episodes practically to themselves, and that others are successively played by different actors, enhances the sense of "scenes from rural life," and the viewer is allowed to surmise that the reason they are strung together in this manner is the narrator's hidden passion for Maria. In other respects, there is no resemblance to a soap opera of either the *Dallas* or *Coronation Street* variety, even if the village setting might make a British public immediately think of *The Archers*. HEIMAT does not have an open-ended narrative, no sub-plots that can be developed separately, and no cliff-hanger suspense that makes the viewer fret for the next instalment.

More important, though, HEIMAT is not a soap opera because its sense of time is different. Glasisch's voice-over gives the whole a retrospective tense, right up to the epilogue where, despite Reitz's effort to balance mourning and mirth, everything seems to fall apart and one gets a rather over-the-top vision of West German society drunkenly staggering into the 1980s. In soap operas, despite the cramming of incidents, crises and dramatic reversals, time is dilated, imperceptibly stretched, so as to minimize its effects on the characters' faces or personalities. Soap operas, despite

HEIMAT

their open narratives, take place in a closed world, into which history only penetrates in the form of current affairs or news (that is, in the temporality typical of television itself as a medium).

In HEIMAT, the main protagonist is time itself, eating into the characters' features, bearing down on their bodies and hardening their attitudes. It is not just the quite remarkable physical transformations that Marita Breuer brings to the role of Maria; the choice of actors who play Maria's three sons at different stages in their lives is very revealing. Whereas Anton gets stockier and more thick-set as his devotion to marketing his optical inventions turn into a mixture of business caution and moral complacency, Ernst, an ace Luftwaffe pilot during the war and in top physical condition, gets thinner and more ferret-like when his marriage-for-money goes to pieces and he becomes an antique dealer who scours the region for peasant furniture and farm implements, which he sells to Cologne and Düsseldorf nightclubs for their rustic decor. Hermann, the youngest, turns from a slim, ethereal and utterly vulnerable adolescent troubadour into a stocky, consciously and coldly elegant composer, to all appearances a city-bred intellectual. He returns to the village resentfully and in the event too late to make peace with his mother, who once took out her incestuous feelings on the woman Hermann was in love with by threatening her with prosecution for seducing a minor.

It is through the details of the actors' body language, the objects Reitz surrounds the action with, and especially the role these play in both situating the period and the personalities, that the film comes into its own as cinema. Freed from the commentary and the recaps, the story has a more epic sweep, but unlike other family sagas on the big screen (THE GODFATHER, 1900), whose journeys through time take their (predominantly male) protagonists on quests either into distant parts or towards self-realization, HEIMAT abandons its males once they leave the charmed circle of Schabbach. The only exception is Eduard, the eldest of the Simon brothers, who figures in the episode set in Berlin during the Nazi seizure of power. He, however, is in many ways the least independent, and his stay in Berlin only highlights his need to return to the Hunsrück region. At one point, he voices what is certainly one side of the dialectic on which Reitz has built his film: the feeling that if everything stayed the same as it is now (the year is 1938), they could be happy forever after. His mother Katharina, though, knows better: the new millennium lives on credit: borrowed money, a borrowed creed, and borrowed time.

HEIMAT's leisurely pace, the emphasis on the changing seasons, the idyllic moments of. picnics and outings, are not, as in a Hollywood production, the preludes or counterpoints to dramatic climaxes or scenes of cathartic violence: they *are* the drama. In the sense that the good things in life – which for Katharina means listening to a Christmas choir, for Lucie owning a villa, for Pauline going to the movies, for Martina making raisin and potato pancakes, or for Maria buying her son a model airplane – are undermined not by the dramatic intrusion of political events or even the war, but by the scars that the small sins of commission or omission, petty injustices, moments of cowardice, indecision or opportunism leave on relationships.

Given the century and the country that Reitz is dealing with, such political minimalism may seem excessively conservative. In fact, Reitz might well be accused of telling a revisionist sentimental history of Germany: a film of and for the apolitical 1980s. The ideological climate of even ten years ago would not have allowed such a project to pass as anything but apologetic: abroad, because Schabbach seems to have few Nazis and even fewer who are anything worse than fellow-travelers, and at home, because West Germans would have been too afraid of not having the "correct" attitude to their own political past. In other words, it is a film that celebrates certain German virtues of sociability, fortitude, *Gemüt*, rather than criticizing, as is more often the case, German vices of character, conviction, self-righteousness, while drawing a rather sharp line between then and now. Reitz implicitly criticizes the West Germany of today for its corruption and its cynicism, in the light of which the misguided idealism of the 20s and 30s, or the spirit of survival and reconstruction of the 40s and early 50s (including currying favor with the Americans), seems at least understandable, if not pardonable.

Ironically, this exoneration of a Germany that is now definitely extinct (lamented also by Syberberg in OUR HITLER as Germany's soul: the triad *Sehnsucht, Wahnsinn, Heimweh*) seems to have been received gratefully and enthusiastically. It comes, however, at a time when the guilt feelings of the last generation still to be morally implicated are no longer in need of being appeased. One can tell that HEIMAT took a long time to make. The gestation and preparation show in the locations, the domestic appliances: Clothes and tools are there not just as objects, period pieces, psychological accessories of the characters and the narrative; they seem to bring with them their own duration, their own survival through use. Usually in historical reconstructions, the props look too expensive because they have been brought in from antique shops, and the decor becomes pure period style, not sufficiently lived in. It is perhaps against the temporality of the objects which the characters handle every day (which is after all a human time) that Reitz would want the spectator to measure and evaluate the different time sense of the land at one end, and history at the other. Eduard, for instance, missed his appointment with history when he slept through the night the Führer marched into Berlin with a torchlight parade, but what he remembers all his life is the casual atmosphere in the brothel where he met his future wife.

The film opens with Paul coming home after walking all the way from a French POW camp in the spring of 1919. As he turns into the yard, he hears and sees his father working at the open forge repairing a wagon wheel. Without a word, he drops his knapsack, picks up his blacksmith's hammer, and fits himself into the job at hand. The harmony of the two men's movements sets a rhythm of gesture as aesthetically pleasing as it is evocative of a certain historical stage of the family as a productive unit.

The same is true of the subsequent scene, when Paul falls asleep at the dinner table, and everybody is talking at once. But whereas the men rock on their chairs or just sit there, crossing their arms and legs, the women ebb and flow around them in an incessant bustle of activity that consists of work, work, work – feeding the men folk, telling the children off, folding the washing or simply standing up to their elbows in a bucket of pig swill – all the while carrying on the banter and the conversation. Far from depicting an idyll, these scenes establish the interactive, productive and reproductive time that knits the families together, and give the spectator a point of reference by which to follow and observe change itself, as the moral impact internal and external events have on the characters.

At this level, HEIMAT's apparently anecdotal and loosely chronological narrative is quite deceptive. For one of the advantages of watching it in the cinema is

EDGAR REITZ

that one becomes aware of the subtle moral and physical reversals, the many echoes and repetitions that create the film's structure, because one is much more conscious of the movement and also the sediment of experience in a house or a landscape. One feels, through the sheer duration of the film, the weight of history on the lives of a group of people whom a less patient sensibility than that of a filmmaker with Reitz's perseverance would probably accuse of having escaped from history into biology and nature: the HEIMAT of family and the land.

(1985)

Note

1.   Edgar Reitz, 'Statt Holocaust – Erinnerungen aufarbeiten', *medium*, May 1979, pp. 21-22.

Discourse and History

One Man's War – An Interview with Edgardo Cozarinsky

Thomas Elsaesser: You made One Man's War *in France at a time when there had already been an extensive public discussion about the French and their collective memory of the Second World War and German occupation,* The Sorrow and the Pity, Lacombe Lucien *and* The Last Métro *among others had very much fixed the critical debate around the question of collaboration and resistance. Your film deliberately displaces these terms, and one could imagine an equally important debate around the use you make of documentary material – in your case, newsreels of the period – and the choice of a German writer, Ernst Jünger, as intimate witness. Does the question of Jünger's complicity, his attitude to the historical events he observed, engage you more than "the truth" about the French?*

Edgardo Cozarinsky: Whether the majority of the French collaborated or resisted is a question of statistics and a neuralgic point in the national conscience. What mattered to me was the question of Jünger the writer, and the quality of his look at history. He approaches current history with a precise surgical hand, almost as if the events he is describing are part of natural history. He works hard at having a perspective. He puts himself at a distance from what he is experiencing as if he were a visitor from another planet.

No doubt, for you, One Man's War *is also part of a different history, if only that of your other films.*

The question of perspective relates to something I tried to do in my previous film. The Sorcerer's Apprentices, where it is present in the use of "inserts" from a future point in time. It was introduced by the use of titles: "let's try and remember what it was like in the last third of the 20th century," an introduction which proposed a point of view to the spectator, the vision of an unknown, unforeseeable future which was established only in those written inserts. The action itself was superficially realistic, according to the conventions of the film noir, but it occasionally opened up to include excerpts of Büchner's *Danton's Death*, excerpts which are themselves fragments from the myth of the Revolution. This kind of formal relationship did not actually come to mind when I was working on One Man's War; only afterwards when I was trying to work out the fascination of Jünger's perspective.

Once again, a writer's attempt to make literature a reference point outside politics and history?

It represents what I believe to be the capacity of most intellectuals – to be cool, to look at things from a distance. Being aware of it, and often having a bad conscience about it, they have shown themselves, in the last half century, overzealous to "commit" themselves, to take a stand, to do anything that might cancel that distance. To the point of wanting to be the stars of History, not its chroniclers. And that distance, when repressed, only comes back the more strongly, in the midst of political engagement. For instance, hundreds of European writers signed the protest for Régis Debray when he was imprisoned in Bolivia, and he knew they were signing for him, not for the hundreds of other people imprisoned in the same jail. The case of Jünger is extreme – a Reich officer in occupied Paris allowed himself to write from the point of view of an intellectual analyzing extraordinary moral, social, and historical upheavals in contemporary society as if he was not a part of it.

EDGARDO COZARINSKY

Are you saying that the exceptional circumstances of Jünger finding himself in Paris, and the disavowal of this exceptionality in his journals, manifest a general predicament of the intellectual in the face of politics?

I feel it to be exemplary because it is so extreme. It casts light on our own experience, and I personally feel it as an Argentinean. When I lived in Argentina under successive but similar military regimes, there was always this understanding in intellectual circles that everybody was against the Regime. At the same time being almost a question of manners, this agreement represented an extraordinary level of passive collaboration – it meant that you did nothing about the situation. And yet, literature seems to thrive under such circumstances ...

If Jünger's look as a writer was that of an alien from another planet, of someone who perceived events and upheavals as part almost of natural history, does this hard, mineral quality of his commentary not stand in a very deliberate, not to say cruel opposition to the sometimes frivolous, frothy material you have chosen from the newsreels, at least in the first "movement" of the film?

When I first started on the project I had an "experimental" attitude to the work. I had the newsreels on the one hand and the Jünger journals on the other and I wanted to see what happened when they came together. Most of my preoccupations were formal (if I had no interest in form I would be doing TV reportage or magazine articles instead of films). I did not know exactly what the end result would be but I knew it would reveal something, I trusted my instinct in choosing as well as in editing: I watched the material in the archives in November and December 1980, I began editing in May 1981 for twelve weeks. After a moment of despair when I thought it would be a five-hour film, I felt the material asked to be grouped in four different units, the four movements of the film. I became very involved in the material during this time and I connected the emotional agitation I felt with my distrust of documentary and the ideology of *cinéma vérité* or direct cinema (I am only interested in "cinéma indirect," if it exists). The material was very much connected with my personal background in Argentina as well as my approach to the cinema.

One might say that the intellectual Right during this century has been preoccupied with the "disappearance of history," whereas the Left, sensing that history was very much in the making, has been obsessed with causes and effects, with instrumentality. Is your film concerned with what has happened to our concept of history during the last fifty years?

I began to feel that the film was as much about today as about the past. And not simply because of the fact that I was watching the material for so many hours a day that it became a part of reality – I didn't see daylight at all! The first association I made was with the attitude of French intellectuals on the left, that "turncoat" quality of French intellectual life which is a kind of farce accepted by everybody. Nobody feels they have to justify it, changing sides and changing factions just out of a feeling that they have to move with the times. Paris fashion, which is an industry, is a model for all kinds of cultural activities, people wear certain ideas which change as fashions change. Look at the shifts of position of magazines like *Tel Quel*, the whole itinerary from promoting the Cultural Revolution, to supporting Soviet dissidents is not based on political analysis or gruesome discoveries but derived from a deeply ingrained intellectual frivolity.

Do you want to be more specific?

Look at Sartre. He spent the Occupation writing his philosophical magnum opus and trying his hand at the theatre (I wonder if he had to sign one of those affidavits, quoted in *The Last Métro*, stating that to his knowledge there was no Jewish blood in the family ... they were asked, it seems, from everybody connected with show business). Then, as if to make up for lost time, he engaged in a non-stop series of public utterances, trying in vain to leave an imprint on the making of History, being wrong more often than not, incarnating the "next-revolution-will-be-the-good-one" syndrome. Of course, he was deadly serious about it all, but the results were not too far from the flippancy of the *Tel Quel* ideologues.

Could it not be said that a preference for Jünger over Sartre today is itself an effect of fashion? Not so long ago, on the occasion of his 87th birthday, Jünger was the subject of a two-page interview in Libération, *the post-'68 newspaper that Sartre himself helped to found.*

My choice of Jünger's point of view was not a question of preference for a Right-wing perspective, but of quoting a patently "foreign" point of view on the Paris I knew and felt I would have approached, more normally, from the Left. It was always in proportion to the capacity I knew so well to be a silent accomplice on the Left that I related to Jünger's experience, not because there is an exact parallel, but because he represents something that always disturbed me deeply on the Left. The "gruesome" dramatic quality of wearing a German uniform from the Third Reich makes Jünger a *figure maudite* par excellence. To relate it to my own experience – there was the widespread complicity of silence about Cuba which persisted until a few years ago. In Argentina, as in every country with a Right-wing government, it was a question of keeping silent about it in order not to play into the hands of the Regime.

The price of Jünger's rock-steady gaze: isn't it always a kind of nihilism, a stoic-heroic defeatism?

Yes. And the Left developed a romance with Power. Jünger, instead, has no illusions whatsoever about power, which is facile in another way – you don't react because evil is impossible defeat, except on individual terms ... I have no answer myself, which perhaps accounts for the deep sense of malaise in the film.

In opposition to Jünger's totally pessimistic, end-of-the-world attitude, you concentrate strongly on the malaise the French officials felt – making speeches expressing the hope that if the French followed the Germans' wishes, there would at least be an amelioration in conditions.

Things that politicians today would never dare say. So much rhetoric that politicians could still afford at the time ... Laval saying "if the French would only trust me ..." I can't imagine Pinochet or Jaruzelski saying it in this age of marketing techniques.

The opposition between the ideology and illusions of the Third Reich and Jünger's pessimism is played down in favour of the image which fashion and the kaleidoscopic newsreels give of contemporary life, against the almost linear narration from Jünger. It struck me that the visual and aural material you have chosen from the archives is as worked on as Jünger's shaping of his experiences in the journals. The journals are very self-reflexive, an inner distance negating his own role, as you say. Likewise, the newsreel material does not strike one as actualité *but rather as so many voices appearing from another perspective. What is interesting about the politicians is that they too, seem to speak from a distance, although it may be the distance of someone who has lost his grip on events. The malaise the film provokes stems from the sense that, as a spectator, we cannot orient ourselves. We are not given an opposition, we cannot work on simple irony, as the basis for our perspective.*

I'm glad you say that because one of my lines of work during the editing was to wipe out every possible "gag." I think there is a constant sense of humor in the film but no gags. The closest I came was in the sequence showing the hats made of new synthetic material presented as a triumph of collaboration, between German I.G. Farben chemists and French fashion designers. There are also a number of "rhymes" which only become apparent on further viewings. For instance, Jünger says that the army had to make ovens because the officials forced to shoot the Jews in the back of the head suffered mental disorders. Later, the propaganda in the French newsreels states that the police officers, found in a common grave, were shot Moscow style in the back of their necks by terrorists, i.e., resistance fighters. Several such interior rhymes occur where opposite voices and opposite propaganda plays reflect themselves.

The malaise is nonetheless never released, the irony never leaves the audience in a position of knowledge.

That is why I felt that the film should end as it does. That the liberation in '44 should be seen as a kind of wake, a funeral ceremony and that at this point there should be a lyrical outburst where image and soundtrack, often following different ways throughout the film, should part forever, to the elegiac music of Strauss.

You must have thought a lot about the "voice" of the camera, as it were, because there is already heterogeneity, an area of friction between the voice-over commentary of the newsreel and the point of view from which the material is shot, without even considering Jünger's voice or that of Pfitzner's or Strauss' music.

One of the reasons for my deep distrust of documentary *vérité* is that I'm never sure what it is a document of. The newsreels were basically very truthful about what they captured; only, they were truthful about things other than what they thought they were saying. Time, in a sense, is the great flashlight because now you see through the lie and everything seems obvious and apparent. There are moments when I repeat the same images but in a very different context, an example is the arrival of Heydrich in Paris. Once it is there with the original newsreel commentary, presented as the arrival of a German personality in Paris, on a par with the arrival of Winifred Wagner or Franz Lehar. He is greeted in much the same way that the others are greeted and he meets French personalities, like Darquier de Pellepoix (who surfaced later in Spain), and

Bousquet, the personalities of the collaboration. Then I took some shots from the sequence containing the Heydrich arrival, intercut them with black leader and put on them Jünger's comments about the fauna to be seen at the German Institute, individuals "he wouldn't touch with a barge pole." Repeating the same shots with a different editing and soundtrack shows them to be both continuous and discontinuous, constructed.

Only once or twice do you show the face of a name which Jünger mentions. Voice and image in general do not come together, or rather, a literary image and a photographic image of the same referent persist side by side, each with its own connotations and provoking subtle delays in the passage from perception to idea.

I knew since I first thought about the film that the soundtrack and the image should be distinct, meeting occasionally at certain points but in general diverging, even where the sound track carries the commentary of the original newsreel. I wanted to have the image and soundtrack in counterpoint, each commenting on the other. What I was most afraid of, on aesthetic grounds, was that the film would be systematic in the wrong sense, in that it would become obvious to the viewer from the start how it worked, the rest following on the same principle. I was very much afraid that the film would have a method which people could pinpoint. Even if the counter-pointing of image and soundtrack could be considered a method, it works in different ways. I was very careful when organizing the film into four movements that you could never predict at the beginning of a section how it was going to develop.

A lot of photographic images have been appropriated by our period as the Image of Paris in the thirties and Paris under the Occupation. A certain "Paris" has been constructed anew, history has been rewritten through these images. Were you conscious of not giving too many iconographic references or points of recognition to your audiences?

The only such point of reference occurs very near the beginning. After the parade on the Champs Elysées there is a series of shots of German street signs which follow a kind of itinerary from the Place de la Concorde to the Opéra. I kept them as a travelogue of Paris in 1940. Instead of

One Man's War

having the traditional kind of travelogue: "here we see these charming natives" etc., instead of a voice-over stressing the difference of the "invader" from the French population, you have one of those invaders telling how happy he is to be back in Paris. He says that perhaps he should take this opportunity to settle down in Paris, since it has been offered to him freely. He is speaking as a writer who had been a frequent visitor to the city, who has friends there, favorite places, and doesn't seem to see much difference in the fact that now he is in the German army wearing a German uniform.

It is as if he is on a travel grant from the German government!
Exactly. Isn't it extraordinary that this *"flâneur"* in Benjamin's sense should be an army officer during the occupation? He is still speaking like a man of culture of the 18th century, like Voltaire going to Prussia.

There is a strong theme concerning Europe in the film. Would you connect this to contemporary thoughts about Europe?
When I was editing the film I began to think about and listen to a certain discourse of fascism in its everyday manifestations. I had previously only read literature on fascism and by fascists and, of course, I have lived in Argentina most of my life. I had always seen the aspect of caricature in fascism.

Frothing at the mouth, hectoring rhetoric, ham acting …
Yes, and even less directly, the idea of fascism as the counter-revolution par excellence, or some Reich-inspired idea about mass hysteria. Anyway, I suddenly saw that these people were dealing with the same problems as France today and other countries too: unemployment, workers from poor countries going to and being exploited by developed countries – the colonizers. There are aspects of the film which are disturbingly close to contemporary Europe. What the Third Reich tried to do – the idea of a unified Europe – was doomed because it was based on the ideas of racial superiority and a millennium mystique which were unacceptable. The idea of a unified Europe has succeeded with the EEC because it has been grounded on mutual economic interest and the ideology of neo-capitalism which has obviously worked, up to a point.

Do you agree with the assessment that fascism will be seen as the ideology of the 20th century because it did what capitalism was going to do anyway but it tried to do it too fast and with a neo-feudal rather than a corporate-technological orientation. That in a sense German fascism anticipated what we are now living through but with means that were inappropriate?
When I first saw the completed film I felt that there was something about it which disturbed me besides the question of fascist ideology. It was a feeling I relate to the fact that I let myself go much more in this film than in my previous work, even though it is a documentary or perhaps because it is a documentary. I let certain emotions into the film much more openly than with films I have shot myself when I was controlling things in another way. I felt the film was about the defeated, in an emotional sense – the German officers, the people of Paris,

the Russian soldiers, etc. All these people were defeated. But by what? Perhaps on one level they were defeated as individuals; even the people who are rejoicing at the liberation are not going to achieve power, they will be the victims of power. Also it's because they are Europeans, which connects with the constant predicament of Europe, for me the only possible place to live and yet at the same time a condemned territory. I wondered also if this period from the late 1950s to the late 70s, of cultural liberality and relative lack of economic stress in Western European life, may not eventually be seen in the years to come as a *belle époque*. And before it, this Third Reich, hideous, but at the same time realistic beyond what I would like to accept as possible. It was a very confused feeling but at the same time very acute. The images, when finally brought together, disturbed me much more, and in a way that I had not expected. I thought that they would say something about the relation of an individual to his position in history and in society, and how he could deceive himself about what he was really doing. I found instead that it was saying something much wider, not so precise, but profoundly disturbing about the post-Cambodia present we're living in.

Are you referring to the technological-industrial character that military engagements, especially in Latin America and Asia, have assumed in the last decade, or to the fact that the superpowers now export their wars, like their weapons and consumer goods, to countries which cannot afford them?

At the end of the film, when Jünger speaks of the attempted suicide of a fellow aristocrat and officer, he says that up to the First World War the old code of honor was still alive, but that now, the war is run by technicians. If I mention Cambodia as a turning point it is because I think it marks the end of a period when intellectuals and politically conscious individuals could feel safe, siding with the Left. Suddenly Kissinger and China were working side by side putting the Khmer Rouge regime in power and letting it conduct the most rational genocide of recent times, and one invoking a Marxist discourse. For intellectuals, wars have always taken place elsewhere, even when they happen in their own country, but Cambodia was perhaps too much.

ONE MAN'S WAR *is a film by an exile about an invader, both looking at Paris from an inner distance. The newsreel material you have put together is light and ephemeral, and perhaps because of Jünger's relentlessly self-centered commentary, shot through with ironies at every point. His was an analytical mind which nonetheless doesn't necessarily believe that there is "truth," which is why the question of perspective and the look – in its widest sense – is so crucial. You emphasize this in your film, for instance, by several shots of people filming, notably in the beginning, where we see a German officer – not Jünger, of course, but in some sense his double, a Jünger alter ego – taking pic-*

tures with a camera. Does this not suggest that despite the polyphonic organization of
many voices and multiple perspectives, the film privileges the individual voice, even if
this is obviously not the voice of truth?

The individual voice, of course. Jünger's – not necessarily. His journals were available and the fact that his predicament (a writer and army officer, an accomplice of henchmen caring for the victims) is exceptional made him richer, more upsetting and revealing as a counterpoint. But the voices I would have liked to listen to are not those of such "stars," however engrossing their account, but those of the nameless "extras." I have frozen the image on their faces (literally, faces in the crowd) to let us fantasize what roles they could have played, what their "one-man's-war" may have been like ...

It seems that despite the fact that we now live in a society of the spectacle and of the
image, the literary word retains a powerful aura. Especially in films made by writers, I
have been struck by a curious effect of reversal, where the function of the images is to
create a space around the words – the equivalent of the silent white margin in the
printed page in a book of poems, perhaps.

I find myself, in all my films so far, using black leader rather often. Sometimes for rhythm, as a caesura, or to let the previous image linger a little longer on the mind, at other times to let words or music stand by themselves.

In your film, too, the individual voice inevitably transforms the crowd of faces into
objects of a certain look, into signs for something else. Perhaps it is at this point that
documentary film-making becomes a question of écriture: on the few occasions when
you freeze an image, as if to point at something, you make sure that what you point to,
by the technical process of interrupting the flow, retains all the ambiguity, all the irre-
ality that such an impossible image provokes.

I see the frozen images in the film as "details," such as you may find illustrating an art book. They try to stop the flow (the editing is quite fast throughout) and call attention to a gesture, to an incident, but never as explanation, rather as unexpected windows opening on something unknown. Most times I worked with them according to the music, and the music was the great organising principle of the film, not only its choices but also whether it was left under, or over, the Jünger voice or the newsreels voices, whether it runs freely for minutes or is broken into tiny units. The music suggested also that a shot be frozen at the end (the smiling girl asking a German for a cigarette) or at the beginning (the boy looking at the camera is like a still photograph suddenly brought to life – he leaves with his pushcart a bombed-out *quartier*); in another case, a freeze frame in the middle of a pan shot (the close-up of a Russian prisoner looking at the sky) was placed as to coincide with a certain musical phrase.

Isn't there a kind of paradox here? We do admit to a fascination of the image, where the documentary image speaks to us in an intense way, in an intimate way, which is more erotic than any fictional image. The word speaks to us, too. Yet in a sense though we are committed to a medium which speaks to us directly, it does so in an irresponsible way – we never need to know why the soldier looked, he may have been looking at a gun, etc. We have, in our fascination with the image, no responsibility to what the image "in reality" might have signified. We appropriate the image in a way that perhaps writing does not allow itself to be appropriated, for when language is used in such an appropriable way, we call it bad writing, verbal kitsch, propaganda.

I said to myself from the beginning that I wanted to rescue the faces of these people and preserve them. Why? To keep them for myself, perhaps. I allowed myself to engage in some kind of necrophilia by making them the object of my desire.

Do you think this is an obsession which has always been in the cinema?

For me its best expression is to be found in "The Oval Portrait," the Poe story. In a sense that is most extraordinary thing ever to be written about the cinema.

It is of course, also Fritz Lang's obsession; the creation and un-creation of those who appear on the screen. Lang, as it were, conceals his own creation in the abstractness of his mise-en-scène which is a way of starting with a blank and ending with a blank. Renoir might be seen as working in an opposite manner. He is director who uses the cinema to actually preserve a certain mode of life, a certain sensibility and vitality. He is, as it were, on the side of life perceiving the cinema as a legitimate way of preserving it. On the other hand, Fritz Lang is on the "daimonic" side, the side of power and pessimism; his cinema is about the power of the image and the power of undoing the reality which the image presumes to preserve.

I did indeed feel this desire to possess – the frozen images. I started to fantasize about these people and to wonder what their lives might be like. I knew this was pointless but I couldn't prevent myself, it was a kind of sorcery. I think it, too, reflects this Lang quality, cinema as a "daimonic" art. It is something, which as I said, I relate very much to Poe. I saw a film not long ago, a medium-length film made in France by the Vietnamese filmmaker Lam-Le, entitled LA RENCONTRE DES NUAGES ET DU DRAGON. It is a story about a man who embellishes the photographs of dead people so that they may enter eternal life looking their very best. For the occupation forces in Vietnam, the French in the 1950s and the Americans in the 1960s, this practice is tantamount to falsification of documents and identity papers. He goes to jail. The film tells the story of his revenge on the people who sent him to jail, using his magic brush. It's an extraordinary film, considering it was made in France on a very tight budget – it was all shot in Paris, and the *banlieue* becomes Saigon in the 1960s. Everything is believable in the sense that von Sternberg's China and Spain (on the other end of the production scale) are believable. The story is at once about an individual's revenge and the revenge of a repressed culture on the occupying forces. But it is also a story about the cinema, the power of the image; the embellishing power, not just of an actor's face but the fact that the cinema creates out of that image an immortality. As in Poe, the cin-ema in general changes the people who work on it and the image does destroy the owner in the end.

This even affects documentary.

Yes. As far as documentary is con-cerned, I always feel that fiction films are the best documentaries of any period for they allow the imaginary to speak, which in the bad sense of documentary is forbidden.

One Man's War

But, of course, in documentaries them-selves, what really speaks is the imaginary.

The stock footage of any period is meant to be a recording of reality but it is completely open to the imagination. For me there is a kind of displacement of roles, the fiction film becomes a document and the would-be document opens itself to the imaginary.

Both the war years and the pre-war period have undergone an extraordinary revival in all forms. Maybe because we also live in a world of public spectacle using roles, images, signs, self-display, and in many ways the 1930s and 1940s were a self displaying, nar-cissistic period on a massive scale but more naively so; perhaps the spectacle of those years holds an attraction because even aesthetically it anticipates our own, more guilty or more provocative narcissism.

I decided to make this film on negative and not just on video, as the I.N.A. (Institut National de l'Audiovisuel) people wanted ... On the one hand I desired to see the images as they were once seen on a film screen in 35 mm black and white, but also because those were pre-TV days and audiences were less used to seeing images of daily life and current affairs, and so the public image worked much stronger than today. People are now saturated with images, and however uncritical, they are familiar with their operation, whereas in the 1930s and 1940s I think people would still say: "It's true, I've seen it on the screen." Everybody is aware now that images can be manipulated. Then images had a much stronger capacity to impress people's imagination. Also there was the fact that people had to leave home to go to the cinema, whereas TV is in the house, the space of daily life. I think this made looking at images akin to a religious experience – you went to the cinema like you went to church and communicated with another world. I think this experience has been lost from watching films on TV. People only go on special occasions or for particular films, whether it is the intellectual cinema-goer or the STAR WARS spectator, it's no longer a weekly event, a ritual.

I would say that the religious dimension is much stronger today. When a large audience goes to the cinema, it is always the end of the world they have come to watch. But perhaps there is, after all, a secret complicity between this desire and a writer's perspective, such as Jünger's. Borges recently quoted Mallarmés: "everything exists to take shape in a book," and added: "a writer knows that whatever he does, he does for his writing."

I cannot think of the relationship between, to put it at its bluntest, Art and Life, if not as a vampiric one. The "committed" films about the Third World exploit the misery that gives them a reason for being and in the end reassure their enlightened audiences in rich countries; when I want to allow people to really see the face of a prisoner about to die, my film feeds on his victimization. And I know that being aware of this is not enough. Jünger was aware of it all and didn't raise his little finger ... So what? Stop caring? Stop writing and making films? Again – I don't know the answer, and those offered to me look banal or obsolete. And I know I can't stop caring, or writing, or making films. Or just putting questions.

(1984)

Rendezvous with the French Revolution

Ettore Scola's THAT NIGHT IN VARENNES

Paris 1792, a Venetian troupe of actors performs on the banks of the Seine, enacting the Fall of the Bastille and other momentous events, thanks to a new technical gadget, the magic lantern. Elsewhere in the city, the notorious publisher, lecher, bon vivant and writer Restif de la Bretonne returns home from the brothel at dawn, to find his assets seized and his books confiscated. But instead of consoling his daughter with the more than fatherly attention she seems accustomed to, he heads for the coach station: Paris is rife with rumors of the King and Marie Antoinette having fled east, in the direction of the German border. Restif's journalist instinct tells him to follow, but he narrowly misses the coach for Metz, on which the writer Tom Paine, American Revolution participant and here observing the French one, makes his way to Alsace, in search of the steel he needs to build a new type of iron bridge. Also among the travelers are a former magistrate with his Italian opera singer mistress, an Alsace industrialist, an Austrian countess, her black maid and her hairdresser, a widow from Champagne and a student going back to his village.

Restif hires a horse to catch up with the party, but after falling off while overtaking another coach has to be rescued by its occupant, an elderly gentleman by the name of Chevalier de Seingalt, who turns out to be Casanova, himself fleeing from his patron who has sent his servants after him. At each stop the party can observe the commotion that the passage of the mysterious carriage traveling a few hours ahead of them is causing. Opinions are divided about the Revolution, the monarchy, the rights of man and the future of France, but it soon becomes apparent that the Austrian countess and her retinue have a more than passing interest in the King: the countess is one of the Queen's ladies in waiting. Interest, however, focuses on Casanova, his exploits and reputation, with all the ladies making him offers he politely declines on account of advanced age. The mood is light-hearted, the peasants from the fields wave, and the student seduces the black maid high up on the coach. A brief stroll while the coach is being pulled up an incline allows Casanova and the countess to renew an acquaintance one of them never knew existed.

As the day wears on, news reaches the countess that the King's plan has come unstuck. At their next stop, a messenger arrives from Paris telling them that the National Assembly had issued a writ against the King. Tempers begin to fray and an argument breaks out between Tom Paine and the Countess. She storms out, walks over to the stables, and into the arms of a lascivious beggar. Her screams are heard by Paine who rescues her, but to little thanks. Only Casanova remains calm, demolishing a five course meal. He makes his exit with a flourish, passing a credit note to the innkeeper as payment and kissing the Countess' hairdresser on the mouth. Restif, starved for news, bribes the villagers, and ends up at Nanette's, patroness of the local tavern. There he meets up with Casanova once more: Restif is introduced as the husband of Nanette's daughter, as whose father she introduces Casanova. The two men are amused to find themselves thus related. Later, in Casanova's coach, Restif confesses that his deceased wife, though bearing the name of Nanette's daughter had no connection with her. To this Casanova replies that he strongly suspects that until this evening, he had never laid eyes on Nanette, but that he had played the part, because of his sense of theatre, and because he had not wished to ruin the reputation of a woman past her prime in front of her customers. The men again are highly amused.

Suddenly, news arrives that the King and his entourage have been detained in Varennes by the postmaster from St. Menehoud, and are staying with M. Sauce, the local chandler and spice merchant. The party makes its way there, but such is the throng of villagers and sightseers that they have to make the last part of the journey on foot. The Countess is able to enter M Sauce's house, but can only get to the top of the stairs. She faints and is carried out. Restif joins them, and intrigued by two parcels he saw them carry from the coach, asks whether he could see what they contained. The countess unpacks them, and it turns out to be the King's dress uniform. They dress the garments over a clothes dummy, on which they finally place the King's hat: so overwhelmed is the countess at the sight that she kneels to pay her respects. Meanwhile, the villagers have begun a torch procession and are turning the occasion into a popular entertainment.

We cut back to the framing story of the theatrical presentation. The balladeer announces the execution of Citizen Louis Capet, and a toy guillotine severs a dummy's head. Restif takes over the narration again, and recites from a book he had written in 1793 where he looks into the future and predicts the United States of Europe. As he walks up the embankment, one sees the Paris of today appear, with traffic in front of the Hotel de Ville and Notre Dame. Restif's figure gradually disappears from sight, into the crowded street.

Thomas Carlyle, in his *History of the French Revolution*, had already made much of the King's (or as he was by then called, Louis Capet's) unhappy and bungled flight to Varennes, a small town in the Lorraine region, from which he returned to Paris only to be imprisoned and eventually guillotined. In the farcical events and the King's ignominious role, Carlyle saw an example of the naiveté of Louis XVI and his innocence, which was perhaps the real culpability of the French monarchy. Scola and his scriptwriter follow this tradition; they depict a Paris prior to the Terror: careless, disorderly, hedonistic, and a countryside where the peasants toil just as hard as they have always done, where the food is good, the

revolutionary hotheads are young, inexperienced, full of bluster, and the women grateful to be recognized by their former lovers on return visits. Since on
this occasion history was a non-event, the ingratiating busybody and professional pornographer Restif serves as guide, chronicler, and buffoon, with the
side show of the coach party becoming the main event. This, of course, has
been a classic device ever since Walter Scott discovered that the best way to tell
history is through minor characters who always just miss the action. And a
stagecoach full of passengers from all walks of life can travel almost as successfully to Varennes for Ettore Scola as it did to Lordsburg for John Ford.

Almost. The film is quite wordy, and given its subject, has to get through a lot
of political philosophy, moral debate, witty repartees, name dropping and
world-weary wisdom before it can let its famous names get on with the situation at hand rather than filling us in on their biographies. Sometimes it does this
quite amusingly, when, for instance, Casanova explains in an aside that his
name did not mean much to the average Frenchman, since the memoirs that
made him famous were yet to be published – after his death. He also indulges
in mild anachronisms: before jabbing a stick into his horse's backside, as he tries
to overtake a rival coach, he tells his travelling companion to fasten his seatbelt,
and after breaking down with a split axle he puts out a triangular traveling bag
as a warning sign. And at the end, as Restif, having returned us to the framing
story of the Venetian theatre troupe, goes up the steps of the embankment, he
has a vision of the future – the year 1992 to be precise, in which "Europe gives
itself a new government." The camera tracks back, cars appear, buses and pedestrians, and Restif is lost in the crowd on the rue de Rivoli as the end titles
come up.

But despite a bit of time travel and a glimpse into the future, THAT NIGHT IN
VARENNES is anything but forward looking. It is a film about the Revolution for
the cynical and resigned late-20th century, in which the young are uniformly
unsympathetic: ignorant and rude, loud and dogmatic, pompous and arrogant,
they strut through villages, read proclamations they do not understand, or
show off by kissing a black girl on top of a coach. While the king (whom we
never see, of course, except his feet, from the point of view of a royalty-struck
Hanna Schygulla) is made to seem a harmless imbecile, his pursuers are dangerous fools. Humor, courage, warmth and candor are all on the side of the women. Whether aristocratic ladies in waiting, mistresses keen to get into a singing
career in opera, brothel madams, or rich widows with a vineyard in the Champagne, they are the only ones who know the true meaning of democracy and
solidarity. At one point, Harvey Keitel (Tom Paine) tells Hanna Schygulla off
for putting the duties of obedience before the rights of man. And although he
rescues her from a very nasty shock, she shouts at him that he is worse than the
beggar salivating at her sight who just tried to rape her in the stable. He seems

to recognize the error of his ways because soon after he asks to see her collection of medallions with portraits of the royal family. The peasants are sly and talkative when bribed, and *en masse* they make a torch-brandishing mob, ready to do anything. As Casanova discusses the Prague premiere of Mozart's *Don Giovanni* and the eternal problem of servants wanting to be masters, the Alsace industrialist recounts the most terrifying sight of his life: a workman, in bright daylight, putting down his tools and crossing his arms defiantly.

And yet, history is made that night: there is a Revolution in Scola's film. It is not about politics, but about sex, and not about the Rights of Man, but the rights of men, and in particular, the rights and privileges of old men. THAT NIGHT IN VARENNES seems a veritable panegyric to old age, with its heroes as sentimental and naively sexist as John Ford's are in DONOVAN'S REEF, with male bodies as self-indulgently decaying, vain and drying to the bone as Orson Welles' Falstaff and his cronies were in CHIMES AT MIDNIGHT. Restif, feasting his eyes on a virgin prepared for him like a meal or climbing into an incestuous bed, has a prayer about the Almighty become Flesh on his lips, until gossip and scandal distract him, and draw him to another kind of promiscuity, that of the snoop and the newshound. Casanova, on the other hand, celebrates his famous name by resolutely refusing all offers made to him, and graciously accepting the confessions of the ladies, that he had been their "first love" although they well understood he would not possibly remember them. What he does recognize, at a glance, even without his glasses, and from a mere fragment left carelessly by the wayside, is the vintage of a bottle of wine from the cellar of the King of France. After all, had he not sat at the King's table a mere twenty years ago?

THAT NIGHT IN VARENNES

Played by Marcello Mastroianni, Casanova is not only a reckless blade when it comes to coach chases, and a hothead when the taste of pork a la St. Menehould is at issue. He is also the true King, naturally regal, without having to evoke either the Divine Right or the Will of the People. In his coach, and before paying for his meal, he makes the innkeeper take off his hat and shout: *"Vive la dignité!"* Like the King, he too, travels incognito, but his true identity is soon recognized, and his reputation precedes him like a fanfare. Unlike the King, disguised as a Majordomo, and his heir dressed up as a girl, Casanova is always himself, for everyone to see, the tallest man in any gathering. Like the King, he his pursued and finally captured: but Casanova is wanted by his patron and benefactor, the Count Wallerstein, who cannot do without his stories, wit, and company.

In THAT NIGHT IN VARENNES the epic form, the stagecoach and the Revolution are a kind of disguise: they protect a fantasy of old age as vigorous, virtuous and seductive all at the same time. Set against a monarch deserting his country and apprehended by a postmaster, the wit, grace and wisdom of Casanova seems sheer self-evidence, surrounded as he is by an audience of adoring women. As one of the characters says, summing up the lesson of the Revolution: We must find the ideals that suit us.

(1989)

Joseph Losey's The Go-Between

Leo Colston, a middle-aged Englishman, played by Michael Redgrave, returns to a Norfolk country estate, recalling the events of a summer, when he was barely in his teens. Young Leo (Dominic Guard) keenly observes the intrigues among the adults in the household, most of whom seem oblivious to his presence, except for Marian Maudsley (Julie Christie), the fiancée of a supercilious aristocrat, on whom she cheats with the farm hand Ted Burgess (Alan Bates). Leo is infatuated with both, and they, aware of his burning curiosity, enlist the boy as their go-between, with tragic consequences. As the story unfolds we come to understand why Leo has never married, and just what psychological damage the illicit passion, the secrecy, a child's trust and the adults' casual use of that trust has inflicted on Leo's life. The Go-Between *won the Palme d'Or at the 1971 Cannes Film Festival.*

Losey, in a good many of his works, likes to draw the lesson that spontaneity is often not the exercise of freedom, but simply the sign of ignorance about the true emotional and social determinants of our lives. Films like M, Time Without Pity, Blind Date or King and Country are concerned with the way a man unwittingly, and yet in retrospect necessarily, entangles himself in different social and private worlds which seem at first to have nothing to do with him, but nonetheless fatally exhaust his strength or destroy his life. Throughout his work, furthermore, Losey has been interested in the worlds within worlds, and his later films trace the properly ideological fabric into which a subjective intelligence is woven. Inevitably, once aware of itself between these worlds, this intelligence experiences life as exile.

From the opening shot, with Colston's voice-over saying "the past is a foreign country, they do things differently there," The Go-Between (as the title suggests) makes the coexistence of different worlds and the sense of being exiled its dominant theme. The ostensible subject – taken from the L.P. Hartley novel – is the loss of spontaneity and innocence through an act of adult selfishness. Leo, a sensitive and intelligent boy of thirteen becomes the accomplice in the desperate and therefore ruthless love affair between Marian, daughter of a Norfolk country gentleman and Ted, the robust farmer who works part of the Maudsley estate. In love with Marian himself, Leo consents to being their messenger boy, but in the event he has to compromise the Maudsleys whose guest he is and betray the lovers. The double breach of loyalty, as much as the confrontation with the sexual act, staged as a Freudian scene (the couple are in some ways Leo's substitute parents) has a traumatizing effect. In the inserted flash-forward scenes Leo appears as a stiff, reserved bachelor visiting the "country of the past" at Marian's request.

Several aspects must have attracted Losey to the subject. There is the theme of intrusion: Leo is a visitor at Brandham Hall rather like Anna is a visitor at Oxford in ACCIDENT. Both introduce a new element into a network of human relationships which respond to this intrusion, in both films to produce fatal results. One remembers the Dirk Bogarde figure in THE SLEEPING TIGER or Robert Mitchum's role in SECRET CEREMONY, and one realizes how much the visitor as intruder has been a constant feature in Losey's work, already present before he collaborated with Pinter (who prefers a similar initiating situation, e.g., THE CARETAKER, THE HOMECOMING). It is furthermore a theme that links Losey with one of the chief dramatic devices of Hollywood, where the solitary outsider so often is the dynamic agent whose intervention forces the community to reveal itself.

In THE GO-BETWEEN, however, the emphasis is not so much on the way the intruder accelerates or catalyzes by his presence the natural momentum of the configuration. He appears more as the reflective recipient (not to say victim) of the different stages in the equilibrium and disequilibrium of the Maudsley household, which is going through a latent crisis. From the moment Marian takes Leo to Norwich, he is being used, manipulated, a pawn in a game he is unable to comprehend. The crisis is primarily an emotional one (Marian is forced to marry a man she does not love), but Losey defines it also in terms of a class conflict and a clash of life-styles. Beneath the domestic crisis we sense an imminent historical change: by taking literally the metaphor of the "Edwardian summer" which came to an end in 1914, Losey revitalizes the cliché with a more directly thematic symbolism. Also, the characters talk about war and mean the Boer war but the audience readily associates World War I. "Do you think this is the end of the summer?" Leo asks Marian on the morning of his birthday as the storm clouds draw up, and it is as if since that day the rainy season had never stopped for Colston.

Because it is conceived as a sustained reminiscence punctuated by flash-forwards in which a Biblical wind "bloweth where it listeth," the film quite naturally amplifies the portrait of a historical period and a social class with the subjective dimension of an individual consciousness, recalling a particularly painful and vivid childhood experience. The narrative thus directly suggests the subjective-objective nexus in which the story is cast (an important change from book to film), and in order to mark the peculiar intensity of memory Losey constantly uses the evidence of a hot summer to play on the ambiguities of light, heat and brilliance," ("You flew too near the sun and you got scorched" the narrator comments as Leo is sitting next to Marian on the coach to Norwich).

In one sense, Leo's presence is an intrusion, into an essentially closed world provoking it to make explicit its behavior, attitudes, and self-understanding.

Subjectively, however, it is also an initiation into another Losey theme since THE BOY WITH THE GREEN HAIR, THE BIG NIGHT up to FIGURES IN A LANDSCAPE. Leo undergoes a threefold rite of passage into the adult world: a different social milieu (the middle-class boy getting his first taste of upper class mores as he is ceremoniously led to the dinner table by the hostess), a new emotional awareness (the feeling of love and the secrets of sex), and entry into world of moral ambiguity, about right and wrong, and the mental anguish of conflicting loyalties.

THE BOY WITH THE GREEN HAIR

On a dramatic level, the double movement of intrusion and initiation provides the inner dialectic of the film, and the subjective-objective "polarity" (which is a unity on a deeper level) articulates the individual parts into a consecutive narrative flow. The introductory prologue illustrates this very well. Leo is led into the house and up the stairs to his friend's room, but at every opportunity he looks out of the window onto the lawn, the croquet game, he glimpses Marian in her hammock, or sees the father waving to them from the park. To penetrate into Brandham Hall is literally and metaphorically to have different vantage points from which to observe other worlds outside, and the scene is constructed in such a way that there is an immediate sense of inner complexity (the angles at which the interior, the staircase, the landings are framed) offset by the seemingly idyllic vistas leading the eye to project itself beyond – a thematic conjunction of distance and desire, proximity and emotional turmoil, which the film develops in the direction of a dualism between the need to belong and the awareness of being excluded, in short, the dilemma that the voyeur shares with the exile.

The movement is continued when the boys leave the house to go into the garden, for here one has an "objective" view of Leo, the boys in the middle distance, Marian in the foreground, with the sense of intrusion conveyed by the voice over (one of Marian's admirers) reading to her from a novel and suddenly interrupting himself to ask "who's that?" Cut to the boys on their way to the outhouses, and Marcus voicing Leo's subjective thoughts by saying "my sister is very beautiful." Finally, a medium shot of Leo followed by a counter shot of Marian in close-up completes the exposition: Losey conceives his narrative strictly in accordance with the emotional logic of the themes, ensuring that every thematically important moment has its double articulation – a subjective vision (Leo's consciousness in action and evolution) confronting the objective existence of worlds outside this vision, mediated by the ordering intelligence of the camera, which never breaks the continuity of a universe at once visibly created, instantly present and reflected upon.

It would be superfluous to show how this principle throughout the film regulates the narrative rhythm, with its *temps morts*, its digressions, repetitions and final acceleration, and determines the montage (the way Losey suggests subjective time in the scene where Leo catches the ball, without having recourse to slow-motion is in itself worth a detailed study). Suffice it to say that it also allows him, in the most classical manner, to frame for instance a threshold, doors, gates, open fields or a straight country lane so as to chart minutely the stages in Leo's exploration of the moral and emotional *terrain vague* around him and within him. A haystack becomes the summit of exultation and the vantage point of boundless freedom, from which Leo-Hermes/Mercury-Icarus lets himself fall in abandon, to be brought back to reality with the sharp pain of an injury that will leave his sensibility scarred for life; and the bark of an oak tree somewhere in the Norfolk countryside conveys the harsh truth of another tree of knowledge about a suffering and misery that nothing can mitigate. Perhaps it is this sense of the palpably physical, communicating in the very feel and texture of phenomena the universals of a cultural heritage and the recurrent crises of emotional life that gives Losey's film a place, paradoxically, not within the British cinema (where he is a toweringly isolated figure) but in the larger perspective of English literary and poetic tradition. And this is not only because the book from which the film is taken is something of a modern classic. Partly, Losey's own ethical outlook – which has always focused (where his films did not describe desperate struggles for psychological, sexual and social supremacy over others, as in EVE, or THE SERVANT) on the tragically wasteful effort of discovering one's moral identity and preserve one's self-respect at the price of emotional barrenness and self-denial – is a very "British" one, and in the mainstream of English literature, especially amongst its foreigners (close to the ironic stoicism of Conrad, in fact).

More directly, however, the phenomenological realism that Losey has retained from his Hollywood background, which works by gesture and inflexion, and depends as much on the turn of a head as on the turn of a phrase, has been (in its literary equivalent) the customary domain of the English realist novel and the strength of English poetic diction since the Romantics. It is the particular achievement of what is generally meant by the Great Tradition, for it implies a certain belief in the stability as well as the transparency of modes and codes of behavior, a belief in the existence of a social life intact, functioning, normative and formative alike on a variety of distinct social levels, and thus presupposing a degree of national identity, a consensus of values and objectives, where discrepancies in behavior and pretension, lapses of language and intonation could be interpreted as a reliable guide to an individual's background and mentality, and where the social and linguistic performance of a person was a conclusive index to his intentions. It meant that no inner life, no mental reality, existed which could not be made manifest through behavioral or linguistic mimesis.

These assumptions Losey acknowledges at the same time as he turns them inside out, by relativizing their historical and aesthetic validity. THE GO-BE-TWEEN, above all, defines bourgeois social life as socializing ritual, and the country house with its pursuits of leisure as a field-exercise in upper-class ideology. The oblique angle under which the Maudsleys are viewed – oblique both because seen through Leo, the outsider, and because within the flow of ordinary

THE GO-BETWEEN

life, the summer holiday clearly assumes the nature of an interlude – exposes how church-going, cricket, the village fete or even bathing are demonstrations of class solidarity and lessons in class consciousness. A trespasser, does one chase him off or put him at his ease? A school cap just isn't worn at a private match, a gentleman cricketer (which Ted is not) doesn't bat in such a way as to endanger the ladies and it's slightly more in order to call someone Trimingham than Mr. Trimingham if he is also a Viscount.

In all this, Pinter is surely for something – a dramatist who in his own work has been undermining the positivist assumptions that ordinary language is the measure of all valid thought, and who has traced the rough edges of banal and everyday conversation, pointing up the crack and gaps where it gives way to another reality altogether. Thus a Pinter line of dialogue is as maliciously trimmed with the grotesque fringes from the civilities of social discourse as a Losey track or pan may be subtly revelatory of fundamental contradictions in the smooth tissue of a visual surface. The projects on which they have collaborated, in addition, seem to reflect a major predilection: to create situations where a certain reality, however preposterous it may seem to an outside observer is nevertheless accepted by the protagonists at face value. As they are vainly struggling within their limited awareness to make sense of the only kind of life the characters know, this limited conception of reality is dialectically shown to have its own justification, if only in that it confers a certain remote rectitude and stature to those thus failing.

A particularly moving example of such irony is the smoking room episode. Responding to Leo's baffled question about sexual fidelity, Trimingham bends forward with impeccable composure to pronounce on the secret borne by the men of his class: that "a lady is never at fault." Both, Leo and he have been betrayed by Marian, yet somehow each is only dimly aware of the pain inflicted upon the other.

That Trimingham can bear his burden with equanimity obviously indicates a heroic dignity of sorts, but it also explains why Marian would feel the need to be unfaithful or reject him altogether. Sexuality is here only a means of rebelling against a social order, which in the realm of personal relationships at least, crucifies both men and women. In the same scene a remark falls about Ted having a woman up these parts. "I know," says Leo, "but she doesn't come on Sundays," thinking of Ted's char. The men show an indulgent slightly pained smile. But the irony is of course that despite Leo being the victim of a semantic confusion which makes him look ridiculous and naive, he knows more about Ted's "woman" than either Trimingham or Mr. Maudsley.

At times Pinter's dialogues seem merely to furnish with a quaint phrases the different worlds created by Losey's mise-en-scène, like the period bric-a-brac that fills the rooms of the house. The public-school slang between the boys, the quips about ladies being gathered rather than seized, or Trimingham, having been "gored by the Boers" are arabesques decorating, however, a quite solid thematic architecture: the language of the Maudsleys gives a recognizable value to the things that surround them and which they dominate, yet it also protects them from life outside and it ultimately hides them from each other. They assume it as a code – to define and defend themselves against ever manner of intrusion. Thus, the different linguistic worlds are brought into sharp contrast by Losey not only to give expression to the poignant inadequacies of language in the effort towards emotional adulthood (Leo's difficulties when trying to grasp the reality behind the word "spooning" and Ted's final "mind you get it told right"), but to draw attention to the whole process of naming as a way of appropriating reality, with its inherent distortion of experience. Losey lets no false nostalgia subsist about Edwardian idylls, for Marian's closing words to Leo Colston about the affair having been a thing of beauty are unmasked by the film as the gross insensitivity of a person used to dispose over words and people alike. In Marian's world Colston is a man robbed of his own experience, because there seems no, language in which he could affirm it. Almost always seen from behind glass and windows, or enveloped in a rainy mist, he inhabits a subaquatic world of silence.

It is here that Losey undercuts most clearly the assumptions of L.P. Hartley's original: the character of Colston, all bitter-stoic resignation to an empty life and choking on his memories, "belongs" in his Wordsworthian preference for enjoy-

ing feelings through contemplation (or quietly suffering them), "to the sentimental standbys of the modern English novel," as Adorno once said of an
Aldous Huxley hero. In comparison with the book, Losey has not reduced the
presence of Colston, but changed his function, making him the furtive shadow,
looming ahead of, and so to speak, "rising to meet" the actual Leo of thirteen
"at evening," rather than the reflecting and thereby dominating narrator. Instead, the controlling function falls unambiguously to the camera, for by weaving the dualism of subjective and objective points of view into a cinematic unity
where one perspective comments and interprets the other, and by showing that
the worlds existing side by side are essentially closed, Losey achieves a perspective with a different depth, in a process of distanciation which allows him to
reinterpret critically the moral position of his characters and his own aesthetic
position as the director. Because the action is seen from Leo's point of view, the
camera shares with Leo the stance of an outsider, but on the far side of Leo's
subjective involvement. The result is a complex aesthetic relativism, by which
Losey is able to comment on the limits of his own mise-en-scène.

The analogies and parallelisms which can be drawn between the closed social
situation which the film depicts and the equally "closed" symbolic style where
nothing is random, perhaps explain why there is a sense that something is hollow at the core of the film, or rather, that there is a very strong (and it seems to
me intentional) feeling of absence created: we are aware of another reality,
which if we knew it would restore our balance as spectators, but which Losey
never shows and the Maudsleys as a matter of course would not and could not
acknowledge as existing. And that reality is evidently Marian and Ted's affair
seen "from outside." Only when Mrs. Maudsley, still wearing her paper hat,
seizes Leo by the sleeve and drags him out into the pouring rain to surprise the
lovers in the act, does she break "form," in the same sense as the film at the end
breaks its form, and would have broken its form had it, say, shown Ted talking
to his charwoman or had attempted to explain what the affair was "really" like.
And this is not only because in order to be consistent, Losey, could in any case
show no more than what Leo himself had witnessed, but because these things,
within the framework that the film sets itself, belong to a different (dis-)order of
reality.

This is also why Ted's suicide is a dramatic and metaphoric, rather than a
psychological, necessity, and why seeing Ted and Marian together in the hayloft
is precisely timed to produce a traumatic (but for the spectator also cathartic)
climax. The sudden acceleration, with frayed tempers at the birthday party, the
growing tension of Mrs. Maudsley, the thunderstorm, the sense of an almost
apocalyptic disaster, which fragments the narrative at the end into a series of
explosive flashes, results from a perfect convergence of style and theme: the
forces of sex explode the Maudsleys' world, while the direct representation of

the sexual act makes the process of "symbolization" redundant: repression of sexuality created the void in Colston's life, but its emergence in his childhood destroys the magic universe of innocent sublimation, which is indeed also the universe of art. Knowledge, Losey seems to be saying – as in so many of his films – is always accompanied by loss, and a diminution of creativity.

Losey's mastery of the fluid transitions between Leo's and the Maudsleys' points of view is thus made possible by the fact that both still belong essentially to the same world, and furthermore, both live on the assumption (which the film disproves) that they have control over their environments: Leo by his magic and the Maudsleys by their social status. The dialectic of subjective-objective vision operates between a voyeur whose desire it is to belong, be part of, and a world which either ignores him or merely lectures him on its own absolute standards – not between the rebel opposing his own vision of reality to the temptations of a form of life as beautiful and deadly as an *atropa belladona* growing in a horticultural decay which is almost wilderness again. Leo, outsider and a child, is in no position to develop his own form of revolt, and he, like the Maudleys "cannot bear much reality," to paraphrase T.S. Eliot.

If there is, therefore, good reason why the contingent has no room in Brandham Hall and ultimately none in the life of Leo Colston – what about Losey's mise-en-scène? Can it do more than exorcise it with the magic of style, can it accommodate a non-symbolic image of the world and still communicate something? Losey has shown a consistent preference for depicting closed social or psychological situations, and no doubt this is partly why a man with left-wing sympathies and intelligence is as an artist profoundly attached to the "style," the rituals and the fictions of the British bourgeoisie, a class that in its upper echelon is still the most cohesive and insular national bourgeoisie anywhere. Losey escapes from insularity like all highly self-aware artists by setting up the mirrors of reflection within his own work.

The strength of THE GO-BETWEEN lies therefore in the fact that it is also a meditation about the freedom and restriction of a cinematic form at a moment of historical closure. In the way his fictional procedures, his treatment of consciousness, time and reality constantly emphasize the limits of the world he depicts, the director also affirms the existence of other worlds not least by marking so clearly the boundaries of this one. Another Britain, another battle of the sexes, another cinema are clearly waiting in the wings. For Losey the exile, not only the past, even the present is another country.

(1972)

Games of Love and Death

Peter Greenaway and Other Englishmen

Chronology as Topography

Like all good readers of Borges and Calvino, Greenaway has a notion of the past that is more topographical than temporal, and so chronology need not dictate causality. DROWNING BY NUMBERS, it appears, was a script finished right after

PETER GREENAWAY

THE DRAUGHTSMAN'S CONTRACT, but at the time the project "failed to get off the ground."[1] Now that it follows A ZED AND TWO NOUGHTS and THE BELLY OF AN ARCHITECT, any similarity with the film that made the director famous becomes vastly more suggestive with the hindsight of an intervening history. Is DROWNING BY NUMBERS a return to home ground – the English countryside – after two foreign forays that had a mixed reception? Or a heroic – Greenaway might say "gay" – effort, in the teeth of his previous protagonists' pessimism and failure, to finish unfinished business and not leave drafts unexecuted?

It might even be a film that interrogates his own work's obsessions, this time not merely through a fictional stand-in for the filmmaker (the coroner joining the cartographers, surveyors, draughtsmen, animal behaviorists and architects) but for what his personal obsessions mean within that part of English culture he willy-nilly "represents." Because Greenaway has become an international auteur he now has to suffer the attendant ambiguities: celebrated abroad, but deeply dividing the critics at home. Shunned by a mass public, though not without a devoted following who tend to use him as the stick with which to beat a (typically English?) parochialism that complains of his emotional "coldness," his cerebral gymnastics, his treatment of actors as pegs on which to hang esoteric ideas. Abroad, especially in France, it is his "Englishness," his eccentricity and yes, his parochialism that is prized, recognized and that, finally, constitutes a major part of his assets.

Contracts and Conspiracies

But what secures Greenaway his claim to loyalty and an audience is that, like any other "serious" artist, his vision is shaped by robust and non-trivial antinomies, on which he has, simultaneously, a tragic and a comic perspective. Whether the subject is decay, man's rage for order, nature's indifference to violence, pedantic love of detail, or sudden death in an idyllic setting ("Murder in an English garden"), Greenaway has the talent to conceive of his themes as double-sided, and to sustain two contradictory insights with equal conviction. This gives his films a kind of inner drama, an intellectual movement and passion, belied by the apparent banality of a plot that in DROWNING BY NUMBERS, is without surprise or suspense. Generated by simple series of three, familiar from fairy tales, nursery rhymes and children's counting rounds, DROWNING BY NUMBERS is not as flashy as THE DRAUGHTSMAN'S CONTRACT, with its court intrigues, verbal duels and power politics. Indeed, it is not at all obvious what could be the intellectual tension in the set piece games, or could make the tableau-like compositions more than the designer's delight they evidently are.

A static, closed universe, jerked into mechanical life by rules, games, and witticisms: this side of the coin is almost too easy to fault, as if the director was in advance disarming the critics by playing even more openly his customary hand. But Greenaway always keeps a powerful motive up his sleeve to propel his figures into narrative: that of the contract and the conspiracy, antithetical and warring principles in one's dealings with the world. For the hapless but willing victims of Greenaway's films (Mr. Neville, the Deuce twins, Kracklite, Madgett) the contest leads to death (suicide, murder: the differences – here between Smut's and Madgett's end – seem to matter little). To the metaphysician in Greenaway, behind the draughtsman's as much as the coroner's contract lies a Faustian wager: to lure Nature into showing her true face, which is evidently not that of Darwinian evolution, or the anthropomorphism of ecological or wild life documentaries, but a more sinister though also serene exchange between life and death, maggot-fermenting pullulation and the night sky's cold, cosmic nothingness.

Sex and food, pregnancy and decay are the manifest agents of the terrestrial side of this trade. It highlights the fundamental asymmetry between masculine and feminine destinies where Greenaway's males seek the solace of sex in direct relation to their anxious, personal intimations of mortality and loss, as illusory tokens of self-preservation, the women's predatory behavior is governed by the need to preserve the species (A ZED AND TWO NOUGHTS, THE BELLY OF AN ARCHITECT, the youngest of the Cissie Colpitts), or produce an heir and pass on property (as in THE DRAUGHTSMAN'S CONTRACT), in each case with sublime indifference to paternity.

Ordinary Misogyny and Male Subjectivity

If the contract binds the men and leads them to their death, the conspiracy is generally hatched by women. They are often the survivors, sometimes "excellent swimmers," who in DROWING BY NUMBERS literally pull the plug on Madgett. He professes envy at their spontaneous solidarity, but the film shows them amoral, voracious, shameless (the Colpitts), promiscuous (Nellie/Nancy) or capricious and teasing (the star-counting skipping girl): a monstrous regiment. They giggle while a corpse is examined by the coroner, crack jokes with the eyewitnesses of a fatal accident, ridicule male sexual anxieties and are erotically stimulated by the sight of death. Alice in Wonderland, nubile nymphomaniac, sentimental good-time girl, bored brassy housewife, comforting maternal bosom: Greenaway has assembled an array of "strong" women characters who are none the less all clearly identified male projections, emanating from longing and loathing in roughly equal parts. As examples of ordinary misogyny, Greenaway's stereotypes are, compared to the *femmes fatales* of recent vintage (BLUE VELVET or FATAL ATTRACTION), positively nostalgic and old-fashioned. What clings to them are the perplexing questions of puberty and adolescence. DROWNING BY NUMBERS is perhaps best seen as belonging to a loose and as yet not very well defined cycle, among them Dennis Potter's THE SINGING DETECTIVE, John Boorman's HOPE AND GLORY and Terence Davies' DISTANT VOICES, STILL LIVES. All are acts of exorcising male childhood traumas, all involve a highly ambivalent reckoning with the mother's sexuality, and in the course of this testify to a cautious, if knowing encounter – for the sake of biographical or collective self-scrutiny – with psychoanalysis (and religion). This is a relatively new and perhaps overdue phenomenon in British cinema (*pace* Nicolas Roeg) which has had the effect of opening out film narrative towards more adventurous forms of fiction. A heightened, emblematic or dream-like realism has appeared, for which the implements, objects, customs, the visual (and often musical) remnants of a bygone popular culture have become the icons of subjectivity, allowing these films to move into the area of male fantasy and anxiety in ways perhaps comparable to the function that the New Gothic (from Angela Carter to Fay Wheldon) has had for women.

"Incest as an Art Form"

It seems that DROWNING BY NUMBERS, a quintessential Greenaway film according to every auteurist criterion of style and theme, is in fact not entirely *sui generis*, but part of a symptomatic use of heavily stylized autobiography. If there is a more specifically personal note to the film, one would expect it to point to the director as intellectual loner, someone who can draw for a character like Smut on childhood memories of playing by himself, populating (and also ruling over) an entire imaginary universe. In this respect, DROWNING BY NUMBERS shares a quest for origins with quite divergent works (admittedly, a somewhat paradoxical claim, seeing how Greenaway is ostensibly concerned with endings, finalities, exhausting alphabets and series), and it might be time to try and rescue the filmmaker from his own auteurist ghetto, where opinion is so sharply polarized about a "Greenaway film."

Boorman's HOPE AND GLORY is a good benchmark for comparison, mainly because it so clearly belongs to the genre of nostalgic evocation, and also because, despite being about an auteur's personal past, its narrative is close enough to mainstream form to be a recognizable, if mildly satirical version of precious national mythologies: about childhood, the Blitz, suburbia, crusty grandfathers, cricket on sunny summer days. It earned Boorman an Oscar nomination and angered the surviving residents of the Surrey Street thus immortalized. Boorman himself sees HOPE AND GLORY rooted in his "admiration, affection and indeed awe for my mother and her three sisters." In the film, William's erotic bond with his mother is quite muted, not least because the boy's curiosity is displaced onto the elder sister and her precocious affair with a Canadian soldier. At one point, however, Boorman makes us share the thrill of witnessing adult indiscretions. With the camera taking Bill's perspective no more than three feet from the ground, and peering out from behind a rack full of blouses, we see two women in their underwear – his mother and her friend – trying on wartime fashion and talking saucily about sex. The scene strained the credulity of a fastidious *TLS* critic, who complained that "the womenfolk seem an unbuttoned lot for those days, and young Bill's nose is forever being rubbed in their intimacies." But HOPE AND GLORY touches here on a fantasy, which is nonetheless grounded in historical experience. The diary published to accompany the film gives a clue: "When my father went to war, he left me with a house full of women, with no male to curb their female excesses. The inexplicable and sudden tears, then the crass conspiratorial laughter at some sexual allusion in shocking carelessness of their mystery ... and the stifling embraces when a boy's face was pressed into that infinite softness, falling, falling, inhaling all those layers of odor only scantily concealed by lily of the valley; acute, knotted, scarlet-blushing, shameful embarrassment."

Boorman keeps these memories at arm's length with a set piece of a scene and passages of purple prose. Not so Terence Davies: his films are, in a sense, agonized hymns to just such "shameful embarrassment." Already the opening shot of DEATH AND TRANSFIGURATION had the middle-aged Tucker run his hands along a row of hangers in his mother's closet, sobbing uncontrollably as he buries his face in her clothes. In DISTANT VOICES STILL LIVES, the mother is such a monument to mute suffering and brutal humiliation that this seems to swallow whatever other emotions the son may feel towards her. But here, too, much of the sexuality is displaced on the sisters, as women, but even more in their dealings with the oppressive, violent father. Religious ceremonies and rituals are called upon, not unlike in Greenaway's films, to dignify nameless pain. One sister's wedding and the father's funeral are disturbingly intercut, confusing the linear narrative, perhaps in order to bring out an inner logic: that only with the father dead can there be a wedding. Yet such is the father's hold over the film, and thus over the subjectivity that informs every image, that it is the sisters who, each in turn, curse him and wish him dead. The son merely gets himself a bloody fist smashing the front room window, and nearly breaks his neck falling through a glass roof.

DISTANT VOICES STILL LIVES may appear to be made up of a series of barely connected incidents, fixed in place and class but difficult to locate in their chronological sequence. What the nostalgic evocation of fifties' pub songs and romantic hits from the radio throws into even sharper relief, however, is the domestic mixture of violence and affection, and the question of what emotional identity corresponds to such a schizophrenic family life. Davies is unusual in that he takes the sisters' point of view – they dominate the image, even where they seem to give in to their boisterously inconsequential husbands. Nonetheless, the film is still narrated through a character, whom the story marginalizes: that of the son. Tony's shadowy existence has to do with his inability to provoke his father either to friendship or overt violence, such as is handed out to his sisters. In a curious reversal we see them constantly challenge their father's authority, and it is they who are slapped, beaten, and loved – not the boy. Each vows to kill him, and each mourns his death. The narrative seems unable to define Tony similarly around this love and hate of the father, and the film's perspective is split between identification with the mother, as abject victim, often enough absent from a scene, but implied by the frontal position of the camera (as in the scene around the Christmas table), and with the figure of Monica/Mickey, the sisters' best friend who occupies the place of a third daughter, as if she was a stand-in for the son.

Despite its artless minimalism, Distant Voices Still Lives is quite a complex "psychoanalytic" narrative, insofar as it is a drama of identifications, of a subjectivity refusing to settle into an identity and hence pervasive and unfocused on a single character. Its floating point of view compares interestingly with the multiple perspectives of Dennis Potter's The Singing Detective, a more flamboyant use of psychoanalysis for the purposes of piling on fictional doubles and generating out of them a many-layered narrative. At first sight the diametrical opposite of Davies' spare, formal snapshot memories of nightmares and traumas, The Singing Detective, with its overt play on TV and movie genres, does share with Distant Voices Still Lives an equally intense vision of boyhood anguish and emotional confusion around sex, death and domestic violence. For The Singing Detective coheres not so much around the various incarnations of Phillip Marlow now, then and as his own wish-fulfilling projection, but around the incomplete identification of a boy with his father – this time a weak, ineffectual one – in order to work out erotic ambivalences towards the mother – this time not victim of male violence but sexually active temptress and femme fatale. It may be argued that Potter uses this version of the Oedipal trauma (with the

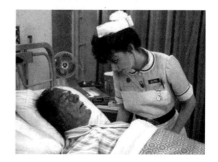

The Singing Detective

scope it gives to verbal aggression and paranoia) as no more than a narrative ploy, a sort of Rosebud motif, signaling a mother's betrayal, constantly activated by scenarios of violent death. But what seems significant is that in both films the emotional appeal of popular music can be joined to the most basic of psychoanalytical plots.

In Distant Voices Still Lives the outcome is a narrative about the narrowness and emotional intensity of working class lives as stylized as a medieval mystery play. In The Singing Detective it results in a structure of projections and narrative doublings credible and coherent enough to dovetail the most disparate of genres: film noir, emergency ward drama, wartime memoir and thriller spoof. Some powerful unifying fantasy seems to be at work, which the non-linear narratives of Potter, Davies and, I would add, Greenaway can explore without naming it outright. That the issue may have to do with male narcissism, and with the possibilities of identification across both gender and generation is even hinted at by Boorman, when he describes what would have been his ideal casting for Hope and Glory: "My own daughters would play the aunt's parts, and when they told stories of me, my son Charley would act me as a boy. I would do the role of their father, my own grandfather. It would be incest as an art form."

The Son's Seduction and the Sphinx's Riddle

For this dimension to come into view, Greenaway's film seems to me exemplary. But in order to "read" the narrative of DROWNING BY NUMBERS for its emotional tensions and the inner logic of events, one has to accept that the boy Smut and Madgett the coroner might be one and the same person, just as the three Cissy Colpitts are manifestly three stages/phases of a woman's life, *in relation to men*. The fiction works through a fantasy in which the son imagines himself seduced by the mother, in order to help eliminate the father. In one sense the "son" yields and complies, as Madgett does, forever in hope of the desired union with the Cissie Colpitts. But he also identifies too much with the "father" to make this solution to the Oedipal dilemma a lasting one. The first murder, of Jake in his tin bath "naked as the day I was born" is both the killing of a drunken old lecher and an act of maternal infanticide. No wonder Smut (a child grown age-less with adult knowledge) tries to protect himself with rituals, obsessively re-hearsing his own anticipated fate. His elaborate animal and insect funerals are particularly telling, because at once archaic and transparent attempts at master-ing, through repetition, the anxieties of loss, the fear of the mother. Greenaway leaves in no doubt what sort of fetish mastery is at stake: to please his teasing and inquisitive playmate, Smut not only sets about circumcising himself with a pair of scissors; at his funerals he also lights phallic rockets stolen from one of the symbolic fathers, who is drowned as punishment for brandishing – in a scene that dispenses with symbolic ambiguity – a yellow (!) ice lolly in place of his member.

By the logic of this Oedipal fantasy, the triple murders are not perpetrated by the women (which rather improbably would associate them with the law of numbers and the comfort to be found in series). Instead, Madgett's complicity in the drownings complements Smut's funerals, and projects the compulsion to repeat onto the Other as a way of getting a grip on his own manhood. After all, the nature of the son's desire dictates that he should want to rub out his rival(s). But in order for the narrative to have its cake and eat it too, agency is displaced, guilt feelings transferred, and fear is recovered as the pleasure of acquiescing in the inevitable. Smut ceremoniously invents a final game whose beauty lies in the fact that the winner is also the loser, and Madgett, abandoned in his boat, awaits his fate, abundantly prefigured throughout – not least in the many characters, places and incidents associated with the dying words of artists and kings.

As a consequence of these moves and subterfuges – and this may account for a measure of unease and bafflement – the Colpitts' actions seem necessarily gratuitous. The fantasy attributes mysterious powers to women, in fact, knowledge of the Grand Design itself, but the plot leaves their motivation whimsical, scurrilous, irrational: a vague and arbitrary conjunction of dissatisfaction and opportunity. As soon as each has fulfilled her role as agent of Madgett's secret fear and wish, Greenaway dismisses them into mythology. It is at this point that the motif of death by drowning merges with its opposite: undoing birth, returning to the womb, trying to reconcile the woman's desire for the "son" with her indifference towards the "father." She is the vessel of impartial and violent Nature, a solicitous and even sorrowful executioner, the guardian of life no less, whose element is water, the coastal regions and the tidepools of invertebrate existence. Indeed, a reading of the names leaves all the main protagonists confined to the lower rungs of the evolutionary ladder: Madgett/maggot, Cissie Colpitts/cesspits, Smut ...

Clerical Necrophilia

Greenaway may be reviving the sentimental romantic antinomies of life versus art, creative chaos versus rational order, and investing them with an equally romantic gender division, but he knows that he is implicated, and shows it. His trademark as a filmmaker after all are clever conceits, grids, numbers, exhaustive taxonomies, invented statistics, serial permutations – drawing by numbers indeed. Greenaway would probably agree with Raymond Queneau: "the secret vices of my life are erudition and bad puns."[2] In DROWING BY NUMBERS such mental binges are, more self-deprecatingly than in previous work, laid bare and opened for inspection.

"Games help his insecurity," says the eldest of the Colpitts about Madgett, and spells out why he and Smut are such obsessive players. In their bachelor household, unable to sustain a productive rapport with the environment, they play competitive games with Nature, as in the one called "Tide and Sheep," where Madgett tries to master, anticipate and replicate, in a grand and self-condemning gesture, the rhythm that epitomizes the female cycle. Likewise, Madgett's "Dead Man's Cricket" is played as a diversionary maneuver, to detract, during the youngest Cissie's wedding party, from various sexual antics and murderous appetites. Both occasions make game playing gender specific, the somewhat pitiful, pathetic response to the unruly rule of conspiracies, asso-

ciated directly and indirectly with female demands. Thus, another reading of
the names hints at how women become the objects of male fear and aggression:
the Madgett/magic that makes them into Colpitts/culprits is the law of numbers,
the rules of the game – what the production notes, in a phrase one assumes is
Greenaway's, call the "clerical necrophilia" of both father and son. Self-appointed administrators of death, they play games, accept coincidence even
when it comes in series, indulge the scientific or the taxonomic impulse in order
to hold on to the notion that what escapes them – women, nature, and sex – can
be controlled by rules, if only they are spelled out clearly.

Cadavres Exquis

Exposing his intellectual vices to the conflicts of male fantasy must have seemed
for the director a tempting impulse of exorcism, or an even subtler form of self-
satisfaction. For the spectator, perhaps, this only works if Greenaway shows
himself as vividly committed to the beauty of his visual material as he is to the
colder eroticism of his heroes' bachelor machines, dismantled with such brittle
sarcasm but also melancholy in both A ZED AND TWO NOUGHTS and DROWNING
BY NUMBERS. In this his incurable romanticism for rural England – here the seascapes, the Suffolk idylls, the windswept, eerily lit night scenes – stand him in
good stead. If the modernist apotheosis of romanticism was indeed surrealism,
then one can see why Greenaway qualifies for French enthusiasm. Superficially,
it is the Delvaux landscapes, the de Chirico still lifes, a beach house as fantastic
as a Magritte, or dead fish tagged with numbers that evoke surrealist imagery.
But there is more than a hint that Greenaway can distil some truth beyond the
painterly pastiche out of situations that appeal to a surrealist imagination of
matter, when for instance, one of the Colpitts pours lemonade over her husband's manual typewriter and then dusts it with sugar. The incident of two cy-
clists falling over a mound of bovine carcasses that suddenly block the road
could – together with the seduction that ensues – have come out of a story by
Bataille, and cinematically harks back to the Bunuel of L'AGE D'OR, as do the
snails (from DIARY OF A CHAMBERMAID) and the self-strangulation with a skipping rope (from VIRIDIANA).

What, however, makes this sensibility less urbanely cinephile and cosmopolitan, and the more haunting and disturbing for it, is the residue of boyhood anguish and raw hurt, underlying the ironic stoicism so ostentatiously on show. In
Greenaway's world, a loner, a solipsist, invents for himself a paranoid world –
his heaven and hell – where everything connects, but the design, once revealed,
points inexorably towards the self's own undoing. If the draughtsman's grid,

the games and rituals, the architect's blueprints or Madgett by numbers, are so many ways of demanding a stay of execution, and keeping at bay some darker agents of chaos (be they the double-headed monsters of fertility and decay, or the mafia-like machinations of the art world and the film business), what is more terrible and at the same time reassuring than to discover beneath the chaos a deeper rationality, intentionality and design? They can, it seems, only be faced, as in Borges' *The Garden of the Forking Paths*, Kafka's *The Castle*, if the flash of recognition illuminates a scene of sacrifice. In DROWNING BY NUMBERS the final firework lights up a funeral: a doubly apt metaphor, recalling another filmmaker's definition of his craft, Jean Cocteau's "the cinema, death at work."

(1988)

Notes

1. "Interview with Peter Greenaway" *Monthly Film Bulletin*, December 1985, 365.
2. Raymond Queneau, *Chene et Chien* (Paris: Gallimard, 1937); vi. Greenaway's games and puns also call to mind W.D. Auden's opinion that "good poets have a weakness for bad puns."

Border-Crossings

Filmmaking without a Passport

Peter Wollen's FRIENDSHIP'S DEATH

Amman, Jordan, "Black September" 1970: the Jordanians are determined to dislodge the PLO from its city-center strongholds. Among the journalists caught in the crossfire is Sullivan (Bill Paterson). Sympathetic to the PLO cause, he is asked to identify a woman (Tilda Swinton) picked up without passport or papers. Sullivan pretends to know her, and takes her to his hotel, where she discloses that she is an extra-terrestrial, code-named Friendship, and sent from the galaxy of Procryon to make contact with advanced members of the human species. Due to a malfunction during atmospheric entry, she lost contact with her base, and landed in Amman, instead of at the Massachusetts Institute of Technology.

After some hesitation, Sullivan decides to accept her story, alternately plying her with alcohol and pumping her for information, intrigued by his feelings for a creature who is a perfect simulation of a white Anglo-Saxon woman.

Friendship, meanwhile, less and less interested in her mission, becomes absorbed in the street life of Amman and the moral paradoxes arising from an incident at the historic ruins of Jedash, where her Palestinian guide is taken hostage by the Jordanian army.

Sullivan uses her absence to search her room, where he takes a handful of colored crystals, which that night begin to glow and emit sounds. Friendship, alerted by him, explains that the crystals are electronic note-pads, and lets him keep one as a memento. The following day, the house-to-house fighting has

FRIENDSHIP'S DEATH

reached the hotel, and Sullivan is able to obtain two passes for Damascus. But Friendship refuses to go: as a robot without a home or a recognized history, her closest kin are the dispossessed Palestinians, whose fate – whatever it might be – she wants to share.

It is in fact a meeting years later back in London with his friend Kubler from the International Red Cross (Patrick Bauchau) that has reminded Sullivan of Friendship, whose death during the September massacres he assumes as certain. His teenage daughter, a computer wizard, asks for the crystal and is allowed to test it with some new equipment. One day, she plays it to her father as a videotape: body-scan images, shots of Amman, strange colors and shapes come together in Friendship's accidental testament: a message without a code, from a sender without an addressee.

In the early 1990s, at a conference in Vancouver about avant-garde, modernist, anti-narrative and neo-narrative filmmaking, Peter Wollen proposed a new category: films without a passport. What at the time was may be a lassitude with labels seems in retrospect to have been a programmatic announcement. Wollen's first solo film as a director is literally about existence without a passport, and is much more an exploration of the attendant state of mind, than a psychological study of two characters or of the generic complications resulting from a sci-fi plot in a polit-thriller. The alien is first of all a presence, a being not (yet) mapped onto the usual grid of coordinates, and by that very fact calling these coordinates the more forcibly to mind. Friendship – the creature and the concept – asserts a reality "in-between": the human and the extraterrestrial, the sentient and the programmed, between male and female, political ally and lethal enemy, but also between voice and image, living memory and recorded, reproducible data. She/it promises a bond, a relationship capable of overcoming the antinomies.

The story development is minimal, and once the initial situation is established, the film concentrates on the philosophical paradoxes and speculative possibilities of a world where despite palpable and ubiquitous warfare and violence the image and the simulacrum are the sole reality. If Friendship's "fully axiomatized ethics" are no help when she realizes that all her "programs have crashed," she does develop a peculiarly terrestrial sensitivity which puts her in agony every time Sullivan pounds the keys of his portable typewriter, and makes her phobic at the sight of room-service wielding a vacuum cleaner.

Maybe a little too much of the film is taken up by verbal exchanges about history and geo-politics ("politics has nothing to do with people, and all to do with maps – a war is the romance of territory") into which machine-gun wielding snipers burst, firing rounds out of the hotel room window, forcing the couple to raise their voices in order to remain audible. These "Brechtian" strategies leave as a marginal filigree the two (non-convergent) trajectories: that of the man, in whom a momentary intellectual confusion gives way to erotic fascination, culminating in the (inevitable) search for the sexed body and its secrets; and that of the "woman," self-contained and detached towards the man, amused by the human physiological apparatus. As she gradually works her way from intellectual puzzles to the micro-political reality of her situation, hers becomes, as one would expect, the more interesting transformation. Apart from learning about male facial hair, body fluids, and the ingesting of liquids (where she shows herself a keen student of Levi-Strauss rather than Chomsky, picking up the semiotic potential and social codes attached to drinking tea or whiskey), Friendship collects objects which she finds in the bazaar, such as crafted bric-a-brac, tourist souvenirs, a bicycle pump. The no-longer-quite-contemporary commodities of our culture in the Third World appear as the trophies of a kind of archaeological dig, seen through alien eyes ("back home we have earth-experts who love every detail about your planet").

Yet this alien gaze is also very familiar; it recalls the nostalgic-surrealist sensibility of a Walter Benjamin ("I thought ruins are the past, but now I see that they belong to the present" Friendship says), when matched with contemporary tastes in domestic decor. After only a few days in Amman, for instance, Friendship's hotel room looks uncannily (and no doubt deliberately) like a SoHo loft or the modest but discerning Islington flat. Much of her story, however, is told through her clothes. First appearing to Sullivan in the PLO tent nattily dressed in a sensible blouse and a pair of well-cut trousers, she quickly "orientalizes" herself, acquiring an extensive wardrobe of ethnic dress, until she finally bids him farewell in the khaki guerrilla outfit made famous by Leila Khaled. Wollen's camera, with much respect and discretion towards Tilda Swinton, who effortlessly conveys the gradations between college innocence abroad, ironic fairy godmother and fiercely independent spirit, plays on a whole history of pictorial eroticism, from the Flemish masters via Ingres to the androgynous extravaganzas of early 20th-century set design.

TOPAZ

Filmic references abound, too. The "war-and-philosophy" passages recall 1970s-Godard, the motif of the journalist in an identity crisis is reminiscent of Antonioni's THE PASSENGER (co-scripted by Wollen), and the sudden overhead shots in the hotel room evoke the oppressive vertigo of similar shots in Hitchcock's DIAL M FOR MURDER, NORTH BY NORTHWEST and TOPAZ. Given this cinematic progeny, FRIENDSHIP'S DEATH is anything but mere cinephile pastiche. At first glance deceptively simple and even austere in its *kammerspiel* format, with detached scenes and confined interiors more like the adaptation of a play than the short story from which it is taken, Wollen's film is a concept piece rather than a chamber piece, a crystalline structure for which film, like the video-tape into which Friendship's image-block is decoded, must remain a rather inadequate material support. Hence perhaps the more pertinent parallels are with that other film without a passport, Chris Marker's SANS SOLEIL. Perhaps less poetic in its interplay of voice and image, but equally committed to a political vision of life, FRIENDSHIP'S DEATH gives a rare glimpse of what an English tradition in this most difficult of genres, the film essay, might be capable of.

(1987)

Andy Engel's MELANCHOLIA

On a dull Friday afternoon, in a smart flat somewhere in London, the German art critic David Keller (Jeroen Krabbé), morose and slightly drunk, receives a mysterious phone call from a man claiming to be an old acquaintance. Intrigued, David calls back later that day from a public phone, to discover that "Manfred," a fellow political activist from '68, needs David's assistance in a political assassination. A Chilean military doctor and former torturer, Adolfo Vargas, is visiting London for a conference, and his death is meant to protest against the reprieves recently given to known torturers in Argentina and Chile. David is too taken aback to refuse. Books, pamphlets, and documents about Chile under Pinochet arrive at his publisher's which stir and trouble his conscience.

A week later, he meets his ex-lover Catherine (Susannah York) for dinner who, for reasons of her own, encourages him to take up again his project of writing a novel. She even offers him the use of her banker husband's farmhouse in Tuscany and an allowance. His publisher, too, supports the idea ("as long as it's not a fat best seller"), and David calls "Manfred" to receive details of Vargas' intended movements.

On the third Friday, "Manfred" (Ulrich Wildgruber) turns up in London and accosts David outside the ICA. He tells him the assassination is off because Vargas, to save his skin, is prepared to expose details of US involvement and is therefore more valuable to the cause if left alive, especially since he will probably be eliminated by the people he has betrayed. David seems relieved. He meets Catherine at Harrods' and later that evening is driven back to his flat by Catherine's teenage daughter, an anti-vivisectionist, who asks him what he thinks of direct action. David replies that he used to support "violence against property" but now believes it only achieves the opposite aim.

The next morning, he is awoken by a call from Sarah Yelin, the widow of one of Vargas' victims and Manfred's Chilean contact. After hearing that the plan was to be abandoned, she had flown to London and now demands to see David. They meet at the Serpentine Gallery, and Sarah (Jane Gurnett) accuses David of moral cowardice, giving him a harrowing account of how Vargas had forced her to watch her husband being tortured to death. David tries to comfort her and agrees to go ahead with the plan.

On the fourth Friday, David watches Vargas (Saul Reichlin) arrive at the airport, follows him to his hotel near the Tower of London, and contrives to gain entry into Vargas' room, by posing as room service. He kills Vargas with a metal pipe previously removed from some scaffolding near Tower Bridge. Making it seem like burglary, David, after replacing the piece of scaffolding, escapes undetected. With Vargas' money he buys a ticket to Florence, but in fact seems to have taken the train to Hamburg, where he arrives on a Sunday morning. He calls the number given to him by Sarah, and arranges *to meet "Manfred" at his office, a law firm where he is a senior partner. "Manfred" harangues David for his stupidity and sentimentality, before ordering him to leave. David picks up a marble ashtray and brings it down hard on "Manfred"'s head, killing him instantly. Having carefully removed all fingerprints, he makes his way out of the deserted building. In Florence, he meets up with Sarah who is horrified when she hears what happened in Hamburg. David leaves her, and the next morning, another Friday, sees him, by himself and not answering the phone, closing the shutters of the windows in the otherwise deserted farmhouse.*

"Einmal dem Fehlläuten der Nachtglocke gefolgt – es ist niemals gutzumachen" (Following a false alarm even once, it can never be undone). With this quotation, from Kafka's *A Country Doctor*, over the persistent ringing of a telephone, Andi Engel closes his first film. This is an evocative sentence, resonant with irony, at the end of a stylish, elegant and quite enigmatic film. Is the false alarm the siren call of '68 and the promise of the Revolution, or more literally, is it the ringing of the telephone, which starts off and drives the narrative, recalling the hero to his own past: student activist, lover, a person of compassion for the suffering of others and a passion for Joseph Beuys? Why the division into a near week of Fridays? Christ, Judas, and the stations of the cross? Maybe the phone is trying to summon David Keller back to life, to face the consequences of having shut himself up, at first in his well-appointed gallery ghetto of art criticism, and then in the Tuscany writer's retreat?

MELANCHOLIA raises serious and timely questions: about politics, individual morality, history, and memory, action and contemplation, loyalty to ideals, and the courage to admit to error. It talks about principles and expediency, means and ends, tactics and strategy, private sacrifice for the sake of shaking the public's conscience, and not least about the morals of the media, including the cinema. Melancholy in the past has been the privilege of kings, and the curse of men of action, in Burton it is the master-builder of utopias, and in Baudelaire it's the boredom that swallows the world in a yawn; for Freud it is over-identification with a lost love object and for sociologists it is alienation and anomie – a disease of the over-civilized.

What is not quite clear, however, is how seriously the film takes its hero, whether it finally throws him to the black dog of his misanthropic self-destructive introspection, or whether it accepts David's own identification with the stoic and possibly tragic figure of Dürer's engraving. The title, and the camera's fascination with Jeroen Krabbé's rugged and at the same time anguished face suggest the latter. Yet his surly self-pity and the fact that he has so little to say for himself in any of the key confrontations with the smooth strategist Manfred or the grieving but fiercely righteous Sarah, make it hard to give him the benefit of a genuine moral dilemma, or the nobility of an intellectual's *Weltschmerz*. In a sense, the real conflict is not between the art-lover and the activist, between Van Gogh and Chile, but between David, the sentimental nihilist, and those who think politically, whether Manfred, the smart lawyer in a tracksuit and a fat Mercedes, or Sarah, the front line activist of memory and suffering. These two political animals would appear to have a lot more to say to each other than either has to David, perhaps because they both use him as a tool. So why does he fall for it? Self-disgust, or morality's last stand? One wonders if he does not kill Vargas merely because he is too squeamish for what Sarah tells him about torture (the strongest scene in the script and impressively acted), and cracks Manfred's skull because he simply cannot stand to listen to more home truths about himself.

On these points, MELANCHOLIA is in something of a quandary: Chile, torture, and terrorist violence are "hot" issues, but this is a "cool" film. As such, it does not want to be another MISSING, UNDER FIRE or THE OFFICIAL STORY, with a

MELANCHOLIA

love interest, throat-choking emotions, and crowds of extras filling the locations; on the other hand, it is not satisfied simply exploring the hero's existential nausea, as it bleeds into post-modern indifference (which would mean leaving the threats vague, the conspiracies half-imagined and the torture mental). It is a problem one also feels in Chris Petit's or David Hare's recent films: plenty of atmosphere, spare, stylish sets, an excellent score and superb photography, but a story a bit too topical not to leave one hungry for tighter plotting, and pointed exchanges, like good old-fashioned TV-drama. What is the stuff that Vargas has on the US administration, what is the conference he is attending on? The film is also too focused on the central hero not to make one curious about judgements, values and motives (what was the relationship between David and Manfred when they were students, what would David have said to Catherine's husband, if he had stayed for dinner). Of course, these are illegitimate questions, but they do not creep up on one in the films of Wim Wenders, a major model for Engel, as it was for Petit. Engel manages to do for London what Wenders did for Paris and Petit for Berlin: make the landmarks of the capitals of Europe seems eerie and uncanny in their very familiarity. Like THE AMERICAN FRIEND, MELANCHOLIA goes to Hitchcock (via Highsmith) for its central device: the exchange of a crime for the sake of distracting from its detection. It also has the same ironic moral: the wrong man is usually the right one after all. At its best, there is indeed a sense of Kafka and Dostoevsky because once aware of his situation, David tries to make the crime fit the punishment.

But the thriller format has its drawbacks. It is very deftly handled, with moments of intense suspense. Yet the more efficient the suspense, the more the political and moral questions tend to evaporate. The film seems to side with David: it settles for violence when it cannot work out the issues. Hitchcock would not have missed giving the victim a chance to meet his killer, in order to show the shock of recognition at the moment of death, nor would he have spared the killer the embarrassment of murdering someone who had shown him a kindness or a courtesy a few moments earlier. Vargas by contrast is dispatched with the anonymous efficiency of an ox felled with a mallet. Engel no doubt did not want to make a Hitchcock film, or involve us in awkward kinds of identification. Instead, the ending recalls Antonioni's THE PASSENGER, in the way the camera abandons the hero. But by then, one suspects, that the director had abandoned him long ago. Let us hope that Andi Engel does not feel the same way about filmmaking, and that Kafka's bell means there is no turning back for him from this new calling.

(1989)

On The High Seas

Edgardo Cozarinsky's Dutch Adventure

Search the mind regarding Rotterdam, and what do you find? The biggest port in Europe, the spot market in oil, once in a while news of a spectacular drug bust. And since 1972, it is the location of the annual Rotterdam festival, haven for avant-garde, independent, and Third World films.

Rotterdam, 14 May 1940: The old town is practically wiped out by a German air attack. The fire is so fierce that even the canals are burning. Newsreel footage shows a lion calmly walking the streets, a refugee from the bombed-out zoo. Three years later, Allied bombers inflict more damage; and in 1944, already retreating, the German army mines the port and blows up more than four miles of docks and almost a quarter of the warehouse capacity. Today, the rebuilt center of Rotterdam resembles nothing more than the rebuilt center of any Western or German provincial capital: banks, pedestrian shopping streets and mournfully empty trams circling in front of the railway station. The reverberating ironies of the city's history have not escaped Edgardo Cozarinsky, author of the much acclaimed ONE MAN'S WAR. He has recently been making VOLLE ZEE (High Seas), shot mainly on location in Rotterdam and Amsterdam. But despite bizarre newsreel images and the choice of a country which can certainly contribute an oblique angle to recent European history, Cozarinsky's latest film is not Rotterdam, Open City. Nor is it an "archive film" as was ONE MAN'S WAR or the "do-commentary" he has just completed for the Paris Institut National de l'Audio-Visuel (INA) as a contribution to the forthcoming centenary of Jean Cocteau's birth (JEAN COCTEAU: AUTOBIOGRAPHY OF AN UNKNOWN, 1983). HIGH SEAS is a fiction film, a fantasy, one man's adventure on a journey of self-discovery or possibly self-destruction.

A Swiss insurance salesman finds himself in Rotterdam with his wife. After a quarrel at the hotel, they tour the harbor. Among the container vessels, tugs and oil tankers the hero spots a three-masted schooner, rocked by the wash of the incoming tide. But what catches his eye is the figure in the rigging – a woman with flowing red hair. She becomes the mystery and the obsession for whom he gives up wife, job, and firm land. Who is she? "The Flying Dutchwoman," as the production team jokingly calls her? An international arms dealer hovering offshore in a deceptively nostalgic craft? A bored rich widow with a weakness for handsome would-be sailors? Or simply the hero's projection, to compensate for a life that consists of guaranteeing against risks rather than taking them?

It is unlikely that the film will want to give a clear answer. As a story with sailors, and a European art film, HIGH SEAS makes one think of Welles' THE IMMORTAL STORY, of Demy, even perhaps of Fassbinder. In Wenders' THE AMERICAN FRIEND, the Dennis Hopper character has a tag line to the effect that he is going to bring the Beatles back to Hamburg.

Edgardo Cozarinsky, if pressed, might say that it is the spirit of Baudelaire or Rimbaud, of *Invitation au Voyage* or *Le Bateau Ivre* that he hopes to bring to Rotterdam. "If I wanted to be intellectual," he says, "I'd mention Karen Blixen. She was a much loved author when I grew up in Argentina. But actually, it's the memory of those Tay Garnett films from the 30s and 40s – HER MAN or SEVEN SINNERS – which gave me the idea of trying something that is simple, almost archaic, and at the same time suggestive of the images and emotions that filled our adolescence, when it was easy to grow restless after seeing a film and hunger for more."

Is he thinking of Technicolor matinées, Gregory Peck holding Ann Blyth in THE WORLD IN HIS ARMS, or Tourneur's ANN OF THE INDIES? "Everyone can bring his own favorite

HIGH SEAS

fantasies, the film won't get in the way of them, but I'm not aiming for a pastiche or a remake of anything. On the high seas, your sense of the horizon changes, and in the cinema anything is possible beyond the frame. I think of La Capitaine, which is what the woman is called in the film, as neither young nor old, but ageless. She's played by Willeke van Ammelrooy, an actress very well known in Holland. She was recently in Raoul Ruiz's ON TOP OF THE WHALE. For one of the other female parts I wanted a kind of younger Lotte Lenya, to suggest something of a Pirate Jenny atmosphere; luckily, they found me an actress from the opera, Cristina Hoving, who is in fact a completely different type, but as I now realize just right for the part. The one choice I absolutely insisted on was for the male lead to be played by Andrzej Seweryn, a Polish actor now working in Paris. He has a quite remarkable screen presence, and the film was very much conceived with him in mind."

Since coming to Paris, Seweryn has mainly acted in the theatre. He was in Patrice Chéreau's PEER GYNT, a production of Bulgakhov's MASTER AND MARGHERITA, and is currently rehearsing for the new Peter Handke play which

Wim Wenders originally directed in Austria. He has worked with Andrzej Wajda both in Poland and in France. He was a secret police officer in MAN OF IRON; acted in THE CONDUCTOR, and had a part in DANTON. He speaks French with great assurance, though there will be a moment in HIGH SEAS when, as a naturalized Swiss, he will revert to his native Polish. "But it's not going to be a political gesture or refer to recent events. The character I am playing is in search of freedom, and that is a very general concept. He has come to a dead end in his life, so he needs to explore himself in different ways. Being hired as a sailor by La Capitaine is a bit like the Forest of Arden or the Sea Coast of Bohemia in Shakespeare. Not a real place, but in the imagination."

HIGH SEAS is a Franco-Dutch co-production. By another deliberate and perhaps provocative irony, the French contributions – the director and the male star – are thus an Argentinian and a Pole. INA will mainly act as distributor in France and also hold television rights. All the other actors and the crew are

ON TOP OF THE WHALE

Dutch, as are the executive producers and the production company. The dialogue will be in English, translated from the French by Don Ranvaud. And to add another story to this Tower of Babel the company is called La Production du Tigre. Under its previous name, Film International, it produced Raoul Ruiz's ON TOP OF THE WHALE, and under its present name – possibly signaling a more aggressive strategy out of the festival and art-house ghetto and into the high streets – it is about to launch a one-hundred per cent English-speaking comedy with music called NAUGHTY BOYS, in the spirit of and with many songs by Noël Coward, written and directed by Eric de Kuyper. The moving spirits behind La Production du Tigre are Monica Tegelaar and Kees Kasander. They are part of a new breed of independent film producer which seems to thrive in Europe, putting together the most unlikely "packages" with immense resourcefulness, very little money, but occasionally with a gambler's instinct for what pays off.

The most successful of the "naughty boys" in the profession are no doubt Paolo Branco and Pierre Cottrell. Like them, Monica Tegelaar is finally convinced that the way ahead lies in making "studio system" films, with production values and box-office appeal, but on low budgets and tight schedules. Her happiest experience has been ON TOP OF THE WHALE, not only because it represented the Netherlands at more international festivals than any other Dutch film ever, but because "the shooting was so economical, fast and relaxed." Monica Tegelaar is Argentinian by birth and went to school in Geneva. For ten years she worked with the Rotterdam Film Festival and Film International before founding her own production company. Apart from La Production du Tigre, she also has a stake in two other companies, Springtime Films and a distribution company, Classic Films. Through the latter, she is reissuing Godard's films in the Benelux countries, and Springtime Films are due to produce a video film with Godard as well as a documentary of Robert Wilson working on his massive performance piece *Civil War(s)*.

Why is she involved in so many different companies? "It makes raising money just a little easier, now that government subsidies for independent film-makers are drying up, and not only in Holland. I can put money into production as an advance on distribution and thereby attract other co-producers. We can still make films quite cheaply in Holland, because many of our young film school graduates are keen to work in feature films and not just for television." It also helps those who do not want to go into the industry to keep their artists' bursary – a part of the Dutch government's cultural policy which the recession has not altogether eroded. HIGH SEAS, with its three-week shooting schedule, enthusiastic young crew and relatively expensive location shooting (the schooner alone cost £ 1,500 a day to hire), is the Tiger's biggest leap so far. It should certainly make it across the Channel and, who knows, maybe across the Atlantic as well.

(1983)

Third Cinema/World Cinema

An Interview with Ruy Guerra

Ruy Guerra was born in Mozambique and went to film school in Paris. He did much of his early film work in Brazil, becoming one of the founders of Cinema Novo. Even though his first film, Os Cafajestes *(1962), a key document of Brazil's cinematic renewal and the manifestation of a major directorial talent, was never publicly shown in Britain, his second film* Os Fuzis *(1963) was immediately recognized as a landmark and turning point. It succeeded in achieving the seemingly impossible: to present a fiction that is unambiguously political in its impact, articulated by means of a linear narrative that loses none of its dialectical logic for being cast in the mould of strict documentation. By contrast,* Sweet Hunters *(1969) met almost everywhere an uncomprehending audience, unprepared for a film that made no reference to cinema novo or Latin American politics.*

Using behavioral realism against itself, so to speak, in order to demonstrate the inescapably social nature and class character of apparently spontaneous behavior or of an

Ruy Guerra

emotional gesture, Guerra has been able to work within the mainstream tradition of the fiction film, while radically subverting the ideological context of that tradition. His films do not stop at reinstating the political dimension which Western narrative art over the past two centuries had carefully eliminated from its psychological and interpersonal picture of human existence, but – conscious no doubt of his responsibility towards a Latin America, which he made his second home – he creates, notably in The Gods and the Dead *(1970), the necessary climate of action. There, magical and mythological forces can assume the role of shaping values and structuring moral responses, indicative of the determining power of the imagination, which any political analysis ignores at its peril. Ruy Guerra still seems exemplary because he stands on the front line of directors capable of making the narrative cinema yield a complex and analytical filmic discourse whose reflexivity and cinematic intelligence underscore a political urgency rather than relativizing his commitment to action.*

The interview was conducted during the Cannes Film Festival of 1970.

Os Cafajestes (1962)

Thomas Elsaesser: Your first film was called Os Cafajestes. *What exactly does the title mean?*
Ruy Guerra: The word is difficult to translate. A "cafajeste" is somebody who flouts accepted moral values, who attacks a given morality by his anti-social or criminal behavior. "Cafajestada" refers to a mean and nasty trick.

Can you say a little more about the social background of the "cafajestes" in your film, because it seems that the actual dramatic conflict hinges very much on social and class differences.
That's quite correct. The plot is really about an attempt at blackmail which doesn't come off. One of the guys, played by Jece Valadão, is a typical "cafajeste", he belongs to the urban proletariat, and he goes round in a borrowed American car, so that he can at least pretend he is something better. He needs the car as a status symbol for his trade as a black-mailer. The "cafajestes" at a certain time were al-most a group with their own codes of behavior, dress, places they hung out in Rio. The interesting thing is that from a sociological point of view, their origins were very heterogeneous, there were young louts and layabouts who didn't have regu-lar jobs, there were professional criminals, pimps, but also millionaires, playboys, sons of the upper bourgeoisie. A lot of people who had somehow not managed to enter the circles of the old landed aristocracy. Oddly enough their aggressiveness

Os Cafajestes

and violence was almost always directed against women – either prostitutes, or women from the haute bourgeoisie. Most of these guys were very good-looking and had chances with women anyway, but they often picked them up just for the fun of humiliating them in front of the gang. A "cafajeste" was something of a specialist in knowing the emotional and sexual hang-ups of women from a certain social class and he was able to exploit them. The "cafajeste" in my film is determined to make the blackmail work because he wants to buy the car, so that he can mix with polite society and wouldn't have to hang round cafes any more. For him the car is a way of climbing socially.

What is the relation between him and his friend who takes the photographs?

The friend comes from a different social milieu, the bourgeoisie, he is weak and he obviously admires the causal ruthlessness of the other man and goes along with him. One thing one must bear in mind is the role of the beach in these circles. The beach democratizes enormously. People go to the beach in the morning and stay there until nightfall. It isn't segregated, it's open and accessible to everyone, and a lot of young men, many from the interior of the country, who come to the city to find work end up on the beach, because if they are good-looking they can make a living as professional male prostitutes and hustlers. Again, that gives them a certain social mobility, they get invited to fashionable parties.

What about the two young women?

They, too, come from different classes. One of them, played by Norma Benguell, is pretty well the exact counterpart of the "cafajeste", with only one difference that she has made it, or so the guy thinks when he tries to blackmail her, because she is the mistress of a rich bourgeois, her "uncle." And the other girl is the cousin of the guy who takes the photos, she is a well looked-after, sheltered girl, with a taste for adventure. The men are the aggressors, as it were, they take the initiative, but in the long run they are shown up by the woman who are both morally and emotionally stronger. Even when the women are the victims, they unmask the men in the process of being victimized, and this often defines the psychological relation between the sexes.

The film begins with the humiliation of a prostitute by the "cafajeste" who takes her home in his car and then throws her out at 2 a.m., so that she gets picked up by the police. Again, the central scene in the film is the humiliation of the girl when the "cafajeste" takes her to the beach, and after seducing her, takes away her clothes, so that they photograph her in the nude and use the pictures for blackmail. In what sense does she feel degraded by this?

She is being humiliated, but not because she's being photographed in the nude. What is humiliating to her is that despite the mutual degradation, she really did feel a certain deep affection for the guy, perhaps because she recognizes how alike they both are. She gives herself to him quite spontaneously, full well knowing what kind of person he is. On the other hand, she is strong enough as a woman – and beautiful enough – not to feel disgraced by being seen naked.

What comes across very strongly in OS CAFAJESTES is the sense that the characters are imprisoned in their social situation as well as in their very limited awareness of themselves. Their only course of action seems to be to torment and exploit each other emo-

tionally, in a rather savage manner, yet this nonetheless makes up their day-to-day rea-
lity and determines their outlook and their reactions.

Yes, and it is also the way they express whatever tenderness and affection they feel. Personally, I don't see a rigid division between good and evil in emotions and actions. The moral value of the characters depends very much on their motivation at a particular moment, the actual circumstances. In a sense, all the characters in Os Cafajestes are "degraded," but that is simply their primary condition, as it were, and it is only within this condition that good and evil take on any moral significance. Similarly, the character of the "Gaucho" in Os Fuzis is morally speaking a bastard, he cheats the unemployed peasants of their money, he enjoys humiliating the father who is forced to sell his daughter, but as the film progresses, other sides of him also become apparent, he comes to realize how much closer his own life is bound up socially – not morally, because he still despises them – with the villagers rather than with his former buddies, the soldiers. What interests me is how feelings of friendship, of love even, are born out of what in terms of ordinary values are morally depraved relationships. I also very much believe in a class-morality. But at the same time, I'm convinced that class-morality doesn't wholly define the moral stance of an individual. True, people are more defined by their class morality than by their individual morality. For example, when he is a lorry-driver and making a living, the "Gaucho's" behavior is very much that of his profession, but as circumstances make him slide down the social scale, a different moral behavior appears. This, obviously, cuts both ways. One has to guard against a certain moral populism. One can't say that the rich are automatically evil and the poor are good, what one can say, however, is that the rich, given their position, have a greater opportunity and perhaps even tendency to do evil than those who are poor. It is a question of class and not of morality. But here we touch a theme which stands behind all this, the question of power relations, and how they develop unconsciously.

Os Fuzis (1963)

Is Os Fuzis based on a historical incident, or how is one to take the subtitle "Nordeste,
1963"?

The film was made in 1963, and that's what it primarily refers to. The history of the holy man and the bull lies back quite some time, it happened in 1924, and the bull was eventually killed not by the peasants, but by the army. Nonetheless, the situation does correspond fairly accurately to a certain streak of mysticism and superstition still very characteristic of the Nordeste today. And the holy man who accompanies the bull was a man who had a definite political influence in the region, a kind of rival to the local politicians, because he promised a miracle, namely that rain would come and end the drought. These droughts, of course, are notorious in the area, and I wanted very much to convey the idea that the circumstances and conditions depicted didn't refer to some historical situation, but belonged very much to the present.

The structure of Os Fuzis *is very carefully worked out. Did the idea of a parallel action develop during the actual shooting?*

No, this is the way I planned it from the start. In Os Fuzis I was particularly conscious of the importance of the narrative structure, I wanted to find a form where I could integrate material which has an almost documentary character.

Os Fuzis

The paralleled action, with its two radically different dramatic rhythms does in fact, when taken together, suggest a political consciousness arrived at dialectically by the implicit rapport between waiting for the miracle that never happens and waiting for the lorries that take away the stockpiled grain and thus the peasants' hope of escaping starvation.

Obviously I thought a lot about this and I tried to convey it mainly through the film's structure. I attach a great importance to the structure of a film, and I work very hard on it, since it carries an essential part of the film's significance. I improvise a good deal on the set, depending on the decor, the material circumstances, the actors, and therefore I have to have a structure which is very solid and well worked out. Even though after the shooting I invariably consider the whole material anew in the cutting room.

Together with Rosi's Salvatore Guiliano, Os Fuzis *is often mentioned as the model of a "political" film, in the sense of a "politicized intelligence." It is often said that a narrative film cannot embody a critical awareness, and yet* Os Fuzis *seems to possess an undoubtedly dialectical movement and is nonetheless quite linear in its structure.*

First of all, I'm always very flattered when people compare me with Rosi, because I think he is an absolutely first-rate director, though I haven't seen that many of his films. Secondly, I think the argument about the impossibility of the narrative form is often wrongly put. For example, when Os Fuzis was first shown in 1963 people thought it a very difficult film, they thought the narrative was terribly devious, complex, and needlessly obscure. That's why it got into the cinemas only three or four years later. And yet the film today seems very clear, not to say simple. But at the time even I thought it was complex and complicated – the film really did cause me a lot of headaches. And because it was thought so obscure, I had a pretty serious disagreement with the producer. He wanted to cut out the bull altogether, and just leave the story of the "Gaucho" and the soldiers, make a straight action movie out of it, rather like a Western. It might have looked quite beautiful, but it didn't make sense to me anymore, there wouldn't have been any justification for making it, because the story of the soldiers and the village only takes on a significance in the context of the bull and vice versa. And for that reason the structure had to be linear and the form had to be narrative.

One often confuses in a film that which takes place in the character and that which the audience notices. It is not possible or even desirable that a character should have an awareness of a given situation which goes beyond what is psychologically or intellectually plausible. Or inversely, even if the character has, let's say, a fairly advanced understanding of the situation, this doesn't mean that the spectator can always follow. The action of the character give rise to something, admittedly, but in the spectator maybe it evokes quite a different reaction. And that's for example, what happened with most of the Italian neo-realist films, which show a really quite serious intellectual confusion. At the end of the film, there would always be a character who asserted that society was bound to change, whereas the spectator may not believe this at all, or at any rate have his doubts whether the guy in the film really knows what he is talking about. I always ask myself what is the rapport between the spectator and the character on the screen. I don't like characters who go beyond their own possibilities. If they do, they become false, and the emotional current between spectator and character is broken. In the case of Os Fuzis I did try to keep a certain political vision in mind, but its manifestations are necessarily complex and occasionally oblique.

In view of the ideological elements which make up a person's consciousness or psychology, what is your conception of "character" in a film?

I think there is a definite need to overcome a purely psychological cinema. I don't mean that there shouldn't be any account taken of what one might call the behavioral psychology of the characters. On the contrary, there is an emotion based on the psychological rapport between spectator and the character, and this rapport must be respected. The character must exist, he must have a mind, a sensibility, reflexes which transmit a whole range of emotions, and those emotions one has to take account of. What has to be questioned is the psychological interpretation of human structures and of society as a whole, which is too narrow and special an angle even when it comes to explaining certain specific and intimate human relationships. I try nonetheless to make my characters exist within a framework of psychological responses, that is, they can be accounted for psychologically in some measure, even if they cannot be interpreted and analyzed fully within this framework. What is dangerous is to reduce all action to the level of individual psychology. In Os Fuzis the characters are psychologically complex, and yet it isn't a psychological film.

How do you see the significance of the "Gaucho' in political terms, especially his act of revolt at the end?

It seems to me that the "Gaucho" in Os Fuzis is in the last analysis an example of false leadership. First of all, he doesn't belong to the masses, except under the conjunction of external circumstances, because from the moment he no longer has any money he has also run out of credit, and once he has lost credit he can't buy his drinks anymore, and it is at this point that he joins the masses, takes the side of the villagers, out of a sense of personal humiliation. But he isn't really someone who belongs to the people. Secondly, his revolt starts from a purely emotional gesture, he does not care whether the others might follow him or not, to be a real leader he would have to assume some kind of responsibility, and not just precede the villagers by a tiny step. That's why his gesture is a suicidal one, it's an act purely on the level of a moral conscience, so to speak, and not of revolutionary consciousness, and that's why he gets himself killed. At the time I was reproached for having given the film such a "negative" ending. People wanted to see the peasants follow the "Gaucho", take up arms, overturn the lorries, burn them, have a big shoot-out and so on., And I said, sure I'd like to see that too, but it has got to happen in reality, not in my film. Because in the film it isn't possible, it's false, given what the people are and the situation. That's how you get false revolutionary cinema, where things are shown on the screen which are not possible or not yet possible in real life. In a sense, too, such films are in danger of giving a false leadership.

SWEET HUNTERS (1969)

On the face of it, SWEET HUNTERS is a film very much concerned with "psychological" themes, the family, the more and more strained relationships between a bourgeois couple, their grown-up daughter on an isolated island. And yet, you have said that it isn't a psychological film. How do see it?

It isn't psychological for me in the sense that the characters do not communicate with each other, they don't try to comprehend each other on the purely psychological level. They all sense that what motivates them to act in the way they do lies deeper, they obscurely sense an unconscious charge that determines their attitudes and emotions. The woman, for example, without entirely being aware of it, follows a course, in her mind as well as in her actions, which converges and fuses with a whole network of cultural patterns whose existence within herself she had hardly suspected. She does things, she ritualizes her gestures without being aware of it, but in the last instance it's they that determine her as a human being. She goes further than the purely psychological, her impulses come from a deeper layer of her being. And in the case of Sterling Hayden the husband, it's rather similar. He is a man who has a theory about the migration of birds and is determined to prove it. But he comes to distrust somewhat his own motives and the utility of his theory, and therefore his behavior is tinged with a certain irony towards himself and his situation, he consciously adopts certain values which he knows belong to the past. That is why I used the Orff score, to emphasize the irony, the humor, and at the same time the way he takes things over-seriously. In the end he is obliged to act in a very definite way, which wasn't at all what he initially intended, his plans for himself, his conception of himself had been rather different. He suddenly has to make the relationship with his wife more important than his theory about the birds.

Do you see it as a film about the bourgeoisie?

No. Not about the bourgeoisie as such. It's a film about a bourgeois couple, true, but it's more a film about dissatisfaction – maybe about the kind of dissatisfaction that comes with being bourgeois? For me, it's ultimately a film about freedom – and love, or rather about the way these two things are connected. The couple are people who are enclosed in a bourgeois way of thinking, even on their island, outside their normal circumstances, and unconsciously, they are trying to break out, escape from their own situation. They are both deeply dissatisfied. He about his birds and the way he is not getting anywhere with his theory, and she is obsessed by an idea of love which she is not so much unable to realize physically – because she does eventually – but to make palpable, assume consciously and with conviction. So that the search for freedom joins that for love, but in this love there is a definite element of the vampire. Vampirism and love are closely allied for me, by the idea of blood, also destruction, even it's something new that arises, it passes through a stage of destruction of which the woman in SWEET HUNTERS is very conscious. She uses the fugitive quite deliberately, she tries to possess him, and even though he rejects this, she makes him almost cruelly dependent on her. Her impulse is so strong that in a sense she couldn't care less whether what she does is evil or not. Love in this film has a perfectly destructive side, and I wanted to bring out this egotism, which however isn't a moral one, it goes deeper.

I noticed that in your films people are always waiting, and the action is structured around the tension inherent in waiting. In Os Cafajestes *the two men are waiting at the fortifications for the girls to arrive, and you shoot the scene so that we feel their boredom as well as their restlessness. They are smoking, swallowing pep pills, wandering around, and all the time there is this tension, which is the more memorable for not being strictly "dramatic." In* Os Fuzis *the peasants are waiting for the rain and the soldiers for the lorries to arrive, and there the tension engendered by the two kinds of inactivity finally explodes in the "Gaucho" running amok. Finally, in* Sweet Hunters *the strain on the couple partly derives from the seemingly endless and to the wife also pointless waiting for the migrating birds to arrive. Is this in any way a personal theme, or do you use it as narrative device to produce this kind of potentially revealing tension?*

It's true, though I've so far never been quite conscious of it, that waiting plays an important role in my films. Individuals have quite different conceptions of time, the conditions of waiting draws out the impulse towards changing their life, or their situation, but I guess some people just wait in the hope that things do change of their own accord, and in this sense, the theme of waiting has a certain social basis, in that the people I'm most often concerned with in my films, large parts of their lives consist of waiting, there is a certain apathy which can suddenly erupt into violence. And maybe it has something to do with myself. Whatever the film one is making, whatever its subject – and even if one is making a so-called "political" film, say, like Os Fuzis, the themes one is treating are always pretty well the same, the same way of looking at the world, one's feeling for things and for people.

The imposed situation of waiting, then, seems very often to come into conflict with the inner drive of the characters to manifest themselves in action, so that there is dialectic in such situations between the objective social and historical conditions which you portray (which may be contradictory to the point of appearing static) and the subjective "psychological" experience of it by the protagonists. Is this a conscious differentiation you are making there?

I think so. The waiting has to come from the action itself, from the overall situation, and this makes for a very sustained emotional charge which I try to mobilize in the characters.

The Gods and the Dead (1970)

Your films contain a very striking use of music, not only the score in Sweet Hunters, *but also the music in* The Gods and the Dead. *What role does music assume in your films?*

Music for me is never used descriptively, but rather figures as a character in his own right. This is particularly true of the Orff score which was written to be performed and therefore already contained very visual element. Furthermore, Orff had done research on the rhythms, it's very telluric music, very much tied to the earth and the soil, and in a sense very African, and we tried to put the music as a kind of chorus, which looks at the characters, it ironizes them a little, while at the same time showing concern for their fate. Hence the music intervenes in the action with a great deal of violence, not so much to underline things, but to open up a character, as it were, and to give the spectator another angle on him.

I was struck by the scene in The Gods and the Dead *when Othon Baston kills the piglet. As the knife goes down the music sets in and the effect is to take the film into a different register, change its level of significance, modulate the flow of the action while it continues visually.*

Yes, that is it, it is as if the film was all of a sudden changing color or something like that. In The Gods and the Dead the music has again this function of a character, and except for one occasion, the music never terminates with the scene, but stops prior to it. This is because I always sense the need to get back into a more "natural" feel, in order to facilitate the change of scene or set-up. With music one is automatically in a more interior world. So the sequences always end on a "concrete" register, that is the physical action of the characters.

You seem to attribute a great importance to the rhythm of your films.

Yes. Partly because I have a great interest in music, partly because it's what gives a film its life. I work very intensively on the montage, at the same time very quickly, because I believe that the rhythm of work, i.e., the amount of time one takes over the cutting, will somehow be reflected in the film itself. If I give myself too much time, I come to posing myself false problems, and I often work 18 hours a day on the montage, so as to stay inside the film while I'm cutting it.

Mise-en-Scène

There is a certain fondness in your films of the straight line: a corridor, railway tracks, a deserted street which give your images an almost geometric shape. Has this any larger, structuring significance?

I work very hard on the individual shot, in its graphic pictorial sense. An image for me is a surface and an extension, which have to be organized by means of framing, getting the perspective lines worked out and so on. This affects the use of decor in relation to the action. But at the same time, there is a rather intuitive element involved. I have to respond positively to the decor, the environment before I can do anything with it, I have to feel a certain pleasure, things have to fall into place, and only when somehow this feeling doesn't produce itself, then I start thinking. And then I notice, say, that the perspective isn't right, that the background is flat, when in fact it ought to have an opening somewhere out on to an exterior, or that there is depth when what you want is an enclosed space, that sort of consideration gets a lot of my time. Decor for me is an interior dimension, which the action "exteriorizes." By this I mean that the behavior of a character manifests itself in concrete terms in the decor, even when he is immobile. And conversely, I use the decor in such a way that it achieves a maximum of rapport precisely with the "psychology" of the characters, without thereby making this behavior necessarily psychological.

In other words, your style, your mise-en-scène is a consequence of your themes, your dramatic intentions at any given point. I was very struck by the way you thematize the graphic elements in your film, for example, the way a straight line often corresponds to a certain impulse towards action, directed action, but then these lines also lose themselves on an indistinct horizon, as if this impulse towards efficient action was somehow annihilated by the vastness of the space surrounding it.

When I'm setting up a scene, there is a whole graphic pattern about the movements of the camera in relation to the action in my head. There are, so to speak, straight lines, crossed lines, tangents, curves, movements developing along one or several axes, so that both the action and the camera obey a certain graphic design. And this design results from the interaction of decor and character, locale and action.

You also seem to have a fairly pronounced preference for scenes where there is first a background, then a character enters the frame in the foreground from the side. What is the significance for you of this?

All my camera movements, except in very special cases, are *on* the characters, in other words, if there are two characters, the camera would never pass from

one character to another through an empty space, the camera never has a life of
its own, it's always linked either to a human field of vision or a movement. The
camera always follows something. This concretizes and gives at every point a
'full' action – even in the dialogue passages. I'm very conscious of plastic
values, of the value of space and matter. That's why I like to take my characters
from very close and at the same time place them in a real context, I don't like to
do a scene wholly in close-ups, because it gives a sense of abstraction which
bores me. Of course, there are always exceptions for special cases, where such
an abstraction is what one is looking for. My whole vision of things is to be very
close to the characters and very close to the decor at the same time. Hence the
fluctuations, the to-and-fro of the camera between long-shots and medium to
close-ups. Also, speaking of the distribution of volume and mass, I often frame
characters in outline, because I think shape and size can sometimes say more
than a glance. You see, in this respect, I'm not at all psychological. I think a
facial expression may tell the spectator less than, say, the outline of someone's
shoulders.

*Does this correspond in your opinion to two levels of the image – the level of presence
and that of consciousness, as one finds it in certain American films, where the background, as it were, exteriorities the characters' inner life?*

   Given that I always try to escape from individual psychology and to render
an emotion, I'm inevitably obliged to think about how to portray the reflective
dimension of a character. I very much like to accentuate an idea which happens
inside the characters with something real in the exterior world which can render
this idea in a direct and immediate manner. Giving the knife to somebody is
giving him death and in THE GODS AND THE DEAD I show a dead guy in the
corner of the room. This is concretizing an interior aspect. If I can find something in the decor which can give me that, be it a geometrical line, or a perspec-
tival alignment, or an opening to a door, or on the level of color, say I work with
the red of the girl in THE GODS AND THE DEAD, then that's fine. I'm very rigorous on the level of the shooting script, I never make a camera-movement or
shoot a shot which is simply descriptive, for which I don't feel the inner necessity. That's why I never simply pan because that's what I would call descriptive.
I only make camera-movements which are linked to a structure of thought.

*You mentioned that you are interested in rendering emotion. It seems to me that the
'emotion' you are interested in not only plays between the characters on the screen, but
sometimes, even aggressively, between the film and the spectator. I'm thinking in particular of the scene OS CAFAJESTES, when the two characters drive endlessly in circles
round the naked girl. The scene is particularly revealing, I think, because in a certain
sense, it is almost a metaphor of the whole film; just as the car – and the camera – circle*

interminably round the girl prostrate on the ground, so the film seems to dig itself deeper and deeper into this situation of a pointless emotional violence which finds no issue in action. The scene seems quite deliberately to go on beyond its point of maximum dramatic or psychological impact, it becomes to the audience a kind of poignant anticlimax, which implicitly defines the mood of the rest of the film.

I'm glad that the scene comes across like this, because I wanted that its primary connotation should be a physical one, and people at the first showing were in fact almost squirming in their seats, saying stop, stop, that's enough. But I wanted to translate the psychological significance of the situation into actual duration.

There is one scene in Os Fuzis, where I think this ambiguous physical involvement of the spectator conveys perfectly the contradictory nature of the experience portrayed. The scene I'm referring to is the love scene between Mario and the girl, and to me it's one of the most complex and at the same time "realistic" love scenes in the cinema. The girl, torn between the most violently conflicting feelings, driven along this barren corridor between two houses, feeling disgust at Mario's complicity with the casual murder of the shepherd, and yet also a strong physical attraction and an infinite need to have some human contact in her bleak world, the innate sense of class solidarity, of moral identification with her people, battling with the assertion of her emotional rights as an individual and woman, all this creates a powerful dialectic which the film translates into movement and duration.

I'm also very fond of this scene, I think it says precisely what it is intended to say. Obviously it's no accident that the episode takes place in the context of the wake for the guy, with all the contradictions implicit in this wake.

Brazil and the Cinema Nôvo

Like so many other scenes in Os Fuzis one gets a strong sense of how necessarily interrelated are the economic situation, military and political institutions, religion, the social and the sexual basis of power structures. The film as a whole seems to be saying that these are all "values" that count in the progress and change in a given society.

I don't think one can imagine a transformation of Brazil, either of society as a whole or in respect of personality structures, without for instance taking into account the religious and mystical factor. I, for one, am not a believer, I'm an atheist and I've never had a religious crisis in my life. Nonetheless there is definitely a mystical streak in my nature, because I'm fascinated by what goes on the level of non-rational cognition, and I'm very attracted by magic and the whole spectrum of values associated with it. Ordinarily, these values are narrowed and reduced by organized religion, for in actual fact the manifestations of religious knowledge are much more diversified. The Brazilians have a religion, a black, "tropical" religion, and it is still deeply embedded in Brazilian society, even in the upper bourgeoisie. It implies a way of seeing things which one might call intuitive, but which I prefer to regard as part of the unconscious, the unconscious of the people. Obviously, in the unconscious of the Brazilian people, the mystical coordinate so to speak is very powerful and it's also the impulse that is most immediately present.

This may be one of the reasons why our films are occasionally rather difficult, because we often make films which do not solely start from rational events, but from the collective unconscious. Of course, this collective unconscious is very difficult to grasp and even more difficult to represent – it manifests itself in things that seem arbitrary or that lend themselves to different interpretations. From a certain perspective, our films seem a little hazy, but that is also their richness. They are rich, but at the same time a bit out of focus, as it were.

What has struck me about a number of Brazilian films I have seen is that they are very much concerned with bringing out a sense of vitality, an almost visceral optimism in the characters – but which doesn't easily find an adequate cinematic expression. To me it is often indistinguishable from rather theatrical hamming. In your own films this sense of a sustained inner dynamic appears far more integrated cinematically, an element of the mise-en-scène and the overall structure, rather than as something directly transmitted by the play of the actors and gestural histrionics.

In some ways I proceed in an inverse manner from that practiced by most other Brazilian filmmakers. They normally have their script written and then proceed to find a suitable location. I personally can't even start to write a scene until I have already found the setting. A scene exists to me – prior to finding the location – only on the level of the theme, everything else develops from the concrete setting. Dialogues change, gestures and movements change according to whether a scene takes place in a bathroom or the living room, because after all, in a film it is the actual material presence which shapes the rest, including the words.

One of the things which must change when Brazilian films are shown abroad is the nature of the communication between film and audience. There is, apart from a different gestural language also a different rhythm, often a rather languid one, which tends to go against the grain of conventionalized cinematic expectations. Are there other than temperamental reasons for this?

It is difficult for me to answer this, but I think it comes both from a different conception of the cinema, i.e., a deliberate protest against certain forms of cinematic discourse and from a different idea of life itself.

When you make your films, do you have a very clear idea of the expectations which the public will bring to the film?

When I started making films, I said to myself – up to the fifth film you'll experiment and after that it's for real. I still think this is somehow true. There has to be a kind of personal research, there are things one has to get out of one's system. So far, I have always made the kind of film I wanted to make and in the manner in which I wanted to make it. Even if this manner of working has proven to be very costly for me. I have always stuck to it nonetheless because filming gives me an enormous pleasure, and I'd very much like to leave it that way and not turn it into a professional chore. Right now I feel that I have acquired a cinematic language which belongs to me in that it conveys efficiently what I want it to express. Also, I now know the technicians and the crew with whom I can work in this direction, which is very important. In other words, I feel I have the human material and a lived experience that allows me to make films the way I want.

Presumably, the Brazilian public, like any other public, is rather habituated to the Hollywood cinema?

That's for sure. Mind you, on a certain level, the Brazilian public has other keys of comprehension and communication as well, but nonetheless, it remains equivalent to the "international" public created by Hollywood. As far as I am concerned, I have certainly been influenced by this tradition to some extent, especially the films of the 30s and 40s, which was really an astonishing period. When I went to the movies in South America, naturally it was mostly Hollywood films, and what I learned was a certain efficaciousness on the primary level of characterization, a certain economy in the dramatic narrative, a great justness of tone ... all the vitality of a cinema of action – and these are things that the Americans seem to be losing under the influence of the European cinema. The great names of the 30s – say Raoul Walsh or King Vidor – these were directors who had a sense for the natural qualities of the decor and the material and that is what they embodied in their narrative. There is something else (I'm currently trying to re-see some of the movies of that period) which strikes me very forcibly. Normally one thinks of the American cinema as given over entirely to action, but as a matter of fact, these films are often based very much on the spoken word, and the mise-en-scène is so dynamic that it virtually absorbs the word, so that even in the most verbal scenes, one's feeling is that of a very sustained and continuous action. There is no doubt that this cinema not only has a very strong appeal for me, it has also to a considerable extent formed me as a filmmaker.

*I think the sense of a sustained and at the same time carefully controlled inner dyna-
mism is what communicates strongly in your own films, even when, as in* THE GODS
AND THE DEAD, *because of the language problem, a lot of the plot escaped me. One
immediately feels that what is happening is important, not because it creates a field of
energy to which the whole composition and the setting responds. Maybe this electrify-
ing quality partly reflects your interest in the machinations of power and the psychological rapport of force between individuals, and of course there is also the strong erotic
undercurrent in your films. At times in* OS CAFAJESTES, *especially in the night scenes
on the beach, I was somehow reminded of Dorothy Malone in a film by Douglas Sirk ...*

... oh yes, the one with the stunt fliers. And there is another one, with the
same actors, in color, a magnificent film – WRITTEN ON THE WIND. When *Cahiers*
reviewed OS CAFAJESTES at the time, they compared it to Vidor, and they mentioned RUBY GENTRY, which isn't altogether off the mark, since RUBY GENTRY is
a film I like a lot, the way it is constructed like a musical score round the piece
played by Walter Brennan on the harmonica. And then the scene of Jennifer
Jones and Charlton Heston in the car – it's the kind of love I was aiming at in
OS CAFAJESTES.

*Do you see a conflict between your interest in "political" cinema and your love for the
cinema of action?*

The misunderstanding about "political" cinema comes, I believe, from a
"symbolic" conception of hero and action, whereas the real problem for a filmmaker is to do his political thinking by way of perceiving inherently cinematic
material politically. In this sense, the American cinema is in fact "materialist" –
even if from an ideological point of view it is a very debatable cinema. A director as "reactionary" as, say John Ford, on the level of his cinematic language, his
portrayal of human relationships, in the justness of his treatment of the material,
he is a 'materialist'.

*In some of Glauber Rocha's films one finds that the rapport between the characters
themselves, and the logic of the action, too, are structured according to ideological or
anthropological categories of analysis, which for me, at any rate, leave the films paradoxically (given the director's manifest political involvement) quite non-committal.*

I'm convinced that what is important in the cinema is the emotion in the
spectator. It's part of the film-maker's material. And emotion, for the majority
of the public, cannot be given politically, not in a pure state. Intellectual understanding is no substitute for emotional comprehension. However, in a film like
THE LION HAS SEVEN HEADS I find that the "political emotion" so to speak, has
a direct echo in me, but I can well see that a lot of people are not susceptible
along this spectrum of values and responses.

What are the conditions, at present, under which the Cinema Nôvo directors can work in Brazil?

In view of the rapid development of the Brazilian film industry in recent years, with something like 120 feature films being made each year, there is now considerable aid being given to the cinema from official sources, but this aid is channeled above all into entertainment films for home consumption. On the other hand, the money is fairly intelligently distributed, so that we, the directors usually grouped as Cinema Nôvo (though this is by now merely a historical label), who after all have a certain reputation both at home and abroad – which is very valuable for the Brazilian government – have access to funds, in spite of the fact that our work is none too kindly viewed by the authorities for what we say about Brazil and the image we give of it. This leaves us a somewhat ambiguous freedom, especially since the money is merely advanced. It has to be repaid, and if we can't find distribution or we are having trouble with the censor, then the credits can be stopped and pressure be put on us. So there is a definite economic censorship on top of the political one which limits one's room for maneuver. But so far there have always been ways of overcoming this, and as long as we can, we carry on.

(1972)

Ruy Guerra's ERENDIRA

In the desert, the tombstones of Amadis and Amadis Jr. Nearby, the mansion where orphaned Erendira is the domestic slave and companion to her tyrannical grandmother. The two women are the sole survivors of a once-powerful dynasty of robber barons and smugglers. A litany of daily chores comes to a sudden end the night Erendira leaves the candelabra too close by the open window and a desert storm sets the curtains on fire. The mansion burns to the ground. As she sells the remains to passing traders, the grandmother vows that Erendira will have to repay her every peso of the loss. Erendira's only assets being her youth and beauty, the grandmother decides to sell the girl's virginity to the highest bidder. She then sets up a tent, in front of which an even longer line of men take their turn.

Erendira's fame soon becomes legend, and the grand-mother announces that a mere eight years seven moths and eleven days will cancel the debt. But as fate has it, Ulises, son of a Dutch farmer and an Indian mother, falls in love with her, pleading with Erendira to plot her escape. The lovers are caught by the combined forces of a vengeful grand-mother, Ulises' father and the police chief. Eventually, Erendira finds refuge in a convent, learning to be a bride of Jesus. Bribed by the grandmother, a young man enters the convent and marries Erendira during the nuns' Holy Communion. Once more the main attraction of the fairground tent show which has sprung up in the desert around the shrewd matriarch who buys immunity and influence, the padlocked Erendira becomes the gift for a night for the mel-ancholy commandant of the nearby town. Ulises, in the meantime, has stolen three of his father's golden oranges, each containing a huge diamond. But Erendira does not

ERENDIRA

want to escape and she challenges her lover to kill the grandmother. A birthday cake filled with rat poison gives the old woman even more unusually vivid dreams at night, while the only visible effects are the large tufts of hair clinging to her comb in the morn-ing. Scolded by Erendira, Ulises places dynamite in the grandmother's piano; the explo-sion destroys the tent and its contents, but the triumphant grandmother merely calcu-lates the damage and adds it to the debt. Shamed by Erendira's contempt, Ulises finally stabs the monstrous woman, who dies in a pool of green blood. By the time Ulises re-

covers from the struggle, Erendira has seized the grandmother's vest with the gold bars and made for the desert, leaving nothing but her footprints in the sand.

Basing himself on Gabriel Garcia Marquez' own adaptation of his short story *Innocent Eréndira and Her Heartless Grandmother*, Ruy Guerra has made a film where the poker-faced political intelligence of a Raoul Ruiz disguises itself in images reminiscent of Fellini's matriarchal fantasies. ERENDIRA is above all a fable of the futility of revolt, the vampirism of love, and the vicious circle of exploitation, violence and betrayal which binds the generations and the sexes to the political status quo. Marquez's cruel fairytale of evil grandmothers, innocent maidens and a Prince Charming who three times bungles the rescue can be interpreted variously as an allegory of a world where innocence only survives corruption once it consents to utter degradation, a postmodern pastiche of all the clichés associated with Latin American machismo popular culture, and even as a feminist rewriting of Western mythologies in the manner of Angela Carter.

The film, on the other hand, opts for a more playful, indulgent and at times even sentimental evocation of Latin Grand Guignol, fleshing out the fable with

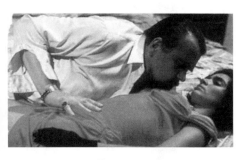

ERENDIRA

bizarre detail and heavily ornamenting the political implications with surrealist dream images and satirical cameos. Michel Lonsdale as the morose town commandant, affects all the languor of a grand bourgeois out of late Bunuel. Irene Papas in the role of the grandmother raving in her sleep like Ophelia, while during the day she is tougher than a drill sergeant and more ferocious with her tongue than the shrew in a Dickens novel, satisfies every schoolboy's idea of female severity and monstrous menopausal power.

ERENDIRA has all the marks of an exile's film: the nightmarish but also tender depiction of a childhood world, staged in the closed and overheated setting of the imagination, lovingly recreating details and situations which, if not recalled from a safe distance, would be too painful to treat with so much pardoning generosity. Ruy Guerra was probably last seen as the proud Indian ruler Pedro de Ursua dispatched to his death by Aguirre in Werner Herzog's 1972 South American epic. He belongs, however, more properly to the Brazilian Cinema Nôvo of the 1960s. Together with Glauber Rocha and Nelson Pereira dos Santos, Guerra initiated a way of making political films without abstracting from the layer of myth and superstition which they saw as constitutive of revolutionary consciousness in an underdeveloped country.

Although more attached to a realist idiom in his early films (Os CAFAJESTES, Os FUZIS) than Glauber Rocha (BLACK GOD WHITE DEVIL, ANTONIO DAS MORTES), Guerra shared especially in THE GODS AND THE DEAD the Cinema Nôvo's awareness that Latin American countries are doubly exploited: materially and through the so-called popular culture purveyed by the mass media. The conviction that political cinema has to work with and through the stereotypes of a sedimented, adulterated and now largely synthetic popular imagination is still present in ERENDIRA, but mellowed by an ironic awareness of the failure of Cinema Nôvo to make an impact anywhere other than at international film festivals and with European art cinema audiences.

Subsequently, Guerra worked for many years in Mozambique, helping the newly Marxist state to develop its own educational television and training students in filmmaking. ERENDIRA signaled Guerra's return to France, and the film typically is a French-German-Mexican co-production destined to be used up on television. A luxuriating pictorialism is at work that could easily have become suffocating were it not for the unfailing exactitude in the timing of each scene or gag, where the director's intelligence manifests a cool control even where it lends itself to the obsessions of another man's mind.

(1986)

Hyper-, Retro- or Counter-

European Cinema as Third Cinema between Hollywood and Art Cinema

Flashback to the Sixties

> Fifty years after the Russian Revolution, the American cinema dominates
> everywhere in the world. There is not much to be added to this fact.
> Nonetheless we should, each according to his abilities, start two or three
> Vietnams at the heart of the immense Hollywood-Mosfilm-Cinecitta-Pine-
> wood Empire. Economically and aesthetically, on two fronts, we must fight
> for national cinemas, free, brotherly, comradely and joined in friendship.
>
> Jean-Luc Godard 1967

Even before Jean-Luc Godard urged filmmakers in 1967 not to make political films but to make films politically, the question of an "alternative cinema" was on the agenda of European directors. While some filmmakers were looking to formal, experimental, non-narrative traditions, Godard's notion was that of a counter-cinema, implying a film-politics that would challenge the economic supremacy of Hollywood, its monopolistic distribution and exhibition system in the countries of Europe, but also in the Third World.

The moment for a radical break was opportune: renewed interest in avant-garde filmmaking during the 1960s and 1970s coincided with a period of stagnation and structural changes in Hollywood which led to large-scale mergers, takeover bids and board-room struggles for the control of the industry's assets, acquired by multi-national companies like Gulf and Western or the Kinney Corporation, whose main interests were in oil, canned food or real estate.

Not least because of a general decline in the cinema as a form of mass entertainment, but due also to lighter and cheaper filmmaking equipment, post-war Europe had seen the emergence of a number of "new" national cinemas with an art cinema orientation: Italian neo-realism, the French *Nouvelle Vague*, the New German Cinema, for instance. By the mid-1960s, the moment was also propitious to another kind of cinema in Latin America, partly modeled on European auteurism, but partly also poised to be a political cinema, influenced by Marxist or Maoist perspectives such as those voiced by Godard. As so often in the history of post-colonialism and the liberation struggles, a European-educated intellectual and artistic vanguard sought to forge links with indigenous sources, often a combination of folk culture and the classic 19th-century European novel.

For this independent cinema after 1968, as well as for the political avant-gardes, the relation between Hollywood and Europe, between Hollywood and Latin American cinema tended to be conceived as radically and absolutely antagonistic in both theory and practice. Filmmakers borrowed their metaphors from the vocabulary of oppression and exploitation, and occasionally, as in the case of Godard, from the class-war. In Europe, the revival of political and formalist avant-gardes corresponded to a desire to abandon the notion of a "national" cinema in favor of an international(ist) radical modernism. But in the case of Glauber Rocha and the Cinema Nôvo in Brazil, or the Peronist cinema of Argentina, anti-Hollywood could also mean self-consciously nationalist cinema echoed in Godard's anti-imperialist appeal.

From Anti-Illusionism to Hyper-Realism

But Hollywood, art cinema and Third World cinema are communicating vessels. By the mid-1970s, most of the initiatives – to join forces with political movements on the ground, as in the case of Glauber Rocha in Brazil; to break out of the isolated cottage-and craft manufacturing that is typical of the avant-garde filmmaker, as Godard had tried when he co-founded the Dziga Vertov Group; or to win a cinema-going audience to an alternative practice, as with the New German Cinema – had all suffered setbacks with the remarkable recovery of commercial Hollywood. Indeed, the self-consciously national cinemas of Latin America saw themselves courted mostly at international festivals, where they became part of a European radical chic. Much the same happened to the New German Cinema: a modestly successful export item on the art cinema circuit, it was massively supported by government funds and government agencies, but showed no signs of rallying domestic audiences to its own films. It was American movies, the package deal and post-industrial production methods which became more than ever the dominant model on both European and world markets. The new independent cinemas, whether national, politically internationalist or author-based, gradually found themselves forced into coexistence on the Americans' own terms, or vanish altogether.

Insofar as spectators returned to the cinema (in most Western countries the mid 1970s registered an upward trend in box office receipts), it was to watch

Hollywood blockbusters. With enormous profits for the industry came capital investments in new technologies, notably computerization, special effects, and the improved sound reproduction made possible with the Dolby system. Such technical innovations were themselves the consequence of new promotion and marketing strategies. By borrowing from related entertainment industries like

CLOSE ENCOUNTERS

the music business, Hollywood was able to attract a different generation of spectators, whose pleasures derived from the thrill of film technology itself: these were better served by hyper-realism and simulation than by "Brechtian" anti-illusionism or distanciation. Special effects, displayed in horror movies and sci-fi epics like STAR WARS, CLOSE ENCOUNTERS, ALIENS, or BLADE RUNNER, to a certain extent "deconstruct" classical narrative cinema by shifting the pleasure of representation from verisimilitude and realism to fantasy and the self-referential play of illusionist codes, while eight-track stereo or Dolby are not innovations that create a greater realism for the ear, and instead, they advertise the presence of a separate sound space dedicated to creating a highly charged, imaginary sound experience. It wasn't a counter-cinema that superseded Hollywood, but a New Hollywood whose development was neither governed by the modernist telos of the medium's self-realization through self-reflexivity, nor by the political logic of opposition and confrontation. Instead, it followed the capitalist logic, which demanded the penetration of new markets in the wake of the activity generated by the interplay between technological innovation, media advertising, and mass-produced, cheap consumer electronics. In this strategy, even avant-garde techniques could find profitable uses, and as a consequence, one critical dimension of film theory – reflexivity – was thrown into crisis, overtaken by the dynamic of transformation and change that realized the agenda of self-reflexivity, but devoid of radical political potential, and with sometimes immense popular success.

The International Market

Given the extent of Hollywood's revival, it is clear that the balance of forces between Hollywood and European independent, art or avant-garde cinema could not continue to be represented as pure opposition. If the term "international market" draws attention to the economic realities of film production, in the competition for the world's spectators, national cinema disguises another term because an auteur cinema will often be more opposed to its own national commercial cinema than it is to Hollywood films. The *"politique des auteurs"* or "cinephilia" are based on such preferment. But in other respects, films are commodities like any other. While the Hollywood product dominates most countries' domestic markets, as well as leading internationally, each national cinema is both national and international, though in different areas of the cultural sphere. Nationally, art cinema participates in the popular or literary culture at large (the New German Cinema's predilection for filmed literature, the intellectual cult status of French film directors, the acceptance of Fellini, Antonioni, or Francesco Rosi as "artists" and Italy's sacred monsters). Internationally or transnationally, each national cinema used to have a particular generic function: a French, Swedish or a New German film set different horizons of expectations for audiences, but which are inverse mirrors to the genre expectations suggested by a Hollywood Western, a science fiction film or a comedy, but which are equally essential a prerequisite for name recognition beyond the director: the firmer a national cinema's generic image, the better (for) the brand.

From the perspective of Hollywood, on the other hand, it makes little difference whether one is talking about the Indian cinema or Argentinian cinema, the French cinema or the German cinema: none of them is a serious competitor for America's domestic output, but each national cinema is a "market" for American films, with Hollywood practices and norms having major repercussions on the national production sector. In most countries this has led to different forms of protectionism, bringing into play state intervention and government legislation, but usually to very little avail, especially since the different national cinemas, however equal they seem before Hollywood, are of course emphatically unequal among themselves, and locked into yet another form of competition when they enter an international market.

The situation has often been described as a form of cultural and economic colonisation, whose dialectics have been analyzed in Hegelian terms of master and slave (Jean Paul Sartre, Frantz Fanon, Amilkar Cabral), in terms of a national Imaginary (Anthony Wilden, Benedict Anderson), or as a particular form of miscognition, as in Fredric Jameson's Lacanian formulation of "the politics of otherness". It can even be figured as an unsuccessful Oedipal challenge, where identification and antagonism are two sides of the same coin, competition with Hollywood leading to an emulation of the American model, as with Latin films ironically or lovingly quoting mainstream cinema (Hector Babenca's Kiss of the Spider Woman, or Ruy Guerra's gangster musical, A Opera do Malandro, based on Brecht's *Threepenny Opera*).

The Vernacular Force of Television

In the debates of the avant-garde around hegemonic Hollywood and a counter-cinema, the oppositional tactics elided another crucial term, namely television, which during the period in question had itself become the dominant cultural form of visual representation, in relation to which both Hollywood as well as the avant-garde had to re-orient themselves. While Hollywood did so, re-emerging within television as a major attraction (the recycling of "movie classics," of stars and cult figures: in short the start of a whole new film culture), the avant-garde was unable to mount an effective challenge to television. Video art has had to retreat to the museums and galleries in order to find any public space at all. The national cinemas of developing or post-colonial countries – despite theorists and filmmakers successfully giving them a new identity as "Third Cinema" – have had to struggle even on the festival circuits. Insofar as some filmmakers who had been identified with political, avant-garde or independent cinema were able to secure state funding or the co-production of television, they were able to continue to make films, but perhaps at a price. Sharing a segment of the general movie-going audience, at least in Europe, these filmmakers became international "auteurs" which is to say, double agents for a cinema, which knowingly pastiched or cleverly inverted movie mythology. Though under contract to Britain's Channel Four, Italy's RAI, France's Antenne Deux or Germany's ZDF *Das Kleine Fernsehspiel*, they could upgrade their television co-productions via film festivals to the status of (art) cinema.

The relative failure of the various avant-garde movements to give roots to an "alternative cinema" thus cannot simply be explained in political terms. The demand for a different depiction of reality has, for most people, been fulfilled by television. But the relation of television to the cinema is precisely the one least accepted by the avant-garde, since it is not based on opposition or struggle, not even on competition, but more on co-option and appropriation. Thus, it cannot be seen in categorical terms, but only as shifts, as intertextuality in an expanding, constantly self-differentiating field.

In this field, Hollywood cinema retains its pre-eminent position because of the totalizing effect which Hollywood has had on national as well as international cultural production – be it in the field of information, art or entertainment. It is either a world language because it dominates trade in both film and television, or it is a "universal language" in its period of decline (like Latin during the Middle Ages), of which television represents the vernaculars: feeding off the classical, but also treating it as merely one more specialized language among many others. Such a role is particularly striking in developing countries. US, Italian or Brazilian soap operas watched in the slums of Rio de Janeiro or

Bogota by people who have neither jobs nor homes, can give the illusion of unity, of belonging, cohesion and participation to a social body that in any other sense is utterly dysfunctional, antagonistically divided and segregated where media spectacles become political, by their very negation of the political, while the political becomes a mere variant of televisual forms of participation (game shows, talk shows, quizzes, phone-ins).

One of the consequences might therefore be that the relation of national cinemas to Hollywood, of television to national cinema, and of national cinema to counter-cinema should be thought of as a series of palimpsests, a sequence of texts, each rewriting other cinematic and pre-cinematic spectacles in the form of intertextual narratives, each restaging the "primal scenes" of specularity and self-alienation itself. I want to explore this a little further around what seem to me two exemplary encounters of the European art cinema with Latin America, an encounter across which a whole history of the image as political may be reconstructed. Francesco Rosi's film CHRONICLE OF A DEATH FORETOLD, after a Gabriel Garcia Marquez story, and Werner Herzog's COBRA VERDE (after a novel by Bruce Chatwin) seem to me to illuminate this particularly complex relation quite concisely.

Francesco Rosi and the Death of a Hero

CHRONICLE OF A DEATH FORETOLD, the story of a vendetta killing, is, according to Rosi, "about a crime that is atrocious and unacceptable. Not because of destiny, but because a whole town abdicated the responsibility to prevent it." On the face of it, this is a good description of the genre Rosi has made his own: political thrillers from SALVATORE GIULIANO and HANDS OVER THE CITY to LUCKY LUCIANO and EXQUISITE CORPSES, inexorably revealing beneath the individual case the conspiracy of silence, the cover-up of crimes and corruption by state bureaucracies or even whole communities. But by the same token, it is an odd summary of Gabriel Garcia Marquez's short novel, and even more so of Rosi's own film based on it because there is no sense of moral outrage towards the characters, and no enlightened distance separates the camera's view from the social mores that make their behavior possible. On the contrary, the code of honor which demands an eye for an eye, and a life for a hymen, becomes, in the course of the film, the language of a deeper wisdom, not so long ago regarded as politically reactionary: the necessity to preserve a tragic sense of life.

The twin supports of Latin culture, in Marquez as in Rosi, are male machismo and the power of mothers. Both are in secret collusion with each other, energizing a field of force that, whatever its cruelty and barbarism, appears ennobling because it raises the stakes in the battle of the sexes to the point of giving the illusion of the two being evenly matched. This is the case in Rosi's CARMEN (where the heroine shouts at her suitor: "I tell you, once I love you, José, you're a dead man") and in CHRONICLE, where the fiancée of one of the unwilling avengers declares: "If you fail in your duty as a man, I shall never marry you." Such a predilection for the double-binds of (hetero)sexuality make one wonder whether Rosi's earlier social commitment has mellowed into melodrama? CHRIST STOPPED AT EBOLI and THREE BROTHERS were investigations in which a sense of history emphatically endowed the tales of private passion unfulfilled, of personal memory and inner struggles, with a political place as well as a geography. In CHRONICLE, by contrast, the investigation into the murder (which could have opened up to history and politics) soon peters out, even if auspiciously inaugurated by the heavy-lidded Gian Maria Volonte scanning the faded colonial follies lining the embankment under a gray-blue sky.

There is firstly the fact that Volonte's presence fades before the flashbacks, the reminiscences and images crowding in on the witnesses still willing to talk such as the old housekeeper, the priest, or the retired mayor rescuing the court records after a flood and hanging the pages on a clothes-line to dry. Secondly, the luxuriant vegetation with strange birds breaking cover as a boat drifts past their nesting places seem to turn the characters themselves into exotic creatures whose present is a time of auguries and premonitions, their past the timelessness of myth or the fatality of an ancestral curse. What is enigmatic about the chief protagonists Nasar, Angela, or Bayardo is not some secret they harbor, but their beauty, which makes them mere surface, deflecting any mystery of motive or intent into pure being, at once out of time and doomed, as the clichés about youth, love and death – to which they owe their existence – have it.

Thus disarmed, the investigation shifts to the chronicle, with its different temporality and different causality, and no presiding consciousness pretends to put the events into an orderly procession. So why, even though only a *fait divers*, does the story assume an epic sweep? Thanks to a very complicated chronology, an interweaving of fragments, tableau-like scenes and oneiric set pieces (like Bayardo's overgrown house with his sports car rusted down to the wheel base, where Angela and Bedoia finally meet face to face), CHRONICLE OF A DEATH FORETOLD becomes a Faulknerian "tale told by an idiot," almost a sort of CITIZEN KANE or RASHOMON set in the swamps of Colombia. A dense forest of symbols linking white birds, white pages, and dead letters, a repetition of motifs around the arrival of a stranger, the return of a prodigal son, and the blessings of a bishop, create the impression of messages only half-deciphered and allegorical depths never quite plumbed. Equally plausible, though, is the realization that the complex narrative may have craftily constructed an echo chamber for a single note: that passion has to be utterly spent before it becomes livable, that youth and beauty have to be sacrificed before they become a thing of value, and that the present has to be the past before its sound and fury become significant.

In some respects, this means that CHRONICLE is an old man's film, its moral anger appeased, its traditional truths and fundamentally tragic stance legitimized by the simplicity of its lyricism, and the naturalness and generality of its symbolic conflicts. But the starkness of the folk epic is also deceptive: if, on the one hand, the film depicts the power of honor (archaic, implacable, senseless and therefore impervious to either enlightenment or religion) and, on the other, the power of women (represented as confined to the cunning of biology and reproduction, and therefore strong because capable of crushing both conscience and individuality), the real threat to this world is the power of money, especially new money.

As embodied in the figure of Bayardo, money kills, not so much because it brings corruption, violence and greed to a community, and therefore upsets what one might call the ecological (or feudal) balance between servitude and security in "primitive" economies (a favorite theme of the Spaghetti Western), but because it devalues everything it touches: the lottery and its prize, the rituals of courtship and love, the old man's house and his memories. With this, a deliberate displacement of the political seems to have occurred in Rosi's film. Colonialism and its moral economy are an issue not because an alternative (political) economy can be their judge, but because a First World metaphysics of value implicitly proposes a kind of ironic counter-ecology to the economics of post-colonialism. How else is one to make a film about virginity in Colombia, a country notorious for its export of cocaine, the white substance from the Third World that dominates the Second and First World's black economies?

From Neo-Realism to Magic Realism

One of the more puzzling things about CHRONICLE OF A DEATH FORETOLD is no doubt the presence of Rupert Everett. As a character in a fictional story, he is barely present. Even by the end, we don't know who he is, where he is from, or what he wants. With so passive a part, it is difficult to accept him as the star of a major international production. But as a screen icon, he is almost too present, his image telescoping several generations of Hollywood masculinity. He wears his Stetson and lounges in his rocker like Henry Fonda in MY DARLING CLEMENTINE, the camera lingers on his figure as it does on James Dean in GIANT, or it frames him with the obsessive symmetry reserved for Alan Ladd in SHANE. At times he contemplates his doomed splendor as if he were the Great Gatsby himself. The role dissolves into poses, narcissistic and non-functional in the narrative. Is this a flaw in the acting, the consequence of a production with an eye to the market, using up a face while it's still in the news, or is it a sign of a mutation in the concept of the European anti-hero who has become the clone-hero of jeans ads and beer commercials? In other words, are we watching a European art film, a Hollywood movie, or a Third Cinema poster-modernist co-production? In either case, Rupert Everett is an interference, the element that troubles the codes, which is of course what, in a sense, Rosi's film is all about.

For even though Rosi is not Wim Wenders indulging in cinephile citations, or Martin Scorsese exorcising the ghost of Jerry Lewis or THE HUSTLER by an elaborate mirror game of fictional projections and Oedipal moves (as in films like KING OF COMEDY and THE COLOR OF MONEY), there is a sense in which the older generation of European directors like Resnais or Rosi, look into the same mirror of movie myths, but from the other side, through nostalgia rather than cinephilia, with the myths affirmed because they are irrecoverable, where the younger directors reanimate them by clever pastiche, by ironies and cross-references. When Rosi ends his film with the dead man spread-eagled on the ground in the exact the pose made familiar in his own SALVATORE GIULIANO he seems neither ironic nor playful, merely advertising that a certain language of cinema, as a commitment to, say, critical or investigative realism, has definitively entered into myth. Opting for the "magic realism" of Marquez thus becomes for a European director of Rosi's generation neither a commitment to a political counter-cinema nor a Latin-American director's pastiche of folk-elements, European modernism and Hollywood kitsch, but a complex displacement: revisiting his own (European, Italian) belief in realism and the structure of investigation, he encounters a Latin American mythology across which he hopes to reconcile the fact that the Left in Europe since 1945 has been nostalgic for a past that the Conservative Right had already dismantled. Not unlike Visconti in THE LEOPARD more than two decades earlier, and Bertolucci in NOVECENTO, Rosi, like them a man of the Left, discovered that he understood the values of feudalist regionalism better than those of a national bourgeoisie making common cause with international capital.

SALVATORE GIULIANO

Werner Herzog: Tarzan or Parzifal of the Art Cinema?

Werner Herzog is one of those filmmakers who with rather fewer films than Rosi has created exemplary heroes, even icons, not least because here, too, there is a blurring of the boundaries between actor and role in his films, though apparently quite different from the Calvin Klein pin-up Rupert Everett. Klaus Kinski, an old professional and a trained actor, and Bruno S. the "natural," have both become permanently identified with the parts they play in Herzog's films, a fact that suggests that there is a deeper bond between the meaning of their archetypes. At first sight worlds apart as the eternal underdog and eternal over-reacher, Bruno S. and Klaus Kinski are brothers underneath the blundering and blustering egos: they are the two sides of Kaspar Hauser: one, the child abandoned by the father, the other the child abandoning the father to pre-empt being abandoned. Where Rosi pastiches machismo and matriarchy, Herzog focuses on two complementary aspects of the same crisis of patriarchal values: the failed submission to, but also the failed rebellion against the symbolic order. Whether supermen or victims, however, Herzog's protagonists are always extreme, marginal, and outside, in relation to the center, which is the social world, the world of history, that of ordinary beings. Thus, the existential dimension of his characters seems to take precedence over any social ill against which they might revolt or from which they might suffer.

Behind Herzog's heroes stands the figure of Hercules, doing other people's dirty work, as well as Prometheus, who tried to steal from the Gods, bringing fire down from the heavens to the benefit of mankind. The role of scapegoats, of self-tormented egomaniacs can thus easily be related to the basic Western myths and their derivations. One of his first films, a ten-minute short called, characteristically, Herakles (Hercules) sums up this ambivalence succinctly. A body-building contest is inter-cut with scenes from a scrap metal yard where a huge machine is crushing automobile wrecks into handy parcels. Around this surreal collage, Herzog has packed the basic configuration of practically all his subsequent films: heroic effort and endeavor in a mockingly futile situation. This asymmetry is also what attracts Herzog to Latin American locations and figures, for behind the image of the superman fighting a losing battle with a world dominated by technology is the very possibility or impossibility of revolution, where the choice often seems to be between degeneration into anarchic revolt, or operatic self-display and exhibitionism.

Pauline Kael, aiming her poisoned arrow well, once called Herzog a "metaphysical Tarzan." Yet if the figure refers to Herzog, it is not the man but the manner of his filmmaking that is targeted. Although he never stated it as openly as Rainer W. Fassbinder, Herzog always wanted to be an international director.

Yet at a time when the cost of the average Hollywood movie reaches figures that equal the entire film production volume of most other countries, an independent director shoulders with each film the burden of reinventing not as Herzog is fond of saying, film history but the film industry. His seriousness makes up his capital, and his naiveté is his key production value. The poet Erich Fried, seeing Herzog in action at a New German directors' press conference, once called him "a Parzifal among the Tuis" (Brecht's word for mandarin intellectuals). But also a Siegfried: the preparations for a Herzog film resemble a military campaign, and for them he casts himself as both victor and vanquished.

Thus, it is the very real anachronism of independent filmmaking in the age of global Media Wars that is one of the buried themes of Herzog's work: not the least of the many ironies of championing individuals or groups who eke out their existence on the margins of the capitalist world is that the symbolic opposition between the weak and the strong, the underdogs and the over-reachers splits Herzog himself. The filmmaker has a foot in either camp, and often David is difficult to tell from Goliath.

Two of his increasingly rare feature films from the 1980s are no exception: behind the Aborigines' resistance to the Mining Company determined to drill for minerals in WHERE THE GREEN ANTS DREAM (1982) stood Herzog's determination to make a film about this resistance. And in COBRA VERDE (1987), Kinski's ambiguous pact with Brazilian slave traders and a mad African monarch is like Herzog's wily but also nervous deals with major American studios. Herzog, in a sense, is doing battle on his characters' backs, and they are inevitably also the foot soldiers thanks to whom the machinery of his own filmmaking can fight it out with the juggernauts of the commercial Hollywood industry.

FITZCARRALDO

The extent to which Herzog's filmmaking is both an act of allegorizing and of literalizing a particular situation could already be seen in FITZCARRALDO (1981). The film, it will be recalled, tells the story of an Irish rubber planter in South America, whose enthusiasm for Caruso makes him want to build an opera house in the jungle, if necessary by hauling a boat across a mountain and opening up a waterway that will generate the cash needed to finance such a scheme. Herzog has frequently talked about this project in interviews, ever since he completed KASPAR HAUSER in 1974. Clearly the film existed as a recognizably typical Herzog story well before production was underway. The idea of pulling a full-size river boat across a jungle mountain was entirely in keeping with the absurd and excessive bravado acts associated with Herzog's public persona. FITZCARRALDO furthermore created expectations that this would be a return for Herzog to the thematic terrain and exotic location of earlier Herzog films, such as SIGNS OF LIFE and AGUIRRE. The film could inscribe itself into a pattern of continuity and alternation that had already made the Herzog oeuvre into a coherent and unified project.

The actual filming was accompanied by an unusual amount of pre-publicity, although in the context of Herzog's habitual self-promotion, it was perhaps to be expected. No less than two films were in fact made about Herzog making FITZCARRALDO. The circumstances of the production itself provided ample copy for the newspapers: there was Hollywood type show-business gossip about difficulties with the leading actors, the replacement of Mick Jagger by Jason Robards, and of Jason Robards by – inevitably – Klaus Kinski. This made the film crystallize around Kinski and Herzog's obviously privileged but problematic relationship with this preferred actor, since he had already used him in AGUIRRE, NOSFERATU, and WOYZECK to portray the Herzog persona par excellence. However, more publicity was generated when Herzog came face to face with global concerns about rainforests, land politics and genocide. FITZCARRALDO was political news because it started a minor civil war in Peru, in a scenario only half-written by Herzog himself, touching issues about the debt crisis, the situation of the Amazon Indians, all of which exposed the dilemma of European liberalism when faced with the problems of population explosion, and the extinction of tribal cultures for the sake of "modernization" and economic development in Latin America. When FITZCARRALDO was eventually released, much of this publicity did seem to have an adverse effect, making it difficult to see the film without the accretions it had already accumulated. Some critics thought that one of the documentaries made on location about the film, Les Blank's BURDEN OF DREAMS was actually the more interesting product of the exercise, while the more spectacular scenes of Herzog's film had already been anticipated by the pre-publicity. That the production and its difficulties somehow became the real event, of which the film, when it finally appeared seemed merely the documentation is also par for the course when the cinema becomes infatuated with the reality of its own making of make-believe.

While FITZCARRALDO was thus the object of considerable controversy, Herzog himself seemed to think of it as a German *Heimatfilm* transposed to the jungle, a film about his own homeland Bavaria in other words, with a figure not unlike Mad King Ludwig who had built fantasy castles and had funded lavishly extravagant productions of Wagner's operas. Certainly Fitzcarraldo can be seen as an anti-hero, who, frustrated in his desire for social progress, turns to art and music, on a scale symmetrically inverse to his social standing and professional failure.

But this underlines the ambiguity of Herzog's recourse to Latin American locations: metaphoric constructions of a cultural "other" in order to say something about the "self" cannot be easily distinguished from a genuine concern and sympathy for the world's victims of the West. Meanwhile, beneath it all, there is always an allegory of the director himself. Having hundreds of Amazon Indians move a tugboat over a mountain is not only Herzog's idea of a perfect image for his own filmmaking, but maybe even of cinema in general: an obsolete technology with a (sweaty) human face. The slaver is always also a slave.

FITZCARRALDO was not the only film where Herzog's pre-production (like any Hollywood blockbuster) made headlines and was good copy, not only on the arts pages. The fact that the director had taken a camera crew to Guadeloupe in order to film the outbreak of a volcano was reported with bated breath. Although La Soufrière failed to blow, Herzog did deliver. Jan Dawson in a review of the film, wrote about Herzog that "gratuitousness [is] the single value he consistently celebrates" referring to the director's admiration for those who remained on the island threatened by a volcano, because rescue to them would only have meant another cycle of the exploitation that made up their lives. But if one can call gratuitous those acts of stubbornness and resistance that attract Herzog, one has to see them as a kind of blocking of the all-too-ready transparency of sense-making and sympathy which especially the television discourse bring to news, disasters and to current events.

In many of Herzog's films the poorest of the poor, the most deprived of Western civilization, possess strength of resistance directly proportional to the degree to which they are dispossessed. Is the spiritual freedom that Herzog seems to grant them a mere consolation prize for material rights that no one is prepared to concede, perhaps not even Herzog himself, who moves the Aborigines in WHERE THE GREEN ANTS DREAM before his camera in much the same way the mining company has them moved by the police?

Documenting a Fiction or Fictionalizing a Documentary?

Herzog has been called a visionary filmmaker, mainly because he contrives so often to suggest the possibility of a radically non-communicating, *stupid* relation between people and between things. Sometimes it is the encounter of a solitary character and an object or a scenery that touches off the pathos inherent in a "land of silence and darkness" even under a blazing sun: Aguirre and the jungle, for instance, Kaspar Hauser in the market square, or the woodcarver Steiner alone at the bottom of his ski slope. COBRA VERDE resumes many of these moments from other films, not least because Kinski is so evidently the amalgam of the underdog and the over-reacher, even more so than he had been in NOSFERATU or WOYZECK. One doesn't really need the hunchback in the bar con-firming that he and the bandit are alike in their contempt for the normal and their ca-pacity to dream the extraordinary, or the cripple on the beach shadowing Kinski's fu-tile efforts to launch his boat, in order to re-cognize in Cobra Verde all the Hegelian twists of master and slave, and the clown of power in a colonized imagination's magic realism. Because there can be no develop-ment in these nightmares of real exploita-tion and imagined identification, the heroes Herzog has created are usually more endur-ing than the stories they appear in. But what would Herzog be without Kinski, who is al-ways Kinski, which is to say, the living em-bodiment of the contradictions and collu-sions between Spaghetti Westerns, Cinema Nôvo, and New German Cinema?

KLAUS KINSKI

Insofar as his films are often associated with landscapes, Herzog does not al-ways escape the charge of celluloid tourism. Many of his early documentaries came out of his own experiences of travel which he, as much a child of the 1960s as other more self-conscious German filmmakers who took to the road, under-took to have a vantage point on his own country and its history: Germany being the subject he has conspicuously avoided to treat head-on. He has traveled to the Sudan and West Africa, to Greece and the United States, to Ireland and the Canary Islands, and more recently, to Latin America and Australia. There is, thus, in Herzog's choice locations, a curious and altogether typical mixture of uncivilized, primitive places, and some of the by now traditional holiday spots of affluent Europeans. His landscapes are of an ambiguous other(worldli)ness, most offensive to "political" tourists, but probably Herzog is no different from other filmmakers scouring the continents for natural production values at unna-turally low production costs.

Cinema of Pain and Toil, or a New Theatre of Cruelty

In a *Guardian* lecture promoting COBRA VERDE at London's National Film Thea-tre (7 April, 1988), Herzog confessed to a new passion for opera, hinting that he might follow the track beaten by other German directors to Bayreuth and Bologna, putting on *Lohengrin* for Wolfgang Wagner and Bussoni's *Faust*. He also told his audience that he makes no distinction between a jungle or desert setting for his films and the stage of an opera house. Both oblige a director to think big, and both allow the spectator to step out of reality. COBRA VERDE – being more deadly serious than Fitzcarraldo's rather harmless obsession with Caruso and an opera house in the jungle – provides a rationale for Herzog's startling assertion, insofar as the effort, enthusiasm, and resistance of the early heroes has become a theatre of cruelty and humiliation. The court rituals on the Brazilian haciendas, the military regime in the Fort, the customs and rites of the Royal House in Dahomey: so many ways of taking account of politics as spectacle, and the spectacle as politics. Opera perhaps allows for the self-display of subjectivity, even when the stakes are thus raised.

In an effort to close off one kind of transparency (that which classical narrative gives), a structure of meaning imposes itself on Herzog's images that can

COBRA VERDE

only be called Manichean, because if the level on which his films are meant to work is cosmic, then the issues he chooses are too politically urgent, and the cases too specific for the metaphysical fiction to become convincing. If on the other hand, Herzog documents in COBRA VERDE, even in reconstructed form, an actual case, then the fantastic anthropology of the African kingdom seems an unnecessary and irritating intrusion. The reverse side of Herzog's attempt to subvert the narrative cinema's inherent discursiveness by recourse to a documentary style becomes itself a form of discursiveness, an accumulation of assertions about his material, chief among which is that his characters are unknowable.

Herzog surrounds himself with people, primitive, innocent, or slightly mad, so long as their behavior, their use of language, their reactions and gestures communicate, unconsciously or by default a certain kind of reification, and on whom the pressure of a deformed life becomes visible. Through them he can represent in action the states of alienation, dehumanization and exclusion that are imposed by society. But what is this society? Sometimes it seems that for the sake of his films, Herzog turns himself into the instrument of this society, puts on the mask of ogre or clown, in order to simulate the conditions he sets out to document. There is, in other words, a poetry even of social anomie and alienation which Herzog's cinema cannot but recognize as an aesthetic value and with which it seduces the viewer.

Against a background of temporal decay, Herzog's view of history has always been tragic: he sees the flawed nature of his characters' rebellion, the radical innocence of their deformation, the resilience and perseverance they oppose to their situation. Perhaps it is this complex which attracts him to Latin American themes and settings, allowing him to displace a more personal and national experience, typical of his generation. For it is not difficult to diagnose in this double vision of heroes and victims, rebels and saints the trace of an Oedipal configuration to which Herzog incidentally alludes regularly in interviews. What emerges as its foil and subtext is the Kaspar Hauser complex: that of the fantasy of being abandoned, fatherless or having to survive between a good father and a bad father. The complex was prominent in the 19th century, after Rousseau and the French Revolution, when the "wild child" was a European-wide phenomenon, and it became a motif again after WW II, when many young men were forced to grow up without fathers. There is François Truffaut's gently autobiographical *L'Enfant sauvage*, but among West Germans it became something of a cliché, thanks also to Alexander Mitcherlich's *The Fatherless Society*, a Freudian socio-portrait of those born during or just after the war. Herzog's work shows a profusion of these kinds of good and bad fathers, as it also shows protagonists that embody the two aspects of the Hauser complex, the active and the passive one, or rather, the pre-emptive and the abject one. In Herzog, Kaspar Hauser is the mirror of Aguirre: one the active embodiment who abandons himself by an act of defiance from both God and his country, while the other finds himself abandoned, and draws from his condition the strength of having nothing to lose.

What the evidence of such an Oedipal configuration might clarify is the peculiar tension between the documentary attention to detail and exhibitionist spectacle that Herzog has contributed to contemporary cinema, although the tension is a fragile one and the sensibility it manifests is not in fashion. He substitutes the play of insufficiency and over-explicitness between image and commentary in his early films like FATA MORGANA with the many incongruities and incompatibilities between the natives and their sympathetic exploiter Cobra Verde. At times, COBRA VERDE appears to want to say something about Idi Amin or the Khmer Rouge, about the madness of regional politics under the pressure of the super-powers' global strategies. But Herzog might also pursue his own counter-strategy, detecting in the Third World Politics of the European Left an abused and vulgarized fascination with the imaginary "Other" at too little cost to its own comfort and moral security. As an expert in cultural and social "Others," Herzog has always insisted on the risks involved, and so he is more interested in dramatizing the act of self-representation as one which escapes the speaking

subject's control, than in passing judgement. What is politically intriguingly ambiguous about the figure of Cobra Verde besides the peacock strutting of cere-
monial power is the extent to which Herzog is prepared to read as a resistance
to the regime of signs and thus as a resistance to social deformation, precisely
those signs that speak most clearly of the hold that Western civilization has
even on the bodies of those it marginalizes and rejects. The chorus of young
women at the end of COBRA VERDE, functioning as a carnevalesque mockery of
the male world of both Kinski and his real or imagined adversaries, and as such
a very new element in Herzog's world, are they not performing for a camera
still hungry for exotic spectacle? Yet in Herzog's documentaries from the 1960s
and early 70s, the distrust of signification was always a matter of refusing to
have the handicapped, the blind, or the sick be subsumed under the discourses
of institutionalized medicine, charitable religion, or the welfare worker. Instead
he intended them to have the chance to appear first and foremost as human
beings. Herzog rejected the pieties of liberal politics in the name of human dignity, viewed beyond sentimentality or pathos with an almost Bunuelian, surrealist cruelty. But when his heroes play devil's advocates and instruments of
power politics, this perception of dignity without histrionics is difficult to maintain, and Herzog's cinema appears increasingly to freeze the image, to create a
kind of frame which makes cult icons of Europe's cultural others.

The Spider's Stratagem or the Kiss of the Spider Woman?

How did Italian critical realism or New German Cinema come to this apparent
impasse between the academic and metaphysical, cultivating the hero as icon,
escaping into myth, music and opera? The flashback to the 1960's with which I
started, where Europe saw its "new" national cinemas giving rise to auteurs,
each creating an individual oeuvre but sustained by the nation's popular and
political culture must be considered as one answer because as Hollywood lan-
guished, the art cinema flourished, some of it by playing off the Hollywood of
the 1940s and 50s against the Hollywood of the 1960s. But while a Wenders or
Fassbinder tried to cast a cinephile and necrophilic eye on the maverick Hollywood of Sam Fuller, Douglas Sirk or Nicholas Ray, filmmakers like Rosi and
Herzog in their own very different ways, did not look backwards, but sideways,
to the Latin traditions of literature and folk mythology, to the travelers' tales,
the bad conscience of a Conrad about white colonialism mitigated by their own
principled dissent from the political orthodoxies of their countries. The Latin
settings and subjects become the subtext not only for their non-antagonistic relation to Hollywood (which distinguishes them from Godard or Glauber Ro-

cha), but they also prevent too easy a play with Hollywood's own icons (as in Fassbinder, Wenders and others): displacing but also re-focusing through a non-binary schema their own "coming to terms" not with the old Hollywood of the 1950s, but the new Hollywood of the 1970s.

For it seems that the literature (and, in a wider sense, the visual imagination) of Latin American authors seems to have become increasingly attractive to European filmmakers, wherever they felt they were competing with America over the truth of the image on the one hand, and on the other, where filmmakers – independent or auteurs – could no longer envisage a terrain not already colonized by television. One can see it also in Latin American filmmakers working in Europe, such as Ruy Guerra's adaptation of a Marquez story, ERENDIRA, for a French production company, or Raoul Ruiz, the Chilean director, making films in Lisbon and Rotterdam when not working in Paris. One of the reasons may be the fact that here is a literary culture, which has always been closer to spectacle and carnival as part of radical politics. It has a precise historical experience of "colonization," but also of appropriating the colonial legacy in a vernacular idiom. Rosi's adaptation of Marquez may be a collage of clichés, yet they are hardly folkloristic: if the clichés are having a ball, it is because they are accompanied by strong feelings, clear outlines, bold colors, simple motifs, archaic spaces. The distance is not created by critical irony, or by political allegory, but through a literalism that offers distance. This, as in the case of Herzog, may leave the sophisticated spectator with the task of trying to become naive. It is not the romantic, heroic, or sentimental cliché that speaks the truth, but its repetition: obstinate, desperate, utopian.

(1988/1992)

Conclusion

European Cinema as World Cinema

A New Beginning?

What is European Cinema Today?

What is European cinema? We no longer seem to know. The very idea of it has slipped between the declining relevance of "national cinemas," and the emerging importance of "world cinema." A few decades ago, European cinema connoted films mainly made in Western Europe and based on its dominant postwar – national and transnational – traditions of neo-realism, politically or pop-art inspired new waves. It named an auteur cinema that drew on national (literary or theatrical) traditions, whose style was that of an art cinema, with psychologically complex protagonists, often the alter egos of the director, and thus inviting expressive-autobiographical interpretation. Add the word "popular," and European cinema refers to the sum total of the nationally specific, but widely seen commercial films of a given country. Popular European cinema featured recognizable national stars and concentrated on proven genres such as Austro-German costume dramas, French "polars" and Italian comedies, British CARRY-ON films or German detective films. "European" here helps distinguish these genre cinemas from Hollywood, without implying transnational, i.e., inter-European popularity. On the contrary, many genres, notably comedies, did not export well, and only very few stars became familiar across the national borders: Romy Schneider was popular in France (not least because of her marriage to Alain Delon), Louis de Funès comedies became hits in Germany and Greece, Fernandel did well in Italy (as an Italian priest), but a French superstar like Jean Gabin did not succeed in Germany, which had its own Gabins: Gert Fröbe, for instance, and later, Mario Adorf. The biggest German star for at least five decades, Heinz Rühmann, has remained totally unknown elsewhere; also despite their trying Hardy Krüger, Karlheinz Böhm and Horst Buchholz all have been unable to establish enduring careers in Britain and Hollywood.

On the other hand, "European" just as often identifies films made outside the commercial rewards and constraints of the box office. Instead, they are financed through the nationally specific funding schemes of government subsidy, like the

French *avances sur recettes*, and public service broadcasting funds, like the German television framework agreement. To some, this is a necessary protective
measure to safeguard the creative talent of a country; to others it is a source of
cheap television programming, and to still others, a trade barrier stifling enterprise and competition. In the 1970s, European cinema also referred to politically
or aesthetically avant-garde cinema with minority appeal: films that were prepared to take formal risks, or practiced a politics of intervention in a society felt
to be stagnant and opposed to change. Jean-Marie Straub and Daniele Huillet
were considered European filmmakers, not least because they came from
France, worked in Germany, and finally settled in Italy. Jean-Luc Godard's
Swiss-French background predestined him for a pan-European outlook, and in
a film like PASSION, he gave roles to actors from at least four different European
countries. Wim Wenders is considered European, and not only because he has
shot films in France and Portugal. So, too, is Peter Greenaway, a self-exile on
"the Continent." Greenaway and Godard examine the interface between cinema
and painting, or between architecture and cinema, while Bergman, Rivette,
Rohmer, but also Fassbinder, François Ozon, and Lars von Trier often have the
theatre as their scenic inter-text. Descriptions do not amount to definitions, and
the label 'European' once more seems to make more sense when applied from
without than when given substance from within.

It suggests that, perhaps, it is time to look at European cinema neither from
"within" nor from "without", but as part of a more dynamic as well as fluid
totality – that of world cinema. But before examining what the term connotes
for the new century, I want to summarize for one last time some of the problems
encountered in the study of European cinema.

The Auteur, the Nation and the Avant-garde

As we saw, a look at the readers and handbooks makes clear how impossible it
is to speak of European cinema, while also confirming how inevitable it is. In
this conjuncture, several points emerged, not as criticisms of specific authors or
editors, but as structural constants that sustain the paradox. First, there is a reliance on categories, such as auteur cinema and art cinema, which are treated as
first-order realities, when (I have argued) they function more likely as second-
order compromise formations.[1] Next, there is a predisposition to rely on the
convergence of the nation, the nation-state and a country's indigenous cinematic production: they are assumed to form a unity of sorts. This implied convergence brings forth the problematic, but seemingly indispensable concept
"national cinema," discussed and dissected in an earlier chapter. Third, a mostly

dualistic and invariably antagonistic perception of the relation between European cinema and Hollywood is also taken for granted. It either functions as first cause (Hollywood poses a permanent threat to the existence and viability of cinema in Europe), or as an explanation for various shortcoming and failings: European films are made on small budgets because the Americans monopolize the theatrical release of films and thus block the box office, or European-made films are shunned by European spectators, because their tastes have been ruined by American blockbusters.

If the auteur, national cinema and hostility to Hollywood are the three most central complexes that stand in the way of a new understanding of European cinema, there are further issues I have named. Some are no longer quite so contentious, because their ideological function has become more evident, and therefore just a little less tenable. For instance, the a priori valorization of realism in European cinema as the only valid ontology of the (photographic) image, based on its particular truth-status of time (the indexicality of the moment) and iconicity of place (what appears in the image corresponds to a once-existing pro-filmic reality). The reliance on realism in European cinema used to go hand in hand with a character psychology based on individual subjectivity, interiority, spiritual alienation, and social anomie – at the expense of fantasy, interpersonal conflict, action, and interactive communication, all seen as either "commercial" and low culture, or typical for Hollywood (action, spectacle). The Dogma manifesto has, by seemingly re-affirming realism as Europe's doxa, shown how much in fact it had by 1995 become a mere set of conventions that could be performed, prescribed, or abrogated (thus implicitly doing away with any special ontological status). Similarly, directors as different as Tom Tykwer (WINTER SLEEPER, THE WARRIOR AND THE PRINCESS, RUN LOLA RUN), Roberto Benigni (LA VITA E BELLA) or Jean-Pierre Jeunet (LE FABULEUX DESTIN D'AMÉLIE POULAIN) have made powerful and striking films in modes that range from fantasy to fairytale and live-action animation, without their films being either less European or less concerned with important issues.

To avoid too many misunderstandings, I want to clarify once more why I believe it makes more sense to suspend the traditional definition of European cinema as an *auteur* cinema, as a national cinema, and as implacably opposed to Hollywood, and why I have been treating them as second-order categories. The *auteur* first: there is no doubt that a long line of outstanding directors has shaped the identity of what we understand as European cinema. From Fritz Lang to Jean Renoir, from Sergei Eisenstein to G.W. Pabst, from Luis Bunuel to Roberto Rossellini, from Ingmar Bergman to Jean-Luc Godard, from Michelangelo Antonioni to Joseph Losey, from Bernardo Bertolucci to Neil Jordan, from Robert Bresson to Mike Leigh, from Carl Dreyer to Lars von Trier, from Agnès Varda to Krzysztof Kieslowski, from Wim Wenders to Jean-Pierre Jeunet: each national cinema has in crucial ways across the decades taken its identity and international face from the uniqueness and distinctiveness of its directors' vision. But the claim to such monopoly also comes with historical baggage and political assumptions that once in a while need to be unpacked. Modeled as the film *auteur* initially was on the representative writer, as this figure emerged in 19th-century national literature (Balzac, Dickens, Flaubert, George Eliot, Fontane), it carried the burden of performing as the nation's spokesperson and representative. Consolidated in 20th-century literary modernism (Thomas Mann, Joseph Conrad, James Joyce, T.S. Eliot, André Gide, Marcel Proust), the 'great writer' bequeathed to the film director furthermore the task of being not only a high culture artist, with a unique and often hermetic vision, but also an opponent of industrial society, of the masses and of modernity. The cinema, however, is a direct product of precisely these three historical forces.

There is a second point. In literature, these recognized authors, with their coherent and consistent body of work, their important themes, always had as their alter egos the rebel-bohemians, the *refusés* and the avant-garde groups of pranksters and nihilists. But while the official rhetoric demanded implacable enmity between the great writers and the avant-garde fringe, each side depended on the other, and knew it – united as they were in their common fight against the philistine establishment. But the avant-garde (no less than the bourgeois writers) played by established rules and had their well-rehearsed rituals: the revolutionary postures, transgressive actions, manifestos and formal-aesthetic experiments. What seems remarkable, when moving to the cinema, is how easily these oppositional structures from the 1910s and 1920s that divided representative authors from the avant-garde movements, while secretly uniting them around common enemies, were transferred – more or less spontaneously, more or less identically – to the 1960s and 1970s film scene. It reproduced itself insofar as European *auteurs* stood on one side (the representative *cinema d'auteur*, or self-important *Autorenkino*) and the avant-gardes on the other (Wim Wenders versus Hellmuth Costard, R.W. Fassbinder attacked by Jean-Marie Straub; Christian Ziewer made fun of by Harun Farocki). The common enemy was the commercial film industry, taking the place of the philistines of the turn of the turn of the century. If the pattern is perhaps most evident in Germany, it also applied to France, where the *nouvelle vague* as "national" authors' cinema was shadowed and attacked by several (film) avant-gardes: by the Lettrists and the Situationists in the 1950s and 60s, by the Maoists (Guy Fihman, Claudine Eizykman) and the Zanzibar dandies during the 1970s. In England, *auteurs* like Losey were ignored in the 1960s, David Lean was dismissed in the 1970s, Peter Greenaway was detested in the 1980s by the structuralist materialist avant-garde gathered in the London Co-op and writing for *Screen* (Malcolm Le Grice, Steve Dwoskin, Peter Gidal). *Screen* in turn was attacked by Lindsay Anderson and John Boorman, perhaps the foremost director-critic-*auteurs* the British cinema produced between 1950 and 1990.

National Cinema as Popular European Cinema

As indicated in the chapters on national cinema, though not discussed in detail, during the 1980s (first in Britain, then elsewhere in Europe) a reaction set in against the *auteur* and the implied high culture appropriation of national cinema, but also against the formalism of the avant-garde, perceived as elitist and sectarian. A re-evaluation of popular (i.e., mass, commercial) culture took place, now seen as a strategic tool for political (class, race and gender) emancipation. Spearheaded in Britain, around the Birmingham Centre for Contemporary Cultural Studies, such concepts as negotiated readings and subversive pleasures led to a broadly based recovery movement also of so-called popular European cinema.[2] This includes anything from cheap horror films made in Italy, to the filmed national sagas of Finland, from German Karl May films (Westerns) to French comedies with Jean-Paul Belmondo, from Gainsborough Studio costume melodramas to late-1960s Danish soft-core porn. The sub-categories of European popular cinema are stars and genres, and the mode of production is closely modeled on Hollywood. Popular European cinema historically came to an end in the late 1960s, when almost all film industries collapsed and the audiences (but also the themes and genres) of this national cinema moved to and relocated on television (soaps, series, cop-shows) and the video rental circuits. The critical recovery of popular European cinema thus has something antiquarian and nostalgic, mixed with a camp appreciation of its insouciance, energy and naivety, and bolstered by a righteous indignation at the "neglect" it has suffered too long: by film scholars, avant-garde critics and even by those cinephiles who profess a love of Hollywood. Auteurism played a less prominent part in this revival, but the valorization of star and genre cinema fits into the larger European Union project of preserving the national heritage, for why not add cinematic *lieux de mémoire* to the Tour de France, Marianne or the Larousse dictionary?[3]

The analogies in the cultural politics of the *cinéma d'auteur* between (national) literature and (national) cinema, and the counter-movement of reclaiming for the "nation" the commercial cinema with popular appeal, hopefully help to put in context what was at stake in making auteurism such a persistent criterion for defining European cinema: it kept the popular at arm's length, while claiming representative status. A third reason for the ideological fit of artist and auteur is that it did have the advantage of once more giving the cinema in Europe the cultural capital it had briefly enjoyed in the 1920s, and which it lost during the 1930s and 40s in the early period of sound and its subsequent (ab)uses by the totalitarian regimes in Europe. From being tainted by the double vice of propaganda and mindless entertainment, cinema in Europe could emerge after 1945 as "art," and it gradually won back the prestige, by re-establishing the principle of authorship, but now on a different basis (European *caméra stylo* plus Hollywood auteurism), and by a new stylistics: not only of originality, innovation or experiment, but of mise-en-scène and the *punctum* (understood here as the light personal touches of the metteur en scène, as the "excess" produced by the system itself, or the felicities of chance and contingency). Furthermore, what the mutually attuned sync between author, national cinema and the nation-state also brought about as a necessary corollary was the demand by filmmakers to be treated like other artists and to enjoy the forms of subvention, subsidy and funding given by the nation state to artists and creative individuals working for national institutions such as museums, opera houses, and theatres. The 1960s and 1970s were marked by this non-commercial, non-industrial filmmaking becoming part of officially sponsored art, This was very evident in France and Germany, less so in Italy and Great Britain. The legacy of being at once "official" and "oppositional" art, and the contradictions thus provoked was typical of many of the discourses around the European cinema in those years. In turn, the close alliance of art cinema and the author with the cultural bureaucracies also entailed – perhaps as an unintended consequence – an almost inevitable elision of the problems of the political: who were the filmmakers representing, for whom were they speaking, how could they assume a credible role, without becoming a caricature of the capricious genius? The art cinema, by its very structures of funding, and by the need for legitimation and accountability, was an elitist affair, while the figure of the author did not and could not avoid authoritarian assumptions about his or her speaking position and representative-ness: this may explain the *ex-cathedra* pronouncements made by some of the prominent European directors, such as Jean-Luc Godard or Hans Jürgen Syberberg, on issues of politics, society, history, life.

However similar the political-institutional context was for directors working in the different countries of Western Europe in the 1970s and 80s, there was no sense of the author's cinema developing "European" perspectives, at least not in anything other than biographical or anecdotal form, such as Margarethe von Trotta's predilection for Italy and that of Helma Sanders and Jutta Brückner for France. The predilection was not reciprocated: French directors (with the exception of the Lothringian Jean-Marie Straub) did not seek contacts in Germany, nor did the Italians, with the possible exception of Luchino Visconti, who made a trilogy on "German" themes (THE DAMNED, DEATH IN VENICE, LUDWIG). His trilogy in fact recalls the intense trans-national cross-border activities during the previous period (the 1950s and 60s), when producers of the commercial film industry shuttled back and forth in order to set up co-productions (secured by intergovernmental treaties and consolidated by tax-concessions and other benefits). By contrast, the auteur cinema of the 1980s, with the notable exception of Polish directors, showed little inter-European ambition. The much-maligned commercial producers – nationally based, but operating internationally, such as Carlo Ponti, Luggi Waldleitner, Pierre Braunberger, Claude Berri, Bernd Eichinger – appear to have been the better Europeans, whatever one may think about some of the films ("Euro-puddings") that resulted.[4]

Much of this has changed since the 1990s, not least through the material advantages now accruing to directors and producers when working on a European-wide basis, thanks to potentially handsome EU funding. Co-productions have become the norm, rather than the exception, and contemporary auteurs feel neither called upon to be "artists" nor to play the role of nationally representative figureheads. If for audiences the provenance of a film has diminished in importance as a reception category, insofar as directors are rarely judged by how well they fit into a predefined national cinema, the director as auteur is still a relevant production category. S/he now functions within a different set of determinants than those encompassed by either national cinema or unique stylistic signature. Rather, what matters is how well local/national provenance can communicate with global/transnational audiences. These changes, as we shall see, can be understood within broader frameworks, but they also affect the last of the three complexes that I claim make up the traditional identity of European cinema, the "hostility to Hollywood".

Europe versus Hollywood

My contention has been that the hierarchical model which implicitly aligned the director as author, the art cinema as high culture, and the nation represented through its artists in widening but concentric circles has to be revised, if one wants to understand the present reality of European cinema in its own terms. A similar revision is necessary when it comes to the binary divide that sees Hollywood as the European cinema's implacable antagonist. One can begin by summarizing in schematic forms the "Europe versus Hollywood" dualism, along its five major axes of differentiation: cultural, institutional, economic, spatial, and political.[5] At the cultural level, Europe used to stand for *art* and Hollywood for *entertainment*, personified in Europe by the *author*, and in Hollywood by the *star*; in Europe, the product is a *unique work of art*, in Hollywood it is a *standardized commodity*. At the institutional level, European cinema has its home in the *art-*

house or *program cinema* and on (public service) television, Hollywood is at home in the *multiplex cinema* and on (cable, commercial) television; European cinema is present in the public sphere through *the critic* as arbiter of taste and quality, while Hollywood is present through *advertising and marketing*; European films are *independently produced*, on a *one off* basis, Hollywood films are *made serially* within the *studio system*. Economically, European films are *financed through the government* and the taxpayers, Hollywood films are made with risk capital or *financed by banks* and the studios; European cinemas prove their value by critical acclaim and *cultural capital*, Hollywood films have to prove themselves at the *box office*, through television rights, video rentals and DVD sales; European cinema is based on film-school trained personnel and *artisanal modes of production*, Hollywood has craft guilds and an *industrial mode of production*. The spatial parameters of European cinema are *place-based and context-dependent* so that the films carry clear linguistic boundaries and geographic markers, their reference points are specific in location and time; Hollywood is less a particular place, and (as so often asserted) "more *a state of mind*"; rather than restricting access, its lingua franca is English, and it wants to be a site available to all, its films *accessible from everywhere*. Finally, when considering the political profile, European cinema is still beholden to the *nation state*, while Hollywood is emphatically part of the American *Empire*, and whereas Europe responds to this with *protectionist measures*, Hollywood plays out its *hegemonic position* in the world of information, entertainment and communication.

This scheme is as incontrovertible in its dualism as it seems self-evident in confirming cultural prejudices. But what if one were to look a little closer, and were to take these polarities literally? Supposing one began with the *spatial parameters* and accepted that Europe is constituted by its geographical boundaries. How wide are these boundaries? From 1945 to 1989, they included only Western Europe. Since then, the borders have shifted eastward and further south: if Greece and Portugal used to make up the southern perimeter, and Ireland and Finland the northern one, what about Turkey or Iceland? If Malta is part of the European Union, doesn't Russia have a better claim to be included in European cinema, as the home of one of its most important traditions, with its roster of world auteurs from Eisenstein and Vertov to Tarkovsky and Sokurov, to name just a few? Should the European Union be coextensive with what we understand by European cinema or should we adopt Donald Rumsfeld's division between old Europe and new Europe, as the United States re-evaluates its European allies, and the new accession states pursue their own alliances and alignments, including their film and media policies? Then, take the *cultural parameters*, which, as referred to above, have shown a revaluation of European *popular* cinema and a surge in interest in studying it. Indigenous stars and genre cinema which flourished in all major European countries right up to the 1970s:

should it be excluded from European cinema because it resembles Hollywood too much, or on the contrary, ought it to be called the true European cinema because of its co-productions and the loyalty that the popularity of the films inspires? Not only among its nostalgic first audiences: new generations have learnt to love these black-and-white or Technicolor genre films revived on television as "classics" and "cult films". Finally, is not the antagonistic scheme Europe-Hollywood biased so as to exclude other international players? How long can European cinema flatter itself as the plucky David against Goliath Hollywood? When will it have to measure up to, or re-negotiate its identity vis-à-vis Asian cinema, Australian cinema, or Indian cinema? As argued more extensively in an earlier chapter, even within Europe, these other cinemas are alive and asserting themselves. Britain, thanks to its large and culturally vibrant Asian community, has seen its own national cinema re-assessed across Bollywood, with a string of films that arguably started with Stephen Frears and Hanif Kureshi's My Beautiful Laundrette (1985) and Sammy and Rosie get Laid (1987), shifted gears with Gurinder Chadha's Bhaji on the Beach (1993), Bend it Like Beckham (2002) and has culminated in her Bride and Prejudice (2004), a Bollywood reworking of Jane Austen. In Germany, Turkish-German directors are pressing equally hard to change the way Germans think of their society as mono-cultural and ethnically homogeneous, while the Maghreb influences on French cinema compete with French *beur* films, with Afro-French or Franco-Asian filmmakers, to redefine French cinema not as European cinema, or even as post-colonial cinema, but as part of world cinema.

If Europe is being re-colonized by its own former colonials, one cannot but salute the poetic justice at work here. As a cinema space, Europe has, however, always been "colonized": from the American perspective, it presented itself as a collection of national markets that had in common the strong presence of Hollywood in each of them, and whose film culture was distributed (unevenly) between US product and the respective national output. Internally, Europe has mostly been an archipelago of mutually exclusive cultural-linguistic spheres, where films from neighboring countries rarely if ever succeed in finding a hospitable reception. Success on its home ground does not guarantee a film success in other countries, and rarely if ever has a film been a world success, without also having been a success in the United States, itself one of the most difficult markets to break into. Some European films (notably from Germany) even had to be exported to the art houses of New York and San Francisco, before being re-imported into their own countries for a second (usually more successful) launch, while the highest compliment Hollywood can pay a film from Europe is to re-make it. Witness the remakes of French films, such as Three Men and a Baby (Trois Hommes et un Couffin), The Odd Couple (La Cage aux Folles) and Nikita, or Wim Wenders' Wings of Desire as City of Angels, Alejandro

Amenabars' Abre los Ojos as Vanilla Sky (Cameron Crowe) and George Sluizer's Spoorloos as The Vanishing.

All this is to underline an obvious fact: the dualistic schemes outlined above for the relation Europe-Hollywood can have no objective validity or disinterested status: they are heavily Euro centric and self-interested. They view the overall picture through West European eyes. Were one to take the inverse view, and look at Europe from Hollywood's perspective (as social historians such as Tyler Cowen or Richard Pells have done), the impression would be that the vast majority of cinema audiences in Europe are happy with Hollywood, and that far from stifling diversity, the success of Hollywood films has created niche markets and opportunities for European filmmakers on all levels.[6] From this vantage point, the antagonism is the result of European countries not having sorted out their differences among themselves concerning audiovisual policy, and of producers and directors demanding protectionist measures from their national governments or Brussels, in order not to have to reform antiquated structures of production, lack of audience-research and "backward" notions of cinema as an art form of individual self-expression. Indeed, one might take an even harsher view, and puncture the widely held but perhaps somewhat complacent idea that Europe stands for innovation and experiment while Hollywood merely churns out formulaic material, recycled and repackaged in gaudy wrapping. Considering the enormous technical and aesthetic innovations made in Hollywood over the past twenty-five years in sound technology, radically transforming the aural experience of going to the movies and creating entirely new sound- and body-spaces; the aesthetic innovations of integrating digital technology not just for special effects (though this is impressive enough), but also for "rendering" perceptual and phenomenal reality in novel ways (Industrial Light & Magic); implementing if not always initiating a revolution in animation technique and the graphic arts (Pixar; Dreamworks), it would seem more than a little perverse to dismiss all this as old wine in new bottles, especially since it is difficult to point to possible European innovations (e.g. multi-strand narratives, layered temporalities, frank depiction of sex) that the Americans are not themselves capable of, or have not imported (by giving assignments to European filmmakers like Mike Figgis, Ridley Scott, Paul Verhoeven, Sam Mendes, Anthony Minghella and Christopher Nolan). On the other hand, were one to take a view that is neither Eurocentric nor biased towards US interests, but anti-capitalist, then "Global Hollywood" does not appear as the new avant-garde, except in the military sense of advancing new forms of exploitation. Hollywood is seen as an unmitigated ecological catastrophe, disguising as benign cultural hegemony the tyranny of the code, and camouflaging as "harmless entertainment" the wholesale appropriation of the world's intellectual property rights, both present and past, with Europe still on the side of the winners rather than losers.[7]

Global Hollywood, Asia and Europe

In another sense of course, European cinema has been the big loser. For what has become undeniable is that European cinema of all the categories specified above suffers an identity crisis and has an image problem. With very few exceptions, films from Europe have little direct appeal to audiences, neither as exports on a world scale nor when competing against Hollywood films within their own markets, be these markets national or inter-European. Some figures on the export side: "Hollywood's proportion of the world film market is double what it was in 1990 and the European film industry is one-ninth the size it was in 1945." Trade restrictions, as well as marketing costs have traditionally excluded foreign pictures from screens in the United States. But even so, the decline of European cinema has been spectacular. "In the 1960s, foreign films (mostly from Europe) constituted 10 percent of the US market; by 1986 they made up 7 percent, and by 2003 they were down to an incredible three-quarters of 1 percent."[8]

The most frequently cited factors that have led to the decline are: firstly, the revival of the Hollywood blockbuster cinema and its massive marketing within Europe; secondly, the difficulties European films encounter in the distribution and exhibition sectors; thirdly, the competition for domestic audiences from television, and fourthly (more controversially), the different forms of cultural protectionism and state subsidy policy, said to have made European filmmakers insensitive to audience needs and thus less innovative.[9] And finally, added to the overwhelming presence of Hollywood, there is increasing competition from Asian cinemas among younger audiences, both on the commercial front and from independent art-, auteur- and new-wave national cinemas.

If we take the last point first: Asian cinemas – Japanese cinema, then Hong Kong cinema, then Taiwanese, mainland Chinese and South Korean cinema, and most recently films from Thailand, Singapore, Malaysia and even Vietnam – have achieved a remarkably high recognition value in markets where they formerly were almost unknown, notably the US market and in Europe, even if in the latter case, this market is still mainly restricted to the festival circuit. But movie-house successes like CROUCHING TIGER HIDDEN DRAGON (admittedly a US independent production) or Wong Kar Wai's CHUNGKING EXPRESS and IN THE MOOD FOR LOVE have shown these films to be box office draws as well as critical successes, and thus an exhibition factor to be reckoned with.

On the other hand, from the European perspective, there is a certain déjà vu across a time lag about these Asian cinemas and their successive successes: it is as if, in certain respects, Southeast Asia was merely catching up, and going through the sorts of changes witnessed in Europe between 1950 and 1970 with the rise of a new generation of auteurs, new waves, and new national cinemas: except that now it is taking place in an accelerated tempo with the graduates from (often international, i.e., mostly American) film schools returning to their native lands, sensing that at home they have the best chance to make their mark, or rather, that a home base gives them the cultural credibility that in turn allows them to make their mark on the international festival circuit. They thereby respond to the opening up of new markets, they signal the existence of a new breed of entrepreneurs, who cater to a new middle class and an economically viable youth culture in these "tiger economies," eager to identify with Western leisure pursuits. This surge in prosperity and disposable income since the 1990s has been taking place in countries whose film culture infrastructure – for instance, a centralized exhibition sector – already supports an established Hollywood distribution system, to which it can add outlets for "independents." By contrast, in Western Europe during the 1960s and 70s, Hollywood was faltering and often uncertain in its approach. It may explain why these Asian cinemas are so much more hybrid, "postmodern" and eclectic: they have clearly absorbed Hollywood (and Hong Kong) movie culture when these were at full strength. A similar pastiche style of in-jokes, homage, and film buff references were also the mode that the French *nouvelle vague* brought to the scene in the 1960s, but with reference to movies from a decade or more before. With the decline of Hollywood in the mid-60s, French cinema (and then other nationals cinemas) became more self-consciously concerned with national specificity and cultural identity. The Asian cinemas of the 90s are, by contrast, quite self-referentially Asian, while also being quite unselfconsciously part of "world cinema."

What is World Cinema?

But what is world cinema? Historically, and semantically, world cinema is a reworking of third cinema, which was "third" in relation to Hollywood as "first" cinema, and European national/art cinema as "second" cinema. Third cinema referred initially to politically engaged cinema (mostly from Latin America), which emerged in the 1970s and was closely tied to the post-colonial, often fiercely nationalist liberation struggles. Since then, this neat division has shifted. Third cinema has shed its "political" agenda (as well as its regional base), and has become "world cinema": a term modeled on music (world music) or food (fusion food) to indicate fusion and hybridity of national and international, ethnically specific and globally universal characteristics. World cinema thus no longer comprises (just) the politicized cinema of Latin America in the 1970s, the art and avant-garde cinema in India, or Francophone cinema in

Africa. Now it can refer to emergent indigenous cinema and film cultures all over the world, from Iran and Sri Lanka to Mozambique and Mexico, from Alaska to South Africa and Burkina Faso.

Yet, world cinema is also in danger of being considered simply "the rest": coming after Hollywood, after other commercial cinemas (Bollywood, Hong Kong cinema, Cinema Down Under), and after the remnants of European auteur/art cinema.[10] Once world cinema simply indicates nothing more than "the rest," that is, anything that falls outside Hollywood and the remaining national cinemas, be they at home in Europe or elsewhere, such as India or Southeast Asia, then the term's use becomes severely limited.[11] Therefore, before letting world cinema carry only this negative meaning, or seeing it as an ethnographic-ethnic label for otherwise unclassifiable film fare, it is worth trying to ascribe a more positive identity by indicating a number of broader implications of this development.

For if it is indeed the case that there exists a ranking order in global film culture, then one is tempted to think of world cinema as something more like the club level of regional leagues in football, coming after the champions league and first division. Extending the football analogy, the measure of the de-centering of European cinema in relation to Asia suggests that non-US commercial cinemas are always threatened by their "relegation" to world cinema status, while some world cinemas clearly harbor hopes and aspirations of "rising" into the first division. There would then be a champions league, mainly made up of the blockbuster cinema produced in the US, occasionally in Britain, and the odd English-speaking filmmaker located elsewhere, such as Peter Jackson, making THE LORD OF THE RINGS trilogy in his home town of Wellington, New Zealand, or the Australian Mel Gibson, who with his THE PASSION OF CHRIST realized an "independent" film, while ultimately benefitting from Hollywood distribution and marketing. Below the champions league we have the first division, into which one can, as indicated, be promoted. The cases in point would be the different Asian cinemas that have come to prominence, and within Europe perhaps the Danish cinema embodied by the Dogma group briefly seemed to qualify, while the Spanish cinema around Pedro Almodóvar, Bigas Luna, Alex de la Iglesia, Iciar Bollain, Julio Medem, and Alejandro Amenábar has in recent years also fielded a formidable "team." From this first division of auteur and national cinema, one can also be relegated, as has largely happened with Italian, German, and to some extent even French cinema. On the other hand, important sections of the formerly auteur-centered national cinemas are now increasingly redefined as part of world cinema, for instance, if we think of French *beur* cinema, "Asian," i.e., Indian cinema in Britain, or when we remember how successful films by second-generation Turkish filmmakers in Germany (Fatih Akin, Thomas Arslan) have been at festivals and with audiences. These last examples indicate the limits of the football metaphor, since such "minority" cinemas are, in relation to a national cinema, neither relegations nor promotions, but the addition of a new element altogether. At a stretch, they may be the equivalent of the multi-cultural, multi-national mix of players that has come to prominence in Europe's first division teams!

In several senses, Asian cinema is beginning to inherit the status once enjoyed by European cinema. In the first instance, as indicated, by representing diverse, distinct, and apparently vibrant and innovative "national" cinemas. But also as a potential counterweight and maybe even as a rival to Hollywood in its respective overseas markets. At the same time, there are signs that Hollywood itself recognizes in Asian cinemas potential partners, and even a major league player within and beyond the national and regional borders. It would then be the auteurs, drawn from different national traditions – Chen Kaige, Zhang Yimou, Wong Kar-Wai, Kim-Kii-Duk – who would make up a kind of dream team, for whom the label "international art cinema" was invented. It could include Americans like Quentin Tarantino or Paul Thomas Anderson, British directors like Christopher Nolan and the already mentioned Fatih Akin, who let it be known that he prefers not to be typecast as a hyphenated ethnic director, and if he cannot be Fatih Akin, he would rather be the new Scorsese than represent the German-Turkish constituency.[12]

Asian cinema is not the only contender for major league status because increasing attention is being paid to Bollywood, the popular cinema of the Indian subcontinent. Even if this cinema is not as unified as it often appears to outsiders, its different genres make up what Indian audiences watch – far outstripping Hollywood – and many of its star vehicles also attract audiences in Europe, the United States, and in other regional markets. Then there is Australia's, and most recently, New Zealand's cinema, which has provided a number of outstanding "international" directors, such as Jane Campion, Lee Tamahori, Nicky Caro, and above all, the already mentioned Peter Jackson, who began as an "art cinema" auteur before he re-invented himself as director and co-producer of the LORD OF THE RINGS trilogy, with which he has developed a Hollywood-style franchise while also trying to launch an indigenous, self-sustaining film industry in and around his native city of Wellington.

What all these have in common is that the traditional line between national and international, as well as between art cinema and commercial cinema is no longer as clear-cut as it was during the confrontation between Europe and Hollywood between 1945 and roughly 1990. All these cinemas are more adept at mixing idioms, more transnational in their styles, as well as having more of a crossover appeal. Remarkably, it is still often a star and genre cinema, where the star may be a director, or in typical European fashion, a director and his leading lady (Zhang Yimou and Gong Li, for instance, in the early 1990s, or Olivier Assayas and Maggie Cheung).

Factor Hollywood: Still the Big Other?

No doubt this map or league table is something of a caricature. Especially where it suggests that, whether we like it or not, these cinemas – and the divisions or categories we choose to employ – have their identity and/or success assessed in light of the big other, namely Hollywood. But once one grants that the box office is only one measure of a film culture's success – as most of those taking an interest in European cinema and world cinema know all too well – then the seemingly parlous state of once famous national cinemas heralds a shift with global implications. Measured against a still firmly established position of Hollywood as market leader, and given the combined distribution power of the multi-national conglomerates (News Corp., Sony, Seagram, Time Warner) in the global entertainment sector and over the world's cinema markets (Disney/Miramax, DreamWorks, Paramount), the European film industries as well as the European art cinema may well be in irreversible decline, at least at first glance. The decades of state subsidy and the various partnerships with television have not been able to make European cinema an internationally competitive creative industry. The fact that it is usually regarded as in decline is perhaps the major problem its directors and producers need to face. Being part of something else, such as a sub-set of "world cinema" may open up a different way of thinking about the strengths and virtues of filmmaking outside not only Hollywood, but also the "national cinema" label. What it may not be able to do without is the auteur, even if his or her function has to be redefined as less the bearer of a personal vision, and more as the creator of a body of films that is both diverse in its genres and themes and carries a signature. Or rather: a creator whose signature is able to legitimate these genres and themes. He/she must be able to attract attention on the festival circuit, but otherwise need not be capable of captivating the broad general cinema-going public. The auteur's natural home would then be world cinema, rather than the old national cinemas, thereby signaling a cinema that, while perhaps not suited for the national market, does well in international export markets, reaches the secondary markets of television or even the mass marketing of DVD releases with their vast network of internet-based fan sites and DVD reviews. A world cinema auteur thus can reach across many different countries, and under different reception conditions, can find a niche market with a dedicated audience. French producers, for this reason, like to invest in international auteurs (Abbas Kiarostami, Wong Kar-

Wai) in order to distribute them world-wide. The model here would not be the book, the poem or the play, but popular music, with its fiercely loyal fans keeping "track" of an artist and performer throughout his or her career. Yet herein also lies a dialectical reversal, since popular music and its leading "artists" are, of course, mostly under the control of the international majors, who in turn, control much of the Hollywood movie-making machine.

In order to grasp these developments of world cinema in their dynamic unfolding, we need to return not so much to the second and third but to the first cinema, the American film industry. Since this new Hollywood is no longer so new, it should really be called "Hollywood," but in its second incarnation, whose typical features include those global economic trends that are sometimes called post-industrial. Hollywood, in other words, is not what it used to be, if ever it was, meaning the monolithic studio system. It has, as is often pointed out, undergone major re-structuring and reorganization, both internally and internationally. At first glance it looks as if these changes – adapting itself to the post-Fordist production methods of outsourcing and the package deal, of intensified marketing, cornering worldwide distribution and product re-purposing, as well as seeking new forms of financing – have made it, in the international arena, even more hegemonic, imperial, and dominant. In this sense, it is of course the Hollywood blockbuster that is literally world cinema, since except for Cuba, Iran, Myanmar and North Korea, there is hardly a place on earth where American films do not form a significant if not *the* significant presence in a country's film exhibition sector.

This fact has given rise to intense and controversial debates over globalization and culture. Legions are the publications – above all in the US itself – about American cultural imperialism, some of them widely discussed in bestsellers like Benjamin Barber's *Jihad vs McWorld* and Naomi Klein's *No Logo*. In the field of film and media studies, authors document the seemingly unbroken hegemony of Hollywood in Europe since World War I, and its increasingly tight hold on the rest of the world since the 1970s. "Why Hollywood rules the world" is not only a frequently asked question, but also the title of a chapter in Tyler Cowen's much-discussed book *Creative Destruction*, which asks whether globalization in the culture industries is a force that favors diversity and stimulates creativity, or on the contrary, whether unlimited trade in an uneven power situation, and thus without a level playing field homogenizes cultures, reduces creative options and Disneyfies the world. The arguments against Global Hollywood are well-summarized in the already cited *Global Hollywood*, which adds a polemic against film studies and textual analysis, and focuses especially on labor relations and intellectual property rights as the key battlegrounds for a new activism and policy initiatives.

Drawing on these publications, more or less partisan and polemical, more or less scholarly and backed up by empirical data, one can summarize present thinking about globalized Hollywood, by also asking: what is it that Hollywood has done "right" in the transition, how has it managed change, and what if anything have the other contenders named above learnt or not learnt from Hollywood? One may then wonder what conclusions, if any European filmmakers will draw, and what strategies should they pursue in order to draw level.

Hollywood and the New Economy

One can begin by putting together a list of natural and unnatural advantages, which have sustained the dominance of American cinema. To start with, what are the (natural) advantages of Hollywood? First, there is the location advantage and the creative talent clustering; second, an extended track record and a long tradition; third, deep pockets: more money to invest in a film than any of their potential competitors. Then, what are the (possibly unnatural) advantages of Hollywood? Above all, a sizeable and very sophisticated (because diversified) home market, mostly closed to foreign competition, which used to be able to sustain the industry, without it being dependent on exports. This no longer being so, Hollywood has ensured that it possesses global distribution networks, often operating as trusts and monopolies outside the US. This well-established trading network is supported by a government policy that consistently listens to the lobbying of the MPA and aggressively uses the State Department in order to enforce copyright and intellectual property rights in all foreign markets, however small or developing they might be: "Hollywood's economic, institutional, and political power gives it a competitive advantage that few industries in the world can match. Only Hollywood can afford to spend $200 million on a single film; only Hollywood has the global distribution network and publicity machinery that can get its movies into theatres worldwide and keep them there; and only Hollywood has the US government behind it pushing to open foreign markets even further."[13]

But once again, we need to ask, are we dealing with the cultural imperialism of Hollywood (multimedia and mono-content) or is the infrastructure that Hollywood movies maintain all over the world not the very condition that allows new forces and new cinemas to emerge? It seems fairly obvious that it is only since Southeast Asia has expanded economically and acquired a middle class eager to spend on leisure, that it has been able to sustain both a lucrative market for Hollywood movies and create the conditions for a successful indigenous filmmaking culture.

Many commentators have furthermore pointed out that the internal shifts in Hollywood have necessitated Hollywood itself becoming more responsive to its non-American audiences and, as it were, learn to put on the mimicry of world cinema. On the one hand, as a consequence of rising costs, Hollywood now depends on its overseas markets for almost 60 percent of its revenue; on the other, the evidence of successful commercial film industries outside its control has produced the traditional response of bringing either this new talent or these new film genres into Hollywood's own tent. That John Woo or Jacky Chan make their films in Hollywood, or that Quentin Tarantino shot large parts of his KILL BILL – itself influenced massively by the kung fu film vogue – in Bejing film studios is part of the same trends of talent transfer and labor outsourcing.

The background to these new alliances and crossovers can be analyzed in straightforward business terms, as a result of shifting market shares. For instance, relocating production facilities is not only the quest for cheaper labor:

> This move derives from studio executives' suspicion that Hollywood films may have reached the limits of their overseas appeal. As evidence, they point to the growing popularity of locally-made films around the world. In 2001, for instance, the top grossing films in South Korea, Hong Kong, and Japan were all domestic productions. Hollywood is finding ways to turn a profit on the desire of local audiences to see local films; rather than trying to beat the competition, the studios are joining it. In the last few years, Columbia, Warner Brothers, Disney/Buena Vista, Miramax, and Universal have all created special overseas divisions or partnerships to produce and distribute films in languages other than English – including German, Spanish, French, Italian, Brazilian, Korean, and Chinese. While some of these films are aimed at international markets, others target local audiences – if they can be exported to the US, that's a bonus, but many of them are not being made primarily with American viewers in mind.[14]

If Hollywood is thus in a sense masquerading as "national cinema," it may in fact constitute a new kind of counter-cinema tactic, if national cinemas are now acting as "world cinema." But rather than letting all the boundaries begin to blur when trying to define the attractions and current uses of the term "world cinema," it is useful to remind oneself of the modes of production typical of world cinema. In most though not all cases, the model is that of the European national cinemas in the 1970s and 1980s: world cinema is made up of films that rely on a form of financing that utilize state-funded support schemes or cultural subsidies, with the implication that a country is willing to finance creative talent as part of its "liberal" image or in maintaining the national culture by means of cinema, along with subsidy for the other arts or crafts typical of the nation. However, the difference lies in the fact that the funding may not come from the filmmaker's own state, but is disbursed in the manner of "development aid."

While the classical state-subsidy production funds were originally intended to facilitate nationally representative cinema, today these are intended to produce world cinema.

Thus, it is instructive to realize in how many cases, world cinema is the result of co-productions, often with European countries, whose former colonies are given cultural development aid, so to speak, with no doubt, double or triple agendas operating on both sides. Classic cases are the role of France and Belgium in Francophone Africa, where hardly a single film is being made without some form of European subsidy, or where the major pan-African film festival, that of Ouagadougou in Burkina Faso is not only funded but also organized and administered from Brussels and Paris. Even Germany, which had colonies in Africa for only a relatively brief (albeit quite bloody) period, makes money available for film production in Namibia and Tanzania via its national film fund. Certain film festivals also offer production subsidies: the best-known example is probably the Hubert Bals Fonds of the Rotterdam Film Festival, but there are several other funds that first-time filmmakers or directors from developing countries can tap into. The Berlin Film Festival in 2004 launched its own, so-called World Cinema Fund:

> In cooperation with the German Federal Cultural Foundation (Kulturstiftung des Bundes) the Berlin International Film Festival is setting up the World Cinema Fund to support filmmakers from transition countries. Until 2007, the geographical focus will be on Latin America, Africa, the Middle East, and Central Asia. The World Cinema Fund has an annual budget of about 500,000 Euros at its disposal. The aim of the World Cinema Fund is to help the realization of films which otherwise could not be produced, i.e., feature films and creative feature-length documentaries with a strong cultural identity. Another important goal is to strengthen the profile of these films in German cinemas. The World Cinema Fund will provide support in the fields of production and distribution. Production companies with directors from the above mentioned regions as well as German production companies working with a director from these regions will be able to apply for production funds. The maximum production amount which can be granted to a film for is 100,000 Euros. In order to receive such funds, a German partner is required. However, the film does not necessarily have to be a co-production.[15]

While one may wonder about the neo-colonial aspects of such measures, one also needs to note that film festivals in particular are vitally dependent on a steady supply of world cinema and thus have a specific interest in fostering the production of such films, as well as binding the respective filmmakers to "their" own festival. However, one has to be careful because what has been said so far might imply that when discussing world cinema one is only talking about films that are neither produced by Hollywood nor for the mainstream cinema circuit, and imagining that filmmakers understand themselves as belonging to this genre or category of world cinema. But this is probably an unwarranted assumption, if one remembers that most directors, wherever they are in the world, consider themselves *auteurs*, and want to see their films shown in cinemas and to popular audiences. However, as already indicated, the category of world cinema and that of auteur cinema are not opposed concepts because they imply and even necessitate each other.

World cinema in this respect is probably not a production category at all, and cannot be defined by its mode of production. Or rather, it is a category conceived of and circulating from the point of use of distribution and exhibition which in turn determines the profile of production. For instance, if we look at marketing and distribution, it is evident that the label world cinema gains its primary currency, as already noted, through the international festival circuit such as the "Forum of Young Cinema" in Berlin, the Rotterdam Festival, and the Toronto festival. The Cannes sidebar "Un Certain Regard," as well as the Sundance and Telluride festival in the US have increasingly invested in upgrading the term "world cinema" into a quality label. The Berlin Forum is the oldest in this respect, and its name still reflects the close association of world cinema with new waves, political counter-cinema and the old "thirdness," so to speak. Nowadays, world cinema has become the section where festival directors or programmers can display their nose for new talent, but also extend their political antennae to topical areas and international hotspots, without courting too much risk aesthetically or inviting politically counterproductive controversy.[16]

As already argued in the chapter on film festivals, the festivals in their networked totality appear in the global marketplace as (co-)producers/distributors and exhibitors, thus achieving for the "independent" sector something akin to the horizontal integration which mirrors that of the Hollywood system. The juncture between the two systems, at the point of reception, becomes even more evident when one considers the clearing house function that film festivals have for distributors like Miramax and for the exhibition outlets that have opened up in the new generation of multiplexes, most of which specifically reserve screens for minority interest films, invariably only those that have attracted critical plaudits or prizes at festivals. The traditional art houses share these films with the multiplexes, and in this fashion, generate half a dozen modest but nonetheless international hits per year. In 2004, a film like THE STORY OF THE WEEPING CAMEL (nominated for best foreign documentary by the American Academy) would qualify as an excellent example of "world cinema." Made with German money and by directors with German connections, it nonetheless qualifies as a German/Mongolian co-production thanks to its location, crew, actors and story material. If in 2004 one traveled to Montreal or Sydney, New York or Munich, Rome or London, chances were that in each city one could have caught THE STORY OF THE WEEPING CAMEL (or ETRE OU AVOIR, LOST IN TRANSLATION, or whatever the festival favorite of the season might be, including the odd documentary such as FAHRENHEIT 9/11) at a dedicated art house, or at one of the multi-screen multiplexes. The independent sector, driven by the post-Fordist logic of customized demand and niche markets, increasingly mimics mainstream cinema and tries to reproduce it in all but scale.

Production

How are films made in Europe today? In the absence of a commercial film industry and the exhibition sector dominated by American majors or globally operating companies, a new division of labor obtains also at the level of production. Hollywood considers the independent sector as a relatively cheap and low risk research and development branch of the global film business, where prototypes can be tested for mainstream or niche markets. Successful "indie" directors may find themselves wooed by a studio-assignment or contract, but after peaking in the 1980s, the transfer of talent from Europe in the 1990s has remained relatively flat, with Alejandro Amenábar and Jean-Pierre Jeunet perhaps the major exceptions to a trend that seems to favor directors from Asia, Mexico and New Zealand.[17] Looked at from the European perspective, European films have to be international successes before they can become trans-European, which is why directors and their companies are not targeting specifically European sources of finance. Anne Jäckel, among others, has shown how many of Europe's formerly national film industries now consist of a myriad of small production houses, often regionally based, financing one-off projects by deal-making, ad-hoc co-production agreements, accumulating different types of state-subsidy, public and private financing, or entering into arrangements with national or trans-national television industries.[18] No clear pattern emerges from Jäckel's account, but when one looks at the official entries to the Cannes Film Festival of 2005, one notes that the majority of European films are indeed co-productions: Wim Wenders' DON'T COME KNOCKING, Lars von Trier's MANDERLAY, Amos Gitaï's FREE ZONE or Jean-Pierre and Luc Dardenne's L'ENFANT. Wenders' and Von Trier's films are furthermore in English, while the German-Austrian Michael Haneke (present with CACHÉ, a French-German-Austrian-Italian co-production) only shoots in French. If financing no longer connotes provenance, and language is no guide, then identity (either national or generic) once more accrues to the director-auteur, as has been the tradition in Cannes.

The implications, however, go beyond Cannes. These co-productions, financed at least in part through Eurimages and other European Union bodies, shift the identity of film as a cultural good or commercial product. No longer tied to national identity or to a national media-industry, such films may be increasingly seen as "European", but do they still fall under the protection of culture or should they be seen as part of European high-tech, in the way that – in the aircraft industries – the Airbus consortium is regarded as a successful competitor to Boeing on a world scale? In other words, under the pressure of the popularity of Hollywood, the European Union is actively promoting films that pool funding and transfer talent between different European countries through channels provided by the EU. Without their content being necessarily multi-cultural or trans-national, these national-international films help to make cinema part of the process of European Union integration. However, they tend to prioritize English and French as the dominant languages, reflecting the countries with the strongest film cultural markets and best chances for export. Thus, while such co-productions, encouraged by EU institutions (such as the European Commission or the Council of Europe), are intended to compete with the international art cinema in the global markets, they tend to void or replace the idea of a national cinema, making the director the sole vehicle for connoting pan-European identity, irrespective of whether s/he crosses borders (like Haneke, Wenders, Von Trotta) or not (like Von Trier or the Dardenne Brothers). The key point, however, would be that such films are different from the "Euro-pudding" co-productions of an earlier period, because they gain their legitimacy via the festival circuit and the promotion of the auteur, whereas "Euro-puddings" were banking on stars and literary properties, if one thinks of NAME OF THE ROSE, HOUSE OF SPIRITS, THE OGRE, GERMINAL, ENEMY AT THE GATES, in order to succeed directly at the box-office. The "cultural good" versus "competitive commodity" argument remains unresolved.

One might be able to shift the terms of the debate by comparing these production considerations to the strategies of post-Fordist Hollywood. There, according to the authors of *Global Hollywood*, it is marketing that determines production, which in turn functions on four distinct levels: *sales* (presence in and penetration of all markets, including art cinema next to mainstream, but also computer games, toys, general merchandising /franchising); *advocacy* (promoting Hollywood as a brand, countering negative profiling and raising acceptability), *surveillance* (intensive market research and sophisticated – including illegal – monitoring of audience preferences) and *reassurance* (Hollywood provides a state-of-the-art, quality-controlled product or service). This sales-and-advertising approach to production most sharply differs from the EU model, where "representation" and "identity" however defined, still play, as we saw, key roles. However, the comparison does illuminate the value of the auteur and the festival within the European system, as the elements that correspond most closely to advocacy and reassurance in the Hollywood system, i.e., the promotion of a brand and the promise of a quality product, mediated and guaranteed through the festival circuit seal.

On the other hand, the emphasis on marketing does not fully encompass the Hollywood production system either. It neglects the importance of research and development already alluded to, which is often conducted through separate high-tech firms offering specialized services, such as in sound technology, digital special effects or computer modeling. Here, Hollywood is merely one of the corporate customers for products, skills and patents also in demand by the music industry, the military or the computer games industry – the latter now increasingly the tail wagging the movie industry dog. Typical companies with a strong experimental division are Pixar, Industrial Light & Magic, Rock Star Games, where the mutual appropriations between film formats and game formats continue unabated. Again, similar synergies between game designers and filmmakers are beginning to take place in Europe, even if on a much smaller scale than in the US, Japan, India or South Korea, and with less auteurist participation.[19] But when one looks beyond the multilateral, Brussels-sponsored Media schemes and the remaining commercial companies (Gaumont, Canal+, Working Title, Constantin Films and a few others) one notes that much of European film production is organized around small outfits, coming together for a specific one-off project, or consists of companies that form around an auteur-director or a collective (X-Films, Wüste Films). These in turn can team up with an American company, either directly or via one of their EU subsidiaries, to guarantee worldwide distribution.[20] However, are such firms small because they do not have the resources to be big, or do they see themselves as specialized providers of high-quality niche products? In other words, one can only speak of a distinct EU production model, insofar as it is mixed, small-scale and hybrid (when looked at from the vantage point of the studio system) or insofar as it is a version of a post-Fordist high-tech "outsourcing" model. In case of the latter, one of the most successful attempts to develop a European version of such post-Fordist practice would be found in Denmark: Lars von Trier's and Peter Albek Jansen's production company Zentropa (with Thomas Vinterberg and Lukas Moodysson as further core directors). With its "studio" complex outside Copenhagen, in what is variously described as a "hippie commune" and "Von Trier's family home," Zentropa – ignoring the question of size and scale – could be modeled on George Lucas' Industrial Light & Magic, as well as echoing Peter Jackson's one-man studio in Wellington, New Zealand. The examples provide a basis for comparison along three distinct lines of investigation: ILM as a specialized company for high-tech research and development that made itself indispensable to major Hollywood productions; Zentropa as the production unit of medium-scale films for the niche market of international art cinema (with, in Von Trier's case, often international stars: Emily Thompson, Catherine

Deneuve, Björk, Nicole Kidman), and the exploitation of a single franchise (the LORD OF THE RINGS series) in the case of Peter Jackson's WingNut Films.

World Cinema, Self-Othering and the Post-Colonial Discourse

From what has been said earlier about the common features of a world cinema film, it should be evident that it fully reflects the tensions and potential contradictions one encounters in other cultural and economic practices connected to globalization. A more detailed account or a series of case studies would have to indicate the manner in which the dynamics of globalization affects not only the type of commodity or service "world cinema" represents, but also what subject matters and styles prevail. Marshall McLuhan famously averred about media change and media transfer that the content of a (new) medium is always another (older) medium. This might very well also apply to "world cinema" where categories such as the nation and national identity, or the uniqueness of locality and region become the subject matter of world cinema, precisely because in their commodity form these films address a global audience, and not the "local" constituency they portray or "represent." These constituencies, in most cases, once they become cinema audiences, are also global, and make up the spectators for Hollywood films or for films made with Hollywood money. World cinema films and Hollywood films here also asymmetrically mirror each other. Cosmopolitan audiences watch films about sub-state entities such a tribes, minorities, ethnic or religious groups, diasporas and other communities struggling to emancipate themselves or trying to re-align their sense of identity and belonging within the wider social formations, while the youth of precisely these communities emulate the values and habits of their cosmopolitan counterparts.

Thus, one definition of world cinema would indeed see such films as part of the identity politics that has permeated both developed and developing nations. World cinema highlights the strains of emergent nationalism and its opposite, the re-emergence beneath the nation state of ethnic loyalty, regional affinity, local patriotism. World cinema films feature contested spaces, which speak of aspirations to regional autonomy, which invoke apparently long-forgotten histories and memories, even reviving feudal customs, clan and family values. In each case, they do so not in the form of political manifestos or top-down social programs, but across stories of journeys and discoveries, of everyday lives in harsh natural conditions or under difficult political circumstances. World cinema may deal with issues of Human Rights, explore diasporic identities, and engage in questions of heritage and cultural patrimony. One might expect stories that feature hitherto unheard voices or that bring out of the shadows the lives of the underprivileged. More broadly, one can say that world cinema is often driven by an essentially ethnographic outlook, even where the narratives are fictional and stories drawn from legends or folktales. Discourses of difference, otherness, authenticity, and poetry prevail, just as issues of history and tradition play a major role. In this manner some of the impulses of third cinema return – questions of underdevelopment, exclusion, racism, genocide, poverty, and of the clash between traditional ways of life and the impact of globalization, modernity, and Western habits or lifestyles. Additionally, world cinema deals with topics such as post-colonialism and expressions of national identity; it concerns the constructions of gender and ethnicity, family values and religion, concepts of good and evil, state authority and censorship, and the role/oppression of women in traditional societies.

Yet the dialectic operating here is that these films do so in the form and context of world cinema, which is to say, within the network of festivals, and for the marketplace of art houses and multiplexes. Formally speaking, in many cases, world cinema seems to be art cinema "light." Its treatment of time and space is closer to the mainstream than earlier experimental, avant-garde films or third cinema, and its narratives appropriate or cite conventional rhetorical strategies: for instance, the motif of the journey, quest or chase are almost universal. Indeed, the road movie is said to have made a comeback in world cinema if road movies were not already a reworking of a much older narrative pattern – that of the picaresque, which had served so well in letting the modern novel emerge out of the ancient chronicle. Likewise, the protagonists of world cinema films are usually drawn from the typology of anti-heroes of folk literature and the (picaresque) novel: ordinary folk, children, orphans, peasants, and suppressed women. There is much in world cinema that is reminiscent of other forms of ethnic kitsch, world music, or folkloric clothing made into high fashion, souvenir culture, and hip white chic. In any case, the films are close to popular consumer culture, even where they celebrate traditional customs, vanishing cultures, and the crafts of ancestors. Invariably, world cinema dramatizes conflicts between tradition and modernity, hegemony and the margins, global and local, Westernization and indigenization.

Insofar as this is its condition of existence, one might be forgiven for regarding world cinema as itself a symptom of neo-colonialism in the cultural sphere. Is it not in many respects another name for a cinema that "others" the other, even if the other colludes in the othering, as also happens with ethnic cuisine and world music? This self-othering might in fact stand in the way of encountering the otherness of the other (whether it is fundamentalist faith, different values systems inimical and incompatible with ours, such as women endorsing patriarchy or communities practicing forms of slavery, without feeling the need to reform). World cinema as post-national cinema prior to auteur status is always in danger of conducting a form of auto-ethnography, and promoting a sort of self-exoticization, in which the ethnic, the local or the regional expose themselves, under the guise of self-expression, to the gaze of the benevolent other, with all the consequences that this entails. World cinema invariably implies the look from outside and thus conjures up the old anthropological dilemma of the participant observer being presented with the mirror of what the "native" thinks the other, the observer wants to see.

Nowhere are the dilemmas of world cinema more apparent than in the vexed question of certain world cinemas' relation to diasporic communities, including such communities in Europe. There, the question of different forms of othering, in the form of certain films made for export and then re-imported, have given rise to fierce discussion. For instance, are the vast diasporas and markets for Indian and Chinese films not "depleting the national cultural imaginary by making it profitable to produce films that primarily service the homesickness of the diasporic communities"? [21] Or is this itself a skewed view of these diasporic communities and the manner in which they partake in the modern media and communication revolution? With respect to television, as well as the videotape market, there have been many sociological studies of diasporic media use, and the results give a more mixed and nuanced picture than one might have expected. To quote from Kevin Robins and Asu Aksoi's field work on the use of Turkish television by London diasporic communities:

> What we have tried to suggest is that, in the Turkish case at least, transnational television might actually be working to subvert the diasporic imagination and its imperatives of identification and belonging. But our critique goes further than this. We have also argued that it is necessary to jettison the basic concepts of "identity," "imagined community" and "diaspora." ...[W]e have felt it necessary to go against the grain of the prevailing culturalism, and to... move our agenda away from the "problem" of migrant culture and identity, to consider how it is that migrants experience migration, and how they think and talk about and make sense of their experiences. The point about identities is that they require simplicity. In the case of minds and consciousness, what is important is always their complexity.[22]

What is being asserted here about metropolitan diasporic communities is worth bearing in mind for the issues that concern us here. When asking about European cinema and how to define it, it may also be necessary to jettison the concept of identity. In other words, what makes European cinema "European" would be its capacity for cultural competence, rather than its assertion of cultural identity. More concretely, this cultural competence would be a film's ability to master the registers of address that overcome even the film festival film's strategies of othering, while also intersecting with the Hollywood film's capacity for cultural camouflage. In the chapter on spaces in European cinema I have tried to identify some of the ways in which the "mutual interference in each others' internal affairs" can generate major categories not just of the political, but also of the narratological and the aesthetic, at the same time as it is precisely the level of engagement, where European films speak to Asian films and to Hollywood films, but speak differently, that is at stake. It is as if European cinema first had to learn to be world cinema, with all the dangers of self-othering this entails, before it can be (once more?) European, that is to say, before it recognizes its part in the process of becoming a stranger to its own identity, while no longer understanding this identity only "face to face with Hollywood". It would indicate the point at which the various national cinemas' "historical imaginaries", in which – as the preceding essays have tried to show – the different kinds of self-othering are invariably caught, can leave behind the precariously balanced, but a-symmetrically distributed power-relations with Hollywood. European cinema may be about to enter a different dialogical space, where the voice of the auteur, on the far side of self-expression, but also on the far side of having to represent his or her constituency, can manifest itself as a voice addressing the world, in the world's terms. Perhaps this is the lesson that Europe's diasporic filmmakers have been quicker to learn than the rest. Like Fatih Akin, they are happy to trade in their hyphenated identities as nationals for a place in the world community of those who "interfere in internal affairs": that capacity so unique to the cinema, of seeing through the eyes of others into the mind of the self.

Notes

1. For a more detailed argument about the second-order reality of the labels auteur and art cinema in, for instance, the New German cinema, see the chapter "Cinema as *Kultur*", in Thomas Elsaesser, *New German Cinema: A History* (London: Macmillan, 1989), 28-51, and my chapter on "New German Cinema" in Elizabeth Ezra (ed.), *European Cinema* (Oxford: Oxford University Press, 2004), 194-213.
2. See Richard Dyer and Ginette Vincendeau (eds.), *Popular European Cinema* (London: Routledge, 1992).
3. These are among the French examples in Pierre Nora's monumental study *Les Lieux de mémoire* (Paris: Gallimard, 1984-1992).
4. A useful overview of European co-production practice in the art cinema is Mark Betz, "The Name above the (Sub-)Title: Internationalism, Co-production and Polyglot European Art Cinema", *Camera Obscura* 46 (2001), 1-46.

5. I am borrowing this scheme from a presentation given by my colleague Jan Simons, with whom for several years I taught a course on "Europe-Hollywood-Europe" at the University of Amsterdam.

6. Tyler Cowen, *Creative Destruction: How Globalization Is Changing the World's Culture* (Princeton, N.J.: Princeton University Press, 2002). Richard Pells, *Not Like Us: How Europeans Have Loved, Hated, and Transformed American Culture Since World War II* (New York: Basic Books, 1997).

7. For a summary see Toby Miller, "Hollywood and the World" in John Hill, Pamela Church Gibson (eds.), *The Oxford Guide to Film Studies* (New York: Oxford University Press, 1998), 371-81. An earlier call to arms and of alarm came from a former insider, David Puttnam, *The Undeclared War: The Struggle For Control Of The World's Film Industry*. (London : HarperCollins, 1997).

8. The figures are taken from Toby Miller et al. (eds.), *Global Hollywood* (London: BFI Publishing, 2003).

9. For a more detailed argument against the various subsidy systems as implemented by European countries, see Tyler Cowen, *Creative Destruction* (Princeton: Princeton University Press, 2002), 73-101.

10. "Do you love world cinema (a.k.a. foreign films, or international movies, or auteur cinema, or just about anything that's not made in Hollywood)? Then you've no doubt noticed, as I have, how difficult it is to find information on the Internet about these films. That's why I've created this webpage devoted to international films, directors, and actors." <http://www.geocities.com/Paris/Metro/9384/intro.htm>

11. From the blurb of a recent textbook: "Is there such a thing as 'World cinema'? Is it simply cinema that isn't from Hollywood? Is British or European cinema part of World cinema or is World cinema something other than our own? These are the key questions students need to consider when studying this subject. The aim of this guide is to provide teachers with a comprehensive approach to teaching World cinema topics. It offers opportunities for development of key concepts around case studies of national cinemas. Table of contents: *Key concepts and terms, *Investigation of 'World cinema' as a classification, the role of New Wave cinema, *The concept of a 'national cinema', *Directors and stars, *Finance and distribution issues * Case studies: the cinemas of Hong Kong, Denmark, Sweden and France." Kate Gamm, *Teaching World Cinema* (London: BFI Publishing, 2004).

12. "Heimat ist ein mentaler Zustand: Solino, Scorsese und die Globalisierung": Fatih Akin im Gespräch mit Michael Ranze, *epd Film*, 11 (November 2002).

13. Christina Klein, "The Asia Factor in Global Hollywood: Breaking down the notion of a distinctly American cinema", *Yale Global*, 25 March 2003. See also: Wade Major, "Hollywood's Asian Strategy," *Transpacific*, March 1997, 24-35.

14. Christina Klein, "The Asia Factor in Global Hollywood." <http://yaleglobal.yale.edu/display.article?id=1242>

15. <http://www.berlinale.de/en/das_festival/world_cinema_fund/wcf_profil/index.html>.

16. From the website of the Toronto International Film Festival: "Contemporary World Cinema is the Festival's core programme. Festival programmers scour the globe to find the best of current international filmmaking and the result is a showcase of inspiring new work to thrill Toronto's film-savvy audiences. The rich diversity of world cinema is highlighted in this programme, which consists of approximately 60 films from around the world. It is a lavish collection of films from major directors,

featuring premieres and prize-winning films selected from a variety of film festivals and programming trips." <http://www.e.bell.ca/filmfest/2004/filmsschedules/contemporaryworld.asp >

17. A detailed assessment of the nature and impact of talent transfers from Europe to Hollywood can be found in Melis Behlil, *Hollywood's Global Talent* (PhD Thesis, University of Amsterdam, forthcoming 2006).

18. Anne Jäckel, *European Film Industries* (London: BFI Publishing, 2004).

19. The exceptions might be Luc Besson, Jean Pierre Jeunet, or Lars von Trier. Jan Simons has argued that the Dogma aesthetics is best understood as an extended exploration of games, levels and simulation. See Jan Simons, *Dogmaville* (Amsterdam University Press, forthcoming, 2005).

20. A telling account of working with a UK producer for the US market by Søren Kragh-Jacobsen about his experience with *The Island on Bird Street* (1997) is given in Mette Hjørt/Ib Bjondebjerg, *The Danish Directors: Dialogues on a Contemporary National Cinema*. Bristol: Intellect Books, 2001, 165-169. Kragh-Jacobsen mentions his differences with the screenwriter John Goldman, chosen under pressure from the US investors, and discusses how co-financing and co-production determine key elements of a film, including, for instance, the ending.

21. Ravi Vasudevan, "National Pasts and Futures: Indian Cinema," *Screen* 41, no. 1 (2000), 119-25.

22. Asu Aksoy and Kevin Robins, "Thinking across spaces: Transnational television from Turkey", *European Journal of Cultural Studies* 2000, 3: 343-365 (365).

European Cinema: A Brief Bibliography

General Introductions, Readers and Encyclopaedias

Ian Aitken, *European Film Theory and Cinema: A Critical Introduction* (Edinburgh: Edinburgh University Press, 2001)

Wendy Everett (ed.), *European Identity in Cinema* (Exeter: Intellect, 1996)

Elizabeth Ezra (ed.): *European Cinema* (Oxford: Oxford University Press, 2004)

Angus Finney, *The State of European Cinema* (London: Cassell, 1996)

Jill Forbes and Sarah Street, *European Cinema: An Introduction* (Basingstoke: Palgrave, 2000)

Catherine Fowler, *The European Cinema Reader* (London: Routledge, 2002)

Diana Holmes and Alison Smith (eds.), *100 Years of European Cinema: Entertainment or Ideology?* (Manchester: Manchester University Press, 2000)

Fabian Maray (ed.), *Visages du cinéma européen* (Paris: Éditions Luc Pire, 2003)

Geoffrey Nowell-Smith (ed.), *Television: The European Experience* (London: British Film Institute, 1991)

Duncan Petrie (ed.*), Screening Europe: Image and Identity in Contemporary European Cinema* (London: British Film Institute, 1992)

Pierre Sorlin, *European Cinemas: European Societies 1939-1990* (London: Routledge, 1991)

Ginette Vincendeau (ed.), *Encyclopaedia of European Cinema* (London: Cassell & British Film Institute, 1995

Ginette Vincendeau, "Issues in European Cinema," in John Hill and Pamela Church Gibson (eds.), *The Oxford Guide to Film Studies* (Oxford: Oxford University Press, 1998), 440-448

The European Art Cinema

Roy Armes, *The Ambiguous Image: Narrative Style in Modern European Cinema* (London: Secker & Warburg, 1976)

David Bordwell, *Narration and the Fiction Film* (Madison: University of Wisconsin Press, 1985)

Pamela Falkenberg, "Hollywood and Art Cinema as Bipolar Modelling System," in *Wide Angle*, 7/3 (1985), 44-53

Robert Philip Kolker, *The Altering Eye: Contemporary International Cinema* (Oxford: Oxford Univ. Press 1983)

Steve Neale, "Art Cinema as Institution," in *Screen* 22/1 (1981), 11-39

John Orr, *The Art and Politics of Film* (Cambridge: Polity Press, 2000)

John Orr and Olga Taxidou (eds.), *Post-War Cinema and Modernity: A Film Reader* (Edinburgh: Edinburgh Univ. Press, 2000)

David Pascoe, *Peter Greenaway Museums and Moving Images* (London: Reaktion Books 1997)

Catherine Russell, *Narrative Mortality: Death, Closure and New Wave Cinemas* (Minneapolis: University of Minnesota Press, 1995)

Alan Woods, *Being Naked Playing Dead* (New York: St. Martin's Press, 1997)

The European Avant-gardes

Kees Bakker (ed.), *Joris Ivens and the Documentary Context* (Amsterdam: Amsterdam University Press 2000)

Ian Christie, "The Avant-gardes and European Cinema before 1930" in John Hill and Pamela Church Gibson (eds.), *The Oxford Guide to Film Studies* (Oxford: Oxford Univ. Press, 1998), 449-454

David Curtis, *Experimental Cinema: A Fifty Year Evolution (London: Studio Vista, 1971)*

Paul Hammond (ed.), *The Shadow and Its Shadow: Surrealist Writings on Cinema* (London: British Film Institute, 1978)

Céline Linssen and Hans Schoots and Tom Gunning, *Het gaat om de film! Een nieuwe geschiedenis van de Nederlandsche Filmliga 1927-1933* (Amsterdam: Bas Lubberhuizen / Filmmuseum, 1999)

A.L. Rees, *A History of Experimental Film and Video* (London: BFI, 1999)

Helma Schleif (ed.), *Stationen der Moderne im Film. 1. Film und Foto. Eine Ausstellung des Deutschen Werkbunds, Stuttgart 1929. Rekonstruktion des Filmprogramms. – 2. Texte, Manifeste, Pamphlete* 2 vols. (Berlin: Freunde der Deutschen Kinemathek 1988, 1989)

Martin Stollery, *Alternative Empires: European Modernist Cinemas and Cultures of Imperialism* (Exeter: Exeter University Press 2001)

Paul Willemen, *Looks and Frictions* (London: British Film Institute, 1994)

Peter Wollen, "The Two Avant-gardes," in *Readings and Writings* (London: Verso, 1982)

Europe-Hollywood-Europe

a. Cultural and Aesthetic Histories

Nick Browne (ed.), *Cahiers du Cinéma 3. 1969-1972: The Politics of Representation* (London: Routledge, 1989)

David Ellwood, Rob Kroes (eds.), *Hollywood in Europe* (Amsterdam: VU, 1994)

Thomas Elsaesser *"Holland to Hollywood and Back,"* in J.C.H. Blom and J. Leersen (eds.), *De onmacht van het grote: cultuur in Europa* (Amsterdam: Amsterdam University Press, 1993)

Christopher Frayling, *Spaghetti Western: Cowboys and Europeans from Karl May to Sergio Leone* (London, Routledge & Kegal Paul, 1981)

Deniz Göktürk, *Künstler, Cowboys, Ingenieure* (Munich: Wilhelm Fink 1998)

Victoria de Grazia, *"European cinema and the idea of Europe, 1925-95,"* in G. Nowell-Smith, and S. Ricci (eds.) *Hollywood and Europe: Economics, Culture and National Identity 1945-95* (London: British Film Institute/UCLA, 1998)

T.H. Guback, *The International Film Industry. Western Europe and America since 1945* (Bloomington: Indiana University Press, 1969)

Jim Hillier, *Cahiers du Cinéma 1. The 1950s: Neo-Realism, Hollywood, New Wave* (London: Routledge, 1985)

Jim Hillier (ed.), *Cahiers du Cinéma 2. 1960-1968: New Wave, New Cinema, Re-evaluating Hollywood: An Anthology from Cahiers du Cinema nos. 103-207* (London: Routledge, 1986)

Norman Kagan, *Greenhorns: Foreign Filmmakers Interpret America* (Ann Arbor: Pieran, 1982)

Thomas Kavanagh, *"Film Theory and the Two Imaginaries,"* in T. Kavanagh (ed.), *The Limits of Theory* (Stanford: Stanford University Press, 1988

Robert A. Kolker, *A Cinema of Loneliness* (Oxford: Oxford University Press, 1988)

Peter Lev, *The Euro-American Cinema* (Austin: University of Texas Press, 1993)

Lucy Mazdon, *Encore Hollywood: Remaking French Cinema* (London: British Film Institute, 2000)

Geoffrey Nowell-Smith (ed.), *Hollywood and Europe: Economics, Culture, National Identity 1945-95* (London: British Film Institute, 1998)

John Orr, *Cinema and Modernity* (Cambridge: Polity, 1993)

James Quinn, *The Film and Television as an Aspect of European Culture* (Leiden: Sijthoff, 1968)

Kerry Segrave, *Foreign Films in America. A History* (Jefferson NC: McFarland and Co. Inc Publisher, 2004)

Sarah Street: *Transatlantic Crossings. British Feature Films in the USA* (New York: Continuum, 2002)

Kristin Thompson, "National or International Films? The European Debate During the 1920s," in *Film History*, 8 (1996), 281-296

John Trumpbour, *Selling Hollywood to the World: U.S. and European Struggles for Mastery of the Global Film Industry, 1920-1950* (Cambridge: Cambridge University Press)

Barbara Wilinsky, *Sure Seaters: The Emergence of Art House Cinema* (Minneapolis: Univ. of Minnesota Press, 2001)

David Wilson (ed.), *Cahiers du Cinéma 4. 1973-1978: History, Ideology, Cultural Struggle* (London: Routledge, 2000)

b. Exile, Emigration, Trade

John Baxter, *Hollywood Exiles* (London: Macdonald and Janes, 1976)

Michel Boujut, *Europe-Hollywood et retour* (Paris: Editions Autrement, 1992)

Michel Ciment, *Les Conquerant d'un autre monde* (Paris: Stock, 1986)

Edgardo Cozarinsky, *Cinéastes en exil: exilés, immigrés, les cinéastes deplacés* (Paris: Cinémathèque Francaise, 1992)

Thomas Elsaesser, "William Dieterle and the Warner Bio-pic," in *Wide Angle*, 8/2 (1986)

Thomas Elsaesser, "Heavy Traffic," in Hamid Naficy (ed.), *Home, Exile, Homeland* (New York and London: Routledge, 1998)

Thomas Elsaesser, "A German Ancestry to Film Noir?," in *Iris*, 21 (1996), 129-144

Ursula Hardt, *From Caligari to California. Erich Pommer's Life in the International Film Wars* (Providence: Berghahn, 1996)

Andrew Higson, Richard Maltby (eds.), *"Film Europe' And 'Film America': Cinema, Commerce and Cultural Exchange, 1920 1939* (Exeter: University of Exeter Press, 1999)

Jan-Christopher Horak, "German Exile Cinema, 1933–1950" in: *Film History*, 8/4 (1996), 373-389

James Morrison, *Passport to Hollywood. Hollywood Films, European Directors* (Albany: SUNY Press, 1998)

Hamid Naficy, *An Accented Cinema. Exilic and Diasporic Filmmaking* (Princeton: Princeton University Press, 2001)

Graham Petrie, *Hollywood Destinies: European Directors in America 1922-1931* (London: Routledge, 1985)

John Russsell Taylor, *Strangers in Paradise: the Hollywood Emigres 1933-1950* (London: Faber & Faber, 1983)

Mike Wayne, *The Politics of Contemporary European Cinema: Histories, Borders, Diasporas* (Bristol: Intellect, 2002)

Don Whittemore, Philip Alan Cecchettini et al. (eds.), *Passport to Hollywood: Film Immigrants Anthology* (New York: MacGraw-Hill, 1976)
Martin Zolotow, *Billy Wilder in Hollywood* (London: Allen & Unwin, 1977)

c. Economic Histories

Anne-Maire Autissiers and Bizerns, Catherine, *Öffentliche Fördereinrichtungen für die Film-und audiovisuelle Industrie in Europa.* Band I & II (Strasbourg: Europäische Audiovisuelle Informationsstelle, 1998)
Tino Balio, "A Major Presence in All the World's Markets. The Globalization of Hollywood in the 1990s," in Steve Neale, Murray Smith (eds.), *Contemporary Hollywood Cinema* (London: Routledge, 1998), 58-73
Tim Bergfelder, "The Nation Vanishes: European Co-productions and Popular Genre Formulae in the 1950s and 1960s". In: *Cinema & Nation*, M. Hjort and S.Mackenzie (eds.) (London: Routledge, 2000)
Mark Betz, "*The Name above the (Sub)Title: Internationalism, Coproduction, and Polyglot European Art Cinema.*", in *Camera Obscura*, no. 46 (2000)
Catherine Bizern, *Public aid mechanisms for film and television in Europe* (Centre National de la Cinématographie, 1998)
M. Dale, *The Movie Game. The Film Business in Britain, Europe and America* (London: Cassel, 1997)
Tanja Nadine Ertel, *Globalisierung der Filmwirtschaft. Die Uruguay-Runde des GATT. Eine Analyse zur Oekonomie, Politik und Kultur von Film unter besonderer Beruecksichtigung der Mediengeschichte und der Positionen der Verhandlungspartner EG und UDA* (Europäische Hochschulschriften, 2001)
Claude Forest, *Economiés contemporaines du cinéma en Europe:L'improbable industrie* (Paris: CNRS Editions, 2001)
Victoria de Grazia, "Mass Culture and Sovereignty: American Challenge to European Cinemas, 1920-1960," in *Journal of Modern History,* 61 (March 1989)
Thomas H. Guback, "Cultural Identity and Film in the European Economic Community," in *Cinema Journal,* 23/3 (1974), 2-17
Paul Hainsworth, "Politics, Culture and Cinema in the New Europe." in *Border Crossing: Film in Ireland, Britain and Europe.* Eds. John Hill, Martin McLoone, and Paul Hainsworth, (Belfast: Institute of Irish Studies British Film Institute, 1994)
Aida A. Hozic, "*Hollyworld, Space, Power, and Fantasy in the American Economy*" (Cornell Univ. Press, 2002)
T. Ilott, *Budgets and Markets: A Study of the Budgeting of European Film* (New York and London: Routledge, 1996)
Anne Jäckel, *European Film Industries* (London: British Film Institute, 2003)

Ian Jarvie, *Hollywood's Overseas Campaign: The North Atlantic Movie Trade, 1920-1950* (Cambridge: Cambridge University Press 1992)

Paul Kerr (ed.), *Hollywood Film Industry: A Reader* (London, Routledge & Kegan Paul, 1986)

Albert Moran (ed.), *Film Policy: International, National and Regional Perspectives* (London, New York: Routledge, 1996)

David Puttnam, *The Undeclared War: The Struggle for Control of the World's Film Industry* (London: Harper Collins 1997)

Wilhelm Roth, "GATT, das Ende des Europäischen Kinos?," in *epd Film*, X/11 (november 93)

Tom Saunders, *Hollywood in Berlin* (Berkeley: University of California Press, 1992)

Stefan Toepler and Zimmer, Annette, "Subsidizing the Arts.Government and the Arts in Western Europe and the United States." In: *Global Culture. Media, Arts, Policy and Globalization* Diana Crane et al. (ed.) (London, New York: Routledge, 2002)

Kristin Thompson, *Exporting Entertainment* (London: British Film Institute, 1986)

Ruth Vasey, *The World According to Hollywood* (Madison: Wisconsin University Press, 1998)

Popular European Cinema

Steve Chibnall and Robert Murphy (eds.), *British Crime Cinema* (London: Routledge, 1999)

Pam Cook, *Fashioning the Nation. Costume and Identity in British Cinema* (London: British Film Institute, 1996)

Richard Dyer and Ginette Vincendeau (eds.), *Popular European Cinema* (London: Routledge, 1992)

Dimitris Eleftheriotis, *Popular Cinemas of Europe: Studies of Texts, Contexts, and Frameworks* (Cambridge: Cambridge University Press, 2002)

David Forgacs, "National-Popular: Genealogy of a Concept," in Simon During (ed.), *The Cultural Studies Reader* (New York: Routledge, 1993)

Julia Hallam, *Realism and popular cinema* (Manchester: Manchester University Press, 2000)

Ian Q. Hunter, *British Science Fiction Cinema* (London: Routledge, 1999)

Ernest Mathijs and Xavier Mendik (eds.), *Alternative Europe. Eurotrash and Exploitation Cinema Since 1945* (London: Routledge, 2004)

Jeffrey Richards (ed.), *The Unknown 1930s. An Alternative History of the British Cinema, 1929-1939* (London: I.B. Tauris 1998)

National Cinemas

Yoram Allon, *Contemporary British and Irish Film Directors* (London: Wallflower Press, 2001)

Ruth Barton, *Irish National Cinema* (London: Routledge, 2004)

I. Bondebjerg, *National Cinema, Cultural Identity and Globalization: Bille August and Lars von Trier* (Paper IAMCR Conference Glasgow, 1998)

Edward Buscombe, "Film History and the Idea of National Cinema," in *Australian Journal of Screen Theory*, 9/10 (1981), 141-153

Michel Ciment, "Europa, Europa", *Positif*, 437/438, 1997

Colin Crisp, *Classic French Cinema 1930-1960* (Bloomington, IN: Indiana Univ. Press, 1993)

Stephen Crofts, "Reconceptualizing National Cinema" in *Quarterly Review of Film and Video*, 14/3 (1993), 49-67

Stephen Crofts, "Concepts of National Cinema," in John Hill and Pamela Church Gibson (eds.), *The Oxford Guide to Film Studies* (Oxford: Oxford University Press, 1998), 385-394

Sean Cubitt, "Introduction. Over the Borderlines", Screen, 30(4), 1989.

John Cunningham, *Hungarian Cinema: From Coffee House to Multiplex.* (London: Wallflower, 2004)

Darrell W. Davis, "Re-Igniting Japanese Tradition with *Hana-Bi*." In: *Cinema Journal* 40, 4 (Summer 2001), 58-79

Richard Dyer and Ginette Vincendeau, "Introduction." In: Dyer, Vincendeau (eds.): *Popular European Cinema* (London, New York: Routledge 1992), 1-14

Thomas Elsaesser, *New German Cinema: A History* (London: British Film Institute, 19942)

Thomas Elsaesser: "The Idea of National Cinema." ('De competitie met Hollywood'), in: *Skrien* 186 (Oct/Nov 1992)

Peter Evans, *Spanish Cinema* (Oxford: Oxford University Press, 1999)

Angus Finney, *The State of European Cinema: A New Dose of Reality* (London: Cassell, 1996)

Jill Forbes, *French Cinema Since the Nouvelle Vague* (London: British Film Institute, 1992)

Lester Friedman (ed.), *Fires Were Started: British Cinema and Thatcherism* (Minnesota University Press, 1992)

Marek Haltof, *Polish National Cinema* (Oxford: Berghahn Books, 2002)

Rémi Fournier Lanzoni, *French Cinema from its Beginnings to the Present* (London: Continuum, 2004)

Bill Grantham, "Some Big Bourgeois Brothel," in *Contexts for France's Culture Wars with Hollywood* (Luton: University of Luton Press, 2000)

Naomi Greene, *Landscapes of Loss: The National Past in Postwar French Cinema* (Princeton: Princeton University Press, 1999)

Kerstin Gutberlet, *The State of the Nation. Das britische Kino der Neunziger Jahre* (St. Augustin: Gardez! Verlag, 2001)

Sabine Hake, *German National Cinema* (London: Routledge, 2002)

J. Hallam, Film, *Class and National Identity: Re-imagining Communities in the Age of Devolution* (Manchester: Manchester University Press, 2001)

Paul Hainsworth, "Politics, Culture and Cinema in the New Europe." In John Hill, Martin McLoone, and Paul Hainsworth (eds.), *Border Crossing: Film in Ireland, Britain and Europe* (Belfast: Institute of Irish Studies in association with the University of Ulster and the British Film Institute, 1994)

Susan Hayward, "Framing National Cinemas," in Hjort, MacKenzie (eds.), *Film & Nation*, 88-102

Susan Hayward, Ginette Vincendeau (eds.), *French Cinema* (London: Routledge 1999)

Stephen Heath, "Film and Nationhood," *Cinetracts* 1, 4 (Spring/Summer 1978), 2-12. Reprinted in Ron Burnett (ed.), *Explorations in Film Theory* (Bloomington: Indiana University Press, 1991)

Andrew Higson, "The Concept of National Cinema," *Screen*, 30/4 (1989), 36-46

Andrew Higson, "The Limiting Imagination of National Cinema," in: Hjort, MacKenzie (eds.): *Film & Nation* 2000, 63-74

Andrew Higson, "National Cinemas, International Markets, Cross-Cultural Identities," in Ib Bondebjerg (ed.), *Moving Images, Culture and the Mind* (Luton: University of Luton Press / John Libby Media, 2000)

Andrew Higson, *Waving the Flag: Constructing a National Cinema in Britain* (Oxford: Oxford University Press, 1995)

Andrew Higson, "The Instability of the National," in Justine Ashby, Andrew Higson (eds.), *British Cinema, Past and Present* (London: Routledge, 2000)

Andrew Higson, *British Cinema, Past and Present* (London: Routledge, 2001)

John Hill, "The Future of European Cinema: The Economics and Culture of Pan-European Strategies," in: Hill, J., McLoone, M. and Hainsworth, P. (eds.) *Border crossing and Film in Ireland, Britain and Europe* (Institute of Irish Studies in association with University of Ulster and the British Film Institute, 1994)

John Hill, "From the New Wave to Brit-grit: Continuity and Difference in Working-class Realism." In *British Cinema, Past and Present*. Justine Ashby and Andrew Higson (eds.), (London: Routledge, 2000)

John Hill, "The Issue of National Cinema and British Film Production," in: Donald Petrie (ed.), *New Questions of British Cinema* (London: British Film Institute, 1992), 10-21

John Hill, "British Cinema as National Cinema: Production, Audience and Representation," in: Robert Murphy (ed.), *The British Cinema Book* (London: British Film Institute, 1997), 244-254

Mette Hjort, "Themes of Nation," in: Hjort, MacKenzie (eds.): *Film & Nation* 2000, 103-117

Mette Hjort and Scott MacKenzie (eds.), *Cinema & Nation* (London, New York: Routledge, 2000)

Ian Jarvie, "National Cinema: A Theoretical Assessment," in Hjort, MacKenzie (eds.), *Film & Nation* 2000, 75-87

Marsha Kinder, *Blood Cinema: The Reconstruction of National Identity in Spain* (Berkeley: University of California Press, 1993)

Michel Marie, *The French New Wave: An Artistic School* (Oxford: Blackwell, 2003)

Marcus Millicent, *After Fellini: National Cinema in the Postmodern Age* (Baltimore: John Hopkins University Press, 2002)

Claire Monk, "Underbelly UK: The 1990s Underclass Film, Masculinity and the Ideologies of 'New' Britain," in Justin Ashby, Andrew Higson (eds.), *British Cinema, Past and Present* (London: Routledge, 2001)

Philip Moseley, *Split Screen: Belgian Cinema and Cultural Identity* (Albany: State University Press, 2001)

Luckett, Moya, "*Travel and Mobility: Femininity and National Identity in Swinging London Films,*" in Justin Ashby, Andrew Higson, *British Cinema, Past and Present* (London: Routledge, 2001)

Robert Murphy (ed.) *British Cinema of the 90s* (London: British Film Institute, 2000)

Geoffrey Nowell-Smith, "But Do We Need It?," in: Martyn Auty and Nick Roddick (eds.), *British Cinema Now* (London: British Film Institute, 1985), 147-158

Duncan Petrie (ed.), *New Questions of British Cinema* (London: British Film Institute, 1992)

Phil Powrie, *On the threshold between past and present: alternative heritage,*" in Justin Ashby, Andrew Higson (eds.), *British Cinema, Past and Present* (London: Routledge, 2001)

René Prédal, *50 ans de cinéma français (1945-1995)* (Paris: Nathan, 1997)

René Prédal, *Le Jeune Cinema Français* (Paris: Nathan, 2002)

Guido Rings and Rikki Morgan-Tamosunas (ed.), *European Cinema: Inside Out. Images of the Self and the Other in Postcolonial European Film* (Heidelberg: Winter, 2003)

Philip Rosen, "History, Textuality, Narration: Kracauer, Burch, and Some Problems in the Study of National Cinemas," in *Iris*, 2, 2 (1984), 69-84

Philip Rosen, "Nation and Anti-Nation: Concepts of National Cinema in the 'New' Media Era," *Disapora* 5.3, 1996

Ulrike Sieglohr, *Heroines without Heroes: Reconstructing Female and National Identities in European Cinema, 1945-51* (London: Castell, 2000)

Marc Silberman, "What Is German in the German Cinema? " in *Film History*, 8 (1996), 297-315

Jan Simons, "Het vermijden van pijnlijke zelfportretten," in *de Groene Amsterdammer* (18 December 1985)

Skrien (October/November 1992), special issue: Dutch cinema

Tytti Soila, Astrid Soderbergh-Widding, Gunnar Iverson, *Nordic National Cinemas* (London: Routledge, 1998)

Pierre Sorlin, *European Cinemas, European Societies 1939-1990* (London: Routledge, 1994)

Pierre Sorlin, *Italian National Cinema 1896-1996* (London: Routledge, 1996)

Kristin Thompson, "National or International Films? The European Debate During the 1920s," in: *Film History* 8 (1996), 281-296

Kristin Thompson, "Nation, National Identity and the International Cinema," in: *Film History* 8 (1996), 259-260 (Introduction to special issue of *Film History*)

Nuria Triana-Toribio, *Spanish National Cinema* (London: Routledge, 2003)

Paul Willemen, "The National," in P.W.: *Looks and Frictions: Essays in Cultural Studies and Film Theory* (London / Bloomington, IN: British Film Institute / Indiana University Press, 1994), 206-219

Alan Williams, *Film and Nationalism* (Brunswick: Rutgers University Press, 2002)

Filmmuseum Berlin Deutsche Kinemathek (ed.), *European 60s. Revolte, Phantasie & Utopie* (München: Beck, 2002)

W. Winston-Dixon (ed.), *Re-viewing British Cinema. 1900-1992* (New York: State University of New York Press, 1994)

Space, Time and Place in European Cinema

Ien Ang and David Morley (eds.) *Cultural Studies*, 3/2 (1989 special issue: "European Identities")

Marc Augé, *Non-Place: An Introduction to an Anthropology of Supermodernity* (London: Verso, 1995)

Gilles Deleuze, *Cinema II. The Time Image* (Minneapolis: University of Minnesota Press, 1985)

Fredric Jameson, *The Political Unconscious: Narrative as a Socially Symbolic Act* (Ithaca: Cornell University Press, 1981)

Fredric Jameson, *Signatures of the Visible* (London and New York: Routledge, 1990)

Fredric Jameson, *The Geopolitical Aesthetic* (London: British Film Institute, 1992)

Myrto Konstantarakos (ed.) *Spaces in European Cinema* (Exeter: Intellect, 2000)

Armand Mattelart, *The International Image Market* (London: Verso, 1994)

David Morley and Kevin Robins, "Spaces of Identity: Communications Technologies and the Reconfiguration of Europe," in *Screen* 30/4 (1989), 10-34

Kevin Robins, "Re-imagined Communities? European Image Spaces Beyond Fordism," *Cultural Studies*, 3/2 (1989)

Anthony Wilden, "in Culture and Identity: The Canadian Question," in *Cine-Tracts*, 7/8 (1984)

The Cinematic City / City and Mobility

Donald Albrecht, *Designing Dreams: Modern Architecture in the Movies* (New York: Harper & Row 1986)

Stephen Barber, *Fragments of the European City* (London: Reaktion Books, 1999)

Centre Européen de la Culture (ed.), *Transeuropéennes* (Paris: Centre Européen de la Culture 1993ff.). No. 21: Relier la ville. (2002)

David Clarke (ed.), *The Cinematic City* (London: Routledge, 1997)

Ewa Mazierska, *From Moscow to Madrid: Postmodern Cities, European Cinema* (London: IB Tauris, 2003)

David Morley & Robins, K. *Spaces of Identity. Global Media, Electronic Landscapes and Cultural Boundaries* (London: Routledge, 1995)

Mark Lamster, *Architecture and Film* (New York: Princeton Architectural Press, 2000)

Dietrich Neumann (ed.), *Film Architecture. From Metropolis to Blade Runner* (Munich: Prestel 1996)

François Penz and Maureen Thomas (eds.), *Cinema and Architecture. Méliès, Mallet-Stevens, Multimedia* (London: British Film Institute, 1997)

Mark Shiel (ed.), *Cinema and the City. Film and Urban Societies in a Global Context* (Oxford: Blackwell, 2001)

Edward W. Soja. "Heterologies: A Remembrance of Other Spaces in the Citadel LA" *Postmodern Cities and Spaces*. Sophie Watson & Katherine Gibson (eds.), (Cambridge: Blackwell, 1995)

The Nation, Europe, Identity, Diversity

Benedict Anderson, *Imagined Communities: Reflections on the Origin and Spread of Nationalism* (London: Verso, 1991)

G.J. Ashworth & P.J. Larkham (eds.), *Building a New Heritage: Tourism, Culture and Identity in the New Europe* (London: Routledge, 1994)

Homi K. Bhabha (ed.), *Nation and Narration* (London: Routledge, 1990)

Homi K. Bhabha, *The Location of Culture* (London, New York: Routledge 1994)

L. van den Berg, J. van der Meer Philip, *Urban Tourism: Performance and Strategies in Eight European Cities* (London: Avebury, 1995)

Michael Billig, *Banal Nationalism* (London: Sage 1995)

Pim den Boer, *Europa. De geschiedenis van een idee* (Amsterdam: Ooievaar, 1997)

Manuel Castells, "*The Information Age: Economy, Society, and Culture Volume I: The Rise of the Network Society* (Oxford: Blackwell, 1997)

Robert Cooper, *The Breaking of Nations: Order and Chaos in the Twenty-First Century* (Atlantic Monthly Press, 2004)

Terry Eagleton, Fredric Jameson, Edward Said (eds.), *Nationalism, Colonialism and Literature* (Minneapolis: University of Minnesota Press 1990)

G. Evans, *Cultural Planning and Towards an Urban Renaissance* (London: Routledge, 2000)

Ernest Gellner, *Nations and Nationalism* (Oxford: Blackwell, 1983)

Ernest Gellner, *Nationalism* (London: Weidenfeld 1997)

Marie Gillespie, "Audio-Visual Culture Among South Asian Families," *Cultural Studies*, 3/2 (1989)

B.J. Graham (ed.), Modern *Europe and Place, Culture, Identity* (London: Arnold, 1998)

Liah Greenfeld, *Nationalism: Five Roads to Modernity* (Cambridge: Harvard University Press 1993)

John A. Hall *(ed.), The State of the Nation: Ernest Gellner and the Theory of Nationalism (Cambridge: Cambridge University Press 1998)*

Eric J.Hobsbawn, *Nations and Nationalism since 1780: Programme, Myth, Reality* (Cambridge: Cambridge University Press, 1990)

John Hutchinson, *Modern Nationalism* (London: Fontana, 1994)

Eugene Kamenka (ed.), *Nationalism: The Nature and Evolution of an Idea* (London: Edward Arnold, 1976)

David MacCrone, *The Sociology of Nationalism. Tomorrow's Ancestors* (London and New York: Routledge, 1998)

Tom Nairn, *The Break-Up of Britain* (London: New Left Books, 1977)

—, *Faces of Nationalism: Janus Revisited.* (London: Verso, 1997)

Carl H. Pegg, *Evolution of the European Idea, 1914-1932* (Chapel Hill, University of North Carolina Press 1983)

Anthony D. Smith, *Theories of Nationalism* (London: Duckworth, 1983)

—, *The Ethnic Origins of Nations.* (Oxford: Blackwell 1986)

—, *National Identity.* (London: Penguin / Reno: University of Nevada Press, 1991)

—, *Nationalism and Modernism* (London, New York: Routledge 1998)

Yael Tamir, *Liberal Nationalism* (Princeton: Princeton University Press, 1993)

Transnational Cinema

Arjun Appadurai, Disjucture and Difference in the Global Cultural Economy. In *Modernity at Large. Cultural Dimensions of Globalisation* (Minneapolis and London: University of Minnesota Press, 1996)

Birgit Beumers (ed.) *Russia on Reels: The Russian Idea in Post-Soviet Cinema* (London: I.B. Tauris, 1999)

Sheila Cornelius, *New Chinese Cinema: Challenging Representations* (London: Wallflower, 2004)

Okwui Enwezor (eds.) *Democracy unrealized: Documenta 11, Platform 1* (Kassel: Hatje Cantz, 2002)

Poshek Fu, David Desser (ed.), *The Cinema of Hong Kong: History, Arts, Identity* (Cambridge University Press, 2002)

Kate Gamm, *Teaching World Cinema* (London British Film Institute, 2004)

Denis Göktürk, Migration und Kino – Substantielle Mitleidskultur oder transnationale Rollenspiel? In Carmine Chiellino (ed.): *Interkulturelle Literatur in Deutschland. Ein Handbuch* (Stuttgart/Weimar: Metzler, 2000)

John Hill and Pamela Church Gibson (eds.), *World Cinema: Critical Approaches* (Oxford: Oxford University Press, 2000)

Dina Iordanova, *Cinema of the Other Europe: the Industry and Artistry of East Central European Film* (London: Wallflower, 2003)

Dina Iordanova, *Cinema of Flames. Balkan Film, Culture, and the Media* (London: British Film Institute 2001)

David E. James, Kyung Hyun Kim (ed.), *Im Kwon-Taek: The Making of a Korean National Cinema* (Wayne State University Press, 2001)

Raminder Kaur, Ajay J. Sinhar (eds.), *Bollyworld: Popular Indian Cinema Through a Transnational Lens* (London: Sage, 2005)

Paul S.N. Lee, Three Processes of Dissolving Boundaries. Internationalization, Marketization and Acculturation, in *In the Search of Boundaries.* Joseph Michan, Bryce T. McIntyre (eds.) (Newport,CT: Ablex Publishing, 2002)

Toby Miller, et al. *Global Hollywood* (London: British Film Institute, 2001)

Lucia Nagib, *The New Brazilian Cinema* (London: I.B. Tauris, 2003)

Andrew Nestingen, Trevor Glen Elkington, *Transnational Cinema in A Global North: Nordic Cinema in Transition (Contemporary Approaches to Film and Television)* (Detroit: Wayne State University Press, 2005)

Geoffrey Nowell-Smith, *The Oxford History of World Cinema* (Oxford: Oxford University Press, 1999)

Donald Richie, *A Hundred Years of Japanese Film* (Tokyo: Kodansha, 2001)

Ella Shohat, Robert Stam (ed.), *Multiculturalism, Postcoloniality and Transnational Media* (New Brunswick: Rutgers University Press, 2003)

Naomi Sakr, *Satellite Realms, Transnational Television, Globalization and the Middle East* (London: I.B.Tauris, 2002)

Alexandra Schneider, "Emotion.Fiktion. Identität: Transkulturalität und Geschlechterdifferenz in Filmen von jungen Regisseurinnen", in *Cinema* (Switzerland), no. 46, 2001

M. Mehdi Semati, Soitirin Patty J., "Hollywood's Transnational Appeal. Hegemony and Democratic Potential?" in *Journal of Popular Film Television*, 1999

Cindy Hing-Yuk Wong, "Cities, Cultures and Cassettes: Hong Kong Cinema and Transnational Audiences", *Post Script*, 1999

Esther Yau, *At Full Speed: Hong Kong in a Borderless World* (Minneapolis: University of Minnesota Press, 2001)

Yingjin Zhang, *Chinese National Cinema* (London: Routledge, 2004)

Yingjin Zhang, *Screening China: Critical Interventions, Cinematic Reconfigurations, and the Transnational Imaginary in Contemporary Chinese Cinema* (Ann Arbor: University of Michigan Press, 2002)

Film Festivals

Peter Bart, *Cannes: fifty years of sun, sex & celluloid: behind the scenes at the world's most famous film festival* (Hyperion: New York, 1997)

Cari Beauchamp and Henri Béhar, *Hollywood on the Riviera: The Inside Story of the Cannes Film Festival* (William Morrow and Company Inc.: New York, 1992)

Pierre Billard, *Festival de Cannes: d'or et de palmes* (Gallimard: Paris, 1997)

Export-Union des Deutschen Films (ed.), *Film Festivals in Germany. A Comprehensive Guide* (Berlin: 2001/2002)

Steven Gaydos, *The Variety Guide to Film Festivals: The Ultimate Insider's Guide to Film Festivals Around the World* (New York: The Berkeley Publishing Group, 1998)

Chris Gore, *The Ultimate Film Festival Survival Guide: The Essential Companion for Filmmakers and Festival-Goers* (Lone Eagle Publishing Company: Los Angeles, 1999)

Wolfgang Jacobsen, *Fünfzig Jahre Berlinale Internationale Filmfestspiele Berlin* (Berlin: Nicolai, 2000)

Adam Langer, *The Film Festival Guide: For Filmmakers, Film Buffs, and Industry Professionals* (Chicago: Chicago Review Press, 2nd revised ed. 2000)

The Museum of Modern Art, New York (ed.), *Cannes 45 Years: Festival International du Film* (New York: MoMA, 1992)

Lorry Smith, *Party in a Box: The Story of the Sundance Film Festival* (Salt Lake City: Gibbs-Smith Publisher, 2001)

Julian Stringer, "Global Cities and the International Festival Economy," in M. Shiel and Fitzmaurice, T., *Cinema and the City: Film and Urban Societies in a Global Context* (Oxford: Blackwell Publishers, 2001)

Shael Stolberg (ed.), *International Film Festival Guide* (Sundance: Festival Products, 3rd edition, 2000)

Kenneth Turan, *Sundance to Sarajevo: Film Festivals and the World They Made* (Berkeley: University of California Press, 2002)

Stephan Walker, *King of Cannes: Madness, Mayhem, and the Movies* (New York, London: Penguin Books, 2001)

List of Sources and Places of First Publication

"European Cinema: Conditions of Impossibility", unpublished, 2005

"European Culture, National Cinema, the Auteur and Hollywood", first presented at the "European Cultural Rights" conference, Louisiana Museum of Modern Art, Humlebek (Denmark), June 1994

"ImpersoNations: National Cinema, Historical Imaginaries", presentation at the "Cinema Europe" PhD seminar, University of Amsterdam, February 2002

"Festival Networks: the New Topographies of Cinema in Europe", unpublished, 2005

"Double Occupancy and Small Adjustments: Space, Place and Policy", paper presented at the "Fortress Europe" conference, Department of Romance and Germanic Languages, University of London, April 2005

"Ingmar Bergman – person and PERSONA ", first published as "Ingmar Bergman: Art Cinema and Beyond", *Sight and Sound* (April 1994), 22-27 and as "Ingmar Bergman - Person and PERSONA: The Mountain of Modern Cinema on the Road to Morocco", in H. Perridon (ed.), *Strindberg, Ibsen and Bergman: Scandinavian Film and Drama* (Maastricht: Shaker, 1998), 35-60

"Joseph Losey: Time Lost and Time Found", *Monthly Film Bulletin* (June 1985), 172-175

"Around Painting and the End of Cinema: Jacques Rivette", *Sight and Sound* (April 1992), 20-23

"Peter Greenaway: Out of the Dark and Into the Light", in Philip Dodd, Ian Christie (eds.), *Spellbound: Art and Film* (London: Hayward Gallery/BFI, 1996), 76-84

"The Body as Perceptual Surface: Johan van der Keuken", given as a talk at the Ludwig Museum, Budapest (Hungary), November 2004

"Television and the Author's Cinema: *Das Kleine Fernsehspiel*," first published as "Twee Nieuwe Duitse Cinemas", in M. Dominicus (ed), *Das Kleine Fernsehspiel* (Rotterdam: Filmfestival Rotterdam, 1994), 20-28

"Touching Base: Some German Women Directors in the 1980s", first published as "German Women Filmmakers in the 80s", *Monthly Film Bulletin* (December 1987), 358-361 and "Mother Courage and her Daughters: Margarethe von Trotta", *Monthly Film Bulletin* (July 1983), 176-178

"Two Decades in Another Country: Hollywood and the Cinephiles", first published as "Hollywood and the Cinephiles: Two Decades in Another Country' in C.W.E. Bigsby (ed.), *Superculture* (London, Elek, 1975), 199-216

"Raoul Ruiz's HYPOTHESE DU TABLEAU VOLÉ", *Monthly Film Bulletin* (December 1984), 368-369

"Images for England (and Scotland, Ireland, Wales ...)", *Monthly Film Bulletin* (September 1984), 267–269 and as "Images for Sale" in Lester Friedman (ed.), *Fires were Started: British Cinema and Thatcherism* (Minneapolis: University of Minnesota Press, 1993), 52-69

"'If You Want a Life': The Marathon Man", first published as "The Marathon Man" in Mieke Bal, Jan van Luxemburg (eds.), 'Cultural History: Straddling Borders: John Neubauer zum 70.Geburtstag', *Arcadia* vol. 38, no. 2, 2003, 407-413

"British Television in the 1980s through the Looking Glass", first published as "TV through the Looking Glass" in Nick Browne (ed), *American Television* (Langhorne, PA: Harwood, 1993), 97-120

"German Cinema Face to Face with Hollywood: Looking into a Two-Way Mirror", first published in Alexander Stephan (ed.), *Americanization and Anti-Americanism: The German Encounter with American Culture after 1945* (New York: Berghahn Books, 2004), 166-155

"Of Rats and Revolution: Dusan Makavejev's THE SWITCHBOARD OPERATOR", first published as "The Switchboard Operator", *Brighton Film Review* 2 (1968), 15-17

"Defining DEFA's Historical Imaginary: The Films of Konrad Wolf", co-authored with Michael Wedel and first published in *New German Critique*, 82 (Winter 2001), 3-24

"Under Western Eyes: What does Žižek want?", first published as "Under Western Eyes" in *de Gids* (April 1995), 263-272

"Our Balkanist Gaze", first presented at the "No Man's Land, Everybody's Image" conference, Film Studies Program, Yale University, February 2003

"Is History an Old Movie", first published as "Filming Fascism: Is History Just an Old Movie?" *Sight and Sound* (September 1992), 18-21 and 49-50

"Edgar Reitz' HEIMAT: Memory, Home and Hollywood", first published as "Memory, Home and Hollywood', *Monthly Film Bulletin* (February 1985), 49-51, 72 and in Miriam Hansen (ed.), "Dossier on HEIMAT", *New German Critique* 36 (Fall 1989), 3-24

"Discourse and History: ONE MAN'S WAR – Interview with Edgardo Cozarinsky", first published as "One Man's War", *Framework* 21 (Summer 1983), 19-23

"Rendezvous with the French Revolution: Ettore Scola's LA NUIT DE VAR-ENNES", first published as "The Night of Varennes", *Monthly Film Bulletin* (June 1989), 147-148

"Joseph Losey's THE GO-BETWEEN", *Monogram* 3, (1972), 17-21

"Games of Love and Death: Greenaway and Others", *Monthly Film Bulletin* (October 1988), 290-293

"Peter Wollen's FRIENDSHIP'S DEATH", *Monthly Film Bulletin* (November 1987), 323-324

"Andy Engel's MELANCHOLIA", *Monthly Film Bulletin* (October 1989), 306-307

"On the High Seas: Edgardo Cozarinsky's Dutch Adventure", first published as "High Seas", *Sight and Sound* (Winter 1983/84), 37-39

"Third Cinema/World Cinema. Interview with Ruy Guerra", first published as "Ruy Guerra", *Monogram* 5 (1974), 27-33

"Ruy Guerra's ERENDIRA", *Monthly Film Bulletin* (July 1986), 208-209

"Hyper- Retro- or Counter-: European Cinema as Third Cinema Between Holly-wood and Art Cinema", originally "Chronicle of a Death Retold: Hyper-, Retro-, or Counter-Cinema," *Monthly Film Bulletin* (June 1987), 164-167 and "Werner Herzog: Tarzan meets Parsifal", *Monthly Film Bulletin* (May 1988), 132-134, and first published as "Hyper-, Retro-, or Counter-: European Cinema and Third Cinema Between Hollywood and Art Cinema" in J. King, A. Lopez, M. Alvarado (eds.), *Mediating Two Worlds: The Americas and Europe 1492-1992* (London: BFI Publishing, 1992), 119-135

"European Cinema as World Cinema?", paper presented at the Cinema Europe PhD seminar, University of Amsterdam, December 2004

Index of Names

Index of Film Titles / Subjects

Film Culture in Transition
General Editor: *Thomas Elsaesser*

Double Trouble: Chiem van Houweninge on Writing and Filming
Thomas Elsaesser, Robert Kievit and Jan Simons (eds.)

Writing for the Medium: Television in Transition
Thomas Elsaesser, Jan Simons and Lucette Bronk (eds.)

Between Stage and Screen: Ingmar Bergman Directs
Egil Törnqvist

The Film Spectator: From Sign to Mind
Warren Buckland (ed.)

Film and the First World War
Karel Dibbets and Bert Hogenkamp (eds.)

A Second Life: German Cinema's First Decades
Thomas Elsaesser (ed.)

Fassbinder's Germany: History Identity Subject
Thomas Elsaesser

Cinema Futures: Cain, Abel or Cable? The Screen Arts in the Digital Age
Thomas Elsaesser and Kay Hoffmann (eds.)

Audiovisions: Cinema and Television as Entr'Actes in History
Siegfried Zielinski

Joris Ivens and the Documentary Context
Kees Bakker (ed.)

Ibsen, Strindberg and the Intimate Theatre: Studies in TV Presentation
Egil Törnqvist

The Cinema Alone: Essays on the Work of Jean-Luc Godard 1985-2000
Michael Temple and James S. Williams (eds.)

Micropolitics of Media Culture: Reading the Rhizomes of Deleuze and Guattari
Patricia Pisters and Catherine M. Lord (eds.)

Malaysian Cinema, Asian Film: Border Crossings and National Cultures
William van der Heide

Film Front Weimar: Representations of the First World War in German Films of the Weimar Period (1919-1933)
Bernadette Kester

Camera Obscura, Camera Lucida: Essays in Honor of Annette Michelson
Richard Allen and Malcolm Turvey (eds.)

Jean Desmet and the Early Dutch Film Trade
Ivo Blom

City of Darkness, City of Light: Émigré Filmmakers in Paris 1929-1939
Alastair Phillips

The Last Great American Picture Show: New Hollywood Cinema in the 1970s
Thomas Elsaesser, Alexander Horwath and Noel King (eds.)

Harun Farocki: Working on the Sight-Lines
Thomas Elsaesser (ed.)

Herr Lubitsch Goes to Hollywood: German and American Film after World War I
Kristin Thompson

Cinephilia: Movies, Love and Memory
Marijke de Valck and Malte Hagener (eds.)